BILL MAGRI
621-2708

FINANCIAL
ACCOUNTING
a programmed text

FINANCIAL ACCOUNTING

a programmed text

James Don Edwards, Ph.D., C.P.A.
J. M. Tull Professor of Accounting
The University of Georgia

Roger H. Hermanson, Ph.D., C.P.A.
Research Professor of Accounting
Georgia State University

R. F. Salmonson, Ph.D., C.P.A.
Professor of Accounting
Michigan State University

1978   FOURTH EDITION

RICHARD D. IRWIN, INC. Homewood, Illinois 60430
Irwin-Dorsey Limited Georgetown, Ontario L7G 4B3

The previous edition of this book was published under
the title of *Accounting I: A Programmed Text*.

ISBN 0-256-02010-8
Library of Congress Catalog Card No. 77–89792

Printed in the United States of America

1 2 3 4 5 6 7 8 9 0 K 5 4 3 2 1 0 9 8

LEARNING SYSTEMS COMPANY –
a division of Richard D. Irwin, Inc. – has developed a
PROGRAMMED LEARNING AID
to accompany texts in this subject area.
Copies can be purchased through your bookstore
or by writing PLAIDS,
1818 Ridge Road, Homewood, Illinois   60430.

Preface

This Fourth Edition of *Financial Accounting: A Programmed Text* has all of the features included in any other financial accounting text, but also contains an additional feature. The text includes a simple-to-use programming format which has proven to be effective in assisting students to understand the material. This increased understanding on the part of the student enables the instructor to be more effective in teaching the material.

This volume on financial accounting may be used alone or in combination with its companion volume, *Managerial Accounting: A Programmed Text*. These two volumes contain the essential financial and managerial accounting subject matter covered in the first year accounting course for undergraduate students majoring in either business administration or accounting.

Contents. Part I, consisting of the first three chapters of this volume, covers the accounting cycle. Part II, Chapters 4 through 10, is concerned with various items which appear in the statement of financial position and with their related effects on revenues and expenses. Part III, consisting of the chapters on analysis and interpretation of financial statements and on the statement of changes in financial position deals with analysis of results. Part IV is concerned with the basic theory underlying financial statements and consolidated financial statements.

This fourth edition has been substantially rewritten so as to make it completely up-to-date in coverage and to reduce the reading level from that of previous editions. This latter change should bring about even clearer communication between the text and its users than in previous editions.

Some users have encouraged us to retain the comprehensive coverage of previous editions. Other users have suggested eliminating certain materials to shorten the coverage. We have attempted to satisfy both types of users by moving considerable materials into appendices. (There are 14 appendices.) This should make the text more *flexible* in that those who prefer a comprehensive coverage can assign all chapters and appendices. Those who prefer to concentrate on only essential subject matter can assign the chapters only. Others can select some option between these two alternatives. All end-of-chapter materials relating to the appendices are identified as such so as to avoid confusion.

Three chapters have each been divided into two parts to give some flexibility in covering these chapters. Some users will assign both parts simultaneously while others will assign the parts separately. The end-of-chapter materials are identified as to which part of the chapter they relate.

In our experience, the primary advantages to the student of combining a text and the programmed learning technique are threefold: (1) to require a more active and alert participation by the student to heighten his or her interest in the subject matter; (2) to provide immediate reinforcement of correct understanding and immediate correction of misinterpretations during the reading process; and (3) to enable the student to come to class with a higher level of comprehension so that the instructor can concentrate attention on clarification of difficult points, reinforcement through illustration and expansion, and demonstration of the practical, real-world utility of the knowledge acquired.

A programmed text communicates with the student in the same way the instructor does — on a first person level. While reading a chapter, the student is asked to respond to questions asked at various points in the chapter. The student is then referred to the proper answers (with explanations). Thus the student's understanding of the concepts is immediately tested and is either reinforced or corrected. The student does not have to wait until an examination is given to evaluate the extent of understanding of the material in a chapter.

We believe the following elements increase the effectiveness of each chapter in this book: (1) a clear statement of *learning objectives*, (2) the *text* of the chapter, (3) a *summary* of chapter contents, (4) a *glossary*, (5) a *student review quiz* (with answers and explanations provided), (6) *questions*, (7) *exercises*, and (8) two series of *problems*.

Learning objectives. Each chapter has a set of clearly stated learning objectives. These are intended to prepare the student for learning by expressly stating the major learning objectives to be achieved by study of that chapter.

Student review quiz. A set of questions, exercises, and problems, constituting a self-administered quiz, has been included at the end of each chapter. Students should use these to test their understanding of the material in the chapter just studied.

Questions, exercises, and problems. At the end of each chapter are separate series of questions and exercises, and two sets of problems (Series A and Series B). The questions provide a vehicle for discussing the specific points in theory introduced in the chapter. The exercises and problems are used to apply the theory to specific situations.

Supplementary materials

Study guide and review manual. A study guide and review manual designed to accompany the text is available as a separate volume. It contains a detailed outline of the material in each chapter and a series of questions, exercises, and short problems to be answered by the student. Answers to the questions, exercises, and short problems are provided.

Check list of key figures in answers. As was true for the prior editions, a check list of the key figures in the answers to both Series A and Series B problems is available to instructors in quantity for distribution to students. The purpose of the list is to provide the students with a key figure in each problem against which they can compare their own solutions while doing their homework.

Work papers. The work papers are specially designed accounting forms for use with specific problems in either Series A or Series B of the homework problems in each chapter. In some instances, they are partially filled in to save the student time in completing the homework. Also available within the work papers volume are (1) answer sheets to serve as a permanent record of the student's responses to the questions in each frame, and (2) answer sheets for the student review quizzes.

Acknowledgments

We are indebted to many persons for the comments and constructive criticisms they have made for this edition. Included among them are the following: Shirley Glass, Macomb Community College; Marty Gosman, University of Massachusetts; Robert A. Kelley, Corning Community College; C. B. Stephenson, Ohio University; Martin Taylor, University of Maryland; Doyle Williams, Texas Tech University.

We also wish to express our deep appreciation to our colleagues at Georgia State University, the University of Georgia, and Michigan State University who have contributed to this project both explicitly and implicitly in this and earlier editions.

January 1978

James Don Edwards
Roger H. Hermanson
R. F. Salmonson

Using the programmed text

The method of programming used in this text is simple to use. You begin by reading Frame 1^1 in Chapter 1. At the end of that frame, you will find questions to be answered. You may use the answer form provided for that chapter in the *Work Papers* or a separate sheet of paper. To determine the correctness of your responses, you merely turn the next page and examine the answers given in Answer Frame 1^1. You are told why each answer is right or wrong. You should use your performance on the questions given as a measure of your understanding of the material in Frame 1^1. If you miss any of the questions asked, you are encouraged to restudy Frame 1^1 before continuing on to Frame 1^2. This same procedure should be used throughout the book. Specific instructions are given throughout as to where to turn next to continue working the program.

When you have completed working through a chapter, you will find a glossary of new terms introduced in the chapter. After completing study of the glossary you should continue on to the student review quiz which follows and use it as an immediate self-administered test of your understanding of the content of the chapter. Special answer sheets are provided in the *Work Papers* for use in answering these questions, and the answers are printed at the back of the text. Forms for use in solving the Series A or Series B problems are also provided in the *Work Papers*.

If you need to study the text a second time (as, for example, in reviewing for an examination), the programming questions and answers may be omitted. Since the frames are arranged sequentially on successive pages, the contents of a chapter may be read in the same manner as a nonprogrammed text. Or, you may desire to further test your understanding of the chapters by answering all the programming questions once again and rereading only those frames in which your comprehension is unsatisfactory. Another alternative would be to read again only those frames where you missed any questions your first time through the material. (If you use and retain the answer sheets in the *Work Papers* you will be able to do this.)

Contents

part III
ANALYSIS OF RESULTS

part I

THE ACCOUNTING
CYCLE

1

An introduction to financial accounting

Learning objectives

Study of the material in this chapter is designed to achieve a number of learning objectives. These include an introductory level comprehension of:

1. The possible value to every person in society of some knowledge of accounting.

2. The nature of accounting and its various subfunctions.

3. Accountancy as a professional career field comprising public, private, and governmental accounting, and the areas of specialization lying within each.

4. The need for and use of accounting information in decision making both within and outside a business firm.

5. Basic financial statements prepared for a business firm and the underlying process that yields these statements, including the crucial importance of proper transaction analysis.

6. Some underlying assumptions— entity, duality, transaction, continuity, cost basis of valuation, money measurement, and periodicity.

When undertaking initial study of any discipline, new terms are usually encountered. To assist in the process of becoming familiar with the language of accounting, a glossary of the terms introduced in each chapter is presented at the end of the chapter.

In our daily activities we make many decisions that consist of choosing between alternatives that have different expected outcomes. These decisions may be of a personal, political, social, or economic nature, involving all aspects of life. Often, we are in doubt as to the course of action we should take to achieve a specific goal. This doubt may be reduced by obtaining relevant information.

Many decisions are made daily in our society that have economic consequences, such as whether our savings should be invested in a savings account in a bank, in government bonds, or in the shares of stock issued by business corporations. We may feel that our savings can be quite safely invested in a savings account or in a government bond. But we are far less certain about the outcome of an investment in shares of stock. To make an informed decision we need information about the economic activity of corporations that issue such shares. And it is here that accounting enters the picture, since accounting is a primary source of information on economic activity.

Because economic activity includes the production, exchange, and consumption of scarce goods, it is found everywhere in our society. Accounting is nearly as extensive. Wherever economic resources are employed, an accounting is likely to be required to show what was accomplished at what cost. This is true whether the resources are used by individuals, business firms, or not-for-profit entities such as churches, units of government, and hospitals. But our attention in this text will center on the accounting and reporting by business firms.

Accounting defined

Accounting is a systematic process of measuring and reporting to various users relevant financial information for decision making regarding the economic activity of an organization or unit. This information is primarily financial in nature; that is, it is stated in money terms.

The accounting process consists of a number of rather distinct functions. Accountants *observe* the economic scene and *select* (or identify) those events that are considered evidence of economic activity. (The purchase and sale of goods and services are examples.) Then, through the use of natural numbers, a monetary scale, and certain other general principles, they *measure* these selected events. As the next step, they *record* these measurements to provide a permanent history of the financial activities of the organization. In order to *report* upon what has happened, accountants *classify* their measurements of recorded events into meaningful groups. The preparation of accounting reports will require that accountants *summarize* these measurements even further. Finally, accountants may be asked to *interpret* the contents of their statements and reports. Interpretation may involve explanation of the uses, meaning, and limitations of accounting information. It may also involve drawing attention to significant items through percentage and ratio analysis.

Accounting may also be defined as an *information system* designed to provide, through the medium of financial statements, relevant financial information. In designing the system, accountants keep in mind the types of users of the information (owners, creditors, etc.) and the kinds of decisions they make that require financial information. Usually, the information provided relates to the economic resources owned by an organization, the claims against these resources, the changes in both resources and claims, and the results of using these resources for a given period of time.

On the answer form provided in the *Work Papers* or on a separate sheet of paper, indicate whether each of the following is true or false.

1. The welfare of a prisoner in a state penitentiary is quite likely to be affected by decisions that are based in part on accounting information.
2. Accounting is primarily concerned with providing financial information on the economic activities of an organization.
3. Accounting could be briefly defined as a measurement and communication process.
4. Accounting information is useful in correcting past decisions regarding the use of economic resources.

To check the correctness of your answers, turn to Answer Frame 1[1] on page 6.

Frame 2[1] ————————————————————

Accountancy as a profession

In our society accountants typically are employed in (1) public accounting, (2) private industry, or (3) the not-for-profit sector. Within each of these areas, specialization is possible; an accountant may, for example, be considered an expert in auditing, systems development, budgeting, cost accounting, or tax accounting.

Public accounting

Accountants may offer their services to the general public for a fee as does a doctor or an attorney. Although the business enterprise is the primary client, individuals and not-for-profit organizations are included. If an accountant has passed a rigorous examination prepared and graded by the American Institute of Certified Public Accountants

2¹
continued

(AICPA)—the accounting equivalent of the American Bar Association or the American Medical Association—and has met certain other requirements, such as having a certain number of years of experience, he or she may be licensed by the state to practice as a certified public accountant (CPA). As an independent, professional person, a CPA may offer clients auditing, management advisory, and tax services.

Auditing. When a business seeks a loan or seeks to have its securities traded on a stock exchange, it is usually required to provide statements on its financial affairs. Users of these statements may accept and rely upon them more freely when they are accompanied by an *auditor's report*. This auditor's report contains the opinion of the CPA regarding the fairness of the statements.[1] In order to have the knowledge necessary for an informed opinion, the CPA conducts an audit of the accounting and related records and seeks supporting evidence from external sources.

Management advisory services. As a result of knowledge gained in an audit, CPAs typically offer suggestions to their clients on how to improve their operations. From these as well as other direct contacts, CPAs may be engaged to provide a wide range of management advisory services. Such services may include, for example, executive recruiting and production scheduling. But they are more likely to involve services related to the accounting process—the design and installation of an accounting system or services in the areas of electronic processing of accounting data, inventory control, budgeting, or financial planning.

Tax services. CPAs often are called upon for expert advice regarding the preparation and filing of federal, state, and local tax returns. The objective here is to use legal means to minimize the amount of taxes paid. But of equal importance, because of high tax rates and complex tax laws, is tax planning. Proper tax planning requires that the tax

---

[1] For an example of an actual auditor's report, see the Appendix to Chapter 14. Included in that Appendix is a complete set of financial statements of the type often presented to external users.

effects, if any, of every business decision be known before the decision is made. There may be little opportunity to alter its effects after the decision has been made.

Private or industrial accounting

Accountants employed by a single business are referred to as private or industrial accountants. They may be the employer's only accountant, or one of several hundred or more. They may or may not be CPAs. If they have passed a rigorous examination prepared and administered by the National Association of Accountants—an organization for accountants employed in private industry—they will possess a Certificate in Management Accounting (CMA). As in public accounting, they may be specialists in providing certain services.

They may, for example, be concerned with recording events and transactions involving outsiders and in the preparation of financial statements. Or they may be engaged in accumulating and controlling the costs of goods manufactured by their employer. They may be specialists in budgeting—that is, in the development of plans relating to future operations. Many private accountants become specialists in the design and installation of systems for the processing of accounting data. Others are internal auditors and are employed by a firm to see that its policies and procedures are adhered to in its departments and divisions.

Accounting in the not-for-profit sector

Many accountants, including CPAs, are employed by not-for-profit organizations, including governmental agencies at the federal, state, and local levels. Here again specialization is possible as, for example, in budgeting or systems design. But the governmental accountant is likely to be concerned with the accounting for and control of tax revenues and their expenditure. Accountants are also employed by governmental agencies whose function is the regulation of business activity— for example, the regulation by a state public service commission of public utilities.

Many accountants (including CPAs) are also employed in the academic arm of the profession. Here attention is directed toward the teaching of accounting and to research into the uses, limitations, and improvement of accounting information and of the theories and procedures under which it is accumulated and communicated.

On the answer form provided in the *Work Papers* or on a separate sheet of paper, indicate whether each of the following statements is correct or incorrect.

1. An accountant may be an expert auditor and not be a CPA.
2. To become a CPA, an accountant must be expert in providing management advisory services.
3. A CPA may practice as an independent professional person, or may be employed as an accountant by a manufacturing company.
4. A CPA employed by a mining company would be permitted to express a professional opinion on the fairness of that company's financial statements.

Check your answers in Answer Frame 2¹ on page 10.

Frame 3¹

The need for accounting information

The usefulness of accounting information in making decisions regarding economic resources has been noted. But little has been said about the decision-making process, to which attention is now directed.

The decision-making process

Basically, as shown in Illustration 1.1, any decision-making process involves (1) recognition of the existence of and the formulation of a problem, (2) determination of the alternative courses of action considered solutions to the problem, (3) prediction of the possible outcome of each of the alternatives, (4) selection of the preferred consequence as determined by reference to the decision maker's personal preferences or previously set goals, and (5) taking action to see that the alternative chosen is implemented.

The problem is caused, at least in part, by events occurring in the real world of human activity and scarce resources. Its existence must be recognized or there will be no decision. The nature of the problem must be understood so that alternatives, which are possible solutions to the problem, can be determined.

The list of alternatives should be complete, or the best solution may be overlooked. And the suggested actions should be competing. One

Illustration 1.1   A model of the decision-making process

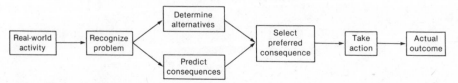

8

need not choose between two approaches to solving a problem if one can have both.

Since they represent future expected happenings, the consequences associated with each alternative must be predicted. Because individuals differ, they are likely to have different personal preferences. Thus, different decision makers may make different decisions even though they predict the same consequences from the same alternatives.

Note that implementing a decision causes new events in the real world, which cause new problems to arise. These problems, in turn, bring about a recycling of the whole process.

As a practical illustration, assume that a bank faces a problem. It has received requests for loans from Company X and Company Y. It is in doubt as to which loan will meet its objectives relative to risk, interest earnings, use of the money, date of repayment, ability to repay, and similar matters.

To solve the problem, the bank gathers information that helps it *predict the outcomes of granting each loan.* The predicted outcome of each loan is based on such factors as the rate of interest that can be charged, how the money will be used, and when it will be repaid. Projected results of the alternatives are compared with established objectives of the bank and a decision is reached. This decision may be influenced by the personal preferences of the person making it. This person may conclude that as far as the bank is concerned, a loan to X does not differ significantly from a loan to Y. But he or she may have a strong preference for loaning money to X because it intends to acquire pollution control equipment, while Y intends to acquire new smelting equipment.

In any event, a decision is made; and whether the loan is granted or not, the bank's relationship with its environment is now changed. This causes new problems requiring new information and further decisions.

In predicting the outcomes of the granting of each of the above loans, the bank relied upon accounting information. Virtually every attempt to predict the future involves a review of the past. And so, in making its predictions, the bank has relied upon the accounting records of the past financial activities of each company.

In this example, the bank is considered an external user of accounting information. But the same decision process is employed, with accounting again supplying part of the information, in reaching a decision on an internal matter. For example, a business manager may have to decide whether or not to begin offering a new line of merchandise. Internal decisions requiring accounting information are now examined briefly.

Internal decisions

In most companies, persons at various levels of management make decisions that require accounting information. These decisions can be classified into four major types:

1. Correct. Many expert auditors employed by large companies as internal auditors are not CPAs and have little reason to seek the CPA certificate.
2. Incorrect. It is demonstrated ability in fulfilling the attest function, not in providing management services, that is required before an accountant can become a CPA.
3. Correct. When licensed by the state, CPAs may practice as independent professional persons. But if they believe their personal prospects for success are greater, they may be employed as accountants by a manufacturing company.
4. Incorrect. An accountant, even though a CPA, is not practicing as a CPA when in the employ of a mining company. He or she would not be considered an independent professional accountant and, consequently, would not be permitted to express an opinion on the fairness of the employer's financial statements. In order to express such an opinion, the CPA must, in addition to being licensed to practice as a CPA, be *independent*.

If you answered incorrectly, read Frame 2¹ again before beginning Frame 3¹ on page 8.

3¹
continued

1. Financing decisions—deciding what amounts of capital are needed and whether it is to be secured from owners or creditors.
2. Resource allocation decisions—deciding how the total capital of a firm is to be invested, such as the amount invested in machinery.
3. Production decisions—deciding what products are to be produced, by what means, and when.
4. Marketing decisions—setting selling prices and advertising budgets; determining where a firm's markets are and how they are to be reached.

Managerial accounting. Managerial accounting is that part of accounting that provides information for the above types of management decisions. It ranges from the very broad (long-range planning) to the quite detailed (why costs varied from their planned levels). The information must meet two tests. It must be useful and not cost more to gather than it is worth. It generally relates to a part of a firm, such as a plant or a department, because this is where most of the decisions are made. It is used to measure the success of managers in, for example, controlling costs and to motivate them to help a firm achieve its goals. And it is forward looking, often involving planning for the future.

Indicate whether each of the following statements is true or false.

1. The decision-making process will vary from firm to firm and according to the type of problem requiring a solution (decision).
2. Management accounting information generally relates to some part rather than the whole of an enterprise.

3. In any situation requiring a decision, the decision maker may forego securing information if it will not be worth its cost.
4. In general, the purpose of information is to reduce doubt.

Check your responses in Answer Frame 3[1] on page 12.

Frame 4[1]

External users and their decisions

The external users of accounting information and the types of questions for which answers are sought can be classified as follows:

1. Owners and prospective owners (stockholders and prospective stockholders in a corporation) and their advisers — financial analysts and investment counselors. Should an ownership interest be acquired in this firm? Or, if one is now held, should it be increased, decreased, or retained at its present level? Has the firm earned satisfactory profits?
2. Creditors and lenders. Should a loan be granted to the firm? Will the firm be able to pay its debts as they become due?
3. Employees and their unions. Does the firm have the ability to pay increased wages? Can it do so without raising prices? Is the firm financially able to provide permanent employment?
4. Customers. Will the firm survive long enough to honor its product warranties? Can a firm install costly pollution control equipment and still remain profitable? Are profit margins reasonable?
5. Governmental units. Is this firm, a public utility, earning a fair profit on its capital investment? How much taxes does it pay? In total, is business activity at a desired level for sound growth without inflation?
6. The general public. Are profit margins too high? Are they an increasing or decreasing part of national income? Are the firms in this industry contributing to inflation?[2]

Except for uses by governmental units, the information needs of the above users are met by providing a set of general-purpose financial statements. These statements are the end product of a process known as financial accounting.

Financial accounting. It is the function of financial accounting to provide statements on a firm's financial position, changes in this position, and on the results of operations (profitability). These statements are published in about a 20- to 60-page document known as the *annual report*. This report contains the auditor's opinion as to the fairness of the

---

[2] For a further discussion of the parties for whom financial statements are primarily intended and the uses made of such information see Chapter 13.

1. False. The decision-making process will not change. It will consist of the recognition and formulation of the problem, determination of the alternative possible courses of action, prediction of the outcomes for each possible alternative, selection of the preferred outcome or consequence (the actual decision), and implementation of the decision. This generalized pattern will hold regardless of the type of firm involved or the nature of the decision to be made.

2. True. Management accounting information is most widely used by internal management personnel who are responsible for a part rather than the whole of an organization.

3. True. As is true in any situation involving a purchasable commodity, the cost of information may exceed its value to some user.

4. True. In brief, this is the purpose of all information.

If you missed any of the above answers, you should read Frame 3¹ again before proceeding to Frame 4¹ on page 11.

4¹
continued

financial statements, as well as other information about the company's activities, plans, and expectations.

Financial accounting information relates to the firm as a whole, since outsiders can make decisions only on matters pertaining to the firm in its entirety, such as whether or not to extend credit to it. Such information is historical in nature, being a report upon what has happened. Because interfirm comparisons are often made, the information supplied must conform to certain standards or principles, called generally accepted accounting principles (GAAP).

But it would be a mistake to assume that a clear-cut distinction can be drawn between financial accounting information and managerial accounting information. Key management officials are keenly aware of the fact that their jobs may depend upon how the figures come out in the annual report. Also, much of what is called managerial accounting information is first accumulated in an accounting system designed with financial reporting in mind.

Indicate whether each of the following statements is true or false.

1. The annual report of a company contains a statement showing the financial condition of the reporting company.

2. Financial accounting information is often called general-purpose information because it is believed that the information needs of different external parties can be satisfied by the same information.

3. As part of the management advisory services rendered, the CPA will express a professional opinion on the fairness of the bulk of the managerial accounting information accumulated by a company.

4. Basically, and in very broad general terms, managerial accounting information is used internally while financial accounting information is used externally.

Check your responses in Answer Frame 4[1] on page 14.

Frame 5[1]

Although accounting information is absolutely essential in the successful management of a not-for-profit organization, primary attention in this text is devoted to business firms.

The development of financial accounting standards

As noted above, the financial statements a business firm issues to external parties must conform to certain standards or principles. These standards and principles have developed largely in accounting practice or have been established by an authoritative body. Brief mention is made at this point of four of the prominent accounting authorities.

American Institute of Certified Public Accountants (AICPA)

The AICPA, an organization of CPAs in public and industrial practice, has been the dominant factor in the development of accounting standards over the past half century. In a 20-year period ending in 1959, its Committee on Accounting Procedure issued 51 *Accounting Research Bulletins* recommending certain principles or practices. From 1959 through 1973, the committee's successor, the Accounting Principles Board (APB), issued 31 numbered *Opinions* which CPAs generally were *required* to follow. These bulletins and opinions dealt with controversial issues. Through its monthly magazine, *The Journal of Accountancy,* its research division, and its other divisions and committees, the AICPA continues to influence the development of accounting standards and practices.

Financial Accounting Standards Board

The APB was replaced in 1973 with a new, independent, seven-member, full-time Financial Accounting Standards Board (FASB). To date (1977), the FASB has issued 16 *Statements of Financial Accounting Standards* and 19 Interpretations of FASB statements of standards. The FASB is widely accepted as the major influence, in the private sector, in the development of new financial accounting standards.

5¹
continued

U.S. Securities and Exchange Commission

Created under the Securities and Exchange Act of 1934, the Securities and Exchange Commission (SEC) administers a number of important acts dealing with the interstate sale of securities. The SEC has the power to prescribe in detail the accounting practices followed by companies required by law to file financial statements with it. This includes virtually every major U.S. business corporation. But rather than exercise this power, the SEC has adopted a policy of working closely with the accounting profession, especially the FASB, in the development of accounting standards.

American Accounting Association

Consisting largely of college instructors of accounting, the American Accounting Association (AAA) has sought to encourage research and study at a theoretical level into the concepts, standards, and principles of accounting. It publishes statements on such matters and supports the research efforts of individuals. In recent years, its quarterly magazine, *The Accounting Review,* has carried many articles reporting on research into the uses of accounting information.

The impact of the federal taxation of income must also be noted as a factor in the development of accounting standards. The accounting required for such purposes, although not usually required for financial reporting, will be discussed and illustrated from time to time in this text.

Indicate whether each of the following statements is true or false.

1. The SEC has, by law, complete authority over the accounting practices of companies required to file financial statements with it.
2. The FASB is the top nongovernmental authority on generally accepted accounting standards.
3. Companies generally must follow tax regulations in their accounting and reporting to external parties.
4. The AICPA has been the major factor in the development of accounting standards over the past half century.

Now check your responses in Answer Frame 5[1] on page 16.

Frame 6[1]

Financial statements of business enterprises

A modern business firm has many objectives or goals. They include providing well-paid jobs and comfortable working conditions for its employees, being a good citizen, generating satisfactory earnings, and maintaining a sound financial position. But the two primary objectives of every business firm are *profitability* and *solvency*. Unless a firm can produce satisfactory earnings and pay its debts as they become due, any other objectives a firm may have will never be realized simply because the firm will not survive.

Investors and creditors are also interested in a firm's profitability and solvency. The return to investors for investing in shares of stock consists of dividends and market price changes in the shares owned. Both of these are influenced, at least in part, by the firm's profitability and solvency. These same factors determine, again at least in part, whether a bondholder will receive interest payments from the firm as well as a return of principal at the bond's maturity date. The financial statements that reflect a firm's solvency (the statement of financial position) and its profitability (the earnings statement) are illustrated and discussed below.

The statement of financial position

The statement of financial position (often called a balance sheet) presents measures of the assets, liabilities, and owners' equity in a business firm as of a specific moment in time. Assets are things of value; they constitute the *resources* of the firm. They have value to the firm because of the uses to which they can be put or the things that can be acquired by exchanging them. In Illustration 1.2 the assets of the Hart Company amount to $35,670. They consist of current assets of cash and accounts receivable (amounts due from customers) and property, plant, and equipment consisting of delivery equipment and office equipment.

6¹

continued

Current assets consist of cash and other short-lived assets that are reasonably expected to be converted into cash or to be consumed or used up in the operations of the business, within a short period, usually one year.³ Property, plant, and equipment refers to relatively long-lived assets that are to be used in the production or sale of other assets or services rather than being sold.

Liabilities are the debts owed by a firm. Typically, they must be paid at certain known moments in time. The liabilities of the Hart Company are both relatively short-lived current liabilities.³ They consist of accounts payable (amounts owed to suppliers) and notes payable (a written promise to pay) totaling $3,600.

Illustration 1.2

HART COMPANY
Statement of Financial Position
July 31, 1979

Assets			Liabilities and Stockholders' Equity		
Current Assets:			Current Liabilities:		
Cash	$12,470		Accounts payable	/ $ 600	
Accounts receivable	700		Notes payable	3,000	
		$13,170			$ 3,600
			Stockholders' Equity:		
Property, Plant, and Equipment:			Capital stock	$30,000	
			Retained earnings	2,070	
Delivery equipment	$20,000				32,070
Office equipment	2,500		Total Liabilities and		
		22,500	Stockholders'		
Total Assets		$35,670	Equity		$35,670

³ Technically speaking, the time period is one operating cycle or one year, whichever is longer. An operating cycle is the length of time that it takes cash spent for merchandise to be sold to come back to the selling company in the form of collections from its customers. Thus, in some industries (distilling, for example) the operating cycle extends for a number of years.

Illustration 1.4

```
                         HART COMPANY
                Statement of Changes in Financial Position
                      For the Month of July 1979

Cash Provided (inflows):
From operations:
    Revenues ...................................................   $ 5,000
    Less cash paid for expenses .............................     3,030
        Cash from operations ..................................              $ 1,970
From other sources:
    Invested by owners...........................................  $30,000
    Borrowed under note payable ...........................      6,000
        Cash from other sources ...............................               36,000
            Total Cash Provided (total inflows)...........               $37,970

Cash Applied (outflows):
Purchased delivery equipment...............................  $20,000
Purchased office equipment .................................    2,500
Repaid note payable...........................................    3,000
            Total Cash Applied (total outflows) ..........               25,500
Increase in Cash for Month...................................               $12,470
```

or it may highlight changes in working capital (defined as current assets less current liabilities). In either case, it provides information not readily obtainable from either the earnings statement or the statement of financial position. For example, it shows that the Hart Company received cash from its customers for services provided in the amount of $5,000 (total revenue of $5,700 less uncollected accounts receivable of $700). Deducting cash paid for expenses of $3,030 (total expenses of $3,630 less unpaid expenses of $600) leaves net cash provided by operations of $1,970. The statement then goes on to explain exactly how the cash increased by $12,470 for the month of July. Understanding the statement of changes in financial position requires some knowledge of accounting. For this reason, discussion is delayed until Chapter 12. The student who wishes to pursue the derivation of the amounts in Illustration 1.4 may turn to Illustration 1.5, page 29.

Indicate whether each of the following statements is true or false.

1. The earnings statement reports on the profit-seeking activities for a period of time.
2. If expenses exceeded revenues for a period, the firm suffered a net loss.
3. The statement of changes in financial position reports on a firm's investing and financing activities for a period of time.
4. By showing cash flows in and out, the statement of changes in financial position shows net earnings for the period.

Check your responses in Answer Frame 7[1] on page 20.

Frame 8¹

The financial accounting process

Having briefly introduced the three principal financial statements, attention is now directed to the process underlying such statements.

The accounting equation

It has been noted that in the statement of financial position presented in Illustration 1.2 the total assets of the Hart Company are equal to its liabilities and stockholders' equity. This equality follows from the basic assumption in accounting that the assets of a business are equal to the equities in those assets; that is, Assets = Equities. Assets have already been defined simply as things of value. In a more sophisticated sense, the accountant designates and records as assets all those economic resources owned by a business which can be measured. And all desired things, except those available in unlimited quantity without cost or effort, are economic resources.

Equities are interests in or claims upon assets. For example, assume that you purchased a new automobile for $5,000 by withdrawing $400 from your savings account and borrowing $4,600 from your credit union. Your equity in the automobile is $400 and that of your credit union is $4,600. The $4,600 can be further described as a liability. Your $400 equity is often described as the owner's equity or the residual equity or interest in the asset. Since, in the case of a corporation, the owners are the stockholders, the basic equation becomes:

$$\text{Assets} = \text{Liabilities} + \text{Stockholders' Equity}$$

This equation must always be in balance. The sum of the interests in assets must always be equal to the assets themselves. It is intuitively logical to hold that all economic resources belong to someone or to some organization.

The right side of the above equation is also looked upon in another manner — namely, it shows the sources of the existing stock of assets. Thus, liabilities are not only claims to assets but they also are sources of assets. And in a corporation, all of the assets are provided by either creditors (liability holders) or owners (stockholders).

As a business engages in economic activity, the dollar amounts and the composition of its assets, liabilities, and stockholders' equity change. But the equality of the basic equation always holds.

Transaction analysis

Our society is characterized by exchange. That is, the bulk of the goods and services produced are exchanged rather than consumed by their producers. From this it follows that much of the economic activity of our society can be observed from the exchanges that take place. In accounting, these exchanges (as well as other changes) are called *transactions*. They provide much of the raw data entered in the accounting system. There are several reasons why this is so. First, an exchange is a readily observable event providing good evidence that activity has occurred. Second, an exchange usually takes place at an agreed-upon price, and this price provides a highly objective measure of the economic activity that has transpired. Thus, the analysis of transactions is a most important part of the financial accounting process.

To illustrate the analysis of transactions and their effects upon the basic accounting equation, the activities of the Hart Company that led to the statements in Illustrations 1.2, 1.3, and 1.4 are presented and discussed below. Assume that the Hart Company was organized as a corporation on July 1, 1979, and that in its first transaction it issued, for $30,000 cash, shares of capital stock to Jim Hart, his wife, and their son. Analyzed, the transaction increased the assets (cash) of the Hart Company by $30,000 and increased its equities (the capital stock element of stockholders' equity) by $30,000. Consequently, the transaction yields a basic accounting equation containing the following:

Assets = Liabilities + Stockholders' Equity
(Cash, $30,000) (Capital stock, $30,000)

As its next transaction, the company borrowed $6,000 from Mrs. Hart's father, giving its written promise to repay the amount in one year.

Which of the following correctly describes the effects of the above transaction upon the company's assets and equities?

1. Assets would increase by $6,000, and stockholders' equity would decrease by $6,000.
2. Assets would increase by $6,000, and liabilities would increase by $6,000.
3. Both assets and stockholders' equity would increase by $6,000.
4. Both assets and liabilities would decrease by $6,000.
   Check your response in Answer Frame 8¹ on page 24.

Frame 9¹

After including the effects of the second transaction, the basic equation is:

Assets   =   Liabilities   +   Stockholders' Equity

(Cash, $36,000)   (Notes payable, $6,000)   (Capital stock, $30,000)

As its third transaction, the Hart Company spent $20,000 for three delivery trucks and $1,500 for some office equipment. In this transaction the Hart Company received delivery equipment priced at $20,000 and office equipment priced at $1,500. It gave up cash of $21,500. This transaction thus does not change the totals in the basic equation, it merely changes the composition of the assets. The equation is as follows:

Assets		=	Liabilities		+	Stockholders' Equity	
Cash..................	$14,500						
Delivery							
equipment.........	20,000		Notes payable...	$6,000		Capital stock...	$30,000
Office equipment...	1,500						
	$36,000	=		$6,000	+		$30,000

Assume that as transaction 4 in the month of July, the Hart Company purchased an additional $1,000 of office equipment, agreeing to pay for it within ten days after it receives a bill for it from the supplier. This transaction increases liabilities in the form of accounts payable (which are amounts owed to creditors for items purchased from them) by $1,000. The items making up the totals in the accounting equation now appear as follows:

Assets		=	Liabilities		+	Stockholders' Equity	
Cash..................	$14,500						
Delivery							
equipment.........	20,000		Notes payable...	$6,000		Capital stock...	$30,000
			Accounts				
Office equipment...	2,500		payable.........	1,000			
	$37,000	=		$7,000	+		$30,000

Revenue and expense transactions

Thus far the transactions presented have consisted of exchanges or of the acquisition of assets either by borrowing or by stockholder investment. But a business is not formed merely to acquire assets. Rather, it seeks to use the assets entrusted to it as a means of securing still greater amounts of assets. This is accomplished by providing customers with goods or services, with the expectation that the value of the assets received from customers will exceed the cost of the assets consumed or surrendered in serving them. This total flow of services rendered or goods delivered (as measured by assets received from customers) has been defined as *revenue*. Thus, revenue is a source of assets. The cost of serving customers is called *expense*. It is measured by the cost of the assets surrendered or consumed. If revenues exceed expenses, net earnings exist. If not, a loss has been suffered.

Assume that as its fifth transaction in July the Hart Company renders delivery services for its customers for $4,800 cash. It is evident that cash has increased by $4,800. But what other change has occurred to keep assets equal to equities?

1. Liabilities would increase by $4,800.
2. Stockholders' equity would increase by $4,800.
3. Other assets would decrease by $4,800.

Check your response in Answer Frame 9[1] on page 24.

Frame 10[1] ————————————————————————————

Incorporating the effects of the revenue transaction upon the financial status of the Hart Company yields the following basic equation:

Assets		=	Liabilities		+	Stockholders' Equity	
Cash..............	$19,300		Notes			Capital	
Delivery equip-			payable...	$6,000		stock.......	$30,000
ment..............	20,000		Accounts			Retained	
Office equip-			payable...	1,000		earnings...	4,800 (service
ment..............	2,500						revenue)
	$41,800 =			$7,000 +			$34,800

Note that the increase in stockholders' equity brought about by the revenue transaction is recorded as a separate item, "Retained earnings." It cannot be recorded as capital stock. No additional shares of stock were issued. The expectation is that revenue transactions will yield net earnings. If net earnings are not distributed to stockholders, they are in fact retained, and the title "Retained earnings" is quite descriptive. Subsequent chapters will show that because of complexities in handling large numbers of transactions, revenues will be shown as affecting re-

Answer frame 8¹

Statement 2 is the only correct response. The company received an additional $6,000 and gave in exchange a written promise to pay this sum at a later date. This written promise to pay is a note payable and is one type of liability. Thus, when this transaction is properly analyzed and recorded, the equation would remain in balance because both sides would be increased by $6,000.

If you missed this question, be sure that you understand why only the second statement is correct before going on to Frame 9¹ on page 22.

Answer frame 9¹

The second response is correct. The stockholders' equity would increase by $4,800. The correctness of this response can be observed by noting that no corresponding increase in liabilities was brought about by the rendering of services. And no specific assets were given up. Thus, by a process of elimination, we reach the conclusion that the rendering of services to customers in exchange for assets increases stockholders' equity. In fact, this is the basic objective of every business corporation.

If you answered incorrectly, you should study Frame 9¹ again before going on in Frame 10¹ on page 23.

10¹

continued

tained earnings only at the end of an accounting period. The procedure presented above is a shortcut used to explain why the accounting equation remains in balance.

Assume that as its sixth transaction in July the Hart Company performs services for customers who agree to pay $900 at a later date. The transaction consists of an exchange of services for a promise by the customer to pay later. It is similar to the preceding transaction in that stockholders' equity is increased because revenues have been earned. It differs because cash has not been received. But a thing of value, an asset, has been received. This is the claim upon the customer, the right to collect from him or her at a later date. Technically, such claims are called *accounts receivable*. But the important point is that accounting does recognize them as assets and does record them. The accounting equation, including this item, is as follows:

Assets		=	*Liabilities*		+	*Stockholders' Equity*	
Cash.................	$19,300		Notes			Capital	
Accounts			payable...	$6,000		stock.......	$30,000
receivable	900		Accounts			Retained	
Delivery equip-			payable...	1,000		earnings...	5,700 (service
ment..............	20,000						revenue)
Office equip-							
ment..............	2,500						
	$42,700 =			$7,000 +			$35,700

To illustrate one more step in regards to accounts receivable, assume that $200 is collected from customers "on account," to use business terminology. The transaction consists of the giving up of claims upon customers in exchange for cash. The effects of the transaction are to increase cash to $19,500 and to decrease accounts receivable to $700. Note that this transaction consists solely of a change in the composition of the assets, not of an increase in assets resulting from the generation of revenue.

Attention may now be directed toward expenses. Suppose (transaction 8) that the Hart Company paid its employees $2,600 for services received in conducting business operations during the month of July. The transaction consists of an exchange of cash for employee services. But what are its effects upon the elements in the basic equation?

1. There is no effect upon the totals of the two sides of the equation.
2. Assets would decrease and liabilities would decrease.
3. Assets would decrease and stockholders' equity would decrease.

Check your response in Answer Frame 10[1] on page 26.

Frame 11[1]

As already noted, the payment of wages consists of an exchange of cash for employee services. Thus, a proper analysis of the transaction appears to indicate an exchange of one form of asset for another. This seems especially true when one recognizes that business corporations generally will surrender assets only for other things of value, for other assets. But, because the value of the services typically has expired by the time payment is made, the accountant engages in a shortcut and treats the transaction as a decrease in an asset and in stockholders' equity. From a purely theoretical point of view, the transaction should be regarded as involving an increase in one asset (labor services) and a decrease in another (cash), and then a decrease in an asset (labor services) and a decrease in stockholders' equity because of the recognition of an expense – wages.

Let us further assume (as transactions 9 and 10) that the Hart Company paid cash of $300 as rent for truck storage space and office space and that it paid its utilities bill for July in the amount of $100. These transactions will be treated by the accountant as having the same effect upon the financial position of the company. They cause a decrease in the asset, cash, of $400 and a decrease in stockholders' equity of $400 because of the incurrence of rent expense of $300 and utilities expense of $100. Incorporating these two items and the wages of $2,600 cumulatively into our accounting equation, it now reads:

25

11¹

continued

Assets		=	Liabilities		+	Stockholders' Equity				
Cash	$16,500		Notes payable	$6,000		Capital stock	$30,000			
Accounts			Accounts payable	1,000		Retained				
receivable	700					earnings	2,700	{	Service revenue	$5,700
Delivery									Less expenses:	
equipment	20,000								Wages	2,600
Office equipment	2,500								Rent	300
	$39,700	=		$7,000	+		$32,700	{	Utilities	100

Because of their similar effects, transactions 11 and 12 of the Hart Company may be treated simultaneously. Assume that the company received a bill for gasoline, oil, and other delivery equipment supplies consumed during the month in the amount of $400 and a bill for $200 for advertising in July. Both transactions would be treated by the accountant as involving an increase in a liability, accounts payable, and a decrease in stockholders' equity because of the incurrence of an expense. The accounting equation depicting the financial position of the Hart Company now reads:

Assets		=	Liabilities		+	Stockholders' Equity				
Cash	$16,500		Notes payable	$6,000		Capital stock	$30,000			
Accounts			Accounts payable	1,600		Retained				
receivable	700					earnings	2,100	{	Service revenue	$5,700
Delivery									Less expenses:	
equipment	20,000								Wages	2,600
Office equipment	2,500								Rent	300
	$39,700	=		$7,600	+		$32,100	{	Utilities	100
									Gas and oil	400
									Advertising	200

Next, (transaction 13) the Hart Company paid the $1,000 balance due on the purchase of the office equipment (transaction 4). This reduced cash by $1,000 and reduced the debt owed to the equipment supplier, recorded as an account payable, by $1,000. Thus, assets and liabilities are both reduced by $1,000.

Finally, (transaction 14) in reviewing his needs for cash at the end of the month, Mr. Hart decided that he would not need as much cash as he now holds. So, he paid $3,000 on the note owed to his father-in-law, plus interest of $30 for the month. What effect does this transaction have on the basic elements in the accounting equation?

1. Assets and liabilities would both decrease by $3,030.

2. Assets and stockholders' equity would both decrease by $3,030.

3. Assets would decrease by $3,030, liabilities would decrease by $3,000, and stockholders' equity would decrease by $30.

Check your response in Answer Frame 11[1] on page 28.

Frame 12[1]

The basic equation as it stands after including the effects of transactions 13 and 14 is shown in Illustration 1.5.

Summary of transactions

The effects of all of the transactions entered into by the Hart Company in the first month of its existence upon its assets, liabilities, and stockholders' equity are summarized in Illustration 1.5. The ending balances in each of the columns are the dollar amounts reported in the statement of financial position in Illustration 1.2. The itemized data in the Retained Earnings column are the revenue and expense items reported in the earnings statement in Illustration 1.3. The reason for each change reported in the Cash column is determined and reported in the statement of changes in financial position in Illustration 1.4. This summary further shows how the basic equation of Assets = Equities is subdivided into the five major elements of financial accounting: assets, liabilities, owners' equity, revenues, and expenses.

The statement of retained earnings

The purpose of the statement of retained earnings is to explain the changes in retained earnings that occurred between two statement of financial position dates. Usually, these changes consist of the addition of net earnings (or deduction of net loss) and the deduction of dividends. Dividends are the means by which a corporation rewards its stockholders for providing it with capital.

The effects of a cash dividend transaction are to reduce cash and retained earnings by the amount paid out. In effect, the earnings are no longer retained but have been passed on to the stockholders. And this, of course, is one of the primary reasons why stockholders organize corporations.

The statement of retained earnings for the Hart Company for the month of July 1979 would be quite simple. Since the company was organized on July 1, there would be no beginning retained earnings balance. Net earnings of $2,070 would be added and, since no dividends were paid, this would also be the ending balance.

Answer frame 11[1]

Statement 3 is the correct choice. The transaction decreased cash by the total amount paid out, $3,030. Of this amount, $3,000 was applied to reduce the principal amount owed on notes payable and the remaining $30 consisted of the payment of interest expense—an element that reduces retained earnings. This transaction serves to illustrate that any given transaction may affect assets, liabilities, and stockholders' equity simultaneously.

If you answered incorrectly, study Frame 11[1] again before continuing in Frame 12[1] on page 27.

12[1]
continued

To provide a more effective illustration, assume that the Hart Company's net earnings for August were $1,500 (revenues of $5,600 less expenses of $4,100) and that it declared and paid dividends of $1,000. Its statement of retained earnings for August is shown in Illustration 1.6.

Indicate whether each of the following statements is true or false.
1. Because dividends and expenses both reduce retained earnings, they are of the same basic nature.
2. Dividends usually consist of a cash distribution to stockholders.
3. Dividends should be deducted from revenues in calculating net earnings.
4. Generally, in order to pay dividends, a corporation should have retained earnings.

Check your responses in Answer Frame 12[1] on page 30.

Frame 13[1]

Some underlying assumptions or basic concepts

The accountant, in seeking to provide useful information on economic activity, relies upon some underlying assumptions or basic concepts. Those covered, explicitly or implicitly, thus far are summarized below.

Entity (*accounting entity*)

The data gathered in an accounting system relate to a specific business unit or entity. This entity is deemed to have an existence separate and apart from its owners, creditors, employees, and other interested parties.

Transaction

Those events or happenings that affect the assets, liabilities, owners' equity, revenues, and expenses of an entity are called transactions and

Illustration 1.5

HART COMPANY
Summary of Transactions
Month of July 1979

Transaction	Explanation	Cash	Accounts Receivable	Delivery Equipment	Office Equipment	Notes Payable	Accounts Payable	Capital Stock	Retained Earnings	
	Beginning balances	$ -0-	$ -0-	$ -0-	$ -0-	$ -0-	$ -0-	$ -0-	$ -0-	
1	Issued stock for cash	+30,000						+30,000		
2	Borrowed money on note	+6,000				+6,000				
3	Purchased equipment for cash	−21,500		+20,000	+1,500					
4	Purchased equipment on account				+1,000		+1,000			
5	Service revenue for cash	+4,800							+4,800	(service revenue)
6	Service revenue on account		+900						+900	(service revenue)
7	Collection on account	+200	−200							
8	Paid wages	−2,600							−2,600	(wages expense)
9	Paid rent	−300							−300	(rent expense)
10	Paid utilities bill	−100							−100	(utilities expense)
11	Bill for gas and oil used						+400		−400	(gas and oil expense)
12	Bill for July advertising						+200		−200	(advertising expense)
13	Paid equipment bill	−1,000					−1,000			
14	Payment on note and interest	−3,030				−3,000			−30	(interest expense)
	Ending balances	$ 12,470	$ 700	$ 20,000	$ 2,500	$ 3,000	$ 600	$ 30,000	$ 2,070	

Assets = $35,670

Liabilities + Stockholders' Equity = $3,600 + $32,070

13¹

continued

Illustration 1.6

HART COMPANY
Statement of Retained Earnings
For the Month Ended August 31, 1979

Retained earnings, July 31	$2,070
Add: Net earnings for August	1,500
	$3,570
Less: Dividends	1,000
Retained Earnings, August 31	$2,570

are recorded in the accounting system. For the most part, transactions consist of exchanges.

Duality

Every transaction has a two-sided or dual effect upon each of the parties engaging in it. Consequently, if information is to be complete, both sides or both effects of every transaction must be included in the accounting system.

Money measurement

Economic activity is recorded and reported in terms of a common unit of measurement—the dollar. If not expressed in a common unit of measurement, accounting reports would be much less useful, if not unintelligible. Changes in the value of the dollar are usually ignored.

Cost

Most of the numbers entered in an accounting system are the bargained prices of exchange transactions. The result is that most assets (excluding cash and receivables) are recorded and reported at their cost of acquisition. Changes in the values of the assets are (with certain exceptions) usually ignored. This practice is usually defended on the grounds of objectivity and the absence of evidence that the acquiring firm would have been willing to pay more. As discussed further in Chapter 13, the historical cost basis of asset valuation has come under severe criticism in recent years, due largely to the "double-digit" inflation experienced.

Periodicity

To be useful, information must be (among other things) timely and current. To provide such information, accountants subdivide the life of an entity into periods and report upon its activities for those periods. The requirement of periodic reporting will require the use of estimates, thus making every accounting report somewhat tentative in nature.

Continuity

Unless strong evidence exists to the contrary, the accountant assumes that the entity will continue operations into the indefinite future. Consequently, assets that will be used up or consumed in future operations need not be reported at their current liquidation values.

The underlying assumptions or basic concepts of accounting will be discussed further in Chapter 13.

Indicate whether each of the following statements is true or false.
1. All events or happenings that affect an entity are recorded in its accounting system.
2. Assets are usually reported at their acquisition cost even though they may have a substantially higher current value.
3. Even though the value of a dollar may change as general price levels change, the accountant uses the dollar as if it were a constant unit of measure.
4. Because of the basic assumption that assets equal equities, the accountant is forced to assume that every transaction has two sides.

Check your responses in Answer Frame 13[1] on page 32.

Summary *chapter* 1

Accounting is a systematic or organized means of gathering and reporting information on economic activity. The information provided

1. False. Many events or happenings occur that affect the well-being of a business. Some of these, such as a strike by the employees of a major competitor, are not recorded in an entity's accounting system simply because their effects cannot be measured. Unless the happening or event has a relatively direct bearing upon the assets and equities of an entity, its effects will not be entered in the entity's accounting system.

2. True. Most assets are recorded and reported at their acquisition cost as reflected in the exchange transaction in which they were acquired.

3. True. No direct reflection of the changing value of the dollar is recognized in accounting systems employed in current practice.

4. True. The notion that a transaction has a dual nature, or has two sides, is directly related to the basic assumption that assets equal equities.

If you answered incorrectly, you should read Frame 13¹ again before continuing with the Summary on page 31.

is used by many external and internal parties, together with other information, for a wide range of decisions.

An accountant may be employed in public, private, or governmental accounting and may be a specialist in one of many fields of expertise such as auditing, budgeting, systems development, taxation, or financial reporting.

Internally, accounting information is used by various levels of management personnel. External users include actual and potential stockholders and creditors and their professional advisers, employees and their unions, customers, suppliers, governmental agencies, and the public at large.

The basic end products of the financial accounting process are the statement of financial position, the earnings statement, the statement of changes in financial position, and the statement of retained earnings.

Most of the information reported in these statements is found originally in the transactions entered into by an entity. These transactions are analyzed and their effects recorded as increases or decreases in assets, liabilities, stockholders' equity, revenues, and expenses—the five basic elements of accounting. The framework for analysis is the basic equation of Assets = Equities expanded to Assets = Liabilities + Stockholders' Equity + Revenues − Expenses.

In providing useful information, accountants rely upon some assumptions including those relating to the entity, transaction, duality, money measurement, cost, periodicity, and continuity.

You have completed the programmed portion of Chapter 1. As the first part of your review, read the Glossary which follows and study the definitions of the new terms introduced in the chapter. Then go to the Student Review Quiz beginning on page 34 as a self-administered test of your understanding of the material in the chapter.

Glossary *chapter* 1

Accounting – a systematic process of measuring and reporting to various users relevant financial information for decision making regarding the economic activity of an organization or unit. *Financial accounting* relates to the process of supplying financial information to parties external to the reporting entity. *Managerial accounting* relates to the process of supplying financial information for internal management use. As a field of employment, accounting is usually divided into *public accounting,* where accounting and related services are offered to the general public for a fee; *private (or industrial) accounting,* where the accountant performs services for one business employer; and *governmental accounting,* where the accountant is employed by and renders services for a governmental agency.

Accounting equation – basically, Assets = Equities; in slightly expanded form for a corporation, Assets = Liabilities + Stockholders' Equity.

Accounting Principles Board – an organization created by the AICPA and empowered to speak for it on matters of accounting principle; replaced by the Financial Accounting Standards Board.

Accounts payable – amounts owed to creditors for items or services purchased from them.

Accounts receivable – amounts owed to a concern by its customers.

American Accounting Association – a professional organization of accountants many of whom are college or university instructors of accounting.

American Institute of Certified Public Accountants – a professional organization of certified public accountants, most of whom are in public accounting practice.

Annual report – a pamphlet or document of varying length containing financial and other information about and distributed annually by a company to its stockholders.

Assets – roughly equatable to things of value or economic resources; things possessing service potential or utility to their owner that can be measured and expressed in money terms.

Auditing – that branch of the accounting profession that is concerned with checking, reviewing, testing, and verifying the accounting work of others, generally with the objective of expressing a formal opinion on the fairness of the resulting information.

Auditor's opinion or report – the formal written statement by a public accountant (usually a CPA) attesting to the fairness of the information contained in a set of financial statements; for an example, see the Appendix to Chapter 14.

Capital stock – the title given to an equity account showing the investment in a business corporation by its stockholders.

Certified public accountant – an accountant who has been awarded a certificate and granted the right to be called a certified public accountant as a result of having passed a special examination and having met other requirements regarding such things as experience and education. In some states, the CPA certificate is a license to practice as a CPA; in others, an additional license must be obtained.

Continuity (going concern) – the assumption by the accountant that unless specific evidence exists to the contrary, a business firm will continue to operate into the indefinite future.

Corporation – a legal form of organization often adopted by businesses; a business which is owned by many stockholders and frequently directed by hired managers.

Cost – the sacrifice made or the resources given up to acquire some desired thing; the basis of valuation of the bulk of the assets of a business.

Dividends – the means by which stockholders share in the earnings of a corporation.

Duality – the assumption by the accountant that every transaction has a dual or two-sided effect upon the party or parties engaging in it.

Earnings statement – a formal array or summary of the revenues and expenses of an organization for a specified period of time.

Entity – a unit that is deemed to have an existence separate and apart from its owners, creditors, employees, and other interested parties and for which an accounting is undertaken.

33

Equities – broadly speaking, all claims to or interests in assets.

Expenses – the sacrifice made, usually measured in terms of the cost of the assets surrendered or consumed, to generate revenues.

Financial Accounting Standards Board (FASB) – the highest ranking nongovernmental authority on the development of accounting standards or principles.

Liabilities – debts or obligations that usually possess a known or determinable amount, maturity date, and party to whom payment is to be made.

Money measurement – expression of a property of an object in terms of a number of units of a standard monetary medium, such as the dollar.

Net earnings – the amount by which the revenues of a period exceed the expenses of the same period.

Net loss – the amount by which the expenses of a period exceed the revenues of the same period.

Note payable – a written promise to pay to another party a definite sum of money at a certain or determinable date, usually with interest at a specified rate.

Periodicity – the assumption that the life of an entity can be divided into periods of time and that useful information can be provided as to the activities of the entity for those periods.

Retained earnings – accumulated net earnings less dividend distributions to stockholders.

Revenues – the flow of goods or services from an enterprise to its customers, usually measured by the flow of assets received.

Statement of changes in financial position – a formal statement summarizing a firm's investing and financing activities for a period of time.

Statement of financial position – a formal statement or array of the assets, liabilities, and owners' equity of an entity as of a specific date; often called a balance sheet.

Statement of retained earnings – a formal statement showing the items causing changes in retained earnings during a stated period of time.

Transactions – recordable happenings or events (usually exchanges) that affect the assets, liabilities, owners' equity, revenues, or expenses of an entity.

U.S. Securities and Exchange Commission – a governmental agency created by the Congress to administer certain acts and having the authority to prescribe the accounting and reporting practices of firms required to file financial statements with it.

Continue with the Student Review Quiz below as a self-administered test of your understanding of the material presented in the chapter.

Student review quiz *chapter* 1

To develop a permanent record of your responses, you may write them on the answer sheet provided in the *Work Papers* or on a separate sheet of paper.

1   If a company has stockholders' equity of $8,900 –
a   A total of $8,900 in capital stock was issued by the company.
b   The business has total assets of $8,900.
c   Net earnings for the year were $8,900.
d   Revenue less expenses equal $8,900.
e   Total business assets less total liabilities equal $8,900.

2   Company Z has assets of $35,000, no liabilities, and stockholders' equity of $35,000. It buys delivery equipment on credit for $4,000. What effect would this transaction have on these amounts?
a   Both assets and stockholders' equity decrease $4,000.
b   Assets stay the same, and stockholders' equity increases $4,000.
c   Both assets and liabilities increase $4,000.
d   Stockholders' equity decreases $4,000, and liabilities increase $4,000.
e   Both assets and stockholders' equity increase $4,000.

3   Revenue is –
a   The flow of products or services provided to customers.
b   Cash received from customers.
c   The difference between the selling price of a product or service and the cost of providing such product or service.
d   A decrease in stockholders' equity.
e   The same as net earnings.

4 The Acme Furniture Company recorded on the last day of the month the $400 of advertising which appeared in the local paper during the month. This advertising was contracted for on an annual basis, with payment required for each month's advertising by the tenth of the following month. Which statement describes the effect of this entry?

a Both assets and liabilities increased by $400.

b Liabilities increased by $400, and stockholders' equity decreased by $400.

c Liabilities decreased by $400, and stockholders' equity increased by $400.

d Liabilities decreased by $400, and assets increased by $400.

e None of the above.

5 Company J collected $800 of its $1,000 of accounts receivable. How is the statement of financial position affected?

a Total assets are decreased, but liabilities and stockholders' equity remain the same.

b Cash increases $800, and stockholders' equity increases $800 because revenue was received.

c There is no change in total assets, liabilities, or stockholders' equity.

d Accounts receivable are decreased $800, and stockholders' equity is decreased $800.

e There is no change in any of the statement of financial position items.

6 Which of the following statements is *incorrect?*

a The earnings statement summarizes revenue and expense transactions for a period of operation between two statement of financial position dates.

b The heading of the earnings statement should clearly indicate the period of operation which the statement covers.

c The earnings statement shows as a final item the net earnings or net loss for the period.

d An earnings statement shows how much of the net earnings or net loss was derived from operations and how much was derived from other sources.

e The earnings statement shows the changes in assets and liabilities which occurred during the period of operation covered by the statement.

7 Given two statements of financial position of the A Company dated December 31, 1978, and December 31, 1979, the retained earnings on the statement dated December 31, 1979—

a Shows the amount of 1979 net earnings less dividends declared.

b Includes the net earnings or net loss for 1979.

c Is equal to the net earnings for 1979.

d Shows the change in total assets in 1979.

e Does none of the above.

8 Which of the following appear on more than one of the three financial statements (statement of financial position, earnings statement, and statement of retained earnings)?

a Cash.

b Net earnings.

c Notes payable.

d Retained earnings.

e All of the above.

f Only (b) and (d).

9 With which of the following is accounting not likely to be concerned?

a Long-range financial planning.

b Cost studies of managerial effectiveness.

c Executive recruitment.

d Design of management information systems.

e Income tax planning.

10 Which of the following is generally the sole province of the CPA?

a Preparation of income tax returns.

b Providing management advisory services.

c Attesting to the fairness of published financial information.

d Auditing.

e Preparation of budgets.

11 Generally, the decision-making process involves all of the following except—

a Determination of alternative courses of action.

b Prediction of the consequence of each alternative course of action.

c Selection of preferred consequence.

d Reporting on actual outcome of the decision.

e Recognition or formulation of the problem.

12 Assets are (choose the best answer) —
a Things of value owned.
b Economic resources owned.
c Desired because of the future benefits they are expected to yield.
d Generally recorded and reported at cost.
e All of the above.

13 As contrasted with financial accounting information, management accounting information is —
a Accumulated only if it is believed to be worth more than it costs.
b Forward looking rather than historical in nature.
c Used internally rather than released to outsiders.
d Likely to be related to a part rather than the whole of an entity.
e All of the above.

14 Financial accounting information is likely to be used for all of the following types of decisions except —
a Deciding whether to add a new product line.
b Deciding whether dividends should be increased.
c Deciding whether an entity should be allowed to purchase goods on a credit basis.
d Appraising the ability of an entity to pay its debts when they mature.
e Determining whether the net earnings for the last year were satisfactory.

15 The statement of changes in financial position (choose the *false* statement) —
a Shows what caused the change in retained earnings from the end of one period to the end of the following period.
b May show cash inflows and outflows for a period of time.
c Is the statement in which the payment of a dividend would be reported.
d Would show the amount of cash received for the capital stock issued for cash.
e Is the statement that would explain why the balance in the equipment account changed.

Now compare your answers with the correct answers and explanations on page 711–12.

Questions *chapter* 1

1 Define accounting. What does the term "relevant" mean when speaking of accounting information? Give an example of relevant information.

2 Accounting has often been called the "language of business." In what respects would you agree with this designation? How might it be argued that it is deficient?

3 What is the relationship between accounting as an information system and economic resources?

4 Define asset, liability, and owners' equity.

5 How do liabilities and stockholders' equity differ? In what respects are they similar?

6 How do accounts payable and notes payable differ? How are they similar?

7 Define revenue. How is revenue measured?

8 Define expense. How is expense measured?

9 How does accounting information usually enter into the decision-making process?

10 Name four organizations that have played or are playing an important role in the development of accounting standards. Describe each briefly.

11 What is a CPA? What are some of the services usually provided by a CPA?

12 What is the role of the accountant in private industry? What are some of the services provided by the industrial accountant?

13 What is a statement of financial position? This statement generally seeks to provide information relative to what aspect of a business?

14 What is an earnings statement? This statement generally provides information on what aspect of a business?

15 What information does a statement of changes in financial position provide? Why must a separate statement for such information be provided? Explain or illustrate.

16 What information does the statement of retained earnings provide?

17 What is a transaction? What use does the accountant make of transactions? Why?

18 What is the accounting equation? Why must it always balance?

19 Give an example from your personal life that you believe illustrates your use of accounting information in reaching a decision.

20 What is the accounting entity assumption? Why is it needed?

21 What is the duality assumption of accounting? Why is it needed?

22 You are a young married person who three years ago purchased a home by borrowing $20,000 on a mortgage. You recently received an inheritance of $25,000 and are considering paying off the mortgage. What types of financial information would you seek in helping you arrive at a decision?

23 You have been elected to the board of deacons of your church. At the first meeting you attend, mention is made of building a new church. What accounting information would the board need in deciding whether or not to go ahead?

Exercises *chapter* 1

1 Give examples of transactions that would have the following effects upon the elements in a firm's accounting system:
a Increase cash; decrease some other asset.
b Decrease cash; increase some other asset.
c Increase an asset; increase a liability.
d Increase an expense; decrease an asset.
e Increase an asset other than cash; increase revenue.
f Decrease an asset; decrease a liability.

2 Assume that retained earnings increased by $24,000 from June 30, 1978, to June 30, 1979. A cash dividend of $2,000 was declared and paid during the year.
a Compute the net earnings for the year.

b Assume expenses for the year were $60,000. Compute the revenue for the year.

3 On December 31, 1978, M Company had assets of $360,000, liabilities of $260,000, and capital stock of $80,000. During 1979 it earned revenues of $120,000 and incurred expenses of $90,000. Dividends declared and paid amounted to $8,000.
a Compute the company's retained earnings amount on December 31, 1978.
b Compute the company's retained earnings amount on December 31, 1979.

4 A Company earned revenues of $100,000 by rendering services on account to its customers. Of the $100,000, $88,000 was collected. Expenses incurred during the period amounted to $60,000 — $40,000 on account, the remainder for cash. Of the $40,000, $33,000 had been paid by year-end. A cash dividend of $3,000 was paid.
Compute the net cash inflow from operations, assuming above data are for the first year of operation.

5 For each of the happenings below, determine whether or not it has an effect upon the basic elements of accounting. For those that do, present an analysis of the transaction showing clearly its two sides or dual nature.
a Purchased some supplies for cash, $1,000. The supplies will be used next year.
b Purchased a truck for $10,000, payment to be made next month.
c Paid $200 cash for the current month's utilities.
d Paid for the truck purchased in (b).
e Employed Don Kettler as a salesperson at $2,000 per month. He is to start work next week.
f Signed an agreement with a bank in which the bank agreed to lend the company up to $200,000 any time within the next two years.

6 Which of the following transactions results in an increase in an expense? Why?
a Cash of $20,000 is paid to employees for services received during the month.
b Cash of $1,000 paid to a supplier in

settlement of a promise to pay given when some advertising supplies were purchased.

c Paid $10,000 of principal plus $400 of interest on a note payable.

d Paid $50 cash as a refundable deposit when an additional telephone was installed.

7 At the start of a year a company had liabilities of $36,000 and capital stock of $100,000. At the end of the year retained earnings amounted to $90,000. Net earnings for the year were $30,000, and $10,000 of dividends were declared and paid. Compute retained earnings and total assets at the beginning of the year.

8 Selected data for the York Company for the year 1979 are as follows (including all earnings statement data):

Revenue from services rendered on account	$ 55,000
Revenue from services rendered for cash	15,000
Cash collected from customers on account	42,000
Stockholders' equity, 1/1/79	80,000
Expenses incurred on account	30,000
Expenses incurred for cash	20,000
Dividends declared and paid	5,000
Capital stock issued for cash	10,000
Stockholders' equity, 12/31/79	105,000

a Compute net earnings for 1979 using an earnings statement approach.

b Compute net earnings for 1979 by analyzing the changes in stockholders' equity between January 1 and December 31, 1979.

Problems, Series A *chapter* 1

1–1–A

Maxwell Company completed the following transactions in September 1979:

Sept. 1 The company is organized and receives $20,000 cash from the issuance of capital stock.

5 The company buys equipment for cash at a cost of $5,400.

7 The company performs services for customers who agree to pay $2,000 in one week.

14 The company receives the $2,000 from the transaction of September 7.

20 Equipment which costs $800 is acquired today; payment is postponed until September 28.

28 $600 is paid on the liability incurred on September 20.

30 Employee services for the month, $700, are paid.

30 Placed an order for new equipment advertised at $5,000.

Required:

Prepare a summary of transactions (see Illustration 1.5, page 29) for the company for the above transactions.

– 1–2–A

The Hanson Company completed the following transactions in June 1979:

June 1 The company is organized and receives $40,000 cash from the issuance of capital stock.

4 The company pays $32,000 cash for equipment.

7 The company borrows $6,000 cash from its bank on a note.

9 Cash received for services performed to date is $3,000.

12 Costs of operating the business so far this month are paid in cash, $2,100.

18 Services performed for customers who agree to pay within a month amount to $3,600.

25 The company repays $2,710 of its loan from the bank, including $10 of interest.

30 Costs of operating the business from June 13 to date are $2,550 and are paid in cash.

30 An order is received from a customer for services to be performed tomorrow, which will be billed at $2,000.

Required:

a Prepare a summary of transactions (see Illustration 1.5, page 29). Include money columns for Cash, Accounts Receivable, Equipment, Notes Payable, Capital Stock, and Retained Earnings.

b Prepare a statement of financial position as of June 30, 1979.

1-3-A

Required:

Use the data in Problem 1-2-A and prepare a statement of changes in financial position that shows cash inflows and cash outflows.

1-4-A

Required:

From the following selected transaction data for the Haner Company, prepare an earnings statement for the month of May 1979:

May   1   Paid May rent on the parking structure, $10,000.
      8   Cash received for eight days' parking services, $4,840.
    15   Cash received for week's parking services, $6,040.
    16   Paid employee wages for the first half of May, $2,400.
    17   Received cash for shares of capital stock issued, $5,000.
    19   Paid advertising expenses for May, $800.
    22   Cash received for week's parking services, $7,920.
    31   Paid wages for last half of May, $3,000.
    31   Cash received for nine days' parking services, $7,040.
    31   Purchased motorized sweeper to clean parking structure, $6,000 cash.
    31   Paid June rent on the parking structure, $10,000.

1-5-A

Following are summarized transaction data for the Lopez Company for the year ending June 30, 1979:

Rent revenue from building owned	$200,000
Interest revenue from bonds owned	36,000
Dividend revenue from stocks owned	28,000
Interest revenue from bank savings accounts	1,800
Building repairs	8,200
Building cleaning, labor cost	9,100
Property taxes on the building	10,300
Insurance on the building	3,500
Commissions paid to rental agent	15,000
Legal fees (for preparation of tenant leases)	3,600
Heating	8,400
Electricity	15,100
Cleaning supplies on hand	3,000
Cost of new awnings installed	5,000

Of the $200,000 of rent revenue above, $10,000 was not collected in cash until July 5, 1979.

Required:

Prepare an earnings statement for the year ended June 30, 1979.

1-6-A

The following data are for the Park-in Corporation whose October 1, 1979, statement of financial position is:

Cash	$68,000	Accounts payable	$18,000
Accounts receivable	6,000	Capital stock	44,000
		Retained earnings	12,000
	$74,000		$74,000

Transactions:

Oct. 1 The accounts payable owed as of October 1 ($18,000) are paid.

7 The company receives cash of $1,400 for parking by daily customers during the week.

10 The company collects $4,800 of the accounts receivable in the statement of financial position at October 1.

14 Cash receipts for the week from daily customers are $2,200.

15 Parking revenue earned but not yet collected from fleet customers, $1,000.

16 The company pays wages of $800 for the period October 1-15.

19 The company pays advertising expenses of $400 for October.

21 Cash receipts for the week from daily customers are $2,400.

24 The company incurred sundry expenses of $280 which will be due November 10.

31 Cash receipts for the last ten days of the month from daily customers are $2,800.

31 The company pays wages of $1,000 for the period October 16-31.

31 Billings to monthly customers total $7,200 for October.

31 The company pays rent for the premises for October, $6,400.

Required:

a Prepare a summary of transactions (see Illustration 1.5, page 29) using column headings as given in the above statement of financial position.

b Prepare an earnings statement for October 1979.

c Prepare a statement of retained earnings for October 1979.

d Prepare a statement of financial position as of October 31, 1979.

1-7-A

Given below are comparative statements of financial position and the earnings statement of the Oakland Company:

OAKLAND COMPANY
Statement of Financial Position

	May 31, 1979	June 30, 1979
Assets		
Current Assets:		
Cash	$10,000	$11,000
Accounts receivable	-0-	4,000
Supplies	6,000	2,000
Total Assets	$16,000	$17,000

41

	May 31, 1979	June 30, 1979
Liabilities and Stockholders' Equity		
Liabilities	$ 4,000	$ 2,000
Capital stock	10,000	10,000
Retained earnings	2,000	5,000
Total Liabilities and Stockholders' Equity	$16,000	$17,000

OAKLAND COMPANY
Earnings Statement
For the Month Ended June 30, 1979

Revenue from services rendered		$16,000
Expenses:		
Salaries	$8,000	
Supplies used	4,000	12,000
Net Earnings		$ 4,000

A cash dividend of $1,000 was declared and paid in June.

Required:

State the probable causes of the changes in each of the statement of financial position accounts from May 31 to June 30, 1979.

Problems, Series B *chapter* 1

1–1–B

The Desmond Company, which provides financial advisory services, engaged in the following transactions during the month of May:

May 1 Received $50,000 cash for shares of capital stock issued upon organization of the company.

2 The company borrows $8,000 cash from the bank on a note.

7 The company buys $45,600 of computer equipment for cash.

11 Cash received for services performed to date is $3,800.

14 Services performed for customers who agree to pay within a month are $2,500.

15 Employee services received in operating the business to date are paid in cash, $3,300.

19 The company pays $3,500 on the note to the bank.

31 Interest paid to the bank for May is $35.

31 Customers of May 14 pay $800 of the amount they owe the company.

31 An order is received from a customer for services to be rendered next week which will be billed at $2,000.

Required:

Prepare a summary of the above transactions (see Illustration 1.5, page 29). Use money columns headed Cash, Accounts Receivable, Equipment, Notes Payable, Capital Stock, and Retained Earnings. Determine balances after each transaction to show that the basic equation balances.

1–2–B

The Veblenn Company engaged in the following transactions in April:

Apr. 1 The company is organized and receives $20,000 cash from the owners in exchange for capital stock issued.
4 The company buys equipment for cash, $10,600.
9 The company buys additional equipment which costs $950 and agrees to pay for it in 30 days.
15 Cash received for services performed to date is $400.
16 Amounts due from customers for services performed total $550.
30 Of the receivables (see April 16), $320 are collected in cash.
30 Various costs of operating the business during the month of $650 are paid in cash.
30 An order is placed for equipment advertised at $3,000.

Required:

a Prepare a summary of transactions (see Illustration 1.5, page 29). Use money columns headed Cash, Accounts Receivable, Equipment, Accounts Payable, Capital Stock, and Retained Earnings.
b Prepare a statement of financial position as of April 30.

1–3–B

Use the data in Problem 1–1–B above. Assume further that a cash dividend of $500 was declared and paid on May 31.

Required:

Prepare a statement of changes in financial position for the month of May that shows cash inflows and cash outflows.

1–4–B

Following are the transactions for August 1979 of Cinema X, a theater:

Aug. 2 Paid current month's rent of building, $8,000.
7 Cash ticket revenue for the week, $4,800.
14 Cash ticket revenue for the week, $5,600.
15 Paid cash dividend, $1,000.
21 Cash ticket revenue for the week, $3,200.
24 Paid month's advertising bill, $3,800.
27 Sundry expenses paid, $1,400.
31 Paid rental on films shown during month, $10,000.
31 Received $12,400 cash from operators of concessions for operating in theater during August.
31 Cash ticket revenue for August 22–31, $8,400.

Aug. 31 Paid $1,500 cash to guarantee receipt of a special film to be shown in September.

31 Paid payroll for the month, $13,200.

Required:

Prepare an earnings statement for August 1979.

1–5–B

Analysis of the transactions of the Mott Drive-In Theatre for the month of June 1979 discloses the following:

Ticket revenue	$26,600
Rent of premises and equipment	5,000
Film rental paid	8,900
Receipts from concessionaires (percentage basis)	5,000
Advertising expense	3,100
Wages and salaries	7,800
Utilities expense	2,350

Statement of financial position figures at June 30 include the following:

Cash	$40,000
Franchise to show movies in area	8,000
Accounts payable	10,400
Capital stock	19,000
Retained earnings, June 1, 1979	14,150

Required:

a Prepare an earnings statement for the month of June 1979.

b Prepare a statement of retained earnings for the month of June 1979.

c Prepare a statement of financial position at June 30, 1979.

1–6–B

MASON SERVICE COMPANY
Statement of Financial Position
April 30, 1979

Assets			*Liabilities and Stockholders' Equity*		
Current Assets:			Current Liabilities:		
Cash	$14,000		Accounts payable		$ 16,000
Accounts receivable	20,000	$ 34,000	Stockholders' Equity:		
			Capital stock	$100,000	
Land		150,000	Retained earnings	68,000	168,000
			Total Liabilities and Stock-		
Total Assets		$184,000	holders' Equity		$184,000

Summarized, the activities for the month of May 1979 are as follows:

a. Issued additional capital stock for cash, $30,000.

b. Collected $20,000 on accounts receivable.

c. Paid $16,000 on accounts payable.

44 d. Sold land costing $50,000 for $75,000 cash.

e. Services rendered to customers: for cash, $40,000; and on account, $30,000.

f. Employee services and other operating costs incurred: for cash, $15,000; and on account, $40,000.

g. Paid dividends of $4,000.

h. Paid building rent for year beginning on June 1, 1979, $24,000.

i. Placed an order for new equipment expected to cost $80,000.

Required:

a Prepare an earnings statement for the month of May 1979.

b Prepare a statement of retained earnings for the month of May 1979.

c Prepare a statement of financial position as of May 31, 1979. (Note: You may wish to prepare, at least in rough form, a summary of transactions; see Illustration 1.5, page 29.)

1–7–B

Given below are the comparative statements of financial position and the earnings statement of the Boston Company:

BOSTON COMPANY
Statement of Financial Position

	April 30, 1979	May 31, 1979
Assets		
Current Assets:		
Cash	$16,000	$18,000
Accounts receivable	24,000	30,000
Prepaid rent	6,000	4,000
Total Assets	$46,000	$52,000
Liabilities and Stockholders' Equity		
Liabilities	$12,000	$10,000
Capital stock	30,000	30,000
Retained earnings	4,000	12,000
Total Liabilities and Stockholders' Equity	$46,000	$52,000

BOSTON COMPANY
Earnings Statement
For the Month Ended May 31, 1979

Revenues from services rendered		$30,000
Expenses:		
Salaries and wages	$20,000	
Rent	2,000	22,000
Net Earnings		$ 8,000

All revenues earned are on account. The liabilities are for unpaid salaries and wages.

Required:

a State the probable cause(s) of the change in each of the statement of financial position accounts from April 30 to May 31, 1979.

b Compute the cash flow generated by operations for the month of May.

2

The basic financial accounting system

Learning objectives

To achieve a working knowledge of the basic design of an accounting system and of the steps taken in accumulating accounting information, this chapter introduces:

1. The account as the basic classificational category and storage unit for information in the accounting system.

2. The technical accounting terms of debit and credit and how the effects of business transactions must first be expressed in these terms before they can be entered into the accounting system.

3. The journal as the original record in which the effects of a business transaction are recorded in the accounting system.

4. The process of journalizing a transaction and then posting the journal entries to the accounts in the accounting system.

5. The use of a trial balance as a partial means of testing the accuracy of the operation of the accounting system.

6. The adjustments required to bring the accounts up to date prior to the preparation of financial statements.

In Chapter 1 the effects of transactions were shown as increases or decreases in the elements in the basic accounting equation. This approach was adopted solely as a means of affording easy understanding of some basic relationships. It is far too cumbersome to be used in actual practice, since even a small business enters into a huge number of transactions every week, month, or year.

The purpose of this chapter is to introduce the basic components of the accounting system—the ledger (book) of accounts and the journal—and to illustrate their use in the information-gathering process. Here again the expectation is that knowledge of the underlying process will yield greater understanding of the end products—the financial statements.

The accounting system

The account

Because a business may engage in thousands of transactions, the data in these transactions must be classified and summarized before they become useful information. Making the accountant's task somewhat easier is the fact that most business transactions are repetitive in nature and can be classified into groups having common characteristics. For example, there may be thousands of receipts or payments of cash. As a result, a part of every transaction affecting cash will be recorded and summarized in an account. An account will be established whenever the data to be recorded in it are believed to be useful information to some party having a valid interest in the business. Thus, every business will have a Cash account in its accounting system simply because knowledge of the amount of cash owned is useful information.

An account may take on a variety of forms, from a printed format in which entries are written by hand to an invisible encoding on a piece of magnetic tape. Every account format must provide for increases and decreases in the item for which the account was established. The account balance, the difference between the increases and decreases, may then be determined.

The number of accounts in a given accounting system will depend upon the information needs of those interested in the business. The primary requirement is that the account provide useful information. Thus, one account may be established for cash rather than separate accounts for cash in the form of coins, cash in the form of currency, and cash in the form of deposits in banks, simply because the amount of cash is useful information while the form of cash is not.

A trend exists, especially in computer-based accounting systems, toward establishing larger numbers of accounts. The primary reason for this is that it is far easier to sum the balances in a number of accounts into a useful total than it is to subdivide a large balance into smaller bits of useful information. In fact, it may be impossible to subdivide a balance without analyzing again every item affecting it.

Indicate whether each of the following statements is true or false. (You may wish to respond on the answer sheet provided in the *Work Papers* or on a separate sheet of paper so that you will have a permanent record of your responses.)

1. An account is a means of classifying the effects of transactions upon an entity.
2. The number of accounts established in the accounting systems of different entities is likely to differ.
3. In designing an accounting system the guiding principle should be: the fewer the accounts, the better.
4. In a large corporation, the accounting system is likely to contain more accounts than are reported in its financial statements.

Check your responses in Answer Frame 1² on page 50.

Frame 2² ————————————————————

The T-account

The way an account functions is shown by use of a T-account. It is used in this text for illustrative purposes only (it is not a replica of a form of account actually used) and derives its name from its resemblance to the letter T. The name of the item accounted for (such as cash) is written across the top of the T. Increases are recorded on one side and decreases on the other side of the vertical line of the T.

Recording changes in assets and equities. Increases in assets are recorded on the left side of the account, decreases on the right side. For reasons to be explained later, the process is reversed for equity in the form of capital stock, for which increases are recorded on the right side. Thus, a corporation would record the receipt of $10,000 for shares of its capital stock as follows (the figure in parentheses is used to tie the two sides of the transaction together):

Cash		Capital Stock	
(1) 10,000			(1) 10,000

The transaction involves an increase in the asset, cash, which is recorded on the left side of the Cash account, and an increase in stockholders' equity in the form of capital stock, which is recorded on the right side of the Capital Stock account.

Because liabilities are a subset of equities, changes in them are recorded in the same manner as for equities—increases on the right side, decreases on the left. Note that the asset amounts are shown on the left

2²
continued

side of the account and the left side of the statement of financial position; equity (liabilities and stockholders' equity) amounts are shown on the right side of the account and the right side of the statement of financial position. But for easy recollection of these rules, all that one need remember is that increases in assets are recorded on the left side of the account and increases in equities are recorded on the right side of the account.

Indicate whether each of the following is a correct or incorrect recording of the transaction described.

1. The purchase of equipment for cash would involve an entry on the left side of the Equipment account and on the right side of the Cash account.
2. The payment of a liability established to record the purchase of a new truck would involve an entry on the right side of the Cash account and the left side of the Automotive Equipment account.
3. The borrowing of money by giving a note would involve an entry on the left side of the Cash account and the right side of the Notes Payable account.
4. The payment of an amount owed a supplier of merchandise would involve an entry on the right side of the Cash account and on the left side of the Accounts Payable account.

Check your responses in Answer Frame 2² on page 52.

Frame 3²

Recording changes in expenses and revenues. To understand the logic behind the recording of changes in expense and revenue accounts recall that all expenses and revenues could be recorded directly in Retained Earnings. Thus, (2) the receipt of $1,000 of cash from customers for services rendered and (3) the payment of $600 of cash to employees as wages could be recorded as follows:

Cash				Retained Earnings		
(2)	1,000	(3)	600	(3)	600	(2)	1,000

But since their amounts are apt to be significant information, separate accounts are maintained for the revenues and expenses. The recording rules for these are:

1. Since revenues increase stockholders' equity (and increases in stockholders' equity are recorded on the right side), it follows that increases in revenues should be recorded on the right side, decreases on the left.
2. Similarly, since expenses decrease stockholders' equity (and decreases in stockholders' equity are recorded on the left side), it follows that increases in expenses are recorded on the left, decreases on the right.

Following these rules, the service revenue and the wages would be recorded in the following manner:

Cash				Service Revenue		
(2)	1,000	(3)	600			(2)	1,000

Wages Expense		
(3)	600	

Debits and credits. The accountant uses the term *debit* in lieu of saying "place an entry on the left side of the account" and *credit* for "place an entry on the right side of an account." Debit (abbreviated Dr.) means simply left side; credit (abbreviated Cr.), right side.

Note that since assets and expenses are increased by debits, these accounts normally have debit (or left side) balances. Conversely, liability, stockholders' equity, and revenue accounts are increased by credits and normally have credit (or right side) balances.

The balance of any account is obtained by summing the debits to the account, summing the credits to the account, and subtracting the smaller sum from the larger. If the sum of the debits exceeds the sum of the credits, the account has a debit balance. For example, the Cash account has a debit balance of $4,000, computed as total debits of $14,000 less total credits of $10,000, in the following T-account:

—————————————————————————————————

1. Correct. The equipment is an asset, and increases in assets are recorded on the left side of an asset account. Cash was given up, and decreases in the asset cash are recorded on the right side of the Cash account.
2. Incorrect. The entry on the right side of the Cash account is correct. But an entry must be made on the left side of the liability account, Accounts Payable, to record the reduction in the liability brought about by the cash payment. This liability was previously increased when the purchase of the truck on a credit basis was entered.
3. Correct. This is the way such a transaction would be recorded.
4. Correct. This is the way such a transaction would be recorded and is the way the transaction described in 2 above should be recorded.

If you missed any of the above questions, you should read Frame 2² again before continuing in Frame 3² on page 51.

3²

continued

Cash			
(1)	5,000	(2)	2,000
(3)	9,000	(4)	8,000

Similarly, the Accounts Payable account has a credit balance of $3,000:

Accounts Payable			
(7)	10,000	(5)	7,000
		(6)	6,000

For the most part, the amounts entered into the accounts are found in the transactions entered into by the business. Business transactions are first analyzed to determine the effects (increase or decrease) that they have upon the assets, liabilities, stockholders' equity, revenues, or expenses of the business. Then these increases or decreases are translated into debits and credits. For example, an increase in an asset is recorded as a debit in the proper asset account. When an asset account is debited, depending upon the transaction, there may be any of five credits:

1. Another asset account may be credited, that is, decreased.
2. A liability account may be credited, that is, increased.
3. A stockholders' equity account may be credited, that is, increased.
4. A revenue account may be credited, that is, increased.
5. An expense account may be credited, that is, decreased.

This double-entry procedure keeps the accounting equation in balance. Every transaction can be analyzed similarly into debits and credits.

The rules of debit and credit may be presented in account form as follows:

Debits	Credits
1. Increase assets.	1. Decrease assets.
2. Decrease liabilities.	2. Increase liabilities.
3. Decrease stockholders' equity.	3. Increase stockholders' equity.
4. Decrease revenues.	4. Increase revenues.
5. Increase expenses.	5. Decrease expenses.

These rules may also be summarized as shown below. Note the treatment of expense accounts as if they were merely subsets of the debit side of the Retained Earnings account. And remember that increases in expenses do tend to reduce what would otherwise be a larger growth in Retained Earnings; and if expenses are reduced, Retained Earnings will increase. The exact reverse holds true for revenues.

Assets = *Liabilities* + *Stockholders' Equity*

An Asset Account		A Liability Account		A Stockholders' Equity Account	
Debit	Credit	Debit	Credit	Debit	Credit
+ In-creases	− De-creases	− De-creases	+ In-creases	− Decreases	+ Increases

Expense Accounts		Revenue Accounts	
Debit	Credit	Debit	Credit
+ In-creases	− De-creases	− De-creases	+ In-creases

Indicate whether each of the following could be a correct or incorrect analysis of a transaction.
1. Plus asset, plus expense.
2. Minus asset, minus liability.
3. Plus expense, plus liability.
4. Plus asset, minus asset.

Check your responses in Answer Frame 3² on page 54.

Frame 4²

The ledger

Accounts are classified into two general groups: (1) the statement of financial position accounts (assets, liabilities, and stockholders' equity) and (2) the earnings statement accounts (revenues and expenses). Whether kept in a bound volume, handwritten in loose-leaf form, or magnetically encoded on plastic tape, the accounts are collectively referred to as the ledger.

1. Incorrect. When analyzed in terms of debit and credit, this statement yields debit asset, debit expense, which is obviously incorrect since there is no credit in the analysis.
2. Correct. A transaction of this type would be the cash payment of a debt, which in debit-credit terminology would be debit liability, credit asset.
3. Correct. A transaction of this type would be the receipt of a bill or invoice for advertising services already received. This would call for a debit (increase) in an expense account and a credit (increase) in a liability account.
4. Correct. Any of a wide variety of cash purchases of assets would yield this type of analysis. Such transactions would call for a debit (increase) in one asset account and a credit (decrease) in another—cash.

If you missed any of the above questions, you should read Frame 3² again before proceeding to Frame 4² on page 53.

4²
continued

The list of the names of the accounts is known as the *chart of accounts*. Each account typically has an identification number as well as a name. For example, assets might be numbered from 100–199, liabilities from 200–299, stockholders' equity items from 300–399, revenues from 400–499, and expenses from 500–599. The accounts would then be arranged in numerical sequence in the ledger. The use of account numbers helps to identify and locate accounts when recording data.

Having completed this introduction to accounts and the recording process, attention is now directed to the journal and to journal entries, as the means whereby data are entered into an accounting system.

The journal

Every business transaction, under double-entry accounting, has a dual effect on the accounts of the business entity. And with the rare exception of transactions such as an exchange of land for land, every recorded business transaction will affect at least two ledger accounts. Since each ledger account shows only the increases and decreases in the item for which it was established, the entire effects of a single business transaction will not appear in any one account. For example, the Cash account contains only data on changes in cash and does not show the exact accounts credited for receipts of cash or the exact accounts debited for cash disbursements.

Therefore, if transactions are recorded directly in the accounts, it is difficult to ascertain the entire effects of any transaction upon an entity by looking at the accounts. To remedy this deficiency, the accountant employs a book or a record known as a journal. A journal contains a chronological record of the transactions of a business. Because each transaction is initially recorded in a journal, a journal is called a book of *original entry*. Here every business transaction is

Illustration 2.1

GENERAL JOURNAL					*Page 1*
Date		Accounts and Explanation	L.F.	Debit	Credit
1979 Jan.	1	Cash	100	5,000	
		Capital Stock	300		5,000
		Capital stock issued for cash.			
	5	Office Equipment..............................	110	1,200	
		Accounts Payable..........................	201		1,200
		Equipment purchased for the office on account.			

analyzed for its effects upon the entity. These effects are expressed in terms of debit and credit – the inputs of the accounting system.

The general journal. The simplest form of journal, the general journal, is illustrated and discussed in this chapter. Other forms or types of journals are discussed in Appendix 4A. As shown in Illustration 2.1, a general journal contains columns for:

1. The date.
2. The name of the account to be debited and the name of the account to be credited, shown on the following line and indented to the right. (Any necessary explanation of a transaction appears below the transaction, indented halfway between the debit and credit entry.)
3. The Ledger Folio (L.F.) column; this will be explained in the section below headed "Cross-indexing."
4. The debit column, in which the money amount of the debit is placed on the same line as the name of the account debited.
5. The credit column, in which the money amount of the credit is placed on the same line as the name of the account credited.

A blank line separates the entries for individual transactions.

Indicate whether each of the following statements is correct or incorrect.
1. Each entry in the journal gives the names of the accounts to be debited and credited, their dollar amounts, and an explanation of the transaction.
2. Since each transaction affects at least two accounts, one cannot perceive the effects of a transaction by looking only at one account.
3. The account to be credited is the first account named in a journal entry.
4. Because it contains a transaction-by-transaction record of the activities of an entity, a journal is very similar to a diary.

Check your responses in Answer Frame 4² on page 56.

Frame 5²

Journalizing

Journalizing is the entering of a transaction in a journal. Information to be journalized originates on source materials or documents such as invoices, cash register tapes, timecards, and checks. The activity recorded on these documents must be analyzed to determine whether a recordable transaction has occurred. If so, the specific accounts affected, the dollar amounts of the changes, and their direction (whether increases or decreases) must also be determined. Then all of these changes must be translated into terms of debit and credit.

Posting

In a sense, a journal entry is a set of instructions. It directs the entry of a certain dollar amount as a debit in a specific account. It also directs entry of a certain dollar amount as a credit in a specific account. The carrying out of these instructions is known as *posting*. In Illustration 2.2, the first entry directs that $10,000 be posted as a debit to the Cash account and as a credit to the Capital Stock account. The three-column balance type of accounts shown in that illustration for Cash and Capital Stock show that these instructions have been carried out. In other words, the entry has been posted.

Postings to the ledger accounts may be made (1) at the time the transaction is journalized; (2) at the end of the day, week, or month; or (3) as each journal page is filled.

Cross-indexing

The number of the ledger account to which the posting was made is placed in the Ledger Folio (L.F.) column of the journal. The number of the journal page *from* which the entry was posted is placed in the Folio

Illustration 2.2

GENERAL JOURNAL					*Page 1*
Date	Accounts and Explanation	L.F.	Debit		Credit
1979 May 1	Cash................................ Capital Stock................ Cash invested in the business.	100 300	10,000		10,000
2	Rent Expense..................... Cash........................... Rent for May 1979.	410 100	500		500
3	Equipment .... Accounts Payable .... Tables and chairs, Diller Company.	110 201	2,200		2,200

GENERAL LEDGER

Cash   *Account No. 100*

Date	Explanation	Folio	Debit	Credit	Balance
1979 May 1 2		J 1 J 1	10,000	500	10,000 9,500

Equipment   *Account No. 110*

Date		Folio	Debit	Credit	Balance
1979 May 3		J 1	2,200		2,200

Accounts Payable   *Account No. 201*

Date		Folio	Debit	Credit	Balance
1979 May 3	Diller Company	J 1		2,200	2,200

Capital Stock   *Account No. 300*

Date		Folio	Debit	Credit	Balance
1979 May 1		J 1		10,000	10,000

Rent Expense   *Account No. 410*

Date		Folio	Debit	Credit	Balance
1979 May 2		J 1	500		500

column of the ledger account. Posting is always from the journal to the ledger account. Cross-indexing is the placing of the account number in the journal and the placing of the journal page number in the account, as shown in Illustration 2.2.

Cross-indexing aids the tracing of any recorded transaction, either from the journal to the ledger or from the ledger to the journal. Cross-reference numbers usually are not placed in the L.F. column of the journal until the entry is posted; thereafter, the cross-reference numbers indicate that the entry has been posted.

By tracing the entries from the journal to the ledger, the reader will understand the posting and cross-indexing process. The ledger accounts need not contain explanations of all the entries, since they can be obtained from the journal. But placing explanations in the ledger accounts may be helpful if the transaction is one of a nonroutine nature.

The explanation of a journal entry should be complete enough to fully describe the transaction and to prove the entry's accuracy and at the same time be concise. If a journal entry is self-explanatory, the explanation may be omitted.

Compound journal entries

The analysis of a transaction often shows that more than two accounts are directly affected. In such cases the journal entry involves more than one debit or more than one credit or both. Such a journal entry is a compound journal entry. An entry with one debit and one credit is a simple journal entry.

Assume that J. T. Stine purchases $8,000 of machinery from the Myers Company, paying $2,000 cash with the balance due on open account. The journal entry for Stine is as follows:

Machinery	8,000	
Cash		2,000
Accounts Payable, Myers Company		6,000
Machinery purchased from Myers Company, Invoice No. 42.		

On a separate piece of paper, write out the compound entry to journalize the following transaction: David Henton owes $5,000 on a note payable. He pays the note, together with interest of $150. Check your response in Answer Frame 5^2 on page 60.

Frame 6²

The functions and other advantages of using a journal are summarized below. The journal—

1. Sets forth the transactions of each day.
2. Records the transactions in chronological order.
3. Shows the analysis of each transaction in terms of debit and credit.

4. Supplies an explanation of each transaction when necessary.
5. Serves as a source for future reference to accounting transactions.
6. Removes lengthy explanations from the accounts.
7. Makes possible posting to the ledger at convenient times.
8. Assists in maintaining the ledger in balance.
9. Aids in the tracing of errors.
10. Promotes the division of labor (for example, one person may enter the journal entries and another may post them).

Indicate whether each of the following statements is true or false.

1. All input into an accounting system must first pass through a journal.
2. The analysis of a transaction in terms of debit and credit is an extremely important step in the journalizing process.
3. It is conceivable that a journal entry to record a complex transaction could contain several debits and several credits.
4. The ledger accounts normally contain a lengthy explanation of the transactions which are posted to them.

Check your responses in Answer Frame 6² on page 60.

Frame 7²

The accounting system in operation

Presented below is an illustration of an accounting system that might be employed by a small merchandising company, the Paxton Company. The company's statement of financial position at December 31, 1978, is as follows:

PAXTON COMPANY
Statement of Financial Position
December 31, 1978

Assets			Liabilities and *Stockholders' Equity*		
Current Assets:			Current Liabilities:		
Cash		$10,000	Accounts payable		$ 2,000
Accounts receivable		4,500	Stockholders' Equity:		
Merchandise inventory		5,000	Capital stock		$30,000
Total Current Assets		$19,500	Retained earnings		3,500
Property, Plant, and Equipment:			Total Stockholders' Equity		$33,500
Furniture and equipment	$ 6,000				
Salesroom fixtures	10,000				
Total Property, Plant, and Equipment		$16,000	Total Liabilities and Stockholders' Equity		$35,500
Total Assets		$35,500			

The required entry is:

Notes Payable	5,000	
Interest Expense	150	
Cash		5,150

    Paid note and interest.

If you answered incorrectly, study Frame 5² again before continuing with Frame 6² on page 58.

Answer frame 6²

1. True. All journals are books of original entry, and all transactions must pass through a journal.
2. True. If the analysis is improper, the data in the accounts can hardly be correct. If the data in the accounts are not correct, it is quite unlikely that reliable financial statements can be prepared. Thus, proper financial reporting depends upon proper analysis of business transactions.
3. True. Not all business transactions can be properly and completely analyzed into a simple entry consisting of one debit and one credit.
4. False. The explanations of transactions are contained in the journal. This permits the removal of lengthy explanations from the accounts.

If you missed any of the above, study Frame 6² again before going on to Frame 7² on page 59.

7²
continued

    The statement of financial position reflects ledger account balances as of the close of business on December 31, 1978. These are, of course, the opening balances on January 1, 1979, and are shown as such in the illustrated ledger accounts.

    The Paxton Company's chart of accounts is as follows:

Account No.	Account title	Account No.	Account title
1	Cash	30	Cost of Goods Sold
2	Accounts Receivable	32	Advertising Expense
3	Commissions Receivable	33	Depreciation Expense – Salesroom Fixtures
4	Merchandise Inventory		
6	Furniture and Equipment	34	Sales Salaries
8	Salesroom Fixtures	35	Salesroom Rent Expense
11	Accounts Payable	36	Other Selling Expense
15	Capital Stock	37	Office Rent Expense
16	Retained Earnings	38	Administrative Salaries
20	Sales	39	Office Supplies Expense
21	Commissions Earned	40	Other Administrative Expense
		41	Depreciation Expense – Furniture and Equipment

Now assume that the following is a complete list (somewhat condensed) of the transactions entered into by the Paxton Company in January 1979:

Jan. 2 Paid January rent: office, $400; and salesroom, $600.
 3 Purchased additional office furniture for cash, $1,500.
 4 Received an invoice from the Burk Agency, $200, for planning January's advertising.
 4 Collected $3,000 on account.
 6 Paid $2,000 on account.
 6 Sales on account for the week, $3,200. Cost of the products delivered to customers, $2,400. (Paxton earns some of its revenue – Sales – by selling and delivering products to its customers. During the week it delivered to its customers products that cost $2,400 in exchange for its customers' promises to pay of $3,200.) Sales would normally be recorded daily, but, for obvious reasons, the illustration must be shortened.
 8 Paid the advertising bill received on January 4.
 9 Purchased merchandise on account, $6,000. (This transaction consists of the receipt of an asset, merchandise inventory, in exchange for a promise to pay for the goods at a later date.)
 9 Purchased office supplies for $120 cash. The supplies are to be used in January.
 10 Collections on account, $1,500.
 13 Sales on account for the week, $4,400. Cost of the products sold, $3,300.
 15 Paid sales salaries of $1,800 and administrative salaries of $2,100 for the first half of the month. (Payroll taxes and deductions are to be dealt with later.)
 16 Paid other administrative expenses, $150.
 17 Paid other selling expenses, $600.
 20 Sales on account for the week, $1,400. Cost of products sold, $1,100.
 23 Received an invoice from the *New York News* for advertising in the first half of January, $300.
 31 Sales on account for the rest of the month, $1,600. Cost of the products sold, $1,200.
 – 31 Purchased $80 of additional office supplies for cash. Supplies are to be used today.
 31 Paid salaries for last half of January (same as on January 15).
 ⌐ 31 Paid sundry other administrative expenses, $250.

The general journal of the Paxton Company for January 1979 is presented below. Some transactions have been completely journalized, others only partially. To test your understanding of the process of analyzing and journalizing transactions, you are to write out on a separate sheet of paper the information that should be inserted in the blank spaces below. Use the chart of accounts presented above for your account titles and numbers. To present the general journal as it would appear when completed, account numbers have been inserted in the L.F. (or reference) column. As already noted, these numbers typically would be inserted only after the posting of the item to the proper ledger account.

Date		Accounts and Explanation	L.F.	Debit	Credit
1979 Jan.	2	Salesroom Rent Expense..	35	600	
		Office Rent Expense...	37	400	
		Cash..	1		1,000
		Rent for January 1979.			
	3	Furniture and Equipment	6	1,500	
		Cash..	1		1,500
		Purchased additional furniture.			
	4	Advertising Expense	32	200	
		Accounts Payable	11		200
		Advertising expense on account.			
	4	Cash..	1	3,000	
		Accounts Receivable.......................................	2		3,000
		Collections on account.			
	6	?	?	2,000	
		?	?		2,000
		Payments on account.			
	6	Accounts Receivable..	2	3,200	
		Sales..	20		3,200
		Sales for the week ended January 6.			
	6	Cost of Goods Sold...	30	2,400	
		Merchandise Inventory.....................................	4		2,400
		Cost of goods sold.			
	8	?	?	200	
		?	?		200
		Paid invoice of January 4.			
	9	?	?	6,000	
		?	?		6,000
		Purchased merchandise on account.			
	9	?	?	120	
		?	?		120
		Office supplies purchased and used.			
	10	?	?	1,500	
		?	?		1,500
		Collections on account.			
	13	?	?	4,400	
		?	?		4,400
		Sales for the week ended January 13.			
	13	?	?	3,300	
		?	?		3,300
		Cost of goods sold.			

GENERAL JOURNAL (*continued*)   *Page 2*

Date		Accounts and Explanation	L.F.	Debit	Credit
1979 Jan.	15	_____?_____	?	1,800	
		_____?_____	?	2,100	
		_____?_____	?		3,900
		Paid salaries for first half of January.			
	16	_____?_____	?	150	
		_____?_____	?		150
		Paid other administrative expenses.			
	17	_____?_____	?	600	
		_____?_____	?		600
		Paid other selling expenses.			
	20	_____?_____	?	1,400	
		_____?_____	?		1,400
		Sales for week ended January 20.			
	20	_____?_____	?	1,100	
		_____?_____	?		1,100
		Cost of goods sold.			
	23	_____?_____	?	300	
		_____?_____	?		300
		Advertising expense on account.			
	31	Accounts Receivable...............................	2	1,600	
		Sales...	20		1,600
		Sales in rest of January.			
	31	Cost of Goods Sold...............................	30	1,200	
		Merchandise Inventory........................	4		1,200
		Cost of goods sold.			
	31	_____?_____	?	80	
		_____?_____	?		80
		Supplies purchased and used.			
	31	Sales Salaries......................................	34	1,800	
		Administrative Salaries............................	38	2,100	
		Cash...	1		3,900
		Paid salaries for last half of January.			
	31	_____?_____	?	250	
		_____?_____	?		250
		Paid other administrative expenses.			

After you have supplied the missing account titles and account numbers for the blank spaces, check Answer Frame 7² on page 66.

Frame 8²

Presented below are the general ledger accounts of the Paxton Company. The accounts are nearly completely posted. You are to write out on a separate sheet of paper the missing items which are indicated by a blank space and a question mark.

GENERAL LEDGER

Cash   +   —   *Account No. 1*

Date		Explanation	Folio	Debit	Credit	Balance
1979						
Jan.	1	Balance				10,000
	2		J 1		1,000	9,000
	3		J 1		1,500	7,500
	4		J 1	3,000		10,500
	6		J 1		2,000	8,500
	8		J 1		200	8,300
	9		J 1		120	8,180
	10		J 1	1,500		9,680
	15		J 2		3,900	5,780
	16		J 2		150	5,630
	17		J 2		600	5,030
	31		J 2		80	4,950
	31		J2 ?		3,900	1,050
	31		J 2		250	800

Accounts Receivable   +   —   *Account No. 2*

Date		Explanation	Folio	Debit	Credit	Balance
1979						
Jan.	1	Balance				4,500
	4		J 1		3,000	1,500
	6		J 1	3,200		4,700
	10		J 1		1,500	1?00
	13		J 1	4,400		7,600
	20		J 2	1,400		9,000
	31		J 2	1,600		10,600

Merchandise Inventory   +   —   *Account No. 4*

Date		Explanation	Folio	Debit	Credit	Balance
1979						
Jan.	1	Balance				5,000
	6		J 1		2,400	2,600
	9		J 1	6,000		8,600
	13		J 1		3,300	5,300
	20		J 2		1,100	4,200
	31		J 2		1,200	3,000

Furniture and Equipment   +   —   *Account No. 6*

Date		Explanation	Folio	Debit	Credit	Balance
1979						
Jan.	1	Balance				6,000
	3		J 1	1,500		7,500

GENERAL LEDGER (*continued*)

Salesroom Fixtures   +   −   *Account No. 8*

Date		Explanation	Folio	Debit	Credit	Balance
1979						
Jan.	1	Balance				10,000

Accounts Payable   −   +   *Account No. 11*

Date		Explanation	Folio	Debit	Credit	Balance
1979						
Jan.	1	Balance				2,000
	4		J 1		200	2,200
	6		J 1	2,000		200
	8		J 1	200		−0−
	9		J 1		6,000	6,000
	23		J 2		300	6,300

Capital Stock   −   +   *Account No. 15*

Date		Explanation	Folio	Debit	Credit	Balance
1979						
Jan.	1	Balance				30,000

Retained Earnings   −   +   *Account No. 16*

Date		Explanation	Folio	Debit	Credit	Balance
1979						
Jan.	1	Balance				3,500

Sales   −   +   *Account No. 20*

Date		Explanation	Folio	Debit	Credit	Balance
1979						
Jan.	6		J 1		3,200	3,200
	13		J 1		4,400	7,600
	20		J 2		1,400	9,000
	31		J 2		*?1600*	*? 10,600*

Cost of Goods Sold   +   −   *Account No. 30*

Date		Explanation	Folio	Debit	Credit	Balance
1979						
Jan.	6		J 1	2,400		2,400
	13		J 1	3,300		5,700
	20		J 2	1,100		6,800
	31		J 2	1,200		8,000

Advertising Expense   +   −   *Account No. 32*

Date		Explanation	Folio	Debit	Credit	Balance
1979						
Jan.	4		J 1	200		200
	23		J 2	300		500

Sales Salaries   +   −   *Account No. 34*

Date		Explanation	Folio	Debit	Credit	Balance
1979						
Jan.	15		J 2	1,800		1,800
	31		J 2	1,800		3,600

The missing account numbers and titles in the Paxton Company general journal for January 1979 are:

Jan.	Account titles	L.F.
6	Accounts Payable	11
	Cash	1
8	Accounts Payable	11
	Cash	1
9	Merchandise Inventory	4
	Accounts Payable	11
9	Office Supplies Expense	39
	Cash	1
10	Cash	1
	Accounts Receivable	2
13	Accounts Receivable	2
	Sales	20
13	Cost of Goods Sold	30
	Merchandise Inventory	4
15	Sales Salaries	34
	Administrative Salaries	38
	Cash	1
16	Other Administrative Expense	40
	Cash	1
17	Other Selling Expense	36
	Cash	1
20	Accounts Receivable	2
	Sales	20
20	Cost of Goods Sold	30
	Merchandise Inventory	4
23	Advertising Expense	32
	Accounts Payable	11
31	Office Supplies Expense	39
	Cash	1
31	Other Administrative Expense	40
	Cash	1

If you missed any of the above answers, you may want to restudy the example in Frame 7² before continuing with Frame 8² on page 64. The above information is used in the continuing illustration.

GENERAL LEDGER (*concluded*)

Salesroom Rent Expense $+$ $-$ *Account No. 35*

Date		Explanation	Folio	Debit	Credit	Balance
1979 Jan.	2		J 1	600		600

Other Selling Expense $+$ $-$ *Account No. 36*

Date		Explanation	Folio	Debit	Credit	Balance
1979 Jan.	17		J 2	600		600

Office Rent Expense $+$ $-$ *Account No. 37*

Date		Explanation	Folio	Debit	Credit	Balance
1979 Jan.	2		J 1	400		400

Administrative Salaries $+$ $-$ *Account No. 38*

Date		Explanation	Folio	Debit	Credit	Balance
1979 Jan.	15		J 2	2,100		2,100
	31		J 2	2,100		4,200

Office Supplies Expense $+$ $-$ *Account No. 39*

Date		Explanation	Folio	Debit	Credit	Balance
1979 Jan.	9		J 1	120		120
	31		J 2	80		200

Other Administrative Expense $+$ $-$ *Account No. 40*

Date		Explanation	Folio	Debit	Credit	Balance
1979 Jan.	16		J 2	150		150
	31		J 2	250		400

Check your responses to the missing items in the above set of ledger accounts in Answer Frame 8² on page 68.

Frame 9²

Control of the recording process

In Frame 2² we promised to explain why accountants record increases in assets (and expenses) as debits and increases in equities (and revenues) as credits. It would be possible to devise a scheme whereby all accounts were increased by entries on the debit side. At the end of any given period, then, all accounts would have positive debit balances.

9²
continued

But, under such a scheme, how would accountants know whether or not the basic equation of Assets = Equities were true? Furthermore, a valuable automatic check for arithmetic errors would be missing. If they wished to check upon the arithmetic accuracy of their work, they would have to repeat virtually every step in the initial recording process. Fortunately, there is an easier way.

Increases in assets (and expenses) are recorded as debits and increases in equities (and revenues) as credits. This yields two sets of accounts — those with debit balances and those with credit balances. If the totals of these two groups are equal, the accountant has some assurance that the arithmetic part of the recording process has been properly carried out. The double-entry system of accounting requires that the debits must equal the credits in the entry to record every transaction. This equality of debits and credits for each transaction will always hold, because both sides of every transaction are recorded. It is this equality of debits and credits, not of increases and decreases, that provides the important control device. If every transaction is recorded in terms of equal debits and credits, it follows that the total of the accounts with debit balances must equal the total of the accounts with credit balances.

The trial balance

The arithmetic accuracy of the recording process is generally tested by preparing a listing of the accounts and their debit or credit balances. Such a listing (called a trial balance) for the Paxton Company is shown in Illustration 2.3. Note the listing of the account titles on the left (account numbers could be included, if desired), the column for debit balances, the column for credit balances, and the equality of the two totals.

The inequality of the totals of the debits and credits columns would automatically signal the presence of an error. But the equality of the two totals does not mean that the accounting has been error-free. In-

Illustration 2.3   *A trial balance*

```
                        PAXTON COMPANY
                          Trial Balance
                        January 31, 1979

                                              Debits      Credits

Cash..................................................  $    800
Accounts receivable ................................     10,600
Merchandise inventory...............................      3,000
Furniture and equipment ............................      7,500
Salesroom fixtures..................................     10,000
Accounts payable....................................                $  6,300
Capital stock.......................................                  30,000
Retained earnings...................................                   3,500
Sales...............................................                  10,600
Cost of goods sold .................................      8,000
Advertising expense ................................        500
Sales salaries......................................      3,600
Salesroom rent expense..............................        600
Other selling expense...............................        600
Office rent expense.................................        400
Administrative salaries.............................      4,200
Office supplies expense ............................        200
Other administrative expense .......................        400
                                                       $50,400      $50,400
```

deed, serious errors may have been made. These include the complete omission of an important transaction or the recording of an entry in the wrong account (for example, the recording of an asset as an expense, or vice versa).

A trial balance may be prepared at any time—at the end of a day, a week, a month, a quarter, or a year. Typically, one is prepared whenever financial statements are to be prepared. Thus, the trial balance provides a listing of the accounts for statement preparation. A trial balance that is out of balance will also indicate the period in which an error was made.

Indicate whether each of the following statements is true or false.
1. An out-of-balance trial balance always signals the presence of an error.
2. A trial balance is one of the financial statements usually published by a business firm.
3. A trial balance may balance even though serious accounting errors have been made.
4. An in-balance trial balance shows only that equal amounts of debits and credits have been entered and that account balances have been correctly drawn.
5. A trial balance will reveal an error in selecting an account title in journalizing a transaction.

Check your responses in Answer Frame 9[2] on page 70.

Frame 10²

Adjusting entries

Continuing the Paxton Company illustration, assume that its management is especially concerned with the profitability of the company for the month. Its instructions that financial statements be prepared for January creates the problem for the accountant of making sure that the accounts properly reflect operations for the month and the financial status at the end of the month. Because economic activity can take place without a transaction occurring, the accounts must be analyzed to determine whether any updating adjustments are required. The entries to record these updating adjustments are called *adjusting entries* and are discussed in depth in Chapter 3.

But, to illustrate briefly here, a study of the Paxton Company's accounts would reveal that no expense is shown for the use of the salesroom fixtures and the furniture and equipment which were acquired on December 31, 1978. Assets such as these will not continue to provide benefits or services indefinitely. Wear and tear resulting from their use will eventually cause them to be disposed of as worthless. Since the assets were used in January, it seems logical to assign some part of the cost of such assets as an expense of the month of January. This expense is called *depreciation*. Assume that by spreading the recorded costs of $10,000 for the salesroom fixtures and $7,500 for the furniture and equipment over their estimated useful lives, the monthly depreciation expenses are $100 and $125. The required journal entry to record these expenses is:

Depreciation Expense – Salesroom Fixtures.................................... 100
Depreciation Expense – Furniture and Equipment............................ 125
    Allowance for Depreciation – Salesroom Fixtures   100
    Allowance for Depreciation – Furniture and Equipment   125
  Depreciation for the month of January.

Note that the depreciation expense is not credited directly to the asset accounts but rather to separate allowance for depreciation accounts. As is explained in Chapter 3, these allowance accounts are special subdivisions of the credit side of the asset accounts established for depreciable assets. They are used primarily because of the tentative nature of the depreciation expense recorded. Illustration 2.6 (page 73) shows how these allowances are reported in the statement of financial position.

Assume that another adjustment is needed to record commissions earned by the Paxton Company, but not yet collected, in the amount of $6,000. Paxton earned these commissions in January by acting as a selling agent for the Brown Wholesale Company, which delivered the merchandise sold by Paxton directly to the customers. The required entry is:

Commissions Receivable... 6,000
    Commissions Earned...   6,000
  Commissions earned in the month of January.

Commissions Earned is a revenue account and will appear in the earnings statement. Commissions receivable is a current asset that will appear in the statement of financial position.

These two adjusting entries are posted in the same manner that every journal entry is posted. The debits would be posted as debits to the named accounts, the credits as credits, and the proper balances brought forward.

Indicate whether each of the following statements is true or false.

1. Commissions receivable is a current asset primarily because it will be converted into cash in the very near future.
2. After the above adjusting entries are posted, the Commissions Receivable account has a debit balance of $6,000.
3. The Depreciation Expense – Salesroom Fixtures account is an expense account that will appear in the earnings statement.
4. Adjusting entries are usually required before financial statements are prepared.

Check your responses in Answer Frame 10² on page 72.

Frame 11²

Financial statements

The financial statements desired by the management of the Paxton Company are presented in Illustrations 2.4, 2.5, and 2.6. As shown by

1. True. Commissions receivable is a current asset for the reason stated.
2. True. Since there is no Commissions Receivable account in the trial balance, the debit to the account from the adjusting entry is the only entry into the account. It must, therefore, have a debit balance of $6,000.
3. True. See Illustration 2.4 for its inclusion as an expense in an earnings statement.
4. True. Some adjustments are usually needed simply because not all economic activity takes place in readily observable business transactions.

If you answered any of the above incorrectly, study Frame 10² again before proceeding to Frame 11² on page 71.

11²
continued

Illustration 2.4   An earnings statement

PAXTON COMPANY
Earnings Statement
For the Month Ended January 31, 1979

Revenues:

Sales	$10,600	
Commissions earned	6,000	$16,600

Expenses:

Cost of goods sold	$ 8,000	
Advertising	500	
Depreciation expense—salesroom fixtures	100	
Sales salaries	3,600	
Salesroom rent	600	
Other selling expense	600	
Office rent	400	
Administrative salaries	4,200	
Office supplies	200	
Other administrative expense	400	
Depreciation expense—furniture and equipment	125	18,725
Net Loss		$ 2,125

Illustration 2.5   A statement of retained earnings

PAXTON COMPANY
Statement of Retained Earnings
For the Month Ended January 31, 1979

Retained earnings, December 31, 1978	$3,500
Net loss for January	2,125
Retained Earnings, January 31, 1979	$1,375

Illustration 2.6   A statement of financial position

PAXTON COMPANY
Statement of Financial Position
January 31, 1979

Assets

Current Assets:

Cash	$ 800	
Accounts receivable	10,600	
Commissions receivable	6,000	
Merchandise inventory	3,000	
Total Current Assets		$20,400

Property, Plant, and Equipment:

Salesroom fixtures	$10,000		
Allowance for depreciation	100	$ 9,900	
Furniture and equipment	$ 7,500		
Allowance for depreciation	125	7,375	
Total Property, Plant, and Equipment			17,275
Total Assets			$37,675

Liabilities and Stockholders' Equity

Current Liabilities:

Accounts payable	$ 6,300

Stockholders' Equity:

Capital stock	$30,000	
Retained earnings	1,375	
Total Stockholders' Equity		31,375
Total Liabilities and Stockholders' Equity		$37,675

the earnings statement in Illustration 2.4, the management of the company has good reason to be concerned about profitability, since the company reports a loss for the month.

The financial accounting process once again is back to its end products, the financial statements. (The fourth major financial statement, the statement of changes in financial position, is discussed in Chapter 12). Thus far, the accounting process has been shown to consist of (1) analyzing economic activity, (2) journalizing transactions, (3) posting to ledger accounts, (4) preparation of a trial balance, (5) adjusting the accounts, and (6) preparing financial statements.

Indicate whether each of the following statements is true or false.
1. Some of the input into the accounting system comes from checks and invoices.
2. The statement of retained earnings ties the earnings statement and the statement of financial position together.
3. The earnings of a company can be determined from its trial balance.
4. Apparently, over its entire life, the Paxton Company has operated profitably.

Check your responses in Answer Frame 11² on page 74.

Summary *chapter* 2

This chapter introduced the basic components of an accounting system and the manner in which data are entered in the system.

An account is a means employed to summarize changes in assets, liabilities, stockholders' equity items, revenues, and expenses. It may be further defined as a classificational category. By convention, asset and expense accounts are increased by entries on the left side of the account (called the debit side) and decreased by entries on the right (credit) side. Liability, stockholders' (owners') equity, and revenue accounts are increased by entries on the credit side and decreased by entries on the debit side. As a result, assets and expenses are usually debit balances and the others credit balances.

Recording increases and decreases in accounts in a manner which provides two groups of accounts—those with debit balances and those with credit balances—provides an automatic check upon the arithmetic accuracy of the accounting process.

Collectively, the accounts are referred to as the ledger. The chart of accounts is a list of the names and numbers of the accounts in an accounting system.

All data are entered in an accounting system by means of a journal, which is a chronological record of business transactions analyzed in terms of debit and credit. Business activity is analyzed and certain transactions recorded in the journal in a process known as journalizing. The amounts journalized are then posted to the accounts. A trial balance is a listing of all of the accounts in the ledger together with their debit or credit balances which, in total, must be equal. After adjusting entries have been prepared and posted, financial statements can be prepared.

Most accounting information is communicated to a wide variety of possible users in financial statements, which are the end products of the financial accounting process. The users find the information communicated useful and relevant in making decisions, which is the basic reason for acquiring any kind of information.

You have completed the programmed portion of Chapter 2. As the first part of your review, read the Glossary which follows and study the definitions of the new terms introduced in this chapter. Then go on to the Student Review Quiz beginning on page 76 for a self-administered test of your comprehension of the material in this chapter.

Glossary *chapter* 2

Account—a device, means, classification category, or storage unit used to classify and summarize money measurements of business activity in an accounting system.

Adjusting entries—journal entries that update the accounts in an accounting system for economic activity that has taken place but has not been reflected in readily discernible transactions.

Chart of accounts—the complete listing of the names (and possibly the account numbers) of all of the accounts in the ledger (or accounting system); somewhat comparable to a table of contents.

Credit—the right side of any account; when used as a verb, to enter a dollar amount on the right side of an account.

Credit balance—the balance in an account when the sum of the credits to the account exceeds the sum of the debits to that account.

Credit entry—an entry on the right side of an account; credits increase liability, stockholders' equity, and revenue accounts and decrease asset and expense accounts.

Cross-indexing—the act of placing in the journal the number of the ledger account to which an entry was posted and placing in the ledger account the page number of the journal on which the entry can be found.

Debit—the left side of any account; when used as a verb, to enter a dollar amount on the left side of an account.

Debit balance—the balance in an account when the sum of the debits to the account exceeds the sum of the credits to that account.

Debit entry—an entry on the left side of an account; debits increase asset and expense accounts and decrease liability, stockholders' equity, and revenue accounts.

Depreciation—that portion of the cost of a long-lived tangible asset used in a business that is allocated to each period of the asset's life. (For further discussion, see Chapter 8).

Journal—a chronological record of business transactions showing the changes to be recorded as a result of each transaction; the simplest form of journal is the two-column general journal.

Journal entry—a complete analysis of the effects of a business transaction as expressed in terms of debit and credit and recorded in a journal. A compound journal entry is a journal entry with more than one debit or credit.

Journalizing—a step in the accounting recording process that consists of entering a transaction in a journal.

Ledger—the complete collection of all of the accounts of an entity; often referred to as the general ledger.

Posting—the transfer of entries from a journal to a ledger.

Rule of double entry—the accounting requirement that every transaction be recorded in an entry that has equal debits and credits.

Trial balance—a list of all of the accounts in a ledger (excluding those with zero balances) at a given point in time, with debit balances listed in one column and

75

credit balances listed in a second column to the right of the first column.

Continue with the Student Review Quiz below as a self-administered test of your understanding of the material presented in this chapter.

Student review quiz *chapter* 2

To develop a permanent record of your responses, you may write them on the answer sheet provided in the *Work Papers* or on a separate sheet of paper. For each of the following questions, select the one best answer.

1 Debits—
a Increase assets and decrease expenses, liabilities, revenue, and stockholders' equity.
b Increase assets and expenses and decrease liabilities, revenue, and stockholders' equity.
c Increase assets and stockholders' equity and decrease liabilities, expenses, and revenue.
d Decrease assets and expenses and increase liabilities, revenue, and stockholders' equity.
e Decrease assets and revenue and increase expenses, liabilities, and stockholders' equity.

2 Expense accounts—
a Eventually increase the balance in the Retained Earnings account.
b Usually have credit balances.
c Show the costs associated with producing revenue during an accounting period.
d Do all of the above.
e Are reported in the statement of financial position.

3 Steno Service, Inc., performed services for customers during the month totaling $1,400, for which it billed the customers. What entry should be made?
a Debit Cash, $1,400; credit Service Revenue, $1,400.
b Debit Accounts Receivable, $1,400; credit Service Revenue, $1,400.
c Debit Notes Receivable, $1,400; credit Service Revenue, $1,400.
d Debit Service Revenue, $1,400; credit Accounts Receivable, $1,400.

e Debit Service Revenue, $1,400; credit Accounts Payable, $1,400.

4 Received a bill for newspaper advertising services received, $25. The bill will be paid in 15 days. What entry is required?
a Debit Advertising Expense, $25; credit Accounts Payable, $25.
b Debit Accounts Receivable, $25; credit Advertising Revenue, $25.
c Debit Cash, $25; credit Advertising Revenue, $25.
d Debit Accounts Payable, $25; credit Cash, $25.
e Debit Advertising Expense, $25; credit Cash, $25.

5 Received $825 from customers in payment of the bills sent to them. What entry is required?
a Debit Cash, $825; credit Accounts Payable, $825.
b Debit Cash, $825; credit Notes Receivable, $825.
c Debit Cash, $825; credit Accounts Receivable, $825.
d Debit Accounts Receivable, $825; credit Cash, $825.
e Debit Accounts Payable, $825; credit Cash, $825.

6 Steno Service, Inc., purchased an electric calculator for $400 and new typists' chairs which cost $120. All items were purchased from the Office Equipment Supply Company on open account. The required entry is which of the following?
a Debit Office Machines, $400; credit Accounts Payable, $400.
b Debit Office Machines, $520; credit Notes Payable, $520.
c Debit Office Machines, $400, and Office Furniture and Fixtures, $120; credit Cash, $520.
d Debit Office Machines, $400, and Office Furniture and Fixtures, $120; credit Accounts Payable, $520.
e Debit Accounts Receivable, $520; credit Office Machines, $400, and Office Furniture and Fixtures, $120.

7 Steno Service, Inc., performed a rush manuscript typing job for S. N. Stowell and received payment in cash of $18.50. The required entry is—
a Debit Accounts Receivable, $18.50; credit Office Supplies, $18.50.

b Debit Cash, $18.50; credit Service Revenue, $18.50.

c Debit Cash, $18.50; credit Accounts Receivable, $18.50.

d Debit Accounts Receivable, $18.50; credit Service Revenue, $18.50.

e Debit Cash, $18.50; credit Office Supplies, $18.50.

8 Steno Service, Inc., paid weekly salaries of $275 in cash. The entry is—

a Debit Salary Expense, $275; credit Salaries Payable, $275.

b Debit Accounts Payable, $275; credit Cash, $275.

c Debit Salary Expense, $275; credit Accounts Payable, $275.

d Debit Cash, $275; credit Salary Expense, $275.

e Debit Salary Expense, $275; credit Cash $275.

9 Which of the following statements regarding a trial balance is *incorrect?*

a A trial balance is a test of the equality of the debit and credit balances in the ledger.

b A trial balance is a list of all of the open accounts in the ledger with their balances as of a given date.

c A trial balance proves that no errors of any kind have been made in the accounts during the accounting period.

d A trial balance helps to localize errors within an identifiable time period.

e A trial balance is useful in preparing the statement of financial position and earnings statement.

10 A ledger is defined as—

a A collection of transactions.

b A collection of all statement of financial position accounts.

c A collection of all earnings statement accounts.

d A listing of all account titles and their balances.

e None of the above.

11 Which of the following statements is *incorrect?*

a The general journal is a record of transactions in chronological sequence.

b Each general journal entry includes the date of the transaction, the title of the account debited, the title of the account credited, the amount of the debit, and the amount of the credit.

c The general journal is the source of postings to the ledger accounts.

d When making entries in the general journal, the accountant need not concern himself or herself with equality of debits and credits.

12 Cross-indexing—

a Provides a link between the journal and the ledger accounts.

b Facilitates the finding of errors.

c Reduces the likelihood of double posting or forgetting to post an item.

d Accomplishes all of the above.

e Accomplishes only two of the above.

13 Posting is the act of—

a Recording entries in the journal.

b Transferring the balances in the ledger to the trial balance.

c Entering amounts in the accounts in the ledger as indicated in the journal.

d Tracing amounts from the journal to the ledger in an attempt to find errors.

e Transferring amounts from the ledger to the journal so that balances may be determined for each account.

14 Which of the following statements is *incorrect?*

a The journal shows all transactions chronologically while the ledger shows only those transactions affecting a given account in chronological sequence.

b Every account title mentioned in the journal over a period of time also appears in the ledger, but accounts appearing in the ledger may not appear in the journal over a period of time.

c The totals of all the debits and all the credits in the journal will equal the totals of the debit and credit balances in the ledger accounts if all entries have been posted.

d The ledger represents a grouping of the amounts for the various accounts mentioned in the journal.

Now compare your answers with the correct answers and explanations on page 712–13.

Questions *chapter* 2

1 How can it be reasonable to state in Chapter 1 that A = L + SE, and then in Chapter 2 to state that A + E = L + SE +

R when it is known that expenses and revenues are usually not equal?

2 Define debit and credit. Name the types of accounts which are—
a Increased by debits.
b Decreased by debits.
c Increased by credits.
d Decreased by credits.
Do you think this system makes sense? Can you conceive of other possible methods for recording changes in accounts?

3 Describe a ledger and a chart of accounts. How do these two compare with a book and its table of contents?

4 Why are expense and revenue accounts used when all revenues and expenses could be shown directly in the Retained Earnings account?

5 What types of accounts appear in the trial balance? What are the purposes of the trial balance?

6 You have found that the total of the debit column of the trial balance of the Burns Company is $100,000 while the total of the credit column is $90,000. What are some of the possible causes of this difference?

7 Store equipment was purchased for $1,500. Instead of debiting the Store Equipment account, the debit was made to Delivery Equipment. Of what help will the trial balance be in locating this error? Why?

8 Differentiate between the trial balance, chart of accounts, statement of financial position, and earnings statement.

9 A student remembered that the side toward the window in the classroom was the debit side of an account. The student took an examination in a room where the windows were on the other side of the room and became confused and consistently reversed debits and credits. Would the student's trial balance have equal debit and credit totals? If there were no existing balances in any of the accounts to begin with, would the error prevent the student from preparing correct financial statements? Why?

10 Are the following possibilities conceivable in an entry involving only one debit and one credit? Why?

Y a Increase a liability and increase an expense.
N b Increase an asset and decrease a liability. *both debits*
N c Increase a revenue and decrease an expense. *both credits*
d Decrease an asset and increase another asset.
Y
e Decrease an asset and increase a liability. *both credits*
N
f Decrease a revenue and decrease an asset.
Y
g Decrease a liability and increase a revenue.
Y

11 Describe the nature and purposes of the general journal. What does "journalizing" mean? Give an example of a compound entry in the general journal.

12 Describe the act of posting. What difficulties could arise if no cross-indexing existed between the general journal and the ledger accounts?

13 Which of the following cash payments would involve the recording of an expense? Why?
N a Paid vendors for office supplies previously purchased on account.
N b Paid an automobile dealer for a new auto for a salesperson.
Y c Paid the current month's rent.
Y d Paid salaries for the last half of the current month.
N e Paid cash and received merchandise that will be sold next month.

Exercises *chapter* 2

1 What debit and credit would be required for each of the following transactions?
a Cash was received for services performed for customers, $600.
b Services were performed for customers on open account, $900.
c Services were performed for customers. The customers were required to sign written promises to pay $700 on a certain date in the future.

2 Give the debit and credit required for each of the following transactions:
a Capital stock was issued for $40,000 cash.
b A loan was arranged with a bank. The bank increased the company's check-

ing account balance by $20,000 after it signed a written promise to return the $20,000, plus interest at 9 percent, six months from the date of the loan.

3 Explain each of the sets of debits and credits existing in the accounts below. There are ten transactions to be explained. Each set is designated by the small letters to the left of the amount. For example, the first transaction is the issuance of capital stock for cash and is denoted by the letter (*a*).

Delivery Equipment

(*b*)	50,000	
(*i*)	10,000	

Delivery Fee Revenue

		(*c*)	600
		(*j*)	4,700

Salaries Expense

(*g*)	1,200	

Cash

(*a*)	70,000	(*e*)	50,000
(*d*)	600	(*f*)	200
		(*g*)	1,200
		(*i*)	10,000

Accounts Payable

(*e*)	50,000	(*b*)	50,000
		(*h*)	400

Rent Expense

(*f*)	200

Accounts Receivable

(*c*)	600	(*d*)	600
(*j*)	4,700		

Capital Stock

		(*a*)	70,000

Delivery Expense

(*h*)	400

4 Assume that the ledger accounts given in Exercise 3 are those of the B. T. Lane Company as they appear at December 31, 1979. Prepare the trial balance as of that date.

5 Assume that the depreciation on the delivery equipment for the year ended December 31, 1979, is $5,000. Prepare the earnings statement for 1979 and the statement of financial position as of the end of 1979, assuming that the data given in Exercise 3 are for the B. T. Lane Company.

6 Give an example of a transaction which would involve the following combinations of types of accounts:
a An asset and a liability.
b An expense and an asset.
c A liability and an expense.
d A stockholders' equity and an asset.
e Two asset accounts.
f An asset and a revenue.

7 Assume that the loan in 2(b) above was paid at maturity date. Give the required entry.

Problems, Series A *chapter* 2

✓ **2–1–A**

The transactions listed below are those of the Sauer Company for the month of April 1979.

Required:

a Mentally analyze each transaction in terms of debit and credit and then enter them directly in suitable T-accounts. To identify each part of each transaction also enter the date of the transaction in the accounts.

b Prepare a trial balance as of April 30, 1979.

Transactions:

Apr. 1   Cash of $30,000 was received for capital stock issued to the owners.

    3   Rent was paid for April, $200.

    6   A delivery truck was purchased for $3,500, cash.

    7   Office equipment was purchased on account from the Barnes Company for $4,800.

  14   Wages were paid, $700.

  15   $2,900 was received for services performed.

  18   An invoice was received from Robb's Gas Station for $25 for gas and oil used.

  23   A loan was arranged with the bank for $5,000. The cash was received, and a note was signed promising to return the $5,000 on May 30, 1979.

  29   Purchased a delivery truck for $4,600 on account.

  30   Unpaid wages for services received amount to $900 and will be paid on May 1, 1979.

(Note: You may ignore depreciation expense for the month.)

2–2–A

Set up the following T-accounts for the Bower Company: Cash; Accounts Receivable; Land; Office Building; Office Equipment; Accounts Payable; Notes Payable, Bank; Capital Stock; Service Sales; Salaries Expense; Office Expense.

Required:

a Enter the transactions given below in the accounts. Date each transaction entry as indicated. Ignore depreciation expense for the period.

b Prepare a trial balance after entering the last transaction.

Transactions:

Apr. 1   The Bower Company was organized, and $40,000 of capital stock was issued for cash.

    1   The company borrowed $25,000 from its bank and issued its note payable to the bank.

    2   Paid $15,000 cash for land.

    2   Paid $47,500 cash for an office building located on the land, above.

3   Purchased $6,000 of office equipment, on account.
4   Paid cash of $400 for office supplies to be consumed in April.
5   Sales of service, on account, were $250.
6   Sales of service, for cash, for the first week, were $1,000.
6   Paid salaries for the first week, $700.

2–3–A

The Dart Corporation entered into the following transactions in August 1979:

Aug. 2   Received cash for capital stock issued to owners, $40,000.
3   Paid rent for August on a building rented, $700.
4   Paid rent for August on a delivery truck, $500.
4   Purchased merchandise on account, $24,000.
6   Sold merchandise costing $4,000 for $6,000 cash.
8   Secured an order from a customer for merchandise with a selling price of $5,000 and a cost of $3,500. The merchandise is to be delivered next month.
13   Sold merchandise costing $5,000 for $8,000 on account to various customers.
15   Received and paid a bill for $87 for gasoline and oil used in delivering goods to customers.
21   Paid cash to suppliers on account, $8,000.
23   Cash collected from customers on account, $5,500.
31   Paid $2,700 to employees for services performed in August.
31   Received the electric and gas bill for the month of August, $75.

Required:

Prepare general journal entries for the above transactions.

2–4–A

Given below is the trial balance of West Company, a computer programming and processing company:

WEST COMPANY
Trial Balance
June 30, 1979

	Debits	Credits
Cash	$ 26,500	
Accounts receivable	17,000	
Office equipment	50,000	
Allowance for depreciation		$ 10,000
Accounts payable		5,400
Notes payable		10,000
Capital stock		20,000
Retained earnings (July 1, 1978)		22,700
Service revenue		60,000
Office rent expense	6,000	
Advertising expense	2,200	
Salaries expense	25,740	
Supplies expense	540	
Miscellaneous expense	120	
	$128,100	$128,100

81

The unrecorded depreciation for the year ended June 30, 1979, on the office equipment is $15,000.

Required:

a Prepare the adjusting journal entry to record the depreciation for the year.
b Prepare the earnings statement for the year ended June 30, 1979.
c Prepare the statement of retained earnings for the year ended June 30, 1979.
d Prepare the statement of financial position as of June 30, 1979.

✓ **2-5-A**

Hi-Speed, Inc., was organized January 1, 1979. Its chart of accounts is as follows:

Account No.	Account name	Account No.	Account name
101	Cash	331	Capital Stock
102	Accounts Receivable	→332	Retained Earnings
106	Unexpired Insurance	441	Delivery Service Sales
107	Prepaid Taxes and Licenses	551	Garage Rent Expense
111	Delivery Trucks	552	Gasoline and Oil Used
112	Garage Equipment	553	Repairs to Delivery Trucks
113	Office Equipment	554	Salaries Expense
221	Accounts Payable	556	General Office Expense
222	Notes Payable		

Required:

a Prepare ledger accounts for all the above accounts except Retained Earnings.
b Journalize the transactions given below for January 1979. (Do not prepare adjusting entries for depreciation expense or other adjustments.)
c Post the journal entries to the ledger accounts.
d Prepare a trial balance as of January 31, 1979.

Transactions:

Jan. 1 The company received $40,000 cash and $20,000 of garage equipment in exchange for $60,000 of capital stock.
   2 Paid garage rent for the month of January, $500.
   4 Purchased office equipment on account, $1,200.
   6 Purchased three delivery trucks at $7,500 each; payment was made by giving cash of $12,500 and a 30-day note for the remainder.
   8 A corrected invoice for the office equipment purchased January 4 showed that the correct total was $1,100, not $1,200.
   10 Paid $150 cash for annual licenses for the delivery trucks and $15 for title registration fees.
   12 Purchased insurance for one year on the delivery trucks. The cost of the policy of $900 was paid in cash.
   15 Received and paid January telephone and electric service bills, $80.
   15 Paid salaries for first half of January, $300.
   17 Cash sales of delivery service to date amounted to $150.
   20 Received bill for gasoline purchased and used in January, $15.

23 Purchased one delivery truck for cash, $9,000. Paid $50 cash for the annual license and $5 for title registration fees.

25 Cash sales of delivery services were $240.

27 Purchased an adding machine on account, $300.

31 Paid salaries for last half of January, $400.

31 Open account sales of delivery service amounted to $950.

31 Paid for repairs to a delivery truck, $10 cash.

2–6–A

The trial balance of the Belle Company at the end of the first 11 months of its fiscal year is given below.

BELLE COMPANY
Trial Balance
May 31, 1979

Account No.	Account name	Debits	Credits
100	Cash	$ 24,120	
102	Accounts receivable	26,400	
106	Merchandise inventory	58,100	
121	Equipment	40,000	
121A	Allowance for depreciation		$ 20,000
210	Accounts payable		12,500
220	Notes payable		10,000
310	Capital stock		40,000
320	Retained earnings (July 1, 1978)		31,200
400	Sales		325,000
500	Cost of goods sold	201,000	
510	Sales salaries expense	33,000	
520	Advertising expense	14,000	
530	Selling supplies expense	1,500	
540	Equipment repairs	700	
550	Office salaries expense	28,500	
560	Building rent expense	4,800	
570	Telephone and utilities expense	1,400	
580	Entertainment expense	580	
590	Depreciation expense	4,400	
600	Interest expense	200	
		$438,700	$438,700

Required:

a Open three-column ledger accounts for each of the accounts in the trial balance. Place the word "Balance" in the explanation space and enter the date June 1, 1979, on this same line.

b Prepare general journal entries for the transactions given below for June 1979.

c Post the journal entries to the general ledger accounts.

d Prepare a trial balance as of June 30, 1979.

e Prepare the adjusting journal entry to record the depreciation on the equipment for June, $400, and post this entry to the ledger accounts.

f Prepare an earnings statement for the year ended June 30, 1979.

g Prepare a statement of retained earnings for the year ended June 30, 1979.

h Prepare the statement of financial position as of June 30, 1979.

83

Transactions:

June 1 Paid building rent for June, $400.
  2 Paid vendors on account, $12,000.
  5 Purchased a new cash register on account, $1,500.
  7 Sold merchandise on account, $18,000; cost, $12,000.
  10 Paid the note payable of $10,000 plus interest of $100.
  13 Cash collections from customers on account, $24,000.
  15 Purchased merchandise on account, $26,500.
  19 Received a bill for equipment repairs, $150.
  24 Paid the June telephone bill, $55, and the June gas and electric bill, $65.
  28 Received a bill for June advertising, $1,100.
  29 Paid the equipment repair bill received on the 19th, $150.
  30 Sold merchandise for cash, $3,000; cost, $2,000.
  30 Paid office salaries, $2,500, and sales salaries, $3,000.
  30 Sales on account since June 7, $12,000; cost, $8,000.
  30 Reimbursed salespersons for costs incurred in entertaining customers in June, $170.

Problems, Series B, *chapter* 2
2–1–B

Required:

a Open T-accounts for the Ruiz Company and enter therein transactions given below for the month of August 1979. Place the date of each transaction in the accounts.
b Prepare a trial balance as of August 31, 1979. (Ignore depreciation expense.)

Transactions:

Aug. 1 Issued capital stock for cash, $15,000.
  3 Borrowed $5,000 from the bank on a note.
  4 Purchased a truck for $5,300 cash.
  6 Services are performed for customers who promise to pay later, $3,600.
  7 Employee services received but not paid for, $700.
  10 Collections are made for the services performed on August 6, $800.
  11 The liability for employee services for the week ending August 7 is paid.
  14 Supplies are purchased for use in future months, $500. They will be paid for next month.
  17 A bill for $100 is received for gas and oil used to date.
  25 Services are performed for customers who pay immediately, $4,500.
  31 Employee services received but not paid for, $1,500.

2–2–B

Required:

a Open proper T-accounts for the Sanders Company and enter therein the transactions given below for the month of July 1979. For identification, place the date of each transaction in the accounts.

b Prepare a trial balance as of July 31, 1979. (Ignore depreciation expense.)

Transactions:

July 2 Cash of $5,000 was received for capital stock issued to the owners.
3 The company paid rent for July, $250.
5 Office furniture was purchased for $3,000 cash.
9 A bill for $500 for advertising for July was received and paid.
14 Cash of $700 was received for fees for services to customers.
15 Wages of $200 for the first half of July were paid in cash.
20 The company sold services on open account to the Hall Company, $400. The account is to be paid August 10.
22 Office furniture was acquired on account from the Mason Company; the price was $400.
30 Cash of $2,250 was received as fees for services to customers.
31 Wages of $200 for the second half of July were paid in cash.

2–3–B

Presented below are the transactions of the Lund Company (partially summarized for the sake of brevity) for the month of March 1979.

a The company was organized and issued capital stock for cash of $60,000.
b Paid $1,800 as the rent for March on a completely furnished store building.
c Purchased merchandise by giving a promise to pay for it later, $55,000.
d Paid $750 as the rent for March on two delivery trucks.
e Paid $300 for delivery supplies received and used in March.
f Sold merchandise costing $30,000 to customers who promised to pay $45,000 for it at a later date.
g Paid suppliers for merchandise purchased on account (see **[c]** above), $40,000.
h Collected cash of $31,000 from customers on account (see **[f]** above).
i Received a bill for $300 for advertising in the local newspaper in March.
j Paid cash for gas and oil consumed in March, $96.
k Paid $1,400 to employees for services provided in March.
l Unpaid wages for services received in March amount to $1,500 at the end of March.
m Received an order for merchandise having a sale price of $10,000 and a cost of $6,000. The merchandise will be delivered in April.

Required:

Prepare the general journal entries that would be required to record the above transactions in the records of the Lund Company. (Ignore depreciation expense.)

2–4–B

The trial balance prepared as of the end of the Amlead Company's calendar year accounting period is as follows:

AMLEAD COMPANY
Trial Balance
December 31, 1979

	Debits	Credits
Cash	$ 4,000	
Accounts receivable	12,500	
Merchandise inventory	12,000	
Delivery equipment	28,000	
Allowance for depreciation – delivery equipment		$ 6,000
Office equipment	8,500	
Allowance for depreciation – office equipment		800
Accounts payable		9,000
Notes payable		10,000
Capital stock		25,000
Retained earnings		1,100
Sales		60,000
Cost of goods sold	27,000	
Rent expense	1,200	
Supplies expense	700	
Advertising expense	1,000	
Wages and salaries expense	17,000	
	$111,900	$111,900

The unrecorded depreciation expense for the year 1979 is $5,000 on the delivery equipment and $800 on the office equipment.

Required:

a Prepare the general journal entries needed to record the depreciation expense for the year.
b Prepare an earnings statement for the year ended December 31, 1979.
c Prepare the statement of retained earnings for the year ended December 31, 1979.
d Prepare the statement of financial position as of December 31, 1979.

2-5-B

Super-Kleen, Inc., was organized July 1, 1979. The following account numbers and titles constitute the chart of accounts for the company:

Account No.	Account name	Account No.	Account name
101	Cash	332	Retained Earnings
102	Accounts Receivable	441	Cleaning Service Sales
111	Office Equipment	551	Salaries Expense
112	Cleaning Equipment	552	Insurance Expense
113	Service Truck	553	Service Truck Expense
221	Accounts Payable	554	Rent Expense
222	Notes Payable	555	Utilities Expense
331	Capital Stock	556	Cleaning Supplies Expense

Required:

a Prepare ledger accounts for all of the above accounts except Retained Earnings.
b Journalize the transactions given below for July 1979. (Ignore depreciation expense.)
c Post the journal entries to the ledger accounts.
d Prepare a trial balance.

Transactions:

July 1 The company issued $30,000 of capital stock for cash.
   5 Office space was rented for July, and $600 cash was paid for the rental.
   8 Desks and chairs were purchased for the office on account, $3,000.
   10 Cleaning equipment was purchased for $4,200; a note was given, to be paid in 30 days.
   15 Purchased a service truck for $18,000, paying $12,000 cash and giving a 60-day note to the dealer for $6,000.
   18 Paid for cleaning supplies received and already used, $300.
   23 Cash cleaning service sales, $1,800.
   27 Insurance expense for July was paid, $450 cash.
   30 Paid for gasoline and oil used by the service truck in July, $60.
   31 Billed customers for cleaning services rendered, $4,200.
   31 Paid salaries for July, $5,400.
   31 Paid utilities bills for July, $550.

2–6–B

Barr Company is a wholesaler of groceries and a canned food broker. Thus, it earns its revenue from sales of groceries and from commissions earned by acting as an agent for a seller who delivers the food sold by Barr directly to the customer. Barr Company's trial balance at the end of the first 11 months of its fiscal year is presented below:

BARR COMPANY
Trial Balance
June 30, 1979

Account No.	Account name	Debits	Credits
1	Cash..	$ 49,160	
2	Accounts receivable.............................	52,400	
6	Merchandise inventory	54,100	
11	Office equipment	35,600	
11A	Allowance for depreciation – office equipment...........		$ 4,000
12	Automobiles	38,600	
12A	Allowance for depreciation – automobiles................		14,000
21	Accounts payable		22,400
31	Capital stock.....................................		50,000
32	Retained earnings August 1, 1978.............		54,000
40	Sales		261,000
41	Commissions earned		128,000
50	Cost of goods sold	160,400	
51	Office salaries expense..........................	43,900	
52	Sales commissions expense	49,600	
53	Advertising expense..............................	12,200	
54	Automobile operating expense	14,600	
55	Office rent expense	10,000	
56	Office supplies expense..........................	800	
57	Telephone and utilities..........................	1,540	
58	Customer entertainment.........................	1,700	
59	Depreciation expense – office equipment..................	2,800	
60	Depreciation expense – automobiles	6,000	
		$533,400	$533,400

Required:

a Open three-column ledger accounts for each of the accounts in the trial balance under the date of July 1, 1979. Place the word "Balance" in the explanation space of each account.

b Prepare general journal entries for the transactions given below for July 1979.

c Post the journal entries to the general ledger accounts.

d Prepare a trial balance as of July 31, 1979.

e Prepare adjusting journal entries to record the depreciation for July: autos, $1,000; and office equipment, $300. Post these entries to the appropriate ledger accounts.

f Prepare an earnings statement for the year ended July 31, 1979. Be sure to include the effects of the adjustments in **(e)**.

g Prepare a statement of retained earnings for the year ended July 31, 1979.

h Prepare the statement of financial position as of July 31, 1979.

Transactions:

July 2   Paid office rent for June and July, $2,000.

      5   Paid the accounts payable of $22,400.

      8   Paid advertising for the month of July, $800.

   10   Purchased a new office desk on account, $700.

   13   Purchased $140 of office supplies on account.

   15   Collected cash from customers on account, $47,200.

   20   Paid for customer entertainment, $50.

   22   The office supplies purchased on July 13 were incorrectly entered; the correct cost was $160.

   25   Collected an additional $4,000 from customers on account.

   26   Paid for gasoline used in the automobiles in July, $180.

   28   Billed customers for commissions earned, $33,000.

   30   Paid July commissions to salespersons, $13,200.

   31   Paid July office salaries, $10,200.

   31   Summarized, the sales for the month (all on account) were $27,000; the cost of goods sold was $15,000.

3

The accounting cycle completed

Learning objectives

Study of the material in this chapter is designed to bring about fulfillment of the following learning objectives:

1. An understanding of the nature of adjusting entries, their four major classes, and the reasons why they must be made.

2. Knowledge of basic characteristics of the accrual and the cash bases of accounting and indication of the circumstances in which the cash basis is found acceptable.

3. A working knowledge of the closing process and the reason why it must be undertaken.

4. Knowledge of the complete accounting functions that are performed as raw data are entered, processed, and transformed into financial statements.

5. A brief introduction to the work sheet for a service company and ways in which it aids in completion of the accounting cycle as described in Appendix 3A.

6. An understanding of the way in which reversing entries may be used (Appendix 3B).

The accounting cycle is completed in this chapter. Previous chapters have discussed and shown how and why the accountant relies upon transactions as the basic source of input data. They have also shown how these transactions are analyzed, journalized, and summarized in accounts.

The need to adjust the accounts prior to the preparation of financial statements was discussed only briefly. This chapter discusses more fully the need for adjusting entries. Adjusting entries are classified into four major categories.

Closing entries and the work sheet are also discussed. The closing of the nominal accounts is necessary at the end of the accounting period. In Appendix 3A the work sheet is introduced as a means of making somewhat easier the tasks of completing the accounting cycle and preparing financial statements.

Appendix 3B discusses and illustrates the possible use of reversing entries. The use of reversing entries is optional.

The need for adjusting entries

The earnings statement of an entity for a certain period must report all of the entity's revenues for the period and all of the expenses incurred to generate those revenues. If it does not, it is certainly incomplete and inaccurate and is quite likely to be misleading. Similarly, a statement of financial position that does not report all of an entity's assets, liabilities, and stockholders' equities may be misleading.

Since interested parties need timely information, periodic financial statements must be prepared. In order to prepare such statements, the accountant must arbitrarily divide an entity's life into time periods and attempt to assign economic activity to specific periods. This requires the preparation of adjusting entries—that is, entries to record economic activity that has taken place but which has not yet resulted in a transaction or other recordable event. Since a transaction has not occurred, adjusting entries are based in part upon estimates which later events may prove to be in error. This is a price that must be paid if timely information is to be secured.

Thus, adjusting entries are necessary under the accrual basis of accounting. They are even required (to a much lesser extent) under cash basis accounting.

Cash versus accrual basis accounting

Some relatively small business firms, such as those engaged in rendering services, may account for their revenues and expenses on a cash basis. This means that (except for depreciation expense) expenses and revenues usually are not recorded until cash is received or paid out. Thus, for example, services rendered to clients in, say, 1977 for which cash was collected in 1978 would be treated as 1978 revenues. Similarly, expenses could be incurred in 1977 but not recorded until 1978 when cash was paid out, at which time they would be treated as 1978 expenses. Because of these improper assignments of revenues and expenses, the cash basis of accounting is generally considered unacceptable. It is acceptable only in those circumstances where the results approximate those obtained under the accrual basis of accounting.

As already illustrated, the accrual basis of accounting recognizes revenues when sales are made even though cash is not yet received. Expenses are recognized as incurred regardless of whether or not cash is paid out. Even under the accrual basis, transactions are the source of input into the accounting system. Thus, adjusting entries are needed to bring the accounts up to date before financial statements can be prepared.

Indicate whether each of the following statements is true or false.
1. Under the cash basis, the cash purchase of a building would be recorded as an expense.
2. Under the cash basis, most expenses and revenues are recorded when cash is paid out or received.
3. When the accrual basis of accounting is properly applied, adjusting entries are not necessary.
4. The demand for periodic financial statements is the basic reason why adjusting entries are made.

Check your responses in Answer Frame 1[3] on page 92.

Frame 2[3]

Time of preparation of adjusting entries

Adjusting entries must be prepared whenever financial statements are to be prepared. Thus, if monthly financial statements are prepared, monthly adjusting entries are required. By custom, and in some instances by law, business firms report to their stockholders at least annually. Consequently, adjusting entries will be required at least annually. In manual accounting systems, adjusting entries may be formally recorded in the accounts only at the end of the annual accounting period. If interim financial reports are to be prepared, the entries may be prepared and entered only on a work sheet—a procedure illustrated in Appendix 3A. On the other hand, in accounting systems employing electromechanical or electronic processing equipment, adjusting entries often are prepared and recorded in the accounts monthly.

2³

continued

Classes of adjusting entries

The adjusting entries illustrated and explained in this chapter can be grouped first into two broad classes. One class consists of those entries that relate to data previously recorded in the accounts. These entries involve the transfer of data from asset and liability accounts to expense and revenue accounts. The second class consists of entries relating to activity on which nothing has been previously recorded in the accounts. These entries involve the first recording of assets and liabilities and the related expenses and revenues. Since each class involves both expenses and revenues, there are four major types of adjusting entries, namely, those involving: (1) asset/expense adjustments, (2) asset/revenue adjustments, (3) liability/expense adjustments, and (4) liability/revenue adjustments.

Indicate whether each of the following statements is true or false.

1. As a minimum, adjusting entries will be entered in every accounting system once a year.
2. In some accounting systems (for example, those employing electronic processing equipment) adjusting entries may be recorded at the end of every month.
3. The preparation of adjusting entries may make accounting information less objective or verifiable and thus more tentative in nature.
4. Although adjusting entries will affect statement of financial position accounts, they are of prime concern because of their effects upon net earnings.

Check your responses in Answer Frame 2³ on page 94.

Frame 3³

Asset/expense adjustments

One of the four major classes of adjusting entries involves the complete or partial expiration of the ability of an asset to render services (thus making it less valuable to its owner) as a result of its use in generating revenues. Because of its relative importance, five examples of this type of adjusting entry are presented below, specifically, for (1) insurance, (2) prepaid rent, (3) depreciation, (4) supplies, and (5) bad debts.

Insurance. When the premium on an insurance policy is paid in advance of the period covered by the policy, an asset is created that expires and becomes an expense with the passage of time. To illustrate, the advance payment of the premium on a one-year insurance policy that runs from August 1, 1979, to July 31, 1980, creates an asset called unexpired, or prepaid, insurance on August 1, 1979, because benefits — insurance protection — will be received in the future. The journal entry to record this transaction is:

```
1979
Aug. 1  Unexpired Insurance...............................................  7,200
            Cash ...........................................................           7,200
            To record payment in advance of annual premium.
```

Assume that the company has a calendar-year accounting period and that it records adjusting entries only at the end of its accounting year. By December 31, a part of the period covered by the policy has expired. Therefore, a part of the asset has expired. It now provides less future benefit than when acquired. This reduction of the ability of the asset to provide services must be recognized. The cost of the services received from the asset is treated as an expense. Since the policy provides the same services for every month of its one-year life, it seems logical to assign an equal amount of cost to each month. Thus, with 5 of the 12 months of coverage provided by payment of the premium having elapsed, 5/12 of the annual premium is charged to expense on December 31. The journal entry and the accounts after posting appear as follows:

```
1979
Dec. 31  Insurance Expense................................................  3,000
             Unexpired Insurance.........................................           3,000
             To record expense for five months, August 1 to
             December 31, 1979.
```

		Unexpired Insurance			*Account No. 104*	
Date		Explanation	Folio	Debit	Credit	Balance
1979						
Aug.	1	Cash paid	J 7*	7,200		7,200
Dec.	31	Adjustment	J 12		3,000	4,200

* Note: in this and all future illustrations, the folio references are assumed.

1. True. Every business firm has a fiscal year (accounting year) for which it presents financial statements. Thus, adjusting entries will be entered in every accounting system at least once a year.
2. True. Because of the speed and efficiency of electronic processing equipment in accepting and processing input data and the automatic printout of financial statements, adjusting entries are usually entered monthly in such systems.
3. True. Some adjusting entries, as will be illustrated later, are based upon estimates and not upon the dollar amounts in actual transactions. The result is the entry of less objective or verifiable data into the accounting system. And because the estimates may be in error, the accounting information is rendered somewhat tentative in nature—that is, subject to correction for error.
4. True. Although not covered specifically in exactly these words, the determination of net earnings has been called the crucial task of the accountant.

If you missed any of the above, read Frames 1³ and 2³ of this chapter again before proceeding to Frame 3³ on page 93.

3³
continued

Insurance Expense   *Account No. 408*

Date		Explanation	Folio	Debit	Credit	Balance
1979 Dec.	31	Adjustment	J 12	3,000		3,000

The insurance expense of $3,000 is reported in the company's earnings statement for the year ended December 31, 1979, as one of the expenses incurred in generating that year's revenues. The remaining amount of the annual premium, $4,200, is reported as a current asset. It is either presented as an individual item or combined with other similar items and reported as "prepaid expenses" in the statement of financial position for December 31, 1979. The $4,200 is a measure of the cost of the asset, unexpired insurance. Unexpired insurance is an asset because it provides future benefits. The $4,200 is shown as a current asset because it will be consumed in the course of normal operations in the next operating cycle of the business or one year, whichever is longer.

. Indicate whether each of the following statements about the above example is true or false.

1. The monthly insurance expense is $600.
2. The $4,200 of unexpired insurance will become an expense in 1980.
3. If a proper adjusting entry had not been made, the company's assets at December 31, 1979, would have been overstated by $4,200.

4. The $4,200 of unexpired insurance is treated as an asset primarily because the policy could be surrendered and a cash refund of that amount received from the insurance company.

Check your responses in Answer Frame 3³ on page 96.

Frame 4³

Prepaid rent. Prepaid rent is another example of the continuous incurrence of an expense and the corresponding using up of a previously recorded asset. When rent is paid in advance for any substantial period of time, the prepayment is debited to the Prepaid Rent account (an asset account) at the date it is paid. Because the benefits resulting from the expenditure are yet to be received, the expenditure creates an asset. Services from the facilities being rented are received *continuously* through time. The expense is incurred *continuously* as time elapses. An entry could be made frequently, even daily, to record the expense incurred. But typically the entry is not made until financial statements are to be prepared. At that time an entry is made transferring from the asset account to an expense account the cost of that portion of the asset that has expired.

The measurement of rent expense usually presents no problems. Generally, the rental contract specifies the amount of rent per unit of time. If the contract states an annual rental, 1/12 of this annual rental is charged to each month. This is true even though there are varying numbers of days in some months. The variations are not considered significant enough to be taken into consideration.

To illustrate, assume that rent was paid in advance in the amount of $1,200 on September 1, 1979, for one year beginning on that date. The entry made at that time was:

```
1979
Sept. 1   Prepaid Rent ..........................................................   1,200
              Cash ............................................................             1,200
          To record advance payment of one year's rent.
```

Assume that adjusting entries are to be prepared and recorded in the accounts as of December 31, 1979. On a separate sheet of paper, prepare the required adjusting entry for the above rent. Then check your response in Answer Frame 4³ on page 96.

Frame 5³

Rent expense is, of course, one of the operating expenses of the business. The balance of the prepaid rent in the example, $800, would be

1. True. With an annual premium of $7,200, the monthly insurance cost is $600.
2. True. Since 7 of the 12 months of coverage fall in 1980, 7/12 of $7,200 will be treated as an expense in 1980.
3. False. The assets would have been overstated by $3,000, the amount that should have been treated as an expense.
4. False. The $4,200 is treated as an asset primarily because it represents a measure of the cost of the benefits expected. In fact, if the policy is surrendered, the amount received as·a refund would generally be somewhat less than $4,200 under typical insurance company practices.

If you missed any of the above questions, you should restudy Frame 3³ carefully before proceeding to Frame 4³ on page 95.

Answer frame 4³

The required adjusting entry would read:

```
1979
Dec. 31  Rent Expense............................................................  400
             Prepaid Rent......................................................          400
         To record rent expense for four months.
```

Since one third of the period covered by the prepaid rent (4 of 12 months) has expired, one third of the $1,200 of prepaid rent is charged to expense. Unless your mistake was arithmetic in nature, you should restudy Frame 4³ if you missed the above entry. Then proceed to Frame 5³ on page 95.

5³
continued

reported as a current asset in the company's statement of financial position for December 31, 1979.

Depreciation. The concept of depreciation was introduced briefly in Chapter 2. Depreciation is another example of the continuous incurrence of an expense which results from the *gradual using up* of a previously recorded asset. The overall period of time involved in using up a depreciable asset, a building for example, is less definite than in the case of an insurance premium or prepaid rent. In the case of a depreciable asset, its life must be *estimated* in advance and individuals are not able to peer 10 to 50 years into the future with any real degree of accuracy. Nevertheless, the pattern of incurring an expense because of the expiration of an asset is basically the same. The cost of the asset (less estimated salvage value) is divided by the estimated number of years in the life of the asset to find the amount of asset cost to be charged as an expense to each time period. This process is called depreciation accounting. The cost allocated to each time period is called depreciation expense. The method discussed and illustrated here is known as the *straight-line method.* (Other methods are presented and discussed in Chapter 8.) The three factors involved in the computation of depreciation are:

1. The cost of the asset.
2. The estimated useful life of the asset.
3. The estimated salvage or scrap value of the asset.

Expressed in equation form, the computation of straight-line depreciation is as follows:

$$\text{Annual depreciation} = \frac{\text{Cost} - \text{Estimated salvage value}}{\text{Number of years of useful life}}$$

The difference between the cost of an asset and its estimated salvage value is sometimes referred to as an asset's *depreciable amount.* This difference is the net cost of using the asset during its useful life. It must be allocated to the various periods in an asset's life.

Depreciation is sometimes expressed as an annual percentage rate determined by dividing the annual amount of depreciation by the cost of the asset.

Indicate whether each of the following statements is true or false with regard to a building purchased at a cost of $200,000 and expected to be sold for $50,000 at the end of 25 years, even though the building will last 50 years.

1. The building's depreciable amount is $150,000.
2. The annual depreciation on the building is $6,000.
3. The annual depreciation rate is 3 percent on acquisition cost.
4. The estimated salvage value is $50,000.

Check your responses in Answer Frame 5³ on page 98.

Frame 6³

THE ALLOWANCE FOR DEPRECIATION ACCOUNT. As introduced in Chapter 2, depreciation is another example of expense as the consumption or using up of an asset. The depreciation expense for a period is not credited directly to the asset account but to a contra (reduction) account called allowance for depreciation (or accumulated depreciation). This account is merely a special subdivision of the credit side of the related plant asset account. The debit balance in the plant asset account minus the credit balance in the related allowance for depreciation contra account equals the cost of the benefits yet to be received from the asset.

Crediting depreciation to an allowance for depreciation account rather than directly to the asset account is justified largely on the grounds that recorded amounts of depreciation are quite tentative due to the use of estimates. In any event, depreciable asset accounts are

6³
continued

maintained at their original acquisition cost. The balance in the related allowance for depreciation increases each year by the amount of depreciation recorded until it finally reaches an amount equal to the cost of the asset (less estimated salvage value), unless the asset is prematurely disposed of.

DEPRECIATION ACCOUNTING ILLUSTRATED. To illustrate the accounting for depreciation, assume that a trial balance at December 31, 1979, includes an account with one delivery truck that cost $4,200. The truck was purchased on January 1, 1979. It is expected to have a useful life of five years; scrap value is estimated at $200. Therefore, the depreciation expense for one year equals ($4,200 − $200) ÷ 5, or $800. This is the amount of depreciation expense allocable to the production of revenue for the year 1979.

Depreciation for 1979 is recorded by the following entry:

```
1979
Dec. 31   Depreciation Expense – Delivery Equipment.....................   800
               Allowance for Depreciation – Delivery Equipment .......          800
          To record the depreciation expense for the year.
```

The ledger accounts will appear as follows:

Delivery Equipment   *Account No. 130*

Date		Explanation	Folio	Debit	Credit	Balance
1979 Jan.	1	One truck	J 8	4,200		4,200

Allowance for Depreciation – Delivery Equipment   *Account No. 131*

Date		Explanation	Folio	Debit	Credit	Balance
1979 Dec.	31	Adjustment	J 14		800	800

Depreciation Expense – Delivery Equipment   *Account No. 418*

Date		Explanation	Folio	Debit	Credit	Balance
1979 Dec.	31	Adjustment	J 14	800		800

At December 31, 1979, after the adjustment, $3,200 of the cost of the truck remains to be converted into expense while the truck is used during future years.

ALLOWANCE FOR DEPRECIATION IN THE STATEMENT OF FINANCIAL POSITION. In the statement of financial position at December 31, 1979, the asset accounts include the following:

Delivery equipment...	$4,200
Less: Allowance for depreciation – delivery equipment...............	800
	$3,400

The portion of the cost of the asset not yet charged to expense at the end of the first year is $3,400. Since expected scrap value is $200, only $3,200 is expected to be charged to expense in future years. Since another $800 of depreciation would be recorded at the end of 1980, the statement of financial position at the end of that year would show:

Delivery equipment..	$4,200
Less: Allowance for depreciation – delivery equipment..............	1,600
	$2,600

At the end of the fifth year, $4,000 of depreciation will have been recorded. If the estimates were correct, the asset will be retired from service and sold for $200. If this occurs, the required entry would read:

Cash...	200	
Allowance for Depreciation – Delivery Equipment	4,000	
Delivery Equipment...		4,200
To record retirement and sale of one delivery truck.		

Depreciation expense is an operating expense and is reported in the earnings statement. Depreciation may be classified as either selling expense or administrative expense.

Indicate whether each of the following statements is true or false.
1. The recording of the expiration of prepaid rent as an expense and the recording of depreciation do not differ conceptually.
2. The depreciation of office equipment could be classified functionally as an administrative expense.
3. The objective of depreciation accounting is to spread the depreciable amount of an asset over its useful life.
4. The account showing the accumulated depreciation on an asset is reported as an operating expense in the earnings statement.

Now turn to Answer Frame 6³ on page 100 to check your responses.

1. True. Both involve the recognition of an expense resulting from the consumption or using up of an asset in the operations of the business.
2. True. Depreciation on office equipment is an expense of operating the office of the business, and this is where the administrative function is usually performed.
3. True. This is indeed the objective of depreciation accounting.
4. False. Depreciation is the operating expense that would be shown in the earnings statement. The account showing the total accumulated depreciation is a contra account to the account containing the cost of the asset being depreciated and would be shown as such in the statement of financial position.

If you missed any of the above, read Frame 6³ again before proceeding to Frame 7³ below.

Frame 7³

Supplies. Every business consumes assets referred to as supplies in its operations. Such supplies may be classified as office supplies (paper, stationery, carbon paper, pencils) or selling supplies (gummed tape, string, paper bags or cartons, wrapping paper) or, possibly, as cleaning supplies (soap, disinfectants). They are frequently bought in bulk and consumed or used gradually through time.

To illustrate, assume that office supplies were bought at various times throughout the year and recorded by debiting an asset account, Office Supplies on Hand, and crediting Cash. At the end of the year, the Office Supplies on Hand account shows a debit balance of $1,400. An actual physical inventory shows that only $400 worth of supplies are on hand. Thus, an adjusting entry is required to bring the accounts up to date. The entry will recognize the reduction in the asset and the incurrence of an expense through the using up of office supplies. From the information given, the asset balance should be $400 and the expense incurred, $1,000. By making the following entry, the accounts will be adjusted to those balances:

```
1979
Dec. 31  Office Supplies Expense............................................  1,000
              Office Supplies on Hand ....................................        1,000
            To record supplies used during the year.
```

While the entry to record the usage of supplies could be made when the supplies are issued from the storeroom, it is usually not worth the expense to account so carefully for such small items.

The Office Supplies Expense account would appear as an operating expense in the earnings statement. Office Supplies on Hand would be reported as a current asset in the statement of financial position, often lumped with similar items and entitled Prepaid Expenses.

Bad debts. No matter how carefully a company screens applications for credit from its customers, if it renders services or sells goods on a credit basis it will encounter the problem of bad debts — uncollectible accounts receivable. Currently, actual bad debts range from a small fraction of accounts receivable to an amount considerably larger, depending, at least in part, upon economic conditions.

To illustrate the problems encountered in accounting for bad debts, assume that the December 31, 1979, trial balance of a company in its first year of operations shows accounts receivable of $50,000. Assume further that the manager of the company, using trade association data, estimates that 4 percent of the accounts receivable will never be collected. This information would require the following adjusting entry:

```
1979
Dec. 31   Bad Debts Expense................................................  2,000
                Allowance for Doubtful Accounts .......................         2,000
          To record estimated bad debts for the year as 4
          percent of accounts receivable.
```

This entry accomplishes two things: (1) it brings about a proper matching of bad debts expense with revenue, since the uncollectible accounts arising from 1979 sales are recognized as an expense in 1979; and (2) the accounts receivable as of December 31, 1979, are properly valued at their net realizable value, the amount of cash expected to be collected. The Allowance for Doubtful Accounts balance is deducted from accounts receivable as follows:

```
Accounts receivable.........................................  $50,000
Less: Allowance for doubtful accounts..............    2,000
                                                         $48,000
```

The topic of accounting for bad debts is covered in greater depth in Chapter 7. The purpose of the discussion here was merely to illustrate it as an adjusting entry.

True or false?

1. Office supplies on hand should be classified as a current asset.
2. If in the entries recording office supplies purchased in Frame 7^3, the debits had been made to Office Supplies Expense instead of to the asset account Office Supplies on Hand, the adjusting entry would have been different.
3. If the entry for Bad Debts Expense had been in the amount of 5 percent of accounts receivable, the amount of the entry would have been increased by $2,500.
4. One reason for making the adjusting entry for uncollectible accounts is to reduce the accounts receivable to their net realizable value.

Now turn to Answer Frame 7^3 on page 102 to check your answers.

Frame 8³

Asset/revenue adjustments

In some instances, agreements are entered into which create a right to collect an increasing amount of assets through time. Periodically, the amounts are collected. Examples of this type of adjustment include the accruals made for commissions earned (discussed in Chapter 2), interest revenue, and rent revenue.

Interest revenue. The interest received periodically on investments such as bonds and savings accounts is literally earned by the lender or investor moment by moment. Rarely is payment of the interest made on the last day of the accounting period. Thus, the accounting records normally will not show the amount of interest revenue earned nor the total assets owned by the investor unless an adjusting entry is made. An entry at the end of the accounting period is needed which debits a receivable account (an asset) and credits a revenue account to record the asset owned and the interest earned.

For example, assume that a company invests some funds in an interest-paying security. The interest is received twice a year on May 1 and November 1 in the amount of $1,800 on each date. If the investment was purchased on May 2, 1979, Interest Revenue is credited with the $1,800 of cash received on November 1. At December 31, 1979, an additional two months' interest of the six months' interest to be received on May 1, 1980, has been earned. An entry must be made to show the amount of interest earned and the asset, the right to receive this interest, at December 31, 1979. The entry, which is said to be an entry to record the accrual of revenue, is:

Accrued Interest Receivable.. 600
    Interest Revenue   600
        To record two months' interest revenue.

The ledger accounts appear as follows:

Accrued Interest Receivable   *Account No. 107*

Date		Explanation	Folio	Debit	Credit	Balance
1979 Dec.	31	Adjustment	J 14	600		600

Interest Revenue   *Account No. 506*

Date		Explanation	Folio	Debit	Credit	Balance
1979 Nov.	1	Cash received	J 13		1,800	1,800
Dec.	31	Adjustment	J 14		600	2,400

The $600 debit balance in Accrued Interest Receivable is reported as a current asset in the December 31, 1979, statement of financial position. The $2,400 credit balance in Interest Revenue is the interest earned during the year. Under accrual basis accounting, it does not matter whether cash was collected during the year or not. The interest revenue earned still is reported in the earnings statement for the year.

ENTRY IN NEXT PERIOD.   The collection of $1,800 of cash on May 1, 1980, is recorded as follows:

```
1980
May 1  Cash.................................................................. 1,800
              Accrued Interest Receivable................................      600
              Interest Revenue ...............................................    1,200
         Collected interest for six months ending May 1.
```

Note how the preparation of the adjusting entry properly assigns the revenue earned to the proper accounting period. The $1,800 collected represents interest earned in the six months ending May 1, 1980. But two of these months fell in calendar year 1979. Therefore, one third of $1,800 should be treated as 1979 revenue and the balance as 1980 revenue. The entries prepared yield exactly these results.

Indicate whether each of the following statements about the above example is true or false.

1. If no adjusting entry had been made, the interest earned in the last two months of 1979 would probably be recorded as 1980 revenue when collected on May 1, 1980.
2. The debit balance in the Accrued Interest Receivable account represents the amount of interest earned but not collected through December 31, 1979.
3. The adjusting entry is made so that the interest earned in November and December of 1979 is recorded as revenue of that year.
4. The credit balance (after adjustment) in the Interest Revenue account shows the amount of interest earned and collected in cash during the year.

Now turn to Answer Frame 8³ on page 104 to check your responses.

1. True. The entry would be likely to consist of a debit to Cash and a credit to Interest Revenue for $1,800.
2. True. The interest for these two months is, by agreement, not payable until May 1; hence, the interest is earned but not collected.
3. True. One of the two reasons for making the entry is to secure a proper assignment to periods of the revenue earned.
4. False. Only $1,800 of cash was received; the remaining $600 was accrued.

Restudy Frame 8³ carefully if you missed any of the above. Then proceed to Frame 9³ below.

Frame 9³

Rent revenue. Rental agreements usually require rent to be paid at the beginning of the rental period. But occasionally a situation may be encountered that requires the accrual of rent revenue and the recognition of an asset.

To illustrate, assume that a company rents the second floor of a building it owns to another party for a monthly rental of $2,400, with the first rental payment due on January 16, 1980. Occupancy is granted on December 16, 1979. Assuming that the company's accounting period ends on December 31, the adjusting entry required on December 31, 1979, is:

Accrued Rent Receivable	1,200	
Rent Revenue		1,200
To record accrual of one half of a month's rent revenue.		

The accrued rent receivable of $1,200 would be reported as a current asset in the statement of financial position, while the rent revenue would be reported in the earnings statement.

ENTRY IN THE NEXT PERIOD. When the first monthly rental payment of $2,400 is received on January 16, 1980, the cash received would be accounted for as a $1,200 collection of the balance in the Accrued Rent Receivable account and $1,200 as a cash collection of January rent revenue. Thus, the adjusting entry provides for the assignment of the first $2,400 of rent earned to the proper periods, as well as correctly stating assets on December 31, 1979.

Liability/expense adjustments

In order to report on net earnings and financial position properly, adjustments involving liability and expense accounts are often required. Discussed below are the adjustments relating to salaries and federal income taxes, although similar adjustments may be required for other forms of taxes, interest, and pension obligations.

Salaries. Employee services are assets when acquired. But the accountant seldom records employee services as assets for two reasons: (1) they are usually recorded when they are paid; and (2) by the time they are recorded, the asset has expired because the benefits have been received. Thus, the recording of employee services usually involves a debit to an expense account and a credit to cash (payroll withholdings and payroll taxes are ignored here but are discussed in Chapter 7). If the receipt of employee services is recognized only when paid, an adjusting entry may be required at the end of an accounting period to record those services received for which payment has not been made.

To illustrate, assume that the Office Salaries Expense account shows a debit balance at the end of January 1979 of $8,800. This consists of four weekly payrolls (Monday through Saturday) of $2,200 each (paid on Saturday). But, assuming the last day of January falls on a Wednesday, the expense account does not show salaries earned by employees for the last three days of the month. Nor do the accounts show the employer's obligation to pay these salaries. If financial statements are to be prepared for January, the following adjusting entry is needed:

Office Salaries Expense 1,100
    Accrued Office Salaries Payable.. 1,100
      To accrue one half of a week's office salaries.

The two accounts involved now appear as follows:

Office Salaries Expense   *Account No. 422*

Date		Explanation	Folio	Debit	Credit	Balance
1979 Jan.	6	1st week cash	J 3	2,200		2,200
	13	2d week cash	J 4	2,200		4,400
	20	3d week cash	J 4	2,200		6,600
	27	4th week cash	J 5	2,200		8,800
	31	Adjustment	J 5	1,100		9,900

Accrued Office Salaries Payable   *Account No. 309*

Date		Explanation	Folio	Debit	Credit	Balance
1979 Jan.	31	Adjustment	J 5		1,100	1,100

The adjusting journal entry brings the month's salaries expense up to its correct amount for earnings statement purposes. The credit records the liability to employees for services for statement of financial position purposes.

Assume that the weekly office payroll in the above example is paid on February 3 in the amount of $2,200. On a separate sheet of paper, write out the entry to record this payment. Then check your answer in Answer Frame 9[3] on page 106.

Frame 10³

Federal income taxes. Profitable corporations are usually subject to federal income taxes. But the tax return will not be filed and the income taxes will not be paid until some time after the end of the accounting year. Consequently, an adjusting entry must be made if expenses and liabilities are to be correctly stated. Assuming that the estimated amount of federal income taxes for the year is $8,400, the required adjusting entry is:

Federal Income Taxes Expense	8,400	
Federal Income Taxes Payable		8,400

To record estimated federal income taxes for the year.

Failure to make such an entry would cause net earnings to be overstated and current liabilities to be understated by $8,400 each. (The topic of income tax allocation is ignored here but is discussed in the Appendix to Chapter 7.)

Liability/revenue adjustments

This class of adjustments covers those situations in which the customer pays assets (usually cash) into the selling company prior to the receipt of merchandise or services. Such receipts are usually credited to an account entitled Prepaid Revenues, Revenues Received in Advance, or Unearned Revenue. Better terminology would be Advances by Customers to show clearly the liability nature of the account. The seller is obligated either to deliver the goods, provide the services, or return the customer's money. The liability is canceled, and revenue is earned by providing the agreed-upon goods or services.

Advance payments could be received for items such as tickets, rent, and magazine or newspaper subscriptions. Because of their similarity, only the advance receipt of subscriptions will be illustrated and discussed.

Subscription revenue. Assume that during 1979 a company received a total of $48,000 at various times as payment in advance for a number of one-year subscriptions to a monthly magazine it sells. The entry debiting Cash and crediting Subscriptions Received in Advance was made to record each amount of cash collected. The liability established when the cash was received is gradually converted into revenue as the magazines contracted for are delivered. Thus, an adjusting entry to update the accounts is usually required before financial statements are prepared. Assuming that 40 percent of the magazines paid for in advance have been delivered by year-end, the required adjusting entry is:

```
1979
Dec. 31  Subscriptions Received in Advance ........................ 19,200
            Subscription Revenue.....................................           19,200
           To record subscription revenue earned in 1979.
```

The subscription revenue of $19,200 is, of course, reported in the earnings statement for 1979. The $28,800 ($48,000 − $19,200) balance in the Subscriptions Received in Advance account is reported as a current liability in the statement of financial position. The $28,800 will be earned in 1980 and transferred to a revenue account in that year.

Assume that on August 1, 1979, a theater company sold all of the tickets for a series of ten plays for $10,000 cash. The cash received was credited to an account entitled Admissions Received in Advance. One play was presented each month, with the first play given in August. Assuming that cash refunds are not paid for unused tickets, on a separate sheet of paper write out the required adjusting entry for December 31, 1979. Then check your response in Answer Frame 10[3] on page 108.

Frame 11[3]

Since the process of preparing financial statements after adjusting entries have been journalized and posted was illustrated in Chapter 2, it need not be dealt with here. Rather, attention will be directed toward the next steps in the financial accounting process.

Closing entries

After adjusting entries have been journalized and posted, up-to-date information of two major types is found in the accounts in an accounting system: (1) information relating to the activities occurring during the period just ended, and (2) information on the financial condition of the entity at the end of the period.

The first type of information is found largely in the expense and revenue accounts. These accounts have already been discussed as temporarily established subdivisions of the Retained Earnings account. The expense and revenue accounts help the accountant fulfill a most

11³
continued

important task—the determination of periodic net earnings. After the financial statements for the period have been prepared, these temporary accounts have served their purpose. They must now be brought to a zero balance in order that information for the next accounting period can be entered in them.

The balance in each expense and revenue account is transferred by journal entry to an account entitled Expense and Revenue Summary. This is a *clearing* account used only at the end of the accounting period to summarize the expenses and revenues for the period. The difference between these two classes of items is the net earnings or loss for the period. Since revenue accounts have credit balances, they are debited and Expense and Revenue Summary is credited. Conversely, expense accounts have debit balances, so they are credited and Expense and Revenue Summary is debited. The Expense and Revenue Summary account now contains either a debit (net loss) or credit (net earnings) balance. It is then debited or credited as required to bring it to a zero balance, with Retained Earnings credited or debited in order to keep the entry in balance. This closing process is often referred to as "closing the books."

Closing entries illustrated

To illustrate the preparation of closing entries, assume that the ledger of a company contains the following earnings statement accounts:

Service Revenue	$196,000	Salaries Expense	$40,000
Depreciation Expense	120,000	Other Expenses	16,000
		Federal Income Taxes	5,000

The required closing entries, assuming a December 31, 1979, closing, are as follows:

1979
Dec. 31   Service Revenue   196,000
         Expense and Revenue Summary   196,000
         To close revenue account.

    31   Expense and Revenue Summary   181,000
         Depreciation Expense   120,000
         Salaries Expense   40,000
         Other Expenses   16,000
         Federal Income Taxes   5,000
         To close expense accounts.

    31   Expense and Revenue Summary   15,000
         Retained Earnings   15,000
         To close Expense and Revenue Summary account
         to Retained Earnings.

Further assume that a Dividends account shows a debit balance of $5,000. It is closed directly to Retained Earnings as follows:

1979
Dec. 31   Retained Earnings   5,000
         Dividends   5,000
         To close dividends.

The above entries are posted in the normal manner and, if properly prepared and posted, will reduce all of the revenue and expense accounts to zero balances so that they can be used to accumulate data needed to determine the next period's net earnings. The Dividends account is also brought to a zero balance so it will be ready to accept entries for dividends in the coming year.

Indicate whether each of the following statements is true or false.
1.   An Interest Revenue account containing a balance of $500 is closed by an entry debiting Interest Revenue and crediting Expense and Revenue Summary for $500.
2.   The net earnings for a period cannot be properly determined if closing entries are not made.
3.   If the Expense and Revenue Summary account has a debit balance, the company has net earnings for the period.
4.   Because annual reporting is the usual practice, closing entries are normally prepared only once a year.

Check your responses in Answer Frame 11³ on page 110.

Frame 12³

The Expense and Revenue Summary and Retained Earnings accounts as they appear after the above closing entries are posted are presented below. The beginning balance of $65,000 in the Retained Earnings account is assumed, as are the account numbers and the posting cross-reference (folio J 15). Note that the Expense and Revenue Summary

12³
continued

account shows clearly the net earnings for the period — the final amount transferred, or closed, to Retained Earnings. The balance in the Retained Earnings account of $75,000 is the amount of retained earnings shown in the statement of financial position for December 31, 1979.

Expense and Revenue Summary   *Account No. 600*

Date		Explanation	Folio	Debit	Credit	Balance
1979						
Dec.	31	Revenues	J 15		196,000	196,000
	31	Expenses	J 15	181,000		15,000
	31	To close	J 15	15,000		–0–

Retained Earnings   *Account No. 317*

Date		Explanation	Folio	Debit	Credit	Balance
1979						
Jan.	1	Balance				65,000
Dec.	31	Net earnings	J 15		15,000	80,000
	31	Dividends	J 15	5,000		75,000

Post-closing trial balance

After the closing process has been completed, the only open accounts in the ledger are the statement of financial position accounts. Since these accounts contain the opening balances for the coming accounting year, they must, of course, be in balance. The preparation of a post-closing trial balance thus serves as a means of checking upon the accuracy of the closing process (the preparation and posting of closing entries and the bringing forward of account balances). At the same time it ensures that the books are in balance at the start of the new accounting period.

As in the case of a trial balance, a post-closing trial balance is simply a listing of all of the open accounts in a system or ledger. The total of the accounts with debit balances must be equal to the total of the accounts with credit balances, or an error has been made.

The accounting cycle summarized

In Chapter 1 the financial accounting process was described as consisting of a number of functions beginning with observation of economic activity and ending with interpretation of reports and statements upon such activity. In this process are a number of steps that relate to the formal accounting system and its use in accumulating, processing, and reporting useful financial information. These steps, which have been illustrated and discussed in this and previous chapters, are referred to collectively as the accounting cycle. These steps are summarized as consisting of the following:

1. Journalizing transactions (and other events) in the journal.
2. Posting journal entries to the accounts.
3. Taking a trial balance of the accounts.
4. Journalizing the adjusting entries.
5. Posting the adjusting entries to the accounts.
6. Preparing financial statements.
7. Journalizing the closing entries.
8. Posting the closing entries to the accounts.
9. Taking a post-closing trial balance.

As is set forth in Appendix 3A, completion of many of the steps that fall at the end of an accounting period may be made somewhat easier through use of a work sheet. Appendix 3B illustrates the use of reversing entries which are used by some accountants.

Indicate whether each of the following statements is true or false.

1. After closing entries have been posted, balances will appear only in the statement of financial position accounts.
2. In automated systems, the Expense and Revenue Summary account is often omitted.
3. A post-closing trial balance contains only statement of financial position accounts.
4. The accounting cycle consists of the specific steps taken in the operation of an accounting system to accumulate, process, and report useful information.

Check your responses in Answer Frame 12[3] on page 112.

Answer frame 12³

All of the statements in Frame 12³ are true. Together, they cover most of the more important points made in Frame 12³. If you missed any of the above questions, you may wish to review Frame 12³ before proceeding to the Summary below.

Summary *chapter* 3

Adjusting entries usually are made to include in the accounts information on economic activity that has occurred but is not evidenced by a specific transaction.

Adjusting entries fall into four major classes, namely, those involving adjustments of (1) asset and expense accounts, (2) asset and revenue accounts, (3) liability and expense accounts, and (4) liability and revenue accounts. In (1) the adjustment involves recognition of an expense as a result of the using up of a previously recorded asset; examples include depreciation, supplies, insurance, bad debts, and rent. In (2) the adjustment involves recognition of the growth of an asset as a result of the rendering of services to customers; examples include commissions and interest. In (3) the adjustment involves recognition of an expense and the corresponding obligation to pay as a result of the receipt of services or the levying of taxes; examples include interest, salaries, and federal income taxes. In (4) the adjustment involves recognition of the earning of revenue and the cancellation of a liability by providing services for which customers pay in advance; examples include subscriptions, tickets, and rent.

In all cases, adjusting entries involve changing account balances from what they presently contain to what they should contain for proper financial reporting.

After the balances in the expense and revenue accounts have been used to prepare the earnings statement (and the Dividends account, if any, reported in the statement of retained earnings), these accounts are brought to a zero balance. They have served their purpose of accumulating useful information for an accounting period. They must be closed in order that information for the next accounting period may be entered in them. The closing of these accounts is accomplished through the preparation and posting of closing entries. The balances in all of the expense and revenue accounts are transferred to an Expense and Revenue Summary account, whose balance in turn (representing net earnings or net loss) is transferred to Retained Earnings. The Dividends account is closed to Retained Earnings. A post-closing trial balance may be prepared to check upon the equality of the debit and credit account balances in the ledger after the closing process has been completed.

The steps undertaken to operate an accounting system are collectively referred to as the accounting cycle and are listed in Frame 12³ on page 111.

Appendix 3A which follows discusses the use of the work sheet in the accounting process. Appendix 3B illustrates the use of reversing entries.

The Glossary and Student Review Quiz for this chapter begin on pages 119 and 120.

APPENDIX 3A: THE WORK SHEET FOR A SERVICE COMPANY

In manually operated accounting systems containing large numbers of accounts, the accounting activities to be completed at the end of a financial reporting period may be organized and handled more efficiently through use of a work sheet. A work sheet is simply a sheet of paper containing a number of columns and lines for recording account titles, item descriptions, and dollar amounts. Since it is used internally only, it can take on a variety of forms. But to be of any real value, it will, as a minimum, contain columns for a trial balance, adjusting entries, an earnings statement, and a statement of financial position. An expanded version of a work sheet is presented in Illustration 3.1 and is discussed below.

The Trial Balance columns

Instead of preparing a separate trial balance, the open accounts in the ledger are entered in the first pair of columns entitled Trial Balance in the work sheet prepared for the Ryder Company for the month ended June 30, 1979. The columns are summed and the equality of the debits and credits in the ledger shown by entering the totals ($26,200) immediately after the last item in the trial balance.

The Adjustments columns

In the next pair of columns, all of the adjustments required to bring the accounts up to date prior to the preparation of financial statements are entered. The assumed adjustments for the Ryder Company are as follows:

Entry (*a*) records $40 of insurance premium paid in advance which relates to coverage for the month of June; the debit and credit keyed with the letter A comprise the entry made to recognize the asset expiration and the related expense.

Entry (*b*) records the fact that supplies costing $600 were used during the month, as determined by a physical inventory.

113

Illustration 3.1

			RYDER COMPANY				
			Work Sheet				
			For the Month Ended June 30, 1979				

Line No.	Acct. No.	Account Titles	Trial Balance		Adjustments	
			Debit	Credit	Debit	Credit
1	101	Cash	14,870			
2	102	Accounts receivable	3,250			
3	102-A	Allowance for doubtful accounts		100		(c) 160
4	112	Store supplies	720			(b) 600
5	114	Unexpired insurance	480			(a) 40
6	120	Furniture and fixtures	2,400			
7	120-A	Allowance for depreciation		200		(d) 20
8	201	Accounts payable		5,100		
9	301	Capital stock		10,000		
10	310	Retained earnings		3,000		
11	311	Dividends	250			
12	401	Service revenue		7,800		
13	514	Salaries expense	1,800			
14	515	Advertising expense	700			
15	517	Other service expense	430			(f) 130
16	521	Office salaries expense	800		(e) 120	
17	525	Other administrative expense	500			
18			26,200	26,200		
19	519	Insurance expense			(a) 40	
20	516	Store supplies expense			(b) 600	
21	520	Bad debts expense			(c) 160	
22	518	Depreciation expense			(d) 20	
23	202	Accrued salaries payable				(e) 120
24	113	Travel advances			(f) 130	
25					1,070	1,070
26		Net earnings				
27						
28		Retained earnings				

Entry (c) increases the allowance for doubtful accounts balance by $160.

Entry (d) records depreciation expense for the month, determined by dividing the cost of the furniture and fixtures ($2,400) by their estimated useful lives of ten years and dividing the result by 12.

Entry (e) records the expense and the liability resulting from the fact that there were unpaid office salaries of $120 at the end of the month.

Entry (f) indicates that at the time it advanced money to an employee to travel on company business, Ryder Company debited the amount advanced to Other Service Expense (and credited Cash). But, since the

Adjusted Trial Balance		Earnings Statement		Statement of Retained Earnings		Statement of Financial Position		Line No.
Debit	Credit	Debit	Credit	Debit	Credit	Debit	Credit	
14,870						14,870		1
3,250						3,250		2
	260						260	3
120						120		4
440						440		5
2,400						2,400		6
	220						220	7
	5,100						5,100	8
	10,000						10,000	9
	3,000				3,000			10
250				250				11
	7,800		7,800					12
1,800		1,800						13
700		700						14
300		300						15
920		920						16
500		500						17
								18
40		40						19
600		600						20
160		160						21
20		20						22
	120						120	23
130						130		24
26,500	26,500	5,040	7,800					25
		2,760			2,760			26
		7,800	7,800	250	5,760			27
				5,510			5,510	28
				5,760	5,760	21,210	21,210	

travel will take place in July, the $130 advanced is not an expense of June. It is an asset, a prepaid expense, and must be removed from the expense account and set up as an asset. The debit and credit, keyed with the letter (*f*), accomplish this.

One advantage of a work sheet is that it assembles all of the accounts in one place, where they may be easily studied to determine the need for possible adjustment. As a result, entries are not likely to be overlooked.

After all of the adjusting entries are entered in the Adjustments columns, the two columns are totaled and their equality noted as a partial check of the arithmetic accuracy of the work completed thus far.

The Adjusted Trial Balance columns

After the adjustments have been entered, the adjusted balance of each account is determined and entered in the Adjusted Trial Balance columns. For example, the Allowance for Doubtful Accounts has a balance of $100, unadjusted, to which was added $160 in adjusting entry (c), leaving a credit balance of $260. This $260 is shown in the credit column of the pair of columns headed Adjusted Trial Balance.

All accounts having balances are extended to the Adjusted Trial Balance columns. Note carefully how the rules of debit and credit apply as to whether an entry increases or decreases the balance in the account. For example, Store Supplies has a debit balance of $720 which is decreased by a credit of $600 to a total of $120 — the correct balance for financial reporting purposes.

The balances in the Adjusted Trial Balance columns are summed. The equality of the accounts with debit balances and those with credit balances is noted as a check upon the arithmetic accuracy of the work completed.

The Earnings Statement columns

All of the accounts in the Adjusted Trial Balance columns that will appear in the earnings statement (the expense and revenue accounts) are now extended into the Earnings Statement columns — revenues as credits, expenses as debits. Each column is subtotaled, revealing expenses (debits) of $5,040 and revenues (credits) of $7,800. This means that the net earnings for the period amounted to $2,760. This amount is entered in the debit column to bring the two column totals into agreement. Note the similarity of the debit here to the debit in the Expense and Revenue Summary account to close or transfer net earnings to the Retained Earnings account. A net loss would, of course, be recorded in the opposite manner — that is, as a credit.

The Statement of Retained Earnings columns

These columns contain the items that appear in the statement of retained earnings, namely: the beginning balance of retained earnings, the net earnings for the period, dividends (if any), and the ending balance of retained earnings. Note that the illustrated columns contain the first three of these items, along with the entry as a credit of the net earnings for the period of $2,760. The columns are subtotaled and the difference between the two subtotals, the ending balance of retained earnings, $5,510, is entered in order to bring the two column totals into balance.

The Statement of Financial Position columns

All of the asset, liability, and the stockholders' equity accounts are extended into the Statement of Financial Position columns — assets as debits and the others as credits. Note that the ending, rather than the beginning, balance in Retained Earnings is carried into these columns. Once again, to check the arithmetic accuracy of the work completed, the columns are totaled and their agreement noted.

The completed work sheet

Some accountants, in completing a work sheet, enter brief explanations keyed to the adjusting entries in the lower left-hand corner of the work sheet. Such a practice is useful for complicated adjustments, but is not necessary for the relatively routine adjustments illustrated here.

When the work sheet is completed, all of the information needed to prepare the financial statements is readily available. It need only be recast into a more formal format.

Note, also, that it would be a relatively routine matter to journalize the adjusting and closing entries in the journal and then post them to the accounts. The adjusting entries can be readily prepared from information in the Adjustments columns, closing entries from the items in the Earnings Statement columns, and the dividends item in the Statement of Retained Earnings columns. But, since financial statements can be prepared from the work sheet, such entries are not likely to be entered formally in the journal and posted to the accounts at any time other than at the formal annual closing of the books. Thus, one of the real advantages of using a work sheet is that interim financial statements can be prepared without going through the work of journalizing and posting adjusting and closing entries.

APPENDIX 3B: REVERSING ENTRIES

For certain types of adjusting entries, reversing entries (given the name because they reverse the effects of the adjusting entry to which they relate) may be prepared as of the first day of the next accounting period. The purpose of a reversing entry is to make simpler the entry relating to that same item in the next accounting period.

To illustrate, we will use the facts presented in Frame 8[3] relating to the accrual of interest. In that discussion a company invested funds in an interest-paying security on May 2, 1979. The interest is to be received on May 1 and November 1 of each year in the amount of $1,800 on each date. The first interest check was received on November 1, 1979, and was properly recorded. An adjusting entry was made at December 31, 1979 (the end of the accounting year), to recognize the interest earned between November 1 and December 31. Below are illustrated the entries from December 31, 1979, through May 1 (1) assuming no reversing entry is used and (2) assuming a reversing entry is used.

<table>
<tr><td align="center">(1)</td><td align="center">(2)</td></tr>
<tr><td align="center">*No reversing entry to be used*</td><td align="center">*Reversing entry to be used*</td></tr>
</table>

1979				1979			
Dec. 31	Accrued Interest			Dec. 31	Accrued Interest		
	Receivable	600			Receivable	600	
	Interest Revenue......		600		Interest Revenue......		600
	To record two months' interest revenue.				To record two months' interest revenue.		

(The closing entries would be the same in either case.)

1980				1980			
Jan. 1	No entry			Jan. 1	Interest Revenue............	600	
					Accrued Interest		
					Receivable		600
					To reverse the adjusting entry made on 12/31/79.		
May 1	Cash	1,800		May 1	Cash	1,800	
	Accrued Interest				Interest Revenue...		1,800
	Receivable		600		Collected interest for six months ending May 1.		
	Interest Revenue...		1,200				
	Collected interest for six months ending May 1.						

You will notice that whether a reversing entry is to be used or not, the adjusting and closing entries for 1979 are identical. The use of a reversing entry (which is the exact reverse of the debit and credit used in the adjusting entry) on January 1 enables the entry made on May 1 to be simpler. The accountant does not have to remember that accrued interest receivable of $600 has already been recorded on this investment. When the $1,800 check arrives, the entry is simply a debit to Cash and credit to Interest Revenue.

When the accounts are maintained on a computer (which is a very common situation), the computer program may have been designed to debit Cash and credit Interest Revenue every time an interest check is received. The use of a reversing entry on January 1 permits the May 1 entry to be recorded in this way.

The end result in the accounts is the same whether a reversing entry is used or not. To prove this, the accounts as they would appear are shown below. The adjusting and closing entries from 1979 are ignored since they were the same under either method.

<table>
<tr><td align="center">(1)</td><td align="center">(2)</td></tr>
<tr><td align="center">*No reversing entry to be used*</td><td align="center">*Reversing entry to be used*</td></tr>
<tr><td align="center">**Cash**</td><td align="center">**Cash**</td></tr>
<tr><td>5/1/80   1,800</td><td>5/1/80   1,800</td></tr>
</table>

Accrued Interest Receivable				Accrued Interest Receivable	
Beg. Bal. 600	5/1/80 600		Beg. Bal. 600	1/1/80 600

Interest Revenue				Interest Revenue	
	5/1/80 1,200		1/1/80 600	5/1/80 1,800

Not all adjusting entries may be reversed on the first day of the next accounting period. Ideal candidates are where cash is going to be paid or received in the following period for an item which accrues over time and resulted in an adjusting entry. Examples of such items would include accrued wages, rent, and interest. Adjustments for items which will not result in a subsequent receipt or payment of cash (such as the adjustment for depreciation) are not candidates for the use of a reversing entry.

Reversing entries are optional and relate to bookkeeping technique. Whether they are used or not has no effect on the financial statements. Students may encounter the use of reversing entries in more advanced accounting courses or in actual practice. An understanding of reversing entries is not essential to a comprehension of the remainder of this text since they will not be utilized.

Glossary *chapter* 3

Accrual basis of accounting – a method of earnings determination under which revenues are recorded when goods are delivered or services are rendered, and expenses are recorded in the same period as the revenues which they helped to create are recognized.

Accrued (assets and liabilities) – those assets and liabilities which exist at the end of an accounting period but which have not been recorded up to the time at which adjusting entries are to be prepared. They represent rights to receive, or obligations to make, payments which are not legally due at the statement of financial position date. Examples are accrued interest receivable, accrued rent receivable, accrued salaries (or wages) payable, and accrued interest payable.

Accumulated Depreciation account – synonymous with Allowance for Depreciation account below.

Adjusting entries – journal entries made to record the accrued effects of economic activity. They are made at the end of the accounting period to bring the accounts to their proper balances before financial statements are prepared.

Allowance for Depreciation account – a contra asset account (defined as an account shown as a deduction from the asset to which it relates in the statement of financial position); an account which shows the sum of all amounts taken as depreciation on the asset up to the statement of financial position date.

Allowance for Doubtful Accounts account – an account showing the estimated amount of outstanding accounts receivable not expected to be collected; a contra asset account shown as a deduction from accounts receivable in the statement of financial position.

Cash basis of accounting – a procedure under which revenue is recorded when cash is received and expenses recorded when cash is paid.

Charge – synonymous with the term "debit."

Closing – the act of transferring the balances in the expense and revenue accounts to the Expense and Revenue Summary account and then to the Retained Earnings account. The balance in the Dividends account, if one is used, is transferred to Retained Earnings.

Deferred costs — one interpretation or definition of assets in which they are viewed as charges awaiting assignment to expense in the determination of net earnings.

Depreciation accounting — the process of allocating and charging to expense the cost of a limited-life, long-term asset (such as a building) over its useful life.

Depreciation expense — the portion of the cost of a depreciable asset charged to expense in a given accounting period.

Depreciation formula — the procedure employed in calculating periodic depreciation, generally cost less estimated salvage value divided by the number of years of expected useful life, which is the procedure employed to determine the annual depreciation charge under the straight-line method.

Expense and Revenue account — a clearing account used to summarize all revenue and expense account balances at the end of an accounting period.

Post-closing trial balance — a trial balance taken after the expense and revenue (and dividend) accounts have been closed.

Prepaid expense — an asset which is awaiting assignment to expense. An example is unexpired insurance.

Revenue received in advance — a flow of assets received from customers in advance of the rendering of services for or the delivery of goods to them; since the revenue has not been earned, it is a liability; often called *prepaid revenue* or *unearned revenue*, although preferred terminology would be *advances by customers*.

Reversing entries — journal entries made on the first day of the next accounting period to reverse the effects of the adjusting entries to which they relate. Their purpose is to make easier the recording of a subsequent transaction relating to those same items. They may only be used for certain types of adjusting entries — usually those accruals where cash is to be paid or received in the next accounting period.

Service potential — the benefits embodied in assets. The future services that as-

sets can render are what make assets "things of value" to a business.

Work sheet — an informal accounting statement used to summarize the trial balance and information needed to prepare the financial statements and the adjusting and closing entries.

Continue with the Student Review Quiz below as a self-administered test of your understanding of the material presented in this chapter.

Student review quiz *chapter* 3

To develop a permanent record of your responses, you may write them on the answer sheet provided in the *Work Papers* or on a separate sheet of paper.

1 Which of the following changes in the accounts is handled through an adjusting entry?

a Gradual conversion of an asset into an expense.

b Equal and gradual growth of an expense and a liability over the accounting period.

c Earning of revenue received in advance.

d Equal and gradual growth of an asset and a revenue over the accounting period.

e All of the above.

2 If the accounts receivable balance is $6,800 and uncollectible accounts are estimated to be 5 percent of accounts receivable, the correct entry to adjust the accounts at the end of the accounting period is —

a Allowance for Doubtful
   Accounts.......................... 360
      Bad Debts Expense......... 360

b Bad Debts Expense 340
      Allowance for Doubtful
         Accounts.................... 340

c Allowance for Doubtful
   Accounts.......................... 340
      Accounts Receivable....... 340

d Bad Debts Expense 360
      Allowance for Doubtful
         Accounts.................... 360

e Accounts Receivable............. 340
      Allowance for Doubtful
         Accounts.................... 340

3 On November 30, the close of an annual accounting period, interest in the amount of $500 has been earned but not received. The correct entry is —

a No entry.

b Cash................................. 500
    Interest Revenue............   500

c Accrued Interest Receivable... 500
    Interest Revenue............   500

d Accounts Receivable............. 500
    Interest Revenue............   500

e Interest Revenue.................. 500
    Accrued Interest
      Receivable..................   500

4 The Unexpired Insurance account shows a balance of $900, representing the payment on July 1 of a three-year insurance premium of $900. The correct adjusting entry on December 31, the close of the annual accounting period in which the policy was purchased, is —

a Insurance Expense............... 150
    Unexpired Insurance.......   150

b Insurance Expense............... 300
    Unexpired Insurance.......   300

c Unexpired Insurance............. 150
    Insurance Expense..........   150

d Unexpired Insurance............. 25
    Insurance Expense..........   25

e None of the above.

5 On June 30, the close of the monthly accounting period, employees of the O'Callaghan Company have earned salaries totaling $921 payable on the payday of July 3. The entry required on June 30 is —

a Salary Expense 921
    Accrued Salaries
      Payable......................   921

b Accrued Salaries Payable....... 921
    Salary Expense   921

c Salary Expense 921
    Cash............................   921

d Salary Expense 921
    Accounts Payable...........   921

e None of the above.

6 Office furniture is purchased on October 1 at a cost of $3,400. Estimated salvage value is $200, and estimated useful life is four years. The entry to record the depreciation on December 31 is (assume this is the close of the annual accounting period) —

a Depreciation Expense —
    Office Furniture................. 850
    Allowance for
      Depreciation — Office
      Furniture....................   850

b Depreciation Expense —
    Office Furniture................. 800
    Allowance for
      Depreciation — Office
      Furniture....................   800

c Allowance for Depreciation —
    Office Furniture................. 800
    Depreciation Expense —
      Office Furniture..........   800

d Depreciation Expense —
    Office Furniture................. 200
    Allowance for
      Depreciation — Office
      Furniture....................   200

e Allowance for Depreciation —
    Office Furniture................. 200
    Depreciation Expense —
      Office Furniture..........   200

7 Company Z pays its employees on the 15th day of each month. The accounting period ends on December 31. If the adjusting entry on December 31, 1978, were neglected, which of the following would be the effect at that date?

a The assets of the company would be understated.

b The stockholders' equity of the company would be understated.

c Net earnings for the period ended would be understated.

d The liabilities of the company would be understated.

e Net earnings for the period ended would be unaffected.

8 Which of the following items is *not* important in the matching of expenses and revenues under the accrual basis of accounting?

a Amortization of patent costs.

b Depreciation of plant assets.

c Estimated allowance for uncollectible accounts.

d Accrual of interest earned.

e Cash receipts.

9 Which type of entry is made necessary because of the employment of the accrual basis of accounting?

a Recording collections of accounts receivable when received.

b Establishing an allowance for uncollectible accounts.

c Recording payments on accounts payable when made.

d Recording the payment of dividends to stockholders when made.

e Recording the interest expense (which has been incurred on bonds which the company has issued in the past) if not paid at year-end.

10 Which of the following accounts is closed by an entry which includes a debit to Expense and Revenue Summary?

a Service Revenue.

b Accounts Receivable.

c Rent Expense.

d Accrued Salaries Payable.

e Retained Earnings.

11 After the accounts have been closed—

a All of the accounts have zero balances.

b The asset, liability, and stockholders' equity accounts have zero balances.

c The revenue, expense, Expense and Revenue Summary, and Retained Earnings accounts have zero balances.

d The revenue, expense, and Expense and Revenue Summary accounts have zero balances.

e None of the above is true.

Questions 12–14 relate to the material on the work sheet contained in Appendix 3A.

12 Which of the following statements is true concerning the work sheet?

a It is a formal accounting statement which is distributed to stockholders and creditors.

b The accounting process could not possibly be completed without preparing a work sheet.

c The work sheet must contain either 8 or 12 columns.

d An explanation of each adjustment must appear toward the bottom of the work sheet.

e Since the work sheet is an informal tool, the accountant can use any format he or she wants to use or choose not to prepare a work sheet at all.

13 The Trial Balance columns of a work sheet show store fixtures of $4,000. Estimated depreciation for the period is $400. The store fixtures amount in the Statement of Financial Position columns of the work sheet will be a—

a $3,600 debit.

b $3,600 credit.

c $4,400 debit.

d $4,000 debit.

e $4,000 credit.

14 Supplies on hand are shown at $315 in the Trial Balance columns of the work sheet. The Adjustments columns show that $290 of these supplies were used during the month. The amount shown as supplies on hand in the Statement of Financial Position columns is a—

a $25 debit.

b $315 debit.

c $290 debit.

d $25 credit.

e $290 credit.

15 (based on Appendix 3B) The purpose of reversing entries is to—

a Reverse the effects of a closing entry.

b Reverse the effects of an adjusting entry for depreciation.

c Record the receipt of accrued interest.

d Reverse the effects of an adjusting entry so as to make easier the recording of a subsequent entry.

e Record the fact that the new accounting period has begun.

Now compare your answers with the correct answers and explanations on page 713–15.

Questions *chapter* 3

1 In what important way do the pre-closing trial balance and the post-closing trial balance differ? Why is the post-closing trial balance prepared?

2 Assuming that the closing process has been accomplished properly, which of the following statements is true? Why?

a After closing, expense and revenue accounts never have a balance other than zero.

b After closing, statement of financial position accounts always have a balance other than zero.

3 Your uncle knows you are taking a course in accounting in college and he asks you to come over and help him. It seems his new bookkeeper has journalized all of the business transactions for the month and has posted the journal entries to the ledger accounts. She now admits that she does not know how to proceed in completing the accounting process for the month. He asks you to tell her what should now be done to complete the process.

4 Why are adjusting entries necessary? Why not treat every cash disbursement as an expense and every cash receipt as revenue when the cash changes hands?

5 Give an example of each of the following:
a Equal growth of an expense and a liability.
b Earning of revenue received in advance.
e Equal growth of an asset and revenue.
d Equal growth of an expense and decrease in an asset.

6 "Adjusting entries would not be necessary if the *pure* cash basis of accounting were followed (assuming no mistakes were made in recording cash transactions as they occurred). Under the pure cash basis, all receipts which are of a revenue nature are considered revenue when received and all expenditures (even for a building) which are of an expense nature are considered expenses when paid. It is the use of the accrual basis of accounting, where an effort is made to match expenses (incurred but not necessarily paid for in the same period) against the revenues (earned but not necessarily received in the same period) they create that makes adjusting entries necessary." Do you agree with this statement? Why?

7 Why don't accountants keep all the accounts at their proper balances continuously throughout the period so that adjusting entries would not have to be made before financial statements are prepared?

8 A fellow student makes the following statement: "It is easy to tell whether a company is using the cash or accrual basis of accounting. When an amount is paid for future rent or insurance services, a firm that is using the cash basis will debit an expense account while a firm that is using the accrual basis will debit an asset account." Correct this misconception.

9 You notice that the Supplies on Hand account has a debit balance of $2,700 at the end of the accounting period. How would you determine the extent to which this account needs adjustment?

10 It may be said that some assets are converted into expenses as they expire and that some liabilities become revenues as they are earned. Give examples of asset and liability accounts for which the statement is true. Give examples of asset and liability accounts to which the statement does not apply.

11 The accountant often speaks of expired costs. Do costs literally expire?

12 What does the word "accrued" mean? Is there a conceptual difference between interest payable and accrued interest payable?

13 It is more difficult to match expenses incurred with revenues earned than it would be to match expenses paid with revenues received. Do you think that the effort is worthwhile? Why are financial statements prepared?

14 (based on Appendix 3A) Describe the purposes for which the work sheet is prepared.

15 (based on Appendix 3A) You have taken over a set of accounting books for a small corporation as a part-time job. At the end of the first accounting period you have partially completed the work sheet by entering the proper ledger accounts and balances in the Trial Balance columns. You turn to the manager and ask, "Where is the list of additional information I can use in entering the adjusting entries?" The manager indicates there is no such list. (In all the textbook problems you have done you have always been given this information.) How would you obtain the information for this real-life situation? What are the consequences of not making all of the adjustments required at the end of the accounting period?

16 (based on Appendix 3B) Describe the nature and purpose of a reversing entry.

Exercises *chapter* 3

1 a If a one-year insurance policy is purchased on July 1 for $2,400 and the following entry is made at that time:

Unexpired Insurance 2,400
    Cash 2,400

what adjusting entry is necessary at December 31?

b Give the adjusting entry which would be necessary if the entry to record the purchase of the policy on July 1 had been:

    Insurance Expense ... 2,400
        Cash 2,400

c Show by the use of T-accounts that the end result is the same under either (**a**) or (**b**).

2 At December 31, 1979, an adjusting entry was made as follows:

    Prepaid Rent 500
        Rent Expense 500

You know that the gross amount of rent paid was $1,200 and it was to cover a one-year period. Determine:
a The opening date of the year to which the $1,200 of rent applies.
b The entry that was made on the date the rent was paid.

3 A building is being depreciated by an amount of $14,000 per year. You know it had an original cost of $155,000 and was expected to last ten years. How must the $14,000 have been determined? Give the entry for the sale of the building at the end of the ten-year period assuming the building was sold for its expected salvage value.

4 Office supplies were purchased for cash on May 2, 1978, for $800. Show two ways in which this entry could be recorded and then show the adjusting entry that would be necessary for each, assuming that $200 of the supplies remained at the end of the year.

5 Prepare the adjusting entry on December 1, 1978, to record estimated bad debts of $1,000.

6 The cash balance at the beginning of the year was $17,000. During the year $80,000 was paid out for assets and expenses and $20,000 was received from the issuance of capital stock. The cash balance at the end of the year was $28,000. The balance in accounts receivable decreased by $6,000 during the year. How much service revenue was earned during the year? There were no receipts or disbursements except those specifically mentioned or implied above.

7 A firm borrows $10,000 on November 1 for 120 days with interest payable at the maturity of the loan at the rate of 6 percent. Prepare the adjusting entry required on December 31. (It should be noted that by December 31, one half of the term of the loan has expired.)

8 A firm buys bonds as an investment. If the semiannual interest amounts to $600 and is paid on March 1 and September 1, what is the adjusting entry required on December 31 to record the interest revenue earned?

9 State the effect that each of the following would have on the amount of net earnings reported for 1977 and 1978. The company's accounting period ends on December 31.
a No adjustment is made for accrued salaries of $800 as of December 31, 1977.
b The collection of $600 for services yet unperformed as of December 31, 1977, is credited to a revenue account. The services are performed in 1978.

10 After adjustment, selected account balances of the Borto Corporation are:

Service revenue	$40,000
Commissions expense (Dr.)	21,000
Advertising expense	4,000
Office expense	13,000

In journal form, give the entries required to close the books for the period.

11 (**based on Appendix 3A**) The three major column headings on a work sheet are: Trial Balance, Earnings Statement, and Statement of Financial Position. For each of the following items, determine under which major column heading it would appear and whether it would be a debit or credit. (For instance, cash would appear under the debit side of the Trial Balance and Statement of Financial Position columns.)
a Accounts receivable.
b Accounts payable.
c Retained earnings.
d Advertising expense.
e Capital stock.
f Fees earned.
g Net earnings for the month.

12 (based on Appendix 3A) If a set of columns were included in a work sheet for the statement of retained earnings, illustrate how it would be used. Assume a beginning balance in retained earnings of $14,000 and net earnings for the year of $6,000.

13 (based on Appendix 3A) In Exercise 12, if there were a deficit of $9,000 as of the beginning of the year and a net loss of $8,000 for the year, show how these would be treated in these columns.

14 (based on Appendix 3B) Using the facts presented in Exercise 8, show how the March 1, 1980, receipt of interest would be recorded assuming (1) no reversing entry is used and (2) a reversing entry is used on January 1, 1980 (show this entry also). Now show by the use of T-accounts that the end result is the same whether a reversing entry is used or not.

Problems, Series A *chapter* 3

3-1-A

Required:

For each of the following cases:

a Prepare the adjusting journal entry, dating it December 31, 1978.

b Set up ledger accounts in skeleton form, enter balances as given, if any, and post the adjusting entries made in part (a).

c Prepare and post closing entries. You will need a separate Expense and Revenue Summary account for each case.

d State the correct figures for the statement of financial position. Show related accounts in each case as they should appear on that statement.

e State the correct figures for the earnings statement.

Account name	Trial balance	Information for adjustments
Case 1: Equipment...	$80,000	Depreciation is computed at the rate of 15 percent per period.
Allowance for depreciation – equipment.........	12,000	
Case 2: Interest expense..	3,000	Unpaid interest incurred on borrowed money amounts to $400.
Case 3: Unexpired Insurance..................................	16,800	Of the unexpired insurance in the trial balance, only $4,400 is for additional protection after December 31.

3-2-A

The trial balance of the Saliba Company at December 31 of the current year includes, among other items, the following account balances:

	Debits	Credits
Unexpired insurance......................................	$ 3,648	
Buildings...	79,000	
Allowance for depreciation – buildings		$15,800
Salaries expense...	55,000	
Prepaid rent	12,000	

Additional information:

a. The debit balance in the Unexpired Insurance account is the advance premium for one year from September 1 of the current year.

b. The buildings are being depreciated at the rate of 4 percent a year, with no salvage value expected.

c. Salaries accrued and payable at December 31 amount to $3,200.

d. The debit balance in Prepaid Rent is for a one-year period that started March 1 of the current year.

Required:

Prepare the adjusting journal entries at December 31.

3–3–A

Among the account balances shown in the trial balance of the Sanford Company at December 31 of the current year are the following:

	Debits	Credits
Office supplies inventory	$ 1,740	
Unexpired insurance	2,400	
Accounts receivable	74,000	
Allowance for doubtful accounts		$ 800
Buildings	42,000	
Allowance for depreciation – buildings		9,750

Additional information:

a. The inventory of supplies on hand at December 31 amounts to $300.
b. The balance in the Unexpired Insurance account is for a two-year policy taken out June 1 of the current year.
c. It is estimated that $1,400 should be added to the Allowance for Doubtful Accounts.
d. The annual rate of depreciation for the buildings is based on the cost shown in the Buildings account, less scrap value estimated at $4,500. When acquired, the lives of the buildings were estimated at 50 years each.

Required:

a Prepare the adjusting journal entries at December 31.
b Open skeleton ledger accounts for each of the accounts involved, enter the balances as shown in the trial balance, post the adjusting entries, and bring down balances.

3–4–A

Required:

a Set up the following three ledger accounts: Accounts Receivable, Bad Debts Expense, and Allowance for Doubtful Accounts.
b Journalize the following transactions and post to the accounts (do not post to accounts not given):

Aug. 1–31 Service revenue on account amounted to $66,000.
     1–31 Cash collected on account amounted to $16,000.
       31 One percent of accounts receivable on August 31 was estimated to be uncollectible.
Sept. 1–30 Service revenue on account amounted to $72,000.
     1–30 Cash collected on account amounted to $30,000.
       30 Increased the balance in the Allowance for Doubtful Accounts account to 1 percent of the balance in the Accounts Receivable account.

3–5–A

The White Company occupies rented quarters on the main street of the city. In order to get this location it was necessary for the company to rent a store larger than needed, so a portion of the area is subleased (rented) to Paul's Restaurant.

Required:

Present the period-end entries required by the statements of fact presented below. Show your calculations of the amounts as explanations of your entries.

The following partial trial balance was taken from the company's ledger as of the close of business December 31, 1978. All of the original entries applicable to the statements of fact were posted to one or more of these accounts.

WHITE COMPANY
Partial Trial Balance
December 31, 1978

	Debits	Credits
Cash..	$20,000	
Accounts receivable...	25,000	
Allowance for doubtful accounts		$ 500
Unexpired insurance	2,850	
Store equipment	22,000	
Allowance for depreciation—store equipment...........		2,400
Notes payable...		5,000
Service revenue...		150,000
Supplies expense	2,700	
Rent expense..	3,600	
Store salaries expense	24,500	
Rent revenue		1,100

Data to be considered:

a. The wages of the store clerks amount to $90 per day and were last paid through Wednesday, December 27. December 31 is a Sunday. The store is closed Sundays.
b. The Allowance for Doubtful Accounts balance needs to be increased by $3,000.
c. An analysis of the Store Equipment account disclosed:

Balance, January 1, 1978...	$16,000
Addition, July 1, 1978	6,000
Balance, December 31, 1978, per Trial Balance...................	$22,000

The company estimates that this equipment will last 20 years from the date it was acquired and that the salvage value will be zero.
d. The store carries one combined insurance policy which is taken out once a year effective August 1. The premium on the policy now in force amounts to $1,800 per year.
e. Unused store supplies on hand at December 31, 1978, have a cost of $180.
f. December's rent from Paul's Restaurant has not yet been received, $100.
g. The note payable is for ten months, has an interest rate of 5 percent, and is dated July 1, 1978.

3–6–A

On June 1, 1978, John Schmidt opened a swimming pool cleaning and maintenance service business. He vaguely recalled the process of making journal entries and establishing ledger accounts from a high school bookkeeping course he had taken some years ago. At the end of June, he prepared an earnings statement for the month of June, but he had the feeling that he had not proceeded correctly. He contacted his brother, Jay, a recent college graduate majoring in accounting, for assistance.

Jay immediately noted that his brother had kept his records on a cash basis. So he set about to bring the books to a full accrual basis.

Required:

a   Prepare the entries for the following transactions as John must have recorded them under the cash basis of accounting.
b   Prepare the necessary adjusting entries as Jay must have prepared them to bring the books to a full accrual basis of accounting.
c   Calculate the change in the net earnings for June brought about by changing from the cash to the accrual basis of accounting.

Transactions:

June 1   Received cash of $9,000 from various customers in exchange for service agreements to clean and maintain their pools for the months of June, July, August, and September.
       5   Paid rent for automotive and cleaning equipment to be used during the period June through September, $2,000. The payment covered the entire period.
       8   Purchased a two-year liability insurance policy effective June 1 for $2,640 cash.
      10   Received an advance of $2,500 from a Florida building contractor in exchange for an agreement to help service pools in his housing development during the months of October through May.
      16   Paid wages for the first half of June, $2,800.
      17   Paid $120 for advertising to be run in a local newspaper for two weeks in June and four weeks in July.
      19   Paid the rent of $4,000 under a four-month lease on a building rented and occupied on June 1.
      20   Borrowed $6,000 from the bank on a 90-day, 6 percent note.
      26   Purchased $1,800 of supplies for cash. (Only $300 of these supplies were used in June.)
      29   Billed various customers for services rendered, $4,200.
      30   Unpaid employee services received in the last half of June amounted to $2,600.
      30   Received a bill for $200 for gas and oil used in June.

3–7–A   (based on Appendix 3A)

Required:

From the following trial balance and supplementary information, prepare:
a   A 12-column work sheet for the year ended December 31, 1978. (See Appendix 3A for illustration of form.)
b   The required closing entries.

Supplementary data:

a.   The building is to be depreciated at the rate of 2 percent per year.
b.   Depreciate the store fixtures 10 percent per year.
c.   The Allowance for Doubtful Accounts account balance is to be increased by $1,365.
d.   Accrued interest on notes receivable is $150.

e. Accrued interest on the mortgage note is $250.

f. Accrued sales salaries are $700.

g. Unexpired insurance is $200.

─*h.* Prepaid advertising is $500.

─*i.* Included in the cash on hand is a check for $25 which was cashed for an ex-employee in 1978 and which is worthless.

SAYKES COMPANY
Trial Balance
December 31, 1978

	Debits	Credits
Cash on hand and in bank	$ 36,350	
Accounts receivable	41,250	
Allowance for doubtful accounts		$ 850
Notes receivable	3,750	
Land	30,000	
Building	55,000	
Allowance for depreciation — building		16,500
Store fixtures	27,800	
Allowance for depreciation — store fixtures		5,560
Accounts payable		18,950
Mortgage note payable		25,000
Capital stock		50,000
Retained earnings		35,090
Service revenue		119,450
Sales salaries	32,000	
Advertising expense	6,000	
Officers' salaries	37,000	
Insurance expense	1,450	
Interest revenue		200
Interest expense	1,000	
	$271,600	$271,600

Problems, Series B *chapter* 3

3–1–B

Required:

For each of the following cases:

a Prepare the adjusting journal entry, dating it December 31, 1978.

b Set up ledger accounts in skeleton form, enter balances as given, if any, and post the adjusting entries made in part (a).

c Prepare and post closing entries. You will need a separate Expense and Revenue Summary account for each case.

d State the correct figure for the statement of financial position. Show related accounts in each case as they should appear on that statement.

e State the correct figures for the earnings statement.

Account name	Trial balance	Information for adjustments
Case 1: Office building	$840,000	Depreciation is computed each period at the rate of 2 percent of cost less salvage value. Salvage is estimated at $40,000.
Allowance for depreciation — office building	160,000	

Case 2: Wages expense .... 98,000 Wages earned by employees since last pay-
day are $1,560.

Case 3: Office supplies inventory .... 5,000 Of the office supplies
purchased, only $1,800
worth remains at the
end of the period.

3–2–B

The trial balance of the Short Company at December 31 of the current year includes, among other items, the following account balances:

	Debits	Credits
Unexpired insurance	$24,000	
Prepaid rent...	28,800	
Accounts receivable....................................	82,000	
Allowance for doubtful accounts		$1,400
Office supplies inventory.............................	5,600	

Examination of the records shows that adjustments should be made for the following items:

a. Of the unexpired insurance in the trial balance, $10,000 is for coverage during the months after December 31 of the current year.
b. The balance in the Prepaid Rent account is for a 12-month period that started October 1 of the current year.
c. It is estimated that $3,000 should be added to the Allowance for Doubtful Accounts balance.
d. Office supplies used during the year amount to $3,600.

Required:

Prepare the adjusting journal entries at December 31.

3–3–B

Tavenner, Inc., has the following account balances, among others, in its trial balance at December 31 of the current year:

	Debits	Credits
Office supplies inventory	$ 1,240	
Prepaid rent	2,400	
Accounts receivable...	25,000	
Allowance for doubtful accounts...........................		$ 600
Service revenues		87,000
Salaries expense..	41,000	

Additional information:

a. The inventory of supplies on hand at December 31 amounts to $90.
b. The balance in the Prepaid Rent account is for a one-year period starting October 1 of the current year.
c. It is estimated that $870 should be added to the Allowance for Doubtful Accounts balance.

d. Since the last payday, the employees of the company have earned additional salaries in the amount of $1,810.

Required:

a Prepare the adjusting journal entries at December 31.
b Open skeleton ledger accounts for each of the accounts involved, enter the balances as shown in the trial balance, and post the adjusting journal entries.

3-4-B

Required:

Given the following information for the Taylor Company, calculate the correct net earnings for 1977 and 1978. The reported net earnings for 1977 and 1978 were $60,000 and $82,000, respectively. No adjusting entries were made at year-end for any of the transactions given below:

a A fire insurance policy to cover a three-year period from the date of payment was purchased on March 1, 1977, for $3,600. The Insurance Expense account was debited at the date of purchase.
b Subscriptions for magazines in the amount of $72,000 to cover an 18-month period from May 1, 1977, were received on April 15, 1977. The Subscriptions Revenue account was credited when the payments were received.
c A building costing $150,000 and having an estimated useful life of 60 years and a scrap value of $30,000 was purchased and put into service on July 1, 1977.
d On September 1, 1977, $10,000 was borrowed from the bank to be repaid on September 1, 1979, with 6 percent annual interest.
e A $3,000 loan was made to a customer on November 1, 1977, to be repaid in three months with 5 percent annual interest.
f On January 12, 1978, wages of $9,600 were paid to employees. The account debited was Wages Expense. One third of the amount paid was earned by employees in December of 1977.

3-5-B

The Toombs Company adjusts and closes its books each December 31. It is to be assumed that the accounts for all prior years have been properly adjusted and closed. Given below are a number of the company's account balances prior to adjustment on December 31, 1978:

	Debits	Credits
Accounts receivable	$66,000	
Allowance for doubtful accounts		$ 170
Unexpired insurance	2,625	
Office supplies inventory	2,150	
Building	85,000	
Allowance for depreciation – building		32,000
Unearned rent revenue		900
Salaries expense	23,000	
Service revenue		92,500

Additional data (*letter your entries to match these items*):

a. It is estimated that $925 should be added to the balance in the Allowance for Doubtful Accounts.
b. The Unexpired Insurance account balance represents the remaining cost of a four-year insurance policy dated June 30, 1976, having a total premium of $4,200.
c. The physical inventory of the office supply stockroom indicates that the supplies on hand had a cost of $675.
d. The building was originally acquired on January 1, 1962, at which time it was estimated that it would last 40 years and have a scrap value of $5,000.
e. Salaries earned since the last payday but unpaid at December 31 amount to $875.
f. Interest earned but not collected on bonds during the year amounts to $75. This interest is not due to be paid to the company until March 1, 1979.
g. The Unearned Rent Revenue account arose through the prepayment of rent by a tenant in the building for 12 months beginning October 1, 1978.

Required:

Prepare the adjusting entries indicated by the additional data. While explanations may be omitted, computations should be included.

3–6–B

The Wiesenhutter Publishing Company began operations on December 1, 1978. The company's bookkeeper intended to use the cash basis of accounting. Consequently, the bookkeeper recorded all cash receipts and disbursements for items relating to operations in revenue and expense accounts. No adjusting entries were made prior to preparing the financial statements for December. You are called in at the end of December to show the bookkeeper how to adjust the accounts to the accrual basis.

Required:

a Prepare journal entries for the following transactions as the bookkeeper prepared them.
b Prepare the adjusting entries necessary at the end of the month to place the books on an accrual basis.
c Compute the increase or decrease in net earnings which results from using the accrual basis of accounting rather than the cash basis.

Transactions:

Dec. 1 Issued capital stock for $10,000 cash.
3 Received $12,000 for magazine subscriptions to run for two years from this date. The magazine is published monthly on the 23d.
4 Paid for advertising to be run in a national periodical for each of six months (starting this month). The cost was $4,500.
7 Purchased an insurance policy to cover a two-year period beginning December 15, $3,600.
11 Borrowed $6,000 from the bank on a 60-day, 6 percent note dated today.
12 Paid the annual lease on the building, $6,000, effective through November 30, 1979.

Dec. 15 Received $18,000 cash for two-year subscriptions starting with the December issue.

15 Salaries for the period December 1–15 amounted to $4,000. Salaries are paid on the 5th and 20th of each month for the preceding half of the month.

20 Salaries for the period December 1–15 are paid.

23 Supplies purchased for cash, $1,800. (Only $150 of these were subsequently used in 1978.)

27 Printing costs applicable equally to the next six issues beginning with the December issue were paid in cash, $12,000.

31 Cash sales of the December issue, $7,000.

31 Unpaid salaries for the period December 16–31 amounted to $4,400.

31 Sales on account of December issue, $3,000.

3–7–B (based on Appendix 3A)

Required:

From the trial balance and additional data given below, prepare:

a A 12-column work sheet for the year ended December 31, 1978. (See Appendix 3A for an illustration.)

b The December 31, 1978, closing entries, in general journal form.

WRIGHT COMPANY
Trial Balance
December 31, 1978

	Debits	Credits
Cash on hand and in bank	$ 35,320	
Accounts receivable	72,520	
Allowance for doubtful accounts		$ 2,760
Notes receivable	85,000	
Store supplies inventory	1,200	
Store equipment	44,000	
Allowance for depreciation – store equipment		8,800
Accounts payable		39,400
Notes payable		12,000
Capital stock		150,000
Retained earnings		60,820
Service revenue		238,680
Interest revenue		500
Interest expense	300	
Sales salaries	69,200	
Advertising	39,000	
Store supplies expense	1,480	
General office expense	4,940	
Fire insurance expense	2,400	
Office salaries	40,400	
Officers' salaries	80,000	
Legal and auditing expenses	5,000	
Telephone and telegraph	2,400	
Rent expense	28,800	
Dividends	1,000	
	$512,960	$512,960

The company consistently followed the policy of initially debiting all prepaid items to expense accounts.

Additional data as of December 31, 1978:

a. Fire insurance unexpired, $700.
b. Sales store supplies on hand, $850.
c. Prepaid rent expense (store only), $3,500.
d. Depreciation rate on store equipment, 10 percent per year.
e. Increase Allowance for Doubtful Accounts account balance to $4,586.
f. Accrued sales salaries, $2,000.
g. Accrued office salaries, $1,500.

part II

FINANCIAL STATEMENT ITEMS

4

Merchandising transactions and introduction to inventories

Learning objectives

Study of the material in this chapter is designed to provide an understanding of:

1. Sales and purchase transactions; the time that each is recorded and why.

2. The nature of, reasons for, accounting for, and reporting of sales (purchase) returns and allowances and sales (purchase) discounts.

3. The characteristics and advantages and disadvantages of perpetual and periodic inventory procedures.

4. The adjusting entries needed to establish the expense account Cost of Goods Sold under the periodic procedure.

5. Common terms under which merchandise is sold, including freight terms; alternative approaches to accounting for purchase discounts; cash discounts distinguished from trade discounts.

6. The earnings statement usually prepared for a merchandising firm.

7. What goods should be included and excluded from inventory and why; the nature of inventory losses.

8. How special journals may be used to reduce posting time and allow for a division of labor (Appendix 4A).

9. The work sheet for a merchandising company (Appendix 4B).

The previous three chapters dealt primarily with accounting for the activities of companies that earned their revenues by rendering services to customers for fees or commissions. This was done to keep the discussion as simple as possible. Net earnings were determined by subtracting the various operating expenses incurred from these revenues. The fact that a company may earn its revenues and net earnings by buying and selling merchandise was introduced in Chapter 2. This chapter and the next one expand upon that initial discussion.

Sales revenue

The amount of sales revenue of a merchandising company indicates the extent to which the company is satisfying its customers' needs. It also gives an approximate measure of the flow of assets from customers into the business. Sales revenue (or net sales) generally consists of gross sales less sales returns, sales allowances, and sales discounts.

Sales

The main revenue of a merchandising company results from sales of merchandise. Basically, a sale consists of the transfer of legal ownership of goods (called passage of title) from one party to another. It is usually accompanied by physical delivery of the goods. Each time a sale is made, a revenue account called Sales is increased (credited) by the amount of the selling price of the goods sold. The accompanying debit is to Cash if the terms of sale are cash or to Accounts Receivable if the goods are sold on account. For example, a $10,000 sale on account would be recorded as follows:

Accounts Receivable	10,000	
Sales		10,000
To record the sale of merchandise on account.		

Typically, the above entry will be based upon a business document called a *sales invoice*, such as is shown in Illustration 4.1. The sales invoice is prepared only after notification from the shipping department of the shipment of the goods to the customer.

Indicate whether each of the following statements is true or false.
1. A sale of goods involves passage of legal title to the goods.
2. Usually, physical delivery of goods accompanies their sale.
3. Sales are credited to a revenue account because they tend to increase stockholders' equity, and a revenue account is a subdivision of the stockholders' equity account Retained Earnings.
4. Net sales is an approximate measure of the assets flowing into a firm from its customers.

Now check your responses in Answer Frame 1⁴ on page 142.

Illustration 4.1 Sales invoice

BRYAN WHOLESALE CO.			*Invoice No.* 1258
476 Mason Street, Detroit, Michigan			*Date* Dec. 19, 1979

Customer's Order No. 218
Sold to   Baier Company
Address 2255 Hannon Street
         Big Rapids, Michigan   *Date Shipped* Dec. 19, 1979
Terms   Net 30   *Shipped by* Nagel Trucking Co.

Description	Quantity	Price per unit	Amount
True-tone CB radios Model No. 5868–24393	100	$100	$10,000
		Total	$10,000

Frame 2⁴

Why record revenue at time of sale? In a merchandising firm, many activities occur both before and after a sale that can be called revenue-producing activities. For example, goods may be bought and stored before a selling season begins, advertising costs may be incurred, salespersons may call upon customers, orders may be received, and costs may be incurred to make good on guarantees. Yet recording revenue at the time of sale can be justified for the following reasons: (1) legal title to the goods has passed and the goods are now the responsibility and property of the buyer; (2) the amount of revenue can be measured—the selling price of the goods has been verified by obtaining assets of that amount from the customer; (3) the revenue has been earned, that is, the seller has completed its part of the contract; (4) the seller has realized revenue in that the goods have been exchanged for other valid assets; and (5) because the seller has completed its part of the contract, its costs can be determined, with the result that net earnings can be calculated.

On the other hand, the selling price of the goods may not be a complete measure of the revenue earned because of sales returns, sales allowances, and sales discounts.

Sales returns

Goods delivered to a customer in the belief that a sale had been made may be returned to the seller for a variety of reasons. These include wrong color, wrong size, wrong style, wrong amounts, or inferior quality. In fact, in some firms such as retail furniture stores, goods may be returned simply because the customer did not like them. The seller's policy may be "satisfaction guaranteed." A sales return is a cancellation of a sale. Conceivably it could be recorded as a debit in the Sales account. But the amount of sales returns may be useful information to

141

2⁴
continued

management, owners, or other interested parties. Thus, they are recorded in a separate account entitled, Sales Returns and Allowances. For example, if $300 of goods sold on account and $150 of goods sold for cash are returned by the customers, the required entry would be:

Sales Returns and Allowances	450	
Accounts Receivable		300
Cash		150
To record sales returns from customers.		

Sales allowances

Sales allowances are deductions from original invoiced sales prices. They may be granted to a customer for any of a number of reasons, including inferior quality or damage or deterioration in transit. As was true for sales returns, sales allowances could be recorded directly as debits in the Sales account because they do cancel a part of the recorded selling price. But, because their amounts may be useful information, they are either recorded in a separate Sales Allowances account or recorded in a combined Sales Returns and Allowances account. In either case, the account is a contra account (a reduction account) to Sales; or it can be viewed as a negative revenue account. It is not an expense account even though it has a debit balance.

To illustrate the recording of a sales allowance, assume that a $400 allowance is granted a customer for damage resulting from improperly packed merchandise. If the customer has not yet paid the account, the required entry would read:

Sales Returns and Allowances	400	
Accounts Receivable		400
To record sales allowance granted for damaged merchandise.		

Indicate whether each of the following statements is true or false.

1. A sales allowance may be granted by a seller for goods sold that possess minor flaws which detract from their salability to the customer.

2. The Sales Returns account is an expense account.
3. If a customer has paid the account, a sales allowance may involve a cash refund to the customer.
4. The accountant justifies recording revenue at the time of sale by arguing that the revenue has been realized.

Check your responses in Answer Frame 2⁴ on page 144.

Frame 3⁴

Sales discounts

Whenever goods are sold on account, the terms of payment are clearly specified on the sales invoice. For example, in the invoice in Illustration 4.1, the terms are stated as "net 30" (which is sometimes written simply as "n/30"). This means that the $10,000 amount of the invoice must be paid on or before 30 days after December 19, 1979, or on or before January 18, 1980. If the terms read "n/10 E.O.M.," the invoice would be due on the tenth day of the month following the month of sale— January 10 in the case of the invoice in Illustration 4.1. Credit terms vary from industry to industry according to trade practices.

In many instances, when credit periods are long, sellers will grant cash discounts in an attempt to induce early payment of an account. Theoretically, cash discounts represent adjustments to gross invoice price to arrive at the actual cost—the cash price—of the merchandise. These discounts, usually ranging from 1 to 3 percent of the gross invoice price of the merchandise, may or may not be taken by the buyer. To the purchaser, they are purchase discounts; to the seller, they are sales discounts.

Cash discount terms are often stated as follows:

2/10, n/30—which is read as "two ten, net thirty." Unfortunately, the statement is misleading. The terms actually offered are a 2 percent discount (2 percent of the gross invoice price of the merchandise) if payment is made within ten days following the invoice date. No discount is allowed after ten days. The gross invoice price is due 30 days from the invoice date. The "n" in the terms should be interpreted as "no discount" rather than as "net." The residual obtained when the discount is subtracted from the invoice price is properly described as "net."

2/E.O.M., n/60—which is read as "two E.O.M., net sixty." The terms actually mean a 2 percent discount may be deducted if the invoice is paid by the end of the month. No discount may be taken after the end of the month, and the gross invoice amount is due 60 days from the date of the invoice.

2/10/E.O.M., n/60—which is usually read as "two ten E.O.M., net sixty." The actual terms offered are a 2 percent discount if the invoice is paid by the tenth of the following month, no discount after this date, and the gross invoice amount is due 60 days from the date of the invoice.

Recording sales discounts. The granting of sales discounts, then, is another factor that reduces the amount of cash actually collected from

1. True. This is perhaps the most common reason for granting a sales allowance.
2. False. Even though the account has a debit balance, it is not an expense account. Sales returns are not costs incurred in generating revenue. They are reductions in the amount of revenue originally recorded because a part of the revenue was canceled when the goods were returned.
3. True. The customer may request, and the seller may grant, a cash refund if a sales allowance is granted subsequent to the time that the customer paid the account balance.
4. True. The act of making a sale to a customer from whom payment is fully expected is often referred to in accounting jargon as an act of realizing revenue.

If you answered any of the above incorrectly, study Frame 2⁴ again before going on to Frame 3⁴ on page 143.

3⁴
continued

the sale of goods. But even when cash discount terms are offered, a seller usually records an invoice at gross invoice price. To illustrate the conventional manner of recording sales discounts, assume that a sale on account of $2,000 was made on July 12; terms are 2/10, n/30. A check in payment of the account was received on July 21 in the amount of $1,960. The required entries are:

July 12	Accounts Receivable	2,000	
	Sales		2,000
	To record sale on account.		
July 21	Cash	1,960	
	Sales Discounts	40	
	Accounts Receivable		2,000
	To record collection on account, less discount.		

The Sales Discounts account is a contra account to Sales and should be shown as a deduction from gross sales in the earnings statement. It is not an expense incurred in generating revenue. Rather, its purpose is to reduce recorded revenue to the amount actually realized from the sale—the net invoice price.

Illustration 4.2 contains a partial earnings statement showing how sales, sales returns and allowances, and sales discounts might be reported.

Indicate whether each of the following statements is correct or incorrect.

1. The data in Illustration 4.2 suggest that the Hanlon Company expects to collect roughly $260,000 of cash from sales made in the year ended June 30, 1979.
2. Theoretically, cash discounts are best viewed as adjustments of recorded amounts of sales (or purchases).

Illustration 4.2   Partial earnings statement

HANLON COMPANY		
Partial Earnings Statement		
For the Year Ended June 30, 1979		
Revenues:		
Gross sales		$282,345
Less: Sales discounts	$ 5,548	
Sales returns and allowances..............................	15,436	20,984
Net Sales..		$261,361

3. A sale on account in the amount of $3,000 made on April 15, terms of 3/10, n/30, on which a sales allowance of $600 was granted, could be settled on April 25 for $2,310.

4. Cash discounts are called purchase discounts by a buyer and sales discounts by a seller.

Now check your responses in Answer Frame 3[4] on page 146.

Frame 4[4]

Interest rate implied in cash discounts.   A simple analysis will show whether money should be borrowed to take advantage of discounts. For example, $10,260 must be paid within 30 days or $10,054.80 must be paid within 10 days to settle an invoice in the amount of $10,260; terms, 2/10, n/30. In other words, by advancing payment 20 days from the final due date, a discount of $205.20 is secured. The interest expense incurred on borrowing $10,054.80 at 8 percent per year for 20 days is $44.69. In this case, management would save $160.51 ($205.20 − $44.69) by borrowing the money and paying the invoice within the discount privilege period.

In terms of an annual rate of interest, the 2 percent rate of discount for 20 days is equivalent to a 36 percent annual rate: $(360 \div 20) \times 2$ percent. All cash discount terms can be converted into their approximate annual interest rate equivalents by this same process. Thus, a firm could afford to pay up to 18 percent on borrowed funds to take advantage of discount terms of 1/10, n/30; up to 7.2 percent for terms of 1/10, n/60; and, as already indicated, up to 36 percent for terms of 2/10, n/30. Thus, unless cash discount terms drop to fractions of 1 percent (as they in fact have in some instances), a firm is likely to benefit by borrowing to take advantage of discounts offered.

Determining cost of goods sold

Basically, there are two methods of determining the cost of the goods sold. One method, called *perpetual inventory procedure,* is usually used

145

1. Correct. Some of the sales discounts and sales returns and allowances recorded might relate to sales of the prior year. A few discounts and returns and allowances might yet be taken on accounts receivable arising from sales of the current year that are still uncollected at year-end. Also, some of the accounts receivable might prove uncollectible.

2. Correct. Any rational buyer in deciding between two or more possible suppliers of goods will take cash discount terms into consideration in making his or her decision. That is, they would be seen as reductions of quoted prices.

3. Incorrect. The account would be settled by payment of $2,328, computed as $3,000 − $600 − (.03 × $2,400). The seller would not allow a discount on a return or an allowance.

4. Correct. Cash discounts are usually described from the viewpoint of the parties to a transaction involving a cash discount.

If you answered incorrectly, review Frame 3⁴ before proceeding to Frame 4⁴ on page 145.

4⁴
continued

by companies selling merchandise that has a high individual unit value, such as automobiles, furniture, and appliances. For items such as these, it is a relatively easy task to maintain records of the cost of each unit of merchandise and in this way determine the cost of each unit sold. The inventory records are designed and maintained in such a manner as to provide close control over the actual goods on hand by showing exactly what goods should be on hand.

The main emphasis in this text will be on periodic procedure rather than perpetual procedure. It is sufficient here to note that the entries required under the perpetual procedure to record the purchase of three identical refrigerators (except for serial number tags) at a cost of $320 each and the subsequent sale of one unit on account for $450 are:

Merchandise Inventory	960	
Accounts Payable		960
To record purchase of three refrigerators on account.		
Accounts Receivable	450	
Sales		450
To record sale on account.		
Cost of Goods Sold	320	
Merchandise Inventory		320
To record cost of refrigerator sold.		

The alternative approach to determining cost of goods sold, called periodic inventory procedure, is described, discussed, and illustrated in the remainder of this chapter. The Appendix to Chapter 5 does deal with perpetual inventory procedure.

Merchandising transactions and introduction to inventories

Cost of goods sold, periodic procedure

Companies selling merchandise that has a low value per unit, such as nuts and bolts, nails, Christmas cards, pencils, and many similar items, often find that the extra costs of record keeping under perpetual procedure more than outweigh the benefits. Close control of such items is not necessary nor is it economically wise. For these firms, periodic inventory procedure is used. Under this procedure the Merchandise Inventory account is not adjusted after each purchase or sale. Adjustment is made only at the end of the accounting period. Quantity records usually are not maintained. The record keeping is reduced considerably, but so is the control over inventory items. At the end of the period, when the physical inventory is taken, there is no account balance against which the physical count can be checked. The Merchandise Inventory account does not show the cost of the goods that should be on hand.

Also under periodic procedure, no attempt is made to determine the cost of the goods sold for each sale at the time of the sale. Instead, the cost of all of the goods sold for all of the sales made in a period is determined at the end of the period. To do so requires knowledge of three items: (1) the cost of the goods on hand at the beginning of the period, (2) the cost of the goods purchased during the period, and (3) the cost of the unsold goods on hand at the end of the period. This information would then be arrayed in the following manner:

Cost of goods on hand at the beginning of the period	$ 24,000
Add: Cost of goods purchased during the period	140,000
Cost of goods available for sale during the period	$164,000
Deduct: Cost of unsold goods on hand at the end of the period	20,000
Cost of Goods Sold during the Period	$144,000

This schedule shows that the firm started the period with $24,000 of merchandise on hand and purchased an additional $140,000, making a total of $164,000 of goods that could have been sold during the period. But $20,000 remained unsold at the end of the period, which implies that $144,000 was the cost of goods sold during the period.

Indicate whether each of the following statements is true or false.

1. The approximate annual interest rate implied in cash discount terms of 3/15, n/60 is 24 percent.

2. Periodic inventory procedure provides tight internal control over inventories by showing at all times the units of merchandise that should be on hand.

3. Under perpetual inventory procedure, the cost of the goods sold for each sale is determined at the time of sale.

4. Under periodic procedure, the cost of the goods sold is determined by subtracting the cost of the goods unsold at the end of the period from the cost of the goods available for sale during the period.

Check your responses in Answer Frame 4⁴ on page 150.

Frame 5⁴ ──────────────────────────────────────

Purchases

When merchandise is purchased, an asset is acquired. Purchases of merchandise which is to be offered for sale to customers are recorded by debits to a Purchases account instead of debits to the Merchandise Inventory account. The Purchases account is increased by debits because it is really a subdivision of the debit side of the asset account Merchandise Inventory. But it is usually listed with the earnings statement accounts in the chart of accounts because the balance in the account is transferred to other accounts at the end of every accounting period. By recording purchases in a separate account, management has knowledge of the cost of the merchandise purchased during the accounting period. This is the only information provided by the account, as it tells nothing about whether or not the goods have been sold.

To illustrate, assume that Antonucci Wholesale Stores purchased $30,000 of merchandise from Wholesaler C on account and $20,000 for cash. The required entries are:

Purchases	30,000	
Accounts Payable		30,000
To record purchase of merchandise on account.		

Purchases	20,000	
Cash		20,000
To record purchase of merchandise for cash.		

All purchases of merchandise are posted to the Purchases account, which appears—with a debit balance—in both the ledger and the trial balance.

Transportation costs

Whenever goods are purchased, costs will be incurred to deliver them to the buyer. Whether or not these costs are given separate recognition in the accounts of the buyer depends upon the terms under which the goods were sold.

The term *f.o.b. shipping point* means free on board at the shipping point; that is, the buyer incurs all transportation costs after the merchandise is loaded on cars or trucks at the point of shipment. The term *f.o.b. destination* means that the seller incurs all transportation charges to the destination of the shipment. In general, title to the goods passes from the seller to the buyer at the point at which the buyer becomes responsible for the transportation charges.

Regardless of which party incurs the freight, when the seller initially *pays* the freight before the goods arrive at their destination, the term "prepaid freight" is used. When the buyer is to initially pay the freight upon the arrival of the goods, the term "freight collect" is used.

Four situations involving transportation costs may exist. They are illustrated below. In each case assume that a purchase of $2,000 of merchandise on account was properly recorded by the buyer as a debit to Purchases and a credit to Accounts Payable. The sale was recorded by the seller as a debit to Accounts Receivable and a credit to Sales.

Case A. If the goods were shipped f.o.b. shipping point, freight collect, the buyer would initially pay the freight bill and would be responsible for the freight costs. The entry on the buyer's books would be as follows (assuming a $100 delivery charge):

Transportation-In	100	
Cash		100
To record payment of freight bill on goods purchased.		

The $100 is actually a part of the cost of the merchandise acquired and could be debited to the Purchases account. But a more complete record of the costs incurred is obtained through use of a separate Transportation-In account. (Under perpetual procedure the debit would have been to Merchandise Inventory.) There would be no entry for freight on the seller's books.

Case B. If the goods were shipped f.o.b. shipping point, freight prepaid, the seller prepaid the freight for the buyer and would charge it to the buyer. The entry on the seller's books (in addition to the entry for the sale) would be:

Accounts Receivable	100	
Cash		100
To charge buyer for freight on goods shipped f.o.b. shipping point, freight prepaid.		

The buyer, in turn, would reimburse the seller when paying the invoice. In this case, the proper entry for the freight on the buyer's books would be:

5⁴
continued

Transportation-In 100
    Accounts Payable 100
To record obligation for freight charges prepaid by seller.

Case C. If the goods were shipped f.o.b. destination, freight prepaid, the seller paid the freight bill and bears the responsibility for it. No separate transportation cost is billed to the buyer. No entry is required on the buyer's books. The transportation cost undoubtedly was taken into consideration by the seller in establishing selling prices. The following entry would be required on the seller's books:

Transportation-Out 100
    Cash.. 100
To record freight cost on goods sold.

The Transportation-Out account is an expense account, showing one of the expenses incurred in making the sale to the customer.

Case D. If the goods were shipped f.o.b. destination, freight collect, the buyer would initially pay the freight bill as a convenience to the seller. The buyer would charge it against the balance in the seller's account payable as follows:

Accounts Payable 100
    Cash.. 100
To record payment of freight bill for seller.

Assuming that the seller knew the amount of the freight cost at the time of shipment, the following entry would be made on the seller's books to reduce the buyer's account balance:

Transportation-Out 100
    Accounts Receivable... 100
To record reduction in buyer's account for freight costs paid on goods shipped f.o.b. destination.

The buyer would pay $1,900 to settle the account with the seller.

Merchandising transactions and introduction to inventories

Purchase returns and allowances

For any of a number of reasons, such as wrong size or color, a buyer may return merchandise to a seller, giving rise to what is known as a purchase return. Similarly, a seller may grant an allowance or reduction in the price of goods shipped to the buyer because of defects, damage, or blemishes. This concession is referred to by the buyer as a purchase allowance. Both returns and allowances serve to reduce the buyer's obligation to the seller and to reduce the cost of the goods purchased. But more importantly, management may be quite interested in knowing the dollar amount of returns and allowances as the first step in controlling the costs incurred in returning unsatisfactory merchandise or negotiating purchase allowances. For this reason, purchase returns and allowances are recorded in a separate account as follows:

```
Accounts Payable.........................................................    350
    Purchase Returns and Allowances.........................................        350
    To record return of damaged merchandise.
```

(Under perpetual procedure the credit would have been to Merchandise Inventory.)

Indicate whether each of the following statements is true or false.
1. A purchase return increases the cost of the merchandise purchased.
2. A purchase allowance reduces the buyer's obligation to the seller.
3. Although the buyer may initially pay the freight company, the seller is responsible for, and ultimately bears the burden of, any transportation costs incurred for goods shipped f.o.b. destination.
4. Under certain circumstances, a freight bill paid by a buyer on goods purchased will not be debited to the buyer's Transportation-In account.

Now check your responses in Answer Frame 5⁴ on page 152.

Frame 6⁴ ——————————————————————————

Purchase discounts

Merchandise is often purchased under credit terms that permit the buyer to deduct a stated discount if the invoice is paid within a specified period of time. Usually, such transactions are accounted for as in the following illustration:

```
May  4  Purchases...............................................  2,000
            Accounts Payable.............................................       2,000
            To record purchase on account; terms, 2/10, n/30.

    14  Accounts Payable.................................................  2,000
            Cash...............................................................       1,960
            Purchase Discounts...........................................         40
            To record payment on account within discount period.
```

1. False. A purchase return, because it in effect cancels a purchase, reduces (rather than increases) the cost of goods purchased.

2. True. By granting an allowance, the seller has agreed to settle an invoice for less than the originally billed amount.

3. True. The term f.o.b. destination means that the seller promises to have the goods delivered to the buyer's location without charge to the buyer. But it is also quite true that the seller, in such circumstances, would take transportation charges into consideration in establishing selling prices. Thus, the buyer is likely to pay the transportation charges as part of a higher selling price.

4. True. When goods are shipped f.o.b. destination, freight collect, the buyer will have to pay the freight bill in order to receive the goods. But this amount will be deducted from the balance in the Accounts Payable account. And the buyer will, of course, deduct the transportation charges paid when making remittance to the seller.

If you answered any of the above incorrectly, restudy Frame 5⁴ before proceeding to Frame 6⁴ on page 151.

6⁴
continued

Note that the purchase invoice is recorded at gross invoice price. The purchase discount is recorded only when the invoice is paid within the discount period and the discount taken. The Purchase Discounts account is looked upon as a contra account to Purchases. (Under perpetual procedure the credit for $40 would have been to Merchandise Inventory.) Its purpose is to reduce the recorded gross invoice cost of the purchase to the price actually paid. It is reported in the earnings statement as a deduction from purchases.

Net price procedure. A theoretically preferable, although not widely used, method of accounting for purchase discounts involves specific recognition in the accounts only of discounts *not* taken. To illustrate, assume that goods with a gross invoice price of $2,000 are purchased under terms of 2/10, n/30. The purchase would be recorded at net invoice price, as follows:

June 4   Purchases 1,960
             Accounts Payable 1,960
             To record $2,000 purchase; terms, 2/10, n/30.

This entry is preferable theoretically because it states the cost of the goods at the amount of cash for which they could be acquired. It also states the liability, accounts payable, at the amount of cash for which it could be settled.

If the discount is taken, the entry is a debit to Accounts Payable and a credit to Cash for $1,960. Note that under this procedure discounts taken do not appear in the accounts.

If the invoice is paid after the discount period has passed, the entry required is:

```
June 30   Discounts Lost .......................................................    40
          Accounts Payable ...............................................  1,960
             Cash .........................................................           2,000
             To record payment of an account and the discount
             lost.
```

With discount rates around 2 percent, effective management of cash calls for establishing procedures so that all invoices are paid within their discount privilege period. The failure to take a discount should be highlighted as a deviation from management policy. Note that the above procedure does exactly this; it calls management's attention to discounts *not* taken by recording them in a Discounts Lost account. The Discounts Lost account then actually contains losses from inefficiency, even though it is reported in the earnings statement among "other expenses."

Indicate whether each of the following statements is correct or incorrect.

1. For many firms, the amount of purchase discounts *not* taken is more useful information than the amount of purchase discounts taken.
2. If recorded, purchase discounts taken should be treated as adjustments of the recorded cost of purchases.
3. Under net price procedure, purchases are recorded at net invoice price regardless of whether the discount is actually taken or not.
4. It can be argued that net price procedure permits overstatement of purchases and accounts payable at the time of the initial recording of an invoice.

Now check your responses in Answer Frame 6⁴ on page 154.

Frame 7⁴

Purchase discounts and transportation charges. Purchase discounts are based on the invoice price of the goods. They are not affected by transportation charges, regardless of whether the buyer or the seller is responsible for freight charges. For example, assume that goods with an invoice price of $2,000 are purchased under terms of 2/10, n/30, f.o.b. shipping point, with freight charges of $100 prepaid. The seller's invoice would show the $2,000 invoice price of the goods, to which would be added the $100 of freight charges prepaid, for a total of $2,100. If the invoice is paid within the discount period, the discount allowed would be $40 (.02 × $2,000), not $42 (.02 × $2,100). A net remittance of $2,060 would be required to pay the invoice.

1. Correct. In well-managed firms, taking discounts may be so much a matter of routine that missing a discount is the exception.
2. Correct. When discounts are taken, the actual cost of the purchases is less than the recorded gross invoice price of the goods.
3. Correct. The cash paid out when a discount is missed is treated as a loss rather than as a part of the cost of the goods purchased.
4. Incorrect. Theoretically, it can be argued that the traditional gross price procedure yields overstated purchases and accounts payable.

If you answered incorrectly, review Frame 6⁴ before going on to Frame 7⁴ on page 153.

7⁴
continued

Merchandise inventories

To determine the cost of the goods sold in any accounting period, information is needed as to the cost of the goods on hand at the start of the period (beginning inventory) as well as the cost of the goods on hand at the close of the period (ending inventory). But the task really consists only of determining the cost of the ending inventory. Because one accounting period follows another, the ending inventory of one period is the beginning inventory of the following period.

Under periodic procedure, the cost of the ending inventory is determined by (1) actually counting the physical units of merchandise on hand, on display, and in the storeroom; (2) multiplying the number of units of each kind of merchandise by its unit cost; and (3) summing the costs of the various kinds of merchandise to obtain the cost of the total inventory.

Once obtained, the cost of the ending inventory is (1) reported in the earnings statement as a deduction from the cost of the goods available for sale to arrive at the cost of the goods sold, (2) entered in the Merchandise Inventory account in the ledger by way of an adjusting entry, and (3) reported as an asset in the statement of financial position prepared at the end of the accounting period. The first two of these uses are illustrated below.

Cost of goods sold. When information is available on the cost of the beginning and ending inventories and on the various elements making up the net cost of purchases, the cost of goods sold in a period can be determined and reported as shown in Illustration 4.3.

Indicate whether each of the following statements concerning Illustration 4.3 is true or false.

1. The ending inventory on June 30, 1978, had a cost of $24,433.
2. The total cost of the goods that could have been sold in the year ended June 30, 1979, was $191,122.

Merchandising transactions and introduction to inventories

3. .It would appear that purchases made by the company were subject to an average cash discount in excess of 2 percent.
4. The net expense for the merchandise sold during the year was $160,112.

Check your responses in Answer Frame 7[4] on page 156.

Illustration 4.3   Determination of cost of goods sold

Cost of goods sold:		
Merchandise inventory, July 1, 1978......................		$ 24,433
Purchases......................................	$167,688	
Less: Purchase returns and allowances............ $8,101		
Purchase discounts............................ 3,351	11,452	
Net purchases................................	$156,236	
Add: Transportation-in................................	10,453	
Net cost of purchases....................................		166,689
Cost of goods available for sale.........................		$191,122
Merchandise inventory, June 30, 1979		31,010
Cost of Goods Sold		$160,112

Frame 8[4]

Adjusting entries for cost of goods sold. To yield the information contained in Illustration 4.3, the underlying ledger accounts and their balances would have to be:

Merchandise Inventory	$ 24,433 Dr.
Purchases	167,688 Dr.
Purchase Returns and Allowances	8,101 Cr.
Purchase Discounts...................................	3,351 Cr.
Transportation-In......................................	10,453 Dr.

Also, the cost of the ending inventory, $31,010, must be known. But until further entries are made, the accounts actually contain raw, unadjusted data. They do not clearly distinguish between that portion of the above items that should be considered an expense for the period and that portion that should be reported as an asset in the statement of financial position prepared at the end of the period. The required additional entries could be prepared in several different ways, one of which is:

June 30	Cost of Goods Sold	191,122	
	Purchase Returns and Allowances.......................	8,101	
	Purchase Discounts	3,351	
	Merchandise Inventory.................................		24,433
	Purchases...		167,688
	Transportation-In		10,453
	To transfer the beginning inventory and the accounts comprising net purchases to the Cost of Goods Sold expense account.		

8⁴
continued

June	30	Merchandise Inventory..	31,010	
		Cost of Goods Sold		31,010

To set up ending inventory and reduce Cost of Goods Sold by the cost of goods not sold.

(As an alternative, the above two entries could be combined with all items remaining the same except that the debit to Cost of Goods Sold would be $160,112 and there would be a net debit to Merchandise Inventory of $6,577.)

The accounts are shown below (with posting references and account numbers omitted) as they would appear after the above adjusting entries were posted. Note that the balance in the Merchandise Inventory account of $24,433 is dated June 30, 1978, which shows clearly that the ending inventory of the prior year is the beginning inventory of the current year. Observe also that this balance remains unchanged throughout the year, a distinguishing feature of periodic inventory procedure.

Merchandise Inventory

Date		Explanation	Folio	Debit	Credit	Balance
1978 June	30	Balance				24,433
1979 June	30	Transfer to Cost of Goods Sold			24,433	–0–
	30	Set up ending inventory		31,010		31,010

Purchases

Date		Explanation	Folio	Debit	Credit	Balance
1978 July	1 to					
1979 June	30			167,688		167,688
	30	Transfer to Cost of Goods Sold			167,688	–0–

156

Purchase Returns and Allowances

Date		Explanation	Folio	Debit	Credit	Balance
1978 July	1 to					
1979 June	30				8,101	8,101
	30	Transfer to Cost of Goods Sold		8,101		–0–

Purchase Discounts

Date		Explanation	Folio	Debit	Credit	Balance
1978 July	1 to					
1979 June	30				3,351	3,351
	30	Transfer to Cost of Goods Sold		3,351		–0–

Transportation-In

Date		Explanation	Folio	Debit	Credit	Balance
1978 July	1 to					
1979 June	30			10,453		10,453
	30	Transfer to Cost of Goods Sold			10,453	–0–

Cost of Goods Sold

Date		Explanation	Folio	Debit	Credit	Balance
1979 June	30	Goods available for sale		191,122		191,122
	30	Set up ending inventory			31,010	160,112

The balances shown in the Purchases, Purchase Returns and Allowances, Purchase Discounts, and Transportation-In accounts are the amounts of each of these items accumulated for the entire year. The balances could result from the posting of dozens of entries to each of these accounts.

Now observe how the first of the adjusting entries given above transfers into the Cost of Goods Sold account the net cost of all of the goods available for sale during the year. The second adjusting entry then removes from the Cost of Goods Sold account the cost of the goods unsold at year-end and establishes this amount as the ending inventory. This entry leaves in the Cost of Goods Sold account the amount of expense incurred during the year for the units of merchandise delivered to customers. The Cost of Goods Sold account is now ready to be closed as follows:

June 30 Expense and Revenue Summary........................... 160,112
          Cost of Goods Sold   160,112
          To close Cost of Goods Sold to the Expense and
          Revenue Summary.

Indicate whether each of the following statements is true or false. When properly prepared, the adjusting entries to enter the cost of the goods sold into the accounts will include:

1. A credit to Transportation-In to reduce this account to a zero balance.
2. A credit to Merchandise Inventory to set up the ending inventory.
3. A debit to Purchase Discounts to reduce this account to a zero balance.
4. A credit to Purchases to reduce this account to a zero balance.

Now check your responses in Answer Frame 8[4] on page 160.

Frame 9[4]

Earnings statement for a merchandising company

The previously presented data on sales and cost of goods sold, together with additional assumed data on operating expenses and other expense and revenue, are shown in the earnings statement in Illustration 4.4 (sometimes referred to as a multiple-step earnings statement). Note that the statement has four sections: (1) operating revenues, (2) cost of goods sold, (3) operating expenses, and (4) nonoperating revenues and expenses.

The term *operating revenues* refers to the revenues generated by the major activities of the business, usually the sale of products or services or both. All other revenues are nonoperating revenues and usually are of an incidental nature, such as those illustrated—gain on sale of equipment and interest revenue.

Operating expenses are those incurred in the normal buying, selling, and administrative functions of a business. In reality, cost of goods sold is an operating expense, the major one in mercantile firms. But it is customary to highlight the amount by which sales revenues exceed the cost of goods sold. The difference is called *gross margin*. Gross margin is often also expressed as a percentage rate and is computed by dividing gross margin by net sales. In Illustration 4.4, it is approximately 38.7 percent. This rate is watched closely by management, since a small fluctuation can cause a large change in net earnings.

Operating expenses are usually classified as either *selling* or *administrative* expenses. Selling expenses are those incurred that relate to the sale and delivery of a product or a service. Administrative expenses are those incurred in the overall management of a business. Examples of both types are given in Illustration 4.4.

Note should also be made of the difference between transportation-in and transportation-out. The latter is an expense incurred to help sell a product, while transportation-in is a part of the cost of the merchandise acquired during the period.

Illustration 4.4   Earnings statement for a merchandising company

HANLON COMPANY
Earnings Statement
For the Year Ended June 30, 1979

Revenues:

Gross sales			$282,345
Less: Sales discounts		$ 5,548	
Sales returns and allowances		15,436	20,984
Net sales			$261,361

Cost of Goods Sold:

Merchandise inventory, July 1, 1978			$ 24,433	
Purchases		$167,688		
Less: Purchase returns and allowances	$8,101			
Purchase discounts	3,351	11,452		
Net purchases		$156,236		
Add: Transportation-in		10,453		
Net cost of purchases			166,689	
Goods available for sale			$191,122	
Merchandise inventory, June 30, 1979			31,010	
Cost of Goods Sold				160,112
Gross margin				$101,249

Operating Expenses:

Selling expenses:

Sales salaries and commissions	$ 26,245	
Salespersons' travel expense	2,821	
Transportation-out	2,729	
Advertising	3,475	
Rent	2,400	
Supplies used	1,048	
Utilities	1,641	
Depreciation—store equipment	750	
Other selling expense	412	$ 41,521

Administrative expenses:

Salaries, office	$ 29,350		
Rent	1,600		
Insurance	1,548		
Supplies used	722		
Contributions	500		
Depreciation—office equipment	600		
Other administrative expense	347	34,667	
Total Operating Expenses			76,188
Net earnings from operations			$ 25,061

Other Revenue:

Interest revenue		$ 256	
Gain on sale of equipment		1,175	1,431
			$ 26,492

Other Expense:

Interest expense		721
Net Earnings (before taxes)		$ 25,771

1. True. The balance in this account is absorbed in determining the proper balance for the Cost of Goods Sold account.
2. False. Merchandise Inventory is debited to set up the ending inventory.
3. True. The balance in this account is absorbed in determining the proper balance for the Cost of Goods Sold account.
4. True. The balance in this account is absorbed in determining the proper balance for the Cost of Goods Sold account.

If you answered any of the above incorrectly, review Frame 8⁴ before proceeding to Frame 9⁴ on page 158.

9⁴
continued

The more important relationships in the earnings statement of a merchandising firm can be summarized in equation form:

1. Net sales = Gross sales − Sales returns and allowances − Sales discounts.
2. Cost of goods sold = Inventory at beginning of period + (Purchases + Transportation-in − Purchase returns and allowances − Purchase discounts) − Inventory at end of period.
3. Gross margin = Net sales − Cost of goods sold.
4. Net earnings from operations = Gross margin − Operating (selling and administrative) expenses.
5. Net earnings = Net earnings from operations + Other revenue − Other expenses.

It is entirely possible that the expenses incurred (operating and nonoperating) will exceed the revenues earned (operating and nonoperating). Then the final result for the period is a net loss rather than net earnings.

Indicate whether each of the following statements is true or false.

1. Although not specifically referred to as such in the earnings statement, the cost of the goods sold is, in reality, an operating expense.
2. It would be quite unlikely that a business would have a negative gross margin.
3. The rent earned from leasing out a part of the building owned would be classified as an operating revenue by a merchandising company.
4. The balance in a Discounts Lost account probably would be reported as an administrative operating expense in the earnings statement.

Check your responses in Answer Frame 9⁴ on page 162.

Frame 10⁴

The fundamental aspects of accounting for and reporting upon the merchandising activities of certain types of businesses have now been presented and discussed. Left for discussion at this time are certain related matters of sufficient importance to merit individual attention. They are trade discounts, items of merchandise that should and that should not be included in inventory, and inventory losses.

Nature and computation of trade discounts

A trade discount is a deduction from the list or catalog price of an article. It is a means employed to determine the actual selling price of an item purchased. The amount of the trade discount probably will be shown on the seller's invoice but not recorded in its records. Nor is it to be recorded on the books of the purchaser. Assume an invoice with the following data:

List price, 200 swimsuits at $6	$1,200
Less: Trade discount, 30%	360
Gross Invoice Price	$ 840

The vendor would record the sale at $840. The purchaser would record the cost of the merchandise at $840.

A policy of quoting trade discounts is followed for several reasons, such as:

1. To reduce the cost of catalog publication. If separate discount lists are given the salespersons whenever prices change, catalogs may be used for a long period of time. Prices may be changed by simply changing the trade discounts without reprinting the entire catalog.
2. To grant quantity discounts. If discounts are increased, customers may be induced to buy in larger quantities.
3. To be able to quote different prices to different types of customers, such as to retailers and wholesalers.

Trade discounts are computed as indicated below. Assume that the list price of an article is $100 subject to trade discounts as indicated:

> On total purchases up to 50 units, 20 percent.
> On total purchases of from 51 to 100 units, 20 and 10 percent.
> On total purchases of from 101 to 150 units, 20, 10, and 5 percent.

The price for 150 units would be quoted as $100 less 20 percent, 10 percent, and 5 percent on each and every unit; this is known as a series of trade discounts, or as a chain discount.

The computation of the gross invoice price of the 150 units is as follows:

List price—150 @ $100	$15,000
Less: 20% of $15,000	3,000
Remainder	$12,000
Less: 10% of $12,000	1,200
Remainder	$10,800
Less: 5% of $10,800	540
Gross Invoice Price	$10,260

1. True. If expenses are classified broadly as operating or nonoperating, the cost of the goods sold can hardly be a nonoperating expense.
2. True. While certain goods may be closed out at selling prices less than cost, only in a firm that is going out of business is it likely that the cost of the goods sold will exceed sales revenue for a period of time.
3. False. It is likely to be incidental to the merchandising operations and classifiable as nonoperating revenue.
4. False. It would be better classified as a nonoperating expense, since it is more in the nature of a loss that did not have to be incurred.

If you answered incorrectly, review Frame 9⁴ before going on to Frame 10⁴ on page 160.

10⁴
continued

The same results can be obtained by multiplying the list price by the complements of the discounts allowed. For example, $15,000 × .80 × .90 × .95 = $10,260. The gross invoice price to be recorded in the accounting records of the seller and the buyer is $10,260. Price-determining trade discounts are not reflected in recorded sales or purchases. But an invoice for the above 150 units could quote terms of 2/10, n/30. And if the invoice is recorded at gross price by the buyer and paid within the discount period, a purchase discount of $205.20 (.02 × $10,260) would be recorded.

Indicate whether each of the following statements is true or false.

1. Trade discounts may be granted to induce customers to buy in larger quantities.
2. Trade discounts are used by a seller to quote different prices to different types of customers, such as wholesalers and retailers.
3. A seller's invoice appears as follows (terms, 2/10, n/30):

List price, 200 pairs of men's socks @ $0.50	$100
Less: Trade discount, 25%	25
Gross Invoice Price	$ 75

    The purchasing company should record a $100 purchase in its records if it employs gross price procedure.
4. In the invoice in statement 3 above, a purchase of $73.50 could be recorded if the buyer employs net price procedure.

Now check your responses in Answer Frame 10⁴ on page 164.

Inventory exclusions and inclusions

In taking a physical inventory, care must be exercised to ensure that all goods owned, regardless of where they are located, are counted and included in the inventory. Thus, goods shipped to a potential customer "on approval" should not be recorded as sold. They should be included in inventory. Similarly, goods delivered on a consignment basis should not be recorded as sold. Here the intent is that the goods remain the property of the shipper (consignor) until sold by the consignee. Such goods must be included in the shipper's inventory.

Merchandise in transit at the end of an accounting period must be recorded as a purchase by the buyer and included in inventory if title to the goods has passed. Generally, whether title has passed can be determined from the freight terms under which the goods were shipped. Goods in the hands of the delivering agent (airfreight line, railroad, or trucking or steamship company) are (1) the property of the seller if shipped f.o.b. destination, or (2) the property of the buyer if shipped f.o.b. shipping point. Briefly stated, the goods belong to the party who must bear the transportation charges.

On occasion, goods may remain in the possession of the seller after they have been sold. Usually, such goods have been packaged and placed in a convenient place awaiting pickup by the buyer. If title has actually passed, the goods must be excluded from the seller's inventory.

Goods which are unsalable due to damage, deterioration, or obsolescence should not be included in inventory. If salable only at a reduced price, the dollar amount attached to the goods must be reduced. As a general rule this amount should not exceed the selling price of the goods less any expected costs of selling the items. This procedure charges the amount of the write-down of the goods to the accounting period in which the loss occurred.

Inventory losses

Under periodic inventory procedure, the general presumption is that the difference between goods available for sale and the ending inventory is the cost of goods sold. In other words, it is assumed that of all of the goods available for sale, those not on hand at the end of the accounting period were sold. But it is not necessarily true that all of the missing goods were sold. Some goods are subject to shrinkage, spoilage, or theft. Losses from shoplifting are estimated at billions of dollars annually in the United States. Under periodic inventory procedure, such losses are automatically buried in the cost of goods sold.

To illustrate, assume that the cost of certain goods available for sale was $200,000 and the actual ending inventory is $60,000. This suggests that the cost of the goods sold to customers was $140,000. But assume

11⁴
continued

further that it is known that $2,000 of goods were shoplifted. If such goods had not been stolen, the ending inventory would have been $62,000 and the cost of goods sold only $138,000. Thus, the cost of goods sold of $140,000 includes the cost of the merchandise delivered to customers and the cost of merchandise stolen.

Appendix 4A covers the topic of special journals which can be used in addition to the general journal. Their use can lead to the more efficient processing of data and can facilitate control.

Appendix 4B illustrates the use of a work sheet for a merchandising company. Its purpose is to show how the merchandising-related accounts are treated in the work sheet.

Indicate whether each of the following statements is true or false.

1. Goods in transit sold under terms of f.o.b. destination are the property of the seller until they reach their destination.
2. Under certain rather rare circumstances, a seller may have goods on hand that are legally the property of a buyer.
3. Goods shipped on consignment are the property of the shipper until sold by the consignee.
4. An advantage of periodic inventory procedure is that it readily permits the determination of losses resulting from stolen goods.

Now check your responses in Answer Frame 11⁴ on page 166.

Summary   *chapter 4*

Sales revenue (net sales, or gross sales less sales discounts and sales returns and allowances) is generally recognized when a sale has been completed. A completed sale involves legal transfer of title to goods and is usually accompanied by physical delivery of the goods. Recognition of revenue at the time of sale is usually justified on the grounds that the revenue has been earned and realized.

Three common adjustments of the gross invoice prices entered in the Sales account are for sales returns, sales allowances, and sales discounts, all of which are recorded in contra accounts to Sales. Net sales shows the approximate amount of assets expected to flow into a firm from its customers.

Theoretically, cash discounts are adjustments of the selling price of goods, although they are often viewed as rewards for prompt payment. A cash discount is a sales discount to the seller and a purchase discount to the buyer. Cash discount terms can be readily converted into equivalent annual interest rates as an aid in determining whether money should be borrowed to take cash discounts.

Under perpetual procedure, the cost of the goods sold is determined at the time of sale. Under periodic procedure, the cost of all sales made during a period is determined only at the end of the period. Periodic procedure involves less record keeping but fails to show the amount of goods that should be on hand at any one time. Under periodic procedure, cost of goods sold is determined as being equal to beginning inventory plus net purchases less ending inventory. Net purchases is equal to purchases less purchase returns and allowances and purchase discounts. Transportation-in is added to net purchases to arrive at the net cost of purchases (see Illustration 4.3). Transportation charges are the responsibility of the seller for goods shipped f.o.b. destination, of the buyer for goods shipped f.o.b. shipping point.

Purchases may be recorded at gross invoice prices, and any discounts taken will be recorded in a Purchase Discounts account. Alternatively, they may be recorded at net invoice prices and purchase discounts *not taken* will be recorded in a Discounts Lost account.

The earnings statement of a merchandising company is likely to have four sections, one each for operating revenues, cost of goods sold, operating expenses, and nonoperating revenues and expenses.

Trade discounts are deductions from list or catalog prices to determine actual selling prices. They are not formally recorded by either the buyer or the seller.

The ending inventory should include all goods owned, regardless of where located. It should exclude all goods not legally owned, as well as all unsalable goods. Goods salable only at reduced prices should normally be written down for inventory purposes.

Cost of goods sold, under periodic procedure, includes the cost of goods missing because of shrinkage, spoilage, and shoplifting—a distinct disadvantage of the procedure.

Appendix 4A covers special journals. Appendix 4B covers the work sheet for a merchandising company.

You have completed the programmed portion of Chapter 4. As the first part of your review, read the Glossary which begins on page 176 and study the definitions of the new terms introduced in this chapter. Then go on to the Student Review Quiz on page 178 for a self-administered test of your comprehension of the material in the chapter.

APPENDIX 4A: SPECIAL JOURNALS

Because of the number of transactions involved, an accounting system which includes only one book of original entry—the general journal—will be inadequate for even a relatively small business. The first step toward more efficient processing of data usually consists of the development of several special journals. These will allow for a division of labor and also for a reduction in posting time because of the grouping of similar types of transactions. Many different formats or types of journals could be used. The ones presented here are illustrative only. The special journals illustrated are the sales, purchases, cash receipts, and cash disbursements journals. Those journals actually used by a particular company are functions of the nature of the transactions encountered by the company and of the imagination of the person designing them.

Special journals are also used to facilitate control. For instance, one of the primary reasons for using specialized journals for sales and purchases is to facilitate the accounting for receivables and payables so that debit-credit information and balances are available for each creditor and each customer. The cash receipts and cash disbursements journals provide handy information regarding receipts and disbursements so that control may exist over these cash flows.

Before discussing these further, it is necessary to review a topic closely related to the posting of amounts from the special journals to the ledger accounts.

Controlling accounts and subsidiary accounts

A controlling account is an account in the general ledger that is supported by a detailed classification of accounting information in a subsidiary record. For example, an up-to-date record must be maintained with each customer to show the business done and the amount owed; therefore, outside the general ledger, an account is maintained with each individual customer, showing the debits and credits to each account and the balance due. The sum of the balances due from all customers equals the balance of the Accounts Receivable controlling account in the general ledger.

The individual account with each customer is known as a subsidiary account; all of the individual customers' accounts constitute the *subsidiary accounts receivable ledger,* or customers' ledger. A subsidiary ledger, then, is a group of related accounts showing the details of the balance of a controlling account in the general ledger. Subsidiary ledgers are separated from the general ledger in order (*a*) to relieve the general ledger of a mass of detail and thereby shorten the general ledger trial balance, (*b*) to promote the division of labor in the task of maintaining the ledgers, and (*c*) to strengthen the system of internal control. A subsidiary ledger may be used whether or not special journals are used.

When a transaction occurs that affects a controlling account and a subsidiary account, it is journalized in such fashion that it will be posted (*a*) to the general ledger and (*b*) to a subsidiary account. The usual way is to enter the transaction in a special column in a journal.

The key to effective operation and control of a subsidiary ledger is found in the posting procedure. The use of special columns in the journals makes it possible to post each transaction to an individual account in a subsidiary ledger during the period. Since the column totals are posted to the controlling accounts at the end of the period (usually a month), a comparison of the controlling account balance with the sum of the individual subsidiary account balances aids in determining that all amounts have been posted to the subsidiary accounts.

A few examples of frequently maintained subsidiary ledgers and the names of the related general ledger controlling accounts are:

Subsidiary ledger	*General ledger controlling account*
Accounts receivable ledger (account with each customer)	Accounts Receivable
Accounts payable ledger (account with each creditor)	Accounts Payable
Equipment ledger (account for each item of equipment)	Office Equipment Delivery Equipment Store Fixtures, etc.

The number of subsidiary ledgers maintained will vary according to the information requirements of each company. Control accounts and subsidiary ledgers generally will be maintained for control purposes where there is a high volume of transactions affecting a given account and where information as to the details of these transactions is needed on a continuing basis.

Grouping of similar transactions in journals

Special journals are designed to systematize the original recording of the major recurring transactions. One journal is set up to record the journal entries for purchases of merchandise on account. Another journal is set up to record the journal entries for sales on account. A cash receipts journal is provided for entry of cash receipts transactions, and a cash disbursements journal is provided for entry of cash disbursements. The general journal remains for all transactions that cannot be entered readily in one of the special journals. All five are records of original entry containing data which will be posted to ledger accounts. In the Folio column of the accounts, abbreviations are used to identify the source of the posting, for example, PJ for the purchases journal and CDJ for the cash disbursements journal as shown:

	Abbreviation
Sales journal	SJ
Purchases journal	PJ
Cash receipts journal	CRJ
Cash disbursements journal	CDJ
General journal	GJ

The sales journal

Normally, sales are for cash or on open account. The sales journal in Illustration 4.5 should be used only for sales of merchandise on account. Cash sales should be recorded in the cash receipts journal. Sales of other assets should be recorded in the cash receipts journal (if cash is received at the time of sale) or in the general journal.

The simplest form of sales journal has only one money column, entitled Accounts Receivable Dr. and Sales Cr. Variations in the sales journal can be made. Special columns could be inserted for items such as state sales taxes, federal excise taxes, and sales returns and allowances. And a departmental breakdown can be obtained by providing a Sales Cr. column for each department in a company.

Posting sales. The posting of sales from the sales journal in Illustration 4.5 involves entering the total of the money column headed Accounts Receivable Dr. and Sales Cr. as a credit to the general ledger Sales account. The folio reference of SJ-1 (sales journal, p. 1) is also entered in the Sales account and the number (301) is written in the sales journal under the total of the money column to show that the $250 was posted as a credit to Sales. Since there generally is no subsidiary sales ledger, the individual items comprising sales are not posted.

Posting accounts receivable. To post accounts receivable from the sales journal in Illustration 4.5, the total of the money column ($250) is posted as a debit to the Accounts Receivable control account in the general ledger with a folio reference of SJ-1. The number (111) is entered under the total of the money column in the sales journal to show that the amount has been posted. The individual amounts in the money

Illustration 4.5

SALES JOURNAL				Page 1	
		Invoice	Accounts Receivable Dr. 111 Sales Cr. 301		
Date	Description	No.	Amount		✓
1979 Apr. 3	Arthur Benson	100	30.00 ←		✓
4	Peter Cote	101	25.00 ←		✓
12	Kenneth Johnson	102	130.00 ←		✓
19	Peter Cote	103	10.00 ←		✓
30	Anthony Demambro	104	55.00 ←		✓
			→ 250.00		
			(111) (301)		

GENERAL LEDGER

Accounts Receivable Control 111

SJ-1 250 ←

Sales 301

SJ-1 250 ←

SUBSIDIARY ACCOUNTS RECEIVABLE LEDGER

Arthur Benson

4/3/79 SJ-1 30 ←

Peter Cote

4/4/79 SJ-1 25 ←
4/19/79 SJ-1 10 ←

Anthony Demambro

4/30/79 SJ-1 55 ←

Kenneth Johnson

4/12/79 SJ-1 130 ←

column are posted to each individual customer's account in the subsidiary ledger so that the account will show the amount currently due from the customer. As each individual amount is posted, a check mark (✓) is placed in the column headed ✓ opposite the amount to show that it has been posted. When the posting of the accounts receivable has been completed, the Accounts Receivable control account will show a balance of $250, which is equal to the sum of the balances in the Accounts Receivable subsidiary ledger accounts, assuming no previous balances in the control account or the subsidiary accounts.

Subsidiary ledger accounts usually are not numbered but are kept in alphabetical order, since their composition is constantly changing.

The cash receipts journal

The cash receipts journal, which might be used in combination with the sales journal, is shown in Illustration 4.6. Any number of different

169

Illustration 4.6

						111 Accounts Receivable Cr.		Sundry Accounts Cr.		
101 Cash Dr.	726 Sales Dis- counts Dr.	Date		Description	301 Sales Cr.	Amount	✔	Acct. No.	Amount	✔
		1979								
10,700.00		Apr.	1	Cash sales	10,700.00					
29.40	.60		6	Arthur Benson – Invoice No. 100		30.00	✔			
10,775.00			7	Cash sales	10,775.00					
6,000.00			10	Sold investments at cost to Wells Corporation				138*	6,000.00	✔
10,600.00			14	Cash sales	10,600.00					
25.00			19	Peter Cote – Invoice No. 101		25.00	✔			
127.40	2.60		20	Kenneth Johnson – Invoice No. 102		130.00	✔			
11,045.00			25	Cash sales	11,045.00					
200.00			26	Dividends received on Krantz Company common stock				303*	200.00	✔
49,501.80	3.20				43,120.00	185.00			6,200.00	
(101)	(726)				(301)	(111)			✔	

CASH RECEIPTS JOURNAL — *Page 5*

* 138 Investments.
* 303 Dividend Revenue.

designs may be used for this journal also. For instance, if some of the items appearing in the Sundry (which means miscellaneous) Accounts Cr. column are frequently credited, it would be advisable to set up a separate column for each of these items.

Since the amounts appearing in the Sundry Accounts Cr. column usually pertain to different accounts, the column total is not posted and a check mark (✔) is placed immediately below the amount. The individual items are posted to the accounts indicated (Accounts 138 and 303 in Illustration 4.6).

A combined sales and cash receipts journal

It is possible to combine the sales and cash receipts journals illustrated earlier. Illustration 4.7 shows the two journals combined. This allows total sales to be posted as one amount rather than two.

But posting and journalizing convenience is not the only consideration. Remember that one of the reasons for creating special journals is so that several persons can work with them at the same time. Having separate sales and cash receipts journals does allow more persons to work with the data in the journals at the same time. A decision in any particular case has to be made so as to maximize the overall efficiency of working with the journals.

Illustration 4.7

COMBINED SALES AND CASH RECEIPTS JOURNAL

101 Cash Dr.	726 Sales Discounts Dr.	111 Accounts Receivable Dr. Amount	✓	Date	Description	Invoice No.	301 Sales Cr.	111 Accounts Receivable Cr. Amount	✓	Sundry Accounts Cr. Acct. No.	Amount	✓
				1979 Apr.								
10,700.00				1	Cash sales		10,700.00					
		30.00	✓	3	Arthur Benson	100	30.00					
		25.00	✓	4	Peter Cote	101	25.00					
29.40	.60			6	Arthur Benson			30.00	✓			
10,775.00				7	Cash sales		10,775.00					
6,000.00				10	Sold investments at cost					138*	6,000.00	✓
		130.00	✓	12	Kenneth Johnson	102	130.00					
10,600.00				14	Cash sales		10,600.00					
		10.00	✓	19	Peter Cote	103	10.00					
25.00				19	Peter Cote			25.00	✓			
127.40	2.60			20	Kenneth Johnson			130.00	✓			
11,045.00				25	Cash sales		11,045.00					
200.00				26	Dividends received					303*	200.00	✓
		55.00	✓	30	Anthony Demambro	104	55.00					
49,501.80	3.20	250.00					43,370.00	185.00			6,200.00	
(101)	(726)	(111)					(301)	(111)			(✓)	

* 138 Investments.
* 303 Dividend Revenue.

The purchases journal

The total in the money column of the purchases journal in Illustration 4.8 (where periodic procedure is assumed) is posted to the Purchases account as a debit and to the Accounts Payable account as a credit at the end of the month. The individual amounts in the column are posted to the accounts in the accounts payable subsidiary ledger.

Most business firms are aware that in order to have an acceptable level of control over cash disbursements they must pay all bills by check. Assuming this to be the case here, all purchases are made on account and are therefore included in the purchases journal (even if the length of delay in payment is only long enough to write the check). The payment is then shown in the cash disbursements journal.

There are, of course, a number of designs which could be used. If there are separate departments, a separate purchases column could be provided for each department.

A column could be inserted for purchase returns and allowances if

Illustration 4.8

PURCHASES JOURNAL					Page 10	
					Purchases Dr. 801 Accounts Payable Cr. 201	
Date	Terms	Invoice Number	Creditor		Amount	✔
1979 Apr. 1	2/10,n/30	862	Smith Corporation		196.00	✔
7	1/15,n/60	121	Lasky Company		99.00	✔
12	2/20,n/60	561	Booth Corporation		4,900.00	✔
15	2/10,n/30	1042	Gooch Corporation		2,940.00	✔
21	3/15,n/60	633	Wyngarden Company		9,700.00	✔
26	2/10,n/30	734	Mertz Company		98.00	✔
30	2/10,n/30	287	Nelson Company		3,920.00	✔
30	2/20,n/60	568	Booth Corporation		1,470.00	✔
					23,323.00	
					(801)(201)	

they are frequently encountered. And since a Purchase Returns and Allowances account normally has a credit balance, an Accounts Payable debit column would have to be included also.

All amounts of purchases have been entered net of discount in the illustration. Any discounts missed should be considered penalties due to inefficiency and recorded in a Discounts Lost account.

The cash disbursements journal

Since it is assumed that all cash disbursements are made by check, the cash disbursements journal in Illustration 4.9 contains a column in

Illustration 4.9

CASH DISBURSEMENTS JOURNAL

201 Accounts Payable Dr. ✔	201 Accounts Payable Dr. Amount	219 Salaries Payable Dr.	821 Discounts Lost Dr.	822 Supplies Expense Dr.	Sundry Accounts Dr. Acct. No.	Sundry Accounts Dr. Amount	✔	Date	Description	Check No.	101 Cash Cr.
				42.00				1979 Apr. 2	Brooklyn Square Paint Company	524	42.00
					123*	1,200.00	✔	3	Insurance policy to cover May 1979 – April 30, 1980	525	1,200.00
					140*	500.00	✔		Furniture – office	526	500.00
					823*	200.00	✔		Rent for April 1979	527	200.00
✔	196.00							4	Smith Corporation – Invoice No. 862	528	196.00
				10.00				6	Allan Park Stationery Company	529	10.00
✔	99.00							8	Lasky Company – Invoice No. 121	530	99.00
✔	4,900.00							14	Booth Company – Invoice No. 561	531	4,900.00
✔	9,700.00							18	Wyngarden Company – Invoice No. 633	532	9,700.00
✔	2,940.00		60.00					21	Gooch Corporation – Invoice No. 1042	533	3,000.00
		1,463.00						27	Clarke Frankson	534	1,463.00
		1,151.15						28	Mead Stacy	535	1,151.15
		788.60						30	Jason Evans	536	788.60
		707.15							Marshall Watson	537	707.15
		395.75							Cleveland Avoy	538	395.75
		334.93							James Jackson	539	334.93
		360.07							Stuart Bently	540	360.07
		370.40							Robert Alco	541	370.40
	17,835.00	5,571.05	60.00	52.00		1,900.00					25,418.05
	(201)	(219)	(821)	(822)		(✔)					(101)

* 123 – Unexpired Insurance.
* 140 – Furniture and Equipment.
* 823 – Rent Expense.

which to record the number of each check written. Payments on accounts payable and salaries payable constitute the majority of items paid in the illustration.

The general journal and other journals

Every transaction that will not fit conveniently into the special journals is entered in the general journal. The general journal would be necessary to record the adjusting and closing entries even if all other entries fit the format of the special journals used.

Various other special journals are conceivable (e.g., purchase returns and allowances journal and sales returns and allowances journal). The proper combination for a particular company depends on the volume of transactions, the types of transactions, management's information needs, and the number of persons having to work with the data at any one time.

Summary of the advantages of using special journals

To summarize, the following advantages are obtained from the use of special journals.

a. Time is saved in journalizing. Only one line is used for each transaction; a full description is not necessary. The amount of writing is reduced because it is not necessary to repeat the account names printed at the top of the special column or columns.

b. Time is saved in posting. Many data are posted as totals of columns.

c. Detail is eliminated from the general ledger. Column totals are posted to the general ledger, and the detail is left in the journals.

d. Division of labor is promoted. Several persons can work simultaneously on the accounting records. This specialization and division of labor pinpoints responsibility and eases the location of errors.

e. Use of accounting machines is facilitated. The mass of routine transactions recorded in special journals frequently makes the use of accounting machines economical.

f. Management analysis is aided. The journals themselves can be useful to management in analyzing classes of transactions (such as credit sales).

APPENDIX 4B: THE WORK SHEET FOR A MERCHANDISING COMPANY

Appendix 3A illustrated the basic structure of a work sheet. It was prepared for a company providing services.

The purpose of Appendix 4B is to show how a work sheet would be prepared for a merchandising company (see Illustration 4.10). The example is simplified to focus on the merchandise-related accounts.

The accounts which appear in the trial balance of a merchandising

Illustration 4.10

LYONS STORE, INC.
Work Sheet
For the Month Ended January 31, 1979

Acct. No.	Account Titles	Trial Balance Debit	Trial Balance Credit	Adjustments Debit	Adjustments Credit	Adjusted Trial Balance Debit	Adjusted Trial Balance Credit	Earnings Statement Debit	Earnings Statement Credit	Statement of Retained Earnings Debit	Statement of Retained Earnings Credit	Statement of Financial Position Debit	Statement of Financial Position Credit
1	Cash	18,663				18,663						18,663	
3	Accounts receivable—Baker Co.	1,880				1,880						1,880	
4	Merchandise inventory, Jan. 1	7,000			(a) 7,000								
6	Accounts payable—Moonbrook Co.		700				700						700
7	Capital stock		15,000				15,000						15,000
8	Retained earnings		10,000				10,000				10,000		
9	Sales		13,600				13,600		13,600				
10	Sales returns and allowances	20				20		20					
11	Sales discounts	44				44		44					
12	Purchases	6,000			(a) 6,000								
13	Purchase returns and allowances		100	(a) 100									
14	Purchase discounts		82	(a) 82									
15	Transportation-in	75			(a) 75								
16	Sales salaries	650				650		650					
17	Rent expense	150				150		150					
18	Dividends	5,000				5,000				5,000			
		39,482	39,482										
	Cost of goods sold			(a) 12,893	(b) 8,000	4,893		4,893					
	Merchandise inventory, Jan. 31*			(b) 8,000		8,000						8,000	
				21,075	21,075	39,300	39,300	5,757	13,600	5,000		28,543	
	Net earnings for January							7,843			7,843		
								13,600	13,600		17,843		
	Retained Earnings									12,843			12,843
										17,843	17,843	28,543	28,543

* If desired, the $8,000 in the Adjustments column and in the Statement of Financial Position column may be placed on the same line as the $7,000 beginning inventory figure.

company which do not appear in the trial balance of a service company are – Merchandise Inventory, Sales, Sales Returns and Allowances, Sales Discounts, Purchases, Purchase Returns and Allowances, Purchase Discounts, and Transportation-In. The balances in the Merchandise Inventory account (representing the beginning inventory), the Purchases account, and all of the purchase-related accounts (such as Transportation-In, Purchase Discounts, and Purchase Returns and Allowances) are transferred to the Cost of Goods Sold account in entry (*a*) in the work sheet. The entry made consists of debits to Cost of Goods Sold, Purchase Discounts, and Purchase Returns and Allowances; and credits to Merchandise Inventory, Purchases, and Transportation-In. The ending inventory (assumed to be $8,000) is established by debiting Merchandise Inventory and crediting Cost of Goods Sold in entry (*b*) in the work sheet. All of these debits and credits should appear in the Adjustments columns of the work sheet.

All revenue accounts in the work sheet are carried to the credit Earnings Statement column. All revenue contra accounts and all expense accounts, including the Cost of Goods Sold account, are carried to the debit Earnings Statement column.

The amount needed to balance the Earnings Statement columns is the net earnings or net loss amount for the period. It is carried to the credit (or debit, if loss) Statement of Retained Earnings column.

The beginning balance in retained earnings is carried to the credit Statement of Retained Earnings column. The dividends balance is carried to the debit Statement of Retained Earnings column. The amount needed to balance the Statement of Retained Earnings columns is the ending retained earnings balance. It is carried to the credit Statement of Financial Position column.

All assets are carried to the debit Statement of Financial Position column. All liabilities and stockholders' equity items are carried to the credit Statement of Financial Position column.

Glossary *chapter* 4

Administrative expenses – operating expenses incurred in the overall management of a business.

Cash disbursements journal – a special journal in which all outflows of cash are recorded.

Cash discount – to the seller, a sales discount; to the buyer, a purchase discount; a deduction allowed from the gross invoice price that can be taken only if the invoice is paid within a specified period of time; typically, cash discounts vary from less than 1 percent to 3 percent.

Cash receipts journal – a special journal in which all inflows of cash are recorded.

Consignment – goods shipped by one party (the consignor) to another (the consignee) who is to pay for the goods only if he or she is able to sell them to a third party.

Controlling account – an account in the general ledger that is supported by a detailed classification of accounting information in a subsidiary record.

Cost of goods sold – an expense incurred consisting of the cost to the seller of goods sold to customers; computed as Beginning inventory + (Purchases + Transportation-in–Purchase returns and allowances – Purchase discounts) – Ending inventory.

Discounts Lost account – an account used to show discounts not taken when purchased merchandise is recorded at net invoice price.

F.o.b. destination – freight terms that mean goods are shipped to their destination without charge to the buyer; in other words, the seller bears the transportation charges.

F.o.b. shipping point – freight terms that mean goods are placed in the hands of the transporting company without charge to the seller; the buyer is responsible for all transportation costs that follow.

Freight collect – terms that require the buyer to pay the freight bill when the goods are delivered; if the terms are f.o.b. destination, the buyer will deduct the amount of freight when he or she remits to the seller.

Freight prepaid – terms that indicate the seller has paid the freight bill at the time of shipment; if the terms are f.o.b. shipping point, the seller will bill the buyer for the amount paid.

Gross margin – Net sales – Cost of goods sold.

Merchandise in transit – goods in the hands of a transport company on an inventory-taking date.

Merchandise inventory – the quantity of goods on hand and available for sale at any given time.

Net earnings – Net earnings from operations + Other revenue – Other expense.

Net earnings from operations – Gross margin – Operating expenses.

Net sales – Gross sales – Sales returns and allowances – Sales discounts.

Nonoperating expenses – expenses incurred that are not related to the acquisition and sale of the products or services regularly offered for sale, for example, interest expense.

Nonoperating revenues – revenues not related to the sale of products or services regularly offered for sale; for example, interest revenue.

Operating expenses – expenses incurred in the normal buying, selling, and administrative functions of a business.

Operating revenues – revenues resulting from the sale of products or services regularly offered for sale.

Passage of title – a legal term used to indicate transfer of legal ownership of goods.

Periodic inventory procedure – a system of accounting for merchandise acquired for sale to customers wherein the cost of such merchandise sold and the amount of such merchandise on hand are determined only through the taking of a physical inventory.

Perpetual inventory procedure – a system of accounting for merchandise acquired for sale to customers wherein the cost of such merchandise sold and the amount of such merchandise on hand can be determined at any time by reference to the Cost of Goods Sold and Merchandise Inventory accounts.

Purchase Discounts account – an account used under periodic inventory procedure to record the amount of discounts taken when payment is made within a specified period of time; properly viewed as a reduction in the recorded cost of purchases.

Purchase invoice – a document prepared by the seller of merchandise and sent to the buyer that contains the details of a sale, such as the number of units, unit price, total price billed, terms of sale, and manner of shipment; a purchase invoice from the seller's point of view is a sales invoice.

Purchase order – a form prepared by a potential buyer ordering merchandise from a prospective seller.

Purchase Returns and Allowances account – an account used under periodic inventory procedure to record the cost of merchandise returned to a seller and to record reductions in selling prices granted by a seller because merchandise was not satisfactory to a buyer; viewed as a reduction in the recorded cost of purchases.

Purchases account – an account used under periodic inventory procedure to record the cost of merchandise purchased during the current accounting period.

Purchases journal – a special journal in which all purchases on account of merchandise for resale are recorded.

Sales allowances – deductions from the originally agreed-upon sales price for merchandise granted by the seller to the buyer because the merchandise sold was not fully satisfactory to the buyer; to the buyer, a purchase allowance.

Sales discounts—a reduction of the amount due from a buyer granted by the seller for prompt payment; theoretically, an adjustment of recorded sales price; to the buyer, a purchase discount.

Sales Discounts account—an account used to record sales discounts taken by customers; a contra account to Sales.

Sales invoice—see purchase invoice.

Sales journal—a special journal in which all sales of merchandise on account are recorded.

Sales returns—from the seller's point of view, merchandise returned by a buyer for any of a variety of reasons; to the buyer, a purchase return.

Sales Returns and Allowances account—a contra account to Sales used to record the selling price of merchandise returned by buyers or reductions in selling prices granted.

Selling expenses—operating expenses incurred in the sale and delivery of merchandise or in the rendering of services to customers.

Subsidiary ledger—a group of related accounts showing the details of the balance of a controlling account in the general ledger.

Trade discounts—deductions from the list or catalog prices of merchandise to arrive at the gross invoice selling price; granted for quantity purchases or to particular categories of customers (e.g., retailers and wholesalers).

Transportation-In account—an account used under periodic inventory procedure to record transportation costs incurred in the acquisition of merchandise; an addition to the cost of the merchandise purchased.

Continue with the Student Review Quiz below as a self-administered test of your understanding of the material presented in this chapter.

Student review quiz *chapter* 4

To develop a permanent record of your responses, you may write them on the answer sheet provided in the *Work Papers* or on a separate sheet of paper. Unless instructed otherwise, select the one best answer for each question.

1 Recording revenue at the time a sale is made is generally considered appropriate because—

a The revenue has been earned—the seller has completed his or her part of the agreement.

b The revenue has been realized—that is, valid assets have been received in an exchange.

c The revenue is measurable with a fairly high degree of precision.

d Legal title to the goods has passed to the buyer.

e All of the above.

2 Choose the one incorrect statement regarding sales discounts.

a They generally range in size from less than 1 percent to 3 percent of the gross invoice price of the goods sold.

b They are usually granted to induce prompt payment of an account.

c Theoretically, they are best viewed as reductions in recorded selling prices.

d They are usually credited to a Sales Discounts account when taken.

e They are deducted from sales to determine or arrive at net sales.

3 Given a list or catalog price of $2,000, trade discounts of 25, 20, and 10 percent, and cash discount terms of 2/10, n/30, the gross invoice price of this merchandise when sold would be—

a $1,080.

b $1,058.40.

c $1,960.

d $1,100.

e $980.

4 Assuming that $1,080 is the correct answer in 3 above, prepare the entry that should be made on the buyer's books at the time of payment, assuming payment within the discount period.

5 A firm received an invoice in the amount of $5,000; terms, 3/10, n/30. It can borrow funds at an 8 percent rate of interest. Compute the equivalent annual rate of interest paid if the invoice is paid on the 30th day. Also compute the dollar amount saved if funds are borrowed on the 10th day to pay the invoice and the loan is repaid 20 days later.

6 All of the following are contra (or reduction) accounts except –
a Sales Discounts.
b Purchase Discounts.
c Transportation-In.
d Sales Returns and Allowances.
e Purchase Returns and Allowances.

7 As between perpetual and periodic inventory procedures of accounting for merchandise, periodic procedure (choose the incorrect statement) –
a Is less costly to apply, since it accumulates less detail.
b Provides better control over inventory.
c Buries losses from shrinkage and shoplifting in cost of goods sold.
d Is more appropriate, economically, for merchandise having a low individual unit value.

8 On June 21 the Bunetta Company purchased merchandise f.o.b. destination, freight collect. Having paid the freight bill on delivery of the goods, the company should, in order to record the payment properly, credit Cash and debit (assume periodic inventory procedure) –
a Transportation-In.
b Accounts Receivable.
c Merchandise Inventory.
d Purchases.
e Accounts Payable.

9 For which of the following purposes are trade discounts typically *not* used?
a To encourage prompt payment of an invoice.
b To facilitate charging different prices to different types of customers.
c To induce purchasers to acquire larger amounts of merchandise.
d To permit the changing of prices without reprinting an expensive catalog.

10 Which of the following should be excluded from inventory?
a Goods salable only at reduced prices.
b Goods out on consignment in the hands of a dealer in a nearby city.
c Incoming goods in transit shipped f.o.b. shipping point.
d Goods delivered to a customer on approval.
e Goods on hand title to which has passed to a customer.

11 Given the following information:

Beginning inventory	$ 5,000
Sales	15,900
Ending inventory	3,000
Purchases	9,000
Sales returns and allowances	600
Transportation-in	700
Sales discounts	300
Purchase discounts	200
Purchase returns and allowances	400

Which of the following statements are correct?
a Net sales are $15,000.
b Net cost of purchases is $9,100.
c Cost of goods available for sale is $14,100.
d Cost of goods sold is $11,100.
e Gross margin is $3,900.

12 On July 1 the following entry was made to record an invoice received on that date:

Purchases	2,000	
Accounts Payable		2,000
To record purchase on which the terms were 2/10, n/30.		

What entry would be correct if the invoice were paid on July 10?

a	Accounts Payable	2,000	
	Cash		2,000
b	Accounts Payable	1,960	
	Purchase Discounts	40	
	Cash		2,000
c	Accounts Payable	1,960	
	Cash		1,960
d	Accounts Payable	2,000	
	Cash		1,960
	Purchase Discounts		40

13 Dori's Dress Shop received from Davis, Inc., merchandise having an invoice price of $4,000; terms, 1/15, n/60, f.o.b. shipping point; and also paid $20 shipping charges to Speedy Delivery Company. If payment of the Davis, Inc., invoice is made within the discount period, the amount of the check should be –
a $4,000 − ($4,000 × .01) = $3,960.
b $4,000 − $20 − ($4,000 × .01) = $3,940.
c $4,000 − $20 − ($3,980 × .01) = $3,940.20.
d $4,000 − ($3,980 × .01) = $3,960.20.
e $4,000 + $20 − ($4,020 × .01) = $3,979.80.

14 If the ending inventory is overstated —

a Cost of goods sold is understated and net earnings for the period are overstated.

b Cost of goods sold is understated and net earnings for the period are understated.

c Cost of goods sold is overstated and net earnings are overstated.

d Cost of goods sold is overstated and net earnings are understated.

e Cost of goods sold is understated and gross margin is understated.

15 Which of the following correctly describes the makeup of the cost of goods sold section of the earnings statement under periodic inventory procedure?

a Beginning inventory + Purchases − Transportation-in − Purchase returns and allowances − Purchase discounts − Ending inventory.

b Beginning inventory + Purchases − Transportation-in − Purchase returns and allowances − Purchase discounts + Ending inventory.

c Beginning inventory + Purchases + Transportation-in + Purchase returns and allowances − Purchase discounts − Ending inventory.

d Beginning inventory + Purchases + Transportation-in − Purchase returns and allowances − Purchase discounts − Ending inventory.

Questions 16–20 are based on Appendix 4A.

16 Which of the following statements is not correct? The use of special journals —

a Facilitates division of labor in journalizing and posting.

b Systematizes the original entries of the major recurring transactions.

c Saves time in journalizing and posting.

d Has the major disadvantage that special journals make the use of accounting machines less feasible.

e Eliminates detail in the general ledger.

17 When special journals are used, adjusting and closing entries are generally recorded in the —

a Cash disbursements journal.

b Cash receipts journal.

c General journal.

d Purchases journal.

e Sales journal.

18 Match each transaction in column A with the appropriate journal in which it would be recorded in column B. Assume each of the journals listed is used as a book of original entry and is designed as illustrated in Appendix 4A.

Column A		Column B	
c 1.	Acquired merchandise on account.	*a.*	Sales journal.
e 2.	Recorded the estimated amount of bad debts.	*b.*	Cash receipts journal.
d 3.	Recorded the payment of wages.	*c.*	Purchases journal.
a 4.	Sold merchandise on account.	*d.*	Cash disbursements journal.
b 5.	Sold merchandise for cash.	*e.*	General journal.
b 6.	Collected cash on account.		
e 7.	Gave a note to a trade creditor.		
e b 8.	Received a cash dividend.		
b a 9.	Sold land and received a note.		
e d 10.	Paid rent for the month.		
d e 11.	Received a credit memorandum from a trade creditor.		
e 12.	Sent a purchase order to a trade creditor.		
d 13.	Paid a trade creditor after the discount period had expired, thereby missing the discount.		

19 Choose the statement that is incorrect.

a An account in the general ledger that is supported by a detailed classification of accounting data in a subsidiary record is known as a controlling account.

b As a general rule, the individual accounts supporting a controlling account appear in the general ledger.

c Individual accounts receivable provide an important source of data for firms which extend credit, and it is thus essential that they be kept up to date.

d More than one controlling account may appear in the statement of financial position.

20 Which of the following figures would not be posted to a ledger account?
a The Cash credit column total in the cash disbursements journal.
b The Sundry debit column total in the cash disbursements journal.
c The Purchases debit column total in the purchases journal.
d The Accounts Receivable debit column total in the sales journal.

21 (based on Appendix 4B.) The Williams Company follows periodic inventory procedure in accounting for the cost of the merchandise it sells. For a particular period, its beginning inventory was $1,200 and its ending inventory $2,000. In a work sheet, which of the following responses *correctly* describe the treatment to be accorded both the beginning and ending inventories?
The beginning inventory appears in the —
a Adjustments debit column.
b Adjustments debit column and Statement of Financial Position debit column.
c Adjustments credit column and Statement of Financial Position debit column.
d Adjustments credit column.
e None of the above.
The ending inventory appears in the —
f Statement of Financial Position debit column and Adjustments debit column.
g Statement of Financial Position credit column.
h Statement of Financial Position debit column.
i Statement of Financial Position debit column and Adjustments credit column.

Now compare your answers with the correct answers and explanations on page 715.

Questions *chapter* 4

1 What account titles are likely to appear in the accounting system of a merchan-

dising company that do not appear in the system employed by a service enterprise?

2 Explain the difference between trade discounts and cash discounts. What are chain discounts and purchase discounts?

3 A financial manager is engaged in explaining his policy to you and states, "Our firm is in a tight financial position. No one will lend us money to take advantage of our discounts. But even though we can't pay within the discount period, I do the next best thing. I pay each bill as soon as I can thereafter." Do you agree that this is the next best approach? Why?

4 Explain the meaning of the terms f.o.b. destination, freight collect, and f.o.b. shipping point, freight prepaid.

5 Determine the effect on net earnings of each of the following:
a Ending inventory is overstated.
b Purchases are understated.
c Purchase discounts are overstated.
d Transportation-in is overstated.
e Beginning-inventory is understated.

6 You find yourself in conversation with a business executive who employs perpetual (rather than periodic) inventory procedure. The executive says, "Sure, it's cumbersome to keep perpetual inventory records, but it's much easier than having to physically count your inventory at the end of every year as you have to under periodic procedure." What would be your response?

7 Is it possible that a firm may use perpetual procedure for some of the products it sells and periodic procedure for others?

8 Perpetual inventory procedure is said to afford control over inventory. Explain exactly what this control consists of and how it is provided.

9 What kind of an account is the Purchases account? What useful purpose does it serve?

10 How can it be argued that the net price procedure of accounting for merchandise acquisitions permits application of the management by exception principle?

11 What are some of the problems encountered in taking a physical inventory? How does the accountant solve them?

12 What is a contra account? Why is it employed? What are some examples?

13 What is gross margin? Why might management be interested in the percentage of gross margin?

14 What is a multiple-step earnings statement? What are the major sections in a multiple-step earnings statement and what is the nature of the items included in each?

Questions 15 and 16 are based on Appendix 4A.

15 Describe the purpose of each of the following journals by giving the types of entries that would be recorded in each: sales, purchases, cash receipts, cash disbursements, and general. Assume the same formats as were illustrated in Appendix 4A.

16 A fellow student remarks, "Whoever first thought of dividing the general journal into special journals did so in an effort to reduce posting time and to make data available to more persons at any one time. The next logical step in the process is to eliminate manual journalizing and posting altogether and use a retrieval system which makes information available to any person in the company at any time. In many firms computerized systems will probably be used to accomplish this." Do you agree?

17 (based on Appendix 4B) Describe how the details in the work sheet differ for a merchandising company as contrasted to a service company.

Exercises *chapter* 4

1 Prepare a table with the following columnar headings: (*a*) name of account, (*b*) increased by (debit or credit), (*c*) decreased by (debit or credit), and (*d*) normal balance (debit or credit). Complete this table for the following accounts: Sales, Sales Returns and Allowances, Sales Discounts, Accounts Receivable, Purchases, Purchase Returns and Allowances, Purchase Discounts, Discounts Lost, Cost of Goods Sold, Accounts Payable, and Transportation-In.

2 (a) The Dorian Company purchased merchandise from the Long Company on account, and before paying its account returned damaged merchandise with an invoice price of $1,050. Assuming use of periodic inventory procedure, prepare entries on both firms' books to record the return. **(b)** Prepare the required entries assuming that the Long Company granted an allowance of $350 on the damaged goods instead of accepting the return.

3 What is the last payment date on which the cash discount can be taken on goods sold on March 5 for $32,000; terms, 3/10 E.O.M., n/60? Assume that the bill is paid on this date and prepare the correct entry on both the seller's and the buyer's books to record the payment.

4 You have purchased merchandise with a list price of $2,000. Because you are a wholesaler you are granted trade discounts of 30, 20, and 10 percent. The cash discount terms are 2/E.O.M., n/60. How much will you pay if you pay by the end of the month of purchase? How much will you pay if you do not pay until the following month?

5 Merchandise with a gross invoice price of $5,000 was purchased by you under terms of 3/10, n/60, on January 2, 1980. You believe that by March 2, 1980, you could pay a loan taken out to take advantage of the discount. What is the highest annual rate of interest you could afford to pay on the loan and be exactly as well off as if you had taken the discount? (Note: 1980 is a leap year.)

6 What is the total difference between the amount to be paid to the seller by the purchaser of goods if the terms are f.o.b. shipping point and the freight of $56 is paid by the seller and if the terms are f.o.b. destination and the freight of $56 is paid by the buyer?

7 The Z Company uses periodic inventory procedure. Determine the cost of goods sold for the company assuming purchases during the period were $4,000, transportation-in was $30, purchase returns and allowances were $100, beginning inventory was $2,500, purchase discounts were $200, ending inventory was $1,300, and sales returns and allowances were $500.

8 The Cattermole Company purchased goods for $2,300 on June 14 under the following terms: 3/10, n/30; f.o.b. destination, freight collect. The bill for the freight amounted to $75. Assume that the invoice was paid within the discount period and prepare all entries required on Cattermole's books.

9 Refer to the data in Question 8 above and assume that the invoice was paid on July 11. Prepare the entry to record the payment made on that date.

10 (based on Appendix 4A) You are employed by a company that has three selling departments. You are asked to design a sales journal which will provide a departmental breakdown of credit sales. Give the column headings that you would use and describe how postings would be made.

11 (based on Appendix 4B) Given the balances shown in the partial trial balance, indicate how the balances would be treated in the work sheet. The ending inventory is $8,000. (The Statement of Retained Earnings columns are not shown since they are not used in this exercise.)

	Trial Balance		Adjustments		Adjusted Trial Balance		Earnings Statement		Statement of Financial Position	
	Debit	Credit	Debit	Credit	Debit	Credit	Debit	Credit	Debit	Credit
Merchandising inventory	10,000									
Sales		70,000								
Sales returns and allowances	4,000									
Sales discounts	1,500									
Purchases	50,000									
Purchase returns and allowances		2,000								
Purchase discounts		1,000								
Transportation-in	3,000									

Problems, Series A *chapter* 4

4-1-A

Compute the annual rate of interest implicit in each of the following terms under the assumption that the discount is not taken and the invoice is paid when due:

a   3/10, n/60.
b   1/10, n/30.
c   2/10/E.O.M., n/90, goods purchased on August 1.
d   2/E.O.M., n/60, goods purchased on January 15.

In view of your computations comment on the desirability of borrowing to take advantage of discounts.

4-2-A

The Faherty Company purchased merchandise with a list price of $10,000, f.o.b. destination, freight prepaid, from Grove, Inc., on August 15, 1979. Trade discounts of 20 and 10 percent were allowed, and credit terms were 2/10, n/30. On August 17 Faherty Company requested a purchase allowance of $470 because some of the merchandise had been damaged in transit. On August 20 it received a credit memorandum from Grove, Inc., granting the allowance.

Required:

Record all the entries required on the books of both the buyer and the seller assuming that both firms use periodic inventory procedure. Also assume that payment is made on the last day of the discount period.

4-3-A

Required:

a   Journalize the following transactions for Company K.
b   Journalize the following transactions for Company D. Both companies follow periodic procedure of recording inventories.

Transactions:

Mar. 12   Company K purchased merchandise from Company D, $13,500; terms, 2/10 E.O.M.
     20   Company K returned $4,500 of the merchandise to Company D.
Apr. 7   Company D received proper payment in full from Company K.
     16   Company K had requested and on this date received a credit memorandum granting a gross allowance of $800 from Company D, due to improper quality of merchandise purchased on March 12.

4-4-A

The purchasing department of the Garretson Corporation asked for and received the following price quotations on 1,400 units of a given product that it wished to buy:

Freeman, Inc. — List price $3.80 each, less 15 percent. Terms: 2/10, n/30, f.o.b. shipping point. (Transportation charges are determined to be $180.)

Goodman Corp. — List price: $3.40 each. Terms: n/30, f.o.b. destination. (Transportation charges are determined to be $175.)

Klein Corp. — List price: $5.50 each, less 20, 15, and 10 percent quantity discount. Terms: 3/10, n/45, f.o.b. destination. (Transportation charges are determined to be $265.)

Heintz Co. — List price: $4.35, less 15 and 10 percent. Terms: n/30, f.o.b. shipping point. (Transportation charges are determined to be $250.)

Required:

State which bid should be accepted and support your conclusion with a schedule showing the net cost of each bid.

4–5–A

Goods costing $4,000 were purchased on January 15, 1979, with terms of 2/10, n/30. Freight charges of $216 were paid on January 15.

Required:

For each of the following cases give the entries that would be made on the books of both the buyer and the seller, assuming both use periodic inventory procedure.

Case A — Terms: f.o.b. shipping point, freight prepaid. The invoice was paid on January 20.
Case B — Terms: f.o.b. destination, freight collect. The invoice was paid on February 10.
Case C — Terms: f.o.b. destination, freight prepaid. The invoice was paid on January 25.
Case D — Terms: f.o.b. shipping point, freight collect. The invoice was paid on February 14.

4–6–A

On August 1, 1979, the Jennings Company sold merchandise to the Lesikar Company, $6,000 list price, f.o.b. shipping point. (The seller prepaid the freight of $80 on August 1, 1979.) Other terms were trade discounts of 30 and 10 percent and cash discount of 2/10 E.O.M., n/60. On August 8, 1979, the Lesikar Company returned $1,000 (at list price) of the merchandise. The balance due was paid on September 9, 1979.

Required:

Journalize all entries required on the books of both the buyer and the seller, assuming that both use periodic inventory procedure.

4–7–A

Required:

From the data given below for the Knowles Company (which uses periodic inventory procedure):

185

a Prepare journal entries for the summarized transactions (omit explanation).

b Post the journal entries to the proper ledger accounts (after entering the balances as of December 31, 1978).

c Prepare and post entries to record cost of goods sold.

d Prepare an earnings statement for the year ended December 31, 1979.

e Prepare a statement of financial position as of December 31, 1979.

KNOWLES COMPANY
Statement of Financial Position
December 31, 1978

Assets		Liabilities and Stockholders' Equity	
Cash	$19,000	Accounts payable	$21,000
Accounts receivable	33,000	Capital stock	25,000
Merchandise inventory	28,000	Retained earnings	34,000
		Total Liabilities and	
Total Assets	$80,000	Stockholders' Equity	$80,000

Summarized Transactions for 1979

Sales for cash	$ 67,000
Sales on account (gross)	148,000
Purchases on account (gross)	160,000
Sales discounts	2,000
Sales returns (charge sales)	4,500
Purchase returns	2,200
Purchase discounts	2,400
Cash collected on accounts receivable	137,500
Cash payments on accounts payable	129,000
Land and building purchased (gave one half in cash and mortgage note for one half)	62,000
Selling expenses incurred and paid for	19,600
Administrative expenses incurred and paid for	18,200
Interest expense on mortgage note on land and building incurred and paid for	1,200

Additional data:

Merchandise inventory at December 31, 1979, per physical listing is $34,400.

4-8-A

Required:

From the following information:

a Journalize the transactions on the records of the Lewis Company.

b Post the entries to the proper ledger accounts.

c Journalize the adjusting entries, assuming the May 31 inventory is $14,000.

d Post the adjusting entries to the proper accounts.

e Prepare a trial balance as of May 31.

f Prepare a partial earnings statement for May, through the gross margin figure.

The company was organized on May 1 and uses periodic inventory procedure.

Transactions:

May 1 Issued 2,000 shares of common stock for $200,000 cash.

1 Purchased merchandise on account from the Linane Company, $13,000; terms, net/10 E.O.M., f.o.b. shipping point.

May 3 Sold merchandise for cash, $8,000.
   6 Paid transportation charges on May 1 purchase, $200 cash.
   7 Returned $1,000 of merchandise to the Linane Company due to improper size.
   10 Requested and was granted an allowance of $500 by the Linane Company for improper quality of certain items.
   14 Sale on account to Roan Company, $5,000; terms, 2/20, n/30.
   16 Cash refund on returns of sales made on May 3, $50.
   18 Purchase on account from White Company invoiced at $8,100, including $100 of transportation charges prepaid by White; terms, 2/15, n/30, f.o.b. shipping point.
   19 Roan Company returned $100 of merchandise purchased on May 14.
   24 Returned $800 of defective merchandise to White Company and requested and was granted a transportation allowance of $10 on the original purchase.
   28 Roan Company remitted balance due on sale of May 14.
   31 Paid White Company for the purchase of May 18 after adjusting for transactions of May 24.

4-9-A

Lubbers Company does not maintain a complete accounting system, but you believe the following account balances are accurate representations of the company's assets and liabilities at the stated dates:

	December 31	
	1978	*1979*
Cash	$ 4,125	$ 8,250
Accounts receivable	14,250	10,500
Merchandise inventory	24,000	30,250
Land	5,750	5,750
Accounts payable	16,250	19,750

An analysis of the company's checkbook for 1979 shows the following:

a Total cash received from customers (the only cash receipts), $102,500.
b Payments to vendors for merchandise purchased, $65,250; the balance of the cash disbursements was for 1979 expenses, all of which were paid in cash in 1979.

Required:

Determine the amount of the 1979 sales, cost of goods sold, total expenses, purchases, gross margin, and net earnings, and the stockholders' equity (in total) as of December 31, 1978, and 1979.

4-10-A (based on Appendix 4A)

On June 30, 1979, the Accounts Receivable controlling account on the books of the Grimes Company was equal to the total of the accounts in the subsidiary accounts receivable ledger. The balances were as follows: Accounts Receivable controlling account

(Account No. 131), $8,590; Ferguson, Inc., $3,300; Hanson Products, Inc., $1,540; and Oliva Company, $3,750.

The purpose of this problem is to illustrate both the controlling account principle and the use of separate sales and cash receipts journals.

Prepare a sales journal (see Illustration 4.5, page 169) and cash receipts journal (Illustration 4.6, page 170). Also set up a general journal.

Required:

Using the following information:
a Completely journalize each of the transactions in the appropriate journals.
b Post only the amounts pertaining to accounts receivable to the subsidiary accounts and to the controlling account. You will have to set up some additional subsidiary accounts. Keep all subsidiary accounts in alphabetical order. You will need accounts for the Cowden Company, Dorsey Company, and Wills Company.
c Prepare a schedule of accounts receivable at July 31, 1979, and compare it with the balance of the controlling account at July 31, 1979.

Transactions (ignore the fact that usually the terms to all customers are the same):

July 1 Sales of merchandise on account to Oliva Company, $600; Invoice No. 306; terms, n/30.
 3 Cash sales, $1,725.
 5 Received cash for land sold at its original cost of $2,500.
 5 Received $2,250 cash as partial collection of amount due today from Ferguson, Inc. No discount was allowed.
 8 Received a 30-day, 6 percent note for $1,050 from Ferguson, Inc., in settlement of its account.
 9 Sold merchandise to the Wills Company, $450; Invoice No. 307; terms, 3/10, n/30.
 11 Received $1,509.20 from Hanson Products, Inc. A discount of 2 percent of the account balance was granted.
 16 Sold merchandise to the Cowden Company, $500; Invoice No. 308; terms, n/30.
 18 Sold merchandise to Hanson Products, Inc., $900; Invoice No. 309; terms, n/30.
 20 Issued a credit memorandum to Hanson Products, Inc., for $125 on goods returned to Grimes on Invoice No. 309.
 22 Sold $600 of merchandise to Ferguson, Inc.; Invoice No. 310; terms, n/10.
 23 Received cash of $2,000 on balance due today from Oliva Company. No discount was taken.
 25 Sold $750 of merchandise to Ferguson, Inc.; Invoice No. 311; terms, n/10.
 27 Allowed Ferguson, Inc., credit of $50 on goods sold July 25 and damaged in transit due to faulty packing by Grimes Company.
 31 Sold $650 of merchandise to the Dorsey Company; Invoice 312; terms, 2/10, n/30.
 31 Cash sales, $10,300.

4–11–A

(based on Appendix 4B)

Required:

From the following trial balance and supplementary information, prepare—

a   A 12-column work sheet for the year ended December 31, 1979. (See Appendix 4B, for illustration of form.)

b   The required closing entries.

Supplementary data:

a.   The building is to be depreciated at the rate of 2 percent per year.

b.   Depreciate the store fixtures 10 percent per year.

c.   The Allowance for Doubtful Accounts is to be increased by one half of 1 percent of net sales. (Round amount up to nearest full dollar.)

d.   Accrued interest on notes receivable is $150.

e.   Accrued interest on the mortgage note is $250.

f.   Accrued sales salaries are $700.

g.   Unexpired insurance is $200.

h.   Prepaid advertising is $500.

i.   Included in the cash on hand is a check for $25 which was cashed for an ex-employee in 1979 and which is worthless.

j.   Cost of merchandise inventory on hand December 31, 1979, $27,750.

WHEELER COMPANY
Trial Balance
December 31, 1979

	Debits	Credits
Cash on hand and in bank	$ 8,600	
Accounts receivable	41,250	
Allowance for doubtful accounts		$ 850
Notes receivable	3,750	
Merchandise inventory, January 1, 1979	20,800	
Land	30,000	
Building	55,000	
Allowance for depreciation—building		16,500
Store fixtures	27,800	
Allowance for depreciation—store fixtures		5,560
Accounts payable		18,950
Mortgage note payable		25,000
Capital stock		50,000
Retained earnings		35,090
Sales		275,750
Sales returns and allowances	1,000	
Sales discounts	1,850	
Purchases	156,450	
Purchase returns and allowances		700
Purchase discounts		1,300
Transportation-in	3,650	
Sales salaries	32,000	
Advertising expense	6,000	
Transportation-out	2,300	
Officers' salaries	37,000	
Insurance expense	1,450	
Interest revenue		200
Interest expense	1,000	
	$429,900	$429,900

189

Problems, Series B *chapter* 4

4-1-B

Compute the annual rate of interest implicit in each of the following terms if the discount is not taken and the invoice is paid when due:

a 2/10, n/30.

b 1/10, n/45.

c 3/E.O.M., n/90, goods purchased on July 16.

d 2/10/E.O.M., n/45, goods purchased on October 2.

4-2-B

On July 2, 1979, the Luecke Corporation purchased merchandise with a list price of $9,200 from the MacEachern Company. The terms were 3/10/E.O.M., n/60; f.o.b. destination, freight collect. Trade discounts of 15, 10, and 5 percent were granted by the MacEachern Company. The Luecke Corporation paid the freight bill of $240 on July 5. On July 6 it was discovered that merchandise with a list price of $800 had been damaged seriously in transit; these items were returned for full credit.

Required:

Assume that the Luecke Corporation makes payment on the last day of the discount period and prepare all the necessary entries. Assume periodic inventory procedure is used.

4-3-B

The following are events and transactions of the Marcelle Company during April 1978:

Apr. 1 The planning department requested the purchasing department to order 1,000 units of a given material.

3 The purchasing department sent out requests for quotations to companies E, M, and W.

7 Quotations received are as follows:

E—List price: $4.20 each, less 30 and 20 percent. On all orders for more than 500 units, an additional 10 percent discount is allowed on the total order. Terms: 3/10, n/30, f.o.b. destination.

M—List price: $4.80 each, less 35 and 30 percent. Terms: 2/10, n/30, f.o.b. shipping point.

W—List price: $2.10 each. Terms: n/30, f.o.b. destination.

(The shipping cost under each bid is determined to be $50, $20, and $30, respectively.)

8 Placed order with lowest bidder.

15 Invoice received covering above merchandise; freight was prepaid.

Apr. 16   Receiving department report stated that merchandise is as ordered. Invoice is checked and found to be correct.

24   Invoice is paid.

Required:

Prepare dated journal entries for the above, where appropriate, including computations showing the actual cost in each bid, assuming that Marcelle Company uses periodic inventory procedure.

4–4–B

Required (assume that both companies use periodic inventory procedure):

a   Journalize the following transactions for Company S.
b   Journalize the following transactions for Company T.

Transactions:

May 18   Company S sold to Company T merchandise with a sales price of $24,000; terms, 2/10 E.O.M.

29   Company T returned $3,000 of the merchandise to Company S.

June 3   Company T requested a gross allowance of $2,000 from Company S due to defective merchandise. Company S issued a credit memo granting the allowance.

7   Company T paid the net amount due.

4–5–B

The McDowell Company purchased merchandise on March 1, 1979, from the Miggans Company at a list price of $5,000, f.o.b. destination. Trade discounts of 30, 25, and 5 percent were granted. Cash discount terms were 2/E.O.M., n/60. The buyer paid the freight of $124 on March 4, 1979. The buyer notified the seller that a $600 credit should be granted against the amount due because of damaged merchandise. The seller agreed and sent the buyer a credit memorandum on March 25, 1979.

Required:

Record all entries, assuming payment on March 26, on the books of both the buyer and seller, assuming that both use periodic inventory procedure.

4–6–B

Required:

From the following information:
a   Prepare an earnings statement for the year ended December 31, 1979.
b   Prepare a statement of financial position as of December 31, 1979.
c   Prepare the adjusting journal entries.

THE PAXTON COMPANY
Trial Balance
December 31, 1979

	Debits	Credits
Cash in bank	$ 10,550	
Accounts receivable	28,500	
Notes receivable, trade	4,000	
Merchandise inventory, January 1, 1979	22,350	
Unexpired insurance	900	
Store supplies inventory	350	
Land	5,000	
Store building	25,250	
Accounts payable		$ 7,000
Notes payable		13,500
Interest payable		550
Common stock		37,500
Retained earnings		25,000
Sales		205,000
Purchases	113,000	
Sales returns	2,850	
Purchase returns		1,200
Sales discounts	3,650	
Purchase discounts		2,050
Sales salaries	32,000	
General selling expenses	1,600	
General administrative expenses	3,950	
Office and officers' salaries	20,250	
Taxes, administrative	4,350	
Taxes, selling	6,100	
Interest revenue		200
Interest expense	1,150	
Delivery expense	4,300	
Heat and light for sales purposes	1,200	
Telephone, office	700	
	$292,000	$292,000

The merchandise inventory on hand December 31, 1979, had a cost of $23,100.

4–7–B

Required:

From the data given below for the Mountain Company (which uses periodic inventory procedure):

a   Prepare journal entries for the transactions.
b   Post the journal entries to the proper ledger accounts.
c   Journalize and post the adjusting entries.
d   Prepare an earnings statement for the month ended May 31, 1979.
e   Prepare a statement of financial position as of May 31, 1979.

Transactions:

1979

May   1   The Mountain Company is organized as a corporation. It issues $170,000 of common capital stock in exchange for $105,000 cash, $40,000 of merchandise, and $25,000 of store fixtures.

May 5 The company purchases and pays cash for merchandise having a gross cost of $45,000, from which a 2 percent cash discount was granted.

8 Cash of $1,050 is paid to a trucking company for delivery of the merchandise purchased May 5. The goods were sold f.o.b. shipping point.

14 The company sells merchandise on open account, $75,000; terms, 2/10, n/30.

16 Of the merchandise sold May 14, $3,300 is returned for credit.

19 Salaries for services received are paid as follows: to office employees, $3,300; to salespersons, $8,700.

23 The company collects the amount due on $30,000 of the accounts receivable arising from the sales of May 14.

25 The company purchases and pays cash for merchandise costing $36,000 gross, less a 2 percent discount.

27 Of the merchandise purchased May 25, $6,000 gross is returned to the vendor, who gives the Mountain Company a check for the proper amount.

28 A trucking company is paid $750 for delivery to the Mountain Company of the goods purchased May 25.

29 The company sells merchandise on open account, $3,600; terms, 2/10, n/30.

30 Cash sales are $18,000 gross, less a 2 percent discount.

30 Cash of $24,000 is received from the sales of May 14.

31 Paid store rent for May, $4,500.

Additional data:

The inventory on hand at the close of business May 31 is $69,700 at cost.

4–8–B

Required:

From the following information for the Reeves Company, prepare:

a Journal entries for the summarized transactions for 1979.
b An earnings statement for the year ended December 31, 1979.
c A statement of financial position as of December 31, 1979.

A suggestion: you may want to set up rough T-accounts and enter the December 31, 1978, balances given below and post your journal entries to arrive at ending balances.

REEVES COMPANY
Account Balances
December 31, 1978

	Debits	Credits
Cash on hand and in banks	$ 47,500	
Accounts receivable	82,500	
Merchandise inventory	70,000	
Accounts payable		$ 52,500
Capital stock		62,500
Retained earnings		85,000
	$200,000	$200,000

193

Cash sales	$167,500
Sales on account at gross invoice prices	370,000
Purchases on account at gross invoice prices	400,000
Accounts receivable collected (net of cash discounts of $30,000)	343,750
Sales returns (from open account sales)	11,250
Purchase returns (from open account purchases)	5,500
Accounts payable paid (net of cash discounts of $6,000)	322,500
Selling expenses incurred and paid	49,000
Store equipment purchased for cash	10,000
Administrative expenses incurred and paid	45,500
Land purchased for cash	20,000
Building purchased (half for cash and half on a mortgage note)	105,000
Interest expense incurred and paid	3,000

Additional data:

The merchandise inventory at December 31, 1979, was $86,000. The company uses periodic inventory procedure.

4-9-B

The owner of Lil's Supply House has asked you for help in preparing financial statements for the year 1979. He does not maintain a ledger of accounts but rather keeps a detailed list of the amounts due from customers, the amounts owed vendors, and all cash received and paid out and the reasons therefor. With this help you are able to develop the following account balances:

	December 31	
	1978	*1979*
Cash	$ 4,000	$ 8,000
Accounts receivable	14,000	10,000
Merchandise on hand	22,000	30,000
Land, at cost	6,000	6,000
Accounts payable	16,000	19,000

Your summary of cash receipts and disbursements for 1979 is as follows:

a. Total cash receipts, solely from customers, $110,000.

b. Payments to vendors for merchandise purchased, $60,000; all other cash payments were for 1979 expenses. There were no unpaid expenses at December 31, 1979.

Required:

Compute the following amounts for 1979: sales, purchases, total expenses, cost of goods sold, gross margin, and net earnings; also, determine the amount of owner's equity at December 31, 1978, and 1979.

4-10-B (based on Appendix 4A)

On June 30, 1979, the Accounts Payable controlling account on the books of the Grimes Company was equal to the total of the accounts in the subsidiary accounts payable ledger. The balances were as follows: Accounts Payable controlling account (Account No. 201),

Merchandising transactions and introduction to inventories

$7,750; Cote Company, $3,525; Larson Corporation, $1,225; and Richards Company, $3,000.

The purpose of this problem is to illustrate both the controlling account principle and the use of separate purchases and cash disbursements journals.

Prepare a purchases journal (see Illustration 4.8, page 172) and a cash disbursements journal (Illustration 4.9, page 173). Also set up a general journal.

Required:

Using the data given below:

a   Completely journalize each of the transactions in the appropriate journal.
b   Post only the amounts pertaining to accounts payable to the subsidiary accounts and to the controlling account. You should arrange all subsidiary accounts in alphabetical order. You will need additional accounts for Aleo Corporation, Ball Company, Hodge Company, and Smith Corporation.
c   Prepare a schedule of accounts payable at July 31, 1979, and compare it with the balance of the controlling account at the same date.

Transactions:

July 1   Purchased merchandise costing $2,500 from the Ball Company; Invoice No. 562; terms, 2/10, n/30. All purchases are recorded net of discount.
      2   Paid the Cote Company $2,500 on account with Check No. 101. No discount was available when the purchase was originally made.
      3   Paid rent with Check No. 102 for the month of July, $300.
      5   Gave the Larson Corporation a 60-day, 6 percent note for the amount owed. A 2 percent discount had been available but was not taken. (The original purchase was for $1,250.)
      6   Purchased merchandise costing $1,250 from the Cote Company; Invoice No. 261; terms, 2/10, n/30.
      9   Paid $1,225 to the Ball Company on the July 1 purchase with Check No. 103.
     11   Paid $500 for a life insurance policy on top executives to cover the period from August 1, 1979, to July 31, 1980. Used Check No. 104.
     14   Paid $1,250 to the Ball Company on the July 1 purchase, Check No. 105.
     17   Purchased merchandise costing $2,000 from the Ball Company; Invoice No. 581; terms, 2/10, n/30.
     21   Received a credit memorandum from the Richards Company for $500 on merchandise returned to it. No discount was available as of the date of purchase.
     23   Purchased merchandise costing $750 from the Aleo Corporation; Invoice No. 1031; terms, n/30.
     25   Paid $1,500 to Richards Company on account with Check No. 106. No discount was allowed as of the date of purchase.
     27   Purchased merchandise costing $1,750 from the Smith Corporation; Invoice No. 328; terms, 2/10, n/30.
     29   Paid the Ball Company $1,000 on the purchase of July 17, Check No. 107.
     31   Purchased merchandise costing $2,000 from the Hodge Company; Invoice No. 168; terms, 2/20, n/60.

4–11–B (based on Appendix 4B)

Required:

From the trial balance and additional data given below, prepare:
a A 12-column work sheet for the year ended December 31, 1979. (See Appendix 4B for an illustration.)
b The December 31, 1979, closing entries, in general journal form.

PETERS COMPANY
Trial Balance
December 31, 1979

	Debits	Credits
Cash on hand and in bank	$ 35,320	
Accounts receivable	72,520	
Allowance for doubtful accounts		$ 2,760
Notes receivable	10,000	
Merchandise inventory, January 1, 1979	42,600	
Sales store supplies inventory	1,200	
Store equipment	44,000	
Allowance for depreciation—store equipment		8,800
Accounts payable		39,400
Notes payable		12,000
Capital stock		150,000
Retained earnings		60,820
Sales		461,180
Sales returns	2,580	
Interest revenue		500
Interest expense	300	
Purchases	250,420	
Purchase returns		2,020
Transportation-in	3,920	
Sales salaries	69,200	
Advertising	39,000	
Sales store supplies expense	1,480	
General office expense	4,940	
Fire insurance expense	2,400	
Office salaries	40,400	
Officers' salaries	80,000	
Legal and auditing expenses	5,000	
Telephone and telegraph	2,400	
Rent expense	28,800	
Dividends	1,000	
	$737,480	$737,480

The company consistently followed the policy of initially debiting all prepaid items to expense accounts.

Additional data as of December 31, 1979:

a. Fire insurance unexpired, $700.
b. Sales store supplies on hand, $850.
c. Prepaid rent expense (store only), $3,500.
d. Depreciation rate on store equipment, 10 percent per year.
e. Increase in allowance for doubtful accounts, $1,826.
f. Accrued sales salaries, $2,000.
g. Accrued office salaries, $1,500.
h. Merchandise inventory, $75,000.

5

Measuring and reporting inventories

Learning objectives

Studying the material in this chapter should help one:

1. Understand the nature of inventory and its importance in both the earnings statement and the statement of financial position.

2. Learn how periodic inventory procedures are applied.

3. Understand which costs are properly included in inventory.

4. Understand the methods of accounting for purchase discounts.

5. Understand the practical and theoretical considerations of the different methods of inventory measurement under varying prices.

6. Learn how to apply the lower-of-cost-or-market rule.

7. Understand the gross margin and retail methods of estimating inventory.

8. Develop an ability to analyze the effect of transactions involving inventory on the financial statements.

9. Learn how perpetual inventory procedures are applied (Appendix).   197

Frame 1[5]

In the preceding chapter the amount of merchandise on hand at any point in time was called the merchandise inventory of a specific business. Cost was used as a basis for measuring and reporting its amount. Illustrations showed (1) how the inventory amount was used in computing cost of goods sold and (2) how inventory was presented as an asset on the statement of financial position. A number of important questions about inventory have not yet been answered. They include: (1) What cost elements should be included in inventory? (2) What methods may be used to determine the cost of ending inventory?

The nature and significance of inventory

Definition of inventory

Inventory is one of the largest and most important assets owned by a merchandising or manufacturing business. In certain companies it may be several times the size of other assets.

What is included in inventory varies with the nature of the business. Retail and wholesale merchandising businesses buy merchandise from others and sell it in the condition in which it is acquired. Thus, they have only one important item of inventory—merchandise held for resale.

Manufacturing companies generally have three inventory items—raw materials, work in process, and finished goods. The finished goods inventory of a manufacturer is similar to a merchandiser's inventory. Both finished goods and merchandise inventory are ready for sale to customers. On the other hand, raw materials and work in process inventories require more processing before they can be sold.

Since current assets are listed in the statement of financial position in order of liquidity (with the most liquid first), inventories are usually listed after accounts receivable. In addition, factory, store, and office supplies are sometimes listed as supplies inventory, even though such items are not actually offered for sale to customers.

Broadly speaking, inventory can be defined as the sum of those items of tangible property which (1) are held for sale in the ordinary course of business, (2) are in process of production for such sale, or (3) are to be currently consumed in the production of goods or services which will be available for sale.[1]

Importance of proper inventory measurement

An accurate measurement of the ending inventory is necessary to reflect the proper net earnings for the period. When the periodic inventory system is used, ending inventory is subtracted from cost of goods avail-

[1] Committee on Accounting Procedure, American Institute of Certified Public Accountants, "Accounting Research Bulletin No. 43," *Accounting Research and Terminology Bulletins, Final Edition* (New York, 1961), p. 27.

able for sale to determine the cost of goods sold. Cost of goods sold is then deducted from revenues to compute gross margin and net earnings. Thus, if ending inventory is misstated, cost of goods sold, gross margin, and net earnings will also be misstated. Also, since the inventory amount is shown as a current asset in the statement of financial position, any misstatement in its measurement means that statement is in error.

If the ending inventory is overstated, then current assets are overstated, and total assets are similarly overstated. At the same time, cost of goods sold is understated with a resulting overstatement of gross margin, net earnings, and retained earnings. To illustrate (assuming periodic procedure):

	For the year ended December 31, 1979			
	Ending inventory correctly stated		*Ending inventory overstated*	
Sales		$800,000		$800,000
Cost of goods available for sale.......	$600,000		$600,000	
Ending inventory	70,000	530,000	80,000	520,000
Gross Margin......:........................		$270,000		$280,000

Since the ending inventory is overstated by $10,000, current assets and total assets will also be overstated by $10,000.

Likewise, an understatement of ending inventory has a number of effects. If ending inventory is understated, the result is to (place "over" or "under" in the blanks below):
1. ___?___ state cost of goods sold.
2. ___?___ state gross margin.
3. ___?___ state net earnings for the period.

Turn to Answer Frame 1⁵ on page 200 to check your answers.

Frame 2⁵

Net earnings, whether misstated or not, are closed to Retained Earnings. If net earnings are misstated, Retained Earnings is misstated in an amount and direction which brings the statement of financial position into balance even though the inventory is misstated. In other words, retained earnings and inventory are both stated incorrectly by the same amount and in the same direction. In the example above, inventory and retained earnings are both overstated by $10,000. Thus, the statement of financial position balances at the wrong amount.

An understated ending inventory would:
1. Overstate cost of goods sold.
2. Understate gross margin.
3. Understate net earnings for the period.

If you answered incorrectly, reread Frame 1⁵ before proceeding to Frame 2⁵ on page 199.

2⁵

continued

Suppose the ending inventory for the year ended December 31, 1979, was overstated. Would this error have an effect on the matching of expenses and revenues in any period other than the year 1979?

1. Yes. It would also affect the net earnings for 1980.
2. No. The only year affected is 1979.

To check your answer, turn to Answer Frame 2⁵ on page 202.

Frame 3⁵

Assuming a correct ending inventory for the next year (ending December 31, 1980), the preceding illustration is continued below (last year's ending inventory is this year's beginning inventory):

	For the year ended December 31, 1980			
	Beginning inventory correctly stated		*Beginning inventory overstated*	
Sales		$850,000		$850,000
Beginning inventory, January 1	$ 70,000		$ 80,000	
Purchases....................................	530,000		530,000	
Cost of goods available for sale.......	$600,000		$610,000	
Less: Ending inventory, December 31	50,000		50,000	
Cost of goods sold		550,000		560,000
Gross Margin.............................		$300,000		$290,000

An overstated beginning inventory understates gross margin by an equal amount. Likewise, an understated beginning inventory overstates gross margin. The overall results of the two periods (1979 and 1980) are summarized as follows:

	1979 and 1980 inventories correct	*1979 ending inventory overstated*
Gross margin, 1979..	$270,000	$280,000
Gross margin, 1980..	300,000	290,000
Gross margin, 1979 and 1980	$570,000	$570,000

The above table shows clearly that inventory errors affect gross margin and net earnings and that an error in one period's ending inventory automatically causes an error in the opposite direction in the next period.

The December 31, 1979, and the December 31, 1980, inventories are reported at $50,000 and $60,000, respectively. If both inventories are overstated by $40,000 (the correct inventories are $10,000 and $20,000), tell whether each of the following statements is correct or incorrect.

1. Net earnings for 1979 are understated by $40,000.
2. Net earnings for 1980 are understated by $80,000.
3. Net earnings for 1981 are understated by $40,000.
4. Total net earnings for the period 1979–81 are not affected.

Check your answers in Answer Frame 3[5] on page 202.

Frame 4[5]

The cost of inventory

Possible inclusions

The cost of inventory includes all outlays that are necessary to obtain the goods and place them in their existing condition and location. Thus, cost includes:

1. The price on the invoice received from the seller.
2. Insurance in transit (when ultimately paid by the buyer).
3. Transportation charges from the seller to the buyer (when ultimately paid by the buyer).
4. Handling costs.

When the periodic inventory system is used, the Purchases account is normally debited for the invoice price of the goods acquired. Preferably, the cost of insurance in transit and transportation-in should be debited to separate accounts.

Inventory and purchase discounts. The method used to account for purchase discounts affects the measurement of inventory and cost of goods sold. The company may record the purchase at the *gross* invoice price at the time of acquisition, with a purchase discount recorded if payment is made within the discount period. Alternatively, the *net* invoice price may be debited to the appropriate account at the time of acquisition and a Discounts Lost account debited for the discount lost if payment is made after expiration of the discount period. These two methods were discussed in Chapter 4 in Frame 6[4]. You may wish to refer back to that discussion to review this concept. Under the net price method, although discounts lost are technically losses, they are usually

201

The first answer is the correct response. The ending inventory of one period is the beginning inventory of the next period. Hence, an inventory error affects the net earnings of two periods. Since the beginning inventory is part of the cost of goods available for sale, when it is overstated the cost of goods available for sale is overstated as shown in Frame 3⁵.

If you answered incorrectly, restudy Frames 1⁵ and 2⁵ before going on to Frame 3⁵ on page 200.

Answer frame 3⁵

1. Incorrect. The overstated 1979 ending inventory means that $40,000 too much was deducted from cost of goods available for sale. Thus, cost of goods sold was understated by $40,000 and gross margin and net earnings for 1979 are overstated by $40,000.

2. Incorrect. The overstated inventory on December 31, 1979, results in an overstated beginning inventory for 1980 which, by itself, would cause net earnings to be understated by $40,000 for the year. But the overstated ending inventory in 1980 has just the opposite effect on net earnings. Since the effects of the two errors exactly offset one another, net earnings are correct even though there are errors in the inventory amounts.

3. Correct. The overstatement of the December 31, 1980, inventory, which is the beginning inventory in 1981, results in a $40,000 overstatement of the cost of goods available for sale in 1981 and consequently an overstatement of cost of goods sold. By deducting $40,000 too much cost from sales revenue, gross margin and net earnings for 1981 are both understated by that amount.

4. Correct. Inventory errors are offsetting, and everything would be worked out by 1981.

If you missed any of the above, restudy Frame 3⁵ before going to Frame 4⁵ on page 201.

4⁵
continued
treated as an element of financial expense. They are classified among the "other expenses" in the earnings statement.

When the net invoice price method is used to record purchases, the Accounts Payable account is credited at the time of purchase with—

1. The gross invoice price of the merchandise.

2. The net invoice price of the merchandise.

3. The gross or net invoice price depending upon whether the discount is taken or not.

Check your answer by turning to Answer Frame 4⁵ on page 204.

Frame 5⁵

Inventory measurement under varying prices

The general rule. Accounting Research Bulletin No. 43 states that the "primary basis of accounting for inventories is cost . . ." and that "a departure from the cost basis . . . is required when the utility of the goods is no longer as great as . . ." their cost. Thus, inventories are usually reported in the statement of financial position at a dollar amount described as *cost or market, whichever is lower.*

But this general rule does not indicate how the cost of goods available for sale should be assigned to ending inventory and cost of goods sold when goods have been acquired at different unit costs. For instance, suppose a retailer has three units of a given product on hand. One unit was acquired at $20, another at $22, and the third at $24. Now the retailer sells two of the units for $30 each. What is the cost of the two units sold? Is it $42, the cost of the first and second units; $44, the cost of the first and third units; or $46, the cost of the second and third units? Or is it $44, determined as two units at an average cost of $22? Four inventory costing methods have been developed to solve this type of problem. They are: (1) specific identification; (2) first-in, first-out (Fifo); (3) last-in, first-out (Lifo); and (4) average.

The data in Illustration 5.1 are assumed with regard to the beginning inventory, purchases, and sales of a given product in order to illustrate the determination of inventory cost. Total goods available for sale consist of 80 units with a total cost of $690. Sixty of the available units were sold, producing sales revenue of $780. Twenty units were left on hand in inventory.

Illustration 5.1   Beginning inventory, purchases, and sales

Beginning inventory and purchases				Sales			
Date	Units	Unit cost	Total cost	Date	Units	Price	Total
Jan. 1	10	$8.00	$ 80.00	Mar. 10	10	$12.00	$120.00
Mar. 2	10	8.50	85.00	July 14	20	12.00	240.00
May 28	20	8.40	168.00	Sept. 7	10	14.00	140.00
Aug. 12	10	9.00	90.00	Nov. 22	20	14.00	280.00
Oct. 12	20	8.80	176.00				
Dec. 21	10	9.10	91.00				
	80		$690.00		60		$780.00

Methods of determining cost

Specific identification. This method can be used when it is known that a particular cost attaches to an identifiable unit of product. It can be easily applied when large items such as automobiles are purchased

The second answer is the correct response. Accounts Payable is credited with the net invoice price at the time of purchase. The entry to record payment of an invoice paid after the discount period has elapsed debits Accounts Payable for the amount previously credited to that account (the net price) and debits the amount of the discount not taken to the Discounts Lost account. It should be noted that the only credit to Accounts Payable is made at the time the invoice is recorded. Whether the company does or does not take advantage of the cash discount does not affect the credit to Accounts Payable.

If you chose the incorrect answer, restudy Frame 4⁵ before going on to Frame 5⁵ on page 203.

5⁵
continued

and sold. When the specific identification method is used, each item is identified by means of a serial number plate or identification tag. Both periodic and perpetual inventory procedures can be used with this method.

To illustrate, assume that the 20 units of product on hand at the end of the year in the above illustration can be identified as 10 from the August 12 purchase and 10 from the December 21 purchase. The ending inventory is shown in Illustration 5.2. The $181 cost of the ending inventory is subtracted from the total cost of goods available for sale of $690 to get the cost of goods sold of $509.

Illustration 5.2 Ending inventory under specific identification

Purchased	Units	Unit cost	Total cost
August 12	10	$9.00	$ 90.00
December 21	10	9.10	91.00
Total	20		$181.00

Assume that the units on hand at the end of the year were identified as five from the March 2 purchase, five from the October 12 purchase, and ten from the December 21 purchase. Under these assumptions, the cost of goods sold for the year is ___?___.

Turn to Answer Frame 5⁵ on page 206 to check your answer.

Frame 6⁵

When the specific identification method is used, cost of goods sold and inventory are stated in terms of the actual cost of the actual units sold and on hand. The method is criticized because it may result in identical units being included in inventory at different prices. For example, television sets may vary only in serial number, but they may be stated at different costs if purchased at different times. Likewise, cost of goods sold may show identical units of product sold entered at different costs. But many people would argue that this is entirely logical under the cost basis of accounting and that this method is the most theoretically sound of all the methods.

It is often stated that earnings can be manipulated when specific identification is used. For example, assume a company has three units of a given product which are identical except for different serial numbers. The three units were acquired at different times at different prices. The first unit cost $2,000, the second, $2,100, and the third, $2,200. Now one unit is sold for $2,800. The units are all alike; therefore, the customer does not care which unit is selected. But the earnings reported on the sale will differ; they will be either $800, $700, or $600 depending upon which unit is shipped. It should be obvious that earnings can be controlled by shipping different units. If higher earnings are desired, ship the unit which cost $2,000. If lower earnings are desired, ship the unit which cost $2,200.

The main disadvantage of the specific identification method is that it cannot be used in many cases. Either the units cannot be identified or trying to identify them would be too costly. For example, it would be too difficult and too costly to apply the method to the nails sold by a hardware store if the nails are purchased in hundred-pound kegs and sold by the pound. It would also be difficult to use the specific identification method in an ice cream parlor that purchases ice cream in five-gallon cans and sells it in cones, pints, and quarts. These difficulties cause the accountant to make assumptions about the flow of costs through a business.

First-in, first-out (Fifo). When this method is used, the accountant assumes that the first units purchased are the first ones sold. In other words, the oldest goods are sold first. In many businesses, the first units in must be the first ones out to avoid large losses from spoilage. Fresh dairy products and fresh vegetables and fruits are excellent examples. In such cases, the assumed first-in, first-out flow of costs corresponds with the actual physical flow of goods. The first-in, first-out method may be used under either periodic or perpetual procedure. (The illustration of Fifo under perpetual procedure is given in the Appendix to this chapter.)

Fifo applied under periodic procedure. When Fifo is used with periodic procedure, inventory is measured by the latest (most recent) purchase prices. The goods on hand are believed to be from the latest purchases. The older goods are the first ones out. That is, they have been sold, while the newer goods are still on hand. But it should be noted that Fifo can be used to measure inventory even when the physical flow of goods is not first-in, first-out.

The first-in, first-out method can be applied to the data in Illustration 5.1 to measure the cost of ending inventory. Begin by listing the latest purchase and move back through the year listing purchases until enough

205

6⁵
continued

units have been listed to agree with the total number of units in inventory. The inventory cost is computed in Illustration 5.3. The ending

Illustration 5.3   Fifo cost of ending inventory under periodic procedure.

Purchased	Units	Unit cost	Total cost
December 21	10	$9.10	$ 91.00
October 12	10	8.80	88.00
Total	20		$179.00

inventory consists of the latest purchases. The Fifo cost of the ending inventory, $179, is subtracted from the total cost of goods available for sale, $690, to get the cost of goods sold of $511.

Assume that the records of the Tarrer Company provide the following information for the month of September 1979:

Inventory on September 1	800 units @ $4.00
Purchases:	
Sept. 4	400 units @ $3.80
13	1,200 units @ $3.50
19	600 units @ $3.90
28	900 units @ $3.70

A physical count shows that there are 1,600 units on hand at the end of September.

The September 30, 1979, inventory priced under Fifo using periodic procedure is—

1. $6,120.
2. $6,020.
3. $5,720.
4. $5,670.

Check your answer in Answer Frame 6⁵ on page 208.

Frame 7[5]

Last-in, first-out (Lifo). Under Lifo the costs of the last units purchased are the first costs charged against revenues. As a result, the cost of goods sold consists of the cost of the most recent purchases while the ending inventory consists of the cost of the oldest purchases. Lifo can be used for federal income tax purposes. But Lifo may be used for tax purposes only if it is used in the general financial statements. Lifo may be used to measure inventory whether or not goods actually flow in a last-in, first-out manner. (Lifo under perpetual procedure is illustrated in the Appendix to this chapter.)

Lifo applied under the periodic procedure. When Lifo is used with periodic procedure, ending inventory is measured by the earliest purchase prices. In fact, ending inventory may consist of costs incurred many years ago. The cost of goods sold, on the other hand, consists of the most recent purchase prices.

The last-in, first-out method can be applied to the data in Illustration 5.1 to measure the cost of the ending inventory. Begin by listing the units in the beginning inventory; continue listing subsequent purchases until enough units have been listed to agree with the total number of units in the ending inventory. Illustration 5.4 shows how the Lifo method is used to measure inventory cost. The Lifo cost of the ending inventory, $165, is subtracted from the cost of goods available for sale, $690, to show a cost of goods sold of $525. Thus the costs charged against revenue are the most recent costs. The ending inventory consists of the oldest costs. It includes the cost of the March 2 purchase and the cost of the beginning inventory which may have been incurred several years ago.

Illustration 5.4   Lifo cost of ending inventory under periodic procedure

Purchased	Units	Unit cost	Total cost
Beginning inventory	10	$8.00	$ 80.00
March 2	10	8.50	85.00
Total	20		$165.00

Assume that Logan-Watkins Company had the following beginning inventory and purchases for 1979:

Inv. on Jan. 1	1,200 units @ $3.10	$ 3,720
May 8	600 units @ $3.00	1,800
July 14	1,800 units @ $3.25	5,850
Nov. 30	900 units @ $3.50	3,150
	4,500 units	$14,520

2. $6,020 is the correct answer. Under periodic procedure, the September 30, 1979, inventory is computed by actual count. Using Fifo, the cost of the 1,600 units in inventory is determined as follows:

Purchases of September 28..........................	900 units @ $3.70 =	$3,330
Purchases of September 19..........................	600 units @ $3.90 =	2,340
Part of purchases of September 13...............	100 units @ $3.50 =	350
Total	1,600 units	$6,020

If you answered incorrectly, restudy Frame 6⁵ before going on to Frame 7⁵ on page 207.

7⁵
continued

There are 1,500 units in the ending inventory.

The cost of goods sold for the year under Lifo is—

1. $9,900.
2. $10,800.
3. $10,395.
4. $4,620.

Check your answer by turning to Answer Frame 7⁵ on page 210.

Frame 8⁵ ——

Fifo and Lifo compared. Much has been written about the relative merits of Fifo and Lifo. Lifo appeals to many companies because prices have risen almost constantly in this country since the early 1930s. An example will make this point clear.

Suppose Company B has one unit of Product Y on hand which cost $20. The unit is sold for $30; other selling expenses total $7. The tax rate is 50 percent. The unit is replaced for $22 before the end of the accounting period. Using Fifo, net earnings are computed as follows:

Net sales	$30.00
Cost of goods sold....................................	20.00
Gross margin...	$10.00
Expenses	7.00
Net operating margin	$ 3.00
Federal income taxes (50% rate).................	1.50
Net Earnings...	$ 1.50

According to the above schedule, the company is selling Product Y at a price which is high enough to produce net earnings. But consider the following:

Cash secured from sale	$30.00
Expenses and taxes paid ($7.00 + $1.50)	8.50
Cash available for replacement and dividends	$21.50
Cost to replace	22.00
Additional Cash Required to Replace Inventory	$ 0.50

Thus, Company B is reporting net earnings of $1.50, but it cannot replace its inventory unless it obtains more cash. Note the different results when Lifo is used to measure inventory:

Net sales	$30.00
Cost of goods sold	22.00
Gross margin	$ 8.00
Expenses	7.00
Net operating margin	$ 1.00
Federal income taxes (50% rate)	0.50
Net Earnings	$ 0.50

Cash secured from sale	$30.00
Expenses and taxes paid ($7.00 + $0.50)	7.50
Cash available for replacement and dividends	$22.50
Cost to replace	22.00
Cash Available for Dividends	$ 0.50

Tax effect of Lifo. We have seen from the above example that the use of Lifo increased cost of goods sold by $2 and decreased taxes by $1. The $0.50 of net earnings can be distributed as dividends because the cost of replacing the inventory has already been deducted from sales revenue. This example shows why many companies have changed to Lifo because of the rather constant price increases experienced in this country.

Those who favor Lifo argue that Lifo tends to match costs and revenues better than does Fifo. When Lifo is used, the earnings statement reports sales and the most current cost of making those sales.

Manipulation possible under Lifo. On the other hand, those who favor Fifo argue that Lifo matches the cost of certain unsold goods against sales revenue. Also, in a period of rising prices, the use of Lifo tends to understate inventory. In addition, the use of Lifo allows management to manipulate net earnings. To obtain smaller net earnings, management purchases an abnormal amount of goods at the end of the current period (at current high prices) for sale in the next period. Under Lifo, these higher costs will be charged to cost of goods sold in the current period. To obtain larger net earnings, management delays making the normal amount of purchases until the next period and charges the older and lower costs to cost of goods sold.

$9,900 is correct. Under Lifo periodic procedure, the ending inventory of 1,500 units is priced:

1,200 units at $3.10............................	$3,720
300 units at $3.00..........................	900
Total....................................	$4,620

The cost of goods sold is:

Total purchases...............................	$14,520
Less ending inventory	4,620
Cost of Goods Sold	$ 9,900

If you did not answer correctly, restudy Frame 7⁵ before going on to Frame 8⁵ on page 208.

───

8⁵
continued

Assume that the purchase price of Product K sold by Colby, Inc., rose steadily throughout the year 1979. Indicate whether each of the following statements is true or false.

1. The sales for 1979 would be higher under Fifo than under Lifo.
2. The December 31, 1979, inventory would be higher if measured by Lifo rather than Fifo.
3. The gross margin would be less if the ending inventory is measured by Lifo rather than Fifo.

Check your answers in Answer Frame 8⁵ on page 212.

Frame 9⁵ ──────────────────────────────────

Average methods. An average inventory cost can be determined under either perpetual or periodic procedure. But the computations differ with the procedure used. Under periodic procedure a weighted-average method is used. Under perpetual procedure a moving-average method is used. (This latter method is shown in the Appendix to this chapter.)

Using periodic inventory procedure, the number of units purchased is added to the number of units in beginning inventory to obtain the total number of units available for sale during the year. The total cost of the purchases is added to the cost of the beginning inventory to arrive at the total cost of goods available for sale during the year. Then the total cost of goods available for sale is divided by the total number of units available for sale to obtain a weighted unit cost. This weighted unit cost is then multiplied by the number of units in the ending inventory to determine the cost of the inventory. Illustration 5.5, using the data from Illustration 5.1, shows how this procedure is applied.

Illustration 5.5   Application of weighted-average method

Purchased	Units	Unit cost	Total cost
Jan. 1	10	$8.00	$ 80.00
Mar. 2	10	8.50	85.00
May 28	20	8.40	168.00
Aug. 12	10	9.00	90.00
Oct. 12	20	8.80	176.00
Dec. 21	10	9.10	91.00
	80		$690.00

Weighted-average unit cost is $690 ÷ 80, or $8.625.
Ending inventory then is $8.625 × 20 .... 172.50
Cost of Goods Sold $517.50

Do you agree that the same result would be obtained by multiplying the number of units in ending inventory by the simple average of the unit costs?

1. Yes.
2. No.

Check your answer in Answer Frame 9[5] on page 212.

Frame 10[5]

Using the weighted-average method, each unit of a product is given the same amount of cost regardless of whether the cost is to be charged to cost of goods sold or carried forward in inventory. Also, when this method is used, the cost of goods sold and the cost of inventory cannot be determined until the end of the period.

Would a company which kept its inventory under periodic procedure have the choice of using Fifo, Lifo, specific identification, or a moving average as the basis for measuring its inventories?

1. Yes; all four of these methods are consistent with keeping inventory records under the periodic procedure.
2. No; although Fifo and Lifo would be acceptable, the specific identification method is not consistent with the periodic procedure.
3. No; although the Fifo, Lifo, and specific identification methods would be acceptable, the moving-average method is used only under perpetual procedure.
4. No; the moving-average and Lifo methods are not applicable under periodic procedure.

Check your answer in Answer Frame 10[5] on page 212.

Answer frame 8⁵

1. False. The amount of sales is not affected by the method of inventory measurement. The amount of sales will be the same under Fifo and Lifo.
2. False. Under Lifo the inventory is measured by the earliest prices. In this case the inventory would consist of the lowest prices since the purchase price of Product K rose steadily throughout the year.
3. True. Under Lifo, cost of goods sold is charged with the most recent costs. In a period of steadily rising prices, this means that the Cost of Goods Sold account is charged with the highest prices paid for the merchandise. Thus, gross margin under Lifo will be less than under Fifo.

If you answered any of the above incorrectly, you should restudy Frame 8⁵ before going to Frame 9⁵ on page 210.

Answer frame 9⁵

No is the correct answer. The method shown in Illustration 5.5 uses a weighted average of the prices paid rather than a simple average. Thus, the number of units purchased at each price affects the unit cost used in computing cost of goods sold and the cost of the ending inventory. In Illustration 5.5, for example, the simple average price per unit would be $8.633. It is computed by summing the six unit costs and dividing by six [($8.00 + $8.50 + $8.40 + $9.00 + $8.80 + $9.10) ÷ 6]. In this case, the difference between the simple average price per unit ($8.633) and the weighted-average price per unit ($8.625) is rather small. It results from stability of quantities purchased. But consider the following example:

200 units @ $2.....................	$ 400
1,800 units @ $3...................	5,400
2,000 units	$5,800

The weighted-average unit cost is $2.90 ($5,800 ÷ 2,000) while the simple average unit cost is $2.50 [($2 + $3) ÷ 2].

If you answered incorrectly, restudy Frame 9⁵ before going on to Frame 10⁵ on page 211.

Answer frame 10⁵

The third answer is the correct response. The Fifo, Lifo, and specific identification methods may be used with either perpetual or periodic inventory procedure. The moving-average method is definitely geared to perpetual procedure, while the weighted-average method is used only under periodic procedure.

If you answered incorrectly, reread Frame 10⁵ before starting Frame 11⁵ below.

Frame 11⁵

Differences in cost methods summarized. Using the data in Illustration 5.1, Illustration 5.6 shows the cost of goods sold, ending inven-

Illustration 5.6   Summary of effects of employing different inventory methods with same basic data

	Specific identifi- cation	Fifo	Lifo	Weighted average
(*Frame which discusses*)...................	(5[5])	(6[5], 8[5])	(7[5], 8[5])	(9[5], 10[5])
Sales	$780.00	$780.00	$780.00	$780.00
Cost of goods sold:				
Beginning inventory	$ 80.00	$ 80.00	$ 80.00	$ 80.00
Purchases.....................................	610.00	610.00	610.00	610.00
Cost of goods available for sale..........	$690.00	$690.00	$690.00	$690.00
Ending inventory	181.00	179.00	165.00	172.50
Cost of goods sold	$509.00	$511.00	$525.00	$517.50
Gross Margin.................................	$271.00	$269.00	$255.00	$262.50

tories, and gross margins of the four basic cost methods of measuring ending inventory.

Note that each of the above methods produces a different inventory measurement and gross margin. Since prices generally increased during the period, Lifo shows the highest cost of goods sold and the lowest gross margin.

Which is the "correct" method? All four methods are acceptable; there is not a single correct one. Different methods look attractive under different conditions. For instance, Lifo results in matching current costs with current revenue. Also, Lifo reduces the amount of taxes payable currently in a period of rising prices.

On the other hand, Lifo often charges against revenues the cost of goods not actually sold. It also allows net earnings to be manipulated by changing the time at which additional purchases are made. Fifo and specific identification result in a more precise matching of historical cost with revenue. But earnings may be manipulated under both the specific identification method and the simple weighted-average method. Under the latter method, the purchase of a large amount of goods at a relatively high price after the last sale of the period will change the average unit cost of the goods charged to the Cost of Goods Sold account. Only under Fifo is the manipulation of earnings not possible.

Would you agree with the following statement? Reducing the amount of taxes payable currently is a valid objective of business management, and since Lifo usually does this, all businesses should use Lifo.

1. Yes.
2. No.

Refer to Answer Frame 11[5] on page 214 to check your answer.

No is the answer we believe is appropriate. Lifo will not always reduce the amount of taxes payable currently because reported net earnings will be higher under Lifo than under other methods if prices decline during the period. Also, Lifo does not seem appropriate for a company dealing in real estate or automobiles, where specific identification of units is readily possible. In addition, there are other uses for accounting information besides reducing the amount of taxes payable currently.

If you did not answer correctly, restudy Frame 11⁵ before going on to Frame 12⁵ below.

Frame 12⁵

Inventories at less than cost

As already noted, *Accounting Research Bulletin No. 43* requires a departure from the cost basis for inventories when the utility of the goods is less than their cost. Such loss of utility may be evidenced by damage or obsolescence or by a decline in the selling price of the goods.

Net realizable value. Damaged, obsolete, or shopworn goods should not be carried in inventory nor reported in the financial statements at more than their net realizable value. Net realizable value is defined as estimated selling price less costs to complete and dispose of the goods. For example, assume that an auto dealer has on hand one auto that has been used as a demonstrator. The auto was acquired at a cost of $4,000 and had an original sales price of $4,800. But, because it has been used and it is now late in the model year, the net realizable value of the auto is estimated at:

Estimated selling price	$3,800
Estimated maintenance and selling costs	300
Net Realizable Value	$3,500

The auto would be written down for inventory purposes from $4,000 to $3,500. In this way, the $500 would be treated as an expense in the period in which the decline in utility occurred. If net realizable value exceeds cost, the item would of course be carried at cost. Accountants generally frown upon recognizing profits before goods are sold.

The lower-of-cost-or-market method. Measuring inventories at the lower of cost or market has long been accepted in accounting. The method assumes that if the purchase price in the market in which the firm buys has fallen, the selling price has also fallen or will fall. But this is not always a valid assumption.

The term "market" as used here means replacement cost in terms of the quantity usually purchased. To apply the method, it is still necessary to determine cost (by specific identification, Fifo, Lifo, or an average method).

Under this method market values are used only when they are less than cost. For instance, if the ending inventory has a cost of $40,000 and a market value of $45,000, this increase in market value is not recognized. To do so would be to recognize revenues before the time of sale.

On the other hand, if market value is $39,600, the inventory can be written down to market value. A $400 loss is recognized on the grounds that the inventory has lost part of its revenue-generating ability. Thus, the write-down recorded anticipates a reduced selling price when the goods are actually sold.

By measuring inventory at the lower of cost or market ($39,600), the loss in the revenue-generating ability of the goods is reflected as a loss —

1. In the period in which the goods were purchased.
2. In the period in which the goods are sold.
3. In the period in which the price decline occurs.

Check your answer in Answer Frame 12[5] on page 216.

Frame 13[5]

APPLICATION OF THE LOWER-OF-COST-OR-MARKET METHOD. In the accounting records, the lower-of-cost-or-market method may be applied to each item in inventory, to each class in inventory, or to total inventory. Illustration 5.7 shows the application of the method to individual items and to total inventory.

Illustration 5.7   Application of lower-of-cost-or-market method

Item	Unit cost	Unit market	Total cost	Total market	Lower of cost or market
1...... 100 units................	$10	$9.00	$1,000	$ 900	$ 900
2...... 200 units................	8	8.75	1,600	1,750	1,600
3...... 500 units................	5	5.00	2,500	2,500	2,500
			$5,100	$5,150	$5,000

13⁵
continued

Fill in the blanks with the correct figures.

1. If each item is priced at the lower of cost or market, the inventory in Illustration 5.7 is $_____?_____.
2. If the total inventory is priced at the lower of cost or market, the inventory is $_____?_____.

Turn to Answer Frame 13⁵ on page 218 to check your answers.

Frame 14⁵

Gross margin method of estimating inventory

The gross margin method can be used to estimate the amount of inventory for the following purposes:

1. To obtain an inventory cost to be used in the monthly or quarterly financial statements.
2. To verify a previously determined ending inventory amount.
3. To determine the amount recoverable from an insurance company when inventory is destroyed by fire or stolen.

The gross margin method is based on the assumption that the rate of gross margin is about the same each period. The method is satisfactory only if this assumption is true.

The gross margin method provides only an estimate of the cost of goods sold and the ending inventory. It is not usable by itself for year-end statements because it assumes that the gross margin rate in the current period is the same as in prior periods. At year-end, it is necessary to use a physical inventory in conjunction with one of the previously described methods of determining the actual inventory, cost of goods sold, gross margin, and net earnings for the current year. Without so doing, the gross margin method is not valid for future years because there would be no way to determine the "normal" rate of gross margin to be used in future computations. But an actual physical count is usually performed only at the end of the year, not during the year.

To illustrate the gross margin method of computing inventory, assume that the Field Company has for several years maintained a rate of gross margin on sales of 30 percent. The following data for 1979 are available: the January 1 inventory was $40,000; purchases of merchandise were $480,000; and sales of merchandise were $700,000. The inventory for December 31, 1979, can be estimated as follows:

Inventory, January 1, 1979		$ 40,000
Purchases		480,000
Cost of goods available for sale		$520,000
Less estimated cost of goods sold:		
Sales	$700,000	
Gross margin (30% of $700,000)............	210,000	
Estimated cost of goods sold		$490,000
Estimated inventory, December 31, 1979..		$ 30,000

Assume that Field Company's sales were $650,000 instead of $700,000. What is its estimated cost of goods sold and what is its estimated ending inventory?

Check your responses by turning to Answer Frame 14[5] on page 218.

Frame 15[5]

Retail method of estimating inventory

Another method of estimating inventory, the *retail method,* is used by a wide variety of companies that sell goods directly to the ultimate consumer. In such companies each item of merchandise usually is marked or tagged with its retail or selling price with the result that the goods are referred to and inventoried at their retail prices.

In skeletal form the retail method consists first of determining the ending inventory at retail prices:

> Beginning inventory at retail prices
> + Purchases at retail prices
> = Goods available for sale at retail prices
> − Sales (which are, of course, at retail prices)
> = Ending inventory at retail prices

To convert the ending inventory at retail prices to cost, the relationship between cost and retail prices must be known. This requires that information on the beginning inventory and purchases be accumulated so that goods available for sale can be expressed in terms of *cost* and *retail prices.* This *cost/retail* price ratio is then applied to sales to determine cost of goods sold and to the ending inventory at retail to reduce it to cost as is shown in Illustration 5.8.

1. If each item is priced at lower of cost or market, the inventory is $5,000.
2. If the total inventory is priced at lower of cost or market, the inventory is $5,100.

If you answered incorrectly, restudy Frame 13⁵ before going on to Frame 14⁵ on page 216.

Answer frame 14⁵

The cost of goods sold is $455,000; the December 31, 1979, inventory is $65,000. These are computed as follows:

Inventory, January 1, 1979		$ 40,000
Purchases		480,000
Cost of goods available for sale		$520,000
Less estimated cost of goods sold:		
Sales	$650,000	
Gross margin (30% of $650,000)	195,000	455,000
Estimated inventory, December 31, 1979		$ 65,000

If you did not answer correctly, reread Frame 14⁵ before going on to Frame 15⁵ on page 217.

15⁵
continued

Illustration 5.8   Inventory calculation using the retail method

	Cost	Retail price
Inventory, January 1, 1979	$ 24,000	$ 40,000
Purchases, net	180,000	300,000
Goods available for sale	$204,000	$340,000
Cost/retail price ratio:		
$204,000/$340,000 = 60%		
Sales		280,000
Cost of goods sold:		
60% of $280,000	168,000	
Inventory, January 31, 1979	$ 36,000	$ 60,000

The $280,000 sales amount is derived from the accounting records. The $168,000 is the cost of the goods sold during the month computed by applying the cost/retail price ratio of 60 percent to the sales of $280,000. Deducting $168,000 and $280,000 from the $204,000 and $340,000 amounts on the "goods available for sale" line yields the January 31, 1979, inventory at cost and at retail.

Now assume the same beginning inventory and sales as in Illustration 5.8 but with January purchases costing $263,000 marked up to a retail price of $370,000. The cost of the January 31, 1979, inventory would then be—

1. $78,000.
2. $91,000.
3. $42,000.

Now turn to Answer Frame 15[5] on page 220 to check your answers.

Summary *chapter 5*

Inventories consist of items which are held for sale to customers (merchandise or finished goods inventories), are being produced for future sale (work in process inventories), or are to be used in the production of goods or services for sale (raw materials and supplies inventories).

In principle, the cost of inventory includes the invoice price of the goods plus all costs required to get them ready for sale (or use, in the case of a manufacturer). Thus, cost of inventory includes insurance in transit and transportation charges (when ultimately paid by the buyer) and handling costs.

In general, inventories should be measured and reported at cost or market, whichever is lower. The four methods for determining cost are specific identification, Fifo, Lifo, and average.

The specific identification method involves the assignment of a known actual cost to an identified unit of product. Both Fifo and Lifo involve assumptions about the flow of costs. Fifo assumes that the cost of the first goods acquired is the cost of goods sold. Thus, the cost of the goods in ending inventory is assumed to be the cost of the last units acquired. Lifo assumes just the opposite. The cost of the last units acquired is the cost of goods sold. The cost remaining in ending inventory is assumed to be the cost of the first units acquired. These two methods can be used regardless of the actual flow of units.

Fifo can be used with either periodic or perpetual procedure, with the same end result. Lifo may also be used with either procedure. (The illustration of perpetual procedure is covered in the Appendix that follows.) If Lifo is used for tax purposes it must also be used for general financial reporting purposes.

The weighted-average method is used with periodic procedure. The total of the number of units purchased plus those in the beginning inventory is divided into the total cost of goods available for sale to derive a weighted-average unit cost. The units in ending inventory are then priced at this weighted-average unit cost.

The moving-average method is applied only under perpetual procedure (covered in the Appendix).

All of the above methods are considered acceptable, and no one of them can be considered the only correct one. Each method possesses an attribute which makes it attractive in certain circumstances.

In applying lower of cost or market, market is defined as current replacement cost. In the accounting records the lower-of-cost-or-market method may be applied to each item of inventory, to each class of inventory, or to total inventory.

The gross margin method can be used to estimate ending inventory. The gross margin method is usually used only for interim statement purposes and as a very rough check on the accuracy of the ending inventory determined by a physical count. It is based on the assumption that the rate of gross margin realized is highly stable from period to period. The method is only as valid as this assumption. To find the ending inventory, the estimated cost of goods sold is deducted from the cost of goods available for sale (the estimated cost of goods is found by subtracting the estimated gross margin from sales). It is advisable to take a physical inventory to determine the year-end inventory, since the gross margin percentage for the current period may have changed from previous years.

The retail method can also be used to estimate inventory. Basically, the ending inventory is determined first at retail prices as follows:

Beginning inventory at retail
+ Purchases at retail
= Goods available for sale at retail
− Sales
= Ending inventory at retail

Records are kept to show the *cost* of the goods available for sale. A ratio (the cost/retail price ratio) is then determined by relating this cost to the retail price of the goods available for sale. The cost of the ending inventory is then determined by applying this ratio to the ending inventory at retail.

You have completed the programmed portion of Chapter 5. As the first part of your review, read the Glossary of new terms introduced in this chapter which is given after the Appendix. Then complete the Student Review Quiz beginning on page 224.

APPENDIX 5: PERPETUAL INVENTORY PROCEDURE

Fifo applied under perpetual procedure

When Fifo is used under perpetual procedure, as merchandise is sold the Inventory account is credited for the cost of the oldest items in stock. After the first lot of merchandise has been sold, the next units sold are charged to cost of goods sold at the cost of the second lot purchased until the second lot is completely gone. The ending inventory will thus consist of the cost of the latest units purchased.

Illustration 5.9 shows how Fifo is applied under perpetual procedure

Illustration 5.9   Fifo cost of ending inventory under perpetual procedure

Date		Units	Unit cost	Cost
Jan. 1	Inventory	10	$8.00	$ 80.00
Mar. 2	Purchased	10	8.50	85.00
	Balance	20:10	8.00	
		10	8.50	$165.00
Mar. 10	Sold	10	8.00	80.00
	Balance	10	8.50	85.00
May 28	Purchased	20	8.40	168.00
	Balance	30:10	8.50	
		20	8.40	$253.00
July 14	Sold	20:10	8.50	
		10	8.40	169.00
	Balance	10	8.40	$ 84.00
Aug. 12	Purchased	10	9.00	90.00
	Balance	20:10	8.40	
		10	9.00	$174.00
Sept. 7	Sold	10	8.40	84.00
	Balance	10	9.00	$ 90.00
Oct. 12	Purchased	20	8.80	176.00
	Balance	30:10	9.00	
		20	8.80	$266.00
Nov. 22	Sold	20:10	9.00	
		10	8.80	178.00
	Balance	10	8.80	$ 88.00
Dec. 21	Purchased	10	9.10	91.00
	Balance	20:10	8.80	
		10	9.10	$179.00

using the data from Illustration 5.1. Note that the ending inventory of 20 units with a total cost of $179 is exactly the same as the ending inventory determined when Fifo was applied under periodic procedure (Illustration 5.3, page 206).

Lifo applied under perpetual procedure

Illustration 5.10 shows how Lifo is applied under perpetual procedure using the data from Illustration 5.1. Note that the amount differs from that achieved under periodic procedure (Illustration 5.4, page 207). When Lifo perpetual is used for financial statement purposes, it is adjusted to the Lifo periodic amount for tax purposes.

Illustration 5.10 Lifo cost of ending inventory under perpetual procedure

Date		Units	Unit cost	Cost
Jan. 1	Inventory	10	$8.00	$ 80.00
Mar. 2	Purchased	10	8.50	85.00
	Balance	20:10	8.00	
		10	8.50	$165.00
Mar. 10	Sold	10	8.50	85.00
	Balance	10	8.00	$ 80.00
May 28	Purchased	20	8.40	168.00
	Balance	30:10	8.00	
		20	8.40	$248.00
July 14	Sold	20	8.40	168.00
	Balance	10	8.00	$ 80.00
Aug. 12	Purchased	10	9.00	90.00
	Balance	20:10	8.00	
		10	9.00	$170.00
Sept. 7	Sold	10	9.00	90.00
	Balance	10	8.00	$ 80.00
Oct. 12	Purchased	20	8.80	176.00
	Balance	30:10	8.00	
		20	8.80	$256.00
Nov. 22	Sold	20	8.80	176.00
	Balance	10	8.00	$ 80.00
Dec. 21	Purchased	10	9.10	91.00
	Balance	20:10	8.00	
		10	9.10	$171.00

Moving-average method. This method can be used only on a continuous basis. After each purchase, a new weighted-average cost is computed by dividing the total cost of units on hand by the number of units on hand. This information is kept in a perpetual inventory record. Only purchases affect the moving-average unit costs; the cost of units sold is always the last-established average unit cost. Using the data from Illustration 5.1, the method is applied as shown on the perpetual inventory record in Illustration 5.11.

Illustration 5.11 *Perpetual inventory record*

	Purchased			Sold			Balance		
Date	Units	Unit cost	Total cost	Units	Unit cost	Total cost	Units	Unit cost	Total cost
Jan. 1..............							10	$8.00	$ 80.00
Mar. 2..............	10	$8.50	$ 85.00				20	8.25	165.00
10..............				10	$8.25	$ 82.50	10	8.25	82.50
May 28..............	20	8.40	168.00				30	8.35	250.50
July 14..............				20	8.35	167.00	10	8.35	83.50
Aug. 12..............	10	9.00	90.00				20	8.675	173.50
Sept. 7..............				10	8.675	86.75	10	8.675	86.75
Oct. 12..............	20	8.80	176.00				30	8.758*	262.75
Nov. 22..............				20	8.758	175.16	10	8.758	87.59
Dec. 21..............	10	9.10	91.00				20	8.929*	178.59
* Rounded.									

Note that with the purchase of March 2, a new unit cost is computed by adding together the cost of the first ten units and the March 2 purchase of ten units to secure a total cost to date of $165. This sum is divided by 20 units to give a unit cost of $8.25. Note also that all units sold are charged out at the previously determined unit cost. The ending inventory in Illustration 5.11 can be compared with the inventory computed under the periodic weighted-average method ($172.50 in Illustration 5.5) to indicate the differences caused by different weights given to the various prices paid. The unit prices in this perpetual inventory record can also be compared with the unit prices under Fifo perpetual procedure in Illustration 5.9, page 221, to see how averaging tends to slow the rise of the unit cost.

Glossary *chapter 5*

Fifo (first-in, first-out) — a method of pricing inventory under which the costs of the first goods acquired are the first costs charged to cost of goods sold when goods are actually sold.

Gross margin method — a method for estimating inventory. Gross margin percentages from previous periods are applied to sales of the current period to arrive at an estimated amount of gross margin and cost of goods sold. Cost of goods sold is deducted from cost of goods available for sale to arrive at estimated ending inventory.

Lifo (last-in, first-out) — a method of pricing inventory under which the costs of the last goods acquired are the first costs charged to cost of goods sold when goods are actually sold.

Lower-of-cost-or-market method — a method of pricing inventory under which cost or market, whichever is lower, is selected for each item, each group, or for the whole inventory.

Moving-average method — a method of pricing inventory under which a new unit cost is determined after each purchase by dividing total cost of units on hand by the number of units on hand. The cost of each sale is recorded at the latest computed unit cost. This method can only be used with perpetual inventory procedure.

Net realizable value — estimated selling price of merchandise less estimated cost of completion and disposition.

Retail inventory method – a procedure for estimating the cost of the ending inventory by applying the ratio of cost to retail price to the ending inventory at retail.

Specific identification – an inventory pricing method which involves the assignment of a known actual cost to a particular identifiable unit of product.

Weighted-average method – a method of pricing inventory under which the total number of units purchased plus those in the beginning inventory is divided into the total cost of goods available for sale to arrive at a weighted unit cost. The ending inventory is carried at this cost per unit.

Continue with the Student Review Quiz below as a self-administered test of your understanding of the material presented in this chapter.

Student review quiz *chapter* 5

To develop a permanent record of your responses, you may write them on the answer sheet provided in the *Work Papers* or on a separate piece of paper.

1 In 1979 the Mooney Company had an ending inventory of $5,600. The following is its trial balance at December 31, 1979:

	Debits	Credits
Cash	$13,500	
Accounts receivable	2,200	
Merchandise inventory, January 1	4,000	
Accounts payable		$ 1,800
Capital stock		13,000
Sales		20,000
Sales returns and allowances	100	
Sales discounts	100	
Purchases	14,000	
Purchase returns and allowances		800
Purchase discounts		150
Transportation-in	350	
Freight-out	400	
Sales salaries	1,100	
	$35,750	$35,750

Considering the above data, the cost of goods sold for the year is –

a $11,450.
b $11,800.

c $12,200.
d $12,350.
e $12,400.
f None of the above.

2 As a matter of proper accounting theory, which of the following costs should not be included in inventory?

a Amount paid to railroad for hauling purchased goods to place of business.
b Amount paid to local trucking company to haul purchased goods to warehouse from railroad station.
c Cost of hauling sold goods from place of business to customers' warehouses.
d Cost of insurance to insure purchased goods while in transit.
e Cost of handling, unpacking, checking, and pricing purchased merchandise received.

3 If the ending inventory on December 31, 1979, is overstated by $100,000, which of the following would result?

a Expenses of 1979 would be understated.
b Net earnings of 1980 would be overstated.
c Net earnings of 1979 would be understated.
d Expenses of 1980 would be understated.
e None of these.

4 The use of a Discounts Lost account implies that –

a The cost of inventory is the gross invoice price of the inventory items.
b Purchase discounts taken are part of the cost of the inventory.
c Purchase discounts lost are a part of the cost of merchandise.
d Purchase discounts lost are penalties for inefficiency rather than additions to cost of merchandise purchased.

5 A company has, for a given year, a beginning inventory of 300 units at $3; purchases of 700 units on May 1 at $4, and 1,200 units on September 5 at $4.50; and sales of 1,000 units and 900 units. What is the cost of the ending inventory under the Fifo method of pricing inventory?

a $900.
b $1,350.
c $1,200.
d $1,150.

6 Which of the following statements is false? When the general price level is rising, the inventory on the statement of financial position at the end of the year —
a Would more nearly approximate current replacement cost under Fifo than under Lifo.
b Would be lower under the Lifo method of costing than under the Fifo method.
c Would be higher under the weighted-average method than under the Fifo method.
d Would be "incorrect" under Lifo.

7 Given the following data, which of the statements below is false? Assume there is no beginning inventory.

Purchases

Feb. 2...............	1,200 units @ $2.00
10...............	800 units @ $2.50
20...............	400 units @ $2.75

Sales

Feb. 12...............	700 units
25...............	600 units

a Under the weighted-average method, the units sold on February 12 would have a unit cost of $2.292 ($5,500 ÷ 2,400).
b Under the Lifo method applied on a periodic basis, the 700 units sold on February 12 would be charged to cost of goods sold at $2.50 each for a total of $1,750.
c Under the Fifo method the 1,200 units purchased on February 2 would be included in cost of goods sold.

8 With respect to the various methods of inventory measurement, which of the following statements is false?
a The application of the Fifo method will usually result in fairly current costs being included in the cost of goods sold.
b A company can manipulate its net earnings to a certain extent if it uses the Lifo method.
c A company can manipulate its net earnings to a certain extent if it uses the specific identification method.
d In applying the lower-of-cost-or-market method, cost must still be determined by using Fifo, Lifo, specific identification or some average method.

9 The Little Company has three different products in its inventory at December 31, 1979, which have costs and current market values as follows:

Item	Cost	Market
A	$4,000	$3,800
B.................	5,000	5,200
C.................	8,000	7,800

With respect to the above inventory, which of the following statements is (are) true?
a The inventory could be reported at $16,800 under the lower-of-cost-or-market method.
b The inventory could be reported at $16,600 under the lower-of-cost-or-market method.
c If item C, which was purchased for sale at a price of $8,500, can still be sold for $8,500, it should be included in inventory at $8,000 under the lower-of-cost-or-market method.
d If item A has a selling price of $4,200 and additional costs of $500 will be incurred in disposing of this item, it should be included in inventory at $3,700 under the lower-of-cost-or-market method.

10 The gross margin method of computing inventory (choose the false statement) —
a Assumes a stable rate of gross margin from period to period.
b May indicate possible inventory shortages when used in conjunction with a physical inventory.
c May be used in place of a physical inventory at year-end.

11 Reed & Melton, Inc., for several years has maintained a 30 percent average gross margin on sales. Given the following data for 1979, what is the approximate inventory on December 31, 1979, computed by the gross margin method of estimating inventory?

	Cost
Inventory, January 1	$12,000
Purchases	65,000
Total................................	$77,000

Sales in 1979 were $90,000.

a $35,100.
b $23,100.

225

c $27,000.
d $14,000.
e $13,000.

12 The Klub Company records show the following information pertaining to a certain department's purchases, sales, and inventory for 1979:

	Cost	Retail
Sales..................		$400,000
Inventory, January 1, 1979...............	$ 28,000	35,000
Purchases, 1979 ...	360,000	450,000

The company uses the retail method of calculating ending inventory. On the basis of the above data, which of the following is the correct ratio of cost to retail price to be used in computing the December 31, 1979, inventory?

a $\dfrac{\$400,000}{\$450,000} = 88.89$ percent.

b $\dfrac{\$388,000}{\$400,000} = 97$ percent.

c $\dfrac{\$388,000}{\$485,000} = 80$ percent.

d $\dfrac{\$488,000}{\$885,000} = 55.14$ percent.

e None of the above.

Now compare your answers with the correct answers and explanations on page 716.

Questions *chapter 5*

1 Why does an understated ending inventory understate net earnings for the period by the same amount?

2 Why does an error in ending inventory affect two accounting periods?

3 What cost elements are included in inventory?

4 How should purchase discounts lost be shown in the earnings statement?

5 What does it mean to "take a physical inventory"?

6 Indicate how a company can manipulate the amount of net earnings it reports if it uses the Lifo method of inventory measurement. Why is the same manipulation not possible under Fifo?

7 What is net realizable value, and how is it used?

8 Why is it considered acceptable accounting practice to recognize a loss by writing down an item of merchandise in inventory to market, but unacceptable to recognize a gain by writing up an item of merchandise in inventory?

9 Under what operating conditions will the gross margin method of computing an inventory produce approximately correct amounts?

10 What are three uses of the gross margin method?

11 How can the retail method be used to estimate inventory?

Exercises *chapter 5*
(Exercises 1 and 2 review concepts covered in Chapter 4.)

1 The Grantham Corporation uses periodic inventory procedure, maintains an account to show discounts lost, and records purchases at their net prices. Prepare entries for the following transactions:

May 1 Received merchandise from the Adam Corporation, $2,000; terms, 2/10, n/30.

3 Received merchandise from the Eve Corporation, $1,200; terms, 2/10, n/30.

8 Paid the Adam Corporation invoice.

15 Paid the Eve Corporation invoice.

2 The Vinson Company uses the net invoice price in its statements and records. Journalize the following transactions:

a Purchased on account and received eight units of merchandise at $100 each; terms, 2/10, n/30.

b Received and paid cash for a large supply of sales tickets, letterheads, and so forth; invoice price, $600 less 2 percent cash discount.

c Ordered six units of merchandise at $150 each; terms, 2/10, n/30.

d Paid cash for one unit of office equipment; terms, 2/10, n/30. The invoice read:

One checkwriter...............	$400	
Less 2% discount	8	$392
Express charges		6
Cash Paid		$398

e Paid transportation charges of $20 on the eight units of merchandise received in (**a**).

f Paid the invoice for transaction (**a**) after the discount period had expired.

g Sold one unit of merchandise acquired in transaction (**a**) for $210 cash.

3 The Charm Company inventory records show a January 1 inventory of 1,000 units at $8 (total $8,000) and purchases of:

	Units	Amount
Feb. 14.............	300	@ $7.40 = $2,220
Mar. 18.............	800	@ $7.25 = $5,800
July 21.............	600	@ $7.70 = $4,620
Sept. 27.............	600	@ $7.40 = $4,440
Nov. 27.............	200	@ $7.85 = $1,570

The December 31 inventory was 1,400 units.

a Present a short schedule showing the measurement of the ending inventory using the Fifo method.

b Do the same using the Lifo method.

4 The Vine Company's inventory of a certain product was 8,000 units with a cost of $11 each on January 1, 1979. During 1979 numerous units of this product were purchased and sold. Also during 1979 the purchase price of this product fell steadily until at year-end it was $9. The inventory at year-end was 12,000 units. State which of the two methods of inventory measurement, Lifo or Fifo, would have resulted in the higher reported net earnings and explain briefly.

5 The Camel Company had the following inventory transactions during 1979:

a January 1 inventory on hand, 200 units at $4 = $800.

b January sales were 40 units.

c February sales totaled 60 units.

d March 1, purchased 100 units at $4.20.

e Sales for March through August were 80 units.

f September 1, purchased 20 units at $4.80.

g September through December sales were 90 units.

Record the journal entries affecting the inventory account assuming periodic inventory procedure is used and a physical inventory on December 31, 1979, showed 50 units on hand. Price the ending inventory at its weighted-average cost.

6 Your assistant has compiled the following schedule to assist you in determining the decline in inventory from cost to the lower of cost or market, item by item:

	A	B	C	D
Units.....	200	200	600	1,000
Unit cost ...	$ 18	$ 8	$ 6	$ 10.20
Unit market	17	9	6	10.40
Total cost ...	3,600	1,600	3,600	10,200
Total market	3,400	1,800	3,600	10,400

Compute the cost of the ending inventory using the cost or market, whichever is lower, method applied to individual items.

7 Royce Company follows the practice of taking a physical inventory at the end of each calendar year accounting period to establish the ending inventory amount for financial statement purposes. Its financial statements for the past few years indicate a normal gross margin of 30 percent. On July 18, a fire destroyed the entire store building and contents. The records were in a fireproof vault and are intact. These records, through July 17, show:

Merchandise inventory, January 1	$ 100,000
Merchandise purchases.............	2,100,000
Purchase returns.....................	40,000
Transportation-in	125,000
Sales.....................................	3,200,000
Sales returns	100,000

The company was fully covered by insurance and asks you to determine the amount of its claim for loss of merchandise.

Problems, Series A *chapter* 5

5-1-A

Farmington Company reported net earnings in 1979 of $130,000, in 1980 of $135,000, and in 1981 of $145,000. Analysis of its inventories shows that certain clerical errors were made so that inventory figures were:

	Incorrect	Correct
December 31, 1979	$40,000	$45,000
December 31, 1980	38,000	35,000

Required:

a Compute the amount of net earnings for each of the three years assuming that the clerical errors in computing the inventory had not been made.

b Determine the total net earnings for the three years with the use of the incorrect inventories and compare this with the total net earnings determined when correct inventories were used.

5-2-A

Following are selected transactions and data of the Lahiri Company:

1979

Mar. 1 Bought merchandise from A Company: invoice amount, $4,000; terms, 2/10, n/30.

5 Bought merchandise from B Company: invoice amount, $5,000; terms, 2/10, n/30.

11 Paid A Company for purchase of March 1.

21 Paid B Company for purchase of March 5.

31 The goods bought from both A Company and B Company make up the complete physical inventory.

Required (you may assume there were no opening inventory and no sales for March):

a Present journal entries to record the above transactions and to set up the ending inventory at March 31, following a procedure which shows discounts taken. Assume periodic inventory procedure is used.

b Repeat (a) above under a procedure which shows discounts lost.

c Which procedure would you recommend, and why?

(Note: This problem reviews concepts covered in Chapter 4. You may wish to refer back to that chapter.)

5-3-A

Following are data relating to the beginning inventory and purchases of a given item of product of the Snow Company for the year 1979:

January 1 inventory	1,400 @ $2.10
February 2	1,000 @ $2.00
April 5	2,000 @ $1.50

June 15 .... 1,200 @ $1.25
September 30 .... 1,400 @ $1.20
November 28 .... 1,800 @ $1.75

During the year 6,600 units were sold. Periodic inventory procedure is used.

Required:

Compute the ending inventory and cost of goods sold under each of the following methods:

a Fifo.
b Lifo.
c Weighted average.

5-4-A

The Staubach Corporation was organized on January 1, 1979. Selected data for 1979–81 are:

Year ended December 31	Inventory		Annual data	
	Fifo	*Lifo*	*Purchases*	*Sales*
1979	$1,600	$1,200	$7,200	$8,100
1980	2,000	1,400	6,000	9,500
1981	3,300	2,000	7,400	8,200

Required:

Compute the gross margin for each of the three years under Fifo and under Lifo.

5-5-A

The Batter Company determines its net earnings using the Fifo method of inventory measurement. It reported net earnings for 1979 of $68,000; 1980, $65,400; and 1981, $67,300. Inventories on the Fifo and Lifo bases were:

Dec. 31	*Fifo*	*Lifo*
1978	$15,000	$14,000
1979	17,200	15,800
1980	16,800	15,600
1981	18,300	16,700

Required:

Compute the net earnings that would have been reported in 1979, 1980, and 1981 by the Batter Company had it used the Lifo method of inventory measurement. Assume that purchases, selling expenses, administrative expenses, and sales are $29,200; $3,000; $2,000; and $100,000, respectively, for each of the years 1979, 1980, and 1981.

5-6-A

Given below are data relating to the ending inventory of the Tucker Company at December 31, 1979:

Item	Quantity	Unit cost	Unit market
1.....................	6,000	$1.00	$0.95
2.....................	12,000	0.80	0.90
3.....................	4,000	0.75	0.80
4.....................	10,000	1.40	1.25
5.....................	8,000	1.25	1.30
6.....................	2,000	0.90	0.80

Required:

a Compute the ending inventory applying the lower-of-cost-or-market method to the total inventory.

b Repeat (a) above applying the method to individual items.

5-7-A

Baily Company employs a fiscal year ending September 30. At this time inventories are usually at a very low level because of reduced activity. The management of the company wishes to maintain full insurance coverage on its inventory at all times. The company has earned around 40 percent gross margin on net sales over the last few years. Given below are data for the seven months ending April 30, 1979:

Sales..	$400,000
Sales returns	40,000
Sales discounts	10,000
Inventory, October 1, 1978.....................	30,000
Purchases	305,000
Purchase returns	23,000
Purchase discounts...............................	7,000
Transportation-in	15,000
Selling expenses....................................	35,000
Administrative expenses.........................	30,000

Required:

a Indicate, in general, how the company can estimate its inventory at any given date.

b State the amount of insurance coverage the company should obtain on its inventory to be fully covered at all times if the inventory is at its highest level on April 30 of each year.

5-8-A

The sales and cost of goods sold for the Blanca Company for the past five years were as follows:

Year	Sales (net)	Cost of goods sold	
1974	$693,400	$464,578	67%
1975	749,600	502,232	67%
1976	857,400	565,884	66%
1977	820,600	558,008	68%
1978	885,600	593,352	67%

For the seven months ended July 31, 1979, the following information is available from the accounting records of the company:

230

Sales..	$645,680
Purchases...................................	382,400
Purchase returns.........................	2,400
Sales returns..............................	14,480
Inventory, January 1, 1979............	79,000

In requesting the extension of credit by a new supplier, the Blanca Company has been asked to present current financial statements. It does not want to take a complete physical inventory at July 31, 1979.

Required:

a Indicate how financial statements can be prepared without taking a complete physical inventory.
b From the data given, estimate the inventory at July 31, 1979.

5–9–A

The following data pertain to a certain department of the Walton Department Store for the year ended December 31, 1979:

	Cost	Retail	
Merchandise inventory, January 1, 1979...............	$ 40,000	$ 60,000	60%
Purchases, net..	440,000	740,000	
Sales		720,000	

Required:

Use the retail method to compute the cost of the inventory on December 31, 1979.

5–10–A

An examination of the records of the Hyslop Company on December 31, 1979, disclosed the following with regard to merchandise inventory for 1979 and prior years:

1. December 31, 1976: Inventory understated $40,000.
2. December 31, 1977: Inventory of $28,000 was included twice.
3. December 31, 1978: Inventory of $25,000 was omitted.
4. December 31, 1979: Inventory is correct.

The reported net earnings for each year were as follows: (including above errors)

1976..	$235,000
1977..	284,000
1978..	307,000
1979..	281,000

Required:

a What are the correct net earnings for 1976, 1977, 1978, and 1979?
b What is (are) the error(s) in each December 31 statement of financial position?

231

Problems, Series B *chapter 5*

5-1-B

Gotham Company reported net earnings in 1979 of $119,200, in 1980 of $128,800, and in 1981 of $108,600. Analysis of its inventories shows that certain clerical errors were made so that inventory figures were:

	Incorrect	Correct
December 31, 1979	$24,200	$28,400
December 31, 1980	28,000	23,400

Required:

a Compute the amount of net earnings for each of the three years assuming that the clerical errors in computing the inventory had not been made.

b Determine the total net earnings for the three years with the use of the incorrect inventories and compare this with the total net earnings determined when correct inventories were used.

5-2-B

Beatle Company, a newly organized corporation, embarked upon an extensive purchasing program in November 1979. It opened its doors for business on December 15, 1979. The company decided to use a calendar-year accounting period, and as of December 31, 1979, its accounts show:

Sales	$ 84,000
Purchases	900,000
Transportation-in	102,000
Purchase discounts	18,000

All purchases were subject to discount terms of 2/10, n/30. The cost of the inventory on December 31, 1979, at vendors' gross invoice prices was $840,000.

Required:

Present a schedule showing the computation of cost of goods sold and the gross margin for the period ending December 31, 1979, assuming that all of the purchase discounts were taken. (Note: This problem reviews concepts covered in Chapter 4. You may wish to refer back to that chapter.)

5-3-B

The purchases and sales of a certain product for the Lawton Company for April 1979 are shown below. There was no inventory on April 1.

Purchases		Sales	
Apr. 3	1,000 units @ $2.50	Apr. 4	600 units
10	800 units @ $2.60	11	500
22	1,600 units @ $2.30	16	500
28	900 units @ $2.40	26	400
		30	600

Required:

a Compute the ending inventory of the above product as of April 30 under each of the following methods: (1) Fifo, (2) Lifo, (3) weighted average, and (4) moving average. (This fourth method is based on the Appendix.) Assume periodic inventory procedure except for method (4).

b Give the journal entries to record the purchases and the cost of goods sold for the month under both Fifo and Lifo methods applied under periodic procedure.

5–4–B

Listed below are the purchases and sales of a certain product made by the Cooper Company during 1979 and 1980. The company had 10,000 units of this product on hand at January 1, 1979, with a cost of $2 per unit.

Purchases		Sales	
1979		1979	
Feb. 20..............	2,000 @ $2.00	Feb. 2..............	3,000 @ $3,00
Apr. 18..............	5,000 @ $1.95	Apr. 23..............	4,000 @ $2.50
Aug. 28..............	5,000 @ $1.90	Sept. 3..............	4,000 @ $2.40
Dec. 22..............	4,000 @ $1.92	Dec. 24..............	3,500 @ $2.45
1980		1980	
Jan. 26..............	3,000 @ $1.95	Jan. 7..............	2,500 @ $2.50
Mar. 6..............	5,000 @ $2.00	Mar. 21..............	4,000 @ $2.60
Aug. 12..............	3,000 @ $2.10	Sept. 8..............	2,500 @ $2.60
Nov. 15..............	4,000 @ $2.20	Dec. 2..............	4,500 @ $2.75

The company uses periodic inventory procedure.

Required:

a Compute the cost of the ending inventory and the cost of goods sold for both years assuming the use of the Fifo method of inventory measurement.

b Repeat (a) above assuming the use of Lifo.

5–5–B

Given below are the net earnings and inventories of the Ashworth Corporation as reported for the years indicated:

December 31	Fifo	Lifo	Net earnings
1979	$360,000	$294,000	$ 950,000
1980	372,000	348,000	980,000
1981	414,000	408,000	1,020,000

The Ashworth Corporation has used the Fifo method of inventory measurement.

Required (ignore the possible effects of federal income taxation):

a State the amount of net earnings that the company would have reported in 1980 and 1981 if it had used the Lifo method rather than Fifo.

b State the amount of net earnings that the company would have reported in 1981 had it changed from Fifo to Lifo in 1981.

5-6-B

The accountant for the Box Corporation prepared the following schedule of the company's inventory at December 31, 1979, and used the lower of the total cost or total market value in determining cost of goods sold.

Item	Quantity	Cost per unit	Market value per unit	Total value Cost	Total value Market
Q	2,500	$2.00	$2.00		
R	1,000	1.50	1.40		
S	3,500	1.00	0.90		
T	3,000	0.75	0.80		

Required:

a State whether this is an acceptable method of inventory measurement and determine the amounts computed.
b Compute the amount of the ending inventory using the lower-of-cost-or-market method on an individual item basis.
c State the effect upon net earnings in 1979 if the method in (**b**) was used rather than the method in (**a**).

5-7-B

As part of a loan agreement with a local bank, the Kirk Company must present quarterly and cumulative earnings statements for the year 1979. The company uses periodic inventory procedure and marks its merchandise to sell at a price which will yield a gross margin of 40 percent. Selected data for the first six months of 1979 are:

	First quarter	Second quarter
Sales	$310,000	$315,000
Purchases	200,000	225,000
Purchase returns and allowances	12,000	13,000
Purchase discounts	3,800	3,900
Sales returns and allowances	10,000	5,000
Transportation-in	8,800	8,900
Selling expenses	31,000	30,000
Administrative expenses	21,000	19,000

The cost of the physical inventory taken December 31, 1978, was $38,000.

Required:

a Indicate how the earnings statements may be prepared without taking a physical inventory at the end of each of the first two quarters of 1979.
b Prepare earnings statements for the first quarter, the second quarter, and the first six months of 1979.

5-8-B

Following are selected transactions and data of the Woods Company for 1979:

June 1 Bought merchandise from the Birch Company: invoice amount, $10,500; terms, 2/10, n/30.

6 Bought merchandise from the Pine Company: invoice amount, $10,000; terms, 2/10, n/30.

12 Paid the Birch Company for the purchase of June 1.

15 Paid the Pine Company for the purchase of June 6.

30 The entire physical inventory consists of the goods bought from the Birch Company and the Pine Company.

Required:

a Assuming use of periodic inventory procedure, present journal entries to record the above transactions and to set up the ending inventory at June 30 following a procedure which shows discounts taken.

b Repeat (a) above under a procedure which shows discounts lost.

c Which method would be of more value to the management of the Woods Company? Why?

(Note: This problem reviews concepts covered in Chapter 4. You may wish to refer back to that chapter.)

5-9-B

The following data pertain to the Little Department Store for the fiscal year ended June 30, 1980:

	Cost	Retail
Merchandise inventory, July 1, 1979	$ 25,000	$ 37,000
Purchases, net	315,000	463,000
Sales		480,000

Required:

Use the retail method to compute the cost of the inventory on June 30, 1980.

5-10-B

As of December 31, 1979, the financial records of the Mott Company were examined for the years ended December 31, 1976, 1977, 1978, and 1979. With regard to merchandise inventory, the examination disclosed the following:

1. December 31, 1976: Inventory of $20,000 was included twice.
2. December 31, 1977: Inventory overstated $10,000.
3. December 31, 1978: Inventory of $22,000 was omitted.
4. December 31, 1979: Inventory is correct.

The reported net earnings for each year were as follows:

1976	$38,400
1977	54,400
1978	67,000
1979	84,600

Required:

a What are the correct net earnings for 1976, 1977, 1978, and 1979?
b What is (are) the errors in each December 31 statement of financial position?
c Comment on the implications of your corrected net earnings as contrasted with reported net earnings.

6

Cash; temporary and stock investments

Learning objectives

Study of the material presented in this chapter is designed to achieve a number of learning objectives. These include an understanding of:

1. The objectives sought by management in administering the cash resources of the company.

2. The nature of cash and the types of bank accounts.

3. The procedures for controlling cash receipts and disbursements.

4. The preparation of the bank reconciliation statement and the necessary actions to take on the basis of the reconciliation.

5. The nature of and accounting for temporary investments in deposit accounts and short-term marketable securities.

6. Accounting for stock investments.

7. How to set up and manage a petty cash fund (Appendix 6A).

8. The nature and operation of a voucher system for controlling cash disbursements (Appendix 6B).

Cash includes currency, coin, undeposited negotiable instruments (such as checks, bank drafts, and money orders), amounts in checking or savings accounts at a bank, and demand certificates of deposit at a bank. Cash does *not* include such items as postage stamps, IOUs, and notes receivable. Cash is usually divided into cash on hand and cash in banks. But in financial reporting these are combined into one amount and reported as "cash."

Many business transactions involve cash. Also, cash is the most useful item for someone to steal since it can be used to obtain anything else. Therefore management must keep close control over cash and account for it carefully.

The objectives of management in regard to cash are:

1. Account for all cash transactions accurately so that management will have correct information regarding cash.
2. Make sure there is enough cash to pay bills as they come due.
3. Avoid holding excessive amounts of idle cash which could be invested in productive assets to increase earnings.
4. Prevent the loss of cash due to theft or fraud.

Most of a firm's cash transactions involve a bank checking account. It deposits its daily receipts into a checking account and writes checks on that account to pay its bills. Periodically, the firm's account and the bank's account are reconciled to make sure that no errors have been made. Therefore, in this chapter significant attention is given to the checking account portion of cash. But first, we examine the procedures used to control cash receipts and cash disbursements to prevent error, theft, and fraud. Other topics include the investing of temporarily idle cash balances and certain long-term investments. The topic of petty cash is covered in Appendix 6A, while the voucher system is covered in Appendix 6B.

Controlling cash receipts

From the moment cash is received until it is deposited in the bank, it should be completely safeguarded. While cash is of no more importance than inventory, it is more easily stolen because it can be concealed and is not readily identifiable.

The methods used to control cash receipts vary with each business. Therefore, the following description of the internal control of cash receipts may be varied in practice to suit the individual needs of each business. A few basic principles for controlling cash receipts follow.

1. A record of all cash receipts should be prepared as soon as the cash is received. Most thefts of cash receipts occur before a record is made of the receipt. Once a record is made, improper uses are more readily traceable.

2. All cash receipts should be deposited intact in the bank, preferably on the next business day or in the bank's night depository on the same day. Cash disbursements should not be made from cash receipts but only by check or from petty cash funds. In many retail stores refunds for returned merchandise are made from the cash register. If this practice is followed, refund tickets should be prepared.

3. The person who handles the cash receipts should not record them in the accounting records, and the company accountant should not have access to the cash receipts.

4. If possible — and it is possible in all but small concerns — the internal function of receiving cash should be separated from the internal function of disbursing cash.

Controlling cash disbursements

The functions of handling cash receipts and cash disbursements should be completely separated. The procedures to control cash disbursements are:

1. With the exception of petty cash disbursements, all disbursements should be by check. No cash receipts should be disbursed.

2. All checks should be prenumbered — consecutively — and all should be controlled and accounted for.

3. Preferably, two signatures should appear on all checks.

4. If possible, the person who approves payment should not be one of those who signs the checks.

5. Each check should be supported by approved invoices or approved vouchers (authorizations to draw the checks).

6. The person authorizing the disbursement of cash should be certain that payment is in order and that it is made to the proper payee.

7. Invoices and vouchers should be indelibly stamped "paid," together with the date and check number. This minimizes duplicate payments of a debt.

8. The person signing the checks should not have access to returned checks paid by the bank.

9. The bookkeeper should obtain the bank statement and the paid checks and prepare the bank reconciliation statement.

10. All voided and spoiled checks should be retained and mutilated to prevent their unauthorized use.

Appendix 6B describes the operation of a voucher system which may be used to provide close control over cash disbursements. The special journals used in such a system are a voucher register and a check register.

Is each of the following statements true or false?

1. Cash includes postage stamps, IOUs, and notes receivable.
2. Management tries to have "just the right amount" of cash available (within a certain range).
3. It is advisable to pay bills out of receipts so as to avoid having to write checks for these items.
4. It is advisable for a company to require that two signatures appear on all checks.

Now go to Answer Frame 1[6] on page 242 to check your answers.

Frame 2[6]

The bank checking account

A bank must account to its depositors for all funds received from and spent for them. Certain business papers are involved.

The signature card

A bank requires a new depositor to complete a signature card giving signatures of persons authorized to sign checks on the account. The signature card is retained at the bank to identify the signatures as they appear on returned checks drawn on the bank.

Bank deposits

When a deposit is made in the bank, the depositor prepares a deposit ticket. Deposit tickets come in many forms but include the name of the account, the account number, the amount of cash deposited, and a listing of the checks deposited. In modern machine-based bank accounting systems, each depositor is given a number of deposit tickets imprinted with the depositor's name and account number. When making a deposit, the depositor receives a machine-imprinted receipt showing the date and the amount of the deposit.

The bank check

There are three parties to every bank check transaction: (1) the depositor issuing the check; (2) the bank on which the check is drawn; and (3) the party to whose order the check is made payable.

A check is a written order on a bank to pay a specific sum of money to the party designated or to his or her order. It is signed by the person issuing the check.

The type of check often used by modern business firms is prenumbered when printed. It is prepared in sets of an original and as many copies as are needed. The lower section of the check is known as a *remittance advice* and is detached prior to the depositing of the check. The remittance advice contains information explaining the check.

The checking account statement

The bank furnishes each checking account depositor with a *bank statement,* one form of which is shown in Illustration 6.1. It is usually issued once each month.

The bank statement shows (*a*) each deposit made during the period, (*b*) each check which cleared during the period, and (*c*) a daily balance of the account whenever it changes. Any debit memoranda (amounts deducted from the account, such as for service charges) and credit memoranda (amounts added to the account, such as for the proceeds' of notes collected for the depositor by the bank) will also be shown.

Copies of the deposit tickets and the checks paid by the bank during the month will also be returned to the depositor with the bank statement.

Reconciling the bank statement and Cash account balances

The balance shown by the bank statement will usually differ from the balance for the same date in the depositor's ledger account for cash in bank. The reasons for this difference include:

1. Items that cause a larger balance to be shown on the bank's statement than in the depositor's ledger account are as follows:
   a. Checks issued by the depositor which are still outstanding; the payees have not presented the checks to the bank for payment.
   b. Deposits made in the depositor's account by the bank for which entries have not been made on the depositor's books. For example, the bank may collect a note for the depositor, add it to the depositor's balance, and advise the depositor of the collection immediately; the depositor may not yet have recorded the amount in its accounting records.
2. Items that cause a smaller balance to be shown on the bank's statement than in the depositor's ledger account are as follows:
   a. Deposits recorded on the depositor's books which are in transit (have not yet been recorded by the bank). They are picked up as deposits on the next period's bank statement.
   b. Bank charges for services rendered by the bank to the depositor which have been deducted from his bank balance but which have not been credited to cash on the books of the depositor. Notice of these deductions is included with the bank statement in the form of debit memoranda. Examples of these deductions are service charges for checks and deposits (when the daily balance in an account is below the minimum required by the bank) and charges for collecting notes.

241

1. False. Cash does not include these items. Instead, it includes currency, coin, checks, bank drafts, money orders, amounts in checking and savings accounts, and certificates of deposit.
2. True. Management does try to have "just the right amount" of cash available. It must be able to pay its bills as they come due, but if too much cash is kept idle, profits will suffer. It could be invested in more productive assets, such as inventory.
3. False. Receipts should be deposited intact. All disbursements (except those out of petty cash) should be made by check. These procedures help establish management control over cash flows.
4. True. This procedure makes it more difficult for a person to steal funds by preparing checks which are not authorized.

If you missed any of the above, reread Frame 1⁶ before starting Frame 2⁶ on page 240.

2⁶
continued

   c. Deductions for N.S.F. (nonsufficient funds) checks. These are checks which were received from customers and were deposited. When the check arrived at the bank which was ordered to pay the funds there were insufficient funds to cover the check. Since the customer has not satisfied the debt, the company needs to reestablish the account receivable.

Incorrect entries on the bank's books or on the depositor's books may cause errors in either balance. As a result of these various items, neither the bank statement nor the depositor's ledger account shows the exact expendable balance of cash that should appear in the statement of financial position. Correcting entries should be made to reflect items 1(*b*), 2(*b*), and 2(*c*) on the depositor's records.

Indicate whether each of the following statements is correct or incorrect.

1. The bank statement is a report sent to a depositor by a bank showing the activity in a firm's checking account for a period of time, usually a month.
2. Deposits in transit will cause the balance shown in the depositor's Cash ledger account to be less than the balance reported in the bank statement, all other things being equal.
3. Bank service charges not yet entered in the depositor's accounting records will cause the balance of cash in the depositor's books to be higher than that reported by the bank, all other things being equal.
4. Outstanding checks of a depositor will cause the balance of the Cash account in the depositor's books to be larger than the balance reported by the bank, all other things being equal.

Now turn to Answer Frame 2⁶ on page 244 to check your answers.

Illustration 6.1 **Bank statement**

THE CITIZENS AND SOUTHERN NATIONAL BANK
ATLANTA, GEORGIA 30302   491-0000

Account Number 023-45-679	ABC COMPANY 123 ELMS STREET	**Date of Statement** 2/28/79
Branch Number 00	ATLANTA, GEORGIA 30301	

Statement Summary

Ending Balance Previous Statement		Total Amount Deposits and Credits		Total Amount Checks and Debits		Balance as of Statement Date
10,500.00	+	159,207.52	—	153,435.12	=	16,272.40

Checks and Debits				Deposits and Credits		Date	Balances
						JAN 31	10,500.00
2,100.00	1,500.75	700.00	NF	6,500.50		FEB 1	12,699.75
75.00	150.28			7,200.22		2	19,674.69
280.50	420.31	600.00		6,200.00		5	
				7,500.00	CM		32,073.88
410.40	270.27	20.00	SC	8,100.00		6	39,473.21
340.30	560.73	14,000.00		4,700.76		7	29,272.94
70.85	105.67	5,000.00	DM	5,800.00		8	29,896.42
530.62				6,100.50		9	35,466.30
710.57	15,500.20			10,200.25		12	29,455.78
840.61	10,961.75	625.40		9,400.40		13	26,428.42
660.83	12,200.00			8,300.60		14	21,868.19
214.14	46.27	10,500.00	DM	8,800.70		15	19,908.48
380.00	8,200.50			7,300.35		16	18,628.33
210.76	10,200.00			7,700.14		19	15,917.71
465.98				6,700.16		20	22,151.89
715.00	68.20	9,472.50		8,200.25		21	20,096.44
840.50	642.10 NF	9,300.00		9,100.41		22	18,414.25
965.45	8,700.00			9,300.37		23	18,049.17
5,210.33	877.50	962.15		8,900.89		26	19,900.08
762.87	7,481.50			5,600.60		27	17,256.31
910.74	7,628.40	45.19		7,600.42		28	16,272.40

Symbols: SC Service Charge. NF Charge for Check on non-sufficient funds. DM Debit Memo. CM Credit Memo. R Reversal of Posted Amount. BP Batch Posted

Member FDIC

1. Correct. It shows the activity which has taken place in the checking account.

2. Incorrect. Deposits in transit have been debited to the firm's Cash ledger account but have not yet been recorded in the bank's records. Thus, they will cause the ledger balance to be greater than the balance reported in the bank statement.

3. Correct. The bank service charges have already been deducted from the depositor's account at the bank, but have not yet been deducted from the Cash account in the depositor's books.

4. Incorrect. Outstanding checks will cause the balance shown in the depositor's Cash account to be smaller, not larger, than the balance reported by the bank. This is because the outstanding checks have already been deducted in the depositor's books (when they were issued) but have not yet been deducted in the bank's records, since they have not yet been presented to the bank and paid.

If you missed any of the above, reread Frame 2⁶ before starting Frame 3⁶ below.

Frame 3⁶

The bank reconciliation statement

A bank reconciliation statement is prepared to explain the difference between the cash balance on the books and on the bank statement. Both the bank statement balance and the balance in the Cash ledger account are adjusted to the true balance of expendable cash that should appear on the statement of financial position, as shown in Illustration 6.2.

The first step in preparing the reconciliation statement is to examine the bank statement and the debit and credit memoranda, if any, returned with the statement. The depositor's accounting records should be examined to see if the items referred to in these memoranda have been recorded. If they have not, they must be added to or deducted from the balance in the Cash account, as shown by the adjustments for $800 for the note collected, $2.50 for bank service charges, and $200 for the N.S.F. check in Illustration 6.2.

The second step is to sort the canceled checks returned by the bank into numerical order. The outstanding checks are identified by a process of elimination. The numbers of the checks which have cleared and been returned by the bank are compared with the numbers of the checks issued. Tick marks (✓) are used in the books to indicate those returned. The checks issued for which no canceled checks have been returned from the bank are the outstanding checks. Checks outstanding at the start of the month which have cleared the bank during the month may be traced to the reconciliation statement prepared at the end of the preceding month. Any checks outstanding at the end of the preceding

Illustration 6.2   Bank reconciliation statement

ATLANTA COMPANY			
Bank Reconciliation Statement			
August 31, 1979			

Balance per bank statement,		Balance per ledger,	
August 31, 1979..................... $23,195.85		August 31, 1979.................... $22,009.85	
Add: Deposit in transit.............. 1,057.05		Add: Note collected	
$24,252.90		by bank 800.00	
		$22,809.85	
Less: Outstanding checks 1,645.55		Less: Bank charges...... $ 2.50	
		N.S.F. check...... 200.00 202.50	
Adjusted Balance,		Adjusted Balance,	
August 31, 1979.................... $22,607.35		August 31, 1979.................... $22,607.35	

month which have not yet been returned during the current month are, of course, still outstanding at the end of the current month.

The next step in preparing the reconciliation statement is to see if there are any deposits in transit to the bank. The receipts for the last day of the month might have been deposited in the night depository box at the bank. Thus, they would be reported as a deposit by the bank as of the next day. The debits to the Cash account can be traced to the individual deposits per the bank statement.

Deposits in transit and outstanding checks, together with the bank service charges indicated on the bank statement, will often account entirely for the difference between the balance in the bank statement and the balance in the Cash account. Any omissions and errors in the depositor's books are corrected by proper entries. These entries should be made prior to the preparation of the financial statements. If any errors made by the bank are discovered in preparing the reconciliation statement (such as charging a check against the wrong account), they should be called to the attention of the bank.

To illustrate the preparation of a bank reconciliation statement, assume that the bank statement of the Atlanta Company at August 31, 1979, showed a balance of $23,195.85; the Cash account balance of the depositor at the same date was $22,009.85. By comparing the canceled checks returned by the bank with the accounting records, the following checks were found to be outstanding at the end of the month:

Check No.	*Amount*
556..............................	$ 840.00
570..............................	354.25
571..............................	451.30
	$1,645.55

An examination of the debit and credit memoranda returned with the bank statement reveals a credit memorandum showing that the bank had collected a customer's note for the Atlanta Company and had credited the amount collected, $800, to the company's account. (A credit memorandum is evidence of an addition to a depositor's account which arises from a transaction other than a normal deposit.) For this service, the bank charged the Atlanta Company $2.50 and so advised the company by including a debit memorandum for that amount with the canceled checks returned on August 31, 1979. There was another debit memorandum in the amount of $200 for an N.S.F. check received from Rook Company on August 10 and deposited on that date.

A tracing of the deposits shown in the accounting records to the bank statement revealed that cash receipts for August 31, $1,057.05, did not appear as a deposit on that date. Examination of the deposit ticket showed that the bank recorded the deposit on September 1.

The statement reconciling the balance per the bank statement with the balance per Cash account as of August 31, 1979 (Illustration 6.2, page 245), shows that the cash available for immediate disbursement is not $22,009.85 or $23,195.85, but $22,607.35. Consequently, the following journal entries must be prepared and posted:

Cash	800.00	
Notes Receivable		800.00
To record note collected by bank.		
Bank Service Charges	2.50	
Cash		2.50
To record bank collection charges.		
Accounts Receivable (Rook Company)	200.00	
Cash		200.00
To record N.S.F. check which was deducted from our account.		

The earnings statement for the period ended August 31, 1979, should include the expense of $2.50. The statement of financial position as of August 31, 1979, should show a cash balance of $22,607.35.

Indicate whether each of the following statements is true or false.

1. An error made by the bank in crediting an amount to a depositor's account requires a correcting journal entry in the depositor's own accounting records.

2. The cash amount shown in a firm's statement of financial position must be the balance reported to the firm in the bank statement.

3. Outstanding checks are the canceled checks which are returned by the bank with each bank statement.

4. Outstanding checks which were included in a bank reconciliation statement at January 31, 1979, must be included in the February 28, 1979, bank reconciliation statement if they are still outstanding.

Now turn to Answer Frame 3[6] on page 248 to check your responses.

Frame 4⁶

The data needed for you to prepare a bank reconciliation statement follow:

Balance per bank statement October 31, 1979	$3,290.00
Balance per Cash account of the Baxter Company at October 31, 1979	3,681.00
Checks outstanding at October 31, 1979	805.00
Receipts of October 31 placed in bank's night depository	480.00
Check of Bixter Company deducted from Baxter Company account in error and included in canceled checks returned by bank	105.00
Credit memorandum covering collection of note by bank for Baxter Company (not recorded by Baxter Company as of October 31)	570.00
Debit memorandum for collection fees charged by bank for collecting above note	3.00
Check of customer (J. Wallis) of Baxter Company deposited on October 25 but returned by bank marked N.S.F. (not sufficient funds). No entry has been made for the return by the Baxter Company	168.00
Baxter Company note payable to bank, charged at maturity by the bank to the Baxter Company's account, including interest of $10	1,010.00

Using the above data and a separate sheet of paper, provide the missing items in the following illustration of a bank reconciliation statement:

BAXTER COMPANY
Bank Reconciliation Statement
October 31, 1979

Balance per bank statement, October 31, 1979		$3,290.00
Add: Check of Bixter Company deducted in error..................	$105.00	
DEPOSIT IN TRANSIT ?	480	? 585
	585	?3875
Less: OUTSTANDING CHECKS ?		? 805.00
Adjusted Balance, October 31, 1979...		$3,070.00
Balance per ledger, October 31, 1979		$3,681.00
Add: _____ ?		? 570
		?
Less: _____ ?	?3.00	
_____ ?	?168	
_____ ?	?1010	?
Adjusted Balance, October 31, 1979...		$3,070.00

Check your answers in Answer Frame 4⁶ on page 248.

Frame 5⁶

The available cash balance is $3,070. The entry to adjust the Cash account in the ledger is:

Collection Fee Expense...	3.00	
Accounts Receivable (J. Wallis)..	168.00	
Notes Payable..	1,000.00	
Interest Expense..	10.00	
Notes Receivable..		570.00
Cash..		611.00

To record adjustments to correct Cash account ($1,181 − $570 = $611 net cash outlay). For details see reconciliation statement for October.

1. False. Since the error was made by the bank, the correction must be made by the bank in its records.
2. False. The expendable cash at the statement of financial position date is the amount that should appear in that statement. Due to such factors as deposits in transit and outstanding checks, this might not be the balance reported in the bank statement.
3. False. Outstanding checks are those checks issued by the firm but which have not yet cleared the bank and been charged against the firm's account.
4. True. The checks are still outstanding, so they still cause a difference between the cash balance on the books and on the bank statement. As such, they must still be included in the reconciliation statement.

If you missed any of the above, reread Frame 3⁶ before beginning Frame 4⁶ on page 247.

Answer frame 4⁶

The completed bank reconciliation is as follows:

BAXTER COMPANY
Bank Reconciliation Statement
October 31, 1979

Balance per bank statement, October 31, 1979		$3,290.00
Add: Check of Bixter Company deducted in error.................	$ 105.00	
Deposit in transit	480.00	585.00
		$3,875.00
Less: *Outstanding checks*		805.00
Adjusted Balance, October 31, 1979.....................................		$3,070.00
Balance per ledger, October 31, 1979...................................		$3,681.00
Add: *Note collected by bank*		570.00
		$4,251.00
Less: *Not sufficient funds check*..	$ 168.00	
Collection fees	3.00	
Baxter Company note charged against account	1,010.00	1,181.00
Adjusted Balance, October 31, 1979.....................................		$3,070.00

If you answered incorrectly, study your errors carefully before proceeding to Frame 5⁶ on page 247.

5⁶
continued

Where more than one checking account is maintained by a company, each account must be reconciled separately with the statement received from the bank covering the account.

Certified checks

Because a check may not be paid when presented to the bank upon which drawn, a payee may demand that the check be certified. A certified check is a regular check drawn by a depositor and taken by the depositor to his or her bank for certification. The bank will stamp "certified" across the face of the check and insert the name of the bank and the date; the certification will be signed by a bank official. The bank will do this only after determining that the depositor's balance is large enough to cover the check, and the check will be deducted from the depositor's balance immediately. The check then becomes a liability of the bank. For this reason it will be accepted without question.

Transfer bank accounts

A company operating in many widely scattered locations and having accounts with many local banks must use special procedures to avoid accumulating too much idle cash. One such procedure involves the use of special-instruction bank accounts. Transfer accounts are set up in the local banks. These banks automatically transfer to a central bank (by wire or bank draft) all amounts on deposit in excess of a stated amount (which may be zero). In this way funds not needed for local operations are quickly sent to the company's headquarters where they can be invested.

Indicate whether each of the following statements is true or false.
1. The company can make a compound journal entry to correct the balance of the Cash account after the bank reconciliation statement has been prepared.
2. A certified check should never be shown as outstanding on a bank reconciliation statement, since it has already been deducted from the company's balance with the bank.
3. A separate reconciliation statement must be prepared for each bank account maintained by a business.
4. Transfer bank accounts which require that excess funds be sent to a central location are used in an attempt to reduce the amount of idle cash held by a company.

Now check your answers by turning to Answer Frame 5^6 on page 250.

Frame 6⁶

Payroll checking accounts

Many firms maintain a separate payroll bank account, especially when many employees are paid by check. In general, a payroll checking account is used in the following fashion. Before each pay date, the net payroll is computed, a check is drawn on the general commercial bank account for that amount, and the check is deposited in the payroll bank account. Individual payroll checks are issued to the employees. When these are cashed they are cleared against the payroll bank account.

The use of a payroll bank account has several advantages, as follows: 249

1. True. The entry made at the beginning of Frame 5⁶ is a compound entry. Alternatively, individual entries could be made to record each item which affects the cash balance.
2. True. Certified checks are deducted from the company's balance at the bank at the time of certification. Therefore, they should not be treated as items that will be deducted from this balance in the future.
3. True. It would make little sense to reconcile a number of bank accounts simultaneously on one reconciliation statement. The data relating to one bank account could become mixed in with data relating to another bank account.
4. True. This is exactly the reason why transfer bank accounts are maintained.

If you missed any of the above, reread Frame 5⁶ before starting Frame 6⁶ on page 249.

6⁶
continued

1. A distinctive payroll check form may be used, with spaces provided on an attached apron for the amounts of gross earnings, the various payroll deductions, and the net cash paid.
2. Payroll checks, identifiable as such, are easily cashed by employees.
3. The work of reconciling the bank balances may be divided among employees. One check is drawn against the general commercial bank account. The hundreds or thousands of payroll checks issued each payday are drawn on the payroll bank account. Occasionally, payroll checks are lost or negotiated many times before clearing the bank. Including these items in the payroll reconciliation simplifies the reconciliation of the general Cash account.
4. Only one authorization is prepared, calling for one check drawn against the general commercial bank account; therefore, payroll checks are issued without separately prepared and signed authorizations.
5. The individual payroll checks need not be entered in the regular cash disbursements record; the payroll check numbers are inserted in the payroll journal or record, and a repetition of the entering of the checks is avoided.

Assume a company maintains a separate payroll bank account. Determine whether each of the following statements is correct or incorrect.

1. Separate authorizations need not be prepared for each payroll check.
2. The payroll checks must be entered individually in the regular cash disbursements record and also in a payroll journal or record.

3. The payroll check form must conform to that of the checks issued for general cash disbursements.

4. The reconciliation of the general Cash account is simplified.

Now check your answers with those in Answer Frame 6[6] on page 252.

Frame 7[6]

Cash short and over

Occasionally, errors are made in returning change to customers. In these cases the amount of cash will be short of, or in excess of, the amount shown by the total of a cash register tape or an adding machine tape total of sales slips for a day.

Assume that a store clerk accidentally shortchanges a cash customer to the extent of $1. Total cash sales for the day were $704.50. At the end of the day, the total actual cash will be $1 over the sum of the sales tickets or the total of the cash register tape. The journal entry to record the day's business is as follows:

Cash	705.50	
Sales		704.50
Cash Short and Over		1.00

The Cash Short and Over account is a miscellaneous expense (debit balance) or revenue (credit balance) account. It is credited if the cash received is greater than the correct amount and debited if the cash received is less than the correct amount. The balance of the account at the end of the period will be treated as an "other expense" or "other revenue."

Indicate whether each of the following statements is true or false.

1. It would be impossible to have a cash overage or shortage if employees were paid in cash rather than by check.

2. The entry to account for daily cash sales for which a small cash shortage existed would include a debit to Cash Short and Over.

3. If the Cash Short and Over account has a debit balance at the end of a period, it is classified as an expense.

4. A credit balance in a Cash Short and Over account should be considered a liability, because the shortchanged customer will demand return of this amount.

Check your answers with those in Answer Frame 7[6] on page 252.

Frame 8⁶

Temporary investments

At times a company may find that it has more cash than that needed for current operations. When this occurs the company is reluctant to leave those funds in a checking account which pays no interest or in a savings account which earns only a very modest rate of return (about 4 or 5 percent). Savings accounts are generally insured up to $40,000 by the federal government. Other resting places can be found which may be as safe or almost as safe and yet pay a higher return. Before utilizing any of these means of earning a return on temporarily excess cash, one should consider three factors — safety (against loss), liquidity (getting the money immediately when it is needed), and rate of return.

Short-term marketable securities

Short-term marketable securities include certificates of deposit, 91-day Treasury bills, Treasury tax anticipation notes, commercial paper of other companies, and other federal, state, and local governmental securities.

Certificates of deposit are purchased at a bank or savings and loan institution. Interest rates vary with supply and demand conditions in the money market. In recent years these certificates have paid between 5¾ percent and 9 percent. They normally are in $1,000 or larger denominations, and the money must be left on deposit for a minimum period of time (for example, three months or two years) in order to earn the stipulated rate of interest. (Early withdrawal results in a significant decrease in the amount of interest earned.) The rate of interest varies with the amount invested and the time to maturity. For example, in the midseventies a major savings and loan institution which paid 5¼ percent interest on regular deposit accounts offered three-month certificates at 5¾ (no minimum amount), one-year certificates at 6½ ($1,000 minimum), and four-year $1,000 certificates at 7½ percent. True annual rates also vary slightly upward when such interest is compounded quarterly, or even daily. Safety and rate of return are at least as good as with regular time deposits, but liquidity may be a problem in that the waiting period for withdrawal of the funds is longer.

Purchases of 91-day Treasury bills may also be made from commercial banks. These bills are normally issued at a discount (at an amount less than face value) and collected at face value, with the difference being interest revenue. For instance, assume that 91-day Treasury bills having a $20,000 face value are acquired at $19,600 on January 1, 1979. The entries required to account for the acquisition and redemption would be:

```
1979
Jan. 1  Marketable Securities—91-Day Treasury Bills ............  19,600
            Cash ..............................................................        19,600


Apr. 2  Cash ................................................................  20,000
            Marketable Securities—91-Day Treasury Bills ......        19,600
            Interest Revenue...............................................           400
```

If a statement of financial position date occurred before the bills matured, it would be necessary to prepare an adjusting entry debiting Marketable Securities—91-Day Treasury Bills and crediting Interest Revenue for the amount of interest earned to that date. For instance, if financial statements were to be prepared on January 31, the following entry would be necessary:

```
1979
Jan. 31   Marketable Securities–91-Day Treasury Bills ..........   131.87
             Interest Revenue.........................................           131.87
          To accrue interest earned on 91-day treasury bills
             (30/91 × $400).
```

Tax anticipation securities are also issued by the U.S. Treasury. They are purchased at a discount, mature shortly after the quarterly due date for corporate income taxes, and are accepted at face value when used to pay these taxes. The accounting for these transactions is similar to that illustrated for the 91-day Treasury bills. Both of these investments provide safety, a fair degree of liquidity, and a reasonable rate of return which varies according to supply and demand conditions in the money markets.

Longer term U.S. government securities may be purchased, but there is greater risk if they must be liquidated before their maturity date. As interest rates fluctuate in the money market, the current prices of these securities fluctuate. Assume that a given security has an interest rate of 5 percent and is selling at face amount ($10,000). If the market rate of interest then goes up to 7 percent, investors would be willing to pay less than $10,000 for this security since the amount it pays is fixed at 5 percent. Thus, market prices vary inversely with the market rate of interest. A given company may have to take a substantial loss in order to obtain its funds when it needs them. It is much more common for companies with temporarily idle cash to stay with 91-day Treasury bills and to "roll them over" (acquire new ones every 91 days) than it is to purchase the longer-term government securities.

Commercial paper (a short-term note) is also available as a temporary investment. This is a form of debt issued by other companies. The interest rate on high-grade commercial paper is only slightly higher than that on 91-day Treasury bills. It is not as safe as U.S. government securities, but safety and rate of return vary depending on the company issuing it. These notes can be sold at any time before maturity, but there is risk of loss since the market prices vary inversely with the market rate of interest.

A company may also choose to invest in securities issued by states and municipalities. Obligations of states and municipalities are generally tax-free, that is, any interest revenue is exempt from federal income taxes. Because of this desirable feature, the interest rates tend to be somewhat lower than on other securities. These securities are not as safe as U.S. government securities, but the degree of risk depends on who issues them. They may be resold in the market before maturity, but once again there is risk of loss since market prices fluctuate.

Determine whether each of the following statements is true or false.

1. Time deposit-type (savings) accounts earn a high rate of return.
2. Certificates of deposit may not be a good vehicle for short-term investment of seasonally idle cash.
3. When marketable securities are purchased at a discount and are collected at face value, the difference between these two amounts is considered interest revenue.
4. Commercial paper paying a 7 percent rate of interest is necessarily more desirable than City of Baltimore bonds yielding 5 percent.

Now turn to Answer Frame 8[6] on page 256 to check your answers.

Frame 9[6]

Stock investments

Sometimes companies invest in the stocks of other companies. Such investments may actually consist of marketable securities in that the stocks may be readily marketable. But these are rarely purchased as temporary investments of idle cash. When acquired, they are more likely to be either long-term investments or an attempt to speculate in the stock market.

The long-term reasons for investing in the securities of others include the desire (1) to establish an affiliation with another business, (2) to acquire control over another business, or (3) to secure a continuing stream of revenue from the investment over a period of years.

Reporting securities in the statement of financial position

The generally stated guides as to how securities should be classified in the statement of financial position tend to emphasize intent and may be summarized as follows.

1. If the securities held are readily marketable, they should be shown as current assets if they *will* be converted into cash in the normal operating cycle of the business. If they will not be converted, they should be considered noncurrent assets and reported in the investments section of the statement.
2. If the securities are not readily marketable, they may not be classified as current assets, unless they mature in the coming operating cycle and there is no doubt as to their redemption.

The primary classification criterion is the intent of management.

9⁶
continued

Valuation of equity securities

The FASB in its *Statement No. 12,* "Accounting for Certain Marketable Securities," describes the method of accounting for marketable equity securities.[1] It requires the use of the lower-of-cost-or-market method for marketable *equity* securities (with certain limited exceptions). Marketable equity securities are to be carried at the lower of total cost or total market for all securities classified as current *taken as a group* and for securities classified as noncurrent *taken as a group.*

Current marketable equity securities. For the securities classified as current any excess of total cost over total market is debited to an account such as Net Unrealized Loss on Current Marketable Equity Securities, which is shown in the earnings statement. The credit is to an asset valuation allowance account such as Allowance for Market Decline of Current Marketable Equity Securities. The entry would appear as follows (assuming cost is $500 above market):

Net Unrealized Loss on Current Marketable Equity Securities......	500	
Allowance for Market Decline of Current Marketable		
Equity Securities		500

Any later recovery in total market price (up to the amount of the original cost) would be debited to the asset valuation allowance and would be credited to an account such as Net Unrealized Gain on Current Marketable Equity Securities, which would be shown in the earnings statement. The entry would appear as follows (assuming market increased by $400):

Allowance for Market Decline of Current Marketable		
Equity Securities..	400	
Net Unrealized Gain on Current Marketable Equity		
Securities		400

[1] Financial Accounting Standards Board, "Accounting for Certain Marketable Securities," *FASB Statement No. 12* (Stamford, Conn., December 1975), pp. 31.

Noncurrent marketable equity securities. Any "temporary" losses on noncurrent equity securities (long-term investments) are charged against a stockholders' equity account (but not deducted from net earnings) and credited to an asset valuation allowance account. The account debited might be entitled, Net Unrealized Loss on Noncurrent Marketable Equity Securities. Thus, the entry might be as follows (assuming cost exceeds market by $1,000):

Net Unrealized Loss on Noncurrent Marketable Equity Securities	1,000	
Allowance for Market Decline of Noncurrent Marketable Equity Securities		1,000

Later recoveries up to cost would be debited to the allowance account and credited to the unrealized loss account as follows (assume market increases by $1,700):

Allowance for Market Decline of Noncurrent Marketable Equity Securities	1,000	
Net Unrealized Loss on Noncurrent Marketable Equity Securities		1,000

Thus, the entry would increase stockholders' equity by $1,000 (not $1,700), but would not increase reported earnings. If a loss on an individual noncurrent security is determined to be "permanent," it is to be written down to market as a realized loss charged against earnings. The entry would be (assuming a permanent loss of $1,400):

Realized Loss on Noncurrent Marketable Equity Securities	1,400	
Investment in Noncurrent Marketable Equity Securities		1,400

Any subsequent recovery in market value would be ignored until the security is sold.

The equity method. When a company holds 20 percent or more of the voting stock (common stock) of another company, it normally can influence the operations of that company. In these situations the company is required[2] to use the equity method of accounting for its investment. Under the equity method, the investor initially records the investment at cost and then adjusts the carrying amount to recognize its share of the other company's earnings or losses after the date of acquisition. Dividends received are deducted from the investment. We shall not deal with this method further. In this chapter we shall assume that investments in the common stock of others represent less than 20 percent of the outstanding shares.

Entry to record acquisition

When the common or preferred stocks of other corporations are acquired, they should be recorded at cost, which is the cash outlay or the fair value of the asset given in exchange. Since the stock acquired will usually be purchased from another investor through a broker, cost will

---

[2] Accounting Principles Board, "The Equity Method of Accounting for Investments in Common Stock," *APB Opinion No. 18* (New York: AICPA, March 1971).

normally consist of the price paid for the stock plus a commission to the broker. For example, assume that Brewer Corporation purchased 1,000 shares of Cowen Corporation common stock at $15 per share through a broker who charged $100 for services rendered in acquiring the stock. Brewer would record the transaction as follows:

Stock Investment	15,100	
Cash		15,100
To record purchase of 1,000 shares of Cowen common at $15 plus $100 broker's commission.		

Cash dividends on investments. The usual accounting for the receipt of dividends on stock investments is to debit Cash and credit Dividend Revenue when the cash dividend check is actually received. This accounting for dividends is acceptable for tax purposes and is widely followed by investors.

An alternative will be required when a dividend is declared in one accounting period which will not be paid until the following period. Assume that the Cowen Corporation declared a cash dividend of 20 cents per share on December 1, 1979, payable on January 15, 1980, to stockholders of record as of December 20, 1979. Under these circumstances an entry should be made either on December 20 or as an adjusting entry on December 31 as follows:

Dividends Receivable	200	
Dividend Revenue		200
To record dividend of 20 cents per share on Cowen common stock due January 15, 1980.		

When the dividend is collected on January 15, the entry would be a debit to Cash and a credit to the Dividends Receivable account. In this manner the dividend is recorded as revenue in the period in which it is earned.

Stock dividends and stock splits. A stock dividend consists of the distribution by a corporation of additional shares of its stock to its stockholders. Usually the distribution consists of additional common stock to common stockholders. Such a distribution is not considered to be a revenue-producing transaction to the holders of the stock. A stock dividend is viewed simply as having the effect of dividing the stockholders' equity into a larger number of smaller pieces. It simply increases the number of shares a stockholder holds, but it does not change his or her percentage of ownership of the outstanding shares.

Thus, the accounting for stock dividends consists only of a notation in the accounts of the number of shares received and a change in the average per share cost of the shares held. For example, if 100 shares of A Company common stock are held, which cost $22 per share, and the A Company distributes a 10 percent stock dividend, the number of shares held is increased to 110 and the cost per share is now $20 ($2,200 ÷ 110 shares = $20 per share).

Similarly, when a corporation splits its stock, the only accounting entry required is a notation indicating the receipt of the additional shares. If Smith Company owned 1,000 shares of Jones Company common stock and Jones Company split its stock on a two-for-one basis, Smith would own 2,000 shares after the split and the cost per share would be halved.

Sale of stock investments. When stock holdings are sold, the gain or loss on the sale is the difference between the net proceeds received and the carrying value of the shares sold.[3] Assume, for example, that 100 shares of Thacker Company common stock are sold for $75 per share. The broker deducted his or her commission and other taxes and charges of $62 prior to making remittance to the seller. If the seller's cost were $5,000, the required entry is:

Cash..	7,438	
Stock Investments		5,000
Gain on Sale of Investments............................		2,438

The realized gain on sale of investments is shown in the earnings statement regardless of whether the securities were classified as current or noncurrent equity securities.

A company can also invest in the bonds of others. If these are marketable securities and will be converted into cash within the normal operating cycle, they should be carried at cost (unless there is a dramatic and seemingly permanent decline in their market value). Interest earned on these obligations will result in a credit to Interest Revenue. Any difference between carrying value and proceeds received upon sale should be recognized as a gain or loss. Chapter 9 deals extensively with bond investments as long-term assets. Much of the discussion in that chapter relates to bonds as temporary investments also. Thus, the discussion here has been kept to a minimum.

Decide whether each of the following statements is correct or incorrect.

1. If securities can be sold easily, they should be reported as current assets.
2. Marketable equity securities should be reported at the lower of cost or market each time financial statements are prepared.
3. If a company holds more than 20 percent of the outstanding shares of a company, it might report this investment at an amount greater than cost.
4. Cash dividends received result in dividend revenue, but stock dividends received do not.

Now turn to Answer Frame 9[6] on page 260 to check your answers.

---

[3] FASB, *Statement No. 12*, p. 5.

1. Incorrect. Only if they will be converted into cash within the normal operating cycle of the business should they be shown as marketable securities among current assets. If they will not be converted within that time, they should be reported among noncurrent assets in the investments section. The primary classification criterion is the intent of management.

2. Correct. The FASB in its *Statement No. 12* requires that marketable equity securities be carried at the lower of total cost or total market. This applies to all marketable equity securities classified as current taken as a group and to all equity securities classified as noncurrent taken as a group.

3. Correct. In situations where a company owns between 20 and 50 percent of the outstanding common shares, it is required by *APB Opinion No. 18* to use the equity method of accounting for its investment. If the company in which it has invested has been profitable since acquisition, the investment would be carried at an amount greater than cost (assuming dividends have not exceeded earnings during this period). If the investment has been unprofitable, or if dividends received have exceeded a proportionate share of earnings, it would be carried at less than cost.

4. Correct. Cash dividends received are viewed as revenue, but stock dividends are not. A stock dividend simply increases the number of shares a stockholder holds but does not change his or her percentage of ownership of the outstanding shares.

If you missed any of the above, reread Frame 9⁶ before beginning the Summary below.

Summary *chapter* 6

Information on cash position and cash movement supplied by the accounting system is used by management in fulfilling its cash management function and by outsiders in appraising the overall financial position of a business firm.

Adequate control over receipts and disbursements is necessary to protect cash. Defalcations are quite numerous and involve stealing cash when it is flowing in or out of the business.

The balance on the monthly statement presented by the bank showing the activity in a checking account will usually differ from the balance shown in the ledger account. The usual causes of this difference are outstanding checks, deposits in transit, and bank service charges which have not been recorded by the depositor. A statement should be prepared reconciling these differences. An entry is often needed to record items uncovered in reconciling the two amounts.

A company operating in many widely scattered locations may establish transfer accounts in local banks which require the immediate forwarding by the bank of any funds in excess of a stated amount to a central bank. There the funds can be quickly invested if not needed for other purposes.

Control over payroll checks is often established, at least in part, through use of a separate payroll checking account. The location of errors is also facilitated if the possible thousands of payroll checks are not intermingled with other checks in one account.

A company may have cash in excess of that needed for current operations. It may decide to invest these funds in temporary short-term securities such as certificates of deposit, 91-day Treasury bills, Treasury tax anticipation notes, commercial paper of other companies, or other government securities. Each of these sources of investment has certain characteristics regarding safety, liquidity, and rate of return which may make it more attractive than others in a given situation.

Stock investments are rarely purchased as temporary investments but rather are purchased for long-term reasons of affiliation, control, or to secure revenue over a period of years. Such securities are to be carried at the lower of total cost or total market. Cash dividends, stock dividends, and stock splits may be received on these investments.

Appendix 6A covers the topic of petty cash. Appendix 6B discusses the use of a voucher system which may be used to provide close control over cash disbursements.

To complete your review of this chapter study the terms in the Glossary on page 270. Then go on to the Student Review Quiz on page 272 for a self-administered test of your comprehension of the material in this chapter.

APPENDIX 6A: PETTY CASH FUNDS

While it is desirable that all disbursements be made by check, most concerns find it convenient to make certain small payments in cash. Disbursements for delivery charges, postage stamps, taxi fares, employees' supper money when working overtime, and other small items usually require a small amount of cash on hand.

To permit such small disbursements to be made in cash and at the same time to maintain adequate control over cash disbursements, firms often establish a petty cash fund of some round dollar amount such as $50 or $100. One individual in the company is placed in charge of the fund and is responsible for the entire sum.

Imprest petty cash funds

A petty cash fund could be established on a basis whereby an entry would be made to record every change in the fund. Thus, when the fund is established, an entry could be made debiting Petty Cash and crediting Cash. If cash is expended for delivery charges, an entry could be made

261

debiting Transportation-In (or Transportation-Out, as the case may be) and crediting Petty Cash. If maintained on this basis, the records of the company would soon be cluttered with numerous entries for small amounts. For this reason, petty cash funds are almost always maintained on an *imprest* basis. This means that only periodically is the petty cash fund reimbursed out of general cash. At the same time, the expenses are recorded. All future discussion will assume the establishment and maintenance of petty cash funds on this basis.

When the petty cash fund is established, a check is prepared, payable to the order of the person who is to be the petty cash cashier, and an entry is made as follows:

```
Petty Cash Fund ...................................................................... 100
      Cash.................................................................................... 100
      To record drawing a check to establish a petty cash fund of $100.
```

The fund should be sufficiently large to care for petty cash disbursements for a reasonable period of time, for example, one month. The check is cashed, and the fund now is ready for disbursements to be made from it.

A *petty cash voucher,* Illustration 6.3, should be prepared for each

Illustration 6.3   Petty cash voucher

PETTY CASH VOUCHER NO. 359		
To Local Cartage, Inc.	Date June 29, 1979	
EXPLANATION	ACCT. NO.	AMOUNT
Freight on parts	27	2 27
APPROVED BY *a. E. L.*	RECEIVED PAYMENT *Ken Black*	

disbursement from the petty cash fund. If the person receiving the cash can furnish an invoice, it should be stapled to the petty cash voucher. The petty cash cashier at all times is accountable for cash and petty cash vouchers totaling to the amount of the fund.

Replenishing the fund

Whenever the balance in the petty cash fund is at a relatively low level, it is replenished. A check is drawn, payable to the cashier of the fund, for the amount of the vouchers. It is charged to the various expense accounts (and occasionally other accounts) indicated by the summarization previously made.

To illustrate, assume that when summarized, the vouchers in a given fund show petty cash fund expenditures of $22.75 chargeable to Transportation-In, $50.80 for postage stamps, and $19.05 chargeable to Delivery Expense, for a total of $92.60. A check in that amount would be drawn, payable to the cashier of the fund, and would be charged to the accounts indicated above. The entry would read:

Transportation-In	22.75	
Stamps and Stationery	50.80	
Delivery Expense	19.05	
Cash		92.60
To record check drawn to replenish petty cash fund.		

After the check for $92.60 has been endorsed and cashed, the amount of cash in the fund is at the established amount, $100.

After the petty cash vouchers have been audited (by someone other than the custodian of the fund) and approved and the fund replenished, the vouchers should be stamped or mutilated so that they cannot be reused.

At the end of the accounting period (assume it is December 31) it is necessary to bring all expenses for the period into the accounts for earnings determination purposes and for proper statement of financial position reporting. This must be done even though the fund is not replenished at that time. Therefore, at the end of the year, if the fund contains $80 of cash and vouchers totaling $20, the following entry should be made:

Dec. 31	Various expense accounts	20	
	Petty Cash		20

The amount of the entry is for the total of the expense vouchers in the petty cash fund. The $80 petty cash balance would be reported as part of the total representing all of the company's cash balances.

Assuming that $10 additional expenditures have been paid out of the petty cash fund prior to January 10, the journal entry to record its replenishment on that date would read as follows:

Jan. 10	Various expense accounts	10	
	Petty Cash	20	
	Cash		30

APPENDIX 6B: THE VOUCHER SYSTEM

In very small companies where the owner has an intimate knowledge of all transactions and where he or she personally signs all checks, there need be no great concern over the proper handling of cash disbursements. In larger companies where the owners or top-management people have no direct part in the payment process, close control over this function should be provided via a formalized system of internal control. While the owner who has an intimate knowledge of all transactions might use special journals to reduce journalizing and posting time, he or she would not have need for the formalized system of internal control over disbursements (called a voucher system) presented here. The voucher system utilizes two special journals which have not yet been described.

With a voucher system, internal control over cash disbursements is achieved in the following way: each transaction that will involve the payment of cash is entered on a voucher and recorded in a voucher register some time before payment is made. A voucher is a form with spaces provided for data concerning the liability being set up (such as invoice number, invoice date, creditor's name and address, description of the goods or services, terms of payment, and amount due). It also has spaces for signatures of those approving the obligation for payment. The voucher usually forms a "jacket" for the invoice and other supporting documents. Each voucher goes through a rigorous process of examination and eventual approval or disapproval. By the time a voucher is approved for payment, one can be quite certain that the liability for payment is legitimate, since various persons have attested to the propriety and accuracy of the claim.

The voucher system eliminates entirely the formal subsidiary accounts payable ledger. The file of unpaid vouchers serves as the subsidiary accounts payable ledger.

When the voucher system is used, the term "vouchers payable" is usually substituted for the term "accounts payable" in the accounts. When financial statements are prepared, however, the more conventional term accounts payable is preferable.

The system of internal control is enhanced by a separation of duties. For instance, the person or persons who authorize the incurrence of liabilities should not also prepare and distribute checks. The receipt of assets or services resulting from a liability incurrence must be acknowledged and approved by (*a*) the receiving department, or (*b*) others who do not have authority to prepare and distribute checks. The persons who have authority to sign checks should do so only when approved vouchers authorizing each check are presented. The possibilities of errors and of recording unauthorized liabilities or cash disbursements are therefore minimized.

Types of vouchers

The voucher system of recording liabilities that will result in cash disbursements is so named because every transaction involving the acquisition of productive factors needed to operate a business will result in the preparation of a voucher. Vouchers usually are numbered consecutively.

In a broad sense a voucher is any written document that serves as a receipt or as evidence of authority to act. In a narrow sense—as applied to the voucher system—a voucher is a form that substantiates a liability and thus serves as the basis for an accounting entry.

One form of voucher is presented in Illustration 6.4. Invoices and receiving tickets are the basis for preparing vouchers. It is assumed in Illustration 6.4 that a separate voucher is prepared for each invoice received from each creditor.

Illustration 6.4   A voucher

ATWELL   SUPPLY   COMPANY
Atwell   Plaza
Atwell,   Texas   78712

VOUCHER

VOUCHER NO. ___141___
OUR P.O. NO. ___2514___
VENDOR'S INVOICE ___416___
PAID BY CHECK NO. ___587___
DATE PAID ___7/18/79___

Payable To: Gregory Corporation
48 Cadillac Square
Detroit, Michigan 48226

DATE		ACCT. NO.	DESCRIPTION	QUANTITY	UNIT PRICE	TOTAL
July	14	126	X-16 Transistors	100	$2.00	$200.00
			TOTAL			$200.00
			DISCOUNT	2%		4.00
			NET PAYABLE			$196.00

TERMS 2/10, n/30
EXPLANATIONS:

AUDITED AS TO CORRECTNESS *a.t.*	APPROVED FOR PAYMENT *L.d.W.*	ENTERED IN VOUCHER REGISTER *R.E.L*	DATE ENTERED 7/14/79

The procedures followed in this basic form of voucher system show clearly that a voucher system is a method of internal control over the *payment* of liabilities. Emphasis is placed on the time of payment rather than on the identity of the creditor. In the administration and control of cash, the primary matters are the time and the amount of the disbursement.

In some lines of business the terms of discount and of payment run from the date of the invoice. When this is the case a voucher should be prepared for each invoice, as in Illustration 6.4, and should be filed according to the date on which the discount period terminates or payment is due. Such a file is called a tickler file.

When discount and payment terms are computed from the end of the month, it is possible to modify the voucher and reduce the number of vouchers prepared and, therefore, the number of entries made in the voucher register. All invoices received from each creditor may be accumulated and listed on one voucher at the month-end, since all will probably be paid by one check. The details of the various invoices may be summarized on one voucher.

Special journals used

Voucher register. A voucher register is a multicolumn journal containing special debit columns for the accounts most frequently debited

Illustration 6.5

VOUCHER REGISTER

Line No.	Voucher Date 1979		Voucher No.	Payee	Explanation	Terms	Date Paid	Check No.	Vouchers Payable Cr. 101	General Ledger Account Name
1	May	2	223	Hanley Company	Ring binders	2/10,n/30	May 12	1350	980.00	
2		4	224	Moore Transport	Transportation, binders		5	1347	13.00	
3		6	225	White Stationery Company	Office supplies	2/10,n/30	12	1351	102.00	
4		8	226	Specialty Advertisers	Advertising		8	1348	1,200.00	
5		10	227	Blanch Company	Note and interest		10	1349	1,010.00	
6		12	228	Internal Revenue Service	Income tax withheld, April 1975		12	1352	2,200.00	
7		14	229	Swanson Company	Filler paper	2/10,n/30	26	1356	3,920.00	
8		16	230	Rizzo Company	Office desk	n/30	25	1355	640.00	
9		18	231	Warren Company	Spiral binders	2/10,n/30	28	1357	4,900.00	
10		20	232	First National Bank	Interest on mortgage note		20	1353	154.00	
11		22	233	Falcone Company	Books	n/30			10,000.00	
12		24	234	Petty cash	Reimbursement		24	1354	132.00	
13		26	235	Swanson Company	Discount lost (No. 229).		26	1356	80.00	
14		28	236	Celoron Company	Drawing sets	2/20,n/30			9,800.00	
15		31	237	Payroll account	Salaries and wages		31	1358	21,600.00	F.I.C.A. Tax Liability
16										Federal Income Tax Withheld
									56,731.00	

when a liability is incurred. Stated in a different manner, a voucher register contains a chronological and serial record of all vouchers prepared. It includes a brief description of the transactions and indicates the accounts involved. One line is allotted to each voucher.

A special Vouchers Payable Cr. column in the voucher register summarizes all vouchers approved. The total of the Vouchers Payable column in the voucher register is posted to the liability controlling account, Vouchers Payable, at the end of each month. The two items appearing in the General Ledger Accounts Cr. column would be posted to the accounts indicated as credits. The column totals of the next seven columns would be posted to the indicated accounts as debits. The three items in the General Ledger Accounts Dr. column would be posted to the indicated accounts as debits.

Illustration 6.5 is presented to show the entry of vouchers in the

Page No. *15*
Month *May 1979*

Accounts Cr.			Dis- counts Lost Dr. 122	Mer- chandise Purchases Dr. 131	Transpor- tation In Dr. 144	Salaries and Wages Dr. 158	Office Expense Dr. 175	Advertising Expense Dr. 262	Interest Expense Dr. 306	General Ledger Accounts Dr.			
Acct. No.	Amount Cr.	✔								Account Name	Acct. No.	Amount Dr.	✔
				980.00									
					13.00								
							102.00						
								1,200.00					
									10.00	Notes Payable	103	1,000.00	
										Federal Income Tax Withheld	108	2,200.00	
				3,920.00									
										Office Equipment	42	640.00	
				4,860.00	40.00								
									154.00				
				10,000.00									
					31.88		60.12	40.00					
			80.00										
				9,800.00									
107	400.00					24,000.00							
108	2,000.00												
	2,400.00		80.00	29,560.00	84.88	24,000.00	162.12	1,240.00	164.00			3,840.00	

special journal for vouchers payable in cases where one voucher is prepared for each invoice. As each voucher is prepared and entered in the voucher register (Illustration 6.5), the voucher is placed in the *unpaid voucher file*. As each is paid, the voucher (or a duplicate copy of it) is transferred to the *paid voucher file*. A notation of the payment is made in the Date Paid and Check Number columns of the voucher register as illustrated.

Check register. A check register (or check record) is a special journal containing a chronological and serial record of all checks issued. One line is allotted to each check. An efficient system of internal control over cash requires that all disbursements be made by check. No check may be issued unless it is authorized by an approved voucher; therefore, the interrelationship of the voucher register and the check register is established. Rigorous compliance enhances the close control over cash disbursements.

A special debit column in the check register summarizes all vouchers paid. After the total of this column is posted as a debit to the Vouchers Payable controlling account in the general ledger, the balance of the account should equal the total of the vouchers in the unpaid vouchers file. The voucher register and the check register are the two primary journals in a voucher system from which postings are made to the Vouchers Payable controlling account. And when a voucher system is employed, these two registers replace the more traditional purchases and cash disbursements journals.

The check register, Illustration 6.6, sets forth the entry and procedure when a check is issued in payment of each voucher. A check register usually has only one money column. The total of this column is posted as a debit to Vouchers Payable and a credit to Cash. If invoices are entered gross (before discount deductions) in the voucher register, a Purchase Discounts Cr. column should also be provided in the check register. In this latter instance, separate columns would be necessary for the debit to Vouchers Payable and credit to Cash, since the dollar amounts posted to these two accounts would be different by the amount of the discount taken.

When vouchers are prepared for the net amount of an invoice and the invoice is paid after the discount privilege period has expired, another voucher should be prepared for the amount of the discount (see line 13 in Illustration 6.5).

Files maintained in a voucher system

Unpaid and paid voucher files. As stated earlier, two files are always maintained when a voucher system is used: the *unpaid voucher file*, referred to earlier as the tickler file, and the *paid voucher file*.

The unpaid voucher file contains all vouchers that have been prepared and approved as proper liabilities but which have not yet been paid. When credit terms run from the invoice date, they are filed according to their due dates. When credit terms run from the end of the month,

Illustration 6.6

						Vouchers Payable Dr., Cash Cr.
		CHECK REGISTER			Page No. *24*	
					Month *May, 1979*	
Line No.	Date 1979		Payee	Voucher No.	Check No.	Vouchers Payable Dr., Cash Cr.
1	May	5	Moore Transport	244	1347	13.00
2		8	Specialty Advertisers	226	1348	1,200.00
3		10	Blanch Company	227	1349	1,010.00
4		12	Hanley Company	223	1350	980.00
5		12	White Stationery Company	225	1351	102.00
6		12	Internal Revenue Service	228	1352	2,200.00
7		20	First National Bank	232	1353	154.00
8		24	Petty Cash	234	1354	132.00
9		25	Rizzo Company	230	1355	640.00
10		26	Swanson Company	235} 229}	1356	4,000.00
11		28	Warren Company	231	1357	4,900.00
12		31	Payroll account	237	1358	21,600.00
						36,931.00

the invoices of each creditor are grouped and included in one voucher. The vouchers are then arranged by due date. It is important that they are carefully filed, since if one gets out of order an allowable discount may be missed.

The paid voucher file contains all vouchers which have been paid. They are filed by their voucher numbers in numerical order. Filed in this manner, they constitute a permanent and convenient reference for anyone desiring to check the details of previous cash disbursements.

When a voucher system is in use, the unpaid voucher file serves as (or takes the place of) the subsidiary accounts payable ledger. But when credit terms run from the invoice date, so that invoices are not grouped by creditor, it does not provide the information on total amounts owed to particular creditors quickly and conveniently. This information may be obtained by regrouping the vouchers by creditor, but this can often be cumbersome. Sometimes, therefore, it is useful to keep duplicate copies of the invoices filed alphabetically.

Procedure for preparing a voucher

Since the voucher system is a method of recording liabilities that will result in cash disbursements, the preparation of a voucher begins with

269

the receipt of an invoice from a creditor, or with approved evidence that a liability has been incurred and cash will be disbursed. The procedure followed from that point is typically as follows. Basic data such as the invoice number, invoice date, creditor's name and address, description of the goods or services, terms of payment, and amount due are entered on the voucher from the invoice. The invoice, voucher, and receiving report are sent to the persons responsible for verifying the correctness of the description of the goods as to quantity and quality, the dollar amounts, and other details. Each of these persons initials the voucher when he or she is satisfied as to its correctness. When the voucher and accompanying documents are received by the accounting department, a notation is made on the voucher as to the proper accounts to be debited and credited. After a final review by an authorized person, the proper entry is made in the voucher register and the voucher is filed in the unpaid voucher file.

Under the voucher system an invoice or other business document is *not* the basis for making a journal entry; rather, it is the basis for preparing a voucher. The voucher is the basis for making the journal entry in the voucher register. All vouchers are entered serially in the voucher register.

Procedure for paying a voucher

When the voucher comes due for payment, it is removed from the unpaid voucher file. A check is prepared for the amount payable. The check, voucher, and supporting documents are then typically sent to the treasurer. The treasurer (or a representative) examines all of the documents. If they are found in order, the treasurer initials the voucher (to show that final approval has been given) and signs the check. The treasurer then mails the check, and usually a remittance advice showing the details of payment, to the creditor. The voucher is returned to the accounting department.

On receipt of the voucher the accounting department makes an entry in the check register showing the date paid, check number, voucher number, and amount paid. The date paid and check number are also inserted in the voucher register and on the voucher itself. The voucher is then filed in the paid voucher file.

Glossary *chapter* 6

Bank reconciliation statement — a statement which shows the items and amounts which cause a bank's record of a depositor's account balance to differ from the depositor's record.

Bank service charges — amounts deducted by a bank from a depositor's account as payment for services rendered.

Bank statement — a statement issued (usually monthly) by a bank describing the activities in a depositor's checking account.

Certified check – a regular check drawn by a depositor and taken to his or her bank for certification. The check is deducted from the depositor's balance immediately and becomes a liability of the bank. Thus, it will be accepted without question.

Checking account – a balance maintained with a bank subject to withdrawal on demand; a checking account balance.

Check register – a special journal containing a chronological and serial record of all checks issued.

Commercial paper – short-term debt issued by other companies.

Deposit in transit – cash receipts of a depositor recorded as receipts in one month but recorded as a deposit by the bank in a succeeding month.

Deposit ticket – a document showing the name and number of the account into which the deposit is made, the date, and the items comprising the deposit.

Dividends – amounts paid to owners of the shares of stock of a corporation. These are usually paid in cash (called cash dividends) or in additional shares of stock (called stock dividends).

Marketable securities (short term) – securities which can and will be converted into cash within one year or one current operating cycle, whichever is longer. Included among these securities are certificates of deposit, 91-day Treasury bills, Treasury tax anticipation notes, commercial paper of other companies, and other governmental securities.

Money order – a written promise on the part of the U.S. postal system or an express company that it will pay a specified sum of money to a designated party upon demand.

Outstanding checks – checks issued by a depositor which have not yet been paid by the bank upon which drawn.

Paid voucher file – a permanent file where vouchers which have been paid are filed in numerical sequence.

Petty cash fund – a usually nominal sum of money established as a separate fund from which minor cash disbursements for valid business purposes are to be made. When established on an *imprest* basis, the cash in the fund plus the vouchers covering disbursements must always equal the balance at which the fund was established and at which it is carried in the ledger accounts.

Remittance advice – a form attached to a check informing the payee why the drawer of the check is making this payment.

Savings accounts – time deposit accounts with commercial banks and savings and loan institutions which earn interest on the balance.

Stock investments – purchases of stock securities issued by other companies.

Stock split – a procedure by which the owner of stock of a corporation receives some multiple of the number of shares he or she currently holds in place of the original shares. For instance, Mr. X might receive 2,000 shares of Corporation B's shares in place of the 1,000 shares he formerly held.

Temporary investments – see Marketable securities (short term).

Transfer bank account – a bank account controlled by special instructions which require the bank to forward immediately any funds in excess of a stated amount to a central bank.

Unpaid voucher file – serves as a subsidiary accounts payable ledger under a voucher system; unpaid vouchers are filed according to their due dates.

Voucher – a form with spaces provided for data concerning the liability being recorded (such as invoice number, invoice date, creditor's name and address, terms, description of the goods or services, and amount due); also has spaces for approval signatures, the date of the check used for payment, and the check number.

Voucher register – a special journal in which prenumbered vouchers are recorded in numerical sequence. In addition to a credit column for Vouchers Payable, it normally has various columns for debits such as Merchandise Purchases, Salaries, and Transportation-In. See Illustration 6.5.

Vouchers Payable – an account title often substituted for Accounts Payable in the ledger when a voucher system is in use.

Voucher system – a procedure used to ensure tight internal control over all cash disbursements.

Continue with the Student Review Quiz below as a self-administered test of your understanding of the material presented in this chapter.

Student review quiz *chapter* 6

To develop a permanent record of your responses, you may write them on the answer sheet provided in the *Work Papers* or on a separate sheet of paper.

1 Which of the following statements is false?

a Effective cash management includes safeguarding cash from loss.

b Effective cash management embraces supplying sufficient cash to prevent disruptions of normal operations due to a cash shortage.

c Stockholders need a more detailed classification of cash than does top management.

d Management seeks to avoid the accumulation of excessive amounts of idle cash because such cash produces no earnings.

e The establishment of effective controls over petty cash is a part of the plan of effective cash management.

2 Which of the following items is *not* classifiable as cash in the current asset section of the statement of financial position?

a Undeposited checks.

b Savings accounts.

c Time certificates of deposit.

d Demand certificates of deposit.

e None of the above would be excluded.

3 Which of the following are desirable procedures to follow in the management and control of cash?

a The person who authorizes payment of invoices should not be the one who signs the checks.

b The cashier should not record the cash receipts in the customers' accounts.

c The function of receiving cash should be separated from the function of disbursing cash.

d All checks should be prenumbered consecutively.

e All of the above.

4 The bank reconciliation statement—

a Has as its basic purpose the disclosing of errors made by the bank in accounting for the depositor's funds.

b Is prepared monthly by the bank for each of its depositors.

c Begins with the balance per the bank statement and the balance per the ledger for cash and reconciles both balances with the adjusted ledger balance.

d Need not be prepared when a daily cash position statement is prepared.

e Serves no useful purpose in the system of internal control over cash.

5 Which of the following items must be deducted from the bank statement balance in preparing a bank reconciliation statement which ends with adjusted cash balance?

a Bank service charges.

b Outstanding checks.

c Checks returned marked "not sufficient funds."

d Deposits in transit.

e Notes collected by the bank for the depositor.

f None of the above.

6 Given the following information for N. Parkinson & Company, determine which of the journal entries shown is necessary to adjust the Cash account balance.

Balance per bank statement, October 31, 1979......................	$22,220
Balance per Cash account in ledger, October 31, 1979............	13,993
Outstanding checks at October 31, 1979.................................	13,000
Deposit in transit dated September 30, 1979.......................	1,525
Deposit in transit dated October 31, 1979.................................	3,670
Bank service charges for October...................................	3
Check from a customer returned by bank marked N.S.F..............	1,100

a	Accounts Receivable.....	1,100	
	Cash in Bank.........		1,100
b	Accounts Receivable.....	1,100	
	Bank Service Charges ...	3	
	Cash in Bank.........		1,103
c	Cash in Bank..............	3,670	
	Accounts Receivable		3,670
d	Cash in Bank..............	1,103	
	Accounts Receivable		1,100
	Bank Service Charges..............		3

e None of the above

7 The accountant for the Anselman Company was able to prepare the bank reconciliation statement for August 31, 1979, using the unadjusted ledger balance for cash and the following information:

Deposit in transit........................	$1,200
Balance per bank statement.............	2,750
Bank service charges......................	5
Checks outstanding........................	1,625
N.S.F. check returned....................	500
Deposit of $550 recorded by company as $505........................	45

What must have been the unadjusted balance in the Cash account in the ledger?
a $2,325.
b $2,875.
c $2,830.
d $3,630.
e None of the above.

8 Which of the following statements is false?
a A certified check is a liability of the bank certifying it.
b A certified check will be accepted by many persons who would not otherwise accept a personal check.
c A certified check is one drawn by a bank upon itself.
d A certified check which has not been returned with the canceled checks at the end of the month need not be included in the outstanding checks.

9 Which one of the following temporary investments could not result in Interest Revenue being credited?
a Savings account in a commercial bank.
b Ninety-one-day Treasury bills.
c Andrews Company capital stock.
d Another company's commercial paper.
e Certificates of deposit.

10 Which of the following statements regarding temporary investments is false?
a Savings accounts are insured against loss up to a certain amount by the federal government.
b Long-term commercial paper may be held by a company as a short-term marketable security.
c Treasury tax anticipation notes are purchased at a discount and may be used to pay corporate income taxes.
d There is little or no risk of loss when long-term commercial paper is held

for short-term purposes, since one can always wait and realize the maturity value.
e Marketable equity securities must be carried at lower of total cost or total market.

11 On August 8, Sugar Candy Company acquired 300 shares of Standard Manufacturing $80 par value capital stock at $98 per share plus a brokerage commission of $700. The proper entry to record this transaction is:

a Investment in Stock—
  Standard Mfg......... 30,100
    Cash 30,100

b Investment in Stock—
  Standard Mfg......... 29,400
  Stock Acquisition
  Expense................ 700
    Cash 30,100

c Investment in Stock—
  Standard Mfg......... 24,000
  Premium on Stock of
  Standard Mfg......... 5,400
  Stock Acquisition
  Expense................ 700
    Cash 30,100

d Investment in Stock—
  Standard Mfg......... 24,000
  Premium on Stock of
  Standard Mfg......... 6,100
    Cash 30,100

e Investment in Stock—
  Standard Mfg......... 24,700
  Premium on Stock of
  Standard Mfg......... 5,400
    Cash 30,100

12 Jefferson Plywood Company holds 500 shares of the capital stock of United Electric Company. On December 1, 1979, United declared a cash dividend of $3 per share and a stock dividend of 10 percent, both payable on January 15, 1980, to stockholders of record on December 27, 1979. At the date of declaration, the stock of United was selling in the market at $60 per share. Jefferson Plywood Company must make which of the following entries before closing the books for 1979 to reflect these dividends?

a No entry required.
b Cash.......................... 1,500
    Dividend Revenue... 1,500

273

c Cash........................... 1,500
    Dividend Revenue...   1,500

  Stock Investments 3,000
    Dividend Revenue...   3,000

d Dividends Receivable ... 1,500
    Dividend Revenue...   1,500

e Dividends Receivable ... 4,500
    Dividend Revenue...   4,500

Questions 13 and 14 are based on Appendix 6A.

13 The Petty Cash account is debited —
a Only when the fund is established.
b When the fund is established and every time it is replenished.
c When the fund is established and when the size of the fund is increased.
d When the fund is established and when the size of the fund is decreased.
e When the fund is established, replenished, or increased in size.

14 J. F. Knauf Company employs an imprest petty cash fund in the amount of $100. On August 14, a count of the fund discloses the following:

Voucher for postage stamps.................	$18
Vouchers for transportation-in	36
Vouchers for sales returns...................	23
Currency.......................................	11
Coins..	9
Total	$97

The correct entry to record replenishing the fund is:

a Postage Expense................... 18
  Transportation-In.................. 36
  Sales Returns and Allow-
    ances 23
      Accounts Payable   77

b Postage Expense................... 18
  Transportation-In.................. 36
  Sales Returns and Allow-
    ances 23
  Cash Short and Over............. 3
      Cash in Bank   80

c Petty Cash.......................... 80
      Cash in Bank   80

d Postage Expense................... 18
  Transportation-In.................. 36
  Sales Returns and Allow-
    ances 23
      Cash Short and Over....... 3
      Cash in Bank 74

e Postage Expense................... 18
  Transportation-In.................. 36
  Sales Returns and Allow-
    ances 23
      Cash in Bank 77

Questions 15–18 are based on Appendix 6B.

15 A voucher system is used in connection with transactions that involve only —
a The receipt of cash.
b The payment of cash.
c The purchase and sale of merchandise.
d Revenue and expense.
e Bonds and capital stock.

16 Which of the following statements is not correct? A file of unpaid vouchers —
a May be used to replace the accounts payable subsidiary ledger.
b Is controlled by the Vouchers Payable account in the general ledger.
c Shows during the year the total amount of all recorded outstanding liabilities for goods and services.
d Shows only the total amount of outstanding liabilities for merchandise purchased.
e Frequently shows the net discounted amounts due on the individual invoices payable.

17 The voucher is prepared and filed in the unpaid voucher file —
a As soon as the goods are requisitioned.
b As soon as the purchase order is sent out.
c As soon as the invoice is received.
d After the receipt of the materials has been verified by the receiving department and the prices and extensions on the invoice have been verified.
e When payment is made.

18 Use of the Discounts Lost account in a voucher system —
a Helps in implementing the principle of management by exception.
b Requires the processing of a second separate voucher each time a payment is not made in time to take advantage of the cash discount.
c Shows the same information as the Purchase Discounts account would show.
d Does all of the above.
e Does (a) and (b).

Now check your answers with the correct answers and explanations on page 717.

Questions *chapter* 6

1 What are the three objectives sought in effective cash management?

2 Cite four essential features in a system of internal control over cash receipts.

3 The bookkeeper of a given company was stealing remittances received from customers in payment of their accounts. To cover the theft, the bookkeeper made out false credit memoranda indicating returns and allowances made by or granted to the customers. What feature of a system of internal control, if operative, would have prevented this defalcation?

4 Cite six essential features in a system of internal control over cash disbursements.

5 The difference between a company's Cash ledger account balance and the balance in the bank statement is usually a matter of timing. Do you agree or disagree? Why?

6 Indicate the manner in which a payroll bank account is operated.

7 Why might a company's management wish to determine the cash position daily?

8 Explain how the use of transfer bank accounts can bring about effective cash management.

9 Discuss the alternatives a company has to leaving temporarily idle cash in a checking account.

10 If certificates of deposit generally pay a higher rate of interest than deposit-type accounts, why does anyone leave his money in a savings account?

11 What risk is there in making a temporary investment in marketable securities, such as commercial paper, which matures in the distant future (over one year from date of purchase)?

12 Explain the main problem encountered in classifying marketable securities in the statement of financial position.

13 The December 31, 1979, statement of financial position of the BMI Corporation shows, under a section heading entitled "investments and advances," U.S. government securities (at cost less amortized premium) in the amount of $100,780. What might be the reason for classifying these securities as "investments" rather than as "current assets"?

14 Describe the valuation used for marketable equity securities.

15 Explain briefly the accounting for stock dividends and stock splits from the investor's point of view.

16 (based on Appendix 6A) Indicate the method of operation of and the advantages obtained through the use of an imprest petty cash fund. Be sure to indicate exactly how control is effected through the use of the imprest system.

(Questions 17 and 18 are based on Appendix 6B).

17 What can be accomplished with a voucher system that is not accomplished through the use of a purchases journal and cash disbursements journal?

18 What should the relationship be between the balance in the Vouchers Payable account, the "open" items in the voucher register, and the total of all vouchers in the unpaid voucher file?

Exercises *chapter* 6

1 The Baker Company's Cash account balance was $70,175 at the end of August. The bank statement showed a balance of $68,600 for the same date. Checks outstanding totaled $21,000, and deposits in transit totaled $30,500. If these are the only pertinent data available to you, what was the correct amount of cash against which the Baker Company could have written checks as of the end of August?

2 From the following data prepare a bank reconciliation statement and determine the correct available cash balance for the Sikes Company as of October 31, 1979:

Balance per bank statement,
October 31, 1979.................... $4,658
Ledger account balance 3,676
Note collected by bank not
yet entered in ledger................. 1,000
Bank charges not yet entered
by Sikes Company.................. 6
Deposit in transit........................... 560
Outstanding checks:
No. 327 128
No. 328 96
No. 329 240
No. 331 84

3 From the following information for the Clerk Company:

a Prepare a bank reconciliation statement as of September 30, 1979.

b Give the necessary journal entries to correct the Cash account.

Balance per bank statement,
September 30, 1979.................. $16,300
Ledger account balance as of
September 30, 1979.................... 14,650
Note collected by bank 1,000
Bank charges............................... 10
Deposits in transit........................ 924
N.S.F. check deposited and
returned 84
Check of Clark Company
deducted in error 50
Outstanding checks 1,718

4 As of March 1 of the current year the Pate Company had outstanding checks of $15,000. During March the company issued an additional $57,000 of checks. As of March 31 the bank statement showed that $51,000 of checks had cleared the bank during the month. What is the amount of outstanding checks as of March 31?

5 The Dexter Company's bank statement as of August 31, 1979, shows total deposits into the company's account of $25,670 and a total of 14 deposits. On July 31 deposits of $1,350 and $1,050 were in transit. The total cash receipts for August amounted to $26,375, and the company's records show 13 deposits made in August. What is the amount of deposits in transit at August 31?

6 On March 1, 1979, $10,000 face value, 91-day Treasury bills are acquired at $9,810. Give the entries required to show the purchase and the conversion back to cash on the maturity date, May 31.

7 Wells Company purchased 100 shares of Tinker Company stock at a total cost of $1,050 on July 1, 1979. At the end of the accounting year (December 31, 1979) the market value for these shares was $950. As of December 31, 1980, the market value had risen to $1,100. This is the only marketable equity security that Wells Company owns. The company classifies the securities as noncurrent assets. Give the entries which would be necessary at the date of purchase and at December 31, 1979, and 1980.

8 Bentley Company purchased on July 1, 1979, 100 shares of Pool Company capital stock at $47 per share plus a commission of $50. On July 15 a 10 percent stock dividend was received. Bentley received a cash dividend of 50 cents per share on August 12, 1979. On November 1 Bentley sold all of the above shares for $58 per share, less commissions and taxes of $55. Prepare entries to record all of the above in Bentley Company's accounts.

9 The Delex Company has marketable equity securities which have a market value that is $800 below their cost. Give the required entry if—

a The securities are current assets.

b The securities are noncurrent assets and the loss is considered to be temporary.

c The securities are noncurrent assets and the loss is considered to be permanent.

Exercises 10 and 11 are based on Appendix 6A.

10 On August 31, 1979, the Mark Company's petty cash fund contained:

Coin and currency $42.50
IOU from office boy 5.00
Vouchers covering expenditures for:
Postage..................................... 20.00
Taxi fares.................................. 8.50
Entertainment of a customer......... 23.00

The Petty Cash account shows a balance of $100. If financial statements are prepared for each calendar month, what journal entry is required on August 31?

11 Use the data in Exercise 10 above. If the fund were replenished on August 31, 1979, what journal entry would be required? Which of the accounts debited would not appear in the earnings statement?

Exercises 12–15 are based on Appendix 6B.

12 You are the chief accountant of the Magnuson Company. An invoice has just been received from the Arnott Company in the amount of $2,000, with terms of 2/10, n/30. List the procedures you would follow in processing this invoice up through the point of filing it in the unpaid vouchers file.

13 Refer to the situation described in Exercise 12. Assume that the time for payment of the voucher has arrived and the payment is to be made within the discount period. List the actions that would be taken if the company uses a Discounts Lost account.

14 What would be a reasonable procedure had the discount period elapsed before payment was made in Exercise 13 above?

15 List the posting steps that would be used to post the data shown in Illustration 6.5 (pages 266–267). How many numbers would actually be posted?

(6) 3-1   MARKETABLE SECURITIES   9810

      CASH   9810

5-31   CASH   10,000

     MARKETABLE SECURITIES   9810

     INTEREST REVENUE   190

(8) 7-1   STOCK INVESTMENTS   4750

      CASH   4750

7-15   NO ENTRY

8-12   CASH   55

      DIVIDEND REVENUE   55

11-1   CASH   6325

     STOCK INVESTMENTS   4750

     GAIN ON SALE OF STOCK   1575
               INVESTMENTS

Problems, Series A *chapter* 6

6–1–A

The bank statement for the Wesson Company's general checking account with the First National Bank for the month ended August 12, 1979, showed an ending balance of $5,309, service charges of $10, an N.S.F. check returned of $210, and the collection of a $1,000 note plus interest of $10. Further investigation revealed that a wire transfer of $1,800 from the bank account maintained by a branch office of the company had not been recorded by the company as having been deposited in the First National Bank account. In addition, a comparison of deposits with receipts showed a deposit in transit of $2,100. Checks outstanding amounted to $1,506, while the cash ledger balance was $3,313.

Required:

a Prepare a bank reconciliation statement for the Wesson Company account for the month ended August 12, 1979.
b Prepare all necessary journal entries.

6–2–A

The following data pertain to the Mellis Company:

a. Balance per the bank statement dated June 30, 1979, is $40,760.
b. Balance of the Cash in Bank account on the company books as of June 30, 1979, is $11,980.
c. Outstanding checks as of June 30, 1979, are $20,000.
d. Bank deposit of June 30 for $3,140 was not included in the deposits per the bank statement.
e. The bank had collected a $30,000, 6 percent, 30-day note and the interest which it credited to the Mellis Company account. The bank charged the company a collection fee of $20 on the above note.
f. The bank erroneously charged the Mellis Company account for a $14,000 check of the Meliss Company. The check was found among the canceled checks returned with the bank statement.
g. Bank service charges for June, exclusive of the collection fee, amounted to $100.
h. Among the canceled checks was one for $690 given in payment of an account. The bookkeeper had recorded the check at $960 in the company records.
i. A check of Mr. Crosley, a customer, for $4,200, deposited on June 20, was returned by the bank marked N.S.F. No entry has been made to reflect the returned check on the company records.
j. A check for $1,680 of Mr. Moran, a customer, which had been deposited in the bank, was erroneously recorded by the bookkeeper as $1,860.

Required:

Prepare a bank reconciliation statement as of June 30, 1979. Also prepare any necessary adjusting journal entries.

6–3–A

The following data pertain to the Tennis Company. The reconciliation statement as of June 30, 1979, showed a deposit in transit of $1,350 and three checks outstanding:

No. 553	$ 600
No. 570	1,100
No. 571	800

During July the following checks were written and entered in the Cash account:

No. 572	$ 750	No. 578	$1,150
No. 573	825	No. 579	1,410
No. 574	1,410	No. 580	180
No. 575	635	No. 581	2,427
No. 576	1,263	No. 582	2,400
No. 577	845	No. 583	924

As of July 31, all the checks which were written, except No. 578, were mailed to the payees. Check No. 578 was kept in the vault pending receipt of a statement from the payee. Four deposits were made at the bank as follows:

July 7	$7,500
14	9,600
14	5,700
28	6,900

The bank statement, which was received on August 2, correctly included all deposits and showed a balance as of July 31 of $25,260. The following checks were returned: Nos. 570, 571, 572, 573, 574, 575, 576, 577, 580, and 581. With the paid checks there were three debit memoranda for:

a. Fee of $4 for the collection on July 30 of a $1,100 noninterest bearing note payable to the Tennis Company for which a credit memorandum was enclosed.
b. Monthly service charge of $5.
c. Payment of $750 noninterest bearing note of the Tennis Company.

The bank statement included a credit for $3,000 dated July 29. The bank telephoned the company on the morning of August 3 to explain that this credit was in error because it represented a transaction between the bank and the Tenist Company.

The balance in the Cash account on the books of the Tennis Company as of July 31 is $15,435.

Required:

Prepare a bank reconciliation statement for the Tennis Company as of July 31, 1979. Also prepare any necessary adjusting entries.

6–4–A

Burch Company's bank reconciliation statement of July 13, 1979, included the following information:

Bank balance, July 13, 1979		$22,850
Balance per books, July 13,1979....................		19,245
Outstanding checks:		
No. 423..	$ 350	
No. 425..	1,225	
No. 430..	1,400	
No. 442..	1,505	4,480
Deposit in transit		2,875

Burch Company's records show the following receipts and disbursements for the month ended August 13, 1979:

Cash receipts		Cash disbursements	
July 18.................	$2,350	Check No. 443.................	$1,750
26.................	3,500	No. 444.................	2,100
Aug. 10.................	7,000	No. 445.................	1,575
13.................	5,250	No. 446.................	1,500
		No. 447.................	1,750

The bank statement covering the month ended August 13 showed:

Balance, July 13, 1975		$20,850
Deposits (4)		15,725
		$36,575
Checks deducted (6)	$8,505	
Service charges.................................	7	8,512
Balance, August 13, 1975....................		$28,063

The checks returned by the bank were Nos. 423, 425, 442, 443, 444, and 445.

Required:

a Compute the unadjusted cash balance per books as of August 13, 1979.
b Prepare a bank reconciliation statement as of August 13, 1979.
c Prepare any necessary adjusting journal entries as of the same date.

6–5–A

The outstanding checks of the Barnes Company at November 30, 1979, are:

No. 229........................	$250.00
No. 263........................	272.25
No. 3678........................	169.75
No. 3679........................	201.00
No. 3680........................	350.50

During the month checks numbered 3681–3720 are issued and all of these checks clear the bank except Nos. 3719 and 3720 for $240.75 and $181.50, respectively. Checks No. 3678, 3679, and 3680 also clear the bank.

The bank statement on December 31 shows a balance of $5,986. Service charges amount to $5 and two checks are returned by the bank, one marked N.S.F. in the amount of $28.50 and the other marked "No account" in the amount of $500.

Mr. Salinas recently retired as the office manager–cashier–bookkeeper for the company and was replaced by Mr. Clark. Mr. Clark noted the absence of a system of internal control but was momentarily deterred from embezzling for lack of a scheme of concealment. Finally, he hit upon several schemes. The $500 check marked "No account" by the bank is the product of one scheme. Mr. Clark took cash receipts and replaced them with a check drawn upon a nonexistent account to make it appear that a customer had given the company a worthless check.

The other scheme was more subtle. He pocketed cash receipts to bring them down to an amount sufficient to enable him to prepare the following reconciliation statement:

Balance, Cash account, Dec. 31, 1979		$6,806.70	Balance per bank statement, Dec. 31, 1979			$5,986.00
			Add: Deposit in transit............			709.45
						$6,695.45
Deduct:						
Worthless check	$500.00		Deduct: Out-			
N.S.F. check............	28.50		standing			
Service charges........	5.00	533.50	checks:			
			No. 3719	$240.75		
			No. 3720...........	181.50	422.25	
Adjusted balance		$6,273.20	Adjusted balance.......			$6,273.20

Required:

a State the nature of the second scheme hit upon by Mr. Clark. How much in total does it appear he has stolen?

b Prepare a correct bank reconciliation statement as of December 31, 1979.

c Suggest procedures which would have defeated the attempts of Mr. Clark to steal funds and conceal these actions.

6–6–A

The treasurer of the Dexter Corporation prepared the following bank reconciliation statement as of April 30, 1979:

Balance per bank statement, April 30...................................		$58,795	Balance per books, April 30		$45,380
Add: Deposit in transit......................................		3,670	Less: N.S.F. check...................	$1,000	
		$62,465	Service charges	15	1,015
Deduct: Outstanding checks...........		18,100			
Adjusted balance............................		$44,365	Adjusted balance		$44,365

The bank statement for the month of May shows:

Balance, May 1, 1979		$ 58,795
Deposits		110,400
		$169,195
Checks cleared	$165,040	
Service charges..............................	35	165,075
Balance, May 31, 1979.....................		$ 4,120

The May deposits include the proceeds of a $30,000 note payable drawn by the treasurer of the Dexter Corporation payable to the bank in 60 days. The total cash receipts as shown by the Dexter Corporation records amount to $81,800, and the total checks recorded amount to $76,640. This latter total does not include one check drawn and signed by the treasurer payable to himself. The treasurer has disappeared. No record of this check appears anywhere in the company's records. Checks outstanding on May 31, 1979, total $16,700.

Required:

a Compute the corrected cash balance as of April 30.

b Compute the unadjusted cash balance as of May 31 shown by the company's records.

c Compute the amount of the undeposited receipts, if any, as of May 31.

d Compute the amount of the check drawn payable to the treasurer.

e Prepare a bank reconciliation statement as of May 31.

f Prepare any necessary adjusting entries.

g State the particular feature of a good system of internal control which is designed to prevent abstractions of funds such as illustrated here.

6-7-A

First Corporation uses an imprest payroll checking account, with a $1,000 balance. This balance is used for payroll advances and to pay employees whose services are terminated between payroll payment dates. Following are selected transactions of the First Corporation during 1979:

June 15 Payroll department determines that the payroll and payroll deductions for the first half of the month of June are:

Officers' salaries		$21,000
Office salaries		19,000
Sales salaries and commissions		31,000
Sales office salaries		15,000
		$86,000
Payroll deductions:		
Federal income taxes withheld	$11,000	
F.I.C.A. taxes withheld	2,000	
Community Fund contributions withheld	3,000	16,000
Net Payroll		$70,000

17 A check in the amount of the net payroll is drawn on the general checking account and deposited in the payroll checking account.

20 Payroll checks are issued.

24 One employee's services are terminated. The salary of this office employee for the partial period is $300, and the only deduction is for $45 of income taxes to be withheld. A payroll check is issued.

The bank statement for the payroll account shows a balance of $1,350.63. Checks outstanding are for $278.25 and $327.38.

Required:

a Prepare general journal entries to record those transactions which would be formally recorded in the records of the First Corporation.

b Determine the actual (not the book) balance in the payroll checking account at June 30. Why is it not the imprest balance of $1,000?

c Prepare a bank reconciliation statement for the payroll checking account as of June 30, 1979.

6–8–A

Walter Green was set up in business by his father, who purchased the business of an elderly acquaintance wishing to retire. One of the few changes in personnel made by Walter was to install a college classmate as the office manager–bookkeeper–cashier–sales manager.

During the course of the year, Walter found it necessary to borrow money from the bank (with his father as co-signer) because although the business seemed profitable, there seemed to be a continuous shortage of adequate cash. The investment in inventories and receivables grew substantially during the year. Finally, after a year had elapsed, Walter's father employed a certified public accountant to audit the records of Walter's business. The CPA reported that the office manager–bookkeeper–cashier–sales manager had been stealing funds and had been using a variety of schemes to cover his actions. More specifically he had:

a   Pocketed cash receipts from sales and understated the cash register readings at the end of the day or altered the copies of the sales tickets retained.
b   Abstracted checks mailed to the company in payment of accounts receivable, credited the proper accounts, and then created fictitious receivables to keep the records in balance.
c   Issued checks to fictitious suppliers and deposited them in accounts bearing these names with himself as signer of checks drawn on these accounts; the books were kept in balance by charging the purchases to the inventory account.
d   Abstracted petty cash funds by drawing false vouchers purporting to cover a variety of expenses incurred.
e   Prepared false sales returns vouchers indicating the return of cash sales to cover further thefts of cash receipts.

Required:

For each of the above items, indicate at least one feature of a good system of internal control which would have prevented the losses due to dishonesty.

6–9–A

The Bruns Company acquired on July 15, 1979, 200 shares of Reetz Company $100 par value capital stock at $97 per share plus a broker's commission of $120. On August 1, 1979, Bruns Company received a cash dividend of 60 cents per share. On November 3, 1979, it sold 100 of these shares at $105 per share less a broker's commission of $80. On December 1, 1979, the Reetz Company issued shares comprising a 100 percent stock dividend declared on its capital stock November 18.

On December 31, 1979, the end of the calendar-year accounting period, the market quotation for Reetz's common stock was $46 per share. The decline was considered to be permanent.

Required:

a   Present journal entries to record all of the above data, assuming the securities are considered temporary investments and are to be valued at the lower of cost or market.   283

b If the remaining shares are to be held for affiliation purposes—Reetz Company has become a major customer—indicate how they should be shown in the statement of financial position.

6-10-A (based on Appendix 6A)

Following are selected transactions of the Richter Company during 1979:

Mar. 1   Established a petty cash fund of $500 which will be under the control of the assistant office manager and is to be operated on an imprest basis.

Apr. 3   Fund is replenished on this date. Prior to replenishment, the fund consisted of the following:

Coin and currency	$284.58
Payroll check issued by Richter Company to part-time office boy, Joe Johnson, properly endorsed by Johnson	27.98
Petty cash vouchers indicating disbursements for—	
Postage stamps	70.00
Supper money for office employees working overtime	24.00
Office supplies	21.80
Window washing service	40.00
Flowers for wedding of employee	10.00
Flowers for hospitalized employee	10.00
Employee IOU	10.00

The employee's IOU is to be deducted from his next paycheck.

Required:

Present journal entries for the above transactions.

6-11-A (based on Appendix 6B)

The Netter Company was organized January 1 of the current year. It uses a voucher register and a check register with the same column headings as in Illustrations 6.5 and 6.6 (pages 266–69), except that there are only four debit columns headed Merchandise Purchases, Transportation-In, Discounts Lost, and General Ledger Accounts.

Required:

Enter the following approved transactions for the month of January in these registers. Total and rule the registers. Start with Voucher No. 1 and Check No. 1. Vouchers are prepared for the net amount of the invoice. For discounts lost, a new voucher is prepared for the amount of the discount.

Transactions:

Jan. 1   Received an invoice from the Modern Company in the amount of $2,400 for office equipment. Terms were 2/10, n/30, f.o.b. shipping point.

     3   Received an invoice from the Bailey Company for merchandise in the amount of $4,200. Terms were 2/10, n/30.

     5   Received an invoice from the Simpson Company for merchandise in the amount of $2,700. Terms were 2/10, n/30.

Jan. 7   Paid $360 to the Lund Advertising Service for services received in January.

     10   Paid $270 of freight charges to the James Company. Of this, $60 was applicable to the office equipment received on January 1 and the rest to merchandise received from the Bailey Company.

     14   Paid the Simpson Company the amount due.

     20   Paid the Bailey Company the correct amount due.

     31   Paid the Thomas Company the net amount of $24,210 for merchandise received today.

Problems, Series B *chapter* 6

6–1–B

The bank statement for Turner Company's account with the First National Bank for the month ended April 14, 1979, showed a balance of $10,886. On this date the company's Cash account balance was $9,527. Returned with the bank statement were (1) a debit memo for service charges of $10; (2) a debit memo for a customer's N.S.F. check of $100; and (3) a credit memo for a $2,200 wire transfer of funds on April 14 from the State Bank, the local bank used by the company's branch office. Further investigation revealed that outstanding checks amounted to $1,300, the cash receipts of April 14 of $1,621 did not appear as a deposit on the bank statement, and the canceled checks included a check for $410 (drawn by the president of the company to cover travel expenses on a recent trip) which the company has yet to record.

Required:

a   Prepare a bank reconciliation statement for the month ended April 14, 1979.

b   Prepare any necessary journal entries.

6–2–B

The following information pertains to the Harris Corporation. The June 30 bank reconciliation statement was:

	Cash account	Bank statement
Balances on June 30	$25,524.48	$25,744.48
Add: Deposit not credited by bank		371.40
Total		$26,115.88
Deduct: Outstanding checks:		
No. 724	$ 24.60	
No. 886	20.00	
No. 896	191.40	
No. 897	250.20	
No. 898	105.20	591.40
Adjusted Cash Balance, June 30	$25,524.48	$25,524.48

285

The July bank statement was as follows:

Balance on July 1		$25,744.48
Deposits during July		6,370.52 $32,115.00
Canceled checks returned:		
No. 724	$ 24.60	
No. 896	191.40	
No. 897	250.20	
No. 898	105.20	
No. 899	25.14	
No. 900	1,914.00	
No. 902	1,262.56	
No. 904	58.68 $ 3,831.78	
N.S.F. check of Manley Company..................	72.04	3,903.82
Bank Statement Balance, July 31....................		$28,211.18

The cash receipts deposited in July, including receipts of July 31, amounted to $7,904.40.
Checks written in July:

No. 899	$ 25.14
No. 900	1,915.00
No. 901	37.00
No. 902	1,262.56
No. 903	79.60
No. 904	58.68
No. 905	1,458.00
No. 906	20.00

The cash balance per the ledger on July 31 was $28,573.90.

Required:

Prepare a bank reconciliation statement and any necessary adjusting entries.

6-3-B

The following information is taken from the books and records of the Shenton Company.

Balance per ledger, July 31, 1979..	$23,242
Collections received on the last day of July and debited to "Cash in Bank" on books but not entered by bank until August	5,312
Debit memo for customer's check returned unpaid (uncollectible check is on hand but no entry for the return has been made on the books)	500
Debit memo for bank service charge for July..	15
Checks issued but not paid by bank	5,034
Credit memo for proceeds of a note receivable which was left at the bank for collection but which has not been recorded on the books as collected ($8 of this is interest revenue).......	800
Check for an account payable entered on books as $480 but issued and paid by the bank in the correct amount of $840.	
Balance per bank statement, July 31, 1979	22,889

Required:

Prepare a bank reconciliation statement and the necessary journal entries to adjust the accounts.

6–4–B

The following data for March 1979 are summarized from the accounts of Norwood, Inc. The accountant also acts as cashier.

Cash receipts		Cash disbursements	
Mar. 2........................	$1,100	Check No. 911........................	$ 884
4........................	3,200	No. 912........................	1,226
5........................	1,300	No. 913........................	1,458
11........................	2,800	No. 914........................	888
13........................	3,500	No. 915........................	1,614
14........................	4,200	No. 916........................	2,400
19........................	1,000	No. 917........................	3,800
20........................	800	No. 918........................	2,700
27........................	60	No. 919........................	750
29........................	320	No. 920........................	700

At March 1 the checks outstanding were:

No. 209.....................	$ 90
No. 792.....................	1,600
No. 796.....................	558
No. 910.....................	1,262

There were no deposits in transit. The balance of the Cash in Bank account per books was $15,350 at March 31. The bank statement for the month of March is as follows:

BANK STATEMENT

Date	Checks	Deposits	Balance
Mar. 1			17,000
3		1,100	18,100
4	884		
4	1,226		15,990
6		4,500	20,490
9	1,614		
9	888		17,988
16		10,500	28,488
19	2,400		
19	2,700		23,388
24		1,800	25,188
25	558		
25	1,262		23,368
26	3,800		
26	1,000 N.S.F.		18,568
27	1,000 D.M.		17,568
29		380	17,948
31	4 D.M.		17,944

The debit memoranda (D.M.) are for the payment of a company note and for the monthly service charge.

Required:

a Prepare a bank reconciliation statement as of March 31, 1979.
b Journalize the entry or entries necessary to correct the books.
c Comment on the company's control of cash receipts.

6-5-B

The following information pertains to the bank reconciliation statement to be prepared for the Barker Company as of May 31, 1979:

a. Balance per bank statement as of May 31, 1979, was $10,980.
b. Balance per the Barker Company's Cash account at May 31, 1979, was $11,914.
c. A late deposit on May 31 did not appear on the bank statement, $950.
d. Outstanding checks as of May 31 totaled $1,100.
e. During May the bank credited Barker Company with the proceeds, $1,510, of a note which it had collected for the company. Face of the note was $1,500.
f. Service and collection charges for the month amount to $4.
g. Comparison of the canceled checks with copies of these checks reveals that one check in the amount of $234 had been recorded in the books at $342. The check had been issued in payment of an account payable.
h. A review of the deposit slips with the bank statement showed that a deposit of $500 of Borker and Company has been credited to the Barker Company account.
i. A $60 check received from a customer, R. Perry, was returned with the bank statement marked N.S.F.
j. During May the bank paid a $3,000, 6 percent, 60-day note of the Barker Company and charged it to the company's account per instructions received. Barker Company had not recorded the payment of this note.
k. An examination of the cash receipts and the deposit tickets revealed that the bookkeeper erroneously recorded a customer's check of $324 as $432.

Required:

a Prepare a bank reconciliation statement as of May 31, 1979.
b Prepare the journal entries necessary to adjust the accounts as of May 31, 1979.

6-6-B

The bank reconciliation statement for the Minoza Corporation for April 30, 1979, was as follows:

	Cash account	Bank statement
Balance as of April 30, 1979	$ 65,252	$107,424
Deposit in transit		2,900
		$110,324
Outstanding checks		52,400
Service charges	$ 48	
Note paid on demand	7,280	7,328
Adjusted Balance on April 30, 1979	$ 57,924	$ 57,924

The bank statement for May shows:

Balance, May 1, 1979		$107,424
Deposits		141,448
		$248,872
Checks cleared	$243,800	
Service charges	60	243,860
Balance, May 31, 1979		$ 5,012

The total cash receipts for May amount to $140,836. The total checks drawn amount to $155,000. This total does not include one check drawn and signed by and payable to the treasurer of the company, who has disappeared. No record of this check appears anywhere in the company's records. Checks outstanding on May 31 total $36,600.

Required:

a Compute the balance in the Cash account as shown by the company's records, excluding the check drawn payable to the treasurer.

b Compute the amount of receipts for May not deposited, if any.

c Compute the amount of the check drawn payable to the treasurer.

d Prepare a bank reconciliation statement as of May 31, 1979.

e Prepare any required adjusting entries.

f What one procedure, if followed, might have prevented the theft of funds by the treasurer?

6-7-B

West Company employs a special checking account upon which its payroll checks are drawn. Employees are paid on the 5th and the 20th of each month the salaries earned in the preceding half-month. The following transactions occur in December:

a. A check for $1,000 is drawn and deposited in the payroll checking account to cover advances to employees and checks issued to employees whose services are terminated. The payroll checking account is to be operated on an imprest basis.

b. The payroll for the last half of November consists of the following:

Gross wages of employees		$26,200
Less: Income taxes withheld......................	$3,500	
F.I.C.A. taxes withheld	400	3,900
Net Payroll...		$22,300

c. On December 4 a check is drawn in the amount of the net payroll and deposited in the payroll checking account.

d. Payroll checks aggregating the amount of the net payroll are issued to employees.

e. A payroll check in the amount of $40 is issued to John Jackson as an advance on the wages he will be receiving on December 20.

f. The payroll for the first half of the month of December is the same as given above. The advance to John Jackson is deducted from his payroll check.

g. A general account check is drawn and deposited in the payroll account.

h. The payroll checks are issued.

Required:

Present in general journal form all entries which must be journalized in the records of the West Company as a result of the above transactions.

6-8-B

The bank statement of the Lumkin Corporation's checking account with the First National Bank shows:

Balance, June 30, 1979.................................		$24,610
Deposits...		36,400
		$61,010
Less: Checks deducted...........................	$36,000	
Service charges.............................	10	36,010
Balance, July 31, 1979		$25,000

The following additional data are available:

a. A credit memorandum included with the canceled checks returned indicates the collection of a note by the bank for the Lumkin Corporation, $2,000.

b. An N.S.F. check in the amount of $920 is returned by the bank and included in the total of checks deducted on the bank statement.

c. Deposits in transit as of July 31, $5,000, and as of June 30, $2,400.

d. Checks outstanding as of June 30, all of which cleared the bank in July, $3,400; checks outstanding as of July 31, $8,200.

e. Balance per ledger account as of July 31, $19,094.

f. Deposit of Lumpkan Corporation credited to Lumkin Corporation account by bank, $2,000.

g. Check of Lumpkan Corporation charged against Lumkin Corporation account by bank, $400.

h. Deposit of July 21 recorded by the company as $637, and by the bank at actual amount of $673. The receipts for the day were from collections on account.

Required:

a Prepare a bank reconciliation statement as of July 31, 1979, for the Lumkin Corporation.

b Determine the amount of cash receipts for the month of July shown by the Lumkin Corporation's accounts prior to adjustment.

c Determine the amount of checks drawn by Lumkin in the month of July.

d Prepare any adjusting journal entries needed at July 31, 1979.

6–9–B

Brezina Corporation purchased on July 2, 1977, 100 shares of East Company $50 par value capital stock at $80 per share, plus broker's commission of $60. A 20 percent stock dividend was received on December 15, 1978.

On July 15, 1979, a dividend of $1 per share was received. On September 15, 1979, the East Company split each of its $50 par value shares of capital stock into two $25 par value shares of capital stock.

On November 2, 1979, the Brezina Corporation sold 100 shares of East capital stock at $50, less commissions and taxes of $40.

Required:

a Present journal entries to record all of the 1979 transactions.

b In light of the above information, how would you recommend that the remaining shares of stock be classified in the December 31, 1980, statement of financial position if still held at that date?

6–10–B

On September 1, 1979, Landry Company purchased the following securities as long-term investments:

a. One thousand shares of Hi-Flyer Company capital stock at $61 plus broker's commission of $400.

b. Five hundred shares of Turkey Company capital stock at $98 plus broker's commission of $350.

Cash dividends of $1.25 per share on the Hi-Flyer capital stock and $1 per share on the Turkey capital stock were received on December 7 and December 10, respectively.

Market prices at December 31, 1979, are Hi-Flyer stock, $65; and Turkey stock, $91.

Required:

a Prepare journal entries to record the above transactions.

b Prepare the necessary adjusting entry(ies) at December 31, 1979, to adjust the carrying values assuming that market price changes are assumed to be permanent.

c Explain what factor(s) may have caused the price of the capital stock to go up in one case and down in the other.

6–11–B (based on Appendix 6A)

The following data pertain to the petty cash fund of the Hardman Company:

Nov. 2   A $400 check is drawn, cashed, and the cash placed in the care of the assistant office manager to be used as a petty cash fund maintained on an imprest basis.

Dec. 17   The fund is replenished. An analysis of the fund shows:

Coins and currency	$ 98.27
Petty cash vouchers for—	
Delivery expenses.....................................	115.65
Freight-in..	174.08
Postage stamps purchased	10.00

31   The end of the accounting period falls on this date. The fund was not replenished. Its contents on this date consist of—

Coins and currency	$334.70
Petty cash vouchers for—	
Delivery expenses.....................................	21.10
Postage stamps..	24.20
Employee's IOU.......................................	20.00

Required:

Present journal entries to record the above transactions.

6–12–B (based on Appendix 6B)

The Gustav Company was organized January 1 of the current year, 1979. It uses a voucher register and a check register with the same column headings as in Illustrations

6.5 and 6.6, pages 266–269, except that there are only four debit columns headed Merchandise Purchases, Transportation-In, Discounts Lost, and General Ledger Accounts.

Required:

Enter the following approved transactions for the month of January in these registers and total and rule the registers. Start with Voucher No. 1 and Check No. 1. Vouchers are prepared for the net amount of the invoice. For discounts lost, a new voucher is prepared for the amount of the discount.

Transactions:

Jan. 2 Received merchandise from the Lind Company on terms of 2/10, n/30. The invoice received was in the amount of $10,400.

3 Paid transportation charges to Moyer Trucking Company on purchase of January 2, $174.

6 Paid Wilson Display Company $6,600 for billboard advertising for a three-month period beginning February 1, 1979.

15 Paid the Lind Company for the purchase of January 2.

17 Received merchandise from Bradly Company on terms of 2/10, n/30. The invoice received was for $8,400.

18 Received merchandise from Burns Company on terms of 2/10, n/30. The invoice received was for $36,400. Paid net amount today to establish a good credit rating.

23 Received invoice for $3,600 from Office Equipment, Inc., for office equipment recently received. Terms are 2/10, n/30.

7

Accounting for receivables and payables

Learning objectives

Study of the material in this chapter is designed to achieve various learning objectives. These include an understanding of:

1. The nature of receivables and payables and their related accounts.

2. The process of accounting for bad debts.

3. The nature of and accounting for notes payable, notes receivable, and notes receivable discounted.

4. Accounting for payables which arise from income taxes, sales taxes, and property taxes.

5. Payroll accounting and the various payables that arise from having employees (Appendix 7A).

6. An understanding of the need for, and mechanics of, income tax allocation (Appendix 7B).

Frame 1⁷

The term "receivables" is often used in a broad sense in accounting to include any sum of money due to be received from any party for any reason resulting from a past transaction.

The term "payables" similarly is used to describe any amount of money due to be paid to any party for any reason resulting from a past transaction.

The purpose of this chapter is to discuss those receivables and payables which are not discussed in other parts of this text. Special attention is given to Allowance for Doubtful Accounts, which is a contra account to accounts receivable, notes receivable and notes payable (and the interest receivable and interest payable which result from them), taxes payable, and payroll accounting (in Appendix 7A).

Illustration 7.1 summarizes receivables and payables which commonly appear in statements of financial position. All of the items mentioned except the bonds, some of the notes, and the Deferred Federal Income Taxes Payable would normally appear as current assets or liabilities in the statement of financial position. Of course there are other receivables and payables that could have been included, but they are less common and are left to texts designed for more advanced courses.

Determine whether each of the following statements is correct or incorrect.

1. There are usually contra accounts for both accounts receivable and accounts payable.
2. Notes payable and notes receivable result only from loans involving a bank or an individual and are long term.
3. Interest receivable and interest payable normally result from notes and bonds; while dividends receivable, dividends payable, and subscriptions receivable result from the existence of capital stock.
4. The employment of persons creates several liabilities on the books of the employer.

Now turn to Answer Frame 1⁷ on page 296 to check your answers.

Frame 2⁷

Accounts receivable

Revenue from sales is usually recorded at the time of the completion of the sale. This point of sale is generally assumed to be the time of delivery of the goods to the customer. There are two main reasons for this: (1) the revenue is earned, that is, the seller has usually completed or substantially completed his or her part of the agreement; and (2) the revenue is realized, that is, an exchange has taken place with an outsider

Illustration 7.1   Summary of receivables and payables

Receivables	Payables	Comments
Accounts receivable	Accounts payable	Result from the sale of goods or performance of services where payment is deferred. These were discussed in Chapters 3 and 4. This chapter focuses on the contra account, the Allowance for Doubtful Accounts, to accounts receivable. There is no such contra account to accounts payable.
Notes receivable	Notes payable	May result from the sale of goods or performance of services, but may also be the result of loans involving a bank or an individual. A note is a formal document signed by the maker. These may be short term or long term.
Bond investments	Bonds payable	Bonds are almost always long term and are discussed in Chapter 9.
Interest receivable	Interest payable	Interest normally results from notes and bonds.
Dividends receivable	Dividends payable	Dividends result from the existence of capital stock and are discussed in Chapter 10.
Subscriptions receivable		Result from the issuance of capital stock and are discussed in Chapter 10.
Rent receivable	Rent payable	Result from the use of a building or other asset by someone other than the owner; covered in Chapter 3 and elsewhere.
	Deferred federal income taxes payable and federal income taxes payable	Result from federal income tax legislation.
	Sales taxes payable	Many states (and some cities) levy a flat rate tax on retail sales.
	Real and personal property taxes payable	Result from taxation of property by local (and some state) governmental units.
	Payroll liabilities: Salaries and wages payable F.I.C.A. taxes payable Employees' income tax withheld Federal unemployment taxes payable State unemployment taxes payable	These all result from the employment of persons by the entity.

2⁷

continued

and the amount of revenue is known because of the receipt of cash or the customer's promise to pay cash. The asset usually received is an account receivable, although cash or, occasionally, a note may be received.

The recording of revenue at the time of the receipt of a promise to pay is the source of a number of special accounting aspects not found in companies selling for cash only. These include sales discounts and uncollectible accounts, as well as the expenses of operating a credit and collection department. Also, any company selling merchandise is likely to have sales returns and sales allowances. Many of these items may not arise until the period following the period of sales. A question arises as to how to properly match these items against the recognized sales revenue which causes them to come into existence.

Uncollectible accounts or bad debts

For companies doing business on a credit basis, certain accounts will not be collected. The desired matching of uncollectible accounts or bad debts against sales revenue is accomplished through making an adjusting entry at the end of the period. The entry debits Bad Debts Expense and credits Allowance for Doubtful Accounts.

The purpose of the debit to Bad Debts Expense is to bring about a proper matching of the bad debts against revenue. For example, this proper matching consists of matching against the revenues of 1979 all accounts arising from 1979 sales which will ultimately prove uncollectible in 1979, 1980, or some other year. The purpose of the credit to Allowance for Doubtful Accounts (a contra account to Accounts Receivable) is to reduce accounts receivable to their proper amount for statement of financial position purposes; that is, the amount that will ultimately be collected—their net realizable value.

There are two basic methods of directly or indirectly estimating the amount of bad debts to be charged to a given accounting period.

Percentage of sales method. This method involves calculating the amount which has proven uncollectible from each year's credit sales. This ratio of uncollectible accounts to credit sales is then used in estimating the amount for the bad debts adjusting entry. If cash sales are small or are a fairly constant percentage of total sales, the entry may be based on total net sales.

To illustrate, assume that the Rankin Company has found that 1 percent of its net sales is uncollectible. On the basis of this experience, each period the company may charge an amount equal to 1 percent of the net sales for the period to expense and add a like amount to the Allowance for Doubtful Accounts. If net sales for 1979 are $400,000, the entry will read:

Bad Debts Expense	4,000	
Allowance for Doubtful Accounts		4,000
To record bad debts expense.		

Assuming that the gross amount of accounts receivable is $100,000 and there was no previous balance in the allowance account, net accounts receivable would appear as follows on the statement of financial position:

Accounts receivable	$100,000
Less: Allowance for doubtful accounts	4,000
Net Accounts Receivable	$ 96,000

The gross and net amounts of accounts receivable should be shown in the current asset section of the statement of financial position. The gross amount is equal to all customers' accounts with debit balances. (The total of all accounts with credit balances, if any, should be shown under current liabilities under the caption "Credit balances in customers' accounts.")

At the date of setting up the allowance, the specific accounts that will become uncollectible are not known. The use of the allowance permits charging expense at the end of the period for open accounts that may become uncollectible in the future.

Sometimes the Allowance for Doubtful Accounts account has a balance before adjustment. Under this first method any existing balance in the allowance account will *not* influence the size of the bad debts adjusting entry.

This method is theoretically preferable because it bases the estimate of expense solely on the sales revenue of the same period and gives the most precise matching of expense and revenue.

Percentage of accounts receivable method. This method is designed to adjust the Allowance for Doubtful Accounts balance to a certain percentage of accounts receivable. It may use one overall percentage or may use a different percentage for each age category of receivable. To illustrate the use of one overall percentage, assume that on the basis of past experience the Jax Company estimates that 5 percent of its outstanding receivables of $100,000 as of December 31, 1979, will ultimately prove to be uncollectible. The Allowance for Doubtful Accounts has a *debit* balance of $1,000. The journal entry to adjust the balance in the allowance account to its required $5,000 *credit* balance is as follows:

Bad Debts Expense 6,000
    Allowance for Doubtful Accounts   6,000
    To adjust allowance for possible uncollectible accounts.

Illustration 7.2

DARCY COMPANY
Analysis of Accounts Receivable
December 31, 1979

Customer	Debit Balance	Not Due 1%	1–30 5%	31–60 10%	61–90 25%	91–180 50%	Amount Needed in Allowance
X	$ 8,000					$ 8,000	$ 4,000
Y	16,000		$ 12,000	$4,000			1,000
Z..............	4,000				$800	3,200	1,800
All others...	800,000	$560,000	240,000				17,600
	$828,000	$560,000	$252,000	$4,000	$800	$11,200	$24,400

Alternatively, an aging schedule may be used so as to apply a different percentage for each age category of receivable. An aging schedule is presented in Illustration 7.2, showing how the age of each customer's account is determined. As can be seen from Illustration 7.2, under this method the age of the accounts is the basis for estimating uncollectibility. For example, only 1 percent of the accounts not yet due (sales made less than 30 days prior to the end of the accounting period) is expected to be uncollectible. At the other extreme, 50 percent of all accounts 91–180 days past due is expected to become worthless.

Assume that the Allowance for Doubtful Accounts in the December 31, 1979, trial balance of the Darcy Company (Illustration 7.2) already has a credit balance of $8,000. Prepare the entry needed to adjust the allowance account *up to* the required credit balance and to recognize the bad debts expense.

Check your answer by turning to Answer Frame 2[7] on page 300.

Frame 3⁷

Write-off of uncollectible accounts

Once a company has established an Allowance for Doubtful Accounts, accounts which are identified as being uncollectible are charged against the allowance. Using the assumed account receivable of Smith (which arose in 1979) as an example and assuming that $4,000 of the account is identified as being uncollectible, the entry to record this fact in January 1980 is:

```
Allowance for Doubtful Accounts ..........................................  4,000
    Accounts Receivable.....................................................          4,000
```

Posting this entry does not change the estimated net collectible amount of the asset, accounts receivable. To illustrate: If accounts receivable amount to $20,000 and the allowance is $2,000, the net receivables are $18,000. If a $1,000 account is written off, the receivables and allowance balances are $19,000 and $1,000, respectively, or $18,000 net.

It should also be noted that it is quite possible for the Allowance for Doubtful Accounts account to have a debit balance if it is adjusted only once a year. Companies do not often carry accounts receivable which are one year or more old in their accounts. Consequently, by the end of 1979, all accounts which arose from 1978 sales will have been collected or written off. If estimates were exact (which is not likely), the allowance balance would be zero. But it may develop a debit balance if previous estimates were too small. Also, some accounts arising from 1979 sales have probably been charged off. The result is very likely to be a debit balance in the Allowance account before adjusting.

In the above entry charging off $4,000 of Smith's account, an expense is *not* recognized because (choose the correct answer):
1. The customer may still pay the account later in the year.
2. The expense will be recognized when the adjusting entry is made to record bad debts expense at the end of 1980.
3. The expense was recognized sometime prior to 1980.

Now turn to Answer Frame 3⁷ on page 300 to check your answer.

Frame 4⁷

Bad debts recovered

The first indication that an account has been charged off in error usually occurs when a check applying to that account is received in the mail. The cash receipt will be recorded by debiting Cash and crediting

Answer frame 2[7]

The required entry to record the information presented is:

Bad Debts Expense	16,400	
Allowance for Doubtful Accounts		16,400

To adjust the Allowance for Doubtful Accounts of $8,000
to the estimated necessary balance of $24,400.

Under this method any existing balance in the allowance account is considered in determining the amount of the entry. If there had been no existing balance, the above entry would have been made for $24,400.

If you answered incorrectly, reread Frame 2[7] before beginning Frame 3[7] on page 299.

Answer frame 3[7]

The third answer is correct. The original sale was made in a prior year. Under the accrual basis of accounting, the expense element was recorded in the same period as the sale. At that time, possible uncollectible accounts were estimated and an entry was made debiting Bad Debts Expense and crediting the Allowance for Doubtful Accounts. To do so again would be double counting.

If you answered incorrectly, reread Frames 2[7] and 3[7] before beginning Frame 4[7] on page 299.

4[7]

continued

Accounts Receivable. To illustrate, assume that on October 8, 1980, Smith's check for $4,000 is received in the mail. The entry is:

Cash	4,000	
Accounts Receivable		4,000

When it is discovered that Smith's account had been written off to the allowance, the following entry to correct the error is required:

Accounts Receivable	4,000	
Allowance for Doubtful Accounts		4,000

If only a part of a previously written off account is collected, the preferable procedure is to reinstate only that portion of the account actually collected, unless there is evidence that the entire account will be collected.

The entry charging off the account as uncollectible is reversed for two reasons. Which of the following is *not* a reason for this action?

1. The write-off of the account resulted from an incorrect assumption that it was uncollectible; the ultimate collection of the account is evidence that it should not have been written off.

2. After the above entries are posted, the customer's account reflects the actual history of the transactions entered into with him or her.

3. The allowance for doubtful accounts was incorrectly estimated on December 31, 1979.

Now check your answer in Answer Frame 4[7] on page 302.

Frame 5⁷

Notes receivable and notes payable

A promissory note is an unconditional promise in writing, made and signed by the borrower (the maker), obligating the borrower to pay the lender (the payee) or someone else who legally acquires the note a certain sum of money on demand or at a definite time. Normally, only the maker and the payee are parties to the instrument, but sometimes others who legally acquire the note or guarantee payment also become parties.

A company may have notes receivable or notes payable arising from transactions with suppliers or customers. Notes may also arise from loans involving a bank or an individual. The accounting for these transactions is covered in this section.

Most notes bear an explicit charge for interest. Interest is the fee charged for use of money through time. It is an expense to the maker of the note and revenue to the payee of the note. For the sake of convenience (and possibly profit), in commercial transactions interest is commonly calculated on the basis of 360 days per year. The elapsed time in a fraction of a year between two stated days is computed by counting the exact number of days, omitting the day the money is borrowed but counting the day it is paid back. A note falling due on a Sunday or a holiday is due on the following business day.

Assume that we desire to calculate the interest on a $1,000 note; the interest rate is 6 percent, and the life of the note is 60 days. The calculation is as follows:

$$\text{Principal} \times \text{Rate of interest} \times \text{Time} = \text{Interest}$$
$$\$1,000 \times 6/100 \times 60/360 = \$10$$

Notice that when the interest rate is 6 percent and the life of the note is 60 days, you can find the amount of interest by moving the decimal point in the principal two places to the left. This is often referred to as the 6 percent, 60-day rule. For instance, assuming that the following notes are all 6 percent, 60-day notes, the interest on each is:

Principal	*Interest*
$ 1,000..........................	$ 10.00
1,250..........................	12.50
168,000..........................	1,680.00

Now assume that a $2,000 note is a 6 percent, 30-day note. Show:

1. How the interest would be calculated using the formula.
2. The calculation using the 6 percent, 60-day rule. (This method can be used even if the note is not a 6 percent, 60-day note.)

Now turn to Answer Frame 5⁷ on page 302 to check your answers.

Statement 3 is the one which is not valid. The fact that Smith happened to pay his account does not mean that the allowance was incorrect. It merely means that Smith's account is not one of those which proved to be or will prove to be uncollectible.

If you answered incorrectly, restudy Frame 4[7] before beginning Frame 5[7] on page 301.

1. Using the formula, the calculation is as follows:

$$\text{Principal} \times \text{Rate of interest} \times \text{Time} = \text{Interest}$$
$$\$2,000 \times 6/100 \times 30/360 = \$10$$

2. Using the 6 percent, 60-day rule, the reasoning is as follows:

Interest on $2,000 at 6 percent for 60 days = $20
Interest on $2,000 at 6 percent for 30 days = $10 (since 30 days is one half of 60 days)

If you do not understand these answers, restudy Frame 5[7] before starting Frame 6[7] below.

Determination of maturity date

The maturity date may be found by one of several methods depending on the wording used in the note:

1. On demand. "On demand, I promise to pay. . . ." In this case, the maturity date is at the option of the holder and cannot be computed.

2. On a stated date. "On July 18, 1980, I promise to pay. . . ." The date is designated, and a computation is not necessary to determine it.

3. At the end of a stated period. (*a*) "One year after date, I promise to pay. . . ." If the maturity is expressed in years, the note matures on the same day of the same month as the date of the note in the year of maturity.

(*b*) "Four months after date, I promise to pay. . . ." If the maturity is expressed in months, the note will mature on the same date in the month of maturity. For example, one month from July 18, 1980, is August 18, 1980, and two months from July 18, 1980, is September 18, 1980. If a note is issued on the last day of a month and the month of maturity has fewer days than the month of issuance, the note matures on the last day of the month of maturity. A one-month note dated January 30, 1980, matures on February 29, 1980.

(*c*) "Ninety days after date, I promise to pay. . . ." If the maturity is expressed in days, the exact number of days must be counted. The first day (date of origin) is omitted and the last day (maturity date) is included in the count. For example, a 90-day note dated October 19, 1980, matures on January 17, 1981.

Life of note (days)		90 days
Days remaining in October not counting date of origin of note:		
Days to count in October (31–19)	12	
Total days in November	30	
Total days in December	31	73
Maturity date in January		17

Notes arising from business transactions

Sometimes a note results from the conversion of an open account. To illustrate, assume that on October 6, 1979, Cooper (the payee) receives from Price (the maker) a 60-day, $18,000 note; the interest rate is 9 percent, and the note results from the earlier sale (on October 4) of merchandise by Cooper to Price. The interest will be earned over the life of the note and will not be paid until maturity, December 5, 1979. The entries for both the payee and the maker are as follows:

Cooper, payee

Oct. 4	Accounts Receivable	18,000	
	Sales		18,000
	To record sale.		
Oct. 6	Notes Receivable	18,000	
	Accounts Receivable		18,000
	To record receipt of note.		
Dec. 5	Cash	18,270	
	Notes Receivable		18,000
	Interest Revenue		270
	To record receipt of principal and interest.		

Price, maker

Oct. 4	Purchases	18,000	
	Accounts Payable		18,000
	To record purchase.		
Oct. 6	Accounts Payable	18,000	
	Notes Payable		18,000
	To record giving of note.		
Dec. 5	Notes Payable	18,000	
	Interest Expense	270	
	Cash		18,270
	To record payment of principal and interest.		

Dishonored note. A note is dishonored if the maker fails to pay it at maturity. The payee of the note may debit either Accounts Receivable or Dishonored Notes Receivable and credit Notes Receivable for the face of the note. If interest is due, the uncollected interest should be debited to the same account to which the dishonored note is debited and credited to Interest Revenue. The maker should merely debit the amount of interest incurred to Interest Expense and credit Interest Payable.

To illustrate, assume that Price did not pay the note at the maturity date. The entries on the books of the payee and the maker are as follows:

Cooper, payee

Dec. 5	Dishonored Notes Receivable	18,270	
	Notes Receivable		18,000
	Interest Revenue		270

Price, maker

Dec. 5	Interest Expense	270	
	Interest Payable		270

Sometimes when a note cannot be paid at maturity, the maker either pays the interest on the original note or includes it in the face of a new note given to take the place of the old note. When it becomes obvious that the maker will never pay the note, the amount in the Dishonored Notes Receivable account pertaining to that note should be written off to Bad Debts Expense, Loss on Dishonored Notes, or some similar account. If notes were taken into account when making the annual provision for doubtful accounts, the debit should be to the Allowance for Doubtful Accounts account.

Assume that Arens gives a $10,000, 6 percent, 60-day note to Taylor on June 1. On the maturity date the note is dishonored. Give the entry required on each set of books on that date.

Now turn to Answer Frame 6⁷ on page 306 to check your answers.

Now turn to Answer Frame 6⁷ on page 306 to check your answers.

Frame 7⁷ ————————————————————————————

Notes payable arising from need for short-term financing

There are various reasons why a business may need short-term financing. Included among these are: (1) delay in the receipt of cash caused by granting customers credit terms on amounts due (although this is at least partially offset by the use of credit on its purchases to delay the payment of cash); (2) seasonal buildup of inventory, such as that occurring in department stores just before the Christmas holidays; and (3) expansion in operations caused by the expectation of a future increase in sales. We shall discuss some of the ways in which a business can acquire short-term financing.

Noninterest bearing notes. In instances when a company presents its noninterest-bearing note to a bank with a request for a loan, the bank computes the amount of interest it charges for the use of its money on the face value of the note, deducts the amount computed from the face value, and gives the balance, the proceeds, to the company. The amount deducted is often called a bank discount. The process of computing the amount is referred to as discounting. To illustrate this process, assume that a bank discounts a company's $20,000, 90-day, noninterest-bearing note at 9 percent. The 9 percent interest is the bank's charge for the use of its money. The discount is $450, and this sum is deducted from the $20,000 and the remainder of $19,550 given to the company.

If the above transaction occurred on December 1, 1979, it would be recorded by the company as follows:

Dec. 1	Cash...	19,550	
	Notes Payable – Discount..	450	
	Notes Payable		20,000

Note that the company does not receive $20,000 but $19,550. Since the company will pay $450 for the use of this sum for a period of 90 days, a rate of interest higher than 9 percent is actually being paid. (If $450 is the interest on $20,000 at 9 percent for 90 days, then $450 is more than 9 percent on $19,550 for 90 days.) Note also that the bank must discount this note in order to introduce interest into the transaction. At maturity the bank will receive $20,000. The Notes Payable – Discount account is used as a valuation contra account to reduce notes (traditionally carried at face value) to their net present value.

Assuming that December 31, 1979, is the end of the company's accounting period, interest expense for the month of December is recorded as follows:

Dec. 31	Interest Expense...	150	
	Notes Payable – Discount		150

In the current liability section on the December 31, 1979, statement of financial position, the note and the discount appear as follows:

Notes payable	$20,000
Less: Discount..	300
	$19,700

When the note is paid at maturity, the entry is as follows (maturity date is February 29, 1980):

Feb. 29	Notes Payable...	20,000	
	Interest Expense...	300	
	Cash..		20,000
	Notes Payable – Discount		300

This entry reduces the Notes Payable – Discount and Notes Payable accounts to zero balances. Notice that the difference between the cash paid out ($20,000) and that originally received ($19,550) is equal to the total interest expense ($450). The interest related to a 90-day period,

The required entries are as follows:

Taylor, payee

July 31	Dishonored Notes Receivable	10,100	
	Notes Receivable		10,000
	Interest Revenue		100

Arens, maker

| July 31 | Interest Expense | 100 | |
| | Interest Payable | | 100 |

If you answered incorrectly, restudy Frame 6⁷ before beginning Frame 7⁷ on page 304.

7⁷

continued

30 days of which fall in the year ending December 31, 1979, and 60 days in the following year. Thus, the amount charged to interest expense should be $150 in 1979 and $300 in 1980.

Interest-bearing notes. The company could alternatively have given a $20,000, 90-day, 9 percent interest-bearing note. At the date of borrowing, the required entry is as follows:

| Cash | 20,000 | |
| Notes Payable | | 20,000 |

At maturity the company pays both the face amount of the note and interest at the rate stated in the note on the face amount (a total of $20,450). When this method is used, the company also is paying the actual stated percentage rate of interest.

Assuming that the note was dated January 1, 1979, what would be the entry to record the repayment on the maturity date?

Now check your answer in Answer Frame 7⁷ on page 308.

Frame 8⁷

Discounting notes receivable. When a company issues its own note payable to a bank, it is directly liable to the bank at the maturity date of the loan. Such notes payable are shown in the statement of financial position as liabilities.

Instead of borrowing directly, a company may use another method of obtaining short-term financing from a bank. It may select a note receivable held by it, endorse it, and receive cash by discounting it at a bank. Thus, a note receivable discounted arises. A company which discounts a note receivable is contingently, instead of directly, liable to the lending bank. It must pay the bank the amount due at maturity only if the maker of the note fails to pay the obligation.

The cash proceeds of notes receivable discounted are computed as follows:

1. Determine the maturity value of the note (face value plus interest).
2. Determine the discount period; that is, count the exact number of days from the date of discounting to the date of maturity. Exclude the date of discounting but include the date of maturity in the count.
3. Using the rate of discount charged by the bank, compute the bank discount on the maturity value for the discount period.
4. Deduct the bank discount from full value at maturity. The result is the cash proceeds.

The contingent liability is usually shown in the accounts by recording the note discounted in a Notes Receivable Discounted account at the face value of the note, even though the contingent liability extends to the interest also. If the original maker does not pay the bank at the maturity date, the borrower who discounts the note will have to pay the principal and interest.

EXAMPLE. Assume that on May 4, 1979, Clark Company received a $10,000 note from Kent Company bearing interest at 9 percent and maturing in 60 days from May 4. On May 14, 1979, Clark Company discounted the note at the Michigan National Bank at 10 percent. The discount and the cash proceeds are determined as follows:

Face value of note	$10,000.00
Add: Interest at 9% for 60 days	150.00
Maturity value	$10,150.00
Less: Bank discount on $10,150 at 10% for 50 days	140.97
Cash Proceeds	$10,009.03

The entry is as follows:

May 14 Cash	10,009.03	
Notes Receivable Discounted		10,000.00
Interest Revenue		9.03

If the proceeds had been less than the book value of the note, the difference would have been debited to an Interest Expense account.

The required entry is:

Apr. 1	Notes Payable	20,000	
	Interest Expense	450	
	Cash		20,450

If you answered incorrectly, reread Frame 7⁷ before beginning Frame 8⁷ on page 306.

8⁷

continued

Now assume that on June 1 Fuller Company receives a $20,000, 9 percent, 90-day note dated June 1. The company discounts it at the bank on July 1. The bank's rate of discount is 8 percent.

1. What is the note's maturity value? 20,450
2. What is its maturity date? AUG.30
3. What is the discount period? 60 days
4. What is the discount amount charged by the bank? 272.67
5. How much are the cash proceeds? 20,177.33
6. What is the entry to record the receipt of the proceeds?

Now check your answers in Answer Frame 8⁷ on page 310.

CASH	20177.33	
N/R DISC.		20,000
INT. REV		177.33

Frame 9⁷

Statement of financial position presentation of notes receivable discounted. In the Clark Company example, a statement of financial position prepared for Clark Company as of June 30, 1979, should show a contingent liability in the amount of $10,000 for notes receivable discounted. Assume that the total of all notes receivable is $70,000. One acceptable method of presenting this information in the statement of financial position is:

Assets

Current Assets:

Cash	$xx,xxx
Accounts receivable	xx,xxx
Notes receivable (Note 1)	60,000

Notes to Financial Statements:
Note 1: At June 30, 1979, the company is contingently liable for $10,000 of customers' notes receivable (in addition to the $60,000 shown) which it has endorsed and discounted at the local bank.

Discounted notes receivable paid by maker. When a note receivable has been discounted, it is usually the duty of the endorsee (the holder) to present the note to the maker for payment at maturity. If the maker pays the endorsee (the bank in the above illustrations) at maturity, the endorser (the company which discounted the note) is thereby relieved of its contingent liability. If the note is not paid at maturity, the endorsee can collect from the endorser which, in turn, can try to collect from the maker.

Assume that Kent Company (in the example) pays the $10,000 note plus interest of $150 to the Michigan National Bank on July 3, 1979, the note's maturity date. Clark Company, which discounted the note at the bank, can no longer be held liable on the note and, therefore, will make the following entry:

July 3	Notes Receivable Discounted	10,000	
	Notes Receivable		10,000

This entry reduces the balance of each of these accounts to zero.

Discounted notes receivable not paid by maker. If Kent Company dishonors its note, the Michigan National Bank will collect the principal ($10,000), interest ($150), and any protest fee (assume it to be $5) from Clark Company. Clark Company will have to make two entries as follows:

July 3	Notes Receivable Discounted	10,000	
	Notes Receivable		10,000
	To remove the note and the contingent liability from the accounts.		
3	Dishonored Notes Receivable	10,155	
	Cash		10,155
	To record the cash deducted from our account by the bank on the note dishonored by Kent.		

Clark Company will then try to collect $10,155 from Kent Company. If this cannot be done, the $10,155 will be removed from the Dishonored Notes Receivable account and treated as a loss from bad debts.

Assume that Smith Company (the maker) dishonors a $5,000 note that Piaza Company had discounted at the bank. On August 20 the bank deducts $5,060 (maturity value plus interest and protest fee) from Piaza Company's account at the bank. Give the entries that Piaza Company would make on its books.

Now check your answers in Answer Frame 9⁷ on page 310.

Now check your answers in Answer Frame 9⁷ on page 310.

Frame 10⁷ ————————————————————————————

Long-term notes

Notes may be either short term or long term. They are usually short term. But when they are long term (have maturities exceeding approxi-

Answer frame 8[7]

The correct answers are as follows:

1. The maturity value is the face value plus the interest, or $20,450.

$$\text{Interest} = \$20,000 \times 9/100 \times 90/360 = \$450$$

2. The maturity date is August 30.

Days in June	30	
Less date of note	1	29
Days in July		31
Days in August needed to total 90 days		30
Total		90

3. The discount period is 60 days.

Days in July	31	
Less date of discounting	1	30
Days in August, including maturity date		30
Total		60

4. The discount charged by bank is $272.67.

$$\text{Maturity Value} \times \text{Discount Rate} \times \frac{\text{Discount Period}}{360}$$

$$\$20,450 \quad \times \quad 8/100 \quad \times \quad 60/360 \quad = \$272.67$$

5. The cash proceeds are $20,177.33 — the maturity value, $20,450, less the discount, $272.67.

6. The required entry is:

July 1 Cash	20,177.33	
Notes Receivable Discounted		20,000.00
Interest Revenue		177.33

If you answered incorrectly, reread Frame 8[7] before beginning Frame 9[7] on page 308.

Answer frame 9[7]

The required entries are:

Aug. 20 Notes Receivable Discounted	5,000	
Notes Receivable		5,000
20 Dishonored Notes Receivable	5,060	
Cash		5,060

If you answered incorrectly, restudy Frame 9[7] before starting Frame 10[7] on page 309.

mately one year) they are to be recorded at their present cash value.[1] To illustrate, assume the existence of a $1,000 face value note, bearing no explicit rate of interest, which is due one year from its date. (Even though this does not "exceed approximately one year" and technically would not have to be recorded at its present value, it is assumed the company chooses to do so.) Assume that the rate of interest to be used in reducing this note to its present value is 6 percent. To solve for the present value one should ask the following question: What amount if invested at 6 percent would grow to $1,000 one year from now? If x equals that amount, the calculation is:

$$x + .06x = \$1,000$$
$$1.06x = \$1,000$$
$$x = \frac{\$1,000}{1.06} = \$943.40$$

Assuming the note payable results from the purchase of a machine on December 31, 1979, it is recorded as follows:

Machinery	943.40	
Notes Payable – Discount	56.60	
Notes Payable		1,000.00

At the due date, $1,000 is paid to the payee and $56.60 is recorded as interest expense. The required entry at the due date, December 31, 1980, is:

Notes Payable	1,000.00	
Interest Expense	56.60	
Notes Payable – Discount		56.60
Cash		1,000.00

The accounting for the interest in this type of transaction is quite similar to that used when a company discounts its own note at the bank.

Most long-term notes do bear an explicit rate of interest. When such a note arises from an arm's-length transaction, it is assumed that the rate of interest stipulated by the parties represents fair and adequate compensation to the supplier of funds. In these instances, the note payable is recorded at the purchase price of the asset acquired. An example of such a transaction is the mortgage note payable.

Mortgage note payable. Sometimes companies give their own notes to finance the acquisition of a plant asset. Such a note is usually a long-term liability and is secured by a mortgage on the property acquired. A mortgage is an obligation to give up the property that has been pledged to the payee in case the maker defaults on the payments. Most of us become familiar with this form of financing when we purchase a home.

[1] Accounting Principles Board, "Interest on Receivables and Payables," *APB Opinion No. 21* (New York: AICPA, August 1971).

Business firms also sometimes use this method of financing when they acquire assets such as buildings.

This form of financing can be illustrated by looking at a situation where a business is acquiring a building. The borrower makes a constant lump-sum payment each month (exclusive of real estate taxes), which at first pays mostly interest and very little principal. Assume that the mortgage is $35,000, the interest rate is 8 percent, and the life of the note is 25 years. There are mortgage payment schedule books which indicate that the monthly payment for principal and interest is $271. Here is how the first two months' and the last month's payments are applied:

	Monthly payment	Interest	Principal	Principal balance
Date of purchase..................	—	—	—	$35,000.00
First month........................	$271	$233.33	$ 37.67	34,962.33
Second month.....................	271	233.08	37.92	34,924.41
300th month.......................	271	2.00	269.00	–0–

Notice that interest is calculated on the latest principal balance. For instance, when the first $271 payment is made interest is calculated as follows:

$$\frac{\$35,000 \times .08}{12} = \$233.33$$

It is necessary to divide by 12 because the interest rate is 8 percent per year and the calculation of the amount is for one month. The excess of the payment over the interest is applied against the principal ($37.67 in the first payment above). Thus, the principal balance decreases slowly (but more rapidly each month), so that the last $271 payment at the end of 25 years pays interest (approximately $2) on the remaining principal balance (approximately $269) and reduces the principal balance to zero.

Assume that on January 1, 1979, Company X acquires a building for $35,000 and gives its 8 percent note payable to a bank to finance the purchase. The January entries pertaining to the mortgage note would be as follows (see table above):

Jan. 1	Building..	35,000.00	
	Mortgage Note Payable..........................		35,000.00
31	Interest Expense	233.33	
	Mortgage Note Payable................................	37.67	
	Cash		271.00

What entry is made at the end of February 1979?

Now check your answer in Answer Frame 10[7] on page 314.

Frame 11[7]

Other payables

The remaining payables which will be discussed all arise from tax legislation in one form or another. A business is subject to various taxes. For some taxes the concern is with the provisions of the law levying them so that proper entries can be made to record any expense and the liability for payment. Sales taxes, property taxes, and payroll taxes generally fall into this category. There is little opportunity for minimizing or delaying any expense associated with these taxes. And for certain of these taxes the business merely performs a collection function since the taxes are levied on employees and customers.

Income taxes are in a different category and are the subject of this first section. Federal income taxes came into being in 1913 and have been used to stimulate or dampen the economy and to encourage or discourage certain activities as well as to raise governmental revenues.

Income taxes

The rates of taxation on earnings of corporations by the federal government alone have in the recent past been 48 percent for certain portions of income. Because of the relatively high rate (and also the increased possibility of legally avoiding or delaying the incurrence of these taxes), the business executive is concerned not only with correctly accounting for these taxes but also with making decisions which will minimize their effects on earnings.

Every corporation organized for profit must file a federal income tax return and pay a corporation tax on its taxable income. Since proprietorships and partnerships are not taxable entities, their owners report their share of business earnings on their individual returns.

A corporation reports information and is taxed as shown in Illustration 7.3.

Net earnings versus taxable income. Net earnings (as shown on the earnings statement) and taxable income (as shown in the corporation's tax return) need not necessarily agree. There are various reasons why they might differ. Some of these are:

1. Certain items of revenue and expense included in the computation of business earnings are excluded from the computation of taxable income. For instance, interest earned on state or municipal bonds is not subject to tax.
2. Only "ordinary" and "necessary" business expenses and "reasonable" amounts of salaries can be deducted for tax purposes.
3. Life insurance premiums are not deductible if the corporation is the beneficiary, and proceeds received from life insurance policies are not taxed.
4. Costs of attempting to influence legislation are not deductible.

The required entry on February 28, 1979, is:

Interest Expense	233.08	
Mortgage Note Payable	37.92	
Cash		271.00

This can be seen from the sample mortgage schedule book in Frame 10^7. If you answered incorrectly, reread Frame 10^7 before starting Frame 11^7 on page 313.

11^7

continued

5. The most obvious item is the federal income tax expense itself. It is deducted in arriving at net earnings but not in arriving at taxable income.

6. Certain items may be included as revenue or deductions for tax purposes which are not included in the computation of business earnings. For instance, oil and other extractive industries have been granted percentage depletion allowances which permit them to charge against taxable income an amount in excess of the cost of the natural resources consumed in production.

7. The timing of recognition of items of revenue and expense often varies for tax purposes from the timing used in determining business earnings. Interpretations of the tax code have generally held that revenue received in advance is taxable when received and that current expenses based on estimates of future costs (such as costs of performance under service contracts) are not deductible until actually incurred. An exception is bad debts expense.

8. Different elective methods may be used for tax purposes than are used for financial statements. For instance, the corporation may be using straight-line depreciation for financial reporting purposes and a different method for tax purposes.

In its tax return a corporation must explain the difference between net earnings as reported in its financial statements and taxable income as reported on its tax return.

Is each of the following correct or incorrect?

1. Since both the tax code and the earnings statement are designed to measure business earnings, one must conclude that one of them is incorrect in its income concept.

2. Interpretations of the tax code have generally held that revenue received in advance is taxable when received.

3. It is conceivable that a corporation will show a net loss on its earnings statement for a given year and still have to pay federal income taxes on operations for that year.

Check your answers by turning to Answer Frame 11^7 on page 316.

*Illustration 7.3   Corporation
tax formula*

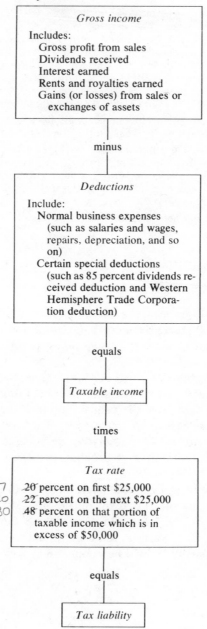

Gross income

Includes:
 Gross profit from sales
 Dividends received
 Interest earned
 Rents and royalties earned
 Gains (or losses) from sales or
  exchanges of assets

minus

Deductions

Include:
 Normal business expenses
  (such as salaries and wages,
  repairs, depreciation, and so
  on)
 Certain special deductions
  (such as 85 percent dividends received deduction and Western
  Hemisphere Trade Corporation deduction)

equals

Taxable income

times

Tax rate

 20 percent on first $25,000
 22 percent on the next $25,000
 48 percent on that portion of
  taxable income which is in
  excess of $50,000

equals

Tax liability

315

1. Incorrect. The purposes of the tax code and of the earnings statement are not the same. The earnings statement is designed to measure business earnings, but the tax code is not primarily concerned with this. A major purpose of federal income taxation is to collect revenue to finance government activities in a way that will not cause runaway inflation. (The federal government has the power to print money so it would not have to tax to spend.) Another purpose of income taxation is to promote the national welfare. Special tax benefits, therefore, are granted to certain taxpayers.

2. Correct. Interpretations generally have applied the cash basis rather than the accrual basis of accounting for these items.

3. Correct. Expenses included in the earnings statement may be disallowed for tax purposes. For instance, part of the salary paid to the president of the company who owns all of the outstanding stock may have been deemed by the taxing authorities to be unreasonably large and actually a dividend rather than an expense.

If you missed any of the above, reread Frame 11[7] before going to Frame 12[7] below.

Frame 12[7]

For corporations, the maximum rate of tax on all net long-term capital gains is 30 percent. Capital gains result from the sale of property owned by the corporation, including real or depreciable property used in the business.

Corporations are also permitted to deduct 10 percent of the cost of acquisition of machinery and equipment (under certain conditions) from their tax liability in the year of purchase. This latter provision is called the *investment credit*. The amount deducted does not reduce the cost of the asset to use for calculating depreciation for tax purposes. Under certain circumstances a speedup in allowable depreciation deductions can also be taken.

As shown in illustration 7.3, an ordinary business corporation is subject to a tax of 20 percent on the first $25,000 of taxable income, 22 percent on the next $25,000, and 48 percent on all amounts over $50,000. For example, if a corporation has taxable income of $80,000, the tax payable would be computed as follows:

$$20\% \times \$25,000 = \$\ 5,000$$
$$22\% \times \ \ 25,000 = \ \ 5,500$$
$$48\% \times \ \ 30,000 = \ \underline{14,400}$$

Total tax $\underline{\underline{\$24,900}}$

A procedure called "income tax allocation" must be applied in recording the tax liability. This procedure is covered in Appendix 7B.

Sales taxes

Many states (and some cities) levy a flat rate tax upon retail sales, with the tax usually levied upon the consumer but collected by the retailer. Entries can readily be made to record the collection of sales taxes on such big-ticket items as automobiles, where each sale is recorded separately. Even retail stores selling numerous smaller items can account for the taxes on sales by ringing such taxes up separately in a cash register. Thus, the register readings for Department K of a given department store for a particular day might require that the following entry be made:

Cash	4,124.68	
Accounts Receivable	6,094.68	
Sales – Department K		9,826.48
Sales Tax Liability		392.88

Property taxes

Legally, property is divided into two categories: real property and personal property. Real property includes land and all other items permanently attached to the land, such as buildings, sewers, fences, and sidewalks. Personal property includes furniture, machinery, delivery equipment, inventories, and in many states such items as security investments and accounts and notes receivable.

Most local governmental units – counties, townships, and cities – depend upon real and personal property taxes as their chief source of revenue. In some cases, states levy real property taxes. In other cases, states participate in the distribution of revenues raised through the levying of personal property taxes. Real and personal property taxes are expenses of the owner of the property and would be recorded in the following manner:

Property Tax Expense	480	
Property Taxes Payable		480

Payroll accounting

Payables arising from payroll accounting include: salaries payable, federal (and sometimes state and city) income tax withheld, F.I.C.A. tax liability, federal unemployment tax liability, and state unemployment tax liability. These are discussed in Appendix 7A.

Indicate whether each of the following statements is true or false.
1. For corporations the maximum rate of tax on all net long-term capital gains is 25 percent.
2. The tax on $70,000 of taxable corporate income would be $27,100.
3. Sales taxes are levied by states and cities rather than by the federal government.
4. Real property includes land and all items permanently attached to the land.

Now turn to Answer Frame 12[7] on page 318 to check your answers.　　317

1. False. The maximum rate is 30 percent rather than 25 percent.
2. False. It would be $20,100, calculated as follows:

$$
\begin{array}{ll}
20\% \text{ of } \$25,000 = & \$\ 5,000 \\
22\% \text{ of } \$25,000 = & \ \ 5,500 \\
48\% \text{ of } \$20,000 = & \underline{\ \ 9,600} \\
& \$20,100
\end{array}
$$

3. True. This is one principal source of revenue for many states and some cities. But most cities rely most heavily on property taxes.
4. True. And personal property includes such items as furniture, machinery, and inventories.

If you missed any of the above, review Frame 12⁷ before beginning the Summary below.

Summary *chapter* 7

Receivables are any sum of money due to be received from any party for any reason resulting from a past transaction. Included among receivables are such items as accounts receivable, notes receivable, interest receivable, rent receivable, dividends receivable, and subscriptions receivable.

Payables are amounts to be paid to any party for any reason resulting from a past transaction. Included among payables are such items as accounts payable, notes payable, bonds payable, interest payable, rent payable, dividends payable, and various types of taxes payable.

The Allowance for Doubtful Accounts is a contra account to accounts receivable. The other side of the entry establishing the allowance is a debit to Bad Debts Expense. Two methods of establishing the amount of the entry are the percentage of sales method and the percentage of accounts receivable method. The latter method may involve the use of one overall percentage or the aging technique.

Notes receivable and notes payable may arise from business transactions or from borrowing or lending for some specific purpose. When in need of short-term financing, borrowers either issue their own note to a bank or may discount a note receivable. They are directly liable for paying their own note, but are only contingently liable for paying the note receivable discounted (they must pay if the maker does not).

Long-term receivables and payables should be recorded at their present cash values.

Various payables arise from taxes levied by governmental units.

Examples are payables arising from income taxes, sales taxes, property taxes and payroll taxes.

Corporations are taxed as a separate entity. Gross income less normal business deductions and special deductions is equal to taxable income. The first $25,000 of taxable income is taxed at 20 percent, the next $25,000 at 22 percent, and the portion of taxable income which exceeds $50,000 is taxed at 48 percent.

Net earnings as shown on the earnings statement and taxable income as shown in the corporation's tax return need not agree. Certain items of revenue and expense included in business earnings are excluded from taxable income, and vice versa. Also, the timing of the recognition of items of revenue and expense often varies for tax purposes from the timing used in determining business earnings.

The estimated amount of income taxes payable for a period as taken from a company's tax return may not be the proper amount of income taxes to report in the earnings statement. Appendix 7B explains the nature of permanent and timing differences and how these apply to income tax allocation.

Payroll accounting exists whenever an entity hires employees. Appendix 7A covers payroll accounting.

To complete your review of this chapter, study the definitions of new terms contained in the Glossary on page 325. Then complete the Student Review Quiz beginning on page 327.

APPENDIX 7A: PAYROLL ACCOUNTING

Federal income tax withheld

Under the federal pay-as-you-go income tax collection system, most individuals must pay (partially or in full) their federal income taxes on wages as they are received throughout the year rather than waiting until they file an income tax return. The tax is withheld by the employer from the wages of employees at the time wage payments are made. The withheld taxes are periodically remitted by the employer to a depository bank or to the Internal Revenue Service.

The amount of the income tax to be withheld from the pay of each employee depends upon (1) the amount of the employee's earnings, (2) the frequency of the payroll period, and (3) the income exempt from taxation as determined by the number of exemptions claimed by the employee. The amount of each personal exemption is built into the withholding tax rates and tables.

Every employer is required to maintain payroll records for the employees, setting forth (among other items) the names and addresses of persons employed during the year, their social security numbers,   319 exemptions, gross wages earned, taxes withheld, other deductions, and dates and amounts of net take-home pay.

After the end of each calendar year, an employer must furnish each employee certain information necessary to aid in preparing his or her personal federal income tax return. This information also serves the purpose of providing the Internal Revenue Service with data for determining whether or not taxpayers have filed proper income tax returns.

Accounting for federal income tax withheld. To illustrate the accounting entries for federal income tax withheld from employees, assume that there is one employee whose gross wages during the first six months of 1979 are $1,000 per month, and that the tax to be withheld is $110.40 each month, determined from a withholding table supplied by the Internal Revenue Service. The monthly accounting entries will be as follows:

Salary Expense...	1,000.00	
Accrued Salaries Payable..		889.60
Federal Income Tax Withheld.......................................		110.40
Accrued Salaries Payable..	889.60	
Cash...		889.60

The correct entry to be made when the tax withheld is remitted to a depositary bank or to the Director of the Internal Revenue Service is:

Federal Income Tax Withheld	110.40	
Cash		110.40

Federal Insurance Contributions Act taxes

The basic plan for management of the F.I.C.A. fund is simple. During their years of employment covered by the Act, employed persons, their employers, and self-employed persons pay a certain percentage of their earnings (up to the limit specified in the Act) into a special fund. This fund is used to pay retirement and other benefits to the covered persons. When earnings stop because the covered worker has retired or died, or in certain cases has been disabled, benefit payments are made from the fund to take the place of the earnings the worker has lost. Certain hospital and post-hospital care costs for almost everyone over 65 also are payable out of social security funds. Additional voluntary medical insurance is also available for those individuals 65 and over who enroll for it.

F.I.C.A. taxes are levied against both the employer and the employee. The amount of tax withheld from the salary of each covered employee for 1977 was 5.85 percent of the first $16,500 of wages paid in any one year. This rate (5.85 percent) and base ($16,500) are subject to frequent change but will be used in our discussion.

The employer must bear a tax equal to that withheld from each employee. Thus, the total F.I.C.A. tax in 1977 amounted to 11.7 percent of the first $16,500 of the wages of each covered employee — half borne by the employee and half by the employer. If eligible for coverage under the Act, a self-employed person pays the entire F.I.C.A. tax at a rate approximately one and one-half times that paid by an employee. But the program, rates, coverage, and benefits may — at any time — be changed. As of this writing, the base is scheduled to rise as follows: 1978, $17,700; 1979, $22,900; 1980, $25,900; 1981, $29,700. Thereafter it will rise in line with wage inflation.

Accounting entries required for F.I.C.A. taxes.   To illustrate the accounting entries for F.I.C.A. taxes, assume that an employee receives a salary of $1,000 per month, paid monthly. The amount to be deducted from the salary of the employee each month is 5.85 percent of $1,000 ($58.50). Also assume that the income tax withholding is $110.40. The entries to record the accrual and payment of the employee's salary on the records of the employer are:

Salary Expense	1,000.00	
F.I.C.A. Tax Liability		58.50
Federal Income Tax Withheld		110.40
Accrued Salaries Payable		831.10
Accrued Salaries Payable	831.10	
Cash		831.10

Both the F.I.C.A. Tax Liability account and the Federal Income Tax Withheld account represent amounts owed to the federal government which are payable to the Internal Revenue Service.

In addition to the amounts withheld for each employee, the employer is liable for its portion of the F.I.C.A. tax. In this case, the employer's expense also is 5.85 percent of $1,000 or $58.50. To record the employer's portion of the F.I.C.A. tax, the following entry is made:

F.I.C.A. Tax Expense	58.50	
F.I.C.A. Tax Liability		58.50

This entry normally is part of the month-end adjustment procedure.

The F.I.C.A. Tax Liability account accumulates both the employer's and the employee's portions of the tax. The balance in the account is carried on the records as a current liability until remittance is made to the Internal Revenue Service.

The journal entry that would be made when the taxes are remitted is:

F.I.C.A. Tax Liability	117.00	
Federal Income Tax Withheld	110.40	
Cash		227.40

Unemployment taxes

The Federal Unemployment Tax Act (F.U.T.A.) provides for a cooperative federal-state system of unemployment compensation. The federal unemployment tax is a tax imposed on salaries and wages to help finance the joint federal-state unemployment program.

Unemployment benefits to qualified unemployed persons are paid by each of the states and territorial governments. The unemployment laws of the several states and territories vary only in minor respects; their general similarity is due to the fact that the Federal Unemployment Tax Act sets forth certain minimum standards that must be met by each state.

Federal unemployment tax rate. The federal unemployment tax rate generally has varied between 3 and 3.5 percent. As of January 1, 1978, it was 3.4 percent, levied on the first $6,000 of earnings per employee. This rate will be used as an example in all further discussion. The Federal Unemployment Tax Act provides that each employer may have a credit of up to 2.7 percentage points against its federal unemployment tax for amounts paid to the state. This, in effect, leaves the federal unemployment tax at .7 of 1 percent on the first $6,000 of wages paid to each employee. The entire federal unemployment tax is borne by the employer; no tax is levied on the employee.

State unemployment taxes. Most states set the state unemployment tax rate at 2.7 percent of the first $6,000 of earnings per employee. This rate and base will be used in this text. Almost all state unemployment insurance tax laws levy a state unemployment tax only against the employer.

Each pay period, or once each month, the employer should prepare accounting entries for the federal and state unemployment taxes in the following form:

```
Federal Unemployment Tax Expense ...........................................  xxx
State Unemployment Tax Expense...............................................  xxx
     Federal Unemployment Tax Liability....................................          xxx
     State Unemployment Tax Liability .......................................          xxx
```

Summary of taxes based on employee earnings

Tax	Paid by	Rate
Social Security (F.I.C.A.)	Both employer and employee pay at current rate	5.85% of first $16,500 each employee earns annually*
Income tax†	Employee	Varies with earnings and exemptions
State unemployment	Employer	2.7% of first $6,000 each employee earns annually‡
Federal unemployment	Employer	.7% of first $6,000 each employee earns annually§

* This rate and base are for 1977. The base is expected to increase in subsequent years.

† If combined F.I.C.A. and withholding taxes exceed $100 per month, they must be deposited monthly with a federal depository bank.

‡ Some states have a higher rate and/or base than this. Also, most states allow a reduction from the basic rate to firms with low labor turnover.

§ The federal rate varies, but in this text an assumption is made that it is 3.4 percent. An allowance of 2.7 percent is granted for amounts paid to the state, thus reducing the effective rate to .7 percent.

APPENDIX 7B: INCOME TAX ALLOCATION

As discussed in the chapter, taxable income and net earnings before income taxes (for simplicity, pretax earnings) may differ sharply for a number of reasons — in fact, the tax return may show a loss while the earnings statement shows positive net earnings. This raises questions as to what amount of income taxes should be shown in the earnings statement. The answer lies in the nature of the items causing the difference between taxable income and pretax earnings. Some of the differences are *permanent* — interest earned on municipal bonds is never taxable but is always included in net earnings. Such differences cause no problem — the estimated actual amount of income taxes payable for the year is shown on the earnings statement even if this results in reporting only $1,000 of income taxes on $100,000 of pretax earnings.

The reasons for other differences between taxable income and pretax earnings are called *timing differences* — that is, items which will be included in both taxable income and in pretax earnings but in *different periods*. The items involved thus will have a tax effect, and when this is true, generally accepted accounting principles require that *tax allocation* procedures be applied to prevent the presentation of possibly misleading information.

To illustrate, assume (1) that a firm acquires for $200,000 a machine whose estimated life is four years with no salvage value expected, (2) that it uses the straight-line depreciation method for financial reporting purposes and the sum-of-the-years'-digits method (to be described in Chapter 8) for tax purposes, (3) that net earnings before depreciation and income taxes for each year of the machine's life will be $150,000, (4) that there are no other items which cause differences between pretax earnings and taxable income, and (5) that the tax rate is 50 percent.

Under these circumstances, the actual tax liability for each year will be:

	1979	1980	1981	1982	Total
Earnings before depreciation and income taxes ...	$150,000	$150,000	$150,000	$150,000	$600,000
Depreciation (sum-of-the-years'-digits basis)*	80,000	60,000	40,000	20,000	200,000
Taxable Income	$ 70,000	$ 90,000	$110,000	$130,000	$400,000
Income Taxes	$ 35,000	$ 45,000	$ 55,000	$ 65,000	$200,000

* Do not be concerned about how the depreciation is calculated. It is explained in Chapter 8.

If the amounts of income taxes computed above were shown in the earnings statements for the years 1979–82, the reason becomes apparent for the requirement that taxes be allocated where timing differences are the cause of a difference between taxable income and pretax earnings. Without allocation, net earnings would be:

	1979	1980	1981	1982	Total
Earnings before deprecia- tion and income taxes...	$150.000	$150,000	$150,000	$150,000	$600,000
Depreciation (straight- line method)...............	50,000	50,000	50,000	50,000	200,000
Earnings before income taxes.........................	$100,000	$100,000	$100,000	$100,000	$400,000
Income taxes	35,000	45,000	55,000	65,000	200,000
Net Earnings..................	$ 65,000	$ 55,000	$ 45,000	$ 35,000	$200,000

To report net earnings as declining this sharply in the circumstances described would be quite misleading. Especially objectionable is the reporting of sharply increased net earnings for 1979 brought about by deducting only $35,000 of income taxes on $100,000 of pretax earnings when the current tax rate is 50 percent and all of the items making up the $100,000 will appear on the tax return. Under such circumstances it is contended that the income taxes should be $50,000. And this is supported by drawing attention to the fact that there is no actual reduction in taxes. Total income taxes for the four years will be $200,000. Therefore, any taxes not paid in the early years of the machine's life will be paid later—note the $65,000 of taxes in 1982—when, as the accountant puts it, the timing differences reverse, that is, in this case when depreciation is less per tax return than for financial reporting purposes.

Consequently, tax allocation procedures should be applied in the above circumstances. Under such procedures, the earnings statement for each of the four years would show:

	Each year	Total for four years
Earnings before depreciation and income taxes.....................	$150,000	$600,000
Depreciation..............................	50,000	200,000
Earnings before income taxes	$100,000	$400,000
Income taxes.............................	50,000	200,000
Net Earnings	$ 50,000	$200,000

Under tax allocation, reported net earnings are $50,000 per year. Note especially that reported income taxes in the earnings statements are $50,000 in each year. This seems logical since pretax earnings are $100,000 and the tax rate is 50 percent.

The entries to record the income tax expense, the income taxes payable, the income taxes paid, and the changes in the deferred income taxes payable are summarized in the T-accounts below. The (9) refers to 1979, the (0) to 1980, and so on.

324

Federal Income Tax Expense		Federal Income Taxes Payable				Deferred Federal Income Taxes Payable			
(9) 50,000		(9a) 35,000	(9) 35,000			(1) 5,000	(9) 15,000		
(0) 50,000		(0a) 45,000	(0) 45,000			(2) 15,000	(0) 5,000		
(1) 50,000		(1a) 55,000	(1) 55,000						
(2) 50,000		(2a) 65,000	(2) 65,000						

The entries keyed with the letter *a* indicate the debits made to record the actual cash paid in settlement of the federal income tax liability. Note that the amount of expense recognized remained constant at $50,000 even though the actual tax liability increased from $35,000 for 1979 to $65,000 for 1982 by $10,000 increments. The normalizing of the tax expense for each year was accomplished by entries in the Deferred Federal Income Taxes Payable account. As can be seen, the tax expense for the four years is $200,000, and the tax payments for the four years also sum to $200,000. The only difference is that the tax expense is not charged to the year in the same amount as the actual liability for the year. Note, also, that in our simplified example the Deferred Federal Income Taxes Payable account has a zero balance at the end of four years.

But actual business experience has shown that once a Deferred Federal Income Taxes Payable account is established it is seldom decreased or reduced to zero. The reason is that most businesses acquire new depreciable assets, at perhaps higher prices. The result is that depreciation for tax purposes continues to be greater than depreciation for financial reporting purposes and the balance in the Deferred Federal Income Taxes Payable account also continues to grow. For this reason, many accountants seriously question the validity of tax allocation in circumstances such as those described above. But discussion of this controversial issue must be left to a more advanced text.

In some instances, taxable income will be greater than pretax earnings because of timing differences such as when rent collections received in advance are taxed before they are considered earned revenue for accounting purposes. Application of tax allocation procedures in such circumstances will give rise to a balance in an asset account entitled Deferred Federal Income Taxes or possibly Prepaid Federal Income Taxes.

Glossary *chapter 7*

Aging (of accounts receivable) – a process of classifying accounts receivable according to their age in appraising the accounts for purposes of establishing or adding to the balance in an Allowance for Doubtful Accounts account.

Allowance for Doubtful Accounts – a contra account to accounts receivable designed to reduce gross accounts receivable to their net realizable value.

Assessed value – a valuation placed on property by a tax assessor or commission. It serves as a base upon which to calculate the amount of real (and sometimes personal) property taxes due.

Bad debts expense – an operating expense

a business incurs when it sells on credit. It results from nonpayment of accounts receivable.

Discounting notes receivable — the act of transferring a note receivable with recourse to a bank. The proceeds are equal to the maturity value less the discount (amount charged by the bank). The discount is computed as the maturity value times the annual discount rate times the number of days the bank must hold the note to maturity divided by 360. In computing the number of days, the maturity date is included while the date of discount is excluded.

Dishonored notes receivable account — an account showing notes which the makers failed to pay at maturity and which have not yet been written off.

Earnings record — a record showing details such as number of exemptions, time worked, gross earnings, deductions, and net pay for an employee.

Exemption — an amount which may be deducted from gross earnings (gross income) in arriving at taxable income.

Experience rating — a measure of a firm's history with respect to the number and periods of time its employees draw unemployment compensation; used in reducing unemployment taxes for firms with a stable history of employment.

F.I.C.A. — the Federal Insurance Contributions Act.

Income taxes — taxes based upon taxable income and levied by governmental bodies on individuals and firms.

Maker — the person preparing and signing a promissory note.

Maturity value — the amount the holder of a negotiable instrument is entitled to receive at the due date. Included in the amount are the principal and accrued interest, if any.

Note, promissory — an unconditional promise made in writing by one person to another, signed by the maker, engaging to pay on demand or at a definite time a sum certain in money to order or to bearer.

Notes Payable — Discount — a contra account used to reduce Notes Payable to their net present value. The amount in the discount account is converted into interest expense as time passes.

Payable — any amount of money due to

be paid to any party for any reason resulting from a past transaction.

Payee — the person to whose order payment is promised or ordered on a note or other negotiable instrument.

Percentage of accounts receivable — a method of determining the desired size of the allowance for doubtful accounts and, indirectly, the bad debts expense for the period. This method has two variations. One is to use an overall percentage, and the other is to use the aging technique.

Percentage of sales — a method of estimating the expected amount of uncollectible accounts from a given period's credit sales and, indirectly, of determining the balance in the Allowance for Doubtful Accounts account.

Permanent differences — differences between taxable income and pretax earnings caused by tax provisions which exclude an item of expense or revenue or gain or loss as an element of taxable income.

Personal property — property such as furniture, machinery, delivery equipment, inventories, and in many states such things as security investments and accounts and notes receivable.

Property taxes payable — obligations which arise from taxes on real property and personal property.

Real property — land and all other items permanently attached to land, such as buildings, sewers, fences, and sidewalks.

Receivable — any sum of money due to be received from any party for any reason resulting from a past transaction.

Tax allocation — a procedure whereby the tax effects of an element of expense or revenue, loss or gain, which will affect taxable income are allocated to the period in which the item is recognized for accounting purposes, irrespective of the period in which it is recognized for tax purposes.

Taxable income — that amount to which the applicable tax rate is applied to arrive at tax liability for the period.

Timing differences — items that will affect taxable income and pretax earnings but in different periods.

Continue with the Student Review Quiz below as a self-administered test of your understanding of the material presented in this chapter.

Student review quiz *chapter 7*

To develop a permanent record of your responses, you may write them on the answer sheet provided in the *Work Papers* or on a separate sheet of paper.

1 Which of the following methods of determining bad debts expense most closely matches expense to revenue?

a Charging bad debts only as accounts are written off as uncollectible.

b Charging bad debts with a percentage of sales for that period.

c Estimating the allowance for doubtful accounts as a percentage of accounts receivable.

d Estimating the allowance for doubtful accounts by aging the accounts receivable.

2 In March 1979, after trying unsuccessfully to collect for nearly two years, Ellis Sport Shop wrote off the $87.50 account of John F. Poole as uncollectible. In August 1979, Mr. Poole remitted a check for $50 with the terse notation "had a good day at the track." Which of the following entries should be made on the books of the Ellis Sport Shop?

a Cash........................... 50.00
  Accounts Receiv-
    able (Poole) 50.00

b Cash........................... 50.00
  Allowance for
    Doubtful
    Accounts............   50.00

c Cash........................... 50.00
  Accounts Receiv-
    able (Poole) 50.00
  Accounts Receivable
    (Poole)..................... 50.00
  Allowance for
    Doubtful
    Accounts............   50.00

d Cash........................... 50.00
  Accounts Receiv-
    able (Poole) 50.00
  Accounts Receivable
    (Poole)..................... 87.50
  Allowance for
    Doubtful
    Accounts............   87.50

e Cash........................... 50.00
  Bad Debts
    Expense.............   50.00

3 The accounts of the Jellis Corporation on December 31, 1979, show Accounts Receivable, $202,000; Allowance for Doubtful Accounts (Cr.), $500; Sales, $980,000; and Sales Discounts, $13,500. At this time, the company decides to write off the account of the Backus Corporation, $2,000. The Allowance for Doubtful Accounts account is then to be adjusted to 2 percent of the outstanding receivables. The amount of bad debts expense recognized for the year is —

a $19,330.
b $19,600.
c $4,040.
d $3,540.
e $5,500.

4 Which of the following items should not be classified as a current asset in the statement of financial position?

a A $5,000, five-year note receivable which matures in six months for which there is no ready market. Collection at that time is expected.

b An amount due from an officer of the company for merchandise purchased on account.

c A wage advance to an employee.

d Semiannual rent receivable on a building owned and leased to another party.

e A note receivable from an officer of the company who has left the company and cannot be traced.

5 The maturity date of a 90-day note dated February 15, 1979, is —

a April 15, 1979.
b May 14, 1979.
c May 15, 1979.
d May 16, 1979.
e On demand.

6 The Lambert Company issued an $1,800, 60-day, 8 percent note to Omsted Wholesalers for merchandise purchased. The journal entry at time of sale on the books of the *payee* is —

a Notes Receivable 1,800
    Sales   1,800

b Notes Receivable 1,824
    Sales   1,800
    Interest Revenue   24

327

c Purchases.................... 1,800
    Notes Payable........   1,800

d Purchases.................... 1,800
    Interest Expense   24
    Notes Payable........   1,824

e Notes Receivable 1,800
    Interest Receivable.......   24
    Sales   1,800
    Interest Revenue.....   24

7 Drehmel & Company accepted a 90-day, 10 percent note having a face value of $400 from T. R. Baxter in settlement of his account receivable. The note was dishonored at maturity. The correct entry on the books of Drehmel & Company to record the default on the note is —

a Dishonored Notes
    Receivable.................... 400
    Notes Receivable   400

b Dishonored Notes
    Receivable.................... 410
    Notes Receivable   400
    Interest Revenue.........   10

c Dishonored Notes
    Receivable.................... 440
    Notes Receivable   400
    Interest Revenue.........   40

d Notes Payable.................. 400
    Accounts Payable—
    Drehmel & Company...   400

e Notes Payable.................. 400
    Interest Expense   10
    Accounts Payable—
    Drehmel & Company...   410

8 Referring to Question 7, prepare the entry on Drehmel's books which would be correct if T. R. Baxter subsequently —
a Gave a new note for the amount owed.
b Paid cash for the amount owed.

9 V. R. Graves arranged a loan at the bank. He gave the bank a 60-day note on which both the face value and the maturity value are $18,000. The bank discounted the note at 9 percent. Which of the following statements is not correct?
a Mr. Graves received $17,730 in cash ($18,000 − $270).
b This type of note is often called a non-interest-bearing note.
c The effective rate of interest on the loan is greater than 9 percent.
d The effective rate of interest on the loan is less than 9 percent.

10 On April 1 Lubenow Brothers received a $300, 60-day, 9 percent note from J. I. Holden. On May 10 they discounted it at the bank at 10 percent. Which of the following statements regarding this set of transactions are *true?*
a Face value of the note is $300.
b Maturity value of the note is $304.50 [$300 + ($300 × .09 × 60/360)].
c The discount period is 20 days.
d The discount is $300 × .10 × 20/360.

11 On June 10 Bradley Shops received a $1,000, 60-day, 9 percent note from Mrs. C. L. Weber. This note was discounted at the bank at 10 percent on the day it was received. The journal entry to record the discounting transaction is —

a Cash.......................... 998.08
    Interest Expense 1.92
    Notes Receivable
    Discounted..........   1,000.00

b Cash.......................... 1,000.00
    Interest Expense 15.00
    Notes Receivable.....   1,015.00

c Cash.......................... 983.08
    Interest Revenue 16.92
    Notes Receivable
    Discounted..........   1,000.00

d Cash.......................... 1,000.00
    Interest Expense........... 15.00
    Notes Receivable
    Discounted..........   1,000.00
    Interest Revenue 15.00

e Cash.......................... 998.08
    Interest Expense 16.92
    Notes Receivable
    Discounted..........   1,000.00
    Interest Revenue 15.00

12 At the date of discounting a note receivable from R. T. Johns, the Arbuckle Company made the following entry:

Cash............................. 2,950
Interest Expense.............   50
    Notes Receivable
    Discounted...........   3,000

The maturity value of the note is $3,050. R. T. Johns did not pay the note. The bank deducted the amount due from the Arbuckle Company's account. The protest fee was $10. Which of the following *correctly* records the default transaction on Arbuckle Company's books?

a Dishonored Notes
    Receivable 3,010
    Cash   3,010

b Dishonored Notes
　　Receivable 3,060
　　　Cash .... 　　　　3,060

c Accounts Receivable...... 3,010
　　　Cash .... 　　　　3,010

d Dishonored Notes
　　Receivable 3,060
　　　Cash .... 　　　　3,060
　　Notes Receivable
　　Discounted 3,000
　　　Notes Receivable ... 　　　　3,000

e Notes Receivable
　　Discounted 3,050
　　　Notes Receivable ... 　　　　3.050
　　Dishonored Notes
　　Receivable 3,060
　　　Cash .... 　　　　3,060

13 The net earnings before income taxes and the taxable income of a corporation may differ. Which of the following could be a cause of a difference between these two amounts?

a Interest on state or local government bonds.

b Political contributions.

c Life insurance premiums.

d Certain revenues received in advance of performance of the required service.

e All of the above.

Questions 14 and 15 are based on Appendix 7A.

14 The January 18, 1979, gross payroll for salaries of the Mateer Corporation is $1,600. The total federal income tax withheld is $325. The employees' share of F.I.C.A. taxes withheld is $93.60. Which of the entries would be correct at the time of payment, assuming no prior recording of salaries?

a Salary Expense 1,217.00
　　　Cash...................... 　　　　1,217.00

b Salary Expense 1,600.00
　　　Cash...................... 　　　　1,600.00

c Salary Expense 1,600.00
　　　Federal Income
　　　Tax Withheld .... 　　　　325.00
　　　F.I.C.A. Tax
　　　Liability .... 　　　　93.60
　　　Cash...................... 　　　　1,181.40

d Salary Expense 1,600.00
　　F.I.C.A. Tax Expense..... 　93.60
　　　F.I.C.A. Tax
　　　Liability .... 　　　　93.60
　　　Federal Income
　　　Tax Withheld .... 　　　　325.00
　　　Cash...................... 　　　　1,275.00

e Salary Expense 1,600.00
　　F.I.C.A. Tax Expense..... 　93.60
　　　F.I.C.A. Tax
　　　Liability .... 　　　　187.20
　　　Federal Income
　　　Tax Withheld .... 　　　　325.00
　　　Cash...................... 　　　　1,181.40

15 Harold Jackson is trying to decide whether to hire four workers at $18,000 each per year, or 12 workers on a part-time basis at $6,000 each per year, to operate four of the concessions at his amusement park. The employees' wages will be subject to F.I.C.A. and unemployment tax expense in 1977 under the two alternatives. (Assume the state unemployment tax rate is 2.7 percent and the federal rate is 3.4 percent, both on $6,000.) The difference in payroll tax expenses is—

a $5,012.

b $3,180.

c $1,983.

d $1,364.

16 (based on Appendix 7B) The pretax earnings of the O Corporation, including $10,000 of interest revenue on City of Detroit bonds, is $150,000. Its taxable income for the same year is only $120,000 because it recorded a greater amount of depreciation for tax purposes than for accounting purposes. If the applicable federal income tax rate is 50 percent, which of the following statements is true?

a O's actual tax liability for the year is $55,000.

b O should report federal income tax expense of $75,000 for the year.

c Entries made by O for the year will include a debit to a deferred taxes account of $15,000.

d O should report federal income tax expense of $70,000 for the year.

Now compare your answers with the correct answers and explanations on page 718.

Questions *chapter* 7

1 What are the two major purposes to be accomplished in establishing an allowance for possible uncollectible accounts?

2 In view of the fact that it is impossible to estimate the exact amount of uncollectible accounts receivable for any one year in advance, what exactly does the Allowance for Doubtful Accounts account contain after a number of years?

3 How might information in an aging schedule prove useful to management for purposes other than estimating the size of the required allowance for doubtful accounts?

4 In view of the difficulty in estimating future events, would you recommend that accountants wait until collections are made from customers before recording sales revenue? Or wait until known accounts prove to be uncollectible before charging an expense account?

5 The credit manager of a company has established a policy of seeking to eliminate completely all losses from uncollectible accounts. Is this a desirable objective for a company? Explain.

6 For a company using the allowance method of accounting for uncollectible accounts, which of the following affects its reported net earnings: (1) the establishment of the allowance, (2) the writing off of a specific account, (3) the recovery of an account previously written off as uncollectible?

7 Explain why an account receivable might have a credit balance. What is the proper treatment of such an item in the financial statement?

8 Differentiate between dishonored notes receivable and notes receivable discounted. How is each shown in the statement of financial position?

9 Describe two ways involving a note payable in which amounts can be borrowed from a bank.

10 Why might a situation arise in which the bank rate of discount is less than the rate in a customer's note which the holding company discounts at the bank?

11 At what amount should long-term notes payable be recorded?

12 How is interest calculated on a mortgage note payable each month?

13 What factors might cause net earnings on a corporation's earnings statement to differ from its taxable income?

Questions 14 and 15 are based on Appendix 7A.

14 What are the various payables that arise from payroll accounting?

15 Which payroll taxes are incurred by the employer? What are the applicable rates and bases for computation of these taxes?

16 (based on Appendix 7B) Classified among the long-term liabilities of the A Corporation is an account entitled, Deferred Federal Income Taxes Payable. Explain the nature of this account.

Exercises *chapter* 7

1 How should the following situation be shown in the statement of financial position? The subsidiary accounts receivable ledger of the Matson Company shows a total of $124,000. An examination of the accounts shows one account of $15,000 due from the president of the company. The composition of this account is as follows:
a Due from sale of merchandise, $4,000.
b A loan of $5,000.
c Stock subscriptions receivable of $6,000 (amounts due on the sale of stock).

2 How should the following appear in the statement of financial position of the Bee Corporation on December 31, 1979? Why?

Accounts receivable (including
  credit balances of $700)............ $123,000
Accounts payable (including
  advance payments to vendors
  of $500)................................ 87,000

3 On December 28, 1979, Jordan Corporation received a check for $2,500 as a 10 percent down payment on an order for merchandise from the Argonne Company. Argonne is not indebted to Jordan at this time. The receipt was recorded by debiting Cash and crediting Argonne's Accounts Receivable account. The merchandise was not delivered until January 5, 1980. On December 31, 1979, the trial balance amount of accounts receivable was $172,000. Indicate the proper statement of financial position presentation of the above data.

4 The accounts of the Baldon Company as of December 31, 1979, show Accounts Receivable, $90,000; Allowance for Doubtful Accounts, $500; Sales, $540,000; and Sales Returns and Allowances, $10,000. Prepare journal entries to adjust for possible uncollectible accounts under each of the following assumptions:

a Uncollectible accounts are estimated at one half of 1 percent of net sales.
b The allowance is to be increased to 3 percent of accounts receivable.

5 On April 1, 1979, Brackton Company, which employs the allowance method of accounting for uncollectible accounts, wrote off Bill Combs' account receivable of $352. On December 14, 1979, the company received a check for that amount from Combs marked "in full of account." Prepare the necessary entries for all of the above.

6 Compute the required size of the Allowance for Doubtful Accounts account for the following receivables:

Accounts receivable	Age (months)	Probability of collection
$100,000	Less than 1	.95
40,000	1 to 3	.80
20,000	3 to 6	.70
5,000	6 to 12	.40
1,000	12 and over	.10

7 You have read the rule that when the terms of an obligation are 6 percent for 60 days you can look at the face amount of the obligation and move the decimal point two places to the left to find the dollar amount of interest. Prove that this rule is true.

8 Bauer gives his 90-day, $15,000, 8 percent note to Beebe in exchange for merchandise. Give the entry that each will make on the maturity date, assuming payment is made.

9 Give the entries that Bauer and Beebe (see Exercise 8) would make at the maturity date assuming that Bauer defaults.

10 Determine the maturity dates for notes with each of the following lives:

Issue date	Life
January 13, 1980	1 year
January 31, 1980	1 month

June 4, 1980	30 days
December 1, 1980	90 days

11 Austin Company gives a 120-day, $5,000, 6 percent note to Chase Company on July 6, 1980. Chase Company discounts the note at the bank on August 20, 1980. The rate of discount is 6 percent. Determine the entries each company would make on the date of discounting.

12 In Exercise 11, if Austin Company fails to make payment on the maturity date, what entry is required on the books of each company?

13 Day Kreuzburg goes to the bank and asks to borrow $1,000 at 6 percent for a 60-day period. Give the entry which should be made to record the proceeds received for each of the following alternatives:

a He signs a note for $1,000. Interest is deducted from the face amount in determining the proceeds.
b He receives $1,000 and signs a note for that amount. The interest is to be paid at the maturity date.

14 Give the entry or entries which would be made at the maturity date for each of the alternatives given in Exercise 13 assuming the loan is repaid before the end of the accounting period.

15 The A and B Partnership has net earnings of $40,000. Determine the tax liability of the partnership.

16 Wexley Corporation has taxable income of $10,000, $25,000, and $60,000 in its first three years of operations. Determine the amount of federal income taxes it will incur each year. *1980 rates*

Questions 17 and 18 are based on Appendix 7A.

17 John Ryans earns $20,000 during one year. Using the rates in the text, how much will be paid to the federal government for F.I.C.A. taxes on John?

18 You live in a state that imposes a 2.7 percent unemployment tax, levied on the same amount of income as is taxed by the federal government under F.U.T.A. During 1979 you employ ten persons and pay each of them $7,500. How much do you incur as federal and state unemployment tax expense? How much would the employees' share normally be?

331

— **19 (based on Appendix 7B)** The pretax earnings of the R Corporation for a given year amount to $200,000 while its taxable income is only $160,000. The difference is entirely attributable to additional depreciation taken for tax purposes. If the current income tax rate is 40 percent, give the entry to record the income taxes chargeable to the year and the tax liability for the year.

Problems, Series A *chapter* 7

7–1–A

Presented below are selected accounts of the Robinson Company as of December 31, 1979. Prior to closing the accounts, the $2,000 account of Lake Company is to be written off (this was a credit sale of February 12, 1979).

Accounts receivable..	$ 160,000
Allowance for doubtful accounts........................	2,000 Dr.
Sales...	1,120,000
Sales returns and allowances	20,000

Required:

a Present journal entries to record the above and to record the bad debts expense for the period, assuming the estimated expense is 2 percent of net sales.

b Give the entry to record the estimated expense for the period if the allowance is to be adjusted to 5 percent of outstanding receivables instead of as in (a) above.

7–2–A

The accounts receivable (all arising under sales terms of n/30) of the Bently Corporation at December 31, 1979, total $200,000. The age composition of $180,000 of these accounts is:

Age	*Amount*
Not yet due..	$142,000
1–30 days past due......................................	18,000
31–60 days past due	8,000
61–90 days past due	6,000
91–120 days past due...................................	4,000
Over 120 days past due................................	2,000
	$180,000

Given below are the four other accounts which account for the remaining $20,000 of accounts receivable:

Company A

Date		Explanation	Folio	Debit	Credit	Balance
1979						
Jan.	1	Balance forwarded (12/27/78 sale)				2,000
Feb.	7		S 14	8,000		10,000
	10		CR 3		2,000	8,000
Mar.	1		CR 6		2,000	6,000
July	5		S 17	1,200		7,200
	8		CR 20		2,000	5,200
Nov.	3		CR 31		400	4,800

Company B

Date		Explanation	Folio	Debit	Credit	Balance
1979						
Jan.	10		S 5	5,000		5,000
Feb.	1		CR 3		2,500	2,500
Mar.	4	Allowance granted 1/10 sale	J 5		1,000	1,500
June	2		CR 16		500	1,000
	6		S 16	300		1,300
July	3		CR 19		500	800
Sept.	12		S 30	900		1,700
	15		CR 22		200	1,500
Nov.	30		CR 32		400	1,100

Company C

Date		Explanation	Folio	Debit	Credit	Balance
1979						
July	5		S 17	1,500		1,500
Aug.	2		CR 20		500	1,000
	28		S 28	1,000		2,000
Sept.	5		CR 21		500	1,500
Oct.	5		CR 28		500	1,000
	6		S 32	12,700		13,700
Nov.	3		CR 31		2,000	11,700

Company D

Date		Explanation	Folio	Debit	Credit	Balance
1979						
Aug.	22		S 26	1,000		1,000
Sept.	5		CR 21		1,000	-0-
	12		S 30	1,200		1,200
	30		S 31	500		1,700
Oct.	5		CR 28		1,700	-0-
	28		S 34	1,300		1,300
Nov.	2	Adjustment granted	J 17		100	1,200
	7		CR 31		1,000	200
	10		S 36	1,800		2,000
Dec.	5		CR 34		1,800	200
	11		S 38	2,200		2,400

Note: The abbreviations in the Folio column stand for the following: CR = Cash Receipts Journal; S = Sales Journal; J = General Journal. These journals are illustrated in Appendix 4A.

Required:

a Prepare an aging schedule for the accounts receivable of the Bently Corporation. Compute the required Allowance for Doubtful Accounts balance assuming estimated percentages of uncollectible accounts of $1/2$, 1, 2, 5, 10, and 25 percent, respectively, for the six classifications given above.

b Prepare the necessary adjusting journal entry assuming the allowance has a debit balance of $600.

✳ 7-3-A

The Rymer Company received on July 24, 1980, a note from the Watt Company with the following description:

Face amount	$30,000
Life of note	90 days
Date of note	7/24/80
Interest rate on note	10%
Date of discounting note at the bank	8/23/80
Rate of discount charged by the bank	12%

Required:

Determine:

a   The maturity date of the note.

b   The maturity value of the note.

c   The number of days from the discount date to the maturity date.

d   The dollar amount of the discount.

e   The cash proceeds received by the company.

f   The entry to record the receipt of the proceeds at the date of discount.

7-4-A

Using the simplified method illustrated in the text on page 301, compute the interest when the terms are as follows:

	Interest rate	Life	Face amount
a	6%	60 days	$ 7,245
b	2	90 days	10,000
c	1	50 days	3,000
d	9	40 days	8,000
e	12	20 days	4,500

7-5-A

The Reetz Company has an accounting period of one year, ending on July 31. On July 1, 1980, the balances of certain ledger accounts are: Notes Receivable, $24,800; Notes Receivable Discounted, $12,000; and Notes Payable, $40,000. The balance in Notes Receivable consists of the following:

Face amount	Maker	Date of note	Life	Interest rate	Date discounted	Discount rate
$12,000	May Co.	5/15/80	60 days	12%	6/1/80	12%
4,000	Brad Co.	6/1/80	60 days	12	—	—
8,800	Ross Co.	6/15/80	30 days	10	—	—
$24,800						

The note payable is a 60-day bank loan dated May 20, 1980. Interest Expense was debited for the discount, which is at a rate of 6 percent.

Required:

Prepare dated journal entries for the following transactions and necessary July 31 adjustments.

Transactions:

July 1 The Reetz Company discounted its own $12,000, 60-day, noninterest-bearing note at the State Bank. The discount rate is 10 percent and the note is dated today.

3 Received a 20-day, 12 percent note, dated today, from the Jones Company in settlement of an account receivable of $2,400.

6 Purchased merchandise from the May Company, $19,200, and issued a 60-day, 12 percent note, dated today, for the purchase.

8 Sold merchandise to the Wood Company, $16,000. A 30-day, 12 percent note, dated today, is received to cover the sale.

14 The $12,000 note discounted on June 1, 1980, is paid by the May Company directly to the holder in due course.

15 The Ross Company sent a $4,000, 30-day, 12 percent note, dated today, and a check to cover its note of June 15, 1980, and interest in full to this date.

18 The Wood Company note of July 8 is discounted at the State Bank for the remaining life of the note. The discount rate is 12 percent.

19 The note payable dated May 20, 1980, is paid in full.

23 The Jones Company dishonored its note of July 3, due today.

26 The Jones Company sent a check for the interest on the dishonored note and a new 30-day, 12 percent note dated July 23, 1980.

30 The Brad Company note dated June 1, 1980, is paid with interest in full.

7-6-A (based on Appendix 7A)

a The Daly Company has 36 employees and an annual payroll in 1977 of $275,600: 8 employees earn $18,000 each per year, and 28 employees earn an equal amount each per year. What is the annual F.I.C.A. tax (1) for the employees and (2) for the employer?

b What is the amount of the federal and state unemployment tax per year, assuming a federal rate of 3.4 percent and a state rate of 2.7 percent for this employer?

c Which of the preceding items would constitute expenses on the records of the Daly Company?

7-7-A (based on Appendix 7A)

Throughout the first quarter of 1977 the Thuss Company employed seven machinists at $3,600 each per quarter year and an assistant manager at $4,500 per quarter year. The monthly payroll was paid on the last day of each month. On January 31 the company withheld $1,230 of federal income taxes from the employees, along with the proper F.I.C.A. tax.

Required:

Journalize:

a The payroll for January.

b The employer's F.I.C.A. tax for January.

c The employer's federal and state unemployment taxes, assuming a federal rate of 3.4 percent and a state rate of 2.7 percent for this company.

d The entry or entries to record payment of the various taxes.

7–8–A [Part (c) is based on Appendix 7B]

The records of the Skyridge Corporation show the following for the calendar year just ended:

Sales	$400,000
Interest earned on—	
State of New Jersey Bonds	3,000
City of Miami Bonds	1,500
Essex County, Ohio, School District No. 2 Bonds	375
Cost of goods sold and other expenses	315,000
Loss on sale of capital asset	3,000
Gain on sale of capital asset acquired two years ago	7,500
Allowable extra depreciation deduction for tax purposes	4,500
Dividends declared	15,000
Revenue received in advance, considered taxable income of this year	3,000
Contribution made to influence legislation (included in the $315,000 listed above)	300

Required:

a Present a schedule showing the computation of taxable income.

b Compute the amount of the corporation's tax that was payable for the current year. (Assume tax rates mentioned in the text. Also assume the company acquired $100,000 of new equipment during the year and qualified for the full amount of investment credit as a reduction in taxes.)

c Prepare the adjusting entry necessary to recognize federal income tax expense assuming income tax allocation procedures are followed. (The reduction in taxes caused by the investment credit is to be deducted from federal income tax expense and federal income tax currently payable.) The permanent differences are the contribution to influence legislation and the interest earned on state, county, and city bonds.

Problems, Series B *chapter* 7

7–1–B

As of December 31, 1979, the Bridges Company's accounts prior to adjustment show:

Accounts receivable	$ 84,000
Allowance for doubtful accounts	3,000
Sales	900,000

Bridges Company follows a practice of estimating uncollectible accounts at 1 percent of sales.

On February 23, 1980, the account of Don Cole in the amount of $3,200 is considered uncollectible and is written off. On August 12, 1980, Cole remits $500 and indicates that he intends to pay the balance due as soon as possible. By December 31, 1980, no further remittance has been received from Cole.

Required:

a Prepare journal entries to record all of the above transactions and adjusting entries.
b Give the entry necessary as of December 31, 1979, if the Bridges Company estimated its uncollectible accounts at 8 percent of outstanding receivables rather than at 1 percent of sales.

7–2–B

The accounts receivable (all arising under sales terms of n/30) of the Potts Corporation as of December 31, 1979, total $280,000. The age composition of $250,000 of these accounts is:

Age	Amount
Not yet due	$205,000
Past due:	
1–30 days	30,000
31–60 days	8,000
61–90 days	2,000
91–120 days	1,000
Over 120 days	4,000
	$250,000

Given below are the three other accounts which account for the remaining $30,000 of accounts receivable:

James, Inc.

Date		Explanation	Folio		Debit	Credit	Balance
1979							
Jan.	1	Balance forward (12/28/78 sale)					3,000
	8		CR	1		3,000	–0–
	11		S	1	4,000		4,000
Feb.	5		CR	2		4,000	–0–
Sept.	18		S	9	5,000		5,000
	26	Adjustment granted	J	9		700	4,300
Oct.	5		CR	10		4,000	300
	8		S	10	2,500		2,800
Nov.	3		CR	11		2,500	300
	15		S	11	3,200		3,500
Dec.	4		CR	12		3,200	300
	18		S	12	4,300		4,600
	21		S	12	2,000		6,600

Knobloch Company

Date		Explanation	Folio	Debit	Credit	Balance
1979						
Apr.	5		S 4	2,200		2,200
May	5		CR 5		2,200	–0–
Aug.	3		S 8	2,100		2,100
Sept.	5	Return	J 9		500	1,600
	11		CR 9		1,600	–0–
Oct.	15		S 10	6,300		6,300
Nov.	7		CR 11		1,500	4,800
	10		S 11	500		5,300
Dec.	15		CR 12		1,000	4,300

Kyle Company

Date		Explanation	Folio	Debit	Credit	Balance
1979						6,200
Jan.	1	Balance forward				
	8		CR 1		6,200	–0–
Feb.	18		S 2	11,000		11,000
Mar.	6		CR 3		11,000	–0–
May	19		S 5	2,200		2,200
June	1		S 6	1,100		3,300
	7		CR 6		2,200	1,100
	23		S 6	20,500		21,600
July	5		CR 7		21,600	–0–
Oct.	15		S 10	23,000		23,000
Nov.	3		CR 11		4,000	19,000
	9		S 11	5,400		24,400
	18	Return 10/15 sale	J 11		300	24,100
Dec.	5		CR 12		8,000	16,100
	17		S 12	3,000		19,100

Note: The abbreviations in the Folio column stand for the following: CR = Cash Receipts Journal; S = Sales Journal; J = General Journal. These journals are illustrated in Appendix 4A.

Required:

a Prepare an aging schedule classifying the accounts as per the age groups given above.

b Assuming the Allowance for Doubtful Accounts has a debit balance of $2,100, prepare the necessary adjusting journal entry for estimated uncollectible accounts as of December 31, 1979, if the amount of uncollectible accounts is estimated at $\frac{1}{2}$, 1, 2, 5, 10, and 25 percent, respectively, of the age groups given above.

c What has apparently happened with regard to $300 of the balance of the James, Inc., account? What is the probability of collecting this balance?

7–3–B

On June 1, 1980, the Stevens Company received a $6,000, 120-day, 8 percent note from the Thomas Company dated June 1, 1980. On August 15, 1980, the note was discounted at the bank. The rate of discount was 12 percent.

Required:

Determine:

a   The maturity value of the note.

b   The number of days from the discount date to the maturity date.

c   The dollar amount of the discount.

d   The cash proceeds received by the company.

e   The proper entry to record the receipt of proceeds at the date of discount.

7-4-B

Following are selected transactions of the Brown Company:

Oct. 31   Discounted its own 30-day, $10,000, noninterest-bearing note at the First State Bank at 12 percent.

Nov. 8   Received a $5,000, 30-day, 9 percent note from the Best Company in settlement of an account receivable. The note is dated November 8.

15   Purchased merchandise by issuing its own 90-day note for $4,800. The note is dated November 15 and bears interest at 12 percent.

20   Discounted the Best Company note at 12 percent at the First State Bank.

30   The First State Bank notified the Brown Company that it had charged the note of October 31 against the company's checking account.

Required:

Assume that all notes falling due after November 30 were paid in full on their due dates by the respective makers. Prepare dated journal entries for the Brown Company for all of the above transactions (including the payment of the notes after November 30) and all necessary adjusting entries assuming a fiscal year accounting period ending on November 30.

7-5-B

The Giersch Company is in the power boat manufacturing business. As of September 1, the balance in its Notes Receivable account is $46,000. The balance in the Notes Receivable Discounted account is $14,000, and the balance in Dishonored Notes Receivable is $10,110. A schedule of the notes (including the dishonored note) is as follows:

Face amount	Maker	Date	Life	Interest rate	Comments
$20,000	C. Davis Co.	6/1/80	120 days	12%	
12,000	A. Box Co.	6/15/80	90 days	8	
14,000	C. Bean Co.	7/1/80	90 days	10	Discounted 8/16/80 at 6%
10,000	Y. Sole Co.	7/1/80	60 days	12	Dishonored, interest, $100;
$56,000					Protest fee, $10

Required:

Prepare dated journal entries for the following transactions.

Transactions:

Sept. 5 The C. Davis Company note is discounted at the Fulton County Bank. The discount rate is 10 percent.

10 Received $6,110 from the Y. Sole Company as full settlement of the amount
due from it. The company does not charge losses on notes to the Allowance for
Doubtful Accounts account.

? The A. Box Company note is collected when due.

? The C. Davis Company note is not paid at maturity. The bank deducts the balance from the Giersch Company's bank balance. A protest fee of $8 is also
deducted.

? C. Bean Company pays its note at maturity.

30 Received a new 60-day, 12 percent note from the C. Davis Company for the
total balance due on the dishonored note. The note is dated as of the maturity
date of the dishonored note. The Giersch Company accepts the note in good
faith.

7–6–B

The records of the Temple Corporation show the following for the calendar year just
ended:

Sales	$850,000
Interest earned on—	
State of New York Bonds	6,000
City of Detroit Bonds	3,000
Howard County, Ohio, School District No. 1 Bonds	750
Cost of goods sold and other expenses	630,000
Loss on sale of capital asset	6,000
Gain on sale of capital asset acquired two years ago	15,000
Allowable extra depreciation deduction for tax purposes	9,000
Dividends declared	30,000
Revenue received in advance, considered taxable income of this year	6,000
Contribution made to influence legislation (included in the $630,000 listed above)	600

Required:

a Present a schedule showing the computation of taxable income.
b Compute the corporation's tax for the current year. (Assume the tax rates mentioned
in this chapter apply.)

7–7–B (based on Appendix 7A)

The Smith Company has an annual payroll of $480,000 in 1977. There are 10 employees
who earn $18,000 each and 40 part-time employees, each of whom earns an equal amount.

Required:

a What are the total employee and employer portions of the F.I.C.A. tax for the year?
b What are the amounts of federal and state unemployment tax per year, assuming that
the federal rate is 3.4 percent and the state rate is 2.7 percent for this company?
c What is the total expense incurred by the employer for these items?

341

7–8–B (based on Appendix 7A)

The Olson Company pays its employees once each month. The payroll data for October are as follows:

Gross payroll .... $41,200 (One employee is above the $6,000 limit. Prior to October his gross salary was $18,000 and his gross October salary was $2,000.)

Income tax withheld........ 4,400
F.I.C.A. tax.................... ?
State income tax .... 3% of gross salary

Required:

Prepare entries to record:

a The October payroll.
b The employer's F.I.C.A. tax for October (use 1977 rates).
c The employer's federal and state unemployment taxes assuming that the federal rate is 3.4 percent and that the state rate is 2.7 percent.
d Payment of the various taxes.

7–9–B [Parts (b) and (c) are based on Appendix 7B]

On January 1 of year 1, Taylor Corporation acquired a machine for $100,000 which is expected to have a four-year life and no salvage value. The company decided to use the sum-of-the-years'-digits method of depreciation for tax purposes and the straight-line method for book purposes. Under the sum-of-the-years'-digits method, the amounts of depreciation are $40,000, $30,000, $20,000, and $10,000, respectively. There are no other timing differences. Net earnings before depreciation and income taxes are $100,000 for each of the four years.

Required:

a Prepare a schedule showing taxable income and income taxes due for each of the four years (assuming a 40 percent tax rate for the sake of simplicity).
b Prepare a schedule showing the amount of net earnings after taxes as it will appear on the earnings statement assuming that income tax allocation procedures are followed.
c Prepare the year-end adjusting entry required at the end of each of the four years to recognize federal income tax expense.

8

Measurement and reporting of long-lived assets*

Learning objectives

Study of the material in this chapter is designed to achieve these learning objectives:

1. A basic understanding of the nature and general characteristics of the various types of long-term assets.

2. An understanding of the nature of depreciation, depletion, and amortization, especially the similarities and differences among these concepts.

3. An understanding of the nature of the transactions involving long-term assets.

4. Theoretical and practical knowledge of the various methods of determining depreciation.

5. Development of the student's ability to trace the effects of transactions involving long-term assets.

*This chapter has been divided into two reading sections to offer flexibility in assigning the chapter. All end of chapter questions, exercises, and problems have been identified as to the reading section to which they relate.

Frame 1[8] ————————————————————————————————

General nature of long-lived assets

In this chapter we will discuss long-lived assets (assets whose useful lives are expected to last over several accounting periods) and their effects on periodic net earnings. To match periodic revenues and related expenses as accurately and logically as possible, it is necessary to measure the part of the service-rendering abilities of these assets which expired during the period. While it is often difficult to determine the exact length of the useful lives of these assets, some estimate must be made so that the amount of expense (the amount of the service) may be determined.

Long-lived assets are made up of plant assets and intangible assets. Plant assets are tangible assets obtained for use in business operations instead of for resale. Intangible assets also have this characteristic but cannot be seen or touched.

Types of plant assets

Plant assets may be classified as follows:

1. Land. This classification includes land currently being used and land held for future use. Land also includes sites bought for natural resource value, residential or speculative value, rights of way, and land purchased for farming. Because land does not deteriorate with age or use, it is not depreciable or depletable. Farmland is an exception to this rule because it may lose its fertility or suffer from erosion.

2. Natural resources. Mines, quarries, oil deposits, gas deposits, and timber stands are known as *wasting assets*. They are used up through the physical removal of part of the resources and are thus subject to depletion.

3. Depreciable plant assets. Buildings, machinery, tools, delivery equipment, office equipment and furniture, and leasehold improvements are also plant assets. They are all tangible, and their usefulness is reduced through wear and tear or obsolescence.

Types of intangible assets

Intangible assets are usually classified as follows:

1. Those that are specifically identifiable and can be acquired individually as well as in groups of assets such as patents, trademarks, and franchises.
2. Those that are not individually identifiable and may be acquired only as part of a group of assets. Because they cannot be identified individually, they are often lumped together and called goodwill.

These intangible assets have no physical characteristics. They have value because they give business advantages or exclusive privileges and rights to their owners.

Expenses related to plant and intangible assets

Plant assets, except land and natural resources, are subject to depreciation. Depreciation in accounting is an estimate, usually expressed in terms of cost, of the amount of service potential of an asset which expired in a given period. It is caused by wear and tear, obsolescence, inadequacy for future needs, physical deterioration, the passage of time, and the action of the elements. Depreciation accounting distributes in a systematic and rational manner the cost of a plant asset, less its salvage value, over the asset's estimated useful life. To record the periodic depreciation, one should debit the depreciation account and credit the allowance for depreciation account. The later accounting treatment of the amounts of depreciation recorded depends upon the type of services which the asset provides. If the services received are classified as selling or administrative, the depreciation is usually expensed in the period recognized. If manufacturing services are received, the depreciation may be treated as a part of the manufacturing cost. In such an instance, it becomes an expense (as part of cost of goods sold) when the manufactured goods are sold to customers. The depreciation recorded on one asset may be considered part of the cost of another—for example, when a truck is used in the construction of a building.

Depletion is the exhaustion of a natural resource such as a mine. It results from the physical removal of part of the resource (ore). Because such resources are usually recorded at their cost, the amount of depletion which is recognized in a period is an estimate of the cost of the amount of the resource which is removed during the period. It is recorded by debiting the depletion account and either crediting the resource account directly or an allowance for depletion account. This depletion cost is combined with other mining or removal costs to determine the total cost of the resource mined. This total cost is then divided between cost of goods sold and the inventory of ore on hand according to the amount of ore sold. Thus, it is possible that all, some, or none of the depletion recognized in a period will be expensed in that period. The part not considered an expense will be part of the cost of a current asset—inventory.

All intangible assets are subject to amortization. Amortization is an estimate of the services or benefits received from an intangible asset in a given period. It is recorded by debiting an amortization account and crediting the intangible asset account directly. Or an allowance for amortization may be established. The possible treatments of the amortization account are the same as those given above for depreciation.

Plant and intangible assets are generally first recorded at the original cost of acquiring them. Depreciable plant assets are then carried at this cost. The portion of the cost which has been assigned to current and past periods is carried in the corresponding allowance for depreciation account. Depletable plant assets and intangible assets, on the other hand, are usually carried at their acquisition cost less that part of the cost which has been allocated to current and past periods.

Often, plant and intangible assets can be sold at prices which vary greatly from their recorded costs. The accounting requirement of realization does not allow recording market prices greater than cost until the asset is sold. It also is not proper to recognize a loss by writing down the asset to a market value lower than cost if the cost of the asset is expected to be fully recovered from the future revenues the asset will produce. Thus, plant and intangible assets are usually reported at cost or, if of limited life, at cost less the amount of cost that has been depreciated or amortized.

On a separate piece of paper, state whether each of the following statements correctly or incorrectly expresses the purpose of depreciation accounting.

1. To adjust the accounts to show the current market value of plant assets on the statement of financial position.

2. To set up a fund of money from which the plant assets can be replaced at the end of their useful lives.

3. To match the cost of plant assets with the revenue produced by the use of those assets.

4. To measure the amount of physical deterioration of plant assets which has occurred during the accounting period.

Check your answers against Answer Frame 1[8] on page 348.

Frame 2[8]

Plant assets

Cost basis of measurement

Plant assets are usually recorded at cost. Cost includes all outlays necessary to obtain and get the asset ready for use.

Cost of land. The cost of land includes the purchase price, option cost, cost of title search, fees for recording the title transfer, unpaid taxes assumed by the purchaser, cost of grading, and local assessments for sidewalks, streets, sewers, and water mains.

Cost of building. If a building is purchased, its cost includes the purchase price, the costs of repairing and remodeling the building for the purposes of the new owner, unpaid taxes assumed by the purchaser, legal costs, and real estate brokerage commissions. When land and buildings are purchased, the total cost should be divided so that separate ledger accounts may be established for land and for buildings. This may be done by a competent appraiser. One of the reasons for dividing the cost is to establish the proper balances in the appropriate accounts. This is especially important since reported earnings will be affected by the later depreciation recorded only on the buildings. Remember that land is not depreciable.

If a building is constructed, the cost may be more difficult to determine. But it usually includes payments to contractors, architects' fees, building permits, taxes during construction, salaries of officers supervising construction, and insurance during construction.

As part of its expansion program, Whitney Corporation purchased an old farm on the outskirts of Manhattan, Kansas, as a factory site. The company paid $90,000 for this property. An appraisal made shortly before the sale showed that the land was worth two thirds of the total value, the buildings one third. The company also agreed to pay back taxes of $6,000 on this property. The attorneys' fees and other legal costs related to the purchase amounted to $750. The farm buildings were demolished at a net cost of $6,500 (cost of removal less salvage value), and a factory was constructed at a cost of $145,000. Building permits and architects' fees amounted to $15,000. Finally, the company paid an assessment of $4,200 to the city for water mains, sewers, and street paving. What is the depreciable cost of the new factory building?

The correct answer may be found by checking Answer Frame 2[8] on page 348.

Frame 3[8]

Cost of machinery. If machinery is purchased, its cost includes the net invoice price, transportation charges, insurance in transit, cost of installation, and other costs needed to put it into condition and location for use. If a company builds a machine for its own use, the cost includes material, labor, and an amount equal to the increase in factory costs caused by the construction of the machine. This cost of the machine should be recorded in the Machinery account (even if it is less than what the company would have paid if it had purchased the machine) since it represents resources sacrificed to acquire the machine.

Cost of delivery equipment. The cost of delivery equipment includes all costs necessary to place the equipment in use. Included in the cost are the f.o.b. shipping point price, transportation charges, accessories' cost, and special paint and decoration costs.

Cost of office equipment. The cost of office equipment includes the net invoice purchase price and all costs necessary to place the equipment in condition and location for use.

1. Incorrect. Depreciation is a process of cost allocation, not a process of valuation. Remember that accounting is usually based on cost.

2. Incorrect. Depreciation accounting does not involve the transfer of any money to a special bank account or to a little tin box in the president's office. While all accounting records are kept in money terms, the only transactions which affect the firm's money holdings are those which include a debit or credit to cash or to some bank account.

3. Correct. The aim of depreciation accounting is to allocate systematically the cost of plant assets to the same period that revenue is produced with those assets.

4. Incorrect. The rate of expected physical deterioration of the asset is one of the factors which determines the expected useful life of the asset. Thus, it has an impact on the rate at which the cost of the asset is charged to expense. But depreciation is not determined solely by the physical deterioration of the asset. Other factors such as obsolescence and inadequacy are equally, and often more, important.

If you answered any question incorrectly, reread Frame 1⁸ before going on to Frame 2⁸ on page 346.

The depreciable cost is $160,000. All of the costs relating to the purchase of the farm and the razing of the old buildings are assignable to the land account in this case, because none of the old buildings purchased with the land is to be used. The real objective was to purchase the land, but the land was not available without taking the buildings also. If, instead of the situation described, one or more of the existing buildings had been remodeled for use by Whitney Corporation, it would have been necessary to determine what part of the cash purchase price of the farm, the back taxes, and the legal fees was allocable to such buildings and what portion of the cost plus remodeling costs would have been included in the cost of the new factory. Land improvements such as sewers, water mains, and paving are usually considered a part of the cost of the land. Thus, the depreciable cost of the factory building is the construction cost of $145,000 plus the architects' fees and building permit costs of $15,000.

If you did not respond correctly, reread Frame 2⁸ before proceeding to Frame 3⁸, on page 347.

3⁸
continued

After pricing machinery of the type needed, the Cover Foundry decided to build its own machine. The cost of construction was $16,000. The f.o.b. shipping point price of a similar machine purchased from the usual source is $18,000, and transportation charges to the Cover Foundry would amount to $950. The machine constructed should be recorded in the accounts at which of the following amounts?

1. $16,000.
2. $18,000.
3. $18,950.

Now check your response in Answer Frame 3⁸ on page 350.

Frame 4⁸ ————————————————————————

Noncash exchanges and gifts of plant assets

Plant assets are usually acquired by purchase. They may also be acquired through an exchange for other assets, or as gifts. When plant assets are acquired under these conditions, it is necessary to determine the amount at which they should be initially recorded. Several possible bases may be used such as book value, fair market value, and appraised value.

Book value. The book value of an asset given up is an acceptable basis for measuring a newly acquired asset only if a better basis is not available. This is true even if some cash is given or received in the exchange.

Fair market value. If noncash assets are received in an exchange for securities having a known market value, the cost of the assets received is considered equal to the fair market value of the securities given up. If the securities given up do not have a known market value, the cash purchase price at which the asset could have been acquired should be used as the cost of the asset. It would also be considered the amount received for the securities.

Appraised value. Noncash assets are sometimes acquired as gifts. Although these assets do not cost the recipient anything, they are usually recorded in the accounts. If similar assets are not regularly traded and a market value cannot be determined for them, they may be recorded at an appraised value determined by a professional appraiser or by management.

When assets are received in a noncash exchange, it is the accountant's job to find the best measure of their value. The general rule followed is to use the fair market value of the assets received or of the assets given up, whichever is more clearly evident.

On July 14, 1979, the Bogart Company acquired land next to its factory for use as a parking lot in exchange for 100 shares of its common stock. At the beginning of negotiations, the owner of the property quoted a price of $8,300 for the land. The common stock of the Bogart Company has a market value of $79 per share on July 14, 1979. Similar plots of land in the city are selling for $7,500. At what amount should this land be recorded in the accounts?

You may check your response in Answer Frame 4⁸ on page 350.

Frame 5⁸ ————————————————————————

Continuing expenditures on plant assets

It is often necessary to make expenditures for plant assets other than when they are acquired. The accounting treatment of such expenditures

Answer frame 3⁸

The correct answer is the first one, $16,000. The accountant uses the actual cost incurred. Estimates of what an item would cost are used only when objective cost figures are not available.

If you answered incorrectly, restudy Frame 3⁸ before going on to Frame 4⁸ on page 349.

Answer frame 4⁸

The land should be recorded at $7,900. Since the stock given in exchange for the land has a known market price at the time of the exchange, that price is the best measure of the cost of the land to Bogart Company. The fact that similar property in the city is selling for less is not important; Bogart Company obviously wanted the property enough to be willing to give up stock which it could sell in the market for $7,900. Also, every tract of land is unique—there is none other exactly like it.

If you did not answer correctly, reread Frame 4⁸ before going on to Frame 5⁸ on page 349.

5⁸
continued

may consist of charging the amount to (1) an asset account, (2) an allowance for depreciation account, or (3) an expense account.

Expenditures which are added to the asset account or charged to the allowance for depreciation account are often called capital expenditures. These expenditures increase the net book value of the plant or capital assets. On the other hand, expenditures immediately expensed are called revenue expenditures. The differences between these two are developed below.

Expenditures capitalized in asset accounts

Expenditures for new or used assets, additions to existing assets, and betterments or improvements to existing assets are called capital expenditures. They are properly chargeable to asset accounts because they add to the service-rendering ability of the assets. For example, the $25,000 cash cost of a used press plus the $450 transportation cost for hauling the press to the company's plant are properly charged to an asset account, Machinery.

Shortly after the purchase, the company spent $3,200 to recondition the press and $750 to install it. These expenditures should be charged to the Machinery account. They are part of the total costs incurred to obtain the services from the press throughout its entire life.

Assume that a few weeks later, the company spent $850 for additional electrical controls for the press. This expenditure has the effect of increasing the efficiency of the asset. What is the correct entry to record the expenditure?

The correct entry is presented in Answer Frame 5⁸ on page 352.

Frame 6⁸

Assuming this press has an estimated life of ten years and no expected salvage value at the end of that time, what is the annual depreciation on this item of machinery under the straight-line method?

Turn to Answer Frame 6⁸ on page 352 to check your answer.

Frame 7⁸

Expenditures capitalized as charges to allowance for depreciation

Occasionally expenditures are made on plant assets which will extend the life of the assets but not the quality of services they produce. Because they will benefit future periods, these expenditures are properly capitalized. But because there is no visible, tangible addition to or improvement of the asset, they are often charged to the allowance for depreciation account. Such expenditures are viewed as canceling a part ·of the accumulated depreciation.

Expenditures for major repairs which do not extend the life of the asset are also often charged to the allowance for depreciation (which increases future depreciation charges). This avoids distortion of net earnings which might result if such expenditures were expensed. In this way the cost of major repairs is spread over a number of years.

To illustrate, assume that after operating the press for four years, the company in the preceding illustration spent $3,750 to recondition it. The effect of the reconditioning is to increase the life of the machine to a total of 14 years from an original estimate of 10 years. The journal entry to record the major repair is:

Allowance for Depreciation – Machinery	3,750	
Cash (or Accounts Payable)		3,750
Cost of reconditioning press.		

When it was acquired, the press had an estimated life of ten years with no expected salvage value. At the end of the fourth year the balance in its allowance for depreciation account under the straight-line method is $12,100 [($30,250 ÷ 10) × 4]. After the $3,750 debit to the allowance for depreciation account, the balances in the asset account and its related allowance for depreciation account are:

Cost of press	$30,250
Allowance for depreciation	8,350
Net Book Value (end of four years)	$21,900

The remaining book value of $21,900 is divided equally among the ten remaining years in amounts of $2,190 per year under the straight-line

Answer frame 5[8]

The correct entry to record the installation of additional electrical controls on the press is:

Machinery... 850
    Cash (or Accounts Payable) 850
Electrical controls installed on press.

If you do not understand that such expenditures should be capitalized, reread Frame 5[8]. Then go on to Frame 6[8] on page 351.

Answer frame 6[8]

The annual straight-line depreciation on the press is $3,025. This is computed by summing the invoice price, transportation charges, reconditioning, installation costs, and the cost of the electrical controls ($25,000 + $450 + $3,200 + $750 + $850 = $30,250) and dividing by ten years.

If you answered incorrectly, restudy this answer frame before going on to Frame 7[8] on page 351.

7[8]
continued

method. The effect of the expenditure, then, is to increase the carrying amount of the asset by reducing its contra account, the allowance for depreciation.

If the expenditure did not extend the life of the asset but, because of its size, was still charged to the allowance for depreciation, the $21,900 would be spread over the remaining six years of life. Annual charges would be $3,650 ($21,900 ÷ 6) under the straight-line method.

This procedure of charging the cost of major repairs to the allowance for depreciation is valid in theory only when the annual depreciation charges are increased to take such expected costs into consideration. For example, assume a company purchased a machine at a total cash cost of $12,000. Assume further that this machine would last ten years if it were given a major overhaul at the end of five years, and that the cost of the overhaul is estimated to be $6,000. Under these circumstances, an entry debiting depreciation and crediting the allowance for depreciation for $1,800 is appropriate [($12,000 + $6,000) ÷ 10 = $1,800]. The only proper treatment of the costs of the major overhaul is to charge them to the allowance for depreciation account.

But it is often difficult to estimate the cost of future repairs. In this case, techniques as precise as the one described above cannot be used. The actual methods used may be closer to the illustration regarding the $3,750 repair to the press.

Expenditures charged to periodic expense

Recurring expenditures that neither add to the service-rendering abilities of the asset nor extend its life are treated as periodic expenses. Thus, regular maintenance (lubricating a machine) and ordinary repairs (replacing a broken fan belt) are expensed immediately as revenue expenditures. For example, if the company above spends $190 to repair the press after using it for some time, the journal entry is:

Maintenance Expense..	190	
Cash..		190
To record payment of repair cost on press.		

Distinguishing between capital and revenue expenditures

It is often very difficult to distinguish between capital and revenue expenditures because the distinction lies mainly in the length of time that the expenditure will be beneficial. If a revenue expenditure is improperly capitalized during a period, asset costs are overstated, expenses are understated, and net earnings and retained earnings are overstated. During the rest of the asset's life, net earnings will be understated because of incorrect depreciation charges. If a capital expenditure is improperly charged to an expense account, the book value of the asset is misstated. In addition, expenses are overstated for that period, and net earnings and retained earnings are understated. In the periods that follow, expenses will be understated and net earnings overstated because depreciation expense will be understated in those periods.

On January 2, 1979, Zee Company purchased a machine for cash at an invoice price of $22,000. In addition, the company paid $317 freight charges and a $425 installation charge. The invoice price of the machine was charged to the Machinery account, while the freight and installation costs were debited to Maintenance Expense. This machine has an estimated life of seven years. If this error is not discovered and corrected, which of the following correctly states the effect on net earnings for 1979 and 1980?

1. Net earnings for 1979 will be understated by $742; net earnings for 1980 will be unaffected.
2. Net earnings for 1979 will be understated by $742; net earnings for 1980 will be overstated by $106.
3. Net earnings for 1979 will be understated by $636; net earnings for 1980 will be overstated by $106.
4. Net earnings for 1979 will be overstated by $848; net earnings for 1980 will be overstated by $106.

Now check your response in Answer Frame 7[8] on page 354.

Answer 3 is correct. The $742 overstatement of maintenance expense caused by charging to expense some of the costs of the new machine will cause 1979 net earnings to be understated by that amount. But the asset account has been understated. Hence depreciation has been based on too small a figure. If the asset costs were properly capitalized, the depreciation charge for 1979 would be $106 larger ($742/7 = $106). Net earnings for the year are therefore understated by the net amount of $742 − $106 = $636. Of course the 1980 depreciation also will be understated by $106 if the error is not corrected, thus resulting in a $106 overstatement of 1980 net earnings.

If you did not respond correctly, restudy Frame 7⁸ before continuing to Frame 8⁸ below.

Frame 8⁸

Depreciation of plant assets

As stated in Frame 1⁸, depreciation is the allocation of the cost of a plant asset to expense over its useful life in a reasonable and systematic manner. Depreciation is one of the costs of operating a business. The use of plant assets in the operation of a business represents the change from a plant asset cost to an operating cost. Depreciation is a noncash cost because it does not require the actual outlay of cash. It is assumed that the asset being depreciated is not being paid for in any way which corresponds to the depreciation expense appearing on the earnings statement.

Factors affecting depreciation estimates. To estimate periodic depreciation, the following three factors must be considered:

1. Cost.
2. Estimated salvage value. Salvage or scrap value is the amount estimated to be recoverable (less disposal cost) on the date the asset will be disposed of or retired.
3. Estimated life. This may be expressed in years, months, working hours, or units of production.

When depreciation is recorded, a depreciation expense account is debited. The depreciation expense account appears in the earnings statement as one of the expenses of generating revenue. The periodic depreciation is credited to an allowance for depreciation account. The allowance for depreciation account is used so that the original cost of the asset will continue to be shown in the asset account. The total accumulated depreciation will be shown separately in the allowance account.

Depreciation is recorded only for that portion of the year during which the asset is available for use. If an asset is purchased on May 1 and the accounting period ends on December 31, only eight months depreciation should be recorded.

Straight-line depreciation. There are many ways to compute depreciation. One of the methods most commonly used is the straight-line method which we introduced earlier. The straight-line method distributes the same dollar amount of depreciation to expense each period. Under this method the passage of time is considered to be the main factor in allocating cost. It assumes that wear, obsolescence, and deterioration of the plant assets are directly proportional to elapsed time. This assumption may not be true.

The formula for computing depreciation under the straight-line method is:

$$\text{Depreciation per period} = \frac{(\text{Cost} - \text{Estimated salvage value})}{\text{Number of accounting periods in estimated life}}$$

To illustrate, for a machine costing $27,000 with an estimated life of ten years and an estimated salvage value of $2,000, the depreciation per year is ($27,000 − $2,000) ÷ 10, or $2,500. The schedule in Illustration 8.1 presents the annual depreciation entries, the balance in the allowance for depreciation accounts, and the book (or carrying) value of this machine. Book value is the difference between original cost and the balance of the allowance for depreciation account.

Illustration 8.1   Depreciation schedule — straight-line method

End of year	Depreciation expense Dr.; Allowance for depreciation Cr.	Total allowance	Book value
			$27,000
1	$ 2,500	$ 2,500	24,500
2	2,500	5,000	22,000
3	2,500	7,500	19,500
4	2,500	10,000	17,000
5	2,500	12,500	14,500
6	2,500	15,000	12,000
7	2,500	17,500	9,500
8	2,500	20,000	7,000
9	2,500	22,500	4,500
10	2,500	25,000	2,000*
	$25,000		

* Estimated salvage value.

On the basis of Illustration 8.1 indicate whether each of the following statements is true or false in regard to the straight-line method of depreciation.

1. The annual depreciation charge is a constant amount.
2. Book value at the end of the last year of an asset's estimated life should be equal to the estimated salvage value.
3. The credit balance in the allowance for depreciation account at the end of the tenth year is equal to the cost of the asset.

Now check your responses in Answer Frame 8[8] on page 356.

1. True. The charge for depreciation is a constant—in this case, $2,500 each year over the life of the asset.
2. True. The depreciation charge is computed on the basis of cost minus salvage. It follows that total depreciation will equal this difference, and the final book value must be equal to the salvage value.
3. False. The credit balance in the allowance account at the end of the tenth year is the total amount of depreciation charged over the life of the asset, which is equal to cost less estimated salvage value. In this case the balance of the account is $25,000 ($27,000 − $2,000), not the $27,000 original cost of the asset. But the statement would be true if the estimated salvage value were zero.

If you answered any of the above incorrectly, restudy Frame 8[8] before going on to Frame 9[8] below.

Frame 9[8]

Units-of-production depreciation. If usage is the main factor causing the expiration of the asset, depreciation may be based on physical output. The depreciation charge per unit of output may be found by dividing the original cost of the asset, less any salvage value, by the estimated number of units to be produced during the asset's life. The periodic depreciation is then obtained by multiplying the rate per unit by the actual number of units produced during the period.

For example, on March 1, 1979, a corporation purchased a stamping machine at a total cost of $27,000. The machine is expected to have a ten-year life and a $2,000 salvage value, during which time it will produce approximately $12\frac{1}{2}$ million units of product. During 1979, this machine processed 800,000 units of product. Depreciation for the year under the units-of-production method is:

1. $2,500.
2. $2,083.
3. $1,600.

The correct answer is in Answer Frame 9[8] on page 358.

Frame 10[8]

Accelerated depreciation. The 1954 Revenue Act permitted taxpayers to use a fixed percentage declining-balance method or a sum-of-the-years'-digits method of computing depreciation. These methods are often called accelerated depreciation and are still used. Under these methods, larger amounts of depreciation are recorded in the earlier years of an asset's life than in the later years. Business managers often prefer these methods because the increased depreciation in the early

Illustration 8.2   Double-declining-balance method depreciation schedule

End of year	Depreciation expense Dr.; Allowance for depreciation Cr.	Total allowance	Book value
			$27,000.00
1. (20% of $27,000)	$5,400.00	$ 5,400.00	21,600.00
2. (20% of $21,600)	4,320.00	9,720.00	17,280.00
3. (20% of $17,280)	3,456.00	13,176.00	13,824.00
4. (20% of $13,824)	2,764.80	15,940.80	11,059.20
5. (20% of $11,059.20)	2,211.84	18,152.64	8,847.36
6. (20% of $8,847.36)	1,769.47	19,922.11	7,077.89
7. (20% of $7,077.89)	1,415.58	21,337.69	5,662.31
8. (20% of $5,662.31)	1,132.46	22,470.15	4,529.85
9. (20% of $4,529.85)	905.97	23,376.12	3,623.88
10. (20% of $3,623.88)	724.78*	24,100.90	2,899.10

* This amount could be $2,529.85 so as to reduce the book value down to the estimated salvage value of $2,000.

years reduces taxable earnings. This in turn reduces the amount of federal income taxes which must be paid in those years.

There is also theoretical support for these methods. Their use seems especially appropriate when the service-rendering or revenue-producing ability of the asset declines over time, when the value of the asset declines more in early years and less in later years of its life, and when repairs and other maintenance costs increase over time.

Double-declining-balance method of depreciation. Under this method the straight-line rate of depreciation is doubled, and the doubled rate is applied to the declining balance of the asset—its net book value. Salvage value is ignored. Illustration 8.2 gives an example of an asset costing $27,000 with an estimated life of ten years and a salvage value of $2,000. In this example, the 10 percent straight-line rate of depreciation (100 percent ÷ 10 years = 10 percent per year) is doubled, giving a depreciation rate of 20 percent.

When the double-declining-balance method is used to compute the annual depreciation amount, the annual amount is allocated to the months within the year on a straight-line basis. For example, the depreciation per month in the first year for the asset in Illustration 8.2 is $450.00 ($5,400 ÷ 12). In the second year, it is $360.00 ($4,320 ÷ 12) per month.

Indicate whether each statement is correct or incorrect. Under the double-declining-balance method, the annual depreciation charge:

1. Is constant over the life of the asset.
2. Increases over the life of the asset.
3. Is computed by multiplying the book value of the asset at the beginning of the year by a fixed percentage.
4. Is computed by multiplying the original cost of the asset by a smaller and smaller percentage each successive year.

Check your responses in Answer Frame 10[8] on page 358.   357

Answer frame 9[8]

Answer 3, $1,600, is correct. The 1979 depreciation on the machine is computed as follows: (the cost of the machine less salvage value) divided by estimated total output is the depreciation per unit; depreciation per unit times output per period is the depreciation expense for the period. Thus, for 1979:

$$\frac{\$27,000 - \$2,000}{12,500,000 \text{ units}} = \$0.002 \text{ per unit; } \$0.002 \times 800,000 = \$1,600$$

$2,500 is the regular straight-line depreciation based on years of life, not usage. The second answer ($2,083) correctly recognized that the machine was in use for only ten months, but is still based on time rather than usage.

If you did not get the correct answer, reread Frame 9[8] before going on to Frame 10[8] on page 356.

Answer frame 10[8]

1. Incorrect. It decreases over the life of the asset.
2. Incorrect. It decreases over the life of the asset.
3. Correct. Salvage value is not deducted. But notice one more thing. When using the fixed percentage on a declining-balance method, there will always be a remaining book value—an "automatic" salvage value. In Illustration 8.2 this amounts to $2,899.10 at the end of the tenth year (unless the decision is made to reduce it to $2,000).
4. Incorrect. The same percentage is used each year.

If you missed any of the above, reread Frame 10[8] before going on to Frame 11[8] below.

Frame 11[8]

Sum-of-the-years'-digits depreciation. This method also produces larger depreciation charges in the early years of an asset's life. The years of estimated life of an asset are added together and used as the denominator in a fraction. The number of years of life remaining at the beginning of the accounting period is the numerator. Cost, less estimated salvage value, is then multiplied by this fraction to compute the periodic depreciation. This is illustrated below for a plant asset which costs $27,000, has an estimated useful life of ten years, and salvage value of $2,000.

Sum-of-the-years' digits: $1 + 2 + 3 + 4 + 5 + 6 + 7 + 8 + 9 + 10 = 55$.

Depreciation:

Year 1:	10/55 of $25,000	$4,545.45
Year 2:	9/55 of $25,000	4,090.91
Year 2:	8/55 of $25,000	3,636.36
Year 4:	7/55 of $25,000	3,181.82
Year 5:	6/55 of $25,000	2,727.27
Year 6:	5/55 of $25,000	2,272.73
Year 7:	4/55 of $25,000	1,818.18
Year 8:	3/55 of $25,000	1,363.64
Year 9:	2/55 of $25,000	909.09
Year 10:	1/55 of $25,000	454.55
	Total Depreciation	25,000.00

At the beginning of Year 1 there are ten years of life remaining. Thus, the ratio used to compute the depreciation charge for Year 1 is 10/55.

The mathematical formula for finding the sum-of-the-years' digits for any given number of periods is:

$$S = \frac{n(n + 1)}{2}$$

where S is the sum-of-the-years' digits and n is the number of periods in the asset's life. Thus the sum-of-the-years' digits for 10 years is 55, computed as follows:

$$\frac{10(10 + 1)}{2} = \frac{110}{2} = 55$$

If, on January 2, 1979, a company purchased an asset costing $80,000 with an estimated life of ten years and salvage value of $8,000, under which of the following methods would the 1979 depreciation be the largest?

1. Straight-line method.
2. Double-declining-balance method.
3. Sum-of-the-years'-digits method.

To check your response, turn to Answer Frame 11[8] on page 360.

Frame 12[8]

Rose Corporation channels production through the newest machinery in the plant whenever possible. The most recently acquired machinery is used most fully, the next oldest is used almost as much, and so on until finally the oldest machinery is placed in a standby capacity. If you were asked to decide whether the Melrose Corporation should use the straight-line or the sum-of-the-years'-digits method for depreciating machinery, which method would result in the best matching of its costs and revenues?

Check your answer in Answer Frame 12[8] on page 360.

Frame 13[8]

Revisions of life estimates

When it is found that the estimate of the life of an asset is incorrect, the annual depreciation charge under the straight-line method may be changed as follows: the net book value (less salvage) of the asset at the

359

Answer frame 11⁸

Answer 2, double-declining-balance method, is correct. The 1979 depreciation for the plant asset computed under each of the three methods is:
1. Straight-line method: $80,000 less $8,000, divided by ten years, is $7,200.
2. Double-declining-balance method: 20 percent of $80,000 is $16,000. The straight-line depreciation rate is 10 percent (100 percent ÷ 10 years = 10 percent); 20 percent is used because it is double the straight-line rate.
3. Sum-of-the-years'-digits method: 10/55 × $72,000 = $13,090.91.

If you answered incorrectly, reread Frames 8⁸–11⁸ before turning to Frame 12⁸ on page 359.

Answer frame 12⁸

The sum-of-the-years'-digits method is correct. The aim of matching costs and revenues is better accomplished by one of the accelerated methods in this case. The machines are used more during their early years and presumably produce more revenue in the first few years and successively less revenue as they grow older. The sum-of-the-years'-digits method results in matching a larger proportion of the cost of the machine to the first year's revenue, with successively smaller charges for depreciation in the following years. This pattern approximates the revenue-producing pattern of the machines owned by the Rose Corporation.

If you answered incorrectly, reread Frames 8⁸–12⁸ before going on to Frame 13⁸ on page 359.

13⁸
continued

beginning of the current period is divided by estimated remaining life of the asset. The result is the new annual depreciation charge to be used in the current and future years.

For example, assume that a machine has a cost of $21,000, an estimated salvage value of $3,000, and that the balance in the allowance for depreciation account (based on a life estimate of ten years) is $9,000 at the end of the fifth year of the asset's life. At the beginning of the sixth year it is estimated that the asset will last another ten years (salvage value remains at $3,000). What is the revised annual depreciation charge?

Check your computation in Answer Frame 13⁸ on page 362.

SECTION 2

Frame 14⁸

Disposition of plant assets

Sale of plant assets. When a plant asset is sold, the balances in the asset account and the related allowance for depreciation account must be taken off the records. The difference between the net book value (cost less allowance for depreciation) of the asset and the amount received from its sale represents a gain or a loss on the sale.

For example, assume that at the date of the sale the account balances, selling price, and gain are as shown below:

Machine cost...	$30,000
Allowance for depreciation...........................	12,000
Book value..	$18,000
Sales price..	20,000
Gain Realized..	$ 2,000

The journal entry to record the sale is:

Cash	20,000	
Allowance for Depreciation – Machinery...............................	12,000	
Machinery...		30,000
Gain on Sale of Plant Assets..		2,000

If an asset is sold for less than its net book value, there is a loss on the sale. Thus, if the machine above were sold for $16,500, a debit of $1,500 ($18,000 − $16,500) would be entered in a Loss on Sale of Plant Assets account.

Accounting for depreciation. When a plant asset is sold or disposed of, it is important to record the depreciation to the date of sale. For example, if an asset were sold on July 1 and depreciation was last recorded on December 31, depreciation for six months (January–June 30) should be recorded. If depreciation is not recorded for that period, operating expenses will be understated and the gain on the sale of the asset understated or the loss overstated.

On December 31, 1979, the Office Equipment account of Company X had a balance of $6,000 and the Allowance for Depreciation – Office Equipment account had a balance of $2,500. The rate of depreciation is 10 percent per year. The office equipment was sold for $3,200 cash on February 28, 1980. The following entry was made to record the depreciation for January and February 1980:

Depreciation – Office Equipment	100	
Allowance for Depreciation – Office Equipment		100
Depreciation on $6,000 at 10 percent for 2 months.		

What is the journal entry to record the sale?

Turn to Answer Frame 14[8] on page 362 to check your answer.

Frame 15[8] —————————————————————————————————————

Asset retirements without sale. When an asset is retired but is not sold, it is necessary to remove the asset from the plant asset accounts.   361

The computation of the revised annual depreciation charge is:

$$(\$21{,}000 - \$9{,}000 - \$3{,}000) \div 10 = \$900$$

The book value at the beginning of the sixth year is $12,000 ($21,000 − $9,000), salvage value is still $3,000, and the life of the asset remaining at the beginning of the sixth year is ten years, which results in the revised annual depreciation charge of $900.

If you did not answer correctly, reread Frame 13⁸ before advancing to Frame 14⁸ on page 360.

Answer frame 14⁸

The journal entry to record the sale is:

Cash	3,200	
Allowance for Depreciation — Office Equipment	2,600	
Loss on Sale of Plant Assets	200	
Office Equipment		6,000

The debit to Cash, of course, is equal to the cash received; the credit balance in the Allowance for Depreciation — Office Equipment account is eliminated by the debit to that account; and Office Equipment is decreased by the cost of the machine. Since the selling price of the asset ($3,200) was less than the book value of the asset at date of disposition ($6,000 − $2,600 = $3,400), the company incurred a loss of $200 on the sale.

If you did not record the correct journal entry, reread Frame 14⁸ before going on to Frame 15⁸ on page 361.

15⁸
continued

If the asset is scrapped for salvaged material — even though the material will not be sold immediately — the value of the material should be debited to a Salvaged Materials account. To illustrate, assume that a machine with an original cost of $7,000 and an allowance for depreciation of $6,200 is retired and the scrap value of the machine is estimated at $375. The journal entry to record the retirement is:

Salvaged Materials	375	
Allowance for Depreciation — Machinery	6,200	
Loss on Retirement of Plant Assets	425	
Machinery		7,000

Assets destroyed. Assume that an uninsured building costing $40,000 with an allowance for depreciation of $12,000 is completely destroyed by a fire. The journal entry is:

Fire Loss	28,000	
Allowance for Depreciation — Building	12,000	
Building		40,000

If the building were insured, only the net fire loss in excess of the amount to be recovered from the insurance company would be debited to the Fire Loss account. To illustrate, assume that in the example above the building was partially insured and that $22,000 was recoverable from the insurance company. The journal entry is:

Receivable from Insurance Company	22,000	
Fire Loss	6,000	
Allowance for Depreciation – Building	12,000	
Building		40,000

Asset exchanges. Certain plant assets, such as automobiles and trucks, are often acquired by trading in an old asset. In these cases, it is necessary to determine the amount at which the new asset is to be recorded and the amount of gain or loss, if any, to be recognized.

To illustrate, assume that Delivery Truck No. 1, which cost $15,000 and on which $13,000 of depreciation has accumulated, is exchanged for Delivery Truck No. 2 which has a suggested list price of $20,000. Delivery Truck No. 1 and $19,000 cash are given in exchange. Using the suggested list price as a base, the exchange might be recorded as:

Delivery Trucks (No. 2)	20,000	
Allowance for Depreciation – Delivery Trucks	13,000	
Loss on Exchange of Plant Assets	1,000	
Delivery Trucks (No. 1)		15,000
Cash		19,000

The loss is the difference between book value, $2,000 ($15,000 − $13,-000), and the trade-in allowance granted by the dealer, $1,000 ($20,000 − $19,000). Depreciation on the new truck would be based on the $20,000.

When assets which are not similar (such as a computer and a delivery truck) are exchanged, both gains and losses are recognized. But when similar assets are exchanged (as in the Delivery Truck No. 1–Delivery Truck No. 2 example), losses are recognized but gains are not recognized. Suppose Delivery Truck No. 1 and $17,000 cash had been given in exchange for Delivery Truck No. 2. Then the exchange would be recorded as:

Delivery Trucks (No. 2)	19,000	
Allowance for Depreciation – Delivery Trucks	13,000	
Delivery Trucks (No. 1)		15,000
Cash		17,000

The asset received is recorded at the book value of the asset given up ($2,000) plus the amount of cash paid ($17,000). A gain is not recognized on the exchange of similar assets.

The Internal Revenue Code does not allow recognition of gains or losses for tax purposes when similar productive assets are exchanged. The amount at which the new asset is recorded is the sum of the net book value of the asset given up plus any additional cash paid. The additional cash expenditure is called "boot." The entry to record the first exchange above in accordance with tax law is:

Delivery Trucks (No. 2)	21,000	
Allowance for Depreciation – Delivery Trucks	13,000	
Delivery Trucks (No. 1)		15,000
Cash		19,000

In the past few years, especially (but not only) in the automobile industry, suggested list prices have been poor indicators of actual selling prices. Discounts of up to 20 percent have been available though they were often hidden by granting large trade-in allowances. Suppose that in the first example, the fair cash value of the truck traded in was $800. By granting a $1,000 trade-in allowance for the old truck, the dealer has actually given a $200 discount on the purchase of the new truck. Ignoring federal income taxes, the entry to record the transaction would be:

Delivery Trucks (No. 2)...	19,800	
Allowance for Depreciation – Delivery Trucks.......................	13,000	
Loss on Exchange of Plant Assets	1,200	
Delivery Trucks (No. 1)...		15,000
Cash		19,000

This is the theoretically preferred approach for recording this exchange. Under this method the asset received (Delivery Truck No. 2) is recorded at the fair cash value of the old asset at the time of exchange plus the amount of cash given as boot: $800 + $19,000 = $19,800.

On June 16, 1979, the Monitor Company traded office equipment which originally cost $10,000 for newer models having a suggested total list price of $14,000. The equipment dealer agreed to allow $5,000 on the trade so Monitor issued a check for $9,000 for the balance due. The old equipment had a cash market value of $3,800 at the time of the trade. Its book value adjusted to June 16, 1979, was $4,500. Calculate the amount at which these new assets would be shown on the Monitor Company books under:

1. The income tax method.
2. The theoretically correct accounting method.

Check your answers in Answer Frame 15[8] on page 366.

Frame 16[8]

Leaseholds and leasehold improvements

A lease is a contract by which the person acquiring the lease (the lessee) makes payments to the person granting the lease (the lessor) in exchange for the right to use property for the amount of time stated in the lease.

Under certain circumstances, a lease transaction may be regarded as a purchase and should be recorded as one. This type of lease is called a capital lease and is discussed in Appendix 9B.

If the lease does not meet the criteria for a capital lease, it is called an operating lease. Operating leases are not shown on the lessee's books unless an initial lump-sum payment is made when the lease is signed. An advance payment is recorded in a Leasehold account and is amortized over the life of the lease by a debit to Rent Expense and a credit to Leasehold. Straight-line amortization is commonly used.

On July 1, 1979, Sliger Company leased a building for 20 years at an annual rental of $8,000 payable each June 30. The first annual rental will be made on June 30, 1980. In addition, the lessor required Sliger Company to make an initial lump-sum payment of $40,000 on the day the lease was signed. The lease is an operating lease.

Which of the following entries is the correct journal entry on July 1, 1979?

Leasehold	40,000	
Cash		40,000
Rent Expense	40,000	
Cash		40,000

Turn to Answer Frame 16⁸ on page 366 to check your answer.

Frame 17⁸

On December 31, 1979, two entries will be made, one to accrue rent under the terms of the contract and the other to adjust the Leasehold account. One entry is:

Rent Expense	4,000	
Accrued Rent Payable		4,000

What is the other entry?

Check your response by turning to Answer Frame 17⁸ on page 366.

Frame 18⁸

If the lessee improves the leased property, these improvements will usually become the property of the lessor after the lease has expired. Improvements are assets and should be debited to a Leasehold Improvements account. The useful life of the leasehold improvements to the lessee is the shorter of the life of the improvements or the life of the lease; hence, this is the period over which the cost of the leasehold improvements should be spread. To illustrate, assume that on January 2, 1979, Y leases a building for 25 years under a nonrenewable lease at an annual rental of $20,000 payable on each December 31. Y immediately incurs a cost of $80,000 for improvements to the building, which are estimated to have a life of 40 years. The $80,000 should be amortized over 25 years, since the period of the lease is shorter than the life of the improvements and Y will not be able to use the improvements beyond

Answer frame 15⁸

The cost of the office equipment acquired by Monitor Company under the two methods is:
1. Under the income tax method: $4,500 + $9,000 = $13,500.
2. Under the theoretically correct accounting method: $3,800 + $9,000 = $12,800.

The entry to record the trade-in under each of the methods is:
1. Income tax method:

Office Equipment (new)	13,500	
Allowance for Depreciation — Office Equipment	5,500	
Office Equipment (old)		10,000
Cash		9,000

2. Theoretically correct method:

Office Equipment (new)	12,800	
Allowance for Depreciation — Office Equipment	5,500	
Loss on Exchange of Plant Assets	700	
Office Equipment (old)		10,000
Cash		9,000

Notice again that under the income tax method, no gain or loss is recognized and the dealer's suggested list price is of no significance in computing the cost of the new equipment. It is meaningful only in determining the amount of "boot" required by the seller. But it does not follow that the suggested list price is always to be ignored. In some cases the actual selling price of an asset may be its suggested list price. And it should be recognized that in many exchanges no objective evidence exists as to the fair cash value of the asset given up. Yet the accountant must be alert to the possibility that assets are overstated.

Note also that the income tax method used in the first journal entry above may lead to material misstatements for purposes of earnings determination and asset measurement. This is true because (1) a loss is not recognized and (2) depreciation expense is improperly stated in future periods because it is not based upon the actual cost of the newly acquired asset.

If you answered incorrectly restudy Frame 15⁸ before continuing in Frame 16⁸ on page 364.

Answer frame 16⁸

The first entry is correct. The $40,000 advance payment is recorded as a long-term asset by debiting the Leasehold account. The appropriate portion of this asset is transferred to Rent Expense at the end of each accounting period. The entire lump-sum payment is not an expense for 1979. That portion applicable to 1979 will be recorded as an expense at the end of the accounting period.

If you answered incorrectly, review Frame 16⁸ before going on to Frame 17⁸ on page 365.

Answer frame 17⁸

The December 31, 1979, entry to amortize the Leasehold account is:

Rent Expense	1,000	
Leasehold		1,000

To record as rent expense one half of a year's amortization of
the leasehold down payment [($40,000 ÷ 20 years) × ½].

If you answered incorrectly, reread Frames 16⁸ and 17⁸ before going on to Frame 18⁸ on page 365.

the life of the lease. If only annual statements are prepared, the following journal entries will properly record the expense for the year ended December 31, 1979:

Rent Expense (or Leasehold Improvement Expense)............... 3,200
    Leasehold Improvements... 3,200
  To charge off 1/25th of $80,000.

Rent Expense... 20,000
    Cash 20,000
  To record annual rent of $20,000.

The total rental expense is thus $23,200 per year.

Leaseholds and leasehold improvements are ordinarily shown in the intangible assets section of the statement of financial position.

Assuming the lease cannot be renewed, the balance in the Leasehold Improvements account should be written off to expense over which of the following?

1. The life of the lease.
2. The life of the improvements.
3. Whichever of (1) and (2) is shorter.

Check your response in Answer Frame 18[8] on page 368.

Frame 19[8]

Natural resources

Natural resources, such as mines, quarries, and timber stands should be recorded in the accounts at either (*a*) the cost of acquisition plus the cost of development or (*b*) the discovery value plus the cost of development.

Discovery value may be used when there is no reasonable relationship between the purchase cost and the value of the resources. For tax purposes, discovery value is the fair market value at the date of discovery or within 30 days after the discovery. Discovery value arises when land is bought at the cost of the land alone, followed by the discovery of some natural resource whose value is greater than the cost. For example, assume that land was purchased for $30,000 for cattle grazing purposes. Shortly after the purchase, valuable oil deposits were discovered under the land surface. A geological survey showed that the oil deposits had a market value of $700,000. The discovery value, then, is $700,000. If an asset worth $700,000 was not shown in the financial statements, assets would obviously be understated. Assuming the $30,-000 land cost has already been recorded, the entry to record the discovery value would be:

Answer 3 is correct. The balance in the Leasehold Improvements account should be written off to expense over the shorter of (1) the life of the lease or (2) the life of the improvements.

If you answered incorrectly, review Frame 18⁸ before proceeding to Frame 19⁸ on page 367.

19⁸
continued

```
Oil Deposits – Discovery Value........................................ 700,000
    Capital from Appreciation – Discovery Value
        Increment......................................................... 700,000
```

Depletion charges may be determined by dividing the cost or discovery value by the estimated number of units – tons, barrels, or board feet – in the property. For example, assume that $900,000 was paid for a mine estimated to contain 900,000 tons of ore. The unit (per ton) depletion charge would be $1 per ton ($900,000 ÷ 900,000 tons). If 100,-000 tons of ore were mined in 1979, the depletion charge would be 100,000 × $1 or $100,000. The journal entry to record the depletion charge would be:

```
Depletion ......................................................... 100,000
    Allowance for Depletion – Mineral Deposits................. 100,000
```

The Mineral Deposits account could also be credited directly. The Depletion account contains the material cost of the ore mined. It is combined with labor and other mining costs to arrive at the total cost of the ore mined. This total cost is then allocated to cost of goods sold and inventory. The asset should be shown in the statement of financial position as follows:

```
Mineral deposits............................................ $900,000
    Less: Allowance for depletion...................... 100,000
                                                       $800,000
```

Depreciation of plant assets. Depreciable plant assets erected on extractive industry property are depreciated in the same manner as other depreciable assets. If such assets will be abandoned when the natural resource is exhausted, they should be depreciated over the shorter of (*a*) the life of the physical asset or (*b*) the life of the natural resource. In some cases the periodic depreciation charge is computed on the basis of the units of mineral extracted.

Reese Mining Company owns mining property acquired on May 1, 1979, at a cost of $5,400,000. The mine is estimated to contain ore deposits of four million tons of which 90 percent can be economically removed. The company plans to work the mine for approximately ten years from the date it starts mining operations, which will be January 1, 1980. In January 1980, machines were installed at a cost of $90,000. The machines will have no further value to the company when the ore body is exhausted. The machines have a physical life of 15 years. During 1980, 400,000 tons of ore were mined. The company uses the units-of-production method of depreciation. Which of the following shows the depletion charge and the depreciation charge for 1980?

1. $600,000 depletion and $10,000 depreciation.
2. $540,000 depletion and $9,000 depreciation.
3. $560,000 depletion and $6,000 depreciation.

Check your calculations in Answer Frame 19[8] on page 370.

Frame 20[8]

Intangible assets

Sources of intangible assets. Intangible assets arise from (1) superior management know-how or reputation–goodwill; and (2) exclusive privileges granted by governmental authority–trademarks, patents, copyrights, and franchises.

All intangible assets are nonphysical, but not all nonphysical assets are classified as intangible assets. For example, an account receivable is nonphysical, but it is a current asset.

GOODWILL. Goodwill is best seen as an intangible value of an entity which results chiefly from its management's skill, or know-how, and favorable reputation with customers. The value of an entity may be greater than the total sum of the fair market values of its tangible assets. This means that the company is expected to be able to generate an above-average rate of earnings on each dollar of investment. Thus, the proof of the existence of goodwill can be found only in the ability of a company to produce superior or above-average earnings.

A Goodwill account will appear in the records only if goodwill has been bought and paid for in cash, capital stock, or other property of the purchaser. Goodwill cannot be purchased by itself. An entire business or a part of it must be purchased to obtain the accompanying intangible asset, goodwill.

To illustrate, assume that A Company purchases all of the assets of B Company. These consist of accounts receivable, inventories, land, buildings, equipment, and patents. A Company pays B Company $600,-000 cash and assumes responsibility for $300,000 of debts owed by B Company. With assumed market values (not costs from B's books) as follows, the intangible value attached to B and purchased by A is:

Answer 1 is correct. The computation of the depletion for 1980 is as follows:

$$\frac{\$5,400,000}{3,600,000^*} = \$1.50 \text{ per ton}; \$1.50 \times 400,000 = \$600,000$$

The computation of the depreciation for 1980 is as follows:

$$\frac{\$90,000}{3,600,000^*} = \$0.025 \text{ per ton}; \$0.025 \times 400,000 = \$10,000$$

* Expected total production = 90 percent of 4,000,000 tons = 3,600,000 tons.

If you chose an incorrect answer, restudy Frame 19⁸ before continuing to Frame 20⁸ on page 369.

20⁸
continued

Cash paid		$600,000
Liabilities assumed		300,000
Total price paid		$900,000
Less fair market values of individually identifiable assets:		
Accounts receivable	$100,000	
Inventories	90,000	
Land	150,000	
Buildings	250,000	
Equipment	200,000	
Patents	35,000	825,000
Goodwill		$ 75,000

The $75,000 is called goodwill and is recorded in a Goodwill account. It is treated in this way because it is difficult to identify the specific reasons for the existence of goodwill. The reasons might include good reputation, product leadership, valuable human resources, and a good information system.

AMORTIZATION OF GOODWILL. Goodwill cannot be amortized in determining taxable earnings. But current accounting practice requires the amortization of goodwill over a period not to exceed 40 years. The reasoning behind this requirement is that the value of the purchased goodwill will eventually disappear. Other goodwill may be generated in its place, but the organization is not equipped to value the regenerated goodwill. If A Company in the above example decided that the goodwill attached to B Company would last ten years, it would make annual adjusting entries debiting Goodwill Amortization Expense and crediting Goodwill for $7,500.

Identify whether each of the following statements is true or false.

1. A company may possess goodwill even though it does not show goodwill on the statement of financial position.

2. The existence of goodwill is evidenced by superior earnings of the firm in comparison to the normal average industry earnings.

3. Purchased goodwill is the price paid for expected future earnings at a level above that which is considered normal.

4. The periodic amortization of goodwill to an earnings statement account is not an acceptable accounting practice.

5. Goodwill is one asset which, if purchased, must be acquired as one of a number of assets acquired at the same time.

To check your responses, turn to Answer Frame 20[8] on page 372.

Frame 21[8] ————————————————————————————

TRADEMARKS. Trademarks are symbols, designs, brand names, or any other item which permits easy recognition of a product. Though trademarks are valid under common law, they should be protected by registration. Trademarks may have an indeterminate life. They should be recorded in the accounts at cost. This includes the cost of developing the trademark and the cost of legal protection.

PATENTS. A patent is an exclusive right granted by a government which gives the owner of the patent the exclusive right to manufacture, sell, lease, or otherwise benefit from the patent. The real value of a patent lies in its ability to produce earnings. The legal life of a patent is 17 years. Protection under the patent starts at the time of application for the patent and lasts for 17 years from the date it is granted.

A patent which is purchased should be recorded in the Patents account at cost. The cost of successfully defended patent infringement suits should also be charged to the Patents account.

The cost of a patent which is purchased should be amortized over the shorter of 17 years or its estimated useful life. If a patent cost $40,000 and is to be amortized over a useful life of ten years, the journal entry to record the amortization at the end of each year is:

Patent Amortization Expense	4,000	
Patents		4,000

1. True. Goodwill is shown in the accounts only if it has been purchased. Since the seller of a business often receives a payment for goodwill, this asset must have existed before sale even though it was not shown on the statement of financial position.
2. True. Goodwill is evidenced by the superior earning capacity of an enterprise.
3. True. Goodwill purchased does represent payment for superior earning power.
4. False. Goodwill must be amortized through periodic charges to an earnings statement account.
5. True. How could you purchase the earning power of a business without buying the business itself, or at least a portion of it?

If you missed any of the answers, reread Frame 20⁸ before going on to Frame 21⁸ on page 371.

21⁸
continued

On January 2, 1979, the G. O. Rye Company purchased a patent and incurred a total of $48,000 of legal and acquisition costs. In the same year the company instituted a patent infringement suit which was settled in favor of the Rye Company. The costs related to this suit amounted to $3,000. On the basis of this information, which of the following entries does not represent a possibly correct amortization policy?

1. Patent Amortization Expense... $2,550
       Patents... 2,550
         To charge off 1/20th of $51,000.

2. Patent Amortization Expense.. 3,000
       Patents... 3,000
         To charge off 1/17th of $51,000.

3. Patent Amortization Expense.. 6,000
       Patents... 6,000
         To charge off 2/17ths of $51,000.

The correct answer is in Answer Frame 21⁸ on page 374.

Frame 22⁸

COPYRIGHTS. A copyright gives its owner an exclusive right protecting writings, designs, and literary productions from being illegally reproduced. A copyright has a life equal to the life of the creator plus 50 years. Since most publications have a limited life, it is advisable to charge the cost of the copyright against the first edition published through charges to expense over the period of its publication.

FRANCHISES. A franchise is a contract usually between a government agency and a private company, usually a public utility. It gives the company certain rights, ranging from those of a nominal nature to that of complete monopoly. It also places certain restrictions on the company, especially regarding rates charged. If periodic payments to the grantor of the franchise are required, they should be debited to a Franchise Expense or Rent Expense account. If a lump-sum payment is made to obtain the franchise, the cost should be amortized over the shorter of the useful life of the franchise or 40 years.

Amortization of intangible assets. If an intangible asset legally expires on a certain date, its cost should be amortized over a period no longer than its legal life. *Opinion No. 17* of the Accounting Principles Board requires that an intangible asset acquired after October 31, 1970, be amortized over a period of not more than 40 years.

On January 2, 1979, the Big City Bus Lines, a privately owned company which uses a calendar-year accounting period, obtained a franchise from the city for the use of city streets and designated bus stops. The franchise was granted for a 12-year period at an annual fee of $2,000 payable on January 2 of each year. Which of the following entries for 1979 correctly illustrates the treatment of the franchise in the accounts of the Big City Bus Lines?

1.	Jan.	2	Rent Expense	2,000	
			Cash		2,000
2.	Jan.	2	Franchise	24,000	
			Cash		2,000
			Franchise Rentals Payable		22,000
3.	Dec. 31		Rent Expense	2,000	
			Franchise		2,000

Check your answer in Answer Frame 22[8] on page 374.

SECTION I

Summary *chapter* 8

Plant assets are broadly classified as land, natural resources, and depreciable property. Intangible assets are often classified according to whether they are individually identifiable or unidentifiable. Plant assets, except land and natural resources, are subject to depreciation. Natural resources, and in some instances land, are subject to depletion. All intangible assets are subject to amortization.

The chief means of valuing plant and intangible assets is cost. Cost consists of all expenditures made (or obligations incurred) to obtain the asset and get it ready for use. Assets acquired in noncash exchanges for securities are recorded at the fair market value of the asset received or the securities given up, whichever is more clearly evident. Assets re-

The first entry is one which cannot be correct. The maximum life of any patent is 17 years; hence the cost of the patent is not correctly amortized over 20 years under any circumstances. Amortization of the total patent cost of $51,000 over the legal life of the patent would result in annual amortization of $3,000 of the cost (as indicated in entry 2).

Entry 3 gives a possible correct answer because the problem did not specify the expected useful life of the patent. If the patent is likely to be effective in producing revenue for a period shorter than its legal life, the cost should be amortized over this shorter period. This entry assumes a life of 8.5 years. It could be a correct amortization.

If you did not select the right entry, restudy Frame 21[8] before going on to Frame 22[8] on page 372.

Number 1 is the correct response. Annual payments are treated as rent expense in the period to which they apply. The Franchise account is debited only if a lump-sum payment is made to obtain the franchise. Annual future rental payments are not set up as a liability at the time the franchise is obtained. Each payment is treated like any other rental payment.

If you answered incorrectly, reread Frame 22[8] before continuing to the Summary on page 373.

ceived as gifts are often recorded at appraised values when no clear-cut evidence of their fair market values exists.

Later expenditures on plant assets can be classed as capital expenditures or revenue expenditures. Capital expenditures are charged to the asset or to the allowance for depreciation accounts. Revenue expenditures are charged to expense accounts. Capital expenditures are those which in some way improve an asset or extend its life. Revenue expenditures are the normal, recurring costs which must be incurred to keep the asset in operating condition. They do not increase the service-rendering ability of the asset or extend its life. Theoretically, the amount of depreciation charged to a given period should have some relationship to the services received from the asset during the period. Four commonly used depreciation methods are straight line, units of production, double-declining balance, and sum-of-the-years' digits.

SECTION II

When an existing asset such as an automobile is traded for a new asset, the newly acquired asset may be recorded at (1) its suggested list price, (2) an amount equal to the net book value of the old asset plus the additional cash paid, or (3) an amount equal to the fair market value of the old asset plus the additional cash paid (the preferred alternative).

When similar assets are exchanged, losses are recognized but gains are not. When nonsimilar assets are exchanged, both gains and losses are recognized.

Under certain conditions a lease transaction may be regarded as a sale and should be recorded as such; otherwise, the lease is called an operating lease. Leasehold improvements go back to the owner of the leased property at the end of the lease and for this reason should be amortized over the life of the lease or the life of the asset, whichever is shorter.

Natural resources are usually recorded at the cost of development plus the cost of acquisition or their discovery value. Such resources should be recorded at discovery value if the land containing them was acquired for the cost of the land alone and the resources subsequently were discovered. Depletion charges on natural resources are usually based upon the number of physical units (pounds, tons, barrels) involved.

Goodwill is the intangible value of an entity resulting mainly from the entrepreneurial skill or capacity of its management to produce an above-average rate of earnings on investment. Goodwill is recorded only if it is purchased. Goodwill must be amortized over a period not to exceed 40 years.

Trademarks seemingly do not expire at the end of a time interval, but must be amortized over a period not to exceed 40 years. Patents which are purchased should be recorded at cost—including the cost of an infringement suit, if any—and, since they are of limited life, should be amortized over their useful life or legal life, whichever is shorter.

The cost of a copyright should be amortized over its useful life, which is often considerably shorter than its legal life. If a lump-sum payment were made to secure a franchise, it should be amortized over a period not to exceed 40 years.

To complete your review, study the definitions of new terms introduced in this chapter in the Glossary which follows. Then go on to the Student Review Quiz on page 376 for a self-administered test of your comprehension of the material in the chapter.

Glossary *chapter* 8

Accelerated depreciation—an accounting procedure under which the amounts of depreciation recorded in the early years of an asset's life are greater than those recorded in later years.

Amortization—an estimate, usually expressed in terms of cost, of the service potential of an intangible asset that expired in a period, which is accounted for by periodically charging a portion of the cost of an intangible asset to expense.

Betterment—replacement of an existing asset or part of an asset with a superior or improved asset or part.

Boot—the amount of cash paid in addition to the asset surrendered to acquire another asset.

Capital expenditure—an expenditure made, usually with regard to plant assets, which is to be capitalized because of the benefits it will render in subsequent periods.

Copyright—an exclusive privilege conferred upon the owner protecting writings, designs, and literary productions from unauthorized reproduction.

Depletion—the amount deducted from the cost (or other basis) of an asset of the natural resource type because of a removal of a part of the resource.

Depreciation—an estimate, usually expressed in terms of cost, of the amount of service potential of a plant asset that expired in a period. The double-declining-balance method of computing annual depreciation consists of finding the straight-line rate, doubling it, and applying it to the net book value which the asset had at the beginning of the year. The straight-line method assigns equal amounts of depreciation to equal periods of time. The sum-of-the-years'-digits method assigns depreciation in decreasing amounts to successive periods of time; the formula used consists of multiplying cost (less estimated salvage) by a fraction, the denominator of which is the sum of the numbers from one to the number of years of useful life expected from an asset and the numerator of which is the number of periods of life remaining from the beginning of the year. The units of production method assigns equal amounts of depreciation to each unit of product produced by an asset.

Franchise—a contract usually between a government subdivision and a private company, often a public utility, granting the latter certain privileges (ranging from those of a minor nature to that of complete monopoly to service a given territory) while placing on it certain restrictions, especially in the matter of rates charged.

Goodwill—the intangible value of an entity resulting primarily from the expectation that its management has the ability to produce an above-average rate of earnings per dollar of investment.

Improvement—an alteration or structural change in a depreciable asset which results in a better asset, that is, one which

has greater durability, productivity, or efficiency. Costs of improvements are properly capitalizable.

Lease—a contract under which the owner of property (the lessor) grants to another (the lessee) the right to operate and use the property for a stated period of time in exchange for stipulated payments.

Leasehold—the down payment, other than first year's rent, made at the time the lease agreement is signed.

Leasehold improvement—any physical alteration to leased property from which benefits are expected to be secured beyond the current accounting period.

Obsolescence—the decline in usefulness of an asset brought about by invention and technological progress.

Patent—an exclusive privilege granted by a government conferring on the owner of the patent the exclusive right to manufacture, sell, lease, or otherwise benefit from the patented invention.

Revenue expenditure—a normal, recurring expenditure made on plant assets to keep them in operating condition which is expected to benefit only the current period.

Trademark—a symbol, design, brand name, or any other indication of easy and ready recognition attributed to a product.

Wasting assets—depletable natural resources such as mineral and petroleum deposits and timber stands.

Continue with the Student Review Quiz below as a self-administered test of your understanding of the material presented in this chapter.

Student review quiz *chapter* 8

To develop a permanent record of your responses, you may write them on the answer sheet provided in the *Work Papers* or on a separate sheet of paper.

SECTION I

1 The chief purpose of depreciation accounting is to—

a Provide a fund for financing the replacement of depreciable assets.

b Show conservative figures on the financial statements.

c Provide a deduction for income tax purposes.

d Revalue assets whose value has declined.

e Systematically allocate the service potential of depreciable assets, usually as measured in terms of cost, against the revenue produced over the estimated useful lives of those assets.

2 The Runner Department store purchased land and a building from Susan Ling for the purpose of building a parking ramp for its customers. The purchase contract specified that Runner Department Store would pay Ms. Ling $30,000 in cash and would assume the present real estate mortgage note of $8,000. Runner also agreed to assume payment of $200 worth of property taxes in arrears. The $280 in legal fees incurred by the store in connection with this transaction included: $150 for title search, $50 for drawing up necessary documents, $60 for transfer taxes, and $20 in recording fees. As soon as it gained title to the property, Runner Department Store demolished the existing building and graded the property in preparation for the erection of the parking ramp. The cost of tearing down the old structure and grading was $5,400. On the basis of the above data, at what cost should this land be recorded in Runner's accounts?

a $30,280.
b $38,200.
c $38,280.
d $43,880.
e $38,480.

3 Akins Company owns a tract of land acquired over 40 years ago at a cost of $40,000. On this tract of land stands a fully depreciated building which is still in use and which cost $500,000. Akins Company purchased the adjoining tract of land. It intends to erect one large manufacturing building over both tracts of land. An old, occupied tenement building is located on the adjoining land. With regard to the following statements regarding expenditures made by the Akins Company, choose the one which is incorrect.

a The cost of demolishing the old fully depreciated building should be charged to the Land account.

b The cost of demolishing the old tenement building should be charged to the Land account.

c Payments made to the occupants of the tenement building to induce them to surrender their leases should be charged to the Land account.

d The cost of the fully depreciated building should be removed from the Building and allowance for depreciation accounts when the building is demolished.

e The cost of excavation of the land to construct a basement for the building should be charged to the Building account.

4 Which of the following expenditures made by the New Millwork Company relative to its plant assets should be charged to expense immediately upon incurrence? Assume the company has been operating for a number of years.

a Transportation and insurance costs on a new lathe.

b Sales tax on a new lathe.

c The cost of safety guards installed on all table and band saws.

d Interest paid on an installment contract to purchase a new band saw.

e Cost of testing and breaking in a new machine.

5 On July 1, 1979, the Lymon Toy Company purchased a machine invoiced at $12,000 (terms are 2/10, n/30 f.o.b. shipping point). The invoice was paid within the discount period. Freight charges amounted to $250, and installation costs to $590. The estimated useful life of the machine is ten years, at which time it will have an estimated salvage value of $400. It is estimated that this machine will produce a total of 100,000 units during its lifetime. Assume that 6,000 units have been produced by December 31, 1979, the end of the accounting period. Depreciation for 1979 based on usage would be:

a $12,440 × 1/10 × 1/2 = $622.
b $0.1284 × 6,000 = $770.40.
c $0.126 × 6,000 = $756.
d $0.1244 × 6,000 = $746.40.
e $0.122 × 6,000 = $732.

6 On July 1, 1978, the Gibson Machine Company built and installed a machine for its own use at a total cost of $11,700. The estimated life of the machine was five

377

years; estimated salvage value, $200. It would have cost Gibson Machine Company $12,500 to buy a comparable machine, installed. Which of the following statements are true?

a The charge for depreciation for the year ended June 30, 1979 (first year), would be greater under the double-declining-balance method than under the sum-of-the-years'-digits method.

b The charge for depreciation for the year ended June 30, 1980 (second year), would be greater under the sum-of-the-years'-digits method than under the double-declining-balance method.

c The charge for depreciation for the year ended June 30, 1979 (first year), under the sum-of-the-years'-digits method would be $3,833.

d Statements (a), (b), and (c) are true.

e Only (a) and (c) are true.

SECTION II

7 On January 2, 1976, Clay's Toggery purchased office equipment at a cost of $2,700. The equipment had an estimated life of six years with no salvage value. On March 1, 1980, the equipment is sold for $850 cash. At the close of the annual accounting period on December 31, 1979, the Office Equipment account had a balance of $2,700 and the Allowance for Depreciation—Office Equipment account, $1,800. Which of the following entries should be made on March 1, 1980?

a Cash............................ 850
  Allowance for
    Depreciation—
    Office Equipment........ 1,800
  Loss on Sale of Plant
    Assets...................... 50
      Office Equipment ...   2,700

b Depreciation Expense ... 75
  Allowance for
    Depreciation—
    Office
    Equipment   75
  Cash............................ 850
  Allowance for
    Depreciation—
    Office Equipment 1,875
      Office Equipment ...   2,700
      Gain on Sale of
        Plant Assets........   25

c Depreciation Expense ... 75
  Allowance for
    Depreciation—
    Office
    Equipment   75
  Cash............................ 850
  Allowance for
    Depreciation—
    Office Equipment 1,800

Loss on Sale of Plant
    Assets...................... 50
      Office Equipment ...   2,700

d Depreciation Expense ... 100
  Allowance for
    Depreciation—
    Office
    Equipment   100
  Cash............................ 850
  Allowance for
    Depreciation—
    Office Equipment 1,900
      Office Equipment ...   2,700
      Gain on Sale of
        Office
        Equipment   50

e None of the above.

8 Couch Furniture Company owns one delivery truck, which it purchased on October 1, 1976, at a cost of $6,400. The estimated life of the truck at that time was four years. On June 30, 1979, the close of the fiscal year, the allowance for depreciation account had a balance of $4,400. On July 1, 1979, the company trades this vehicle for a new one having a suggested retail price of $7,400. The dealer allows an $1,800 trade-in for the old truck, and the company pays the balance in cash. The old truck has a fair market value of $1,500. The journal entry to record the trade-in (using the theoretically correct accounting method) is:

a Delivery Truck No. 2 ... 7,400
  Allowance for
    Depreciation—
    Delivery Truck.......... 4,400
  Loss on Exchange of
    Plant Assets.............   200

378

Delivery Truck
No. 1 6,400
Cash 5,600

b Delivery Truck No. 2 ... 7,100
Allowance for
Depreciation—
Delivery Truck 4,400
Loss on Exchange of
Plant Assets 500
Delivery Truck
No. 1 6,400
Cash 5,600

c Delivery Truck No. 2 ... 7,600
Allowance for
Depreciation—
Delivery Truck 4,400
Delivery Truck
No. 1 6,400
Cash 5,600

d Delivery Truck No. 1 ... 7,600
Allowance for
Depreciation—
Delivery Truck 4,400
Delivery Truck
No. 2 6,400
Cash 5,600

e Delivery Truck No. 2 ... 5,600
Allowance for
Depreciation—
Delivery Truck 4,400
Loss on Exchange of
Plant Assets 2,000
Delivery Truck
No. 1 6,400
Cash 5,600

9 On March 15, 1979, the firm of Tweedle, Dee, and Dum traded in an old typewriter for a newer model. The cost of the old machine was $200 and its book value (adjusted to March 15, 1979), $60. The new machine was priced at $500 but was acquired for $400 plus the old machine. According to income tax regulations, the basis for depreciation of the new machine is:
a $500.
b $460.
c $400.
d $480.
e None of these (must know fair market value of the old machine at date of trade-in).

10 Burton, Inc., leased a building for ten years. The operating lease contract called for an advance lump-sum payment of $30,000 (20 percent of the total payments due under the lease) plus $12,000 annual rent payable at the end of each year. The

Burton Company immediately remodeled the building at a cost of $14,000. The building has an estimated useful life of 28 years. Which of the following entries should be made at the end of each year?

a Leasehold Improve-
ment Expense 1,400
Leasehold Im-
provments 1,400
Rent Expense 15,000
Leasehold 3,000
Cash 12,000

b Leasehold Improve-
ment Expense 500
Leasehold Im-
provements 500
Rent Expense 15,000
Leasehold 3,000
Cash 12,000

c Leasehold Improve-
ment Expense 500
Rent Expense 15,000
Leasehold Im-
provements 3,000
Cash 12,500

d Leasehold Improve-
ment Expense 1,400
Rent Expense 15,000
Leasehold 1,400
Cash 15,000

e Leasehold Improve-
ment Expense 1,400
Leasehold Im-
provements 1,400
Rent Expense 12,000
Cash 12,000

11 On August 1, 1978, Payne Metals Company acquired ore deposits estimated at three million tons. 2,600,000 tons are expected to be economically removable. The property on which the ore is situated was acquired at a cost of $1,300,000. In the fiscal year ended July 31, 1979, Payne mined 300,000 tons of the ore. The correct adjusting entry on July 31, 1979, is—

a Depletion 150,000
Allowance
for
Depletion 150,000

b Depletion 130,000
Allowance
for
Depletion 130,000

c Depletion 75,000
Allowance
for
Depletion 75,000

d Depreciation.......... 130,000
    Allowance
      for Depre-
      ciation.........   130,000

e None of the above.

12 Perry Drug Company purchased a patent on a new drug. The cost of the patent was $180,000. Legal fees in securing the patent amounted to $2,000. It was estimated that the patent would have a useful life of about five years. Shortly after the patent was acquired, Perry Drug Company became involved in a lawsuit. It successfully defended itself against the claim of patent infringement. The cost of this litigation was $8,000. The correct journal entry to reflect the patent amortization for each fiscal year is—

a Patent Amortization
    Expense................ 36,000
      Patents   36,000

b Patent Amortization
    Expense................ 36,400
      Allowance for
      Amortiza-
      tion—Patents ...   36,400

c Patent Amortization
    Expense................ 38,000
      Patents   38,000

d Patent Amortization
    Expense................ 11,176
      Patents   11,176

e No entry; patents are not amortized.

13 Which of the following statements is true?
a Goodwill is recorded only when purchased for cash.
b The goodwill of a business can be purchased separately from the rest of its assets.
c Goodwill, once recorded, should not be amortized.
d The existence of goodwill can be determined without reference to the earnings of a business.
e All of the above are false.

Now compare your answers with the correct answers and explanations on page 720.

Questions *chapter 8*

SECTION I

1 Barnes Corporation recently bought, for $200,000, a plot of land on which to construct a new warehouse at some future date. Legal fees connected with the transaction were $2,200. Back taxes on the property amounted to $8,000, for which Barnes Corporation assumed the liability. Estimates from various demolition crews indicate that the cost of razing the old warehouse currently on the property will be $9,000. What is the cost of the land?

2 Why should periodic depreciation, depletion, or amortization be recorded on virtually all plant assets?

3 For each of the following, state whether the expenditure made should be charged to an expense, an asset, or an allowance for depreciation account:
a Cost of installing air-conditioning equipment in a leased building.
b Biennial painting of an owned factory building.
c Cost of replacing the roof on a 10-year-old building which was purchased new and has an estimated total life of 40 years. Replacement of the roof was anticipated in setting the annual depreciation charge on the building.
d Cost of rewinding the armature of an electric motor.

4 a Distinguish between depreciation, depletion, and amortization. Name two assets which are subject to depreciation; to depletion; to amortization. **(b)** Distinguish between tangible and intangible assets and classify the above-named assets accordingly.

5 What four factors might be considered in determining a periodic depreciation charge?

Measurement and reporting of long-lived assets

SECTION II

6 a When plant assets are sold for cash, how is the gain or loss determined? **(b)** Assume that a plant asset is disposed of by exchanging it for a new asset of a similar type. Describe the three different bases at which the new asset may be recorded. Which basis has the most support in accounting theory?

7 What is the difference between a leasehold (under an operating lease contract) and a leasehold improvement? Is there any difference in accounting procedures applicable to each?

8 Brush, Inc., leased a tract of land for 40 years at an agreed annual rental of $10,000. The effective date of the lease was July 1, 1979. During the last six months of 1979 Brush constructed a building on the land at a cost of $250,000. The

building was placed in operation on January 2, 1980, at which time it was estimated to have a physical life of 50 years. Over what period of time should the building be depreciated? Why?

9 You note that a certain store seems to have a steady stream of regular customers, a favorable location, courteous employees, high-quality merchandise, and a reputation for fairness in dealing with customers, employees, and suppliers. Does it follow automatically that this business has goodwill?

10 In any exchange of noncash assets, the accountant's task is that of finding the most appropriate valuation to assign to the assets received. What is the general rule for determining the most appropriate valuation in such a situation?

Exercises *chapter* 8

SECTION I

1 Hrizik Company acquired, for $320,-000 cash, real property consisting of a tract of land and two buildings. The company intended to raze the old factory building and remodel and use the old office building. To allocate the cost of the property acquired, the company had the property appraised. The appraised values were: land, $120,000; factory building, $120,000; and office building, $160,000. The factory building was demolished at a net cost of $16,000. The office building was remodeled at a cost of $32,000. The cost of a new identical office building was estimated to be $180,000. Present a schedule or schedules showing the determination of the amounts at which the assets acquired should be carried in the Hrizik Company accounts. Show calculations.

2 The Hayes Company purchased some office furniture on March 1, 1978, for $6,200 cash. Cash of $100 was paid for freight and cartage costs. The furniture is

being depreciated over a four-year life under the straight-line method, assuming $300 of salvage value. The company employs a calendar-year accounting period and records depreciation for the full month in which an asset is installed. On July 1, 1979, $40 was spent to refinish the furniture. Prepare journal entries for the Hayes Company to record all of the above data, including the annual depreciation adjustments, through 1979.

3 Martin Company purchased a new machine on January 2, 1979, at a cash cost of $60,000. The machine is estimated to have a life of five years, with no salvage value at the end of that time. If federal income taxes are levied at a rate of 50 percent of net earnings, how much would the income taxes payable for the years 1979 and 1980 be reduced if the company chose the double-declining-balance method of computing depreciation rather than the straight-line method?

79 - 6000
80 - 1200

381

4 Plant equipment originally costing $36,000 on which $24,000 of depreciation has been accumulated is sold for $9,000. Prepare the journal entry to record the sale.

5 King Company owns an automobile acquired on July 1, 1977, at a cash cost of $5,200; at that time it was estimated to have a life of four years and $400 salvage value. Depreciation has been recorded through June 30, 1980, on a straight-line basis. On July 1, 1980, the auto is traded for a new auto having a list price of $6,600. The dealer allows a $2,000 trade-in allowance for the old auto, and King Company pays the balance due in cash. The old auto has a cash value of $1,000 on this date. Prepare the journal entry to record the trade-in, using that method which most clearly portrays the current value of the new auto.

6 Ace Company paid $1,000,000 for the right to extract all of the mineral-bearing ore, estimated at five million tons, from a certain tract of land. During the first year, King Company extracted 500,000 tons of the ore and sold 400,000 tons. What part of the $1,000,000 should be charged to expense during the first year?

7 Pebble Company leased a building under an operating lease contract for a 20-year period beginning January 1, 1979. The company paid $80,000 in cash and agreed to make annual payments equal to 1 percent of the first $500,000 of sales and one half of 1 percent of all sales over $500,000. Sales for 1979 amounted to $1,500,000. Payment of the annual amount will be made on January 12, 1980. Prepare journal entries to record the cash payment of January 1, 1979, and the proper expense to be recognized for the use of the leased building for 1979.

8 The Hannah Company purchased a patent on January 1, 1963, at a total cost of $68,000. In January 1974 the company successfully prosecuted an infringement of its patent rights. The legal fees amounted to $15,000. What will be the amount of patent cost amortized in 1979? (The useful life of the patent is the same as its legal life — 17 years.)

Handwritten notes (left margin):

CA$ 9,000
a 24,000
ss 300
QUIP. 36,000

AUTOS 5600
-DA 3600
OSS 600
CASH 4600
AUTOS 5200
old

Handwritten journal entries (bottom):

(7)

1-1 LEASEHOLD   80,000
        CASH   80,000

12-31 RENT EXPENSE   14,000
         ACCRUED RENT PAY.   10,000
         LEASEHOLD   4,000

Problems, Series A *chapter* 8

SECTION I

8-1-A

The Land Building Corporation purchased a two-square-mile farm from the owner under the following terms: cash paid, $325,000; mortgage note assumed, $200,000; and interest accrued on mortgage note assumed, $5,000. Land was to issue to the owner 1,000 shares of its $20 par common stock, which at this time had a market value of $80 per share, although its book value was only $72 per share.

The company paid $46,000 for brokerage and legal services to acquire the property and secure clear title. It planned to subdivide the property into residential lots and construct homes on these lots. Clearing and leveling costs of $18,000 were paid. Crops on the land were sold for $12,000. A house on the land, to be moved by the buyer, was sold for $4,200. The other buildings were razed at a cost of $8,000, and salvaged material was sold for $8,400.

Approximately six acres of the land were deeded to the township for roads, and another ten acres were deeded to the local school district as a site for a future school. After the subdivision was completed, this land would have an approximate value of $1,600 per acre. The company secured a total of 1,200 salable lots from the remaining land.

Required:

Present a schedule showing in detail the composition of the cost of the 1,200 salable lots.

8-2-A

Bunsen Company acquired a machine on July 1, 1979, at a cash cost of $48,000 and immediately spent $2,000 to install it. The machine was estimated to have a useful life of eight years and a scrap value of $3,000 at the end of this time. It was further estimated that the machine would produce 500,000 units of product during its life. In the first year the machine produced 100,000 units.

Required:

Prepare journal entries to record depreciation for the fiscal year ended June 30, 1980, if the company used:
a   The straight-line method.
b   The sum-of-the-years'-digits method.
c   The double-declining-balance method.
d   The units-of-production method.

8-3-A

Fulton Company purchased a machine on January 2, 1978, at an invoice price of $62,-600. Transportation charges amounted to $700, and $1,500 was spent to install the machine. Costs of removing an old machine to make room for the new amounted to $600. $200 was received for the scrapped material from the old machine.

Required:

a State the amount of depreciation that would be recorded on the machine for the first year on the straight-line basis, on the double-declining-balance basis, and on the sum-of-the-years'-digits basis, assuming an estimated life of eight years and no salvage value expected.

b Give the journal entry needed at December 31, 1980, to record depreciation assuming a revised total life expectancy for the machine of 12 years; assume that depreciation has been recorded through December 31, 1979, on a straight-line basis.

8–4–A

When you were hired as manager of the East Street Company on January 1, 1980, the company bookkeeper gave you the following information regarding one of its equipment accounts:

Equipment – Machine C

1979			1979		
Jan. 1	Disposition cost of Machine B	500	Jan. 1	Cash from sale of Machine B	400
1	Material used in building Machine C	15,000	Dec. 31	Depreciation on Machine C for year ended 12/31/79 (10% of $28,000)	2,800
1	Labor used in building Machine C	10,000			
1	Cost of installing Machine C	1,900			
1	Net earnings from building Machine C rather than purchasing it	1,500			

Required:

Construct the theoretically correct equipment account for Machine C.

8–5–A

Trap Company purchased a machine at a cash cost of $35,000. An electric motor was purchased for cash and attached to the machine at a total cost of $26,000. The machine was installed in a production center on the first floor at a cost of $8,000 on July 1, 1978. Its estimated life was 15 years, with no salvage value expected. On July 1, 1983, the machine and motor unit was moved from its first-floor location to the second floor and the entire unit installed at a cost of $16,000. The estimated life of the unit in its second-floor location is ten years, with no salvage value expected.

Required:

Compute the depreciation charge for the year ending June 30, 1984, using the straight-line method.

8–6–A

Grape Company purchased land and a building having appraised values of $120,000 and $200,000, respectively. The terms of the sale were that Grape would pay $163,000 in cash and assume responsibility for a $100,000 mortgage note, $5,000 of accrued interest, and $12,000 of unpaid property taxes. Grape intends to use the building as an office building.

Required:

Prepare journal entries to record the purchase.

SECTION II

8–7–A

Keith Company purchased a new 1979 model automobile on September 1, 1979. The list price of the new car was $5,300, and the company received a trade-in allowance of $1,000 for a 1977 model. The 1977 model had been acquired on September 1, 1977, at a cost of $4,800. Depreciation had been recorded through December 31, 1978, on a double-declining-balance basis, with four years of useful life expected. At the time of the trade, the 1977 automobile had a cash value of $900.

Required:

Prepare journal entries to record the exchange of the automobiles under (a) the tax method and (b) the theoretically correct accounting method.

8–8–A

Barnes Company acquired a mine for $4,500,000. The mine contained an estimated 4.5 million tons of ore. It was also estimated that the land would have a value of $400,000 when the mine was exhausted and that only four million tons of ore could be economically extracted. A building was erected on the property at a cost of $600,000. The building had an estimated useful life of 35 years and no scrap value. Specialized mining equipment was installed at a cost of $825,000. This equipment had an estimated useful life of seven years and an estimated $21,000 salvage value. The company began operating on July 1, 1978. During the year ended June 30, 1979, 400,000 tons of ore were extracted. The company decided to use the units-of-production basis to record depreciation on the building and the sum-of-the-years'-digits method to record depreciation on the equipment.

Required:

Prepare journal entries to record the depletion and depreciation charges for the year ended June 30, 1979. Show calculations.

8–9–A

The Hackett Company purchased a patent for $60,000 on January 2, 1978. The patent was estimated to have a useful life of ten years. The $60,000 cost was properly charged to an asset account and amortized in 1978. On July 1, 1979, the company incurred legal and court costs of $18,000 in a successful defense of the patent in an infringement suit.

Required:

Compute the patent amortization cost for 1979.

Problems, Series B *chapter* 8

SECTION I

8-1-B

White Company planned to erect a new factory building and a new office building in Atlanta, Georgia. Preliminary studies showed two possible sites as available and desirable. Further studies showed the second site to be preferable. A report on this property showed an appraised value of $300,000 for land and orchard and $200,000 for a building.

After considerable negotiation the company and the owner reached the following agreement. White Company was to pay $180,000 in cash, issue to the owner 2,000 shares of its common stock, assume an $80,000 mortgage note on the property, assume the interest accrued on the mortgage note of $3,200, and assume unpaid property taxes of $12,000. White Company's common stock had a book value of $66, a par value of $50, and a market value of $75 per share on the date the agreement was signed. White company paid $33,000 cash for brokerage and legal services in acquiring the property.

Shortly after acquisition of the property, White Company sold the fruit on the trees for $4,400, remodeled the building into an office building at a cost of $64,000, and removed the trees from the land at a cost of $15,000. Construction of the factory building is to begin in a week.

Required:

Prepare schedules showing the proper valuation of the assets acquired by the White Company.

8-2-B

The Broad Company has the following entries in its Building account:

			Debits
1979			
May	5	Cost of land and building purchased	$400,000
	5	Broker fees incident to purchase	18,000
1980			
Jan.	3	Contract price of new wing added to south end of building	110,000
	15	Cost of new machinery, estimated life ten years	400,000
June	10	Real estate taxes for six months ended 6/30/80	9,000
Aug.	10	Cost of landscaping and building parking lot for employees in back of building	12,400
Sept.	6	Replacement of broken windows	400
Oct.	10	Repairs due to regular usage	4,600

Credits

1979
Dec. 31   Transfer to Land account, as per allocation of purchase cost authorized
in minutes of board of directors   60,000

1980
Jan.   5   Proceeds from lease of second floor for six months ended 12/31/79   10,000

The original property was acquired on May 5, 1979. The Broad Company immediately engaged a contractor to construct a new wing on the south end of the building. While the new wing was being constructed, the company leased the second floor as temporary warehouse space to the Goody Company. During this period (July 1 to December 31, 1979) the company installed new machinery costing $400,000 on the first floor of the building. Regular operations began on January 2, 1980.

Required:

a   Compute the correct balance for the Building account as of December 31, 1980. The building is expected to last 40 years. The company employs a calendar-year accounting period.

b   Prepare the necessary journal entries to correct the records of the Broad Company at December 31, 1980. No depreciation entries are required.

8-3-B

The Kash Company's fiscal year ends May 31. The company has its own fleet of delivery vehicles. Included are the following:

Description	Date acquired	Cost	Expected life	Expected resale value
Sedan No. 3.................	June 1, 1977	$ 8,000	4 years	$1,200
Truck No. 2.................	June 1, 1973	12,000	100,000 miles	1,000
Truck No. 5.................	Jan. 1, 1979	28,000	150,000 miles	2,800
Trailer No. 8...............	Apr. 1, 1976	16,000	400,000 miles	–0–

Mileage readings at May 31 show the following:

	1978	1979
Sedan No. 3	15,000 miles	28,000 miles
Truck No. 2	120,000	150,000
Truck No. 5	–0–	20,000
Trailer No. 8	50,000	75,000

Required:

Set up schedules showing in full detail the amount of depreciation to be recorded for the year ended May 31, 1979, on each of the above assets. (Use the straight-line method for Sedan No. 3 and the units-of-production (number of miles driven) method for the other vehicles.)

8-4-B

A machine belonging to the McGraw Company that cost $30,000 has an estimated life of 20 years. After ten years, an extremely important machine part, representing about

387

40 percent of the original cost, is worn out and replaced. The replacement cost is $9,000, and the useful life of the new part is the same as the remaining useful life of the machine.

Required:

a Prepare journal entries to record the replacement of the old part with the new part. (Assume depreciation has already been brought up to date.)
b Compute the annual depreciation charge after replacement, using the straight-line method.

SECTION 2

8–5–B

On January 1, 1979, the Weber Company had the following balances in its plant asset and allowance accounts:

	Asset	Allowance for depreciation
Land	$ 40,000	
Leasehold	50,000	
Buildings	219,600	$18,375
Equipment	192,000	89,100
Trucks	28,800	14,025

Additional information:

a. The leasehold covers a plot of ground leased on January 1, 1975, for a period of 20 years.
b. Building No. 1 is on the owned land and was completed on July 1, 1978, at a cost of $126,000. Its life is set at 40 years. Building No. 2 is on the leased land and was completed on July 1, 1975, at a cost of $93,600. Its life is also set at 40 years.
c. Equipment is depreciated at 12.5 percent per year.
d. Truck A, purchased on January 1, 1977, at a cost of $9,600, was given a life of two and a half years and a scrap value of $600. Truck B, purchased on July 1, 1977, at a cost of $8,400, was given a life of two years and a scrap value of $1,400. Truck C, purchased on July 1, 1978, at a cost of $10,800, was given a life of three years and scrap value of $1,350.

The following events occurred in 1979:

Jan. 2 Rent for 1979 on leased land is paid, $5,600.
Apr. 1 Truck B is traded in on Truck D. List price of the new truck is $9,600. A trade-in allowance of $1,800 is granted ($1,800 is also the cash value of Truck B). The balance is paid in cash. Truck D is given a life of two and a half years and a scrap value of $600. (Do not use tax method.)
      1 Truck A is sold for $1,800 cash.
Dec. 31 At this time, it is decided that Truck C will have a life of only two and a half instead of three years. Its scrap value remains unchanged.

Required:

Prepare journal entries to record the 1979 transactions and the necessary December 31, 1979, adjusting entries, assuming a calendar-year accounting period. Use the straight-line depreciation method.

8–6–B

Young Moving Company purchased a new moving van on October 1, 1979. The list price of the new van was $22,000, and the company received a trade-in allowance of $4,000 for a 1977 model. The balance was paid in cash. The 1977 model had been acquired on October 1, 1977, at a cost of $18,000. Depreciation had been recorded through December 31, 1978, on a double-declining-balance basis, with three years of useful life expected. At the time of trade, the 1977 van had a cash value of $5,000.

Required:

Present journal entries to record the exchange of the moving vans.

8–7–B

The accounts of the Peterson Company with respect to one automobile owned as of September 30, 1979 (the close of the company's fiscal year), show: Automobile, cost, $6,500; and Allowance for Depreciation—Automobile, $5,500. On October 1, 1979, Peterson Company traded this automobile for another having a manufacturer's list price of $8,200. The dealer allowed a $1,500 trade-in allowance for the old car. The company remitted a check for the difference between list price and trade-in allowance, plus $246 of sales taxes and $24 for an auto license for the balance of the calendar year. The old car had a fair market value of $900 at the time of the exchange.

Immediately after purchasing the new automobile, the company installed heavy-duty premium tires on the automobile, exchanging the regular tires on the auto for new ones having a list price of $380. The company received a trade-in allowance for the regular tires of $145. The company could have purchased the new heavy-duty premium tires for $300 in cash. Cash was also paid out in the amount of $150 for special advertising painting on the auto.

Required:

Prepare journal entries to record the acquisition of the new auto and the new heavy-duty tires and to record the cost of the special painting. Do not use the tax method.

8–8–B

The Klay Mining Company, on January 2, 1979, acquired ore deposits at a cash cost of $1,785,000. The ore deposit contains an estimated three million tons. Present technology will allow the economical extraction of only 85 percent of the total deposit. Machinery, equipment, and temporary sheds are installed at a cost of $306,000. These assets will have no further value to the company when the ore body is exhausted; they have a physical life of 12 years. In 1979, 350,000 tons of ore are extracted. The company expects the mine to be exhausted in ten years, with sharp variations in annual production.

Required:

a Compute the depletion charge for 1979.
b Compute the depreciation charge for 1979 under each of the following methods: (1) straight-line, (2) sum-of-the-years' digits, (3) double-declining balance, and (4) units of production.
c Which depreciation method do you believe to be most appropriate in the circumstances cited?

8–9–B

The Monticello Company spent $41,650 to purchase a patent on January 2, 1979. It is assumed that the patent will be useful during its full legal life. In January 1980 the company successfully prosecuted an infringement of its patent rights at a cost of $8,000. Also in January 1980 the company paid $12,000 to obtain patents that could, if used by competitors, make the earlier Monticello patents useless. The purchased patents will never be used.

Required:

Give the entries to record the information relative to the patents in 1979 and 1980.

9

Long-term liabilities and bond investments

Learning objectives

Study of the material in this chapter is designed to achieve these learning objectives:

1. An understanding of the nature of long-term debt.

2. An understanding of the theory and application of financial leverage in the management decision-making process.

3. An awareness of the possibilities of corporate bonds as an investment opportunity.

4. An understanding of the process of accounting for bonds by both the issuing corporation and the investor.

5. An understanding of the nature of bond discount and premium, as well as the methods of accounting for each.

6. A knowledge of the use of sinking funds as a device for debt retirement.

7. An understanding of the concepts of future worth and present value (Appendix 9A).

8. A basic understanding of leases and pensions as long-term debts and the accounting for each (Appendix 9B).

Bonds

A bond is one of the most common forms of long-term debt financing. When bonds are issued by a company, often other companies purchase them as long-term investments. A bond is a written unconditional promise wherein the borrower promises to pay to the holder of the bond (1) the face value of the bond at the maturity date, and (2) interest at a specified rate on the face value at specified dates (usually semiannually).

Bonds may be secured or unsecured. *Secured bonds* are those which have a claim against certain property of the issuer if the bonds are not paid at the maturity date. The property pledged (or mortgaged) may be real estate, machinery, merchandise, investments, or personal property. A *mortgage* is a conditional transfer of certain property given by the borrower (the mortgagor) to the lender of funds (the mortgagee) to secure the payment of a loan. Bonds which have first claim on a certain asset are called *first-mortgage bonds,* while those which have second claim on that same asset are called *second-mortgage bonds,* and so on.

Most *unsecured bonds* are called *debenture bonds* — they are issued against the general credit of the corporation. Another form of unsecured bonds which is quite rare are *income bonds.* They are different from other bonds in that interest need be paid only to the extent of the earnings of the issuer. For instance, if interest on the bonds is $20,000 for a given year and the issuer only earns $5,000 before interest expense is deducted, only $5,000 of interest must be paid. (If there are no earnings or if a loss is sustained, no interest need be paid).

For interest-paying purposes bonds may be either *registered bonds* or *coupon bonds.* Interest is paid to the owner of registered bonds by check. The owner's name is registered on the records of the issuing corporation. Interest is paid on coupon bonds when the appropriate coupon is detached and cashed at the interest date or thereafter. The registered type of bond is most frequently used by corporations today. An unregistered bond is transferred to another party by mere delivery, whereas transfer of a registered bond requires the owner's endorsement, assignment, and registration.

Any type of bond may be *convertible* if such a provision is stated in the *bond indenture* (the contract between the issuer of bonds and the bondholders or the trustee representing the bondholders). Such bonds are convertible, at the bondholder's option and under stated conditions, into stock of the issuing corporation. For example, a $1,000 convertible debenture bond might be convertible (for a stated period of its life) into 20 shares of the issuing company's common stock.

Bonds may also be *callable* if such a provision is included in the bond indenture. This provision entitles a company to call in its bonds before the maturity date. This usually involves payment of an amount in excess of the face value. The amount above the face value is the *call premium.*

Indicate whether each of the following statements is correct or incorrect.

1. Debenture bonds are not secured by a pledge of any specific property.

2. It is easier to transfer an unregistered bond than it is to transfer one that is registered.

3. A bondholder with a bond secured by a second mortgage is in a less favorable position than a first-mortgage bondholder in the event of a seizure and sale of the property (called a foreclosure).

4. The same property may be used as security for more than one issue of bonds.

5. The issuing corporation determines whether it will accept the request of a holder of convertible bonds that the bonds be converted into the stipulated number of common shares.

Turn to Answer Frame 1[9] on page 394 to check your answer.

Frame 2[9]

Why a company might decide to issue bonds

When a corporation needs additional long-term funds, it must decide between the issuance of additional capital stock or borrowing by issuing notes or bonds. The issuance of notes and bonds may be advantageous if the present stockholders prefer not to share ownership and corporate earnings with additional shareholders.

A bondholder is a creditor and a stockholder is an owner, but both can be viewed as investors. Many bonds are secured by the plant assets of the borrower and always rank ahead of the stock as claims on assets in liquidation. Therefore, owners of bonds are provided with greater protection for their investment than are stockholders.

Interest expense on a note or bond is a fixed cost to the borrower. It must be met when it is due if default on the loan is to be avoided. Interest on bonds must be paid on dates specified by the bond contract. Dividends on stock are declared at the discretion of the board of directors.

Advantages and disadvantages of borrowing

The advantages of operating a business with borrowed funds may be illustrated with the use of the data contained in Illustration 9.1. Both companies began operations on January 1, 1979. They were equally efficient in employing assets, as both were able to earn a 20 percent rate of return from operations (before interest and taxes) on assets acquired as of the beginning of 1979 ($4,000,000 ÷ $20,000,000). Com-

9²
continued

Illustration 9.1   Favorable financial leverage

COMPANIES A AND B, CONDENSED STATEMENTS
Statement of Financial Position
January 1, 1979

	Company A	Company B
Total assets	$20,000,000	$20,000,000
Bonds payable, 7%		$10,000,000
Stockholders' equity (capital stock)	$20,000,000	10,000,000
	$20,000,000	$20,000,000

Earnings Statement
Year Ended December 31, 1979

	Company A	Company B
Net earnings from operations for 1979	$ 4,000,000	$ 4,000,000
Interest expense		700,000
Net earnings before income taxes	$ 4,000,000	$ 3,300,000
Income taxes at 50%	2,000,000	1,650,000
Net Earnings for 1979	$ 2,000,000	$ 1,650,000
Number of shares	2,000,000	1,000,000
Earnings per share	$1.00	$1.65

pany B, because of the bonds in its capital structure, earned $1.65 per share while Company A earned only $1 per share.

Financial leverage. The differences can be explained as follows: Company B borrowed $10 million at a rate of 7 percent, which cost the company $350,000 after income taxes. Interest of $700,000 was incurred, but the $700,000 of interest reduced the amount of federal income taxes levied by $350,000. Thus, the net cost after tax is $350,000. Both companies operated equally efficiently, earning $4 million (before interest and taxes) on $20 million worth of total assets. Company B, however, was able to finance one half of its assets at a cost before taxes of 7 percent, while the assets secured through borrowing were earning a return of 20 percent before taxes. This additional return of $1,300,000 ($2,000,000 − $700,000) yielded an additional $650,000 of net earnings after taxes (at a 50 percent rate) to the stockholders of Company B. The additional earnings were sufficient to increase earnings per share in Company B to $1.65 as contrasted to $1 for Company A.

Company B is employing what is known as financial leverage, or is said to be "trading on the equity." That is, it is using the existence of stockholders' equity as a basis for securing borrowed funds, the use of which is intended to enhance the amount of earnings per share of the common stockholders. The situation given above, where the use of leverage increased the earnings per share, is called favorable financial leverage.

Unfavorable financial leverage can exist also, and would for Company B if earnings from operations of each company amounted to only $1 million instead of $4 million. In this case the earnings per share for Companies A and B, respectively, would be $0.25 and $0.15 (you may want to prove this to yourself).

A disadvantage of borrowing is that it reduces the ability of a company to absorb losses. Suppose that both A and B sustain losses amounting to $11 million. Company A will still have $9 million worth of stockholders' equity at the end of the year and can continue operations with a chance to recover. Company B will be insolvent at the end of the year (its liabilities will exceed its assets), and the stockholders of B may lose their entire investment through liquidation proceedings.

State whether each of the following statements is correct or incorrect.

1. Earnings of a company with substantial amounts of debt outstanding are likely to fluctuate more widely than those of a company with little or no debt outstanding.
2. For most levels of earnings, the financial structure of a corporation influences the amount of earnings per share of capital stock.
3. Paying 6 percent dividends on capital stock has the same effect on earnings as paying 6 percent interest on bonds.
4. Issuing bonds has a beneficial effect on earnings per share regardless of the level of earnings from operations.

Now check your answers in Answer Frame 2⁹ on page 396.

1. Correct. Such earnings are subject to greater fluctuation for a leveraged company than for an unleveraged company. At high levels of earnings before interest and taxes, the leveraged company will have higher earnings. At low levels it will have lower earnings than an unleveraged company.

2. Correct. This is one of the points which is apparent from an examination of Illustration 9.1. The firm's financial or capital structure affects the amount of earnings which is available to common stockholders and the number of shares outstanding. Thus it influences the amount of earnings per share of common stock.

3. Incorrect. Bond interest is deductible in arriving at taxable earnings, but dividends on capital stock are not.

4. Incorrect. The deductibility of bond interest expense for tax purposes is often mentioned as one advantage of issuing bonds as opposed to stock. But, if earnings from operations are very low, the fixed interest may even exceed those earnings. Thus, whether or not issuing bonds will increase earnings per share depends on the expected level of earnings from operations.

If you missed any of the above, restudy Frame 2⁹ before continuing in Frame 3⁹ below.

Frame 3⁹

Bonds payable

Accounting for the issuance of bonds

The *bond indenture* (the overall contract between the issuer and the bondholders) sets forth the total amount of bonds that may be issued. The bonds may all be issued at one time or a portion at one date and the remainder later.

Assume that the Southern Company issued on July 1, 1979, $1,000,000 of its $1,500,000 authorized first-mortgage, 9 percent, ten-year bonds (dated July 1, 1979) at face value of $1,000,000. This transaction would be recorded in the accounts as follows:

July 1 Cash.. 1,000,000
               Bonds Payable 1,000,000

Recording bond interest

Interest on most bonds is paid semiannually, as required by the provisions of the bond indenture. We will assume that the interest is paid directly by the borrower to the bondholders and that the accounting year ends on December 31. It would be recorded as follows:

1979
Dec. 31 Bond Interest Expense....................................... 45,000
               Accrued Bond Interest Payable 45,000
               To accrue bond interest expense for the period
               July 1–December 31, 1979.

1980
Jan. 1   Accrued Bond Interest Payable 45,000
         Cash   45,000
         To record the payment of interest for the period
         July 1–December 31, 1979.

The price received for a bond issue

The price a bond issue will bring when offered to investors, or the price at which a bond sells in the market, often may differ from its face or maturity value. Basically, a bond issue will sell at a price higher (lower) than its face or maturity value if the rate of interest offered in the bonds is higher (lower) than that needed to induce investors to buy the bonds at face value. The effect of a premium or discount on a bond is to change the rate of interest offered by the bond to the effective rate desired by the investor.

In purchasing a bond, an investor actually acquires two promises from the issuer of the bond: (1) the promise to pay the stated principal amount on a given date — the maturity date — and (2) a promise to pay periodic interest at stated intervals throughout the life of the bond. Thus, a $1,000, 20-year, 8 percent bond, dated October 1, 1979, which calls for semiannual interest payments on each April 1 and October 1, contains two promises. The issuer promises to pay $1,000 to the holder on October 1, 1999, and to pay $40 each April 1 and October 1 through October 1, 1999, beginning on April 1, 1980.

If an investing company desired an 8 percent rate of interest from such a bond, it would offer to purchase it at face value. It would invest $1,000 and receive $80 of interest per year — exactly an 8 percent rate. But suppose the company would invest in such a bond only if it could earn a 10 percent rate. Since the rate on the face of the bond (the nominal or coupon rate) cannot be changed, the investing company can change the rate at which interest is actually earned only by changing the price paid for the bond. In this instance it would pay less than the face value. The method for determining the price which a company would be willing to pay for a bond is discussed in Appendix 9A.

Indicate whether each of the following statements is true or false.

1. The entry recording the issuance of bonds payable includes a debit to Cash and a credit to Bonds Payable.
2. Usually the interest on bonds payable is paid annually.
3. If the rate of interest offered in a bond issue is higher than that which can be obtained from similar bonds of other issuers selling at face value, the bonds will sell at a price higher than the face value.
4. When purchasing a bond, an investor receives only the promise that the face value will be paid at the maturity date.

Now turn to Answer Frame 3[9] on page 398 to check your answers.

Frame 4⁹

Bonds issued at a discount

To illustrate the accounting for bonds issued at a discount, assume that on July 1, 1979, the Southern Company issued $1,000,000 of first-mortgage, 9 percent, ten-year bonds for $980,000, or at 98 percent of face value. The bonds call for semiannual interest payments and mature on July 1, 1989. At issuance the entry would be:

July 1	Cash	980,000	
	Discount on Bonds Payable	20,000	
	Bonds Payable		1,000,000

Note that in recording bonds payable on the issuer's books, the bonds are carried at their face value in one account and the discount (or premium) in another. It is customary in accounting to record liabilities at the amount expected to be paid at maturity, excluding interest unless it has actually accrued.

Accounting for bond discount

To the issuing corporation, bond discount represents a cost of using funds just as it is a form of additional interest earnings to the investor. Thus the total cost of borrowing includes the total interest paid in cash (ten years times $90,000) plus the total discount ($20,000) which is paid as a lump sum at maturity as part of the face value of $1,000,000. Both items must be spread equitably over the life of the bonds, although no disbursement is made for the amount of discount until the debt is paid at or before maturity.

Thus, the original amount in the Discount on Bonds Payable account should be charged to expense ($2,000 per year) over the period of time between the date on which the bonds were issued and their maturity date. The amount charged to expense is usually computed on a straight-line basis, that is, equal amounts are charged to expense for equal periods of time elapsed. How often this adjusting entry will be made will depend upon how often the company prepares financial statements.

To illustrate, assume that the Southern Company, which issued $1,000,000 of ten-year, 9 percent bonds at 98, uses a calendar-year accounting period and prepares semiannual financial statements. The total discount of $20,000 must be written off over the ten years of life in the bonds. The annual charge is $2,000, and the charge per interest period (six months) is $1,000. The entry required on December 31, 1979, would be (recall that the bonds were issued on July 1, 1979):

Dec. 31	Bond Interest Expense	46,000	
	Discount on Bonds Payable		1,000
	Accrued Bond Interest Payable		45,000

Under the straight-line method illustrated, the total interest cost for each six months is the $45,000 which must be paid currently plus $1,000 of the $20,000 of discount which will be paid at maturity, or a total of $46,000.

The straight-line discount accumulation method shown is widely used because of its simplicity and ease of application. An alternative, and the theoretically correct method which yields slightly different results, embraces the use of the effective rate of interest. This method is covered in Appendix 9A.

Each time a statement of financial position is prepared, the remaining balance in the Discount on Bonds Payable account will be shown as a deduction from Bonds Payable. The bonds payable, except for amounts maturing currently, are usually shown in the long-term liability section of the statement of financial position. At the end of the tenth year of the bonds' life—after 20 interest payments have been made—the balance in the Discount on Bonds Payable account will be zero; the entire amount will have been charged to expense.

Bonds issued at a premium

Bonds are issued at a premium (at more than face value) when the interest rate specified on the face of the bonds is higher than the market rate of interest for similar bonds. Investors are willing to pay a premium because the periodic interest payments are larger than the minimum they would be willing to accept if they purchased bonds of this quality at face value. Thus, investors literally purchase some of the interest to be paid periodically by the issuing company. The total interest cost to the company, then, will not be the total of all of the cash interest payments made but will be this sum less the amount of premium received.

To illustrate, assume that the bonds mentioned above instead had been issued at 102 percent of face value. The total of the periodic interest payments to be made on the bonds is $90,000 per year for ten years, or a total of $900,000. But this will not be the total expense to the company. The investors have actually purchased in advance a part of each periodic interest payment; and in this way, they have invested more capital in the business issuing the bonds than simply the face value of the bonds. And so a part of each periodic payment to the investors must be viewed as a partial return of the investors' capital.

At the date of issuance the required entry is:

```
July 1   Cash..........................................................   1,020,000
            Bonds Payable .......................................              1,000,000
            Premium on Bonds Payable.......................                 20,000
```

Accounting for bond premium

The typical accounting treatment for bond premium is to amortize the original amount by crediting interest expense with an equal amount each accounting period between the issue date of the bonds and their maturity date. This is called straight-line amortization. To continue the above illustration, the amount of premium amortized each year would be $2,000 ($20,000 ÷ 10 years). The following entry would be recorded at the end of 1979:

```
Dec. 31   Bond Interest Expense .........................................   44,000
            Premium on Bonds Payable...................................    1,000
            Accrued Bond Interest Payable .......................              45,000
```

The debit to Premium on Bonds Payable is $1,000. The interest cost recorded is $44,000, which would equal an annual cost of $88,000. This $88,000 can be verified in another manner. The total interest payments over the life of the bonds amount to $900,000; the premium is $20,000; and the net total interest cost is $880,000. Dividing this by ten years, an annual cost of $88,000 is obtained.

When a statement of financial position is prepared, the remaining balance in the Premium on Bonds Payable account will be added to the amount of Bonds Payable. This amount, except for currently maturing amounts in some instances, is shown in the long-term liabilities section.

Indicate whether each of the following statements is correct or incorrect.

1. The amount of cash paid out periodically as interest will be the same regardless of whether bonds are issued at a discount or at a premium.

2. The amount of interest expense will be the same regardless of whether bonds are issued at a discount or at a premium.

3. To find the total amount of interest expense to be reported over the life of the bonds, one can take the cash paid out as interest and add the total discount or deduct the total premium.

4. In either instance illustrated above, the required entry on January 1, 1980, would be:

```
Accrued Bond Interest Payable .....................................   45,000
   Cash ................................................................              45,000
```

Now turn to Answer Frame 4[9] on page 402 to check your answers.

Bonds issued at face value between interest dates

Frequently, bonds are issued between interest dates. In this case, the bond investor usually pays for both the bond and the interest accrued from the last interest payment date to the date of purchase. On the interest date following the interim date of purchase, the accrued interest will be collected by the bondholder when a check is received for the interest for the entire period. The company is obligated, by contract, to pay the bondholders interest for the full six months on the interest payment date *regardless* of how long these holders have owned the bonds. Since the bond purchaser has paid for the interest which had accrued to the purchase date, it would be improper not to recognize this fact in determining the bond interest expense for the first interest period after issuance.

To illustrate, assume that the Carlson Company issues $100,000 of 9 percent bonds on May 1, 1979 (four months after the last interest date), at face value plus accrued interest. The accrued interest is equal to $100,000 \times .09 \times 1/3 = \$3,000$. The entry to record the issuance is:

May 1	Cash	103,000	
	Accrued Bond Interest Payable		3,000
	Bonds Payable		100,000

Assuming no action has been taken to record the interest accrued for the two months prior to the payment of the semiannual interest, the Carlson Company will make the following entry in its accounts at the time of semiannual payment:

July 1	Accrued Bond Interest Payable	3,000	
	Bond Interest Expense	1,500	
	Cash		4,500

The net interest expense to the Carlson Company is $1,500 ($100,000 \times .09 \times 1/6$) which represents interest for the two months from the date of issuance to the succeeding interest date.

Bonds issued at other than face value between interest dates

The most complex situation involving bonds occurs when bonds are issued between interest dates at either a premium or a discount. Accrued interest must be accounted for at the issuance date and a discount must be accumulated or a premium amortized at year-end.

Assume that Issuer Corporation issues ten-year, 12 percent bonds with a face value of $1,000,000 to the Purchaser Insurance Company at 92.2 on March 1, 1979. The bonds are dated January 1, 1979. The necessary entries on the issuer's books during 1979 are:

1. Correct. The amount of cash paid out as interest is based on the face value of the bonds times the stated rate of interest. For instance, the amount of cash paid out as interest on bonds with a face value of $1,000,000 and a stated rate of interest of 10 percent is $100,000 per year regardless of whether the bonds were issued at a discount or premium.

2. Incorrect. In the above examples notice that the interest expense for the six-month period differed by $2,000 ($46,000 − $44,000) because the bonds were issued at a discount in one instance and at a premium in the other.

3. Correct. For instance, in the case of the bonds issued at a discount, the annual interest expense would be $92,000 ($46,000 × 2). For the entire life of the bonds it would be $920,000 (the cash paid out as interest of $900,000 plus the discount of $20,000).

   In the instance of the bonds issued at a premium, the annual interest expense would be $88,000 ($44,000 × 2). The total interest expense over the life of the bonds would be $880,000 ($88,000 × 10 years). This is equal to cash paid out as interest of $900,000 less the premium of $20,000.

4. Correct. This entry would be required to pay the accrued interest payable on January 1, 1980. In both instances, this liability was established at $45,000.

If you missed any of the above, reread Frame 4⁹ before starting Frame 5⁹ on page 401.

5⁹
continued

Mar. 1	Cash		942,000	
	Bonds Payable − Discount		78,000	
	Bonds Payable			1,000,000
	Accrued Interest Payable			20,000
	To record the issue of bonds at 92.2 plus two months' accrued interest.			
July 1	Accrued Interest Payable		20,000	
	Interest Expense		40,000	
	Cash			60,000
	To record the payment of six months' interest.			
Dec. 31	Interest Expense		60,000	
	Accrued Interest Payable			60,000
	To record the accrual of six months' interest.			
	Interest Expense		6,610	
	Bonds Payable − Discount			6,610
	To record the accumulation of ten months' discount at $661 per month.			

With the bonds issued at a discount, entries are required to allocate the discount to the periods of *remaining life of the bonds*. The time over which the discount is spread is 118 months. Thus the amount to accumulate per month is:

$$\frac{\text{Discount}}{\text{Months between issuance and maturity dates}} = \frac{\$78,000}{118 \text{ months}} = \$661 \text{ per month}$$

To test your understanding, assume that the Issuer Corporation had sold the bonds to the Purchaser Insurance Company on March 1, 1979, at 107.8. Using the entries above as a guide, prepare the entries as of March 1, July 1, and December 31.

Now check your answers with those in Answer Frame 5⁹ on page 404.

Frame 6⁹

Redeeming outstanding bonds

At the maturity date the bonds are to be redeemed at their face value. Assuming interest for the last period has already been paid, the redemption of bonds with a face value of $100,000 would be recorded as follows:

Bonds Payable..	100,000	
Cash..		100,000

If bonds are redeemed before their maturity date, any difference between the amount paid and the book value is treated as a gain or loss on retirement. Book value is equal to the face value plus the pro rata share of any remaining premium or minus the pro rata share of any remaining discount. The gains and losses from such transactions are totaled and, if material in amount, are classified as an extraordinary item in the earnings statement, net of the related income tax effect. (This is required under *FASB Statement No. 4*.)

Bonds known as *serial bonds* are redeemed in a series in accordance with the provisions of the indenture. For instance, for ten-year bonds, 1/10 may mature at the end of the first year, 1/10 at the end of the second year, and so on. This allows investors to select a bond with the desired time period to meet their needs. Quite often serial bonds are issued by governmental units, such as cities. No interest accrues on a bond beyond its scheduled redemption date.

Use of a sinking fund to redeem bonds

The manner in which a sinking fund has been employed to redeem bonds has changed through the years. Traditionally, a sinking fund consisted of an accumulation of cash and securities (and earnings thereon) which were readily marketable. The use of these funds was restricted to the redemption of the entire bond issue at the maturity date.

Provisions in modern indentures require that payments be made on or before a given date to a sinking fund which will be used to immediately redeem a stipulated amount of bonds and to pay the accrued interest on them. If a trustee is used in such sinking fund arrangements, the trustee will determine by specific identification which bonds will be called for redemption. The expenses of the sinking fund trustee are not

The correct entries for 1979 are:

Mar. 1 Cash 1,098,000
           Bonds Payable...................................... 1,000,000
           Bonds Payable – Premium........................ 78,000
           Accrued Interest Payable 20,000
           To record the issue of bonds at 107.8 plus
           two months' accrued interest.

July   1 Accrued Interest Payable 20,000
           Interest Expense... 40,000
           Cash 60,000
           To record the payment of six months'
           interest.

Dec. 31 Interest Expense.. 60,000
           Accrued Interest Payable 60,000
           To record the accrual of six months' interest.

           Bonds Payable – Premium............................ 6,610
           Interest Expense..................................... 6,610
           To amortize ten months' premium at $661
           per month.

The entries are quite similar to those for the situation in which there was a discount. The only difference is that the amortization of the premium has an effect on interest recognized opposite to that of the accumulation of the discount. If you answered incorrectly, restudy Frame 5⁹ carefully before going on to Frame 6⁹ on page 403.

6⁹
continued

to be reimbursed from the sinking fund. Thus, the modern sinking fund brings about the serial redemption of outstanding bonds without actually issuing serial bonds.

To illustrate current practices regarding the use of a sinking fund, assume that on October 1, 1975, the Bradley Company issued $1 million of 25-year, 12 percent, semiannual coupon bonds at face value. Under the terms of the indenture, the company is to deliver to the trustee on September 30, 1980, and each September 30 thereafter as long as any bonds are outstanding, an amount sufficient to redeem $50,000 of the principal amount at 100 and to pay any accrued interest on the bonds called for redemption through the sinking fund. The entry to record the required payment on September 30, 1980, is:

Sinking Fund... 53,000
    Cash 53,000
    Payment to trustee of funds to call $50,000 of bonds at face
    value plus accrued interest of $3,000 ($50,000 × .12 × 1/2).

The trustee calls $50,000 of bonds, pays for the bonds and the accrued interest, and notifies the company. Assuming that the accrued interest has been recorded, the entry is:

Accrued Bond Interest Payable	3,000	
Bonds Payable	50,000	
Sinking Fund		53,000

To record payment by trustee of accrued interest on, and redemption of, bonds through sinking fund.

Indicate whether each statement is correct or incorrect.

1. The primary purpose of a sinking fund is the payment of periodic interest on outstanding bonds.
2. During that period of the life of a bond issue when the company is required to make annual payments into a sinking fund, a portion of the bonds outstanding should be shown as a current liability in the statement of financial position.
3. The journal entry made by the company when its sinking fund trustee reports the purchase of securities according to the terms of the indenture consists of a debit to Bond Investments and a credit to Sinking Fund Cash.

To check your responses, turn to Answer Frame 6[9] on page 406.

Frame 7[9]

Statement of financial position illustration

The liabilities portion (current and long term) of the statement of financial position of the Sperry Corporation (Illustration 9.2) presents certain accounts discussed in this chapter.

Illustration 9.2

THE SPERRY CORPORATION Partial Statement of Financial Position December 31, 1979			
Liabilities and Stockholders' Equity			
Current Liabilities:			
Accounts payable		$160,000	
Accrued bond interest payable		4,000	
Current portion of long-term debt		10,000	$174,000
Long-Term Liabilities:			
Debenture bonds, 10%, due 1983	$190,000		
Less: Discount	4,000	$186,000	
First-mortgage bonds, 12%, due 1984	$200,000		
Add: Premium	2,000	202,000	388,000
Total Liabilities			$562,000

405

1. Incorrect. The periodic deposits made with the sinking fund trustee are not primarily for the payment of the bond interest.
2. Correct. If you answered correctly, you are doing quite well, since nothing has been said about the classification of outstanding bonds when periodic sinking fund payments are required. An amount equal to the value of the bonds which will be redeemed through the operation of the sinking fund in the coming operating cycle should be shown as a current liability.
3. Incorrect. The journal entry made when the sinking fund trustee reports the acquisition of securities debits Bonds Payable and credits Sinking Fund. A company cannot invest in its own bonds.

If you did not answer correctly, reread Frame 6⁹ before proceeding to Frame 7⁹ on page 405.

7⁹
continued

With reference to the information pertaining to bonds contained in this partial statement of financial position, indicate whether each of the following statements is true or false.

1. At the time the 10 percent debenture bonds were issued, the prevailing market rate of interest for similar bonds was greater than 10 percent.
2. The semiannual interest payment date of at least one of the bond issues does not fall on December 31, 1979.
3. The stated interest rate of 12 percent on the first-mortgage bonds was lower at the time of their issuance than the prevailing market rate for similar bonds.
4. Both of the corporation's bond issues are secured by pledges of specific property.

Check your answers in Answer Frame 7⁹ on page 408.

Frame 8⁹

Why a company might decide to invest in bonds

A company can only issue bonds when some other party is willing to acquire them. There are both short-term and long-term reasons for deciding to invest in bonds.

The main short-term reason is to earn at least a nominal rate of return on cash that would otherwise be temporarily idle. As emphasized in Chapter 6, there may be vehicles for investment which involve less risk, but regardless of this some companies do acquire bonds as a temporary investment. The primary risk is that the investor will have to sell the bonds at a time when the market price is relatively low (because of an increase in the market rate of interest).

Long-term reasons for investing in bonds include the desire to secure a continuing stream of revenue from the investment over a period of years and the desire to establish a financial affiliation with another company. Insurance companies often acquire bonds for the former reason. They receive insurance premiums from customers and must earn a return on these until the time comes to pay claims. Investing in capital stock is too risky, while investing in bonds is not. The insurance companies can usually wait until the maturity date if need be and collect the face value of the bonds. They can usually refrain from having to sell the bonds before maturity at a temporarily depressed market price. Also, interest on bonds must be paid, while dividends on capital stock need not be declared.

The purpose for which a corporation acquires bonds, which usually must be determined on the basis of management intent, has a determining influence on accounting for the bonds and the way they are shown in the statement of financial position. If bonds are held as a temporary investment they should be classified as current assets. Otherwise, they should be considered to be long-term and reported as noncurrent assets, under the caption "Investments."

This chapter deals primarily with the accounting treatment for the long-term type of investment in bonds by corporations.

Indicate whether each of the following statements is true or false.
1. The marketability of bonds owned is the basis for showing them in the statement of financial position as either a current or noncurrent asset.
2. The purchaser of a bond must hold the bond to its maturity date.
3. One purpose for holding bonds is to secure some revenue from cash that would otherwise be idle.
4. To an insurance company interested in securing a steady stream of revenue for a number of years, an investment in bonds involves less risk than an investment in capital stock of the same company.

Check your responses in Answer Frame 8[9] on page 408.

Frame 9[9]

Accounting for Bond Investments

If bonds are purchased at face value, the entry to record the purchase includes a debit to Bond Investments and a credit to Cash for the face value of the bonds. But bonds are often purchased at a premium or discount for reasons already covered. Recording the acquisition of bonds and the earning of interest revenue are discussed below. Rounded

407

9⁹
continued

dollar amounts are used merely for the sake of keeping the illustrations simple.

Bonds purchased at a discount or premium

Earlier in the chapter when bonds were *issued* at a discount or premium, the discount or premium was recorded in a separate account. But when bonds are *purchased* at a discount or premium, no separate account is used for the discount or premium.

To illustrate, assume that Northern Company on July 1, 1979, purchased $1,000,000 of 9 percent, ten-year, first-mortgage bonds of the Southern Company for $980,000 (this example is the opposite side of the transaction where bonds were issued by Southern Company at this amount in Frame 4[9]). The interest dates are July 1 and January 1. The bond investment would be recorded as follows:

July 1	Bond Investments	980,000	
	Cash		980,000

The total amount carried to the Bond Investments account is the total cost of acquiring the bonds. This usually consists of the price paid for the bonds, broker's commission, and perhaps postage and other miscellaneous delivery charges. (These latter charges are ignored in the example.) No useful purpose is served by recording the face value of the bonds in one account and the difference between face value and total cost in another.

If the bonds are purchased as a temporary investment, there is no need to amortize the premium or accumulate the discount. But *if the bonds are to be held to maturity,* that is, if they are considered long-term investments, the premium is amortized or the discount is accumulated over the remaining life of the bonds. Usually this is done on a straight-line basis. In this example the $20,000 discount is to be accumulated over the ten years that the company will hold the bonds. The annual amount is $2,000, and the amount per interest period (six months) is $1,000. The entry required on December 31, 1979, would be (recall that the bonds were purchased on July 1, 1979):

Bond Investments	1,000	
Accrued Interest Receivable	45,000	
Interest Revenue		46,000

Interest is calculated as follows:

$$\$1,000,000 \times .09 \times \tfrac{1}{2} = \$45,000 \text{ per 6 months}$$

The Northern Company's statement of financial position as of December 31, 1979, would show accrued interest receivable of $45,000 as a current asset. The bonds will be shown in the investments section of that statement at $981,000.

If the bonds had been purchased at a premium of $20,000 instead of at a discount, the entry to record the purchase would have been:

Bond Investments	1,020,000	
Cash		1,020,000

The entry required at December 31 would have been:

Accrued Interest Receivable	45,000	
Bond Investments		1,000
Interest Revenue		44,000

The Northern Company's statement of financial position as of December 31, 1979, would have shown accrued interest receivable of $45,000 and bond investments of $1,019,000.

Is each of the following statements true or false?

1. When a company invests in bonds of another company, any premium or discount is recorded in a separate account.

2. Any premium or discount on a bond investment is to be amortized or accumulated over the remaining life of the bonds in every instance.

3. For bonds which are to be held to maturity, the correct period over which to write off the premium or discount is the entire life of the bonds.

4. In the above example, the entry to record the receipt of an interest check shortly after January 1, 1980 (regardless of whether there was a premium or discount), would be:

```
Cash ................................................................................  45,000
      Accrued Interest Receivable ..........................................         45,000
```

Now turn to Answer Frame 9⁹ on page 412 to check your answers.

Frame 10⁹ _____

Bonds purchased at face value between interest dates

Assume that the $100,000 of 9 percent bonds of the Carlson Company (described on page 401) are purchased by Braxton Company on May 1, 1979, at face value plus four months of accrued interest. (They were purchased four months after the most recent interest date.) The accrued interest is equal to $100,000 × .09 × $\frac{1}{3}$ = $3,000. The entry to record the purchase is:

```
May 1   Bond Investments ..............................................  100,000
            Accrued Interest Receivable ...............................    3,000
                 Cash ......................................................         103,000
```

If no action has been taken to record the interest accrued for the two months prior to the receipt of the semiannual interest, the Braxton Company will make the following entry in its accounts at the time it receives the first interest check:

```
July 1   Cash ..........................................................  4,500
              Accrued Interest Receivable ...............................         3,000
              Interest Revenue .............................................         1,500
```

The net interest revenue is $1,500 ($100,000 × .09 × $\frac{1}{6}$) which is interest for the two months from the date of purchase to the first interest date.

Bonds purchased at a discount or premium between interest dates

When bonds are purchased at a discount or premium between interest dates, it is necessary to allocate the premium or discount over the

410

period running from the acquisition date to the maturity date. It is important to note that you do not write off the discount or premium over the *entire* life of the bonds.

To illustrate, assume that the Purchaser Insurance Company on March 1, 1979, bought bonds of the Issuer Corporation at 92.2. They are 12 percent bonds with a face value of $1,000,000. The bonds are dated January 1, 1979. (The other side of this transaction was given in Frame 5[9]. You may want to refer back to it as you examine the entries required for the purchaser.)

The entries required for 1979 on the Purchaser Insurance Company's books are as follows:

Mar.	1	Bond Investments	922,000	
		Accrued Interest Receivable	20,000	
		Cash		942,000
		To record the purchase of bonds at 92.2 plus two months' accrued interest.		
July	1	Cash	60,000	
		Accrued Interest Receivable		20,000
		Interest Revenue...		40,000
		To record receipt of six months' interest.		
Dec.	31	Accrued Interest Receivable	60,000	
		Interest Revenue...		60,000
		To record the accrual of six months' interest.		
		Bond Investments	6,610	
		Interest Revenue...		6,610
		To record the accumulation of ten months' discount at $661 per month.		

$$\frac{\$78,000}{118 \text{ months}} = \$661.$$

Valuation of debt securities held

Investments in bonds. For investments in bonds, the most common basis of valuation is cost whether classified as current assets or long-term investments. Cost usually consists of price paid plus broker's commission. An exception to this practice is made when a *substantial* and *apparently permanent* decline in the value of the bonds occurs. Then these bond investments are written down to market by debiting Loss on Market Decline of Bond Investments and crediting Bond Investments.

Once bond investments are written down, it is not permissible to write them back up to even their original cost if market prices advance in the future. Gain or loss is simply recorded for the difference between the sales proceeds and the amount at which the bonds are carried in the accounts when they are sold.

The topics of leases and pensions are covered in Appendix 9B.

1. False. The net amount paid is recorded in the Bond Investments account. There is no separate account for the premium or discount.

2. False. Only if the intention is to hold the bonds until maturity should the premium or discount be amortized or accumulated. If the bonds are held for short-term purposes, the accountant would not know the proper period over which to write off the premium or discount.

3. False. The period over which to write off the premium or discount is the period from the *acquisition date* to the maturity date. For instance, if ten-year bonds dated January 1, 1978, are acquired on January 1, 1980, the premium or discount would be written off over the period January 1, 1980, to January 1, 1988.

4. True. On January 1, 1980 (or shortly thereafter), an interest check in the amount of $45,000 would be received and would be recorded as shown.

If you missed any of the above, reread Frame 9⁹ before beginning Frame 10⁹ on page 410.

10⁹
continued

To test your understanding, assume that the Purchaser Insurance Company referred to above had purchased the bonds at 107.8 instead of at 92.2. Using the entries above as a guide, prepare the entries as of March 1, July 1, and December 31.

Now turn to Answer Frame 10⁹ on page 414 to check your answers.

Summary *chapter* 9

A bond is one of the most common forms of long-term debt financing. Because of the interest expense on such debt and its deductibility in arriving at taxable net earnings, the issuance of debt will have an effect, known as financial leverage, on the earnings available for stockholders. Favorable financial leverage results when borrowed funds generate more earnings per share than if the funds had been raised by issuing additional shares of capital stock. When the reverse is true, unfavorable financial leverage is present.

Bonds may be secured or unsecured, and they may or may not be convertible into stock of the issuing corporation. They may also be callable.

The price a bond will bring often differs from its face value and is dependent on the relationship between the contract rate of interest and the current market rate of interest for bonds of the same risk category. The contract (coupon) rate of interest determines how much cash will be paid as interest on each interest date during the life of the bonds. The bonds sell at a premium or a discount to make the effective (or yield) rate of interest equal to the market rate of interest which exists at the time of issuance. Any discount or premium is recorded in a separate account by the issuing company, but the amount paid by the investor is usually recorded in a single account on his books. The discount or premium must be assigned to the time periods within the bond's life.

When bonds are issued between interest dates, the investor will pay for both the bond and the interest accrued from the last interest payment date to the date of acquisition. This is because the issuer is obligated to issue interest checks which cover a full interest period, whereas the investor is entitled to interest only for that period during which he or she holds the bonds.

Bond indenture provisions relative to redemption of the bonds vary. Bonds may be redeemed in their entirety at maturity, or in whole or in part at a date preceding maturity (usually at a specified premium, through the operation of a sinking fund). Any difference between the book value of the long-term bond investment (or liability) and the amount received (or paid) will be treated as either a gain or a loss.

When bonds are issued by a company, other companies often purchase them as long-term investments. Long-term investments in bonds are made to establish an affiliation with another company or to secure a continuing stream of revenue over a period of years. Alternatively, they may be acquired as a temporary investment. The intent of management is the determining factor as to whether an investment in bonds is short term or long term in nature. Any discount or premium will be written off over the time period remaining to maturity only if the bonds are to be held to maturity. The entries made by the investor regarding bond transactions are comparable to those made by the issuer of the bonds. The amounts of accrued interest and accumulation of discount or amortization of premium are often similar.

The concepts of future worth and present value are covered in Appendix 9A. The topics of leases and premiums are covered in Appendix 9B.

To complete your review, study the definitions of new terms introduced in this chapter contained in the Glossary on page 427. Then go on to the Student Review Quiz beginning on page 428 for a self-administered test of your comprehension of the material in the chapter.

APPENDIX 9A: FUTURE WORTH AND PRESENT VALUE

This Appendix discusses the concepts of future worth (or value), present value, and present value of an annuity, their use in determining the price of a bond issue, and the effective rate of interest method for accumulating the discount on bonds payable.

Future worth

Interest is compounded when periodically its amount is computed and added to the base to form a new amount upon which the interest for a

The correct entries are:

Mar.	1	Bond Investments	1,078,000	
		Accrued Interest Receivable	20,000	
		Cash		1,098,000

To record the purchase of bonds at 107.8
plus two months' accrued interest.

July	1	Cash	60,000	
		Accrued Interest Receivable		20,000
		Interest Revenue		40,000

To record the receipt of six months' interest.

Dec.	31	Accrued Interest Receivable	60,000	
		Interest Revenue		60,000

To record the accrual of six months' interest.

		Interest Revenue	6,610	
		Bond Investments		6.610

To amortize ten months' premium at $661
per month.

The entries are quite similar to those for the situation in which there was a discount. The only difference is that the amortization of the premium has an effect on interest recognized opposite to that of the accumulation of the discount.

If you answered incorrectly, restudy Frame 10⁹ carefully before turning to the Summary on page 412.

later period is to be computed. For example, an investment of $1,000 at 3 percent compound interest will grow to $1,060.90 in two periods at compound interest, but only to $1,060 at simple interest. At simple interest, the interest for each period will be $30 for a total of $60. At compound interest, the interest for the first period will be $30 and the amount of the investment at the end of the first period will be $1,030 ($1,000 × 1.03). Interest for the second period will be $30.90 ($1,030 × .03), and the amount of the investment will be $1,060.90 ($1,030 × 1.03) at the end of the second period.

Note that the $1,060.90 amount was derived by multiplying $1,000 × 1.03 × 1.03. Since 1.03 × 1.03 is equal to $(1.03)^2$, a shortcut can be employed in the calculation. The amount of the investment at the end of the second period is simply $1,000 × $(1.03)^2$, which equals $1,000 × 1.0609, or $1,060.90. From this the formula for the compound amount of 1 can be derived as being $(1 + i)^n$ where i is the interest rate per period and n is the number of periods involved.

The task of computing the sum (the future worth) to which any invested amount will grow at a given rate for a stated number of periods is facilitated through the use of interest tables. From Table I (at the end of this Appendix), the amount to which an investment of $1 at 3 percent for three periods will grow can be determined as being $1.092727. The amount to which an investment of $1,000 will grow is simply 1,000 times this amount.

Present value

In the illustrations above, the future worth of a given investment was found by multiplying the investment by $(1 + i)^n$, where i was the interest rate involved and n the number of periods of life. Since present value is exactly the reverse of a future sum, it is found by dividing the future sum by $(1 + i)^n$. Thus, the present value of $1,000 due in one period at 3 percent is equal to $1,000 \div (1.03)$. Or the computation can be expressed as $1,000 \times 1/(1.03)$ which is equal to $1,000 \times .970874$, or $970.87. Thus, $970.87 invested at 3 percent per period will grow to exactly $1,000 in one period.

The present value of $1,000 due in two periods then is simply $1,000 $\div (1.03)^2$. Here again the computation can be expressed as $1,000 \times 1/(1.03)^2$, which simplifies to $1,000 \times .942596$, or $942.60. Table II at the end of this Appendix contains the present values of $1 at different interest rates for different periods of time. The use of the table can be illustrated by determining the present value of $10,000 due in 40 periods at 3 percent. The present value of 1 due in 40 periods at 3 percent per period is given as .306557. The present value of $10,000 due in 40 periods at 3 percent then is $3,065.57 ($10,000 \times .306557$).

Present value of an annuity

An annuity may be defined as a series of equal payments equally spaced in time. The present value or worth of such a series may be desired information for certain types of decisions. The approach to the problem of valuing annuities can be illustrated by finding the present value, at 3 percent per period, of an annuity calling for the payment of $100 at the end of each of the next three periods. It would be possible, through the use of Table II in this Appendix, to find the present value of each of the $100 payments as follows:

> Present value of $100 due in —
> 1 period   is .970874 × $100 = $ 97.09
> 2 periods is .942596 × $100 =   94.26
> 3 periods is .915142 × $100 =   91.51
>   Total Present Value
>   of Three $100
>   Payments................. $282.86

Such a procedure could become quite tedious if the annuity consisted of 50 to 100 or more payments. Fortunately, tables are also available showing the present values of an annuity of $1 per period for varying interest rates and periods. See Table III at the end of this Appendix. Thus, a single figure can be obtained from the table which represents the present value of an annuity of $1 per period for three periods at an interest rate of 3 percent per period. This figure is 2.828611, and when multiplied by $100, the number of dollars in each payment, yields the present value of the annuity as $282.86.

Determining the price of a bond

The concepts discussed above will now be employed to illustrate the computation of the price of a bond issue.

In determining the price of a bond, the life of the bond is always stated in terms of interest payment periods, and the effective rate used in seeking amounts from the interest tables is the annual effective rate divided by the number of interest periods in one year.

Assume that bonds with a face value of $100,000 and an interest rate of 10 percent (semiannual interest payments) are issued at a price which will yield the investor a return of 12 percent. The issue date is July 1, 1979, and the maturity date is July 1, 1982 (this unrealistically short life is used for sake of keeping the illustration simple). The price the investor would pay is calculated as shown:

Present value of the promise to pay principal is $100,000 times the present value of $1 due in 6 periods at 6%, or $100,000 × .704961 (from Table II)	$70,496.10
Present value of the promise to pay periodic interest is $5,000 times the present value of an annuity of $1 for 6 periods at 6%, or $5,000 × 4.917324 (from Table III)	24,586.62
Total Price	$95,082.72

Thus, the amount of the discount is $100,000 − $95,082.72 = $4,-917.28.

The effective rate of interest method for accumulating the discount

The following table shows how this discount would be accumulated over the life of the bonds. The yield rate must be known to make the calculations required under this method. Notice that the amount accumulated increases each period rather than remaining constant as it would under the straight-line method ($819.55 per six-month period under the straight-line method).

Discount accumulated by the effective rate of interest method

Date	Cash Credit	Interest Expense Debit	Discount on Bonds Payable Credit	Carrying value of Bonds Payable
7/1/79				$ 95,082.72
1/1/80	$ 5,000[1]	$ 5,704.96[2]	$ 704.96[3]	95,787.68[4]
7/1/80	5,000	5,747.26	747.26	96,534.94
1/1/81	5,000	5,792.10	792.10	97,327.04
7/1/81	5,000	5,839.62	839.62	98,166.66
1/1/82	5,000	5,890.00	890.00	99,056.66
7/1/82	5,000	5,943.34[5]	943.34	100,000.00[5]
	$30,000	$34,917.28	$4,917.28	

[1] $100,000 × 10% × $\frac{1}{2}$ = $5,000.
[2] $95,082.72 × 12% × $\frac{1}{2}$ = $5,704.96.
[3] $5,704.96 − $5,000 = $704.96.
[4] $95,082.72 + $704.96 = $95,787.68.
[5] Actually this came to $5,943.40, but was reduced to make the carrying value come to $100,000.

APPENDIX 9B: LEASES AND PENSIONS

Leases

During the past 25 years the long-term lease has become a common method of financing operating assets. The contracts usually call for rental payments over a period of years. Often the lease will extend over a significant portion of the expected life of the leased asset, or it may extend over a shorter period with an option to either renew the lease or purchase the asset, sometimes at a nominal price. The terms of the contracts may be individually tailored to the needs of the lessee. Often, such leases stipulate that taxes, insurance, and maintenance costs be paid by the lessee.

Leasing may be advantageous to a particular firm because of its flexibility, tax implications, and the possibility of obtaining financing when other means are not readily available. One of the disadvantages of leasing is that it may cost more than borrowing from other sources. But the total contract and services involved must be evaluated in order to make such a determination.

How leases should be treated on the statement of financial position has been the subject of considerable debate. It has been proposed by some that leasing an asset is no different from purchasing the asset — that only the method of financing differs. This line of argument states that the lease payments should be discounted at the current rate of interest applicable to the firm and their present value recorded as a liability, with a corresponding debit to an asset account. Then as each payment is made, a portion of the recorded liability is canceled, interest expense is recognized, and a credit is made to cash. Proponents of this theory believe that such a treatment shows all assets on a comparable basis in the

417

Table 1 Amount of 1 (at compound interest) $(1 + i)^n$

Periods	2%	2½%	3%	4%	5%	6%
1.....	1.02	1.025	1.03	1.04	1.05	1.06
2.....	1.040 4	1.050 625	1.060 9	1.081 6	1.102 5	1.123 6
3.....	1.061 208	1.076 891	1.092 727	1.124 864	1.157 625	1.191 016
4.....	1.082 432	1.103 813	1.125 509	1.169 859	1.215 506	1.262 477
5.....	1.104 081	1.131 408	1.159 274	1.216 653	1.276 282	1.338 226
6.....	1.126 162	1.159 693	1.194 052	1.265 319	1.340 096	1.418 519
7.....	1.148 686	1.188 686	1.229 874	1.315 932	1.407 100	1.503 630
8.....	1.171 659	1.218 403	1.266 770	1.368 569	1.477 455	1.593 848
9.....	1.195 093	1.248 863	1.304 773	1.423 312	1.551 328	1.689 479
10.....	1.218 994	1.280 085	1.343 916	1.480 244	1.628 895	1 790 848
11.....	1.243 374	1.312 087	1.384 234	1.539 454	1.710 339	1 898 299
12.....	1.268 242	1.344 889	1.425 761	1.601 032	1.795 856	2.012 196
13.....	1.293 607	1.378 511	1.468 534	1.665 074	1.885 649	2.132 928
14.....	1.319 479	1.412 974	1.512 590	1.731 676	1.979 932	2.260 904
15.....	1.345 868	1.448 298	1.557 967	1.800 944	2.078 928	2.396 558
16.....	1.372 786	1.484 506	1.604 706	1.872 981	2.182 875	2.540 352
17.....	1.400 241	1.521 618	1.652 848	1.947 901	2.292 018	2.692 773
18.....	1.428 246	1.559 659	1.702 433	2.025 817	2.406 619	2.854 339
19.....	1.456 811	1.598 650	1.753 506	2.106 849	2.526 950	3.025 600
20.....	1.485 947	1.638 616	1.806 111	2.191 123	2.653 298	3.207 135
21.....	1.515 666	1.679 582	1.860 295	2.278 768	2.785 963	3.399 564
22.....	1.545 980	1.721 571	1.916 103	2.369 919	2.925 261	3.603 537
23.....	1.576 899	1.764 611	1.973 587	2.464 716	3.071 524	3.819 750
24.....	1.608 437	1.808 726	2.032 794	2.563 304	3.225 100	4.048 935
25.....	1.640 606	1.853 944	2.093 778	2.665 836	3.386 355	4.291 871
26.....	1.673 418	1.900 293	2.156 591	2.772 470	3.555 673	4.549 383
27.....	1.706 886	1.947 800	2.221 289	2.883 369	3.733 456	4.822 346
28.....	1.741 024	1.996 495	2.287 928	2.998 703	3.920 129	5.111 687
29.....	1.775 845	2.046 407	2.356 566	3.118 651	4.116 136	5.418 388
30.....	1.811 362	2.097 568	2.427 262	3.243 398	4.321 942	5.743 491
31.....	1.847 589	2.150 007	2.500 080	3.373 133	4.538 039	6.088 101
32.....	1.884 541	2.203 757	2.575 083	3.508 059	4.764 941	6.453 387
33.....	1.922 231	2.258 851	2.652 335	3.648 381	5.003 189	6.840 590
34.....	1.960 676	2.315 322	2.731 905	3.794 316	5.253 348	7.251 025
35.....	1.999 890	2.373 205	2.813 862	3.946 089	5.516 015	7.686 087
36.....	2.039 887	2.432 535	2.898 278	4.103 933	5.791 816	8.147 252
37.....	2.080 685	2.493 349	2.985 227	4.268 090	6.081 407	8.636 087
38.....	2.122 299	2.555 682	3.074 783	4.438 813	6.385 477	9.154 252
39.....	2.164 745	2.619 574	3.167 027	4.616 366	6.704 751	9.703 507
40.....	2.208 040	2.685 064	3.262 038	4.801 021	7.039 989	10.285 718

Table II   Present value of 1 (at compound interest) $\dfrac{1}{(1+i)^n}$

Periods	2%	2½%	3%	4%	5%	6%
1.....	0.980 392	0.975 610	0.970 874	0.961 538	0.952 381	0.943 396
2.....	0.961 169	0.951 814	0.942 596	0.924 556	0.907 029	0.889 996
3.....	0.942 322	0.928 599	0.915 142	0.888 996	0.863 838	0.839 619
4.....	0.923 845	0.905 951	0.888 487	0.854 804	0.822 702	0.792 094
5.....	0.905 731	0.883 854	0.862 609	0.821 927	0.783 526	0.747 258
6.....	0.887 971	0.862 297	0.837 484	0.790 315	0.746 215	0.704 961
7.....	0.870 560	0.841 265	0.813 092	0.759 918	0.710 681	0.665 057
8.....	0.853 490	0.820 747	0.789 409	0.730 690	0.676 839	0.627 412
9.....	0.836 755	0.800 728	0.766 417	0.702 587	0.644 609	0.591 898
10.....	0.820 348	0.781 198	0.744 094	0.675 564	0.613 913	0.558 395
11.....	0.804 263	0.762 145	0.722 421	0.649 581	0.584 679	0.526 788
12.....	0.788 493	0.743 556	0.701 380	0.624 597	0.556 837	0.496 969
13.....	0.773 033	0.725 420	0.680 951	0.600 574	0.530 321	0.468 839
14.....	0.757 875	0.707 727	0.661 118	0.577 475	0.505 068	0.442 301
15.....	0.743 015	0.690 466	0.641 862	0.555 265	0.481 017	0.417 265
16.....	0.728 446	0.673 625	0.623 167	0.533 908	0.458 112	0.393 646
17.....	0.714 163	0.657 195	0.605 016	0.513 373	0.436 297	0.371 364
18.....	0.700 159	0.641 166	0.587 395	0.493 628	0.415 521	0.350 344
19.....	0.686 431	0.625 528	0.570 286	0.474 642	0.395 734	0.330 513
20.....	0.672 971	0.610 271	0.553 676	0.456 387	0.376 889	0.311 805
21.....	0.659 776	0.595 386	0.537 549	0.438 834	0.358 942	0.294 155
22.....	0.646 839	0.580 865	0.521 893	0.421 955	0.341 850	0.277 505
23.....	0.634 156	0.566 697	0.506 692	0.405 726	0.325 571	0.261 797
24.....	0.621 721	0.552 875	0.491 934	0.390 121	0.310 068	0.246 979
25.....	0.609 531	0.539 391	0.477 606	0.375 117	0.295 303	0.232 999
26.....	0.597 579	0.526 234	0.463 695	0.360 689	0.281 241	0.219 810
27.....	0.585 862	0.513 400	0.450 189	0.346 817	0.267 848	0.207 368
28.....	0.574 375	0.500 878	0.437 077	0.333 477	0.255 094	0.195 630
29.....	0.563 112	0.488 661	0.424 346	0.320 651	0.242 946	0.184 557
30.....	0.552 071	0.476 743	0.411 987	0.308 319	0.231 377	0.174 110
31.....	0.541 246	0.465 115	0.399 987	0.296 460	0.220 359	0.164 255
32.....	0.530 633	0.453 770	0.388 337	0.285 058	0.209 866	0.154 957
33.....	0.520 229	0.442 703	0.377 026	0.274 094	0.199 873	0.146 186
34.....	0.510 028	0.431 905	0.366 045	0.263 552	0.190 355	0.137 912
35.....	0.500 028	0.421 371	0.355 383	0.253 415	0.181 290	0.130 105
36.....	0.490 223	0.411 094	0.345 032	0.243 669	0.172 657	0.122 741
37.....	0.480 611	0.401 067	0.334 983	0.234 297	0.164 436	0.115 793
38.....	0.471 187	0.391 285	0.325 226	0.225 285	0.156 605	0.109 239
39.....	0.461 948	0.381 741	0.315 754	0.216 621	0.149 148	0.103 056
40.....	0.452 890	0.372 431	0.306 557	0.208 289	0.142 046	0.097 222

Table II (*continued*)

Periods	8%	10%	12%	14%	16%	18%	20%
1.....	0.926	0.909	0.893	0.877	0.862	0.847	0.833
2.....	0.857	0.826	0.797	0.769	0.743	0.718	0.694
3.....	0.794	0.751	0.712	0.675	0.641	0.609	0.579
4.....	0.735	0.683	0.636	0.592	0.552	0.516	0.482
5.....	0.681	0.621	0.567	0.519	0.476	0.437	0.402
6.....	0.630	0.564	0.507	0.456	0.410	0.370	0.335
7.....	0.583	0.513	0.452	0.400	0.354	0.314	0.279
8.....	0.540	0.467	0.404	0.351	0.305	0.266	0.233
9.....	0.500	0.424	0.361	0.308	0.263	0.225	0.194
10.....	0.463	0.386	0.322	0.270	0.227	0.191	0.162
11.....	0.429	0.350	0.287	0.237	0.195	0.162	0.135
12.....	0.397	0.319	0.257	0.208	0.168	0.137	0.112
13.....	0.368	0.290	0.229	0.182	0.145	0.116	0.093
14.....	0.340	0.263	0.205	0.160	0.125	0.099	0.078
15.....	0.315	0.239	0.183	0.140	0.108	0.084	0.065
16.....	0.292	0.218	0.163	0.123	0.093	0.071	0.054
17.....	0.270	0.198	0.146	0.108	0.080	0.060	0.045
18.....	0.250	0.180	0.130	0.095	0.069	0.051	0.038
19.....	0.232	0.164	0.116	0.083	0.060	0.043	0.031
20.....	0.215	0.149	0.104	0.073	0.051	0.037	0.026
21.....	0.199	0.135	0.093	0.064	0.044	0.031	0.022
22.....	0.184	0.123	0.083	0.056	0.038	0.026	0.018
23.....	0.170	0.112	0.074	0.049	0.033	0.022	0.015
24.....	0.158	0.102	0.066	0.043	0.028	0.019	0.013
25.....	0.146	0.092	0.059	0.038	0.024	0.016	0.010
26.....	0.135	0.084	0.053	0.033	0.021	0.014	0.009
27.....	0.125	0.076	0.047	0.029	0.018	0.011	0.007
28.....	0.116	0.069	0.042	0.026	0.016	0.010	0.006
29.....	0.107	0.063	0.037	0.022	0.014	0.008	0.005
30.....	0.099	0.057	0.033	0.020	0.012	0.007	0.004
31.....	0.092	0.052	0.030	0.017	0.010	0.006	0.004
32.....	0.085	0.047	0.027	0.015	0.009	0.005	0.003
33.....	0.079	0.043	0.024	0.013	0.007	0.004	0.002
34.....	0.073	0.039	0.021	0.012	0.006	0.004	0.002
35.....	0.068	0.036	0.019	0.010	0.006	0.003	0.002
36.....	0.063	0.032	0.017	0.009	0.005	0.003	0.001
37.....	0.058	0.029	0.015	0.008	0.004	0.002	0.001
38.....	0.054	0.027	0.013	0.007	0.004	0.002	0.001
39.....	0.050	0.024	0.012	0.006	0.003	0.002	0.001
40.....	0.046	0.022	0.011	0.005	0.003	0.001	0.001

Table III   Present value of an Annuity of 1 $\dfrac{1 - \dfrac{1}{(1 + i)^n}}{i}$

Periods	2%	2½%	3%	4%	5%	6%
1.....	0.980 392	0.975 610	0.970 874	0.961 539	0.952 381	0.943 396
2.....	1.941 561	1.927 424	1.913 470	1.886 095	1.859 410	1.833 393
3.....	2.883 883	2.856 024	2.828 611	2.775 091	2.723 248	2.673 012
4.....	3.807 729	3.761 974	3.717 098	3.629 895	3.545 951	3.465 106
5.....	4.713 460	4.645 829	4.579 707	4.451 822	4.329 477	4.212 364
6.....	5.601 431	5.508 125	5.417 191	5.242 137	5.075 692	4.917 324
7.....	6.471 991	6.349 391	6.230 283	6.002 055	5.786 373	5.582 381
8.....	7.325 481	7.170 137	7.019 692	6.732 745	6.463 213	6.209 794
9.....	8.162 237	7.970 866	7.786 109	7.435 332	7.107 822	6.801 692
10.....	8.982 585	8.752 064	8.530 203	8.110 896	7.721 735	7.360 087
11.....	9.786 848	9.514 209	9.252 624	8.760 477	8.306 414	7.886 875
12.....	10.575 341	10.257 765	9.954 004	9.385 074	8.863 252	8.383 844
13.....	11.348 374	10.983 185	10.634 955	9.985 648	9.393 573	8.852 683
14.....	12.106 249	11.690 012	11.296 073	10.563 123	9.898 641	9.294 984
15.....	12.849 264	12.381 378	11.937 935	11.118 387	10.379 658	9.712 249
16.....	13.577 709	13.055 003	12.561 102	11.652 296	10.837 770	10.105 895
17.....	14.291 872	13.712 198	13.166 119	12.165 669	11.274 066	10.477 260
18.....	14.992 031	14.353 364	13.753 513	12.659 297	11.689 587	10.827 604
19.....	15.678 462	14.978 891	14.323 799	13.133 939	12.085 321	11.158 117
20.....	16.351 433	15.589 162	14.877 475	13.590 326	12.462 210	11.469 921
21.....	17.011 209	16.184 549	15.415 024	14.029 160	12.821 153	11.764 077
22.....	17.658 048	16.765 413	15.936 917	14.451 115	13.163 003	12.041 582
23.....	18.292 204	17.332 111	16.443 608	14.856 842	13.488 574	12.303 379
24.....	18.913 926	17.884 986	16.935 542	15.246 963	13.798 642	12.550 358
25.....	19.523 457	18.424 376	17.413 148	15.622 080	14.093 945	12.783 356
26.....	20.121 036	18.950 611	17.876 842	15.982 769	14.375 185	13.003 166
27.....	20.706 898	19.464 011	18.327 032	16.329 586	14.643 034	13.210 534
28.....	21.281 272	19.964 889	18.764 108	16.663 063	14.898 127	13.406 164
29.....	21.844 385	20.453 550	19.188 455	16.983 715	15.141 074	13.590 721
30.....	22.396 456	20.930 293	19.600 441	17.292 033	15.372 451	13.764 831
31.....	22.937 702	21.395 407	20.000 429	17.588 494	15.592 811	13.929 086
32.....	23.468 335	21.849 178	20.388 766	17.873 552	15.802 677	14.084 043
33.....	23.988 564	22.291 881	20.765 792	18.147 646	16.002 549	14.230 230
34.....	24.498 592	22.723 786	21.131 837	18.411 198	16.192 904	14.368 141
35.....	24.998 619	23.145 157	21.487 220	18.664 613	16.374 194	14.498 246
36.....	25.488 843	23.556 251	21.832 253	18.908 282	16.546 852	14.620 987
37.....	25.969 453	23.957 318	22.167 235	19.142 579	16.711 287	14.736 780
38.....	26.440 641	24.348 603	22.492 462	19.367 864	16.867 893	14.846 019
39.....	26.902 589	24.730 344	22.808 215	19.584 485	17.017 041	14.949 075
40.....	27.355 479	25.102 775	23.114 772	19.792 774	17.159 086	15.046 297

Table III (continued)

Periods	8%	10%	12%	14%	16%	18%	20%
1......	0.926	0.909	0.893	0.877	0.862	0.847	0.833
2......	1.783	1.736	1.690	1.647	1.605	1.566	1.528
3......	2.577	2.487	2.402	2.322	2.246	2.174	2.106
4......	3.312	3.170	3.037	2.914	2.798	2.690	2.589
5......	3.993	3.791	3.605	3.433	3.274	3.127	2.991
6......	4.623	4.355	4.111	3.889	3.685	3.498	3.326
7......	5.206	4.868	4.564	4.288	4.039	3.812	3.605
8......	5.747	5.335	4.968	4.639	4.344	4.078	3.837
9......	6.247	5.759	5.328	4.946	4.607	4.303	4.031
10......	6.710	6.145	5.650	5.216	4.833	4.494	4.192
11......	7.139	6.495	5.937	5.453	5.029	4.656	4.327
12......	7.536	6.814	6.194	5.660	5.197	4.793	4.439
13......	7.904	7.103	6.424	5.842	5.342	4.910	4.533
14......	8.244	7.367	6.628	6.002	5.468	5.008	4.611
15......	8.559	7.606	6.811	6.142	5.575	5.092	4.675
16......	8.851	7.824	6.974	6.265	5.669	5.162	4.730
17......	9.122	8.022	7.120	6.373	5.749	5.222	4.775
18......	9.372	8.201	7.250	6.467	5.818	5.273	4.812
19......	9.604	8.365	7.366	6.550	5.877	5.316	4.844
20......	9.818	8.514	7.469	6.623	5.929	5.353	4.870
21......	10.017	8.649	7.562	6.687	5.973	5.384	4.891
22......	10.201	8.772	7.645	6.743	6.011	5.410	4.909
23......	10.371	8.883	7.718	6.792	6.044	5.432	4.925
24......	10.529	8.985	7.784	6.835	6.073	5.451	4.937
25......	10.675	9.077	7.843	6.873	6.097	5.467	4.948
26......	10.810	9.161	7.896	6.906	6.118	5.480	4.956
27......	10.935	9.237	7.943	6.935	6.136	5.492	4.964
28......	11.051	9.307	7.984	6.961	6.152	5.502	4.970
29......	11.158	9.370	8.022	6.983	6.166	5.510	4.975
30......	11.258	9.427	8.055	7.003	6.177	5.517	4.979
31......	11.350	9.479	8.085	7.020	6.187	5.523	4.982
32......	11.435	9.526	8.112	7.035	6.196	5.528	4.985
33......	11.514	9.569	8.135	7.048	6.203	5.532	4.988
34......	11.587	9.609	8.157	7.060	6.210	5.536	4.990
35......	11.655	9.644	8.176	7.070	6.215	5.539	4.992
36......	11.717	9.677	8.192	7.079	6.220	5.541	4.993
37......	11.775	9.706	8.208	7.087	6.224	5.543	4.994
38......	11.829	9.733	8.221	7.094	6.228	5.545	4.995
39......	11.879	9.757	8.233	7.100	6.231	5.547	4.996
40......	11.925	9.779	8.244	7.105	6.234	5.548	4.997

statement of financial position and avoids mixing operating expenses with the cost of financing.

But the Accounting Principles Board refused to go so far as to require that all leases be recorded in this manner. Rather the Board, in *Opinions No. 5 and 7*, chose to distinguish between financial (or capital) leases and operating leases.

The FASB has continued this distinction between capital and operating leases in its *Statement*, "Accounting for Leases."[1] The lease is to be considered a capital lease by the lessee (reported as an asset and as a liability) if the lease meets *any one* of the four following criteria:

1. Ownership is transferred to the lessee by the end of the lease term.
2. The lease contains a bargain purchase option (an option to buy the the item at significantly less than its fair market value).
3. The lease term is at least 75 percent of the property's estimated economic life.
4. The present value of the minimum lease payments is 90 percent or more of the fair value of the leased property, less any related investment tax credit retained by the lessor.

When none of these conditions is present,[2] the lessee is simply renting the asset rather than buying it — as one might rent an automobile for several days.

Generally, no liability is recorded for future payments under an operating lease. The cost of the rent is simply charged to the period in which it is incurred. The terms of the lease are disclosed in the footnotes to the financial statements.

The assets and liabilities implicit in capital leases are, on the other hand, generally recorded at the discounted value of the future rental payments. To illustrate, assume that the Brand J Company enters into a noncancellable ten-year lease on January 1, 1979, and agrees to pay $5,000 immediately and another $5,000 at the end of each of the first nine years of the lease. At the end of the tenth year, the company can purchase the machine, which is estimated to have a useful economic life of 15 years, for $1. The lease is to be treated as a capital lease. The company currently has to pay 8 percent on borrowed funds used to finance the purchase of similar assets.

The value to be recorded in the Equipment account is equal to the immediate payment of $5,000 plus the present value of an annuity of $5,000 for nine years at 8 percent. Using Table III, the debit to the Equipment account is computed as:

---

[1] Financial Accounting Standards Board, "Accounting for Leases," *FASB Statement No. 13* (Stamford, Conn., November 1976).

[2] For the lessor, a lease that meets any one of the above four criteria plus two additional criteria is to be treated as a sale of the asset. The two additional criteria are: (1) collectibility of the minimum lease payments is reasonably predictable; and (2) no important uncertainties surround the amount of unreimbursable costs yet to be incurred by the lessor under the lease. A lease that does *not* meet the criteria is to be accounted for as an operating lease. For the lessor, the asset involved in an operating lease is reported among the plant assets and is depreciated. Rental earnings are shown in the earnings statement.

$5,000 + (\$5,000 \times 6.247) = \$36,235$. The appropriate entry on signing the lease and paying the first lease payment of $5,000 is:

Jan. 1	Equipment	36,235	
	Long-Term Lease Liability		31,235
	Cash		5,000

To record the "purchase" of equipment under a
ten-year lease at $5,000 plus the discounted value
(8 percent) of the future lease payments.

The long-term lease liability can be viewed as the balance of the "principal" of a loan obtained to acquire the property which is being leased. To find the interest expense that has accrued on this loan by the end of 1979, it is necessary to multiply 8 percent by the outstanding balance ($31,235) as of the beginning of the year. Since $(.08 \times \$31,235) = \$2,498.80$, this is the amount of interest that is being paid at the end of 1979 when the second lease payment is made. The remainder of the $5,000 payment made on December 31, 1979, is applied against the principal ($31,235) to reduce it as follows:

Principal balance before December 31 payment	$31,235.00
Less portion of $5,000 which is not interest ($5,000 − $2,498.80)	2,501.20
Principal balance after December 31 payment	$28,733.80

Thus the correct entry to record the payment on December 31, 1979, is:

Interest Expense	2,498.80	
Long-Term Lease Liability	2,501.20	
Cash		5,000.00

To record payment on lease in accord with terms of lease.

Also on December 31, 1979, it is necessary to record the adjusting entry for depreciation of the equipment acquired. Assuming that the straight-line rate is to be used and that the estimated salvage value at the end of 15 years is $235, the amount each year is:

$$\frac{\text{Cost} - \text{Salvage value}}{\text{Life in years}} = \frac{\$36,235 - \$235}{15} = \$2,400 \text{ per year}$$

The entry on December 31, 1979, and every year thereafter through the 15th year is:

Depreciation Expense	2,400	
Allowance for Depreciation — Equipment		2,400

To record depreciation expense on equipment acquired under
long-term lease.

It is desirable to construct a table such as that shown in Illustration 9.3 to show the portion of each $5,000 payment that should be debited to Interest Expense and the portion that should be debited to the Long-Term Lease Liability account.

Using Illustration 9.3, the correct entry to record the $5,000 lease payment made on December 31, 1980, would be:

Interest Expense	2,298.70
Long-Term Lease Liability	2,701.30
Cash	5,000.00

To record the December 31, 1980, payment on the
long-term lease.

The amounts for this entry are obtained from the 1980 line in Illustration 9.3. Notice that after the December 31, 1987, entry has been made, the balance in the Long-Term Lease Liability account has been reduced to zero since the "loan" has been completely paid off.

Illustration 9.3

	Entry required on December 31			
	(a)	*(b)*	*(c)*	*(d)*
	Debit to Interest Expense (8% of previous balance in Long-Term Lease Liability account)	*Debit to Long-Term Lease Liability account ($5,000 − amount in Column a)*	*Credit to Cash*	*Balance in Long-Term Lease Liability account after Dec. 31 entry*
Beginning..........				$31,235.00
1979	$2,498.80	$2,501.20	$5,000	28,733.80
1980	2,298.70	2,701.30	5,000	26,032.50
1981	2,082.60	2,917.40	5,000	23,115.10
1982	1,849.21	3,150.79	5,000	19,964.31
1983	1,597.14	3,402.86	5,000	16,561.45
1984	1,324.92	3,675.08	5,000	12,886.37
1985	1,030.91	3,969.09	5,000	8,917.28
1986	713.38	4,286.62	5,000	4,630.66
1987	370.45	4,629.55	5,000	1.11*

* Difference is due to rounding. The difference is eliminated by increasing the debit to Long-Term Lease Liability by $1.11 and decreasing the debit to Interest Expense by this amount.

Pensions

One of the long-term liabilities on the books of some firms is for obligations under an employee pension plan. Pension plans typically provide that each employee with a certain number of years of service can begin receiving a specific sum from a pension fund each year, beginning at a certain age or upon disability. For instance, such a plan may state that an employee with 5 to 10 years of service will receive an amount each year after age 65 which is equal to 30 percent of his or her highest annual salary; an employee with 10 to 20 years of service, 40 percent; and an employee with over 20 years of service, 50 percent. Since these plans are usually the result of extensive bargaining between the firm and a labor union, the provisions of various plans are subject to wide variation.

A pension plan may be funded or unfunded. It is a *funded plan* if periodic payments are made by the firm to a trustee or to some other outside agency, such as an insurance company, which has taken over the obligation to pay benefits when due. Then the firm has no future control over the cash paid into the pension fund. *Unfunded plans* are those where the company retains its obligation to pay future benefits under the plan and, therefore, does not make payments to an outside agency. Under some such plans the firm need not even set aside funds to pay these future benefits. Because of sad stories about 64-year-old workers losing their pensions because they were not funded and the company went out of business, there is an increasing tendency toward funded plans.

Under funded plans the accounting is not very complex. The pension expense to be recognized for a given accounting period is the amount which the firm is obligated to pay into the fund as a result of meeting the terms of the pension plan. For instance, if the pension plan formula is applied and it is determined that $248,000 must be paid into the fund, this is the amount of pension expense for the period. The amount of any pension plan liability is simply the amount that is due to be paid into the fund but has not yet been paid. For firms that are delinquent in their payments, this liability can grow to substantial amounts. Once the amount has been paid, the cash is out of the control of the firm and is usually invested by the outside agency to accumulate enough earnings to meet the payments to former employees when they come due. The benefits to be paid under some such plans depend on the success of the investments made by the trustee (or other outside agency).

The accounting entries for an unfunded plan are more complex. The accountant will usually seek the advice of an actuary in estimating the amounts involved. Such factors as estimates of how long people will work for the company, how long they will live after retirement, and so on, are involved. The pension plan expense is equal to the present value of future pension benefits that have been incurred that year.[3] The Pension Plan Liability account is credited for this amount. When benefits are paid to retired former employees, the Pension Plan Liability account is debited. As long as the present value of the future pension benefits incurred each year exceeds the payment of benefits, the liability continues to grow. The detailed actuarial methods used to arrive at the amounts involved in accounting for unfunded pension plans are beyond the scope of this text.

To illustrate the accounting entries for an unfunded pension plan, assume that the Retire Corporation incurred an obligation to pay future pension benefits with a present value of $160,000 in 1979 and actually paid out benefits of $70,000 during the year. The necessary entries to

---

[3] This is complicated somewhat by the fact that a special problem is encountered initially when a pension plan is adopted. Some method must be used to recognize the pension liability created (which can be substantial in amount). The pension an employee will become eligible to receive is often based on years of service which occurred before and after the plan was adopted. The cost of providing pension benefits for years before the plan was adopted is referred to as past service cost. *APB Opinion No. 8* requires that past service costs be allocated to future periods of not less than 10 nor more than 40 years.

reflect these events (in summary form) are (assuming there is no past service cost to amortize) as described below.

The correct entry on December 31, 1979, is:

Pension Plan Expense	160,000	
Pension Plan Liability		160,000

To record the obligation to pay future benefits under the pension plan at their present value.

The entry for payments to be made at various dates during 1979 is:

Pension Plan Liability	70,000	
Cash		70,000

To record the payment of benefits under the pension plan.

Glossary *chapter* 9

Annuity – a series of equal payments spaced equally in time.

Bond indenture – the overall contract between the issuer of bonds and the bondholders or the trustee representing the bondholders.

Bond redemption fund – a fund established to bring about the gradual redemption of outstanding bonds; usually called a sinking fund.

Call premium – the price in excess of face value which a bond issuer may be required to pay to redeem bonds prior to maturity date.

Compound interest – interest calculated on the principal plus the interest earned in previous periods, as compared to simple interest in which interest is computed only on the principal.

Contract rate of interest – the rate of interest printed on the face of the bonds.

Debenture bonds – unsecured bonds whose value depends upon the general credit of the issuer and which are a general lien against all unpledged property.

Effective interest rate method – a method in which interest expense (revenue) for a period is calculated by multiplying the book value of the bonds payable (investment in bonds) by the effective interest rate at the bond issue (purchase) date. The difference between the actual expense (revenue) and the amount paid (received), based on the nominal bond interest rate, represents the accumulation of discount or amortization of premium for the period.

Effective rate of interest – the rate of interest that an investor can earn on a particular bond issue by paying a certain price for it and that the issuer will incur by issuing it at that price.

Favorable financial leverage – effect on earnings per share resulting from the generation of a larger amount of net earnings by borrowed funds than the cost incurred to use them.

Financial leverage – the effect upon earnings of the introduction, or existence, of long-term debt (or other instrument with a fixed payout) as a means of financing a business; results from the fact that interest on debt is fixed in amount regardless of the level of earnings and is deductible in arriving at taxable earnings.

Income bonds – unsecured bonds for which the payment of periodic interest is contingent upon its being earned.

Lease – a contract calling for periodic rental payments for the use of an asset.

Market rate of interest – the minimum rate of interest which investors are willing to accept on bonds of a particular risk category.

Mortgage – a conditional transfer of title to property to secure a debt.

Present value – the value today of a specified future cash flow (an annuity or a lump-sum amount); determined by discounting such flows at a stipulated rate of interest.

Redemption premium – see call premium.

Registered bonds—bonds for which the names of the owners are recorded by the issuer or trustee.

Senior lien—a first mortgage, or the first claim or lien upon property.

Sinking fund—a fund into which periodic cash deposits are made for the purpose of redeeming outstanding bonds.

Straight-line method—a method of accumulating a discount or amortizing a premium which results in the same amount being assigned to each month of the life of a bond.

Trading on the equity—the securing of a portion of the needed capital of a business through the use of securities which limit the amount of interest (or dividends) paid periodically on them (see financial leverage).

Trustee—usually a bank or trust company selected to represent the bondholders in a bond issue and enforce the provisions of the bond indenture made by the issuing company.

Unfavorable financial leverage—the reverse of favorable financial leverage.

Unsecured bonds—bonds for which no specific property is pledged as security and whose value, as a result, depends on the general credit of the issuer.

Continue with the Student Review Quiz below as a self-administered test of your understanding of the material presented in this chapter.

Student review quiz *chapter* 9

To develop a permanent record of your responses, you may write them on the answer sheet provided in the *Work Papers* or on a separate sheet of paper.

1 A bond issued at a discount indicates that at the date of issue—

a Its contract rate was lower than the prevailing market rate of interest on similar bonds.

b Its contract rate was higher than the prevailing market rate of interest on similar bonds.

c The bonds were issued at a price greater than their face value.

d The bonds are noninterest bearing.

e None of the above.

2 On October 1, 1979, the Heide Company issued $1 million of 12 percent bonds due on October 1, 1989, at a discount of $120,000. The adjusting entry on December 31, 1979, the end of the company's accounting year, is—

a

Bond Interest Expense	33,000	
Bonds Payable —Discount		3,000
Accrued Bond Interest Payable		30,000

b

Bond Interest Expense	30,000	
Bonds Payable— Discount	3,000	
Accrued Bond Interest Payable		33,000

c

Bond Interest Expense	30,000	
Bonds Payable— Discount	3,000	
Cash		33,000

d

| Bond Interest Expense | 30,000 | |
| Cash | | 30,000 |

e

Bond Interest Expense	42,000	
Bonds Payable —Discount		12,000
Accrued Bond Interest Payable		30,000

3 On the day the bonds are dated the Stanhope Corporation issued 12 percent, first-mortgage bonds having a face value of $500,000 for $575,000. What entry is required:

a

| Cash | 500,000 | |
| Bonds Payable | | 500,000 |

b

| Cash | 575,000 | |
| Bonds Payable | | 575,000 |

c

Cash	575,000	
Bond Interest Payable		75,000
Bonds Payable		500,000

d

Cash	575,000	
Bonds Payable— Discount		75,000
Bonds Payable		500,000

e Cash 575,000
    Bonds
    Payable —
    Premium...... 75,000
    Bonds
    Payable 500,000

4 G.K., Inc. issued 20-year bonds at a premium of $40,000. The entry to record the semiannual amortization of the premium is —

a Bond Interest Expense... 1,000
    Bond Interest
    Payable 1,000

b Bonds Payable —
    Premium.................. 1,000
    Bond Interest
    Payable 1,000

c Bonds Payable —
    Premium.................. 2,000
    Bond Interest
    Expense 2,000

d Bonds Payable —
    Premium.................. 1,000
    Bond Interest
    Expense 1,000

e Bond Interest Expense... 1,000
    Bonds Payable —
    Premium............. 1,000

5 The Ebenworth Company issued $100,000 of 12 percent bonds on September 1, 1979, and received a total of $100,-750. Interest on these bonds is payable on January 1 and July 1 of each year. The correct entry to record the issuance of the bonds is —

a Cash 100,750
    Bonds
    Payable 100,750

b Cash 100,750
    Bonds
    Payable 100,000
    Bonds
    Payable —
    Premium...... 750

c Cash 100,750
    Bonds
    Payable 100,000
    Accrued Bond
    Interest
    Payable 750

d Cash 100,750
    Bonds Payable —
    Discount............ 1,250
    Bonds
    Payable 100,000

    Accrued Bond
    Interest
    Payable 2,000

e Cash 100,750
    Bonds Payable —
    Discount............ 1,250
    Bonds
    Payable 100,000
    Interest
    Revenue 2,000

6 Marshall Corporation issued $300,000 of 10 percent, 20-year bonds on July 1, 1979, at 97. The bonds are dated July 1, 1979, mature on July 1, 1999, and call for semiannual interest payments on July 1 and January 1. The bond indenture provides that upon proper notice, the issuing corporation may redeem its bonds, in whole or in part, on any date after December 31, 1981, at 105. In 1989 the corporation notifies holders of $100,000 face value of bonds that their bonds will be called for redemption on July 1, 1989. Interest coupons for the interest payment due on July 1, 1989, are to remain attached to the bonds called for redemption. The company's accounting year ends on June 30. Assuming all of the bonds called are surrendered, the entry to record the redemption of the bonds is —

a Bonds Payable....... 100,000
    Accrued Bond
    Interest
    Payable 5,000
    Loss on Bond
    Redemption........ 5,000
    Cash 110,000

b Bonds Payable....... 100,000
    Accrued Bond
    Interest
    Payable 5,000
    Loss on Bond
    Redemption........ 6,500
    Cash 110,000
    Bonds
    Payable —
    Discount...... 1,500

c Bonds Payable....... 100,000
    Loss on Bond
    Redemption........ 6,500
    Cash 105,000
    Bonds
    Payable —
    Discount...... 1,500

d Bonds Payable....... 100,000
    Accrued Bond
    Interest
    Payable 5,000

429

Loss on Bond
Redemption........ 9,500
Cash 110,000
Bonds
Payable –
Discount...... 4,500

e Bonds Payable....... 100,000
Loss on Bond
Redemption........ 9,500
Cash 105,000
Bonds
Payable –
Discount...... 4,500

7 The Marsohn Corporation issued $100,000 of 10 percent, ten-year bonds at face value. The bond indenture provides that a sinking fund be established by the company through annual payments each June 30 sufficient to enable the trustee to call and retire $10,000 of the bonds at face value plus accrued interest on July 1. The bonds call for semiannual interest payments on January 1 and July 1. The entry to be made by the company at the time of making its first deposit with the trustee is –

a Sinking Fund 10,000
   Cash.................. 10,000

b Sinking Fund 10,000
   Bond Interest
     Payable.................. 500
     Cash.................. 10,500

c Bonds Payable 10,000
   Cash.................. 10,000

d Bonds Payable 10,000
   Interest Expense 500
   Cash.................. 10,500

e None of the above.

8 On July 1, 1979, Cosgrove Corporation issued $500,000 of 10 percent, serial bonds at 100. The bond indenture provides that $50,000 of these bonds mature each July 1, beginning in 1982. The bonds are registered as to the principal and interest, and interest payments are made semiannually directly by the company by check. The company's accounting period ends on June 30. Which of the following entries properly records the transactions entered into by the company on July 1, 1982, assuming that all of the bonds maturing on this date are surrendered for redemption?

a Bonds Payable 50,000
   Accrued Bond
    Interest Payable 25,000
    Cash................. 75,000

b Bonds Payable 50,000
   Cash................. 50,000

c Bonds Payable 50,000
   Accrued Bond
    Interest Payable 2,500
    Sinking Fund 52,500

d Bonds Payable 50,000
   Accrued Bond
    Interest Payable 25,000
    Sinking Fund 75,000

e None of the above.

9 Any balance in a bond sinking fund of a modern business corporation would probably best be classified in the statement of financial position as part of the –
a Current assets.
b Current liabilities.
c Long-term liabilities.
d Long-term assets.
e Stockholders' equity.

10 James Company purchased $100,000 face value of Carol Corporation bonds on April 30. The interest rate was 9 percent, payable semiannually on January 1 and July 1. James Company paid $102,000 in the transaction. The journal entry to record the purchase is:

a Investment in
   Bonds................ 102,000
    Cash 102,000

b Investment in
   Bonds................ 100,000
   Accrued Interest
    Receivable 2,000
    Cash 102,000

c Investment in
   Bonds................ 100,000
   Premium on
   Investment in
    Bonds.............. 2,000
    Cash 102,000

d Investment in
   Bonds................ 99,000
   Accrued Interest
    Receivable 3,000
    Cash 102,000

e Investment in
   Bonds................ 99,000
   Premium on
   Investment in
    Bonds.............. 3,000
    Cash 102,000

11 (based on Appendix 9A) The present value of $1 due in 40 periods at 2 percent is .45289042. The present value of $1 due in 20 periods at 4 percent is .45638695. The present value of $1 due at the end of each of 40 periods at 2 percent is 27.35547924. The present value of $1 due at the end of each of 20 periods at 4 percent is 13.59032634. If $100,000 of 20-year, 5 percent bonds issued and dated on July 1, 1979, and calling for semiannual interest payments on January 1 and July 1 are issued to yield 4 percent, their issue price is —

a $114,027.40.
b $79,614.52.
c $113,677.74.
d $79,264.86.
e None of the above.

12 (based on Appendix 9B) Which of the following statements are incorrect?

a Entering into a long-term lease agreement can result in the recording of an asset and a liability on the books of the lessee.
b When a long-term lease amounts to an installment purchase of a depreciable asset, it is necessary to record interest expense and depreciation expense for the first and several subsequent accounting periods.
c All long-term leases are to be treated as installment purchases.
d Pension plans which are funded are easier to account for than are unfunded pension plans.
e When benefits are paid to persons under an unfunded pension plan, the company should debit Pension Expense and credit Cash.

Now compare your answers with the correct answers and explanations on page 721.

Questions *chapter* 9

1 What is meant by the term "trading on the equity"?

2 What are the advantages of obtaining long-term funds by the issuance of bonds rather than additional shares of capital stock? What are the disadvantages?

3 Ace Corporation was authorized to issue $1.5 million of 7 percent, ten-year

bonds. On a certain statement of financial position date, only $1 million of the bonds had been issued. How should these facts be displayed in the statement of financial position? Why should they be disclosed?

4 When bonds are issued between interest dates, why is it appropriate that the issuing corporation should receive cash equal to the amount of accrued interest in addition to the issue price of the bonds?

5 Why might it be more accurate to describe a sinking fund as a bond redemption fund?

6 Indicate how each of the following items should be classified in a statement of financial position on December 31, 1979:

a Cash balance in a sinking fund.
b Accrued interest on bonds payable.
c Debenture bonds payable due in 1989.
d Premium on bonds payable.
e First-mortgage bonds payable, due July 1, 1980.
f Discount on bonds payable.
g First National Bank — Interest account.
h Estimated accrued pension costs.

7 Why would an investor whose intent is to hold bonds to maturity pay more for the bonds than their face value?

8 (based on Appendix 9A) If a corporation can obtain funds at a net cost of 3 percent to buy an asset which will produce a series of annual net cash flows of $1,000 at the end of each of the next ten years, should it make the investment in this asset if its cost is $8,750? (The present value of an annuity of $1 due for ten periods at 3 percent is 8.53020284.)

9 (based on Appendix 9B) In what way may long-term leases be similar to installment purchases of property?

10 (based on Appendix 9B) Is the pension plan liability likely to be larger at any given time under a funded plan or an unfunded plan? Why?

Exercises *chapter* 9

1 Interest on Martin Corporation's coupon bonds is paid by a trustee, the Third National Bank. Assuming the semiannual

431

interest amounts to $25,000 and all of the coupons are cashed, prepare the entries to record the deposit of the interest with the trustee, the accrual of the interest, and the cashing of the coupons.

2 The Bailey Company issued $100,000 of ten-year, 9 percent bonds dated June 1, 1979, on August 1, 1979, at 99 plus accrued interest. Prepare the entry necessary to record the issuance. Wonder Company bought one tenth of these bonds. Prepare the journal entry to record this long-term investment.

3 Thayer Company issued $200,000 of ten-year, 10 percent bonds at 102 on January 1, 1979, the date of the bonds.
a Was the market rate of interest for these bonds higher or lower than 10 percent?
b What is the amount of bond interest expense for 1979, assuming straight-line amortization of the bond premium?

4 If Baxter Corporation bought $40,000 of the bonds issued by Thayer Company (see Exercise 3) as a long-term investment, what amount of interest revenue was earned in 1979, assuming straight-line amortization was used? Give the journal entry required at December 31, 1979, to amortize the premium.

5 If, in Exercise 3, the bonds were issued at 95, what would the interest expense be for 1979 assuming use of the straight-line method?

6 The Wixon Company, pursuant to provisions of its bond indenture, acquired $20,000 of its outstanding bonds on the open market at 97 plus accrued interest. These bonds were originally issued at face and carry a 6 percent interest rate payable semiannually. The acquisition was made on September 1, and the bonds are dated December 1, 1968. Prepare the entries required to record the acquisition and the accrual of the interest to the acquisition date on the bonds acquired.

7 The K Company is required to make an annual deposit of $40,000 plus accrued interest of $1,200 on April 30, 1980, to the trustee of its sinking fund so that the trustee can redeem $40,000 of the bonds on May 1, 1980. Prepare the entries required on April 30 to record the interest accrual and sinking fund deposit and the entries on May 1 to record the bond retirement, payment of interest, and payment of trustee expenses, assuming the latter amount to be $125. (The bonds were issued at 100.)

8 (based on Appendix 9A) Conceptually, what is the present worth of a lump-sum payment of $10,000 due in five years? If the going market rate of interest on investments of a certain type is 5 percent per year and the present value of $1 due in five years at 5 percent is .78352617, what is its specific worth?

9 (based on Appendix 9A) Conceptually, what is the present worth of a series of annual payments of $1,000 due at the end of each of the next five years? If the going market rate of interest on investments of this type is 5 percent per year and the present value of an annuity of $1 for five periods at 5 percent is 4.32947667, what is its specific worth?

10 (based on Appendix 9B) Equipment is acquired under a long-term lease. The terms of the lease state that $10,000 must be paid on January 1, 1979, and each January 1 thereafter for the next nine years. The equipment has an estimated life of 20 years and no salvage value. The lease is to be accounted for as a capital lease. Give the following:
a The entry to record the initial lease payment (use 6 percent as a reasonable rate of discount).
b The adjusting entries on December 31, 1979, to accrue the interest on the lease and for depreciation on the equipment.
c The entry required for the second lease payment on January 1, 1980.

11 (based on Appendix 9B) Dexter Corporation has a funded pension plan and is obligated to pay $32,250 to the Bengston Insurance Company (the outside agent) for the year 1979. It makes the payment on January 15, 1980. Give the entries to accrue the expense on December 31, 1979, and to record the payment on January 15, 1980.

12 (based on Appendix 9B) Ryberg Corporation has an unfunded pension plan. During 1979 it incurs the obligation to pay future benefits having a present value of $42,536. It also pays $18,400 to retired and disabled employees as pension benefits. Give the entries to record these transactions.

Problems, Series A *chapter* 9

9–1–A

On December 1, 1979, Brooks Company issued $500,000 of ten-year, 9 percent bonds dated July 1, 1979, at 100. Interest on the bonds is payable semiannually on July 1 and January 1. All of the bonds are registered. The company's accounting period ends on March 31. Quarterly financial statements are prepared.

The company deposits a sum of money sufficient to pay the semiannual interest on the bonds in a special checking account in the First National Bank and draws interest payment checks upon this account. The deposit is made the day before the checks are drawn.

Required:

a   Present journal entries to record the issuance of the bonds; the December 31 adjusting entry; the January 1, 1980, interest payment; and the adjusting entry needed on March 31, 1980.
b   The Brown Corporation bought $100,000 of the Brooks Company bonds on December 1, 1979, as a long-term investment. The company's year-end is December 31. Present all journal entries for Brown Corporation for these bonds through December 31, 1979.

9–2–A

Laundon Corporation issued $100,000 of 9 percent, ten-year bonds at 95. Interest is payable semiannually. Mann Company also issued $100,000 of 9 percent, ten-year bonds, but received a price of 105 for its bonds. These bonds also call for semiannual interest payments. Both bond issues are dated and issued on July 1, 1979.

Required:

Prepare journal entries to record the issuance of both bond issues, the interest expense, and the payment of interest for the first semiannual period. Both companies have a fiscal-year accounting period ending on June 30 and straight-line amortization is applicable. (Amortize any premium and accumulate any discount on the interest date.) Which company is actually paying the lower interest rate? Why?

9–3–A

On October 1, 1979, Marsalis Corporation issued $200,000 of ten-year, 9 percent debenture bonds at face value. The bonds are registered, and interest is payable semiannually on October 1 and April 1. The company is required by the bond indenture to deposit with the trustee each September 30 an amount sufficient to retire at face value $20,000 of the outstanding debenture bonds plus accrued interest. Such bonds are to be called for redemption on October 1 of each year, beginning in 1980. The company has the right to deliver bonds acquired in the market in lieu of making a cash deposit, with the required deposit reduced by $1,000 plus interest of $45 for each bond so delivered.

The first three interest payments were made according to provisions of the bond indenture, and the first sinking fund deposit was made as scheduled. The trustee reported on October 1, 1980, that the required number of bonds had been called. Trustee expenses of $100 were paid on December 1, 1980.

On August 1, 1981, the company purchased $20,000 of its outstanding bonds in the market at 99¾ plus accrued interest and delivered these to the trustee in lieu of making a cash deposit on September 30, 1981.

Required:

Prepare journal entries to record all transactions on the above bonds from October 1, 1979, through August 1, 1981, including the necessary adjusting entries. The company has a calendar-year accounting period and prepares quarterly statements.

9-4-A

Dahlberg Company issued $200,000 of 9 percent, ten-year first-mortgage bonds at 102.36 on September 1, 1979. The bonds are dated July 1, 1979, and call for semiannual interest payments on July 1 and January 1.

Lauer Company issued $200,000 of 8 percent, ten-year-first-mortgage bonds at 96.55 on December 1, 1979. The bonds are dated July 1, 1979, and call for semiannual interest payments on July 1 and January 1.

Required:

Assuming that the accounting period ends on March 31 for both companies, present journal entries to record the issuance of the bonds, the payment of the first semiannual interest payment, and the adjusting entries needed on March 31. Use the straight-line method for amortizing the premium and accumulating the discount and do so only at year-end.

9-5-A

Temple Corporation bought $100,000 face value of the bonds of each company in Problem 9-4-A as a long-term investment. Temple's accounting year ends on March 31.

Required:

Present all journal entries necessary to record the purchases, interest payments, and any adjusting entries needed through March 31, 1980. Amortize the premium or accumulate the discount only at the accounting year-end.

9-6-A

Following are selected transactions relating to the bonds of the McPherson Company.

1979

July 1   Authorized issue of $200,000 of 9 percent, ten-year bonds dated July 1, 1979, interest payable semiannually on January 1 and July 1.

Sept. 1   Issued $100,000 face value of the bonds at 92.92.

1980

Jan.   1   Paid the semiannual interest.
Feb.   1   Issued the remaining bonds at 102.26.
July   1   Paid semiannual interest.

Required:

Present journal entries to record all of the above transactions, including the adjusting entry needed at June 30, 1980, the end of the company's accounting period. Also, present the long-term liability section of the company's June 30, 1980, statement of financial position. Use the straight-line method in accounting for the discount and premium, and amortize any premium or accumulate any discount only at the end of the accounting year.

9–7–A

Lauber, Inc., issued $1 million of bonds on January 1, 1979, at 105 percent of their face value. The bonds bear interest at the rate of 9 percent, payable semiannually, and mature on January 1, 1999. The bond indenture provides that the issuing corporation may, on any interest date subsequent to December 31, 1983, redeem all or any part of its outstanding bonds by call by paying a redemption price equal to 105 percent of face value. On January 1, 1984, after due notification as to which bonds are being called, the corporation calls and cancels $400,000 of its outstanding bonds. The company employs a calendar-year accounting period.

Required:

Prepare journal entries to record the issuance of the bonds, the accrual of the first six months' interest expense and the payment thereof (also amortize the premium on this date), and the entries necessary on January 1, 1984.

9–8–A

Knobloch Company issued $200,000 of 9 percent bonds on July 1, 1979, at face value. The bonds are dated July 1, 1979; call for semiannual interest payments on July 1 and January 1; and mature at the rate of $20,000 per year on July 1, beginning in 1984. The company's accounting period ends on September 30.

Required:

a   Present journal entries to record the interest expense and payment for the six months ending July 1, 1984; the maturing of the bonds on July 1, 1984; and the adjusting entries needed on September 30, 1984.
b   Show how the bonds will be presented in the company's statement of financial position for September 30, 1984.

9–9–A (based on Appendix 9A)

Johnston Company issued $100,000 of 8 percent, 20-year bonds on July 1, 1979. Kenimer Company issued $100,000 of 5 percent, 20-year bonds on July 1, 1979. Both   435 bond issues are dated July 1, 1979, call for semiannual interest payments on July 1 and January 1, and are issued to yield 6 percent (3 percent per period).

Required:

a Compute the amount received by each company for the bonds issued. (Use the tables in Appendix 9A.)
b Present entries to record the issuance of the bonds.
c Using the effective interest rate method, present entries to recognize the interest expense and payment of the interest for the first six months. Assume a fiscal-year ending December 31.

9–10–A (based on Appendix 9A)

Joyce Corporation purchased one tenth of the Johnston Company bonds (see Problem 9–9–A) as a long-term investment.

Required:

Present the journal entries for the purchase and the interest payment of January 1, and the adjusting entry required on June 30, 1980, the company's year-end. Use the effective interest rate method to amortize any premium or accumulate any discount, and do so at each interest date and at the end of the accounting period.

9–11–A (based on Appendix 9B)

Bryant Company entered into a lease agreement on January 1, 1979, covering some equipment and calling for payments of $50,000 a year at the beginning of each of the ten years of the lease. The terms of the lease clearly indicate that it is in effect a purchase of the equipment. The company currently is paying 10 percent for borrowing used to finance asset purchases.

Required:

Give the journal entries to record the first lease payment and the signing of the lease on January 1, 1979; the interest accrued for 1979; the depreciation expense for 1979 on the equipment, assuming a 15-year life and no salvage value; and the second lease payment on January 1, 1980.

Problems, Series B *chapter* 9
9–1–B

On June 1, 1979, Ackerman Corporation issued $900,000 of ten-year, 8 percent bonds dated April 1, 1979, at 100. Interest on the bonds is payable semiannually upon presentation of the appropriate coupon. All of the bonds are of $1,000 denomination. The company's accounting period ends on June 30, with semiannual statements prepared on December 31 and June 30.

All of the first coupons on each of the bonds are presented to the company's bank and paid by October 2, 1979. All but two of the second coupons on the bonds are similarly received and paid on April 1, 1980.

Required:

a Present all necessary journal entries for the above transactions, including all adjusting entries needed at June 30, 1979.

b Allen Company purchased $300,000 of Ackerman Corporation's bonds on June 1, 1979, as a long-term investment. The company prepares financial statements on September 30. Present all journal entries for Allen Company relating to the bonds through September 30, 1979.

9–2–B

Yates, Inc., issued $200,000 of 8 percent, ten-year bonds at 98. Interest is payable semiannually. Wyatt Corporation also issued $200,000 of 8 percent, ten-year bonds, but received a price of 102 for its bonds. These bonds also call for semiannual interest payments. Both bond issues are dated and issued on July 1, 1979.

Required:

Prepare journal entries to record the issuance of both bond issues, the interest expense, and the payment of interest for the first semiannual period. Assume both companies have a calendar-year accounting period and that straight-line amortization is acceptable. Which company is actually paying the lower interest rate? Why?

9–3–B

The Allison Company, on July 1, 1979, issued $100,000 of ten-year, 12 percent bonds dated July 1, 1979, at face value. Bond interest coupons are to be submitted semiannually on July 1 and January 1 for payment. The company is required to deposit with the trustee on each June 30, beginning in 1980, a sum sufficient to enable the trustee to call $10,000 face value of bonds for redemption on July 1 at face value plus accrued interest. The company also has the right to deliver bonds acquired in the open market to the trustee in lieu of making a cash payment. The company's accounting period ends on December 31, and semiannual statements are prepared.

The following transactions were entered into by the Allison Company:

1980

Jan. 2 Bank reports that it paid all of the semiannual interest coupons.

June 30 Paid the required deposit to trustee.

July 1 Trustee reports $10,000 of bonds acquired at face value as well as payment of accrued interest on these bonds.

3 Bank reports that it paid semiannual interest coupons in the amount of $5,400.

Dec. 31 Paid $75 of trustee's expenses.

1981

Jan. 2   Report from bank shows that it paid all of the outstanding coupons due for payment on January 1, 1981.

June 1   Purchased $10,000 of outstanding bonds in the market at 99½ and delivered them to the trustee in lieu of the cash deposit required on June 30.

Required:

Prepare journal entries to record the issuance of the bonds and to record the data in the above transactions, including whatever adjusting entries are needed at December 31, 1979, June 30, 1980, and December 31, 1980.

9–4–B

On December 1, 1979, Wright Company issued $200,000 of 9 percent, ten-year, first-mortgage bonds for $193,040 cash plus accrued interest. The bonds are dated August 1, 1979, and call for semiannual interest payments on August 1 and February 1.

Armstrong Corporation issued $200,000 of 9 percent, ten-year, first-mortgage bonds on August 1, 1979, for $209,520 cash plus accrued interest. The bonds are dated July 1, 1979, and call for semiannual interest payments on January 1 and July 1.

Required:

Assume the accounting period ends for both companies on March 31 and present entries to record the issuance of both bond issues, the first interest payment, and the necessary adjusting entries at March 31, 1980. Straight-line amortization is appropriate.

9–5–B

The Wofford Corporation purchased one tenth of the bonds of each company in Problem 9–4–B as a long-term investment. Its year-end is also March 31. Present the journal entries to record the acquisition of the bonds, the first interest payment, and any necessary adjusting entries at March 31, 1980.

9–6–B

Following are selected transactions of the Bailey Company, which employs a fiscal year ending on June 30:

1979

July 1   Received authorization to issue $200,000 of 9 percent, ten-year bonds dated July 1, 1979. Interest is payable semiannually on January 1 and July 1.

Aug. 1   Issued, for cash, $100,000 of the bonds at 103.57.

1980

Jan. 1   Paid semiannual interest.

Mar. 1   Issued the remaining bonds for $97,760 plus accrued interest since the last interest date.

July 1   Paid semiannual interest on all bonds.

Required:

Prepare journal entries to record all of the above transactions including the adjusting entries needed at June 30, 1980. Also present the long-term liability section of the company's June 30, 1980, statement of financial position. Straight-line amortization is acceptable.

9–7–B

On January 1, 1979, Barnes, Inc., issued $100,000 of 7 percent, 20-year bonds dated January 1, 1979, at 106. Interest is payable on January 1 and July 1. The bond indenture provides that the company may retire any or all of the bonds on any interest payment date subsequent to July 1, 1983, at a price equal to 105 percent of face value. On January 1, 1984, Barnes, Inc., redeemed $40,000 of its outstanding bonds. The company's accounting period ends on December 31.

Required:

Prepare journal entries to record the issuance of the bonds, the first semiannual interest payment (the company decided on semiannual, straight-line amortization of the premium), and the entries necessary on January 1, 1984.

9–8–B

Wilkerson Company issued $200,000 of 8 percent serial bonds on July 1, 1979, at face value. The bonds are dated July 1, 1979; call for semiannual interest payments on July 1 and January 1; and mature at the rate of $40,000 per year, with the first maturity falling on July 1, 1984. The company's accounting period ends on September 30, with quarterly statements prepared.

Required:

Present journal entries to record the interest payment of July 1, 1984; the maturing of $40,000 of bonds on July 1, 1984; and the adjusting entry needed on September 30, 1984. Also, show how the bonds will be presented in the company's statement of financial position for September 30, 1984.

9–9–B (based on Appendix A)

Whitley Company issued $100,000 of 7 percent, 20-year bonds on October 1, 1979. The bonds are dated October 1, 1979, call for semiannual interest payments on October 1 and April 1, and are issued to yield 8 percent (4 percent per period).

Boucher Company issued $100,000 of 9 percent, 20-year bonds on October 1, 1979. The bonds are dated October 1, 1979, call for semiannual interest payments on October 1 and April 1, and are issued to yield 8 percent (4 percent per period).

Required:

a Compute the amount received by each company for the bonds issued. (Use the tables in Appendix 9A).

b Present entries to record the issuance of the bonds.

c Present entries to recognize the interest expense and payment for the first six months using the effective interest rate method of allocation of premium or discount to the periods of life in the bonds. Assume a fiscal year accounting period ending May 31.

9–10–B (based on Appendix 9A)

Bray Company bought one tenth of the Whitley Company's bonds (see Problem 9–9–B) as a long-term investment. Record the journal entries for the acquisition of the bonds; receipt of interest on April 1, 1980; and the adjusting entry required on September 30, 1980, the company's year-end. Use the effective interest rate method for the entries required on April 1 and September 30 for amortizing any premium or accumulating any discount.

9–11–B (based on Appendix 9B)

The Whitehead Corporation entered into a long-term lease agreement in which it agreed to pay $60,000 at the end of each year for 25 years for the use of equipment. (Leases usually require advance payment at the beginning of the year, but this one does not). The terms of the lease clearly indicate that the lease agreement is, in effect, a purchase. The company currently is paying interest at 8 percent on some installment contracts.

Required:

Compute the amount at which the equipment is to be recorded. Show the original journal entry recognizing the asset and the liability, and the entry to record the first year's payment. Also, show the entry to record depreciation at the end of the first year assuming the double-declining-balance method is used.

10

Measurement and reporting of owners' equity*

Learning objectives

Study of the material presented in this chapter is designed to achieve several learning objectives. These include:

1. A general knowledge of the nature of corporations.

2. An introductory level comprehension of the nature of capital stock, particularly the distinctions between common and preferred stock.

3. A working knowledge of the theoretical considerations and transaction analysis in the handling of treasury stock.

6. A basic understanding of the nature and accounting treatment of dividends.

7. Knowledge of the accounting treatment of retained earnings, including retained earnings reserves.

8. An understanding of the nature of proprietorships and partnerships and the accounting techniques associated with these organizations (Appendix).

* This chapter has been divided into two reading sections to offer flexibility in assigning the chapter. All end of chapter questions, exercises, and problems have been identified as to the reading section to which they relate.

441

Frame 1¹⁰

The corporation defined

Although fewer in number than single proprietorships and partnerships, corporations possess most of our business capital and supply us with most of our goods and services. A corporation is an association of individuals recognized by law as having an existence separate and distinct from any of these individuals. That is, it is a separate legal entity. It is an artificial, invisible, intangible being or person created by law. It has many of the rights and obligations possessed by natural persons. It can, for example, enter into contracts in its own name; buy, sell, or hold real or personal property; borrow money; hire and fire employees; and sue and be sued.

Advantages of the corporation

The corporation has certain advantages over the proprietorship and the partnership type of organization. These advantages include (1) ease of transfer of ownership; (2) limited liability, that is, the stockholders are not personally responsible for the corporation's debts; (3) continuous existence; (4) professional management; (5) centralized authority and responsibility; and (6) stockholders not being agents of a corporation.

Assume that you are a wealthy person who has agreed to provide the capital for a firm that will manufacture and sell a device developed by a destitute inventor. You and the inventor are each to have half interest in the firm. Indicate whether each of the following statements is true or false.

1. You favor the corporate form of organization for your business enterprise primarily because of the ease with which the corporation's shares can be transferred.

2. The fact that a stockholder's responsibility for corporate debts is usually limited to his or her investment in the capital stock of the corporation is the main reason you favor the corporate form of business organization.

3. If you expected your business to have a very long life, you would prefer the partnership form of organization for your enterprise.

4. The fact that the corporation may secure the services of a team of highly skilled professional managers persuades you to favor the corporate form.

Now turn to Answer Frame 1¹⁰ on page 444 to check your answers.

Frame 2¹⁰

Disadvantages of the corporation

The corporate form of organization has its disadvantages. These include:

1. *Taxation.* Since a corporation is a separate legal entity, its net earnings are subject to taxation.

2. *Government regulation.* Because corporations are created by law, they are subject to greater regulation and control than other forms of organization.

3. *Entrenched management.* Management may become thoroughly entrenched because it can use corporate funds to solicit proxies (votes) from stockholders.

4. *Limited ability to raise creditor capital.* The limited liability of stockholders makes a corporation an attractive device for accumulating stockholder capital. At the same time, limited liability limits the amount of creditor capital a corporation may amass because creditors cannot look to the personal assets of stockholders for satisfaction of their debts if the corporation cannot pay.

The contract between the state and the incorporators and their successors is known as the charter. The application for the charter is known as the articles of incorporation. When the information requested in the application form is supplied, the articles are filed with the proper office in the state of incorporation. Upon approval by this office (frequently the secretary of state), the charter is granted and the corporation exists.

Directing the corporation

The corporation is managed through the delegation of authority from the stockholders to the directors to the officers. The stockholders elect the board of directors. The board of directors formulates the broad policies of the company and selects the principal officers, who carry out the policies.

Stockholders. Stockholders, as such, do not have the right to participate actively in the management of the business, although they may serve as directors or officers, or both. But each stockholder does have certain basic rights. These include the right to (1) dispose of his or her shares, (2) buy additional shares as they are issued on a proportional basis (the preemptive right), (3) share in dividends when declared, (4) share in assets in liquidation, and (5) share in management by voting his or her shares.

Normally, stockholders meet annually. At this meeting each stockholder is entitled to one vote for each share of voting stock held. Stockholders who do not personally attend meetings may vote by proxy. A proxy is a document of authority, signed by the stockholder, giving another person—usually the secretary of the corporation—the authority

443

2¹⁰
continued

to vote his or her shares. At the annual meeting, the stockholders share in the management by voting on such questions as changing the charter, increasing capital stock issues, approving pension plans, selecting auditors, and others.

Determine whether each of the following is true or false.

1. One of a stockholder's basic rights is to dispose of his or her shares of capital stock.

2. Through the use of a proxy, a stockholder gives another person authority to vote his or her shares at a stockholders' meeting.

3. The preemptive right refers to a stockholder's right to receive dividends when they are declared by the board of directors.

4. When a corporation liquidates, stockholders have the right to receive the undistributed assets that are in excess of the claims of creditors.

Turn to Answer Frame 2¹⁰ on page 446 to check your answers.

Frame 3¹⁰

Stockholders elect a board of directors to formulate broad business policies and to protect the interests of stockholders and creditors. The board appoints administrative officers who execute the broad policies established by the board. The officers typically consist of a president, vice presidents, a secretary, and a treasurer.

Code of regulations (bylaws). At its first meeting, the board of directors, authorized by the stockholders, drafts and adopts a code of regulations, also known as the corporation's bylaws. The code contains, along with other information, the following: (*a*) the place, date, and manner of calling the annual stockholders' meeting; (*b*) the method of electing directors and the number of directors; (*c*) the duties and powers of the directors; and (*d*) the method of selecting officers of the corporation.

Determine whether each of the following is true or false.

1. The administrative officers of a corporation are elected by the stockholders.
2. The application for a charter is known as a code of regulations.
3. The board of directors is elected by the stockholders and exercises broad directional control over the affairs of the corporation.

Now turn to Answer Frame 3^{10} on page 446 to check your answers.

Frame 4^{10}

Capital stock

The corporate charter will state the number of shares and the par value, if any, per share of each class of stock that the corporation is authorized to issue. The corporation may not intend to issue all its authorized stock immediately. It may hold some for issuance in the future when more capital is needed. But the total ownership of the corporation is with the holders of the outstanding shares of stock — that is, the shares authorized, issued, and currently held by stockholders. For example, if a corporation is authorized to issue 20,000 shares of common stock but has issued only 15,000 shares, the holders of the 15,000 shares own 100 percent of the corporation. Shares authorized but not issued are called unissued shares. There are 5,000 unissued shares in the example above. These shares carry no rights or privileges until they are issued.

Classes of capital stock

The two ordinary classes of capital stock are (*a*) common stock and (*b*) preferred stock. If only one class of stock is issued, it is known as common stock, and the rights of the stockholder (listed in Frame 2^{10}) are enjoyed equally by the holders of all shares. The interest of common stockholders is usually referred to as the residual equity in the corporation. This means simply that all other claims against the assets of the corporation rank ahead of the claims of the common stockholder.

A corporation may also issue preferred stock with different rights and privileges from those possessed by the common stock. Different classes of preferred stock may exist with slightly different characteristics. 445

Answer frame 2¹⁰

Answer frame 2¹⁰ ──────────────────────────────

1. True. This is one of the stockholder's basic rights.

2. True. A proxy does give another person the authority to vote a stockholder's shares at a stockholders' meeting.

3. False. The preemptive right is the right of the stockholder to subscribe for additional shares from new issues of capital stock of the class owned in proportion to his or her holdings at the date of the additional issue.

4. True. This is one of the basic rights of a stockholder.

If you missed any of the above, restudy Frame 2¹⁰ before beginning Frame 3¹⁰ on page 444.

Answer frame 3¹⁰ ──────────────────────────────

1. False. The board of directors selects the administrative officers of a corporation.

2. False. The application for a charter is known as the articles of incorporation.

3. True. Stockholders do elect the board of directors, which, in turn, represents the stockholders' interest in the overall management of the corporation.

If you missed any of the above, reread Frame 3¹⁰ before beginning Frame 4¹⁰ on page 445.

4¹⁰
continued

Indicate whether each of the following statements is true or false.

1. A corporation may have several classes of preferred stock.

2. The number of shares of stock which a corporation has issued and outstanding may at times exceed the number of its authorized shares.

3. Shares of preferred stock and shares of common stock both represent ownership in a corporation and both always confer the same rights and privileges.

4. The number of a corporation's authorized shares of stock may exceed the number of its shares which are issued and outstanding.

Now turn to Answer Frame 4¹⁰ on page 448 to check your answers.

Frame 5¹⁰ ──────────────────────────────

Common stock

When a corporation issues only one class of stock, it must be common stock. Holders of common stock have full voting rights and privileges in the corporation. Though common stock ranks behind preferred stock in distribution of assets and dividends upon dissolution of the corporation, there is no limit to the amount of dividends which a share of common stock may receive. Common stock also possesses a greater chance of increasing in market value. Thus, while holders of common stock in a corporation assume greater risks than holders of preferred, they also have the potential to realize a greater return on their investment.

Common stock is either with par value or without par value according to the terms of the charter of the issuing corporation. The par value, if any, is stated in the charter and is printed on the stock certificate issued. Par value may be of any amount – 1¢, 10¢, 16⅔¢, $1, $5, $100 or any other amount.

Par value serves two purposes: (1) it is the amount per share that is credited to the capital stock account for each share outstanding, and (2) the par value of the outstanding shares is often the legal or stated capital of the corporation. A corporation is prohibited by law from declaring dividends or acquiring its own stock if such actions will reduce stockholders' equity below the legal capital of the corporation. For this reason, the par value of the outstanding shares does serve as a buffer or cushion of capital to protect creditors from losses.

Par value per share does not indicate the amount of stockholders' equity per share (book value per share, as it is called) that is recorded in the accounting records of the corporation. The stockholders' equity consists of paid-in capital and retained earnings; the latter may be either positive or negative. Par value also does not give any clue to the market value of the stock. Shares with a par value of $5 have sold in the market for well over $600. Many $100 par value preferred stocks have sold for much less than par. Par value is not even a reliable indicator of the price at which shares can be issued. Even in new corporations, shares are often issued at prices much greater than par value.

Indicate whether each of the following statements is true or false.

1. The par value of a share of capital stock is no indication of the market value or of the book value of the share of stock.
2. The par value of a share of capital stock indicates the price at which the share must originally be issued.
3. The par value of a share of common stock must be $100.
4. Losses decrease, and earnings increase, the par value of stock.

Now check your answers by turning to Answer Frame 5¹⁰ on page 448.

Frame 6¹⁰

Common stock without par value.   Laws permitting the issuance of shares of stock without par value (sometimes referred to as no-par value stock) were first enacted in New York in 1912. Similar, but not uniform, legislation has since been passed in many states. Shares of stock without par value may or may not have a stated value assigned to them.

STATED VALUE STOCK.   The board of directors of a corporation issu-

Answer frame 4¹⁰

1. True. There can be several classes of preferred stock, each with different characteristics (such as dividend rates).
2. False. The number of shares which a corporation has issued and are outstanding cannot exceed the number of shares it is authorized to issue.
3. False. Shares of preferred stock and of common stock do not usually confer the same rights and privileges, although both represent ownership in the corporation.
4. True. For various reasons, a corporation may not issue all the stock it is authorized to issue.

If you missed any of the above, reread Frame 4¹⁰ before beginning Frame 5¹⁰ on page 446.

Answer frame 5¹⁰

1. True. The assignment of a par value to a share of stock is meaningless as far as indicating the market value or book value of the stock.
2. False. A share of stock may be issued for more than its par value.
3. False. Par value may be any amount.
4. False. Earnings and losses do not influence the par value of stock. They do, however, affect the book value of stock.

If you missed any of the above, reread Frame 5¹⁰ before beginning Frame 6¹⁰ on page 447.

6¹⁰
continued

ing stock without par value may assign a stated value to each share of capital stock. This stated value usually may be set at any amount by the board. But some state statutes specify a minimum amount such as $5 per share.

When shares without par value but with stated value are issued, the shares are carried in the capital stock account at a uniform amount per share—the stated value. Any amounts received in excess of the stated value per share are also part of the capital of the corporation and should be credited to a paid-in capital account. The stated or legal capital of a corporation issuing shares with a stated value is usually equal to the total of the stated value of the shares issued.

As an illustration, assume that the Peanut Corporation, which is authorized to issue 10,000 shares of capital stock without par value, assigns a stated value of $25 per share to its stock. The 10,000 authorized shares are issued at $28 per share. The stockholders' equity section of the statement of financial position is as follows:

Common stock without par value, stated value,
$25; 10,000 shares authorized, issued, and outstanding................... $250,000
Paid-in capital in excess of stated value 30,000
Total Stockholders' Equity $280,000

The $30,000 received over the stated value of $250,000 is carried permanently as paid-in capital because it is part of the capital originally contributed by the stockholders. But the stated capital of the Peanut Corporation is generally held to be $250,000 – the stated value of the shares issued.

SHARES WITHOUT PAR VALUE OR STATED VALUE. If a corporation issues shares without par value which have not been assigned a stated value, the entire amount received is credited to the capital stock account. Because shares may be issued at different times and for different amounts, the credit to the capital stock account is not at a uniform amount per share. The entire amount received for shares without par value or stated value is the amount of stated capital.

If, in the above illustration of the Peanut Corporation, no stated value is assigned to the shares, the stockholders' equity section of the company's statement of financial position is as follows:

Common stock without par or stated value; 10,000 shares authorized,
   issued, and outstanding $280,000
       Total Stockholders' Equity $280,000

The actual capital contributed by stockholders is $280,000. The legal capital is also $280,000.

Decide whether each of the following statements is true or false.
1. The assignment of a stated value to each share of stock that is without par value results in the receipt of a uniform price per share for the stock.
2. The amount carried in the account Paid-In Capital in Excess of Stated Value represents part of a corporation's permanent capital.
Now turn to Answer Frame 6[10] on page 450.

Frame 7[10]

Preferred stock

Corporations generally issue preferred stock for one or more of three main reasons: (1) With several classes of stock available for issuance, more capital may be attracted from investors who have differing investment objectives. In fact some institutional investors are prohibited by law from owning common stocks but may own preferred stocks. (2) Since preferred stocks may have no voting rights, their issuance does not weaken the control of the common stockholders over the corporation. (3) The return (dividend) on preferred stock is usually fixed. Thus, considerable financial leverage is made possible by its use.

As an example of financial leverage, assume that the organizers of a   449

7¹⁰
continued

corporation have two ways of securing capital: (1) issue 40,000 shares of $10 par value common for $400,000, or (2) issue 20,000 shares of $10 par value common for $200,000 and 2,000 shares of $100 par value, 6 percent preferred stock for $200,000. Net earnings of $60,000 per year are expected. The earnings to the common stockholders on a per share basis (net earnings less preferred dividends divided by number of common shares outstanding) and as a percentage of original investment are:

	With preferred	Without preferred
Net earnings..	$60,000	$60,000
Preferred dividends:		
.06 × $100 × 2,000....................................	12,000	–0–
Net earnings to common stock	$48,000	$60,000
Number of common shares outstanding.............	20,000	40,000
Earnings per share of common stock:		
$48,000 ÷ 20,000....................................	$2.40	
$60,000 ÷ 40,000.....................................		$1.50
Earnings to common as a percentage of original investment:		
$48,000 ÷ $200,000...................................	24%	
$60,000 ÷ $400,000...................................		15%

The use of the preferred stock increases the expected earnings per share on the common stock from $1.50 to $2.40 and the rate of return expected on the original investment from 15 percent to 24 percent. Under these circumstances, the common stock will probably sell at a much higher price if the preferred is issued than if it is not.

Preferred stock almost always has a par value. When it does not, it may be assigned a stated value. Preferred stock may be:

1. Preferred as to dividends. If it is, it may be:
   a. Cumulative.
   b. Noncumulative.
2. Preferred as to assets in the event of liquidation.

3. Convertible or nonconvertible.
4. Callable.

Stock preferred as to dividends. If stock is preferred as to dividends, its holders are entitled to a specified dividend per share before the payment of any dividend on the common stock. The dividend may be stated as a dollar amount per share per year, such as $5, or it may be stated as a percentage of par value. Regardless of the manner in which they are stated, preferred stock dividends are usually paid quarterly. A dividend can be paid on the preferred stock only if it is declared by the board of directors. In some states a preferred dividend can be paid only if the corporation has retained earnings at least equal in dollar amount to the dividend declared.

A stock preferred as to dividends is cumulative if all dividends in arrears (required dividends not paid in prior years) and the current dividend on this stock must be paid before dividends can be paid on the common stock. For example, assume a company has cumulative 4 percent preferred stock outstanding of $200,000, common stock outstanding of $200,000, and retained earnings of $20,000. No dividends have been paid for two years, including the current year. The preferred stockholders are entitled to dividends of $16,000 ($200,000 × .04 × 2) before any dividend can be paid to the common stockholders.

If a preferred stock is noncumulative, a dividend omitted or not paid in any one year need not be paid in any future year. Because omitted dividends are lost forever, noncumulative preferred stocks hold little attraction for investors and are seldom issued.

A corporation has $100,000 par value of 5 percent preferred stock outstanding, $200,000 par value of common stock outstanding, and $50,000 of retained earnings. No dividends were paid last year because a net loss was sustained. Before the payment of any dividends to the common stockholders may be made at the current year-end, the preferred stockholders are entitled to dividends of:

1. How much if the stock is cumulative?
2. How much if it is noncumulative?

Now check your answers by turning to Answer Frame 7[10] on page 452.

Frame 8[10]

Stock preferred as to assets. Most preferred stocks are preferred as to assets in the event of liquidation of the corporation. This means that the preferred stockholders are entitled to receive the par value (or a larger stipulated liquidating value) per share before the common stockholders receive any distribution of corporate assets. If there are cumulative preferred dividends in arrears at liquidation, they usually are pay-

8¹⁰
continued

able regardless of whether there are retained earnings sufficient to meet them. Stock may be preferred as to assets or dividends, or both.

To illustrate the preference-as-to-assets feature, assume a corporation has $100,000 par value of preferred stock outstanding and $200,000 par value of common stock outstanding. After paying its liabilities it has cash of $240,000 remaining to distribute to its stockholders. If the preferred stock is preferred as to assets and there are no dividends in arrears, the preferred stockholders will receive $100,000. $140,000 will be paid to the common stockholders. If the preferred stock is not preferred as to assets, the $240,000 is prorated between the preferred and common stockholders in the ratio of the dollar total of the classes: $80,000 [($100,000/$300,000) × $240,000] to the preferred stockholders and $160,000 to the common stockholders.

Indicate whether each of the following statements is true or false.

1. Shareholders whose stock is preferred as to assets in the event of corporate liquidation are entitled to receive the par value of their shares before any amounts are distributed to creditors or common stockholders.

2. All stock preferred as to dividends is also preferred as to assets.

3. In the event of liquidation, holders of shares preferred as to assets and dividends are entitled to receive only the par value of their stock before common shareholders receive anything, even though cumulative preferred dividends are in arrears.

Now check your answers in Answer Frame 8¹⁰ on page 454.

Frame 9¹⁰

Convertible preferred stock. In recent years large amounts of new preferred stock have been issued by corporations merging with or acquiring other corporations. The preferred stock issued is often convertible; that is, the holder of the stock may exchange it for shares of common stock of the same corporation at a conversion ratio stated in the preferred stock contract.

Preferred stock is often issued in these mergers for two main reasons: (1) to avoid the use of bonds with their fixed interest charges which must be paid regardless of the amount of net earnings, and (2) to avoid issuing so many additional shares of common stock that earnings per share will be less in the current year than in prior years.

Investors find convertible preferred stock attractive because of the greater probability that the dividends on the preferred will be paid (compared to dividends on common shares) and because the conversion privilege may be the source of increased market price. To illustrate, assume that the James Company issued 2,000 shares of 6 percent $100 par value convertible preferred stock at $100 per share. The stock is convertible at any time into four shares of James common stock, which has a current market value of $20 per share. In the next several years the company reports sharply increased net earnings and increases the dividend on the common stock from $1 to $2 per share. The common stock now sells at $40 per share. The holder of one share of preferred stock can convert the stock held into four shares of common stock and increase the annual dividend received from $6 to $8. Or the preferred share can be sold at a substantial gain. The preferred stock will sell in the market at approximately $160, the market value of the four shares of common into which it is convertible. Or the preferred share can be held with the expectation of realizing an even larger gain at a later date.

The issuing corporation may force conversion by calling the preferred stock for redemption. Virtually all preferred stocks, convertible or nonconvertible, are callable by the issuing corporation. This means that the holders of nonconvertible preferred stock must surrender it to the company when requested to do so. Holders of convertible preferred stock may either surrender it or convert it into common shares. The preferred shares are usually callable at a small premium (the call premium) of 3 or 4 percent of the par value of the stock. If the stock is surrendered, the former holder receives par value, plus the call premium, plus any dividends in arrears and a prorated portion of the current period's dividend. If the market value of the common shares that can be obtained by conversion is higher than the redemption value of the preferred stock, the stockholder would be foolish not to convert.

The reasons why a corporation may call its preferred stock include (1) the preferred stock may require a 7 percent annual dividend while capital to retire the stock can be secured by issuing a new 4 percent preferred: (2) the issuing company may have been sufficiently profitable to enable it to retire the preferred stock out of earnings; and (3) the company may wish to force conversion of a convertible preferred because the cash dividend on the equivalent common shares will be less than the dividend on the preferred.

1. False. The claims of the creditors rank ahead of the claims of the stockholders, even those stockholders whose stock is preferred as to assets.
2. False. A stock may be preferred as to assets or dividends, or both. Preferred stock is not automatically preferred as to both assets and dividends.
3. False. If there are cumulative preferred dividends in arrears at liquidation, they must also be paid in full before any distribution can be made to the common stockholders.

If you missed any of the above, reread Frame 8[10] before beginning Frame 9[10] on page 452.

9[10]
continued

Statement of financial position presentation

To illustrate the financial reporting of preferred and common stock, assume that a corporation is authorized to issue 20,000 shares of $100 par value, 7 percent, cumulative, convertible preferred stock, all of which have been issued at par and are outstanding. It is also authorized to issue 400,000 shares of $10 par value common stock of which 210,000 shares have been issued at par and are outstanding. The stockholders' equity section of the statement of financial position (assuming $500,000 of retained earnings) is:

Paid-In Capital:

Preferred stock—$100 par value, 7%, cumulative, convertible; authorized, issued, and outstanding, 20,000 shares	$2,000,000	
Common stock—$10 par value; authorized, 400,000 shares; issued and outstanding, 210,000 shares	2,100,000	$4,100,000
Retained earnings		500,000
Total Stockholders' Equity		$4,600,000

A footnote would disclose the rate at which the preferred stock is convertible into common stock.

Indicate whether each of the following statements is true or false.

1. Use the data in the above illustration and assume that no dividends have been declared or paid for the years 1978 and 1979. If the board of directors declares $350,000 of dividends on January 2, 1980, $280,000 must go to the preferred stockholders.
2. The corporation in the above illustration could safely and properly issue the 190,000 authorized but unissued common shares to its common stockholders for $10 per share.
3. A corporation can often force conversion of its convertible preferred stock even though holders of the stock would prefer not to convert it.

4. A corporation can issue a preferred stock that is cumulative, convertible, callable, and that possesses voting rights.

Now check your answers in Answer Frame 9[10] on page 456.

Frame 10[10]

Recording capital stock issues

When par value stock (common) is issued at par value for cash, the Cash account is debited and the Common Stock account is credited. If par value stock is issued for cash at more than par value, the Cash account is debited for the issue price, the Common Stock account is credited for the par value, and a Paid-In Capital in Excess of Par Value account is credited for the difference between issue price and par value. For example, assume that the Kake Company issues 25,000 shares of $20 par value common stock at $20 each. The entry is:

Cash..	500,000	
Common Stock..		500,000
To record sale and issuance of 25,000 shares at par.		

If the Kake Company issues an additional 20,000 shares at $30, the entry is:

Cash..	600,000	
Common Stock..		400,000
Paid-In Capital in Excess of Par Value—Common		200,000
To record sale and issuance of 20,000 shares at $30.		

Issuance of stock without par value. If 100 shares of stock without par value but with a stated value of $10 per share are issued for $20 each, the Cash account is debited for $2,000, the Common Stock account is credited for $1,000, and the Paid-In Capital in Excess of Stated Value—Common account is credited for $1,000. If 100 shares of stock without par or stated value are issued for $20 per share, Cash is debited for $2,000 and Common Stock is credited for $2,000.

The Stock Subscribed account. In most states, authorized stock becomes legally issued when a subscription is accepted. But for accounting purposes, capital stock is not recorded as issued until the stock certificate is delivered to the shareholder. When the stock certificate is not issued until a shareholder has paid in full for the subscription, a separate account must be kept to show the amount of stock subscribed but not yet outstanding. This is done by setting up a Common (or Preferred) Stock Subscribed account.

To illustrate, assume that the Damon Corporation was authorized to issue 200,000 shares of common stock without par value. On January 2, 1979, the corporation received subscriptions for 20,000 shares at $10 per share. One half of the subscription price was paid in cash immediately. The balance was paid on January 15, and the stock certificates were issued. The journal entries were:

1   True. The preferred stock is entitled to dividends of $140,000 per year. Since the stock is cumulative, two years' dividends must be paid to the preferred before any dividends can be paid to the common stockholders.

2. False. The corporation cannot safely and properly issue the unissued common shares to its common stockholders. Some of the authorized but unissued shares must be reserved for issuance to the preferred stockholders when they present their convertible preferred shares for conversion.

3. True. A corporation can often force conversion of its preferred stock. If the market price of the preferred is largely a reflection of the market value of the common shares into which it can be converted, and if this market price is larger than the call price of the preferred, an investor would be foolish not to convert the preferred when it is called.

4. True. A corporation will usually put into a preferred stock contract those features necessary to make the stock attractive to investors. If all of these features are required to induce investors to acquire the stock, then they may be included. The callable feature permits the corporation to terminate the investment.

If you missed any of the above, reread Frame 9¹⁰ before beginning Frame 10¹⁰ on page 455.

10¹⁰
continued

1979			
Jan. 2	Cash	100,000	
	Subscriptions Receivable — Common	100,000	
	Common Stock Subscribed		200,000
	To record subscriptions to 20,000 shares at $10 per share accompanied by one half the subscription price.		
15	Cash	100,000	
	Subscriptions Receivable — Common		100,000
	To record the collection of balance of subscriptions.		
15	Common Stock Subscribed	200,000	
	Common Stock		200,000
	To record issuance of stock certificates for 20,000 shares.		

To test your understanding, suppose that a company is authorized to issue 4,000 shares of preferred stock with a par value of $100 per share; 2,000 shares are subscribed at $110 per share; 50 percent of each of the subscriptions is subsequently collected; and no stock certificates are issued. The company is also authorized to issue 20,000 shares of common stock with a par value of $100 per share; 12,000 shares are subscribed at $120 per share. Eighty percent of each of the subscriptions is subsequently collected. No stock certificates are issued. Each class of capital stock must be named in the journal entry and in the ledger accounts. In all other respects the entries are similar to those already illustrated. Thus the entries for the preferred stock subscriptions and their partial collection are:

Subscriptions Receivable – Preferred.	220,000	
Paid-In Capital in Excess of Par Value – Preferred		20,000
Preferred Stock Subscribed.		200,000

To record subscriptions to 2,000 shares of $100 par value preferred stock at $110 per share.

| Cash. | 110,000 | |
| Subscriptions Receivable – Preferred | | 110,000 |

To record the collection of 50 percent of the subscriptions.

Prepare the entries to record the subscriptions to the common stock and their partial collection.

Check your answers by turning to Answer Frame 10¹⁰ on page 458.

Frame 11¹⁰

Capital stock issued for property or services. When capital stock is issued for property or services, a question arises: At what dollar amount should the exchange be recorded? In general, accountants record such exchanges at the fair value of (1) the property or services received or (2) the stock issued, whichever is more clearly evident.

As an example, assume that the owners of a tract of land deed it to a corporation in exchange for 1,000 shares of $15 par value common stock. At the time of the exchange, the land has a value of $20,000. The required entry is:

Land	20,000	
Common Stock		15,000
Paid-In Capital in Excess of Par Value – Common		5,000

Indicate whether each of the following statements is true or false.

1. When shares of stock are issued for property other than cash, the exchange may be recorded at the fair value of the shares issued.

2. When shares of stock are issued for property other than cash, the exchange should generally be recorded at the par or stated value of the shares issued.

Now turn to Answer Frame 11¹⁰ on page 458 to check your answers.

SECTION II

Frame 12¹⁰

Treasury stock

Treasury stock is capital stock which has been issued and reacquired by the issuing corporation. It has not been canceled, and it is legally available for reissuance. Treasury stock and unissued capital stock

457

12¹⁰
continued

differ in that treasury stock has been issued at some time in the past.

Treasury stock may be acquired by purchase by the issuing corporation, by donation to the corporation by a stockholder, in settlement of a debt due the corporation, and in other transactions.

The corporation laws of most states consider treasury stock as issued but not outstanding. The treasury shares have at some time in the past been issued to stockholders but they are no longer outstanding; that is, they are no longer held by stockholders. Treasury shares have no voting or dividend rights.

Some states require that acquisitions of treasury stock "be made out of retained earnings." This means that if a corporation acquires treasury stock, retained earnings equal to the cost of the shares are unavailable for dividends until the treasury stock is reissued. The cost of the treasury stock must not exceed the amount of retained earnings at the date of acquisition. Thus, dividends plus treasury stock purchases must not impair the legal (or stated) capital of the corporation. If a corporation is subject to such a law, the retained earnings available for dividends are limited to the amount in excess of the cost of the treasury shares.

Treasury stock in the statement of financial position. Treasury stock should not be shown as an asset since its acquisition reduces the stockholders' equity. An asset is not received when treasury stock is acquired. Instead, the acquisition of treasury stock consists of a return of capital to the stockholder from whom the stock is acquired.

When a corporation acquires its own capital stock as treasury stock, the purpose of the acquisition may be (1) to cancel and retire the stock, (2) to reissue it to employees or others, (3) to reduce the number of shares outstanding and thereby increase earnings per share, or (4) to use the stock in stock option plans. If the intention of the acquisition is cancellation and retirement, the treasury shares exist simply because they have not been retired and canceled by formal reduction of the authorized capital.

When treasury stock is held on a statement of financial position date, it is usually shown in that statement at cost and as a deduction from the sum of the paid-in capital and retained earnings, as follows:

Common stock, authorized and issued, 40,000 shares, par value $10 per share, of which 4,000 shares are in the treasury.........	$400,000
Retained earnings (including $44,000 restricted by acquisition of treasury stock)...	160,000
Total..	$560,000
Less: Treasury stock at cost, 4,000 shares	44,000
Total Stockholders' Equity	$516,000

Indicate whether each of the following statements is true or false.

1. The stockholders' equity section illustrated above indicates that dividends of up to $160,000 may be declared from retained earnings.

2. Since treasury stock has been issued once, it may be reissued without violating the preemptive rights of the stockholders.

3. The cost of treasury stock held should be shown as a deduction in the stockholders' equity section of the statement of financial position.

4. Treasury stock is a corporation's own capital stock which has been issued, reacquired, and canceled.

Now check your responses in Answer Frame 12[10] on page 460.

Frame 13[10]

Acquisition and reissuance of treasury stock. When treasury stock is acquired, the stock is recorded at cost. Reissuances are credited to the Treasury Stock account at the cost of acquisition. The excess of the reissue price over cost is credited to Paid-In Capital—Treasury Stock Transactions because it represents additional paid-in capital.

For example, assume that the Grayson Corporation whose stockholders' equity consists solely of capital stock and retained earnings, acquires ten shares of its outstanding common stock for $60 each and two months later reissues three shares for $65 each. The entries are:

1. False. An amount equal to the cost of the treasury shares acquired, $44,000, is shown as being unavailable for dividends in the parenthetical statement following retained earnings. Therefore, only $116,000 is available for dividends. Certain states require that the retained earnings available for dividends be limited to the amount of retained earnings in excess of the cost of the treasury shares.

2. True. It may be reissued without violating the preemptive rights.

3. True. The acquisition of treasury stock reduces stockholders' equity to the extent of the cost of the stock. The cost of the treasury stock thus should be shown as a deduction in the stockholders' equity section. It is deducted from the sum of paid-in capital and retained earnings.

4. False. Treasury stock is a corporation's own stock which was once outstanding but has since been reacquired by the corporation. But it has not been canceled and thus is available for reissuance.

If you answered incorrectly, reread Frame 12¹⁰ before beginning Frame 13¹⁰ on page 459.

13¹⁰
continued

Treasury Stock — Common	600	
Cash		600

Acquired ten shares of treasury stock at $60.

Cash	195	
Treasury Stock — Common		180
Paid-In Capital — Treasury Stock Transactions		15

Reissued three shares of treasury stock at $65; cost $60 per share.

If the reissue price is less than the acquisition price, the difference is debited to Paid-In Capital — Treasury Stock Transactions. If the Grayson Corporation reissues an additional two shares at $58 per share, the entry is:

Cash	116	
Paid-In Capital — Treasury Stock Transactions	4	
Treasury Stock — Common		120

Reissued two shares of treasury stock at $58, cost $60 per share.

At this point, the balance in the Paid-In Capital — Treasury Stock Transactions account is $11 ($15 − $4). If the remaining five shares are reissued for $56 per share, the entry will be:

Cash	280	
Paid-In Capital — Treasury Stock Transactions	11	
Retained Earnings	9	
Treasury Stock — Common		300

Reissued five shares of treasury stock at $56; cost $60 per share.

It should be noted that the Paid-In Capital — Treasury Stock Transactions account has been exhausted (it cannot have a debit balance). The balance of the excess of cost over reissue price of $9 is regarded as a special distribution to the stockholders involved and is charged to the Retained Earnings account.

The practices illustrated above are also applicable to stock with and without par value, whether with or without stated value.

Assume a corporation acquires one share of its outstanding common stock, which has a par value of $100, for $104. The entry is:

Treasury Stock – Common	104	
Cash		104

Acquired one share of $100 par value stock for $104.

One month later the corporation reissues this share of treasury stock for $104. Which of the following is the correct entry to record this transaction?

1. Cash 104
    Treasury Stock – Common 100
    Paid-In Capital – Treasury Stock Transactions 4

2. Cash 104
    Treasury Stock – Common 104

3. Cash 100
    Paid-In Capital – Treasury Stock Transactions 4
    Treasury Stock – Common 104

4. Cash 104
    Paid-In Capital – Treasury Stock Transactions 104

You can check your response in Answer Frame 13[10] on page 462.

Frame 14[10]

Donated treasury stock. Treasury stock may be acquired by donation as well as by purchase. Capital stock may be donated to the corporation by the stockholders when the corporation's working funds are at a low level. Under such circumstances the stockholders sometimes agree to donate capital stock to the corporation to be reissued to obtain working capital.

If capital stock is donated to a corporation, no journal entry need be made. A memorandum should be made in the Treasury Stock – Common account noting the number of shares received. Retained earnings are not restricted, since the treasury stock was obtained without cost.

If 400 shares of donated treasury stock are reissued for $44,000, the required entry is:

Cash	44,000	
Paid-In Capital – Donations		44,000

To record the reissuance of donated shares.

The second entry is the correct one. The reissue price was equal to the cost of the share of treasury stock. The entry to record the reissuance is thus simply a debit to Cash and a credit to the Treasury Stock—Common account for $104. If you answered incorrectly, reread Frame 13¹⁰ before turning to Frame 14¹⁰ on page 461.

14¹⁰
continued

Assume that 50 shares of $20 par value common stock are donated to a corporation when their market value is $22 per share. Two weeks later these shares are reissued for $1,200. Which of the following entries properly records the reissue of these donated treasury stock shares?

1. Cash... 1,200
       Treasury Stock—Common... 1,100
       Paid-In Capital—Donations... 100

2. Cash... 1,200
       Treasury Stock—Common... 1,000
       Paid-In Capital—Donations... 200

3. Cash... 1,200
       Paid-In Capital—Donations... 1,200

4. Cash... 1,200
       Paid-In Capital... 1,200

Check your answer in Answer Frame 14¹⁰ on page 464.

Frame 15¹⁰

Dividends

Dividends are distributions of earnings by a corporation to its stock-holders. The normal dividend is a cash dividend. But other types of assets, such as marketable securities, may be distributed. A corporation may also distribute notes, other promises to pay cash in the future, or additional shares of its own capital stock as dividends.

Since they are the means by which the owners share in the earnings of the corporation, dividends are usually charged against retained earnings. They must be declared by the board of directors and recorded in the minutes book. The significant dates concerning dividends are the date of *declaration,* the date of *record,* and the date of *payment.* The date of declaration is the date the board takes action in the form of a motion that dividends are payable. The date of record is the date set by the board to determine to whom the dividends will be paid. The date of payment is the date of actual payment of the dividend.

Assume that a quarterly cash dividend on 1,000 shares of $100 par value of 8 percent preferred stock is declared on January 21, 1979, to stockholders of record on February 5, 1979, to be paid on March 1, 1979. The entries at the declaration and payment dates are:

Jan. 21	Retained Earnings..	2,000	
	Dividends Payable..		2,000
	Declared the quarterly cash dividend on the 8 percent preferred stock.		

Mar. 1	Dividends Payable..	2,000	
	Cash...		2,000
	Paid the dividend declared on January 21, 1979.		

When a cash dividend is declared, some companies debit a Dividends account instead of Retained Earnings. At the end of the fiscal year, the Dividends account is closed to Retained Earnings. The Dividends account summarizes the dividends declared for the year in one place. A legally declared cash dividend is a current liability of the corporation.

Decide whether each of the following statements is true or false.
1. The payment of a cash dividend increases a corporation's current liabilities.
2. The date of record follows the date of declaration of a dividend.
3. The date of declaration is the date used to determine to whom the dividends will be paid.
4. The presence of a Dividends Payable account among the current liabilities in a statement of financial position indicates a dividend has been declared but not paid.

You may check your answers in Answer Frame 15[10] on page 464.

Frame 16[10]

Stock dividends

A corporation may declare a dividend consisting of additional shares of its capital stock. Usually more shares of common stock are issued to common stockholders. The effect of a stock dividend usually is to transfer a sum from retained earnings to permanent paid-in capital. The amount transferred for stock dividends is usually the fair market value of the distributed shares.

Stock dividends have no effect on the total amount of stockholders' equity. They merely decrease retained earnings and increase paid-in capital by an equal amount or transfer amounts between paid-in capital accounts. Immediately after the declaration and distribution of a stock dividend, each share of similar stock has a lower book value per share. This is because there are more shares outstanding with no increase in total stockholders' equity.

Answer frame 14¹⁰

The third entry is correct. Since there was no cost to the corporation for the donated stock, the entire proceeds of the reissuance are credited to a Paid-In Capital—Donations account. The credit to the Treasury Stock—Common account in the first two entries is in error. No debit was made to this account when the donated shares were acquired, since no cost was involved. Paid-In Capital, credited in the fourth entry, is not specific enough for use as an account title. There are many sources of paid-in capital and a separate account, properly labeled, should be kept for paid-in capital from each source.

If you answered incorrectly, reread Frame 14¹⁰ before going on to Frame 15¹⁰ on page 462.

Answer frame 15¹⁰

1. False. The declaration of a cash dividend increases a firm's current liabilities. The payment of the cash dividend decreases current liabilities.
2. True. The date of record does follow the date of declaration. If it did not, the company would in some instances be paying dividends to individuals who no longer owned stock at the time the dividend was declared. Both of these dates precede the date of payment.
3. False. The date of record is the date used to determine to whom the dividends will be paid. The date of declaration is the date the liability for dividends payable becomes effective.
4. True. The declaration of a dividend requires the use of the Dividends Payable account. When the dividend is paid, the balance in the Dividends Payable account is eliminated.

If you answered incorrectly, reread Frame 15¹⁰ before beginning Frame 16¹⁰ on page 463.

16¹⁰
continued

Stock dividends have no effect on the total amount of a stockholder's ownership in the corporation. His or her total equity is simply spread over a larger number of shares. For example, if a stockholder owns 2,000 shares in a corporation having 200,000 shares of stock outstanding, he or she owns 1 percent of the outstanding shares. After a 10 percent stock dividend, the stockholder will still own 1 percent of the outstanding shares—2,200 of 220,000 outstanding.

Indicate whether each of the following statements is true or false.

1. The number of shares of capital stock outstanding is increased by the corporation's declaration and issuance of a stock dividend.
2. The declaration and issuance of a stock dividend does not change the total amount of stockholders' equity in the corporation.
3. A stock dividend usually reduces retained earnings and increases permanent paid-in capital.

Now check your responses in Answer Frame 16¹⁰ on page 466.

Frame 17¹⁰ _____

Stock split-ups

A distribution of shares greater than 20 to 25 percent of the previously outstanding shares is assumed to have the effect of reducing the market price of the shares by increasing the number outstanding and is treated as a stock split-up, or stock split.

There are a number of ways to account for a stock split-up, depending on the particular circumstances. If the board of directors reduces the par or stated value of shares, only the number of shares outstanding and the par or stated value need to be changed on the records. Thus, a two-for-one stock split in which the par value of the shares is decreased from $20 to $10 could be recorded as follows:

Common Stock – $20 par value	100,000	
Common Stock – $10 par value		100,000

To record a two-for-one stock split-up. Five thousand shares of $20 par value common stock were replaced by 10,000 shares of $10 par value common stock.

A corporation may wish to double the number of its outstanding shares without changing the par or stated value of the shares. To do this, it declares a 100 percent stock dividend. Whenever a distribution of shares occurs and the par or stated value of the shares is not changed, the distribution is generally described as a stock dividend. But such "stock dividends" of over 20–25 percent of the previously outstanding shares are *accounted for* as stock splits. They are viewed as capital transactions, to be kept in the capital accounts, rather than as dividends that are properly charged against Retained Earnings. The shares issued are credited to the capital stock account in an amount equal to the total par or stated value. The debit is entered in other paid-in capital accounts, to the extent possible, and in Retained Earnings only as a last resort. Thus, the net effect of a 100 percent stock dividend declared and paid by Walt Disney Productions in 1973 on its 14,276,173 shares of $1.25 par value common stock was to transfer approximately $17,845,216 from Paid-in Capital in Excess of Par Value to Capital Stock – Common.

If no other paid-in capital related to the class of shares issued exists, or exists only in an amount less than the par or stated value of the shares issued, the dividend, if larger than 20–25 percent, is charged in its entirety, or in part, to Retained Earnings. The amount so charged need not exceed the par or stated value of the additional shares issued.

Recording stock dividends

Assume a corporation is authorized to issue 40,000 shares of $100 par value common stock, of which 16,000 shares are outstanding. Its board of directors now declares a 10 percent stock dividend (1,600 shares). The market price of the stock is $150 per share immediately

465

1. True. The issuance of a stock dividend increases the number of shares of capital stock outstanding but does not change the individual stockholder's percentage of ownership in the corporation.

2. True. The usual stock dividend merely decreases retained earnings and increases paid-in capital by an equal amount. Thus, there is no change in total stockholders' equity.

3. True. An amount is transferred from retained earnings to paid-in capital.

If you missed any of the above, restudy Frame 16¹⁰ before beginning Frame 17¹⁰ on page 465.

17¹⁰
continued

before the stock dividend is announced. Since distributions of less than 20–25 percent of the previously outstanding shares are to be accounted for at market value, the entry for the declaration of the dividend is (assuming the dividend was declared on August 10, 1979):

Aug. 10	Retained Earnings	240,000	
	Stock Dividend Payable – Common		160,000
	Paid-In Capital – Stock Dividend		80,000

To record the declaration of a 10 percent stock dividend; shares to be distributed on September 20, 1979, to stockholders of record on August 31, 1979.

Can you give the entry to record the issuance of the shares? Turn to Answer Frame 17¹⁰ on page 468 to check your answer.

Frame 18¹⁰

Current liabilities are usually paid out of current assets. A stock dividend payable is not payable with assets; hence, it is not a liability. If a statement of financial position is prepared between the date of declaration of the 10 percent dividend and the date of issuance of the shares, the proper statement presentation of the stock dividend is as follows:

Paid-In Capital:		
Common stock, $100 par value; authorized, 40,000 shares; issued and outstanding, 16,000 shares	$1,600,000	
Stock dividend payable on September 20, 1979, 1,600 shares at par value	160,000	
Total par value of shares issued and to be issued	$1,760,000	
From stock dividends	80,000	
Total Paid-In Capital		$1,840,000
Retained earnings		260,000
Total Stockholders' Equity		$2,100,000

Suppose the market price is still $150 per share on the date of declaration but the common stock is without par value and has a stated value of $50 per share. What are the entries to record the declaration and issuance of the 10 percent stock dividend (1,600 shares) of the same class of stock?

Check your answer by turning to Answer Frame 18[10] on page 468.

Frame 19[10]

Retained earnings

In general, the stockholders' equity or interest in a corporation is made up of two elements: (1) paid-in (or contributed) capital and (2) retained earnings. Retained earnings is the term used to describe the increase in stockholders' equity resulting from profitable operation of the corporation. As such, it indicates the source of certain assets received but not distributed to stockholders as dividends. Thus, both categories indicate the source of assets received by the corporation — actual investment by the stockholders and investment by the stockholders in the sense of dividends foregone.

When the Retained Earnings account has a debit balance, a deficit exists. It is shown under that title as a negative amount in the stockholders' equity section of the statement of financial position. The net effect of having a deficit is that net assets have decreased rather than increased as a result of operations and dividend declarations. The title of the general ledger account need not be changed merely because it contains a debit balance.

Indicate whether each of the following statements is correct or incorrect.

1. The balance in the Retained Earnings account consists largely of the accumulated earnings earned but not distributed to stockholders.
2. The Retained Earnings account describes one source of corporate capital and is properly classified as paid-in capital in the stockholders' equity section of the statement of financial position.
3. A net loss suffered by a corporation during an accounting period increases the total stockholders' equity shown in its statement of financial position.

Check your responses in Answer Frame 19[10] on page 468.

The required entry is as follows:

Sept. 20   Stock Dividends Payable—Common.................... 160,000
           Common Stock.. 160,000
           To record distribution of 1,600 shares of common
           stock as authorized in stock dividend declared
           on August 10, 1979.

If you did not make this entry, reread Frame 17¹⁰ before beginning Frame 18¹⁰
on page 466.

The entry to record the declaration of the stock dividend is:

Retained Earnings... 240,000
    Stock Dividend Payable—Common............................ 80,000
    Paid-In Capital—Stock Dividend............................ 160,000

The entry to record the issuance of the stock dividend is:

Stock Dividend Payable—Common................................. 80,000
    Common Stock....................................... 80,000

If you answered the question incorrectly, review Frames 17¹⁰ and 18¹⁰ before
going on to Frame 19¹⁰ on page 467.

1. Correct. This is basically what the balance in the Retained Earnings account represents.
2. Incorrect. Although a source of corporate capital, retained earnings do not represent paid-in capital, that is, capital contributed by the owners. Retained earnings are classified separately from paid-in capital in the stockholders' equity section.
3. Incorrect. A net loss reduces the credit balance (or increases the debit balance if one exists) in the Retained Earnings account, and this reduces the total stockholders' equity.

If you missed any of the above, reread Frame 19¹⁰ before beginning Frame 20¹⁰
below.

Frame 20¹⁰

Retained earnings reserves (appropriations)

A retained earnings reserve (also called an appropriation of retained
earnings) is a subdivision of retained earnings and is recorded by a debit
to Retained Earnings and a credit to a properly named reserve account.
The reason for the establishment of the reserve is often indicated by the
title of the reserve account. Transferring a part of retained earnings to a
reserve has the purpose and effect of limiting dividend declarations to
the remaining balance—the free or unappropriated retained earnings.

In other words, the creation of a retained earnings reserve informs stockholders that a certain amount of the assets brought into the corporation through the earning process is not to be distributed to stockholders as dividends. But no cash is being set aside by the entry. Retained earnings reserves are established by action of the board of directors, voluntarily or in accordance with the provisions of certain contracts such as bond indentures or loan agreements.

The following entry might be made if a bond indenture requires the restriction of $50,000 of retained earnings:

Retained Earnings	50,000	
Reserve for Retirement of Bonds Payable		50,000

When the retained earnings reserve has served its purpose, it may be returned intact to Retained Earnings at the direction of the board of directors. The entry is simply a debit to the reserve and a credit to Retained Earnings.

Reserves in the statement of financial position

In the statement of financial position, retained earnings reserves should be shown in the stockholders' equity section as follows:

Paid-In Capital:	
Preferred stock, $50 par; 1,000 shares authorized, issued, and outstanding	$ 50,000
Common stock, $10 par; 10,000 shares authorized, issued, and outstanding	100,000
Total Paid-In Capital	$150,000
Retained Earnings:	
Appropriated:	
Reserve for retirement of bonds payable	$ 50,000
Free and unappropriated...	40,000
Total Retained Earnings..	$ 90,000
Total Stockholders' Equity	$240,000

Note that the creation of a retained earnings reserve does not reduce the equity of the stockholders.

The word "reserve" still is used in several different senses by accountants and the general public. Although modern accounting practice tends to limit use of the term reserve to accounts which are reservations of retained earnings, enough exceptions exist to require careful interpretation of "reserves." Retained earnings reserves should not be confused with allowances such as allowances for depreciation and doubtful accounts.

The formal recording and reporting of retained earnings reserves is decreasing and is being replaced by footnote explanations such as the following:

Note 7.   Retained earnings restrictions.
          According to provisions in the bond indenture, dividends are limited to $40,000.

Indicate whether each of the following statements is true or false.

1. A retained earnings reserve account is established by a debit to Retained Earnings and a credit to the reserve account being set up.
2. The creation of a retained earnings reserve increases the amount of the free and unappropriated retained earnings shown in the statement of financial position.
3. The establishment of a retained earnings reserve reduces the total stockholders' equity shown in the statement of financial position.
4. The creation of a retained earnings reserve may reflect an action taken by the board of directors to restrict the amount of dividends which may be declared.

Now check your answers in Answer Frame 20[10] on page 472.

Summary *chapter* 10

SECTION I

A corporation is an association of individuals recognized by law as a separate legal entity. A corporation is granted legal existence when (among other requirements) a proper application for incorporation is submitted to and approved by the appropriate state agency and a charter is granted. The stockholders elect a board of directors to formulate broad policies. The board of directors selects officers to guide the corporation and carry out policies.

The two ordinary classes of stock a corporation may issue are preferred and common. Preferred stock usually has some rights not granted to common stockholders, such as a preference in receiving dividends. As to dividends, a preferred stock may be cumulative or noncumulative. Preferred stockholders frequently do not have the right to vote. Capital is often raised by issuing preferred stock to increase the return to common stock and to keep control of the corporation in the hands of the common stockholders.

Par value is an arbitrary dollar amount assigned to capital stock. It may be more or less than book value or market value. But the stated (legal) capital of a corporation issuing par value shares is usually the aggregate par value of the shares issued.

Stock without par value may be assigned a stated value. Stated value is an arbitrary amount similar to par value. The stated (legal) capital of a corporation issuing shares with a stated value is usually equal to the total of the stated value of the shares issued.

When a stock subscription is received, a subscriptions receivable account and a stock subscribed account will always be needed unless payment in full is received immediately and the stock is issued. Depending on the price agreed upon, an excess over par or stated value account may also be involved.

Capital stock issued for property or services is recorded at the fair market value of either the property or services received or the shares issued, whichever is more clearly evident. When shares are issued for an amount greater than their par or stated value, this excess should be credited to an account called Paid-In Capital in Excess of Par (or Stated) Value, with separate accounts established for each class of stock.

SECTION II

Shares of capital stock which have been issued and then returned to the issuing corporation are called treasury stock or shares. Such shares are issued but not outstanding. The amount of dividends which may be declared out of retained earnings is generally restricted by an amount equal to the cost of treasury stock. The cost of treasury stock is reported as a deduction from total stockholders' equity. If treasury stock is reissued, the difference between cost and reissue price is carried to a Paid-In Capital — Treasury Stock Transactions account. If there is no balance in this account, any excess of cost over reissue price is charged to Retained Earnings upon reissue. Since donated treasury shares have no cost, the only formal journal entry made for them is to credit the entire amount received upon reissue to a Paid-In Capital — Donations account.

The typical dividend is a cash distribution of corporate earnings to stockholders. A corporation may also distribute as dividends other forms of assets, promises to pay, or additional shares of its own capital stock (a stock dividend).

Stock dividends greater than 20 to 25 percent are stock split-ups. The amount transferred to the Capital Stock account is equal to the par or stated value of the shares issued. It is debited to other paid-in capital attaching to the same class of shares, or, if such amounts are not sufficient, to Retained Earnings. Stock dividends of less than 20–25 percent are recorded at market value and are debited to Retained Earnings.

Retained earnings reserves are restrictions on the distribution of retained earnings as dividends. These reserves are created by transfers of retained earnings and are returned intact when they have served their purpose. Retained earnings reserves are reported as a part of retained earnings in the statement of financial position.

Accounting for single proprietorships and partnerships is covered in the Appendix to this chapter.

To complete your review, study the terms introduced in this chapter in the glossary which follows the Appendix. Then go on to the Student

471

Review Quiz beginning on page 484 for a self-administered test of your comprehension of the material in the chapter.

APPENDIX 10: UNINCORPORATED BUSINESSES

There are more unincorporated businesses (single proprietorships and partnerships) than corporations in the United States. Single proprietorships and partnerships are very similar because they do not issue capital stock and their existence is not separated from the owners. The difference is that a single proprietorship is owned by one person while a partnership is an association of two or more persons to carry on a business as co-owners.

Owners' equity accounts

The owners' equity accounts of a single proprietorship consist of a capital account and a drawing account with the owner, as follows:

David Welk, Capital
David Welk, Drawing

The owners' equity accounts of a partnership consist of a capital account and a drawing account with each partner, as follows:

Jenny Reed, Capital
Jenny Reed, Drawing

John Howard, Capital
John Howard, Drawing

Capital accounts are credited with capital investments (contributions) made by the owners, and drawing accounts are debited for withdrawals of cash or other assets made by the owners. For example, assume that Paul Kent invested $31,000 in a sporting goods store on January 2, 1979. The following entry was made:

Cash 31,000
     Paul Kent, Capital   31,000

When Mr. Kent withdrew $1,400 from the business on March 8, 1979, the following entry was made:

Paul Kent, Drawing 1,400
     Cash   1,400

Single proprietorships

The characteristics of the capital account and the drawing account of a single proprietorship are set forth below, based on the trial balance shown in Illustration 10.1.

Illustration 10.1

PAUL KENT Trial Balance December 31, 1979		
	Debits	*Credits*
Cash	$ 17,600	
Accounts receivable	21,000	
Accounts payable		$ 18,000
Paul Kent, capital		31,000
Paul Kent, drawing	10,000	
Sales		117,000
Sales returns	5,000	
Purchases	84,000	
Rent expense	5,200	
Delivery expense	6,700	
Store expense	16,500	
	$166,000	$166,000

The inventory for Paul Kent's business at December 31, 1979, was $16,200. When the trial balance was taken at December 31, 1979, the capital and drawing accounts of Kent were as follows:

Paul Kent, Capital

Date		Explanation	Folio	Debit	Credit	Balance
1979 Jan.	2	Cash investment			31,000	31,000

Paul Kent, Drawing

Date		Explanation	Folio	Debit	Credit	Balance
1979						
Mar.	8	Cash		1,400		1,400
June	17	Cash		2,800		4,200
Sept.	9	Cash		2,600		6,800
Dec.	16	Cash		3,200		10,000

The ending inventory is set up and the expense and revenue accounts are closed to the Expense and Revenue Summary account. The Expense and Revenue Summary account appears as follows:

Expense and Revenue Summary

Date		Explanation	Folio	Debit	Credit	Balance
1979						
Dec.	31	Net sales			112,000	112,000
	31	Expenses		96,200		15,800

The balance of the Expense and Revenue Summary account—$15,800—representing the net earnings for the year, is now closed to the Paul Kent, Drawing account:

Expense and Revenue Summary 15,800
    Paul Kent, Drawing 15,800

Finally, the balance of the drawing account is closed to the capital account:

Paul Kent, Drawing 5,800
    Paul Kent, Capital 5,800

Financial statements for a single proprietorship

The proprietor's equity section of Paul Kent's statement of financial position is shown in Illustration 10.2. As the illustration shows, the

Illustration 10.2

PAUL KENT
Statement of Financial Position
December 31, 1979

Assets			*Liabilities and Proprietor's Equity*	
Current Assets:			Current Liabilities:	
Cash	$17,600		Accounts payable	$18,000
Accounts receivable	21,000		Proprietor's Equity:	
Merchandise inventory	16,200		Paul Kent, capital	36,800
			Total Liabilities and	
Total Assets	$54,800		Proprietor's Equity ...	$54,800

statement of financial position of a single proprietorship differs from that of a partnership or corporation only in the owner's equity section.

The earnings statement of a single proprietorship (Illustration 10.3) is similar to that of any other type of business organization. There is no separation of taxes on the earnings of the business or on the withdrawals. All earnings are taxable to the owner whether he withdraws them or not.

Illustration 10.3

PAUL KENT Earnings Statement For the Year Ended December 31, 1979		
Gross sales		$117,000
Less: Sales returns..		5,000
Net sales		$112,000
Cost of goods sold:		
Purchases...	$84,000	
Deduct: Merchandise inventory, December 31, 1979...............	16,200	
Cost of goods sold		67,800
Gross margin		$ 44,200
Deduct: Operating expenses:		
Rent expense	$ 5,200	
Delivery expense	6,700	
Store expense..	16,500	28,400
Net Earnings...		$ 15,800

Partnerships

The Uniform Partnership Act defines a partnership as "an association of two or more persons to carry on as co-owners a business for profit." The association of two or more persons should be effected by a written contract. The contract is known as the *articles of copartnership*. Any natural person who has the right to enter into a contract may become a partner. Each partner usually has one vote in the management of the business.

Partnerships are formed when (1) business capital requirements exceed the amount that may be raised by a single proprietor, or (2) a single proprietor desires to obtain the talents and services of other persons who will also share in the risks and rewards of the business, or (3) the single proprietor wishes to induce an employee to stay with the business by making the employee a partner.

A partnership is commonly known as a firm. But many partnerships end their names with the word "company," used in the sense of "associates." For example, Frank Henry & Company could be the name of a partnership of certified public accountants.

Accounting for owners' equity of a partnership is similar to that for a single proprietorship. But separate capital accounts and drawing accounts must be kept for each partner. Net earnings of the partnership are divided among the partners according to the earnings and loss ratio set forth in the partnership agreement. This is explained in greater detail later.

The Expense and Revenue Summary account is closed to the partners' drawing accounts according to the earnings and loss ratio. Each drawing account is then closed to the respective partner's capital account.

The following entries will illustrate partnership accounting. Assume Chris Connors and Lisa Burton form a partnership on January 1, 1979. Connors contributes cash of $20,800 and delivery equipment valued at $15,200. Burton contributes cash of $2,000, land valued at $10,000, and a building valued at $50,000.

The journal entries on January 1, 1979, to record the investment of each partner are as follows:

```
Cash ...............................................................................   22,800
Delivery Equipment............................................................   15,200
Land .................................................................................   10,000
Building............................................................................   50,000
        Chris Connors, Capital.................................................              36,000
        Lisa Burton, Capital ..................................................              62,000
    To record the investments of Connors and Burton in the
    partnership.
```

If additional investments are made at a later date, they also are credited to the capital accounts. Assume that on August 1, 1979, additional investments are made as indicated by the following journal entry:

```
Cash.................................................................................   12,300
        Chris Connors, Capital .................................................              6,900
        Lisa Burton, Capital ....................................................              5,400
    To record additional cash investments.
```

The partners agreed that instead of salaries Connors and Burton would withdraw $1,200 and $800, respectively, each month in cash. Thus, each month the following entry is made for actual withdrawals:

```
Chris Connors, Drawing ......................................................   1,200
Lisa Burton, Drawing..........................................................     800
        Cash.........................................................................              2,000
```

The net earnings of the partnership for the year ended December 31, 1979, are $50,000. The earnings and loss ratio of 3:2 indicates that Connors will receive a credit for $\frac{3}{5}$ or 60 percent of the net earnings and that Burton will receive a credit for $\frac{2}{5}$ or 40 percent of the net earnings. The journal entry to close the net earnings to the drawing accounts is:

```
Expense and Revenue Summary ...........................................   50,000
        Chris Connors, Drawing...............................................              30,000
        Lisa Burton, Drawing ................................................              20,000
    To close the net earnings to the drawing accounts.
```

After the Expense and Revenue Summary account has been closed, the drawing accounts have the following balances:

```
        Chris Connors, Drawing [$30,000 − (12 × $1,200)]............   $15,600
        Lisa Burton, Drawing [$20,000 − (12 × $800)]..................   10,400
```

The next step is to close the balance of the drawing accounts to the capital accounts by the following journal entries:

Chris Connors, Drawing..	15,600	
Chris Connors, Capital..		15,600
To close the December 31, 1979, drawing account balance.		
Lisa Burton, Drawing	10,400	
Lisa Burton, Capital		10,400
To close the December 31, 1979, drawing account balance.		

After the entries are posted, the partners' drawing accounts and capital accounts would have the following balances:

Chris Connors, Drawing........................	$ –0–
Chris Connors, Capital.........................	58,500
Lisa Burton, Drawing...........................	–0–
Lisa Burton, Capital	77,800

Financial statements of a partnership

The financial statements for a partnership are very similar in form to the financial statements for a single proprietorship or corporation. But a few differences do exist. The partnership earnings statement contains a section such as the following showing the division of the net earnings between the partners:

Distribution of net earnings

Chris Connors, 60%	$30,000
Lisa Burton, 40%	20,000
Total Net Earnings	$50,000

The statement of financial position for the Connors and Burton partnership at December 31, 1979, would show:

Partners' Equity:

Connors, capital......................................	$58,500	
Burton, capital..	77,800	
Total Partners' Equity		$136,300

At the end of each fiscal period, a statement of partners' capital is prepared to present details that cannot readily be shown on the statement of financial position. See Illustration 10.4.

Division of partnership earnings

The ratio in which partnership earnings and losses are divided is known as the *earnings and loss ratio,* or, as it is frequently called, the profit and loss ratio. The earnings and losses are divided in accordance with the provisions of the partnership contract. If the contract is silent with respect to the division of earnings and losses, the law assumes an

Illustration 10.4

		CONNORS AND BURTON		
		Statement of Partners' Capital		
		For the Year Ended December 31, 1979		

	Connors	*Burton*	*Total*
Investment, January 1, 1979	$36,000	$62,000	$ 98,000
Investment, August 1, 1979	6,900	5,400	12,300
	$42,900	$67,400	$110,300
Add: Net earnings per earnings statement	$30,000	$20,000	$ 50,000
Less: Drawings	14,400	9,600	24,000
	$15,600	$10,400	$ 26,000
Capital Account Balances, December 31, 1979	$58,500	$77,800	$136,300

equal division for all partners; this is true even if there is inequality in investments, ability, time devoted to the business, or risks assumed.

If each of the partners invests an equal amount of assets, has approximately equal ability, devotes the same amount of time to the business, and incurs the same risks, the earnings and losses probably should be divided equally. If variations in the foregoing factors exist between partners, the partner devoting the most time to the business, for example, might be compensated by a salary (out of net earnings) preceding the division of the remaining net earnings. The salary is part of the earnings sharing agreement. It is not considered an expense of the partnership. For example, if A is to be given credit for a salary of $10,000 before the remaining earnings are divided equally with B and net earnings are $50,000, A is credited with $30,000 and B with $20,000 when the Expense and Revenue Summary account is closed. As another illustration, one partner may invest greater capital than another partner, in which case the partner with the greater investment may insist on an inclusion in the partnership agreement that interest be allowed on capital account balances in the division of net earnings before the remainder is divided in accordance with the earnings and loss ratio.

Common methods of dividing earnings are:

1. In a set ratio such as:
   a) Equally.
   b) In an agreed ratio other than equal.
   c) In the ratio of the partners' capital account balances at the beginning of the fiscal period.
   d) In the ratio of the average capital investment.
2. By allowing interest on the capital investments or salaries and dividing the remaining net earnings in an agreed ratio.

Illustrations of distributions of partnership earnings

The illustrations which follow are based on these data about the partnership of Anders and Budd: net earnings for the year ended December 31, 1979, were $60,000. During 1979 Anders' drawings were $14,000 and Budd's drawings were $22,000. The capital account balances of the partners on December 31, 1979, before the accounts were closed, were Anders, $85,000, and Budd, $134,000.

Case 1. Earnings divided only in a set ratio. If the net earnings of $60,000 were divided equally between Anders and Budd, they would each be credited with $30,000 of earnings. If the partnership agreement instead called for a division of earnings of 60 percent to Anders and 40 percent to Budd, the entry to divide the $60,000 net earnings for 1979 would credit Anders with $36,000 and Budd with $24,000.

Sometimes the earnings are divided in the average capital account ratio. Illustration 10.5 contains the assumed details in the partners' capital accounts.

The ratio of average capital amounts is computed by using the total average capital ($50,000 + $90,000 = $140,000) as the denominator of fractions having each partner's average capital as numerators. Thus, Anders is credited with $50,000/$140,000 or 35.71 percent of net earnings, and Budd with $90,000/$140,000 or 64.29 percent.

Illustration 10.5   Computation of average capital

Anders, Capital					
Date	Debits	Credits	Balance	Months Unchanged	Month-Dollars (Weighted Equivalent)
Jan. 1			$40,000	6	$240,000
July 1		$15,000	55,000	5	275,000
Dec. 1		30,000	85,000	1	85,000
				12	$600,000

Average capital of Anders: $600,000 ÷ 12 = $50,000.

Budd, Capital					
Date	Debits	Credits	Balance	Months Unchanged	Month-Dollars (Weighted Equivalent)
Jan. 1			$ 80,000	7	$ 560,000
Aug. 1		$ 4,000	84,000	3	252,000
Nov. 1		50,000	134,000	2	268,000
				12	$1,080,000

Average capital of Budd: $1,080,000 ÷ 12 = $90,000.

Case 2. Interest allowed on investments before dividing the remainder. If interest is allowed on the partners' capital investments (the balance in the capital accounts) at the beginning of the year, or on their average capital amounts for the year, a portion of annual net earnings (equal to the total capital account balances multiplied by the interest rate agreed upon) is divided in a capital investment ratio.

479

The interest allowed is a distribution of part of net earnings for the period rather than an expense to be deducted in arriving at net earnings. It is considered a distribution of net earnings. If there is a net loss for the year, the debit to Expense and Revenue Summary resulting from the distribution will further increase the debit balance in that account to be distributed to the partners.

To follow the illustration of this method of earnings distribution, it is necessary to recall that the partners' capital account balances on January 1, 1979, were Anders, $40,000, and Budd, $80,000, and their average capital investments for 1979 were $50,000 and $90,000, respectively.

If interest at 6 percent per year is allowed each partner on his capital investment at the beginning of the year, the interest allowed is:

Anders, $40,000 at 6%	$2,400
Budd, $80,000 at 6%	4,800
Total	$7,200

If interest at 6 percent per year is allowed each partner on the average of his capital account for the year 1979, the interest allowed is:

Anders, $50,000 at 6%	$3,000
Budd, $90,000 at 6%	5,400
Total	$8,400

Case 3. Salaries allowed before dividing the remainder. Partners also may agree to allow themselves salaries. Salaries may be allowed in order to compensate for differences in time devoted to the business or differences in ability.

Salaries to partners are divisions of net earnings and are not operating expenses as are salaries paid to employees. If a salary agreement is in effect, the salaries are credited to the partners' drawing accounts as distributions of net earnings. The net earnings amount on a partnership's earnings statement is computed without deducting amounts for interest on partners' capital and salaries to partners. These are always considered to be part of the earnings-sharing mechanism instead of expenses to be deducted in arriving at net earnings. Salaries are allowed even if their total exceeds the amount of earnings.

In the case of Anders and Budd, suppose that partnership net earnings are only $20,800, that the earnings-sharing conditions are that Anders is allowed a salary of $16,000 per year and Budd a salary of $10,000 per year, and that the remaining net earnings or net loss is divided equally. What is the correct division of the $20,800 total between Anders and Budd?

The answer is that Anders receives $13,400 and Budd $7,400. This is determined as follows:

	Anders	Budd	Both	Earnings to be distributed
Net earnings......................................				$20,800
Salaries..	$16,000	$10,000	$26,000	(5,200)
Remainder (negative balance)................	(2,600)	(2,600)	(5,200)	−0−
	$13,400	$ 7,400	$20,800	

Notice that the salaries are granted even though earnings are insufficient to cover them. The resulting negative balance is then distributed to the partners in the agreed ratio.

Case 4. Interest and salaries allowed before dividing the remainder. Assume that Anders and Budd are allowed interest at 6 percent per year on their capital account balances at January 1, 1979, and that Anders is allowed a salary of $16,000 and Budd a salary of $10,000; remaining net earnings or net loss is divided equally. Net earnings are $60,000. The division in this case is:

	Anders	Budd	Both	Earnings to be distributed
Net earnings......................................				$60,000
Interest..	$ 2,400	$ 4,800	$ 7,200	52,800
Salary..	16,000	10,000	26,000	26,800
Remainder	13,400	13,400	26,800	−0−
Distribution......................................	$31,800	$28,200	$60,000	

Even if the allowances for salaries or interest exceed net earnings, or if there is a net loss for the period, the partners still are given credit for their full amounts of interest and salary. For example, in the situation above if there were a net loss of $20,000 instead of net earnings of $60,000 for the year, the division would be:

	Anders	Budd	Both	Earnings to be distributed
Net loss...				$(20,000)
Interest..	$ 2,400	$ 4,800	$ 7,200	(27,200)
Salary..	16,000	10,000	26,000	(53,200)
Remainder	(26,600)	(26,600)	(53,200)	−0−
Distribution......................................	$ (8,200)	$(11,800)	$(20,000)	

Glossary, *chapter* 10

Articles of copartnership—see partnership agreement.

Articles of incorporation—the form containing information about the proposed corporation that is filed with the state by incorporators seeking to organize the corporation.

Book value (per share)—stockholders' equity per share; computed as the amount per share each stockholder would receive if the corporation were liquidated without incurring any further expense and if assets were sold and liabilities liquidated at their recorded amounts.

Call premium—the difference between the amount at which a corporation may call its preferred stock for redemption and the par value of the stock.

Capital account—an owner's equity account used in proprietorship and partnership accounting. It is credited with the owner's initial and additional investments and when the drawing account for that owner has a credit balance and is closed to it. It is debited for reductions in the permanent investment of the owner and when the drawing account for that owner has a debit balance and is closed to it. A separate capital account is maintained for each owner.

Capital stock authorized—the stock that a corporation is entitled to issue as specified in its charter.

Capital stock, unissued—capital stock authorized for which stock certificates have not been issued.

Charter, corporate—the contract between the state and the incorporators of a corporation or their successors granting the corporation its legal existence.

Code of regulations (bylaws)—a set of rules or regulations adopted by the board of directors of a corporation to govern the conduct of corporate affairs within the general laws of the state and the policies and purposes stated or implied in the corporate charter.

Contributed capital—all capital paid into a corporation, including that carried in capital stock accounts.

Convertible preferred stock—preferred stock which is convertible into common stock of the issuing corporation.

Corporation—an association of individuals which, at law, is viewed as an artificial person. It is granted many of the rights and placed under many of the duties of a natural person. As viewed through the eyes of the law of a given state, all corporations organized under the laws of that state are domestic corporations: all others are foreign.

Date of declaration (of dividends)—the date on which the board of directors formally states its intention that the corporation will pay a dividend.

Date of payment (of dividends)—the date on which dividend checks are to be mailed or additional shares issued in the case of a stock dividend.

Date of record (of dividends)—the date at which the corporation determines to whom dividends are to be paid.

Deficit—a debit balance in the Retained Earnings account.

Dividend—a pro rata distribution, usually of cash, by a corporation to its stockholders, excluding distributions made in exchange for shares of stock, usually chargeable to retained earnings; legality of a dividend is satisfied if stockholders' equity exceeds stated capital after the act of declaration.

Dividends in arrears—cumulative unpaid dividends on preferred stock.

Donated treasury stock—treasury stock acquired by gift.

Drawing account—an owner's equity account maintained for each owner. It is debited when the owner withdraws assets (usually merchandise or cash) from the business and for the owner's share of a net loss. It is credited for the owner's share of net earnings.

Earnings and loss (profit and loss) ratio—the ratio used to divide earnings and losses in a partnership.

Incorporators—natural persons seeking to bring a corporation into existence.

Liquidation value—the amount to be paid per share of preferred stock upon liquidation of the corporation, often equal to par value, accumulated dividends, and a fixed premium.

Paid-in capital—all of the contributed capital of a corporation, including that carried in capital stock accounts. When the words "paid-in capital" are included in an account title, the account contains capital contributed in addition to that assigned to the shares issued and recorded in the capital stock accounts.

Paid-in Capital—Treasury Stock Transactions—the title of the account credited when treasury stock is reissued for more than its cost. This account is also debited, to the extent of the balance therein, for deficiencies when such shares are reissued at less than cost.

Partnership—an association of two or more persons to carry on a business as co-owners.

482

Partnership agreement—also known as articles of copartnership (when in written form): the conditions or provisions accepted by all of the partners to serve as the basis for the formation and operation of the partnership.

Par value—an arbitrary amount assigned to each share of a given class of stock and printed on the stock certificate.

Preemptive right—the right of a stockholder to subscribe to a proportionate number of additional shares of the same class of stock he or she holds in any subsequent issuance of new shares.

Preferred stock—corporate capital stock which carries certain privileges or rights not carried by all outstanding shares of stock. Preferred stock may be:

Cumulative—the right to receive a basic dividend each year that accumulates if not declared.

Noncumulative—the right to receive a dividend expires if not declared.

Premium on capital stock—the amount by which the subscription price for shares exceeds the par value of the shares.

Redemption value—the price per share at which a corporation may call its preferred stock for retirement.

Reserve (retained earnings)—an account created as a voluntary or contractual restriction upon retained earnings and designed to inform readers of the existence of the restriction.

Retained earnings—that part of stockholders' equity resulting from the retention of earnings; the account to which the results of corporate activity are carried and to which dividends and certain items resulting from capital transactions are charged.

Single proprietorship—a business organization owned by one person.

Stated capital—an amount prescribed by law below which the stockholders' equity of a corporation cannot be reduced through the declaration of dividends or other distributions of corporate assets to stockholders in exchange for their shares of stock.

Stated value—an arbitrary amount assigned by the board of directors to each share of a given class of no-par-value stock.

Statement of partners' capital—a summary of the transactions affecting the capital account balance of each partner and in total for all partners. (For an example, see Illustration 10.4.)

Stock certificate—a printed or engraved document serving as evidence of ownership of shares of capital stock.

Stock dividend—a dividend payable in additional shares of the declaring corporation's stock.

Stock Dividends Payable—that stockholders' equity account credited for the par or stated value, or the value assigned by the board of directors in the case of shares without par or stated value, upon the recording of the declaration of a stock dividend.

Stock preferred as to assets—a stock which is entitled to receive assets in liquidation up to a stated amount before any assets may be distributed to the common stockholders.

Stock preferred as to dividends—a stock which is entitled to receive certain dividends prior to the payment of any dividends to common stockholders.

Stock split-up (stock split)—a distribution of additional shares of the issuing corporation's stock without consideration and for the purpose of effecting a material reduction in the market price per share of the outstanding stock.

Stock without par value (no-par-value stock)—capital stock without par value, to which a stated value may or may not be assigned.

Subscribed stock—stock for which subscriptions have been received, but for which stock certificates have not been issued.

Subscriber—a person contracting to acquire shares, usually in an original issuance of stock by a corporation.

Subscription—a contract to acquire shares of stock, usually in an original issuance of stock by a corporation.

Subscription price—the price at which a subscriber agrees to acquire shares of stock in a subscription agreement.

Treasury stock—shares of capital stock issued and returned to the issuing corporation which have not been formally canceled or retired and are available for reissue.

Uniform Partnership Act—a written law adopted in many states which is applicable in resolving contested matters between partners which are not covered in the partnership agreement.

483

Unlimited liability—a characteristic of single proprietorships and partnerships under which owners are liable for more than merely the amounts invested in the business, as their personal assets may also be taken to satisfy the claims of business creditors.

Continue with the Student Review Quiz below as a self-administered test of your understanding of the material presented in this chapter.

Student review quiz *chapter* 10

To develop a permanent record of your responses, you may answer them on the answer sheet provided in the *Work Papers* or on a separate piece of paper.

SECTION I

1 Which of the following is not a characteristic of a corporation?
a Limited liability of owners to creditors.
b Difficult transferability of ownership.
c Separate legal existence.
d Ability to enter into contracts.
e Right to sue (and to be sued) in its own name.

2 A common stockholder does not possess which of the following?
a The right to share in the earnings of the corporation when dividends are declared.
b The right to vote in the election of the board of directors of the corporation.
c The right of direct ownership of the corporate assets.
d The right to share proportionally in corporate assets in case of liquidation if such assets exceed the claims of creditors.
e The right to transfer his or her ownership in the corporation.

3 The par value of a share of common stock is:
a The amount for which the stock can be sold in the market.
b The amount at which, according to some state laws, the share must be first issued.
c The same thing as stated value.
d A changing amount which varies according to earnings and losses of the issuing corporation.
e Generally of little significance, being merely a nominal and arbitrary amount printed on a stock certificate.

4 P. B. Ames Company is organized with authorized capital stock of $100,000, consisting of 10,000 shares of $10 par value common stock. All of the capital stock is subscribed at par. In the following week, payment is received in full for 70 percent of the shares subscribed. No payment has been received from the persons who subscribed for the other 30 percent of the shares. Which of the following entries should be made to record receipt of the subscription payments?

a Cash 70,000
   Subscriptions Receivable—
    Common......... 70,000
b Cash 70,000
   Common Stock ... 70,000
  Common Stock
   Subscribed 70,000
   Subscriptions
    Receivable—
    Common......... 70,000
c Cash 70,000
   Common Stock ... 70,000
d Cash 70,000
   Subscriptions
    Receivable 70,000
  Common Stock
   Subscribed 70,000
   Common Stock ... 70,000
e Cash 70,000
  Common Stock
   Subscribed 70,000

5 The I. M. Hungry Restaurant Corporation issued 100 shares of common stock (par value $100 per share) to Alfred D. Hogland for real estate having a fair market value of $12,000 at the date of transfer. Which of the following is the required entry?

a Land 10,000
   Common Stock ... 10,000
b Land 12,000
   Common Stock ... 12,000

484

c Land 12,000
    Common Stock ... 10,000
    Paid-In Capital in
    Excess of Par
    Value 2,000

d Land 12,000
    Common Stock ... 10,000
    Paid-In Capital in
    Excess of
    Stated Value ... 2,000

e Land 12,000
    Common Stock ... 10,000
    Discount on
    Stock 2,000

6 Cobbler Furniture Company was incorporated with authorized capital of 100,000 shares of common stock without par value but with a stated value of $20 per share. The company issued 40,000 shares for cash at a price of $50 per share. Which of the following entries should be made?

a Cash............... 2,000,000
    Common
    Stock 800,000
    Paid-In Capital in Excess of
    Stated
    Value..... 1,200,000

b Cash............... 2,000,000
    Common
    Stock 2,000,000

c Cash............... 2,000,000
    Common
    Stock 800,000
    Paid-In Capital in Excess of
    Par
    Value..... 1,200,000

d Subscriptions
    Receivable—
    Common 2,000,000
    Common
    Stock 800,000

    Paid-In
    Capital in
    Excess of
    Stated
    Value..... 1,200,000

e Subscriptions
    Receivable—
    Common 2,000,000
    Common
    Stock 800,000
    Paid-In Capital in Excess of
    Par
    Value..... 1,200,000

7 Tiger Machine Company has outstanding 8,000 shares of 6 percent $100 par value preferred stock (noncumulative) and 10,000 shares of $100 par value common stock. All the shares were issued at $110. Retained earnings are $95,000. No dividends were paid last year. What amount of dividends are the preferred stockholders entitled to at the end of the current year before payment of any dividends to common stockholders?
a $52,800.
b $48,000.
c $77,000.
d $95,000.
e $96,000.

8 Hammer Plumbingware Company has outstanding 9,000 shares of 5 percent, $100 par value, cumulative preferred stock and 100,000 shares of $10 par value common. Retained earnings are $110,000. No dividends were paid last year. Retained earnings available at the end of the current year for dividends on the common stock are:
a None.
b $10,000.
c $18,000.
d $20,000.
e $65,000.

SECTION II

9 An appropriation of retained earnings to a retained earnings reserve account—
a Is used to limit the amount of retained earnings available for dividends.
b Indicates amounts which will be needed to meet contingencies, but has no limiting effect on dividends.
c May be used only when a legal restriction on retained earnings is imposed by creditors.

485

d Results in the building up of a fund of assets to meet specific needs.

e Does none of the above.

10 When the total stockholders' equity is smaller than the amount of paid-in capital, this deficiency is called—

a A net loss.

b A dividend.

c A liability.

d A deficit.

e None of the above.

11 On July 6, 1979, the board of directors of the T. P. Engine Corporation declared a cash dividend of $2 per share on 20,000 shares of outstanding common stock, payable September 1, 1979, to stockholders of record on August 10, 1979. The entry to record the declaration of this dividend is:

a Retained Earnings 40,000
    Cash   40,000

b Retained Earnings...... 40,000
    Dividends
        Payable   40,000

c Dividends Payable..... 40,000
    Cash   40,000

d Retained Earnings 40,000
    Capital Stock......   40,000

e Dividends 40,000
    Dividends
        Payable   40,000

f Either (**b**) or (**e**).

12 Which of the following statements regarding a dividend in common stock to common stockholders is true?

a A stock dividend reduces total corporate capital.

b A stock dividend alters the individual stockholders' percentage of ownership in the corporation.

c A stock dividend has the effect of decreasing the book value per share of that class of stock.

d Stock Dividends Payable is a current liability account.

e None of the above is true.

13 ABC Corporation has outstanding 10,000 shares of common stock, par value $100 per share. The board of directors declares a 10 percent stock dividend on the common stock. The market price of the stock on the date the dividend is declared is $130 per share. The entry to record the declaration of the stock dividend is:

a Retained Earnings... 130,000
    Stock
      Dividends
      Payable—
      Common   130,000

b Retained Earnings... 100,000
    Stock
      Dividends
      Payable—
      Common   100,000

c Retained Earnings... 130,000
    Stock
      Dividends
      Payable—
      Common   100,000
    Paid-In Capital
     —Stock
     Dividend   30,000

d Retained Earnings... 100,000
    Cash..............   100,000

e Retained Earnings... 130,000
    Paid-In Capital
     —Stock
     Dividend   130,000

14 The XYZ Corporation acquired 200 shares of its own $10 par common stock for $2,400 ($12 per share). All of the stock had been previously issued at par. Three weeks later it reissued all 200 of the treasury shares at $11 per share. The entry to record reissuance of these shares, assuming no previous transactions in treasury stock, is:

a Cash.......................... 2,200
    Treasury Stock—
      Common   2,200

b Cash.......................... 2,200
    Treasury Stock—
      Common   2,000
    Paid-In Capital—
      Treasury Stock
      Transactions   200

c Cash.......................... 2,200
    Paid-In Capital—
      Treasury Stock
      Transactions   200
    Treasury Stock—
      Common   2,400

d Cash.......................... 2,200
    Paid-In Capital—
      Treasury Stock
      Transactions   100
    Treasury Stock—
      Common   2,300

e None of the above.

15 In the preparation of a statement of financial position, which of the following statements is true?

a No reference need be made to donated treasury stock, since the acquisition of such stock does not restrict retained earnings.

b Treasury shares and unissued shares can be reported as a total of shares not outstanding with no distinguishing comments.

c Treasury shares should be shown as a deduction, at cost, from the total paid-in capital of the company.

d Treasury shares should be shown as a deduction, at cost, from the total paid-in capital plus retained earnings, and a restriction on retained earnings caused by their acquisition must also be stated.

e Treasury shares should be shown as a deduction, at cost, from retained earnings, since their acquisition usually results in a restriction on retained earnings.

16 The following is the stockholders' equity section of a statement of financial position dated June 30, 1979. (No dividends have been declared or paid in the first half of 1979.)

Stockholders' Equity

Paid-In Capital:

Capital stock—preferred, 5%, $100 par value; authorized and issued, 1,000 shares of which 200 are held in treasury......................	$100,000
Capital stock—common, $10 par value; authorized, 100,000 shares, issued, 60,000 shares of which 500 are held in treasury, including 100 shares donated..................	600,000
Total Paid-In Capital	$700,000
Retained earnings (restricted to the extent of cost of 200 shares of preferred treasury stock, $21,000, and 400 shares of common treasury, $18,000)	200,000
Total.........................	$900,000
Less: Cost of treasury stock: preferred (200 shares), $21,000; common (500 shares, 100 received by donation), $18,000...	39,000
Total Stockholders' Equity	$861,000

Which of the following statements is true?

a A dividend declared on June 30, 1979, of $1 per share on the common stock would involve a total amount of $60,000.

b The cost of the common treasury stock acquired by purchase is $16 per share.

c The corporation has 40,500 shares of common stock (40,000 shares unissued and 500 shares in treasury) available for issuance. It is free to issue these shares to whomever it wishes, since 500 of the shares have previously been outstanding and the stockholders have authorized the issuance of the other 40,000 shares.

d The restriction upon retained earnings by the acquisition of common stock is limited to the cost of the 400 shares acquired by purchase.

e All of the above statements are true.

17 (**based on the Appendix**) Which of the following accounts would appear in the equity section of the annual statement of financial position of a single proprietorship?

a Jack Lee, Drawing.

b Jack Lee, Current.

c Jack Lee, Capital.

d Jack Lee, Capital Stock.

e (b) and (c).

f (a) and (c).

18 (**based on the Appendix**) The partnership agreement between Reeves and Hayes states that earnings and losses are to be divided in the ratio of 4:5 (Reeves and Hayes, respectively). Net earnings for 1979 are $27,000. The entry needed to record the division of earnings for 1979 is:

a

Expense and Revenue Summary	27,000	
Reeves, Drawing...		13,500
Hayes, Drawing...		13,500

b

Expense and Revenue Summary	27,000	
Reeves, Drawing...		12,000
Hayes, Drawing...		15,000

c

Expense and Revenue Summary	27,000	
Reeves, Drawing...		10,800
Hayes, Drawing...		16,200

d

Expense and Revenue Summary	27,000	
Reeves, Drawing...		9,000
Hayes, Drawing...		18,000

e Reeves, Drawing....... 12,000
   Hayes, Drawing........ 15,000
     Expense and
       Revenue
         Summary........   27,000

Now compare your answers with the correct answers and explanations on page 722.

Questions *chapter* 10

SECTION I

1 What are the basic rights associated with a share of capital stock if there is only one class of stock outstanding?

2 What are the differences between par value stock and stock with no par value?

3 Explain the nature of the Subscriptions Receivable account. How should it be classified in the statement of finan-cial position? On what occasions is it debited? Credited?

4 Cite the major advantages of the corporate form of business organization and indicate why each is considered an advantage.

5 With reference to preferred stock, what is the meaning of the terms cumulative and noncumulative?

SECTION II

6 How should a declared but unpaid cash dividend be shown in a statement of financial position? A declared but unissued stock dividend?

7 Why is a dividend consisting of the distribution of additional shares of the common stock of the declaring corporation not considered earnings to the recipient stockholders?

8 What is the effect of each of the following on the total stockholders' equity of a corporation: (a) declaration of a cash dividend; (b) payment of a cash dividend already declared; (c) declaration of a stock dividend; and (d) issuance of a stock dividend already declared?

9 The following dates are associated with a cash dividend of $50,000: July 15, July 31, and August 15. Identify each of the three dates and give the journal entry required on each, if any.

10 What is the purpose underlying the statutes which provide for restriction of retained earnings in the amount of the cost of treasury stock? Are such statutes for the benefit of stockholders, management, or creditors?

11 On May 10, Shiner sold his capital stock in the Tanner Corporation directly to Bright for $10,000 endorsing his stock certificate and giving it to Bright. Bright placed the stock certificate in his safe. On May 8 the board of directors of the Tanner Corporation declared a dividend, payable on June 5 to stockholders of record on May 17. On May 30, Bright sent the stock certificate to the Tanner Corporation for transfer. Who received the dividend? Why?

12 What is the purpose of a retained earnings reserve?

13 (based on the Appendix) Contrast briefly the differences in accounting for capital, earnings and losses, and distributions of earnings in a single proprietorship, a partnership, and a corporation.

14 (based on the Appendix) Richards is currently operating a small printing shop. He is considering forming a partnership with an employee whom he considers an excellent worker and supervisor and with whom it is easy to associate. Prepare a brief list of the advantages and disadvantages to Richards of the potential partnership.

Measurement and reporting of owners' equity

Exercises *chapter* 10

2)(b) issued at 103
     PREFERRED STOCK 100,000
     PIC IN excess of PV 3,000
     RE   2000
              CASH   105,000

SECTION I

1 Blarney Corporation has 500 shares of $100 par value convertible preferred stock outstanding which was issued at par value. Each share is convertible into 3.5 shares of $10 stated value common stock. Give the entry to record the conversion of all 500 shares of preferred.

2 Richie Company called all of its 1,000 shares of outstanding $100 par value preferred stock. The stock was cumulative, entitled to $100 per share plus cumulative dividends in liquidation, and callable at $105. Give the entry to record the calling of the preferred stock, assuming it was originally issued at par value. Give the

entry required if the stock had originally been issued at $103. In each case assume there are no unpaid cumulative dividends.

3 Hilton Company has 3,000 shares of cumulative preferred stock with a $5 annual dividend per share and 8,000 shares of common stock without par value outstanding. No dividends were paid in 1977 or 1978. At the beginning of 1979 the company had a deficit of $5,000. During 1979 it had net earnings of $84,000. If a dividend of $3 per share is declared on the common stock, what is the ending balance in retained earnings?

1) PREFERRED STOCK   50,000
      COMMON STOCK   17,500
      PIC in excess of SV-CS   32,500

2) (a) issued at par value
      PREFERRED STOCK   100,000
      R.E,   5,000
            CASH   105,000

SECTION II

4 Baskin Company received 50 shares of its $20 stated value common stock on December 1, 1979, as a donation from a stockholder. On December 15, 1979, it issued the stock for $3,000 cash. Give the journal entry or entries necessary for these transactions.

5 The statement of financial position of the A Company contains the following:

Reserve for contingencies...... $200,000

a Give the journal entry made to create this account.
b Explain the reason for its existence and its manner of presentation in the statement of financial position.

6 The stockholders' equity section of X Company's statement of financial position on December 31, 1979, shows 100,000 shares of authorized and issued $10 stated value common stock, of which 10,000 shares are held in the treasury. On this date, the board of directors declares a cash dividend of $2 per share payable on January 21, 1980, to stockholders of record on January 10. Give dated journal entries for the above.

7 Johns Company has outstanding 200,000 shares of common stock without

par or stated value which were issued at an average price of $10 per share. Retained earnings total $400,000. The current market price of the common stock is $20 per share. Total authorized stock consists of 500,000 shares.
a Give the required journal entry to record the declaration of a 10 percent stock dividend.
b If, alternatively, the company declared a 30 percent stock dividend, what additional information would you need before making a journal entry to record the dividend?

8 (**based on the Appendix**) Carter, Ford, and Rusk are partners. In 1979 net earnings are $80,000. The earnings and loss ratio is 50–30–20, respectively. Give the entries to record the division of earnings. Also, give the entries to close the drawing accounts assuming that drawings were $20,000, $12,000, and $10,000, respectively.

9 (**based on the Appendix**) Stevens, Hill, and Keller are partners. In 1979 the partnership incurred a net loss of $25,000. The earnings and loss ratio is 40–10–50, respectively. How will the partners share the $25,000 loss?

Problems, Series A *chapter* 10

SECTION I

10-1-A

On July 1, 1979, the Whitten Company was authorized to issue 20,000 shares of $20 par value common stock. On July 7, subscriptions for 2,000 shares at $30 per share were received. The subscription contract required a 10 percent immediate payment, with the remainder due on July 31. No stock certificates were to be issued until the subscriptions were paid in full.

Required:

a Present the entries to record all transactions during July 1979. Subscriptions were collected when due.
b Present the July 1979 entries assuming the stock is without par value.
c Present the entries for July 7, 1979, if the subscriptions for the stock without par value were accompanied with cash payment in full and the stock was issued immediately.

10-2-A

On July 3, 1979, the Gibbs Company was authorized to issue 10,000 shares of common stock. On July 10 subscriptions were received from the general public for 6,000 shares at $9 per share, with one half of the subscription price paid in cash immediately. The balance is due August 10, 1979.

Required:

a Prepare the statement of financial position of the Gibbs Company as of the close of July 10, 1979, assuming the authorized stock has a $5 par value.
b Repeat (a) assuming the stock is without par value but is to have a $8 stated value.
c Repeat (a) assuming the stock is without par or stated value.

10-3-A

On July 1, 1979, the Laurie Corporation received authorization to issue 50,000 shares of common stock without par value. On that date subscriptions were received from the general public for 14,000 shares at $15 per share. The following transactions occurred during the remainder of the month of July:

July 10 Received subscriptions for another 6,000 shares at $16 per share and collected one third of each of the July 1 subscriptions for 14,000 shares.
11 Issued 4,000 shares in exchange for a tract of land.
20 Collected the balance of each of the July 1 subscriptions and issued the shares. Also, collected one half of each of the July 10 subscriptions.
30 Collected the balance of each of the July 10 subscriptions and issued the shares.

Required:

a   Assume that on September 1, 1979, the board of directors placed a stated value of $10 per share on the common stock. Present journal entries to record all of the July transactions and the entry needed on September 1.

b   Prepare journal entries to record all of the July transactions assuming that the stock issued was $10 par value stock.

10–4–A

Part 1. On January 1, 1975, the retained earnings of the Carroll Company were $140,000. Net earnings for the succeeding five years were as follows:

1975.....................	$97,000
1976.....................	61,000
1977.....................	4,000
1978.....................	22,000
1979.....................	91,000

The outstanding capital stock of the corporation consisted of 2,000 shares of $4 preferred stock with a par value of $100 per share, and 8,000 shares of common stock without par value having a stated value of $50 per share. No dividends were in arrears as of January 1, 1975.

Required:

Prepare schedules showing how the net earnings for the above five years were distributed to the two classes of stock if in each of the years the entire current earnings (and only these earnings) were distributed as dividends and the preferred stock was:

a   Cumulative.
b   Noncumulative.

Part 2. In 1980 the board of directors and stockholders decided to dissolve the Carroll Company. All of its assets were sold, its liabilities were liquidated, and $480,000 remained for distribution to stockholders. No dividends were in arrears, and current dividends had been paid.

Required:

Prepare short schedules showing how the cash was distributed to the stockholders if:

a   The preferred stock were preferred as to assets and entitled to $105 in liquidation.
b   The preferred stock were not preferred as to assets.

SECTION II

10–5–A

The stockholders' equity of the Finlay Company on June 30, 1979, consists solely of capital stock of $600,000 and retained earnings of $430,000. The stock is $100 par value common stock, with 10,000 shares authorized and 6,000 issued and outstanding.

The board of directors on June 30, 1979, declares a 10 percent cash dividend and a 10 percent stock dividend, both payable on July 31 to stockholders of record on July 15. The cash dividend applies only to the shares outstanding prior to the stock dividend. The market price of the stock on June 30 is $200 per share.

Required:

Present journal entries to record the declaration of both dividends, the payment of the cash dividend, and the issuance of the stock dividend.

10–6–A

Following are selected transactions of the Warren Corporation:

1974

Dec. 31   By action of the board of directors, $40,000 of retained earnings was appropriated to provide for future expansion of the company's main building.
(On the last day of each of the four succeeding years the same action was taken. You need not make entries for these four years.)

1979

Jan.   3   Obtained, at a cost of $400, a building permit to construct a new wing on the main plant building.

July   30   Paid $212,000 to the Able Construction Company for completion of the new wing.

Aug.   4   The board of directors authorized the release of the sum appropriated for expansion of the plant building.

         4   The board of directors declared a 10 percent common stock dividend on the 25,000 shares of $40 par value common stock outstanding. The market price on this date was $44 per share.

Required:

Present journal entries to record all of the above transactions.

10–7–A

The trial balance of the Wells Corporation at December 31, 1979, contains the following account balances:

Bonds payable, 7%, due May 1, 1981	$1,000,000
Common stock without par value, stated value $10; 200,000 shares authorized, issued, and outstanding	2,000,000
Retained earnings, unappropriated	228,000
Dividends payable in cash declared December 15 on preferred stock	6,000
Reserve for pending litigation	280,000
Preferred stock, 6%, par value $100; 2,000 shares authorized, issued, and outstanding	200,000
Paid-in capital in excess of par value — preferred	4,000

Required:

Present in good form the stockholders' equity section of the statement of financial position.

10–8–A

The stockholders' equity section of Adam Company's December 31, 1978, statement of financial position is:

Paid-In Capital:		
Preferred stock: 5%, $100 par value; authorized, 5,000 shares, issued and outstanding 2,500 shares..		$250,000
Common stock without par or stated value; authorized, 50,000 shares, issued, 25,000 shares of which 500 are held in treasury		375,000
Paid-in capital in excess of par – preferred		5,000
Total Paid-In Capital		$630,000
Retained Earnings:		
Appropriated:		
Reserve for plant expansion...	$ 25,000	
Unappropriated (restricted as to dividends to the extent of $10,000, the cost of the treasury stock held)...	210,000	
Total Retained Earnings...		235,000
		$865,000
Less: Treasury stock, common at cost (500 shares).......................		10,000
Total Stockholders' Equity...		$855,000

Following are selected transactions occurring in 1979:

Jan. 13 Subscriptions are received for 550 shares of previously unissued common stock at $22.

Feb. 4 A plot of land is accepted as payment in full for 500 shares of common, and the stock is issued. Closing market price on this date of the common is $21 per share.

Mar. 24 All of the treasury stock is reissued at $24.50.

June 22 All stock subscriptions are collected in full, and the shares issued.

  23 The regular semiannual dividend on the preferred stock is declared.

  30 The preferred dividend is paid.

July 3 A 10 percent stock dividend is declared on the common stock. Market price on this date is $25.

  18 The stock dividend shares are issued.

Oct. 4 The company acquires 105 shares of its common stock at $24.

Dec. 18 The regular semiannual dividend on the preferred and a $0.40 per share dividend on the common are declared.

  31 Both dividends are paid.

  31 An additional appropriation of retained earnings of $5,000 for plant expansion is authorized.

Required:

a Prepare journal entries to record the 1979 transactions.

b Prepare a statement of retained earnings (showing the unappropriated balance) for the year 1979. The net earnings for the year were $65,125.

c Prepare the stockholders' equity section of the December 31, 1979, statement of financial position.

10-9-A (based on the Appendix)

DAVID LANDON
Trial Balance
December 31, 1979

	Debits	Credits
Cash	$ 29,800	
Accounts receivable	56,000	
Inventory, January 1	22,000	
Land	130,000	
Accounts payable		$ 50,000
David Landon, capital		169,000
David Landon, drawing	15,000	
Sales		210,000
Purchases	75,000	
Purchase returns		4,000
Rent expense	26,000	
Delivery expense	29,000	
Store expense	42,000	
Other expense	8,200	
	$433,000	$433,000

The inventory at December 31, 1979, is $25,000.

Required:

a Prepare necessary adjusting and closing entries at the year-end.
b Prepare an earnings statement for the year.
c Prepare a statement of financial position at the year-end.

10-10-A (based on the Appendix)

Slim and Fat own and operate a partnership. The balances in the capital accounts of Slim and Fat at January 1, 1979, are $25,000 and $32,000, respectively. These balances did not change during the year. Net earnings for the year ended December 31, 1979, amount to $70,000 (the balance in the Expense and Revenue Summary account). The partners' drawing accounts have the following balances before closing entries are made:

Slim, drawing	$20,000
Fat, drawing	11,000

Slim and Fat share earnings and losses in the ratio of 60–40.

Required:

a Prepare journal entries to close the Expense and Revenue Summary and drawing accounts.
b Prepare a statement of partners' capital for the year ended December 31, 1979.

10–11–A (based on the Appendix)

SALT AND PEPPER
Trial Balance
December 31, 1979

	Debits	Credits
Cash	$ 20,500	
Accounts receivable	30,000	
Allowance for doubtful accounts		$ 500
Inventory	18,500	
Equipment	35,000	
Allowance for depreciation of equipment		8,500
Unexpired insurance	455	
Accounts payable		25,500
Salt, capital		18,500
Pepper, capital		36,500
Salt, drawing	500	
Pepper, drawing	6,000	
Sales		275,000
Purchases	220,000	
Selling expenses	20,000	
Administrative expenses	16,500	
Other revenue		2,955
	$367,455	$367,455

The articles of copartnership for Salt and Pepper provide for the distribution of earnings and losses in the following manner:

a. Each partner is allowed 6 percent interest per year on his capital investment as of the beginning of the year.
b. Salt is allowed a salary of $15,000 and Pepper a salary of $18,000 per year as a distribution of earnings.
c. The remaining earnings and losses are divided equally.

Your analysis of the books and records discloses the following data that require your consideration: the ending inventory is $15,500; a total of $1,750 is to be added to the allowance for doubtful accounts; depreciation on the equipment should be recorded at 10 percent of cost. Salt's capital account includes a credit for $2,000 invested on July 15 of the current year. Unexpired insurance at December 31, 1979, is $40.

Required:

You are to prepare the following for the partnership:
a   Adjusting and closing journal entries.
b   An earnings statement for the year.
c   A statement of partners' capital for the year.

Problems, Series B *chapter* 10

SECTION I

10–1–B

In the charter granted January 2, 1979, the Skelton Corporation was authorized to issue 1,000 shares of common stock without par value. On January 5 subscriptions for 500   495 shares at $52 per share were received, and on May 1 an additional 300 shares were subscribed at $70 per share. Subscription agreements called for immediate payment of one half of each subscription, with the remainder due on the first day of the following month. All subscriptions were collected in accordance with the agreements.

Required:

a Present the entries to record all the transactions of January through May 1979, assuming no stock was issued until the subscriptions were paid in full.

b Present the May 31, 1979, statement of financial position, assuming there were no transactions other than those described above.

10-2-B

On January 2, 1978, the date the Jarrett Company received its charter, it issued all of its authorized 2,000 shares of preferred stock without par value at $104 and all of its 8,000 authorized shares of common stock without par value but with a stated value of $1 at $40 per share. The preferred stock had a stated value of $5 per share, was entitled to a basic cumulative preference dividend of $6 per share, was callable at $106 beginning in 1980, and was entitled to $100 per share plus cumulative dividends in the event of liquidation.

On December 31, 1979, the end of the second year of operations, retained earnings were $60,000. No dividends had been declared or paid on either class of stock in 1978 or 1979.

Required:

a Prepare the stockholders' equity section of the Jarrett Company's December 31, 1979, statement of financial position.

b If $50,000 of dividends were declared on December 31, 1979, compute the amount payable to each class of stock.

10-3-B

McCloud, Inc., was authorized to issue 2,000 shares of $2.50 cumulative preferred stock, par value $50, and 20,000 shares of common stock, par value $25.

McCLOUD, INC.
Post-Closing Account Balances
December 31, 1979

Paid-in capital in excess of par—preferred..	$ 5,000
Accounts payable	30,000
Inventory	90,000
Unexpired insurance	3,000
Common stock subscribed, 2,000 shares..	50,000
Subscriptions receivable—common	50,000
Building and equipment...	130,000
Notes payable, due June 30, 1980	15,000
Cash...	70,000
Allowance for depreciation...	30,000
Preferred stock, $50 par value; 2,000 shares authorized	100,000
Paid-in capital in excess of par—common	12,000
Common stock, $25 par value; 20,000 shares authorized................................	200,000
Accounts receivable	142,000
Retained earnings	?

Required:

From the above list of account balances, prepare the December 31, 1979, statement of financial position in good form.

10-4-B

Ray Company, on May 1, 1979, received a charter which authorized it to issue:

a. 4,000 shares of preferred stock without par value to which a stated value of $3 per share was assigned. The stock was entitled to a cumulative dividend of $2.40, convertible into two shares of common stock, callable at $52, and entitled to $50 per share in liquidation.

b. 1,000 shares of $100 par value, $5 cumulative preferred stock which is callable at $125 and entitled to $110 in liquidation.

c. 100,000 shares of common stock without par value to which a stated value of $10 was assigned.

Transactions:

May 1 All of the $2.40 convertible preferred was subscribed for and issued at $51 per share, cash.

2 All of the $5 cumulative preferred was exchanged for inventory, land, and buildings valued at $28,000, $35,000, and $60,000, respectively.

2 Subscriptions were received for 60,000 shares of common at $20 per share, with 20 percent of the subscription price paid immediately in cash.

31 All of the subscriptions to the common stock were collected and the shares issued.

Required:

a Prepare journal entries for the above transactions.

b Assume that retained earnings were $80,000. Prepare the stockholders' equity section of the May 31, 1979, statement of financial position.

c On June 30, 1983, the company called and retired all of the $5 cumulative preferred stock and all of the $2.40 convertible preferred stock was converted into common stock. Give the required journal entries, assuming no cumulative dividends were in arrears.

<h2 style="text-align:center">SECTION II</h2>

10-5-B

Following are selected transactions of the Ashe Corporation.

1974

Dec. 31 The board of directors authorized appropriation of $300,000 of retained earnings to provide for the future acquisition of a new plant site and the construction of a new building.

(On the last day of the four succeeding years the same action was taken. You need not make entries for these four years.)

1977

Jan. 2 Purchased a new plant site for cash, $125,000.

Mar. 29 Entered into a contract for construction of a new building, payment to be made within 30 days following completion.

1979

Feb. 10 Following final inspection and approval of the new building, the Plains Construction Company was paid in full, $1,380,000.

Mar. 10 The board of directors authorized release of the reserve appropriated for the plant site and building.

Apr. 2 A 10 percent stock dividend on the 100,000 shares of $100 par value common stock outstanding was declared. The market price on this date was $110 per share.

Required:

Present journal entries for all of the above transactions.

10-6-B

Following are selected data and accounts of the Mitchell Corporation at December 31, 1979:

Net earnings for the year	$270,000
Dividends declared on preferred stock	40,000
Retained earnings appropriated for future plant expansion during the year	100,000
Dividends received on stock investments	14,000
Excess over stated value received for shares of common stock issued during the year	64,000
Dividends declared on common stock	36,000
Retained earnings, January 1, unappropriated	410,000
Directors ordered balance in "Reserve for bond sinking fund," related to bond issue retired on March 31, 1979, returned to unappropriated retained earnings	200,000

Required:

Prepare a statement of retained earnings (showing the unappropriated balance) for the year 1979.

10–7–B

The only stockholders' equity items of the Kushner Company at June 30, 1979, are:

Common stock, $25 par; 4,000 shares authorized, 2,000 shares issued and outstanding...	$ 50,000
Paid-in capital in excess of par value...	25,000
Retained earnings	40,000
Total Stockholders' Equity...	$115,000

On August 4, a 5 percent cash dividend was declared, payable September 3. On November 16, a 10 percent stock dividend was declared. The shares were issued on December 1. The market value of the common stock on November 16 was $42 per share and on December 1, $44.

Required:

Present journal entries for the above transactions.

10–8–B

The stockholders' equity of the A. Bonetti Company on December 31, 1978, consisted of 1,000 authorized and outstanding shares of $7 cumulative preferred stock, par value $10 per share, which were originally issued at $105 per share; 100,000 shares authorized and outstanding of $5 stated value common stock which were originally issued at $5; and retained earnings of $100,000. Following are selected transactions and other data relating to 1979:

1. The company acquired 2,000 shares of its common stock at $15.
2. One thousand of the treasury shares were reissued at $13.
3. The first quarter's dividend of $1.75 per share was declared and paid on the preferred stock. No other dividends were declared or paid during 1979.

The company suffered a net loss of $20,000 for the year 1979.

Required:

a Prepare journal entries for the numbered transactions above.
b Prepare the stockholders' equity section of the December 31, 1979, statement of financial position.

10–9–B (based on the Appendix)

MICHAEL REED
Trial Balance
December 31, 1979

	Debits	Credits
Cash...	$ 12,500	
Accounts receivable	16,800	
Inventory, January 1	8,900	
Accounts payable..........................		$ 14,500
Michael Reed, capital		12,500
Michael Reed, drawing	8,000	
Sales...		100,000
Purchases...................................	50,000	
Purchase returns...........................		1,000
Rent expense	15,000	
Delivery expense	6,400	
Store expense..............................	10,400	
	$128,000	$128,000

The inventory at December 31, 1979, is $10,200.

Required:

a Prepare necessary adjusting and closing entries at year-end.
b Prepare an earnings statement for the year.
c Prepare a statement of financial position at the year-end.

10–10–B (based on the Appendix)

He and She own and operate a partnership. The balances in the capital accounts of He and She at January 1, 1979, are $15,000 and $18,000, respectively. He invested $20,000 on March 1, 1979. She invested an additional $10,000 on March 1, 1979. The net loss for the year ended December 31, 1979, amounts to $8,000 (the debit balance in the Expense and Revenue Summary account.) The partners' drawing accounts have the following balances before closing entries are made:

He, drawing........................	$6,000
She, drawing......................	7,000

He and She share earnings and losses equally.

Required:

a Prepare journal entries to close the Expense and Revenue Summary account and the drawing accounts.
b Prepare a statement of partners' capital for the year ended December 31, 1979.

10–11–B (based on the Appendix)

Pickle and Onion are partners operating a retail store. Their partnership agreement calls for annual salaries of $12,000 to Pickle and $16,000 to Onion, interest at 6 percent on average capital account balances throughout the year if drawings for the year do not exceed salaries allowed, and the balance of the earnings to be shared equally. Their June 30, 1979, trial balance follows:

	Debits	Credits
Cash	$ 40,400	
Accounts receivable	64,000	
Inventory, July 1, 1978	28,800	
Accounts payable		$ 40,800
Notes payable, Onion		20,000
Pickle, capital		28,000
Onion, capital		20,000
Pickle, drawing	8,000	
Onion, drawing	10,000	
Sales		428,000
Purchases	272,000	
Purchase returns		4,000
Employee salaries and wages	12,000	
Rent expense	52,000	
Delivery expense	16,800	
Store expense	36,800	
	$540,800	$540,800

The $20,000 note payable to Onion is a 90-day note dated May 1, 1979, and calls for interest at 6 percent per year. Interest on this note is an expense of the business rather than a means of sharing earnings and losses. The inventory at June 30, 1979, is $33,200. The only change in the capital accounts during the year was an additional investment by Pickle of $8,000 on January 1.

Required:

a   The necessary adjusting and closing entries.
b   An earnings statement for the year ended June 30, 1979.
c   A statement of partners' capital accounts for the year.
d   A statement of financial position at the end of the year.

part III

ANALYSIS OF RESULTS

11

Analysis and interpretation of financial statements*

Learning objectives

Study of the material in this chapter is designed to achieve a number of learning objectives:

1. An understanding of the nature and purposes of comparative financial statements.

2. The ability to apply the basic analytical techniques used with comparative statements including the use of percentages in the analysis of financial statements.

3. A knowledge of the comparisons, ratios, and computations used by the financial analyst. An understanding of the significance of different comparisons and ratios to different users of financial statements is of primary importance.

4. Recognition of the limitations of financial analysis.

5. An understanding of the effect of changes in the general purchasing power of the dollar on the comparability of financial statements.

* This chapter has been divided into two reading sections to offer flexibility in assigning the chapter. All end of chapter questions, exercises, and problems have been identified as to the reading section to which they relate.

Frame 1¹¹

Objectives of financial statements

Financial statements are issued to communicate useful financial information to interested parties. If this objective is not met, the statements serve no purpose. But careful analyses and interpretations made by the user of financial statements will often clarify and add to their usefulness and thus aid communication. Thus, it is essential that the users of statements become skilled in the use of available techniques for analyzing financial statements. Several of these analytical techniques are presented in this chapter.

Managers, employees, current and prospective investors, current and prospective creditors, business counselors, and executives of trade associations are among those who at one time or another will be interested in the financial statements of a specific firm. For example, a commercial bank loan officer will decide whether or not to grant a loan to a firm after the firm's financial statements have been analyzed. The loan officer will pay close attention to the firm's ability to pay its debts. A current stockholder may decide to sell his or her stock in the company after analyzing the company's financial statements and comparing its earnings history with that of another firm.

The purpose of financial statement analysis is to establish and present the relationships and trends found in the data contained in financial statements. Based upon this analysis, the users will draw their own conclusions and act accordingly.

Comparative financial statements

Nature and purpose

Comparative financial statements present the statements of the same firm for two or more accounting periods so that changes and trends can be analyzed. The usefulness of financial statements is greatly improved when they are so presented. The nature of, and trends in, changes which affect a firm can be seen far more clearly in comparative statements than in the statements for a single period.

To illustrate, a statement of financial position dated December 31, 1980, shows an accounts receivable balance of $500,000. That information by itself tells the statement user only that there is a receivables balance and that it equals $500,000. Suppose the user is also told that on December 31, 1979, the receivables balance was $250,000 and that the balance increased by $250,000 during 1980 — an increase of 100 percent. Then, the balance of $500,000 on December 31, 1980, becomes more meaningful. But neither statement indicates what the balance ought to be.

Methods of comparison—illustrated

Comparisons of financial statement data can be expressed as:

1. Absolute increases and decreases for an item from one period to the next or from a base period which is more than one period removed.
2. Percentage increases and decreases for an item from one period to the next or from a base period which is more than one period removed.
3. Percentages of an aggregate total.
4. Trend percentages.
5. Ratios.

The first three of these methods have been used in preparing the following comparative financial statements which will serve as a basis for the first analyses presented in this chapter. Trend percentages are then discussed. Finally, various ratios are presented and illustrated.

The statements presented are:

Exhibit A: Comparative statements of financial position, Illustration 11.1.

Exhibit B: Comparative statements of earnings and retained earnings, Illustration 11.2.

Schedule B–1: Comparative schedules of selling and administrative expenses, Illustration 11.3.

Schedule B–2: Comparative schedules of other expenses and revenues, Illustration 11.4.

These statements are presented here where they will be easy to find for reference while studying this chapter. The "Other expenses" and "Other revenues" categories include earnings statement items which are not directly related to the regular operations of the business.

The comparative statements of financial position of the Knight Corporation, Illustration 11.1, set forth certain relationships. Management can establish these relationships by means of analysis and use them as guidelines when it makes business decisions. For example, the comparative statements of financial position in Illustration 11.1 show (among other items):

1. The dollar amount of each asset, liability, and stockholders' equity item and the total of each class of assets, liabilities, and stockholders' equity on December 31, 1979, and on December 31, 1980.
2. The increase or decrease in dollar amounts of each of the items listed in (1) above, by comparison of December 31, 1980, balances with those of December 31, 1979. For example, it is shown that on December 31, 1980, as compared with December 31, 1979:
   a. Current assets have increased $37,121, while current liabilities have increased $17,280. This increase in the Knight Corporation's working capital (current assets less current liabilities) could have resulted from (1) retention of earnings, (2) con-

Illustration 11.1

THE KNIGHT CORPORATION						
Comparative Statements of Financial Position						
December 31, 1979 and 1980						*Exhibi*

	December 31		*Increase or decrease** *1980 over 1979*		*Percentage of total ass* *December 31*	
	1980	*1979*	**Dollars**	**Percentage**	*1980*	*1979*
Assets						
Current Assets:						
Cash............................	$ 80,215	$ 54,980	$25,235	45.9	12.6	10.0
Accounts receivable, net.....	124,171	132,550	8,379*	6.3*	19.5	24.0
Notes receivable................	55,000	50,000	5,000	10.0	8.7	9.1
Inventories	110,825	94,500	16,325	17.3	17.4	17.1
Prepaid expenses..............	3,640	4,700	1,060*	22.6*	.6	.9
Total Current Assets	$373,851	$336,730	$37,121	11.0	58.9ᴿ	61.1
Property, Plant, and Equipment:						
Land	$ 21,000	$ 21,000	–0–	–0–	3.3	3.8
Building	205,000	160,000	$45,000	28.1	32.3	29.0
Less: Allowance for depreciation...............	(27,040)	(22,355)	(4,685)	21.0	(4.3)	(4.1)
Furniture and fixtures........	83,200	69,810	13,390	19.2	13.1	12.7
Less: Allowance for depreciation...............	(20,800)	(14,100)	(6,700)	47.5	(3.3)	(2.5)
Total Plant Assets ...	$261,360	$214,355	$47,005	21.9	41.1	38.9
Total Assets	$635,211	$551,085	$84,126	15.3	100.0	100.0
Liabilities and Stockholders' Equity						
Current Liabilities:						
Accounts payable	$ 70,310	$ 64,560	$ 5,750	8.9	11.1	11.7
Notes payable..................	20,000	15,100	4,900	32.5	3.1	2.7
Taxes accrued..................	36,830	30,200	6,630	22.0	5.8	5.5
Total Current Liabilities	$127,140	$109,860	$17,280	15.7	20.0	19.9
Long-Term Liabilities:						
Mortgage notes payable, land and building, 7%, 1981.........................	43,600	60,750	17,150*	28.2*	6.9	11.0
Total Liabilities	$170,740	$170,610	$ 130	†	26.9	30.9
Stockholders' Equity:						
Common stock, par value $10 per share..............	$240,000	$200,000	$40,000	20.0	37.8	36.3
Retained earnings	224,471	180,475	43,996	24.4	35.3	32.8
Total Stockholders' Equity	$464,471	$380,475	$83,996	22.1	73.1	69.1
Total Liabilities and Stock- holders' Equity	$635,211	$551,085	$84,126	15.3	100.0	100.0

† Less than one half of 1 percent.
ᴿ Rounding error.

Illustration 11.2

THE KNIGHT CORPORATION
Comparative Statements of Earnings and Retained Earnings
For the Years Ended December 31, 1979, and 1980   *Exhibit B*

	Year ended December 31		Increase or decrease* 1980 over 1979		Percentage of net sales	
	1980	1979	Dollar	Percentage	1980	1979
Gross sales............................	$995,038	$775,836	$219,202	28.3	100.9	101.3
Less: Sales returns and allowances......................	8,650	10,321	1,671*	16.2*	.9	1.3
Net sales............................	$986,388	$765,515	$220,873	28.9	100.0	100.0
Cost of goods sold:						
Inventories, January 1	$ 94,500	$ 85,150	$ 9,350	11.0	9.6	11.1
Net purchases	639,562	510.290	129,272	25.3	64.8	66.7
	$734,062	$595,440	$138,622	23.3	74.4	77.8
Inventories, December 31	110,825	94,500	16,325	17.3	11.2	12.4
Cost of Goods Sold.......	$623,237	$500,940	$122,297	24.4	63.2	65.4
Gross margin	$363,151	264,575	98,576	37.3	36.8	34.6
Less: Selling expenses, Schedule B–1..........	$132,510	$ 84,898	$ 47,612	56.1	13.4	11.1
Administrative expenses, Schedule B–1..........	120,345	98,642	21,703	22.0	12.2	12.9
	$252,855	$183,540	$ 69,315	37.8	25.6	24.0
Net operating earnings............	$110,296	$ 81,035	$ 29,261	36.1	11.2	10.6
Less: Net other expenses, Schedule B–2..................	3,000	2,800	200	7.1	.3	.4
Net earnings before federal income taxes..................	$107,296	$ 78,235	29,061	37.1	10.9	10.2
Deduct: Federal income taxes.............................	48,300	31,700	16,600	52.4	4.9	4.1
Net earnings, to retained earnings.........................	$ 58,996	$ 46,535	$ 12,461	26.8	6.0	6.1
Retained earnings, January 1.....	180,475	146,440	34,035	23.2		
	$239,471	$192,975	$ 46,496	24.1		
Deduct: Dividends declared and paid	15,000	12,500	2,500	20.0		
Retained Earnings, December 31	$224,471	$180,475	$ 43,996	24.4		

version of plant assets to current assets through sale, (3) long-term borrowing, and/or (4) the issuance of more capital stock. Further examination of the comparative statements of financial position and the earnings statement will reveal that the first and last of these possibilities have caused the improvement in the current position.

b. Total assets have increased $84,126, while total liabilities have increased only $130. Total stockholders' equity has increased $83,996, of which $40,000 represents an increase in outstanding capital stock. Thus, retention of earnings and investments

Illustration 11.3

THE KNIGHT CORPORATION
Comparative Schedules of Selling and Administrative Expenses
For the Years Ended December 31, 1979, and 1980   *Schedule B–1*

	Year ended December 31		Increase or decrease* 1980 over 1979		Percentage of net sales	
	1980	*1979*	*Dollars*	*Percentage*	*1980*	*1979*
Selling Expenses:						
Advertising.............................	$ 28,632	$18,105	$10,527	58.1	2.9	2.4
Salespersons' salaries..................	69,225	45,900	23,325	50.8	7.0	6.0
Rent of sales office.....................	10,150	7,200	2,950	41.0	1.0	.9
Payroll taxes...........................	9,366	4,050	5,316	131.3	1.0	.5
General sales office expense and depreciation	15,137	9,643	5,494	57.0	1.5	1.3
Total Selling Expenses (Exhibit B)....................	$132,510	$84,898	$47,612	56.1	13.4	11.1
Administrative Expenses:						
Officers' and office salaries	$ 90,132	$74,957	$15,175	20.2	9.1	9.8
Bad debts expense	1,100	2,500	1,400*	56.0*	.1	.3
Telephone and light....................	10,300	7,200	3,100	43.1	1.0	.9
Taxes, payroll, and other.............	9,853	7,450	2,403	32.3	1.0	1.0
General administrative office expense and depreciation...........	8,960	6,535	2,425	37.1	1.0	.9
Total Administrative Expenses (Exhibit B).......	$120,345	$98,642	$21,703	22.0	12.2	12.9

Illustration 11.4

THE KNIGHT CORPORATION
Comparative Schedules of Other Expenses and Revenues
For the Years Ended December 31, 1979, and 1980   *Schedule B–2*

	Year ended December 31		Increase or decrease* 1980 over 1979		Percentage of net sales	
	1980	*1979*	*Dollars*	*Percentage*	*1980*	*1979*
Other Expenses:						
Interest expense	$9,325	$10,850	$1,525*	14.1*	.9	1.4
Total Other Expenses..............	$9,325	$10,850	$1,525*	14.1*	.9	1.4
Other Revenues:						
Gain on sales of plant assets.............	6,325	8,050	1,725*	21.4*	.6	1.0
Net Other Expenses (Exhibit B).......................	$3,000	$ 2,800	$ 200	7.1	.3	.4

by stockholders have greatly increased the stockholders' equity in the corporation while the equity of the creditors has increased only slightly.

3. The percentage increase or decrease in each of the items listed in (1) above—December 31, 1980, balances are compared with December 31, 1979, balances. For example, inspection of the comparative statements of financial position shows that—

Current assets have increased by 11 percent, while current liabilities have increased by 15.7 percent. Total assets have increased by 15.3 percent, while total liabilities have increased by less than one half of 1 percent, and total stockholders' equity has increased by 22.1 percent. These percentages express the increases and decreases in terms which have more meaning than do the increases and decreases expressed in dollar amounts.

Trend percentages

Trend percentages (also referred to as index numbers) are a useful means for comparing financial statements for several years. They emphasize changes or trends that have occurred over a period of time. They are calculated by:

1. Selecting a base year.
2. Assigning a weight of 100 percent to the amounts appearing on the base year financial statements.
3. Expressing the amounts shown on the other years' financial statements as a percentage of their corresponding base year financial statement amounts. (In other words, divide the other years' amounts by the base year amounts.)

As an example, assume the following information is given:

	1979	1980	1981	1982
Sales	$350,000	$367,500	$441,000	$485,000
Cost of goods sold	200,000	196,000	230,000	285,000
Gross margin	$150,000	$171,500	$211,000	$200,000
Operating expenses	145,000	169,000	200,000	192,000
Net Earnings before Taxes	$ 5,000	$ 2,500	$ 11,000	$ 8,000

Letting 1979 be the base year, the trend percentages would be calculated as follows:

1. Divide the amounts shown for "Sales" by $350,000.
2. Divide the amounts shown for "Cost of goods sold" by $200,000.
3. Divide the amounts shown for "Gross margin" by $150,000.
4. Divide the amounts shown for "Operating expenses" by $145,000.
5. Divide the amounts shown for "Net Earnings before Taxes" by $5,000.

After all the divisions have been made, the resulting trends would appear as follows:

	1979	1980	1981	1982
Sales	100	105	126	139
Cost of goods sold	100	98	115	143
Gross margin	100	114	141	133
Operating expenses	100	117	138	132
Net earnings before taxes	100	50	220	160

In reviewing the trends, one should pay close attention to the trends for interrelated items. Trend percentages indicate changes and the direction of changes. They do not explain the basic reasons for the changes. But by looking at the trend percentages, management can determine which areas of the business need to be investigated.

On the basis of what has been said about comparative financial statements, indicate whether each of the following statements is correct or incorrect.

1. Comparative financial statements are used to determine in an ideal sense what the balance in a given account or category of accounts ought to be.
2. Comparative financial statements are statements in which the financial data for two or more companies are compared for the same period.
3. Comparative financial statements are statements in which figures for a single company are presented for each of two or more periods.
4. Trend analysis emphasizes changes that have occurred over a period of time.

Check your responses in Answer Frame 1[11] on page 514.

Frame 2[11]

It is generally recognized that logical relationships exist between certain items in the statement of financial position. Logical relationships also exist between certain items in the earnings statement, and between pairs of items of which one appears in one statement and one in the other. Thus, many ratios can be computed from the same set of financial statements. These ratios can be broadly classified as (1) liquidity ratios, (2) tests of equity position and solvency, (3) profitability tests, and (4) market tests.

Liquidity ratios

Current or working capital ratio

Working capital is equal to the excess of current assets over current liabilities. The ratio which relates these two categories to each other is known as the *current ratio* or *working capital ratio*. It measures the ability of a company to meet its current liabilities. It also indicates the strength of a company's working capital position. The dollar amount of working capital does not provide an adequate index of the ability to pay current debts. The current ratio has been designed to provide a better index.

The current ratio is computed by dividing total current assets by total current liabilities:

$$\text{Current ratio} = \frac{\text{Current assets}}{\text{Current liabilities}}$$

The ratio is usually stated in terms of the number of dollars of current assets to one dollar of current liabilities (although the dollar signs usually are omitted). Thus, if current assets total $75,000 and current liabilities total $50,000, the ratio is expressed as 1.5:1 or 1.5 to 1.

To illustrate the superiority of the current ratio over working capital as a measure of debt-paying ability, consider the following example. Assume that Company A and Company B have current assets and current liabilities on December 31, 1979, as follows:

	Company A	Company B
Current assets.....................	$11,000,000	$200,000
Current liabilities..............	10,000,000	100,000
Working capital.................	$ 1,000,000	$100,000
Current ratio.....................	1.1 to 1	2 to 1

Company A has ten times as much working capital as Company B. But Company B has a superior debt-paying ability since it has two dollars of current assets for each dollar of current liabilities. Company A has only $1.10 of current assets for each $1 of current liabilities.

Short-term creditors are especially interested in the working capital ratio. They expect to receive payment from the conversion of inventories and accounts receivable into cash. They are not as concerned with long-range earnings as are investors. Therefore, they concentrate on the current, short-term financial position. They are more interested in the short- and medium-term prospects of a firm and whether it will be able to meet current operating commitments. The current ratios for the Knight Corporation are shown in Illustration 11.5.

Illustration 11.5

	December 31		Amount of increase
	1980	*1979*	
Current assets (*a*).........................	$373,851	$336,730	$37,121
Current liabilities (*b*)	127,140	109,860	17,280
Working capital (*a − b*)..................	$246,711	$226,870	$19,841
Current ratio (*a ÷ b*).....................	2.94:1	3.07:1	

1. Incorrect. Comparative financial statements array data from successive periods and indicate changes. There is no way to determine from these data whether the balance for one year is the "right" balance and for the other year(s) the "wrong" balance. Such a standard cannot be derived from the financial statements themselves.

2. Incorrect. They are statements in which the financial data for the *same* company are compared for two or more different time periods.

3. Correct. The description column and the first two money columns in Illustrations 11.1 through 11.4 are enough to qualify these statements as comparative statements. Additional columns and information may be included, as was done in the examples in Frame 1¹¹, to help the user to interpret the statements.

4. Correct. Trend analysis indicates changes and the direction of changes.

If you answered any of the above inappropriately, reread Frame 1¹¹ before going to Frame 2¹¹ on page 512.

2¹¹
continued

Current assets defined. Current assets consist of cash and any other assets which will be realized in cash, or sold or consumed in the course of normal operations during the normal operating cycle of the business or one year, whichever is longer. Real comprehension of the operations of a business enterprise requires a thorough understanding of this circulation process. Inventories are acquired by the disbursement of cash or the incurrence of current liabilities or both; inventories, upon sale, are converted into cash or trade receivables or both (at a gain, normally); receivables are in turn converted into cash, which is used to pay current liabilities. At the same time, other current liabilities are being created to replenish inventories, and so on. The average time intervening between the time cash is expended to acquire inventories, and the time that it is received from the collection of receivables is an operating cycle.

Provide the missing words in the following statements:

1. Current assets include those assets which are reasonably expected to be realized in cash, or sold or consumed in the course of normal operations during the _____?_____ of the business or one year, whichever is _____?_____ .

2. Current assets minus current liabilities equal _____?_____ .

3. The current ratio is computed by the formula: _____?_____ .

4. Another name for the current ratio is the _____?_____ ratio.

Refer to Answer Frame 2¹¹ on page 516 to check your answers.

Frame 3¹¹ —————————————————————————————

For each of the following transactions, indicate whether the transaction increases, decreases, or has no effect on the amount of working capital.

1. Received cash from a customer in payment of the customers' account. There is no cash discount offered.
2. Purchased equipment on account.
3. Sent a check in payment of the gross amount of an account payable.
4. Issued additional capital stock for cash.
5. Sold marketable securities at their book value for cash.
6. Acquired a parcel of land in exchange for shares of the company's common stock.
7. The board of directors declared a cash dividend payable next month.
8. Purchased raw materials on account.

Turn to Answer Frame 3¹¹ on page 516 to check your responses.

Frame 4¹¹ —————————————————————————————

Quick or acid test ratio

The acid test ratio (or quick ratio) is the ratio of cash, net receivables, and marketable securities (known as quick assets) to current liabilities:

$$\text{Acid test ratio} = \frac{\text{Quick assets}}{\text{Current liabilities}}$$

Inventories and prepaid expenses are excluded from this computation because they might not be readily convertible into cash. Short-term creditors are especially interested in this ratio since it relates the "pool" of cash and immediate cash inflows to immediate cash outflows.

For the Knight Corporation, acid test ratios are presented in Illustration 11.6.

Illustration 11.6

	December 31		Amount of increase
	1980	*1979*	
Quick assets (*a*)	$259,386	$237,530	$21,856
Current liabilities (*b*)	127,140	109,860	17,280
Nét quick assets (*a* − *b*)	$132,246	$127,670	$ 4,576
Acid test ratio (*a* ÷ *b*)	2.04:1	2.16:1	

515

The following are the correct responses for the blanks in Frame 2¹¹:
1. Normal operating cycle; longer.
2. Working capital.
3. Current assets ÷ Current liabilities.
4. Working capital.

If you answered any of the above incorrectly, restudy Frame 2¹¹ before proceeding to Frame 3¹¹ on page 515.

Answer frame 3¹¹

The following are the correct answers for the transactions in Frame 3¹¹:
1. No effect.   One current asset increased, another decreased by the same amount.
2. Decreased.   Current liabilities increased; no change in current assets.
3. No effect.   Current assets and current liabilities decreased by the same amount.
4. Increased.   Current asset (cash) increased; current liabilities not affected.
5. No effect.   Again one current asset decreased (marketable securities) while another (cash) increased.
6. No effect.   This transaction does not affect any current account.
7. Decreased.   Current liabilities increased (dividends payable); the debit is to Retained Earnings, an equity account.
8. No effect   Current assets (inventory) and current liabilities increased by the same amount.

If you answered any of the above incorrectly restury Frame 3¹¹ before going on to Frame 4¹¹ on page 515.

4¹¹
continued

If inventory or prepaid expenses or both are present, will the acid test ratio be larger or smaller than the current ratio?
1. Larger.
2. Uncertain.
3. Smaller.

Refer to Answer Frame 4¹¹ on page 518 to check your choice.

Frame 5¹¹

Accounts receivable turnover

The turnover of accounts receivable is computed by dividing net sales by average net accounts receivable, that is, accounts receivable after deducting the balance of the allowance for doubtful accounts.

$$\text{Accounts receivable turnover} = \frac{\text{Net sales}}{\text{Average net accounts receivable}}$$

Ideally, the divisor should be computed by averaging the end-of-month balances or end-of-week balances of net accounts receivable outstanding during the period. Often though, only the beginning-of-year and end-of-year balances are averaged, which is the method we will use. Sometimes a formula calls for the use of an average balance, but only the year-end amount is available. Then the analyst must use the year-end amount in the calculation. (This comment applies to the accounts receivable turnover and other ratios described in this chapter.) The net sales figure should include only sales on account. But if cash sales are relatively small or if their proportion to total sales remains fairly constant from year to year, reliable results can be obtained by using total net sales. We will use this latter method. Illustration 11.7 shows the computations of the accounts receivable turnover for the Knight Corporation for 1980 and 1979. (Assume that the net accounts receivable on January 1, 1979, was $121,240.)

Illustration 11.7

	1980	1979	Amount of increase or decrease*
Net sales (*a*)	$986,388	$765,515	$220,873
Accounts receivable:			
January 1	132,550	121,240	11,310
December 31	124,171	132,550	8,379*
Total	256,721	253,790	2,931
Average accounts receivable (*b*)	128,361	126,895	
Turnover of accounts receivable (*a* ÷ *b*).........	7.68	6.03	

Which of the following is the correct formula for computing the turnover of accounts receivable?

1. $\dfrac{\text{Gross sales}}{\text{Average net accounts receivable}}$

2. $\dfrac{\text{Net sales}}{\text{Average net accounts receivable}}$

3. $\dfrac{\text{Cost of goods sold}}{\text{Average net accounts receivable}}$

4. $\dfrac{\text{Average net accounts receivable}}{\text{Cost of goods sold}}$

5. $\dfrac{\text{Average net accounts receivable}}{\text{Net sales}}$

Check your answer in Answer Frame 5[11] on page 518.

Answer frame 4[11]

Smaller. Number 3 is the correct answer. Both ratios have total current liabilities in the denominator; thus, the deciding factor as to which ratio is smaller depends on the numerator. Since the current ratio uses total current assets in the numerator and the acid test ratio excludes inventory and prepayments and includes only the "quick assets" (those current assets nearest to being cash), the acid test ratio has a smaller numerator and must, therefore, be smaller than the current ratio.

If you chose an incorrect answer, reread Frame 4[11] before continuing to Frame 5[11] on page 516.

Answer frame 5[11]

The second answer is correct. The turnover of accounts receivable is computed by dividing net sales (preferably net credit sales) for the year by the average accounts receivable figure.

If you did not select this answer, restudy Frame 5[11] before proceeding to Frame 6[11] below.

Frame 6[11]

The turnover of accounts receivable indicates, on the average, how often the accounts receivable were collected. In other words, a turnover of 12 would mean that it takes about one month for accounts to be collected; a turnover of 8 would mean the collection period is longer — about 46 days ($365 \div 8$). The number of days in the year (365) divided by the turnover of accounts receivable is the average life of accounts receivable or the average collection period. The ratio measures the average liquidity of the accounts receivable and gives an indication of their quality.

Assume that a company has an accounts receivable turnover of 5 (which indicates an average collection period of 73 days). The company wants to take action to improve this ratio. Relying on your own logic (since this has not been specifically covered), indicate whether each of the following would be considered in making policy decisions to achieve the desired goal.

1. Collection policies.
2. Terms of sale.
3. Terms of sale offered by other firms in the industry.
4. Salespersons' salaries.
5. Credit screening of potential new accounts.

To check your choices, turn to Answer Frame 6[11] on page 520.

Frame 7[11]

Inventory turnover

The turnover of inventory is obtained by dividing the cost of goods sold for a given period by the average inventory for the same period:

$$\text{Inventory turnover} = \frac{\text{Cost of goods sold}}{\text{Average inventory}}$$

It is advisable to obtain an average of all the month-end inventories of the year plus the beginning of year inventory. But an average of the January 1 and December 31 inventories is often used for practical reasons (which we also use in the illustration). Inventory turnover for the Knight Corporation is shown in Illustration 11.8.

Illustration 11.8

	1980	1979	Amount of increase
Cost of goods sold (*a*)	$623,237	$500,940	$122,297
Inventories:			
January 1	$ 94,500	$ 85,150	$ 9,350
December 31	110,825	94,500	16,325
Total	$205,325	$179,650	$ 25,675
Average inventory (*b*)	102,663	89,825	
Turnover of inventory (*a* ÷ *b*)	6.07	5.58	

In attempting to secure satisfactory earnings, the costs of storage, obsolescence, and implicit interest incurred in owning inventory must be balanced against the possible loss of sales from not owning it. Other things being equal, the management which is able to maintain the higher inventory turnover rate is considered more efficient.

The following selected data are taken from the financial statements of the Gretel Company:

Net accounts receivable, 12/31/79	$117,000
Inventory, 1/1/79	70,000
Inventory, 12/31/79	50,000
Net sales	705,000
Cost of goods sold	348,000

The turnover of inventory for this company in 1979 was ____?____.

Check your answer in Answer Frame 7[11] on page 520.

Answer frame 6[11]

All of the factors mentioned would be considered except salespersons' salaries. Collection policies practiced by the company certainly will have an effect on the collection time, hence the turnover rate. Cash discounts encourage customers to pay more promptly. On the surface, terms of sale offered by other firms in the industry may not seem relevant. But remember that customers can do business with the firm's competitors. Thus, the leniency or stringency of competitors' credit terms and collection policies must be taken into account when making decisions in this area. The turnover ratio is a measure of the quality of the accounts receivable. The quality of those accounts is a function of the credit screening policies of the firm. If it does no screening, for example, and grants credit to anyone who asks, it will probably have a large amount of slow-paying (if collectible at all) accounts, which of course reduces the turnover ratio.

Salespersons' salaries probably have no direct effect on the promptness with which customers pay their accounts and, hence, need not be considered in making a decision to try to bring about faster payments.

If you answered incorrectly, reread Frame 6[11] before turning to Frame 7[11] on page 519.

Answer frame 7[11]

The correct answer is 5.8. The cost of goods sold amount indicates the total amount of inventory sold during the year—at cost prices. Thus, this amount divided by the *average* inventory indicates how many times the inventory turned over. Inventory turnover is therefore 5.8 ($348,000 ÷ $60,000).

If you did not get this answer, restudy Frame 7[11] before continuing to Frame 8[11] below.

Frame 8[11]

Turnover of total assets

The turnover of total assets shows the relationship between dollar volume of sales and average total assets used in the business and is calculated as follows:

$$\text{Total assets turnover} = \frac{\text{Net sales}}{\text{Average total assets}}$$

It measures the efficiency of the use of the capital invested in the assets (assuming a constant margin of earnings on each dollar of sales). The larger the dollar volume of sales made per dollar of invested capital, the larger will be the earnings on each dollar invested in the assets of the business. If available, monthly figures could be used to determine average total assets. Alternatively, the beginning and ending balances can be used. For the Knight Corporation the total assets turnover ratios for 1980 and 1979 are shown in Illustration 11.9. (Assume total assets as of January 1, 1979, were $510,200.)

Illustration 11.9

	1980	1979	Amount of increase
Net sales (*a*)	$ 986,388	$ 765,515	$220,873
Total assets:			
January 1	551,085	510,200	40,885
December 31	635,211	551,085	84,126
Total	1,186,296	1,061,285	125,011
Average total assets (*b*)	593,148	530,643	
Turnover of total assets (*a* ÷ *b*).........	1.66	1.44	

In 1979, each dollar of total assets produced $1.44 of sales; and in 1980, each dollar of total assets produced $1.66 of sales, or an increase of $0.22 of sales per dollar of investment in the assets.

Indicate if each of the following statements is correct or incorrect.
1. The turnover of total assets is affected by the turnover of receivables, inventories, and other assets.
2. Turnover of total assets ideally is determined by dividing net sales by average total assets.
3. The increase in turnover of total assets from 1.44 in 1979 to 1.66 in 1980 indicates clearly that net earnings of the firm increased in 1980.

To check your answers turn to Answer Frame 8[11] on page 522.

Frame 9[11]

Tests of equity position and solvency

Equity ratio

The data shown in Illustration 11.10, taken from the comparative statements of financial position in Illustration 11.1, show the sources of the assets of the Knight Corporation on December 31 of 1980 and 1979. The two sources of assets are owners (stockholders) and creditors. The stockholders of the Knight Corporation have increased their proportionate equity in the assets of the company through additional investment in the company's common stock and through retention of the company's earnings.

The equity ratio is equal to the proportion of owners' (stockholders') equity to total equity (or to total assets) at the end of the period:

$$\text{Equity ratio} = \frac{\text{Owners' equity}}{\text{Total equity}}$$

1. Correct. Total assets include receivables, inventories, and plant assets. Therefore, the turnovers of these assets are automatically included in the turnover of total assets.
2. Correct. Because sales occur throughout the year, the average total assets figure is an appropriate base.
3. Incorrect. The increase in the turnover of assets would not increase earnings if the merchandise were sold below cost. Sales might increase substantially in this instance, but earnings would decline substantially. The turnover of assets computation, then, does not give a very concrete indication as to what happened to the earning power of the firm between two points in time. But because certain expenses are apt to be fixed and because additional sales are apt to be made at prices in excess of the variable costs of such sales, an increase in the rate of turnover of assets is generally viewed as favorable.

If you missed any of the above, restudy Frame 8¹¹ before proceeding to Frame 9¹¹ on page 521.

9¹¹
continued

The Knight Corporation's equity ratio increased from 69.1 percent in 1979 to 73.1 percent in 1980. The equity ratio must be carefully interpreted. From a creditor's point of view, a high proportion of owners' equity is desirable. A high percentage indicates the existence of a large protective buffer for creditors in the event the company suffers a loss. But from an owner's point of view a high proportion of owners' equity may or may not be desirable. If borrowed funds can be used by the business to generate earnings in excess of the net after tax cost of the interest on such borrowed funds, a lower percentage of owners' equity may be desirable. For example, assume that Dorton Company has $10,000,000 of 8 percent bonds payable in its capital structure, which after taxes have a net cost of $400,000 ($10,000,000 × .08 × .5), assuming a 50 percent tax rate. If the Dorton Company can use the $10,000,000 to produce earnings in excess of the $400,000 net after-tax cost of the borrowed funds which will increase earnings per share, it may decide that borrow-

Illustration 11.10

	December 31, 1980		December 31, 1979	
	Amount	Percent	Amount	Percent
Current liabilities	$127,140	20.0	$109,860	19.9
Long-term liabilities	43,600	6.9	60,750	11.0
Total Liabilities	$170,740	26.9	$170,610	30.9
Common stock	$240,000	37.8	$200,000	36.3
Retained earnings	224,471	35.3	180,475	32.8
Total Stockholders' Equity	$464,471	73.1	$380,475	69.1
Total Equity (equal to total assets)	$635,211	100.0	$551,085	100.0

ing is advantageous. Use of borrowed funds to such an advantage is termed successful "trading on the equity" or "favorable *financial leverage.*"

The following is a brief illustration of the effect on the Knight Corporation if it were more highly leveraged (i.e., had a larger proportion of debt). Assume that Knight Corporation could have financed its present operations with $50,000 of 8 percent bonds instead of 5,000 shares of common stock. The effect on earnings for 1980 would be as follows, assuming a marginal federal income tax rate of 50 percent:

Earnings as presently stated (Illustration 11.2)....................	$58,996
Net additional interest on bonds .50 (8% × 50,000)............	2,000
Adjusted earnings...	$56,996

As shown, net earnings would be less. But there would be 5,000 fewer shares outstanding. Therefore, earnings per share would be increased to $3 ($56,996 ÷ 19,000) from $2.46 ($58,996 ÷ 24,000). In recent years many companies have introduced larger portions of debt into their capital structures to increase earnings per share. But these companies will also show a larger drop in earnings per share when earnings go down than will those which are financed largely by common stock.

It should also be pointed out that too low a percentage of owners' equity (too much debt) may be hazardous from the owners' standpoint. A period of business recession may result in operating losses and shrinkages in the values of assets (such as receivables and inventories) leading to an inability to meet fixed payments for interest and principal on the debt. This in turn may cause stockholders to lose control of the company. The company may be forced into liquidation.

Owners' equity/debt ratio

The relative equities of owners and creditors may be expressed in several ways. To say, for example, that creditors hold a 26.9 percent equity in the assets of the Knight Corporation on December 31, 1980, is equivalent to saying that the stockholders hold a 73.1 percent interest. In many cases, the relationship is expressed as a ratio of owners' equity to debt. Such a ratio for the Knight Corporation would be 2.23 to 1 ($380,475 ÷ $170,610) on December 31, 1979, and 2.72 to 1($464,471 ÷ $170,740) on December 31, 1980. (Some analysts relate only long-term debt to owners' equity in these calculations.)

Indicate whether each statement is true or false.

1. A company that is successfully trading on the equity has a higher rate of earnings on its stockholders' equity than it would have if all of its long-term capital has been acquired from equity sources.
2. If a company can earn a 10 percent return on total assets and can borrow funds at 8 percent, it is always desirable for the company to include a high percentage of long-term debt in its capital structure.
3. As a prudent potential investor in Company X, you would be only casually interested in knowing what proportion of Company X's assets is financed through the use of borrowed capital.

To check your responses turn to Answer Frame 9[11] on page 526.

To check your responses turn to Answer Frame 9[11] on page 526.

SECTION II

Frame 10[11]

Profitability tests

Determination of earning power on operating assets

The best measure of earnings performance without regard to the sources of assets is the relationship of net operating earnings to operating assets.

Net operating earnings exclude nonoperating revenues (such as extraordinary gains on the early retirement of debt and interest earned on investments), nonoperating expenses (such as interest paid on obligations), and federal income taxes.

Operating assets are all assets actively used in producing operating revenue. Examples of excluded (that is, nonoperating) assets are land held for future use, a factory building being rented to someone else, and long-term bond investments.

Elements in earning power

There are two elements in the determination of earning power. They are the operating margin and the turnover of operating assets. The operating margin can be expressed in formula form as follows:

$$\text{Net operating margin} = \frac{\text{Net operating earnings}}{\text{Net sales}}$$

The total assets turnover is inadequate as an independent measure of earnings performance. But when slightly changed and used in combination with the net operating margin, it becomes an excellent measure of earnings performance as shown below. If nonoperating assets are excluded (as they should be), this ratio becomes the "turnover of operating assets" represented by the formula:

$$\text{Turnover of operating assets} = \frac{\text{Net sales}}{\text{Operating assets}}$$

The turnover of operating assets shows the dollars of sales made for each dollar invested in operating assets. The operating assets amount used is generally the year-end amount. One could argue that the average balance should be used, but it seldom is (and we will not use it).

The earning power of a firm is equal to the net operating margin multiplied by the turnover of operating assets. The more a company earns per dollar of sales and the more sales it makes per dollar invested in operating assets, the higher will be the return per dollar invested. Earning power may be expressed by the following formula: Earning Power = Net Operating Margin × Turnover of Operating Assets or,

$$\text{Earning power} = \frac{\text{Net operating earnings}}{\text{Net sales}} \times \frac{\text{Net sales}}{\text{Operating assets}}$$

Since the net sales amount appears as both a numerator and a denominator, it can be canceled out, and the formula for earning power becomes:

$$\text{Earning power} = \frac{\text{Net operating earnings}}{\text{Operating assets}}$$

But it is more useful for analytical purposes to leave the formula in the form which shows margin and turnover separately.

Securing desired earning power

Companies that are to survive in the economy must attain some minimum level of earning power. But this minimum can be obtained in many different ways. To illustrate, consider a grocery store and a jewelry store, each with an earning power of 8 percent on operating assets. The grocery store normally would have a low margin and a high turnover while the jewelry store would have a higher margin and a lower turnover:

	Margin	×	*Turnover*	=	*Earning power*
Grocery store	1%	×	8.0 times		8%
Jewelry store	20	×	.4		8

The earning power figures for the Knight Corporation for 1980 and 1979 are calculated in Illustration 11.11.

1. True. But remember that trading on the equity can backfire; hence, the policy must be followed with discretion. If earnings drop below the fixed rate which must be paid on borrowed funds, the earnings per share of stock (net earnings divided by number of shares of stock outstanding) will be less than they would have been if the company had not traded on the equity. A stockholder should, therefore, be interested in the ratio of equity to debt in the company's capital structure.

2. False. The decision to use more debt in the capital structure must be based on more than a comparison of the average expected return and the dollar cost of the borrowed funds. Borrowed funds bring with them a commitment to meet a fixed payment for interest over a long period of time. Thus, one important consideration is whether the company's well-being is highly sensitive to business fluctuations in the economy; another is the future outlook for the company and whether reasonably accurate predictions can be made.

3. False. First of all, consider the fact that interest payments have priority over dividend payments; also in liquidation the stockholders have a claim only to the residual left after creditors have been satisfied.

If you missed any of the above, restudy Frame 9^{11} before continuing to Frame 10^{11} on page 524.

10^{11}
continued

Illustration 11.11

	1980	1979	Amount of increase
Net operating earnings (a)	$110,296	$ 81,035	$ 29,261
Net sales (b)	986,388	765,515	220,873
Net operating margin ($a \div b = c$)	11.18%	10.59%	
Net sales (d)	$986,388	$765,515	$220,873
Total assets (all operating assets) (e)	635,211	551,085	84,126
Turnover of operating assets ($d \div e = f$)	1.55	1.39	
Earning power ($c \times f$)	17.33%	14.72%	

Earning power is the best measure of the profitability of the firm without regard to the sources of the assets. It is concerned with the earning power of the company as a bundle of assets, not with the determination of which sources of the assets are favored in the division of earnings.

Indicate whether each of the following statements is correct or incorrect.

1. An industry with a low turnover of operating assets would be expected to have a lower net operating margin rate than an industry with a high operating asset turnover.

2. An increase in the net operating margin rate may accompany a decrease in operating earnings measured in absolute dollars.

3. The ratio of net earnings to sales is one of the best measures for

comparing the profitability of different companies without regard to the source of assets.

4. Net earnings as a percentage of sales measures the number of cents of net earnings on each unit of product sold.

To check your responses, turn to Answer Frame 10[11] on page 528.

Frame 11[11]

Net earnings as a percentage of net sales

Net earnings as a percentage of net sales is obtained by dividing the net earnings for the period by the net sales for the same period:

$$\text{Net earnings to net sales} = \frac{\text{Net earnings}}{\text{Net sales}}$$

This ratio measures the proportion of the sales dollar which remains after the deduction of all expenses. For the Knight Corporation the computations are shown in Illustration 11.12.

Illustration 11.12

	1980	1979	Amount of increase
Net earnings (*a*)	$ 58,996	$ 46,535	$ 12,461
Net sales (*b*)	986,388	765,515	220,873
Ratio of net earnings to net sales (*a* ÷ *b*)	5.98%	6.08%	

Although the ratio of net earnings to net sales indicates the net margin of earnings on each dollar of sales, a great deal of care must be exercised in its use and interpretation. The amount of net earnings is equal to net operating earnings plus nonoperating revenues and less nonoperating expenses and taxes. Thus, unlike the earning power on operating assets, the ratio of net earnings to net sales is affected by the methods used to finance the assets of the firm.

Net earnings as a percentage of average stockholders equity

From the stockholders' point of view, an important measure of the earnings-producing ability of a company is the relationship of net earnings to stockholders' equity or the rate of return on stockholders' equity. Stockholders are interested in the ratio of operating earnings to operating assets as a measure of the efficient use of assets. But they are even more interested in knowing what part of the earnings remains for them after other capital suppliers have been paid.

1. Incorrect. Just the reverse is true; a low operating asset turnover is generally associated with a higher margin. The assets are turned over fewer times during the year so that a higher rate of return must be earned on each sales dollar in order for those companies to earn a satisfactory return on capital invested in the company.

2. Correct. An increase in the net operating margin rate could be brought about by an increase in the selling price of the product, all costs remaining the same. But such a price increase may cause some customers to turn to other products or other suppliers, reducing the turnover of operating assets and the absolute amount of operating earnings.

3. Incorrect. The earning power ratio is the best measure of the profitability without regard to sources of the assets.

4. Incorrect. It measures the number of cents of profit in each dollar of sales revenue, not on each unit of product sold.

If you missed any of these, restudy Frame 10^{11} before proceeding to Frame 11^{11} on page 527.

11^{11}
continued

Net earnings as a percentage of stockholders' equity is obtained by dividing the net earnings for the period by the average total stockholders' equity for the same period. If available, monthly figures could be used to determine average total stockholders' equity. Alternatively, the beginning and ending balances can be used. The ratios for the Knight Corporation are shown in Illustration 11.13. (Assume that total stockholders' equity on January 1, 1979, was $321,460.)

Illustration 11.13

	1980	1979	Amount of increase
Net earnings (a)	$ 58,996	$ 46,535	$ 12,461
Total stockholders' equity			
January 1	380,475	321,460	59,015
December 31	464,471	380,475	83,996
Total	$844,946	$701,935	$143,011
Average total stockholders' equity (b)	$422,473	$350,968	
Ratio of net earnings to stockholders' equity (a ÷ b)	13.96%	13.26%	

The increase in this ratio from 13.26 percent to 13.96 percent would be looked upon favorably.

Indicate whether each of the following statements is true or false.

1. The return on stockholders' equity is computed by dividing the net earnings for the period by average total paid-in capital.

2. The ratio of net earnings to average stockholders' equity is always equal to or less than the ratio of net earnings to average total assets.

3. The return on average stockholders' equity is the same as the return on average net assets.

4. The return on average stockholders' equity is one of the most meaningful ratios to a banker deciding whether to grant a short-term loan to a company.

Refer to Answer Frame 11[11] on page 530 to check your answers.

Frame 12[11]

Earnings per share

When preferred stock is outstanding, a portion of the net earnings must be assigned to the preferred stock with the remainder left for the common stock. To determine the rate of earnings (or dollars earned per share) on the common stock, the portion of net earnings belonging to the various classes of stock outstanding must be computed.

Most preferred stock issues provide for preference over common stock for a specific limited dividend per share with no dividend rights beyond this amount. In this case it is necessary to deduct from the net earnings for the period only the annual dividends to which preferred stockholders are entitled. The remainder is then divided by the average number of shares of common stock outstanding to compute the earnings per share of common stock:

$$\text{Earnings per share of common stock} = \frac{\text{Earnings available to common stockholders}}{\text{Average number of shares of common stock outstanding}}$$

When extraordinary gains or losses are included in net earnings, *Accounting Principles Board Opinion No. 9* requires that separate per share amounts be shown for net earnings before extraordinary items; for the net amount of the extraordinary items, if any (net of their tax effects); and for net earnings. Thus a company which has suffered a loss on the early retirement of debt might include the following in its earnings statement for the year:

Per share of common stock—
Net earnings before extraordinary loss	$1.75
Loss on early retirement of debt, net of tax	(0.25)
Net Earnings..	$1.50

Annual preferred dividend requirements, if any, must be deducted in computing the $1.75 as well as the $1.50.

For the Knight Corporation, which had no preferred stock outstand-   529

12[11]
continued

ing in either 1980 or 1979, earnings per share of common stock are computed in Illustration 11.14.

Illustration 11.14

	1980	1979	Amount of increase
Net earnings (a)	$58,996	$46,535	$12,461
Average number of shares of common stock outstanding (b)	22,000	20,000	2,000
Earnings per share of common stock (a ÷ b)	$2.68	$2.33	

Effect of shares issued for assets

In interpreting the above illustration it is important to note that although the Knight Corporation increased its outstanding common stock by 4,000 shares in 1980, the increase in the average number of shares outstanding was only 2,000. The above computation assumes that the

4,000 shares were issued on June 30. Having 4,000 shares outstanding for one-half year is equivalent to having 2,000 shares outstanding during all of the year. Hence, the average number of shares outstanding increased by 2,000.

When new shares are issued for assets, or outstanding shares are reacquired by the company, it is best to compute the average number of shares outstanding during the period. Earnings per share of common stock are then reported on an average basis for the entire year rather than being based on amounts which were true for only a part of the year.

To illustrate, assume that as of January 1, 1979, Barnes Corporation had 110,000 shares of common stock outstanding. On October 1, 1979, it issued 40,000 shares for cash. Earnings available to common stockholders for 1979 amount to $480,000. The average number of shares outstanding is computed as follows:

$$(110,000 \times \tfrac{9}{12}) + (150,000 \times \tfrac{3}{12}) = 120,000$$

The computation shows 110,000 shares outstanding for nine months and 150,000 shares outstanding for the last three months.

The earnings per share are:

$$\$480,000 \div 120,000 = \$4$$

Effect of shares issued for stock dividends or stock splits

When additional shares are issued during the period as a result of a stock dividend or stock split, no attempt is made to average the number of shares outstanding at different times during the year as is done when additional shares are issued for cash or other property. The reason is that the stock split or the stock dividend is not viewed as being a change in substance. It is simply a division of the stockholders' interest into more pieces.

When comparing earnings per share before and after a stock split or stock dividend, the earnings per share should be adjusted to the same basis. Assume a company reports earnings per share as follows: 1978, $1; 1979, $1.25; 1980, $0.75. But a two-for-one stock split occurred in 1980. The first two years' figures should be adjusted for the stock split in order to be comparable to the 1980 figure. Thus, earnings per share would be $0.50 for 1978 and $0.625 for 1979. Then the proper trend can be seen:

Year	Earnings per share
1978	$0.50
1979	0.625
1980	0.75

On January 1, 1977, Bailey Corporation had 120,000 shares of common stock outstanding. On September 1, 1979, it issued 30,000 shares for cash. Earnings available to common stockholders for 1979 amount to $540,000. Compute the earnings per share of common stock for the Bailey Corporation for 1979.

Check your answer in Answer Frame 12[11] on page 534.

Frame 13[11]

Number of times interest is earned

Another relationship which focuses attention upon the position of a particular class of investor—in this case, the bondholder—is the ratio of earnings available for bond interest charges to the amount of such charges. For example, if the amount of earnings before interest and income taxes is $100,000 and the bond interest expense for the period is $10,000, the ratio is 10 to 1. In such a case the bond interest is said to have been earned ten times.

Bondholders are interested in knowing whether the company is earning enough so that even if a drop in earnings should occur, it could continue to earn enough to meet its interest payments. It is true that interest must usually be paid regardless of whether earnings are sufficient to cover it. But it is also true that a company probably could not continue to pay interest in excess of net earnings before interest for a long period of time. Thus, the bondholders are interested in knowing the likelihood that they will continue to receive their interest.

The number of times that the present interest is earned is one measure of a company's ability to meet interest payments. And, of course, since bond interest is deductible for income tax purposes, net earnings before bond interest and income taxes is used since there would be no tax if bond interest were equal to or greater than net earnings before interest and taxes. In formula form, the ratio is:

$$\text{Number of times interest is earned} = \frac{\text{Net earnings before interest and taxes}}{\text{Interest expense}}$$

If other interest-bearing obligations are outstanding, the ratio is computed using total interest expense.

Given the following data:

Net earnings before interest and income taxes	$40,000
Bond interest expense	6,000
	$34,000
Federal income taxes	6,540
Net Earnings	$27,460

Which of the following represents the number of times bond interest is earned?

1. 5.67.
2. 4.58.
3. 6.67.
Check your computations in Answer Frame 13[11] on page 534.

Frame 14[11]

Number of times preferred dividends are earned

Preferred stockholders, like bondholders, must usually be satisfied with a fixed dollar return on their investments. They are interested in the company's ability to make preferred dividend payments each year. This can be measured by computing the number of times preferred dividends are earned. It can be computed as follows:

$$\text{Times preferred dividends earned} = \frac{\text{Net earnings after income taxes}}{\text{Preferred dividends}}$$

Suppose a company has earnings after income taxes of $48,000 and has $100,000 (par value) of 8 percent preferred stock outstanding. The number of times the preferred dividends are earned would be:

$$\frac{\$48,000}{\$8,000} = 6 \text{ times}$$

The higher this rate, the higher is the probability that the preferred stockholders will receive their dividends each year. While the analogy is far from perfect, a finance company would be much more likely to expect to continue to receive payments on a loan from an individual who is earnings eight times the required periodic payment than one who is earning only twice the payment.

Given the following data:

Net earnings before income taxes	$50,000
Net earnings after income taxes	30,000
Preferred dividends	6,000

Which of the following represents the number of times preferred dividends are earned?

1. 8.33.
2. 5.00.
3. 9.33.
4. 6.00.
Check your computations in Answer Frame 14[11] on page 534.

The average number of shares outstanding is computed as follows:

$$(120,000 \times {}^{9}\!/_{12}) + (150,000 \times {}^{4}\!/_{12}) = 130,000$$

The earnings per share are:

$$\$540,000 \div 130,000 = \$4.15 \text{ per share}$$

If you did not get this answer, restudy Frame 12^{11} before continuing in Frame 13^{11} on page 532.

Number 3 (6.67) is the correct answer. Bond interest expense is deductible from revenue before computation of federal income tax. Therefore, it is logical to use net earnings before interest and taxes to determine the times interest is earned.

If you chose an incorrect answer, reread Frame 13^{11} before going to Frame 14^{11} on page 533.

Number 2 (5.00) is the correct answer.

$$\text{Times preferred dividends earned} = \frac{\text{Net earnings after income taxes}}{\text{Preferred dividends}}$$
$$= \frac{\$30,000}{\$6,000}$$
$$= 5 \text{ times}$$

If you answered incorrectly, reread Frame 14^{11} before going on to Frame 15^{11} below.

Frame 15^{11}

Market tests

Price-earnings ratio and yield on common stock

A firm's earnings per share are often compared to the current market value of its shares as follows:

$$\frac{\text{Earnings per share}}{\text{Current market price per share}} = \text{Earnings rate (or earnings yield) on market price}$$

Suppose, for example, that a company had earnings per share of common stock of $2 and that the quoted market price of the stock on the New York Stock Exchange was $30. The earnings rate (or earnings yield) on market price would be:

$$\frac{\$2}{\$30} = 6{}^{2}\!/_{3} \text{ percent}$$

This ratio when inverted is called the price-earnings ratio. In the case just cited the price-earnings ratio is:

$$\text{Price-earnings ratio} = \frac{\text{Current market price per share}}{\text{Earnings per share}} = \frac{\$30}{\$2} = 15 \text{ to } 1$$

Investors would say that this stock is selling at 15 times earnings or at a multiple of 15. They might have a multiple in mind as being the proper one that should be used to judge whether the stock were underpriced or overpriced. Different investors will have different estimates of the proper price-earnings ratio for a given stock and also different estimates of the future earnings prospects of the firm. These are two of the factors which cause one investor to sell stock at a particular price and another investor to buy at that price.

Dividend yield and payout ratios

The dividend paid per share of common stock is also of much interest to common stockholders. When the dividend is divided by the current market price per share, the result is called the "dividend yield."

If the company referred to immediately above paid a $1.50 per share dividend, the dividend yield would be:

$$\text{Dividend yield} = \frac{\text{Dividend per share}}{\text{Current market price per share}} = \frac{\$1.50}{\$30.00} = 5 \text{ percent}$$

One additional step is to divide the dividend per share by the earnings available per share to determine the "payout ratio" as follows:

$$\text{Payout ratio} = \frac{\text{Dividend per share}}{\text{Earnings per share}} = \frac{\$1.50}{\$2.00} = 75 \text{ percent}$$

A payout ratio of 75 percent means that the company paid out 75 percent of the earnings per share in the form of dividends. Some investors are attracted by the stock of companies that pay out a large percentage of their earnings. Other investors are attracted by the stock of companies which retain and reinvest a large percentage of their earnings. The tax status of the investor has a great deal to do with this. Investors in very high tax brackets often prefer to have the company reinvest the earnings with the expectation that this will result in share price appreciation which would be taxed at capital gains rates when the shares are sold. Dividends are taxed at ordinary income rates, which may be much higher than capital gains rates.

The following selected data are those of the Daniel Company:

Current liabilities	$ 80,000
Long-term liabilities	130,000
Preferred stock, 4%, cumulative, nonparticipating ($100 par)	100,000
Common stock ($50 par)	200,000
Paid-in capital in excess of par—common	10,000
Retained earnings, 12/31/79	40,000
Net earnings after income taxes	24,000
Dividends declared:	
Preferred stock	4,000
Common stock	9,000

The net earnings per share of common stock are ____?____ .

Check your answer in Answer Frame 15[11] on page 538.

Frame 16[11]

Yield on preferred stock

Preferred stockholders compute yield in a manner similar to the computation of dividend yield for common stockholders. Suppose a company has 2,000 shares of $100 par value, 8 percent preferred stock outstanding which has a current market price of $110 per share. The yield would be computed as follows:

$$\text{Yield} = \frac{\text{Dividend per share}}{\text{Current market price per share}} = \frac{\$8}{\$110} = 7.27 \text{ percent}$$

Through the use of yield rates, different preferred stocks having different annual dividends and different market prices can be compared.

Assume that an investor purchased 100 shares of 6 percent, $100 par value, preferred stock at $96 per share. Compute the investor's expected annual yield.

Check your answer in Answer Frame 16[11] on page 538.

Frame 17[11]

Limitations in evaluating financial position

Financial statements presented in comparative form for several accounting periods facilitate analysis of changes and possible trends. Generally, three to five years is a minimum time period necessary for evaluation. There is no substitute for informed judgment in financial analysis. Percentages and ratios are useful *guides* to aid comparisons. The sophisticated financial analyst uses these tools to uncover potential corporate strengths and weaknesses. The analyst should try to discover the *basic causes* behind apparent changes and trends. For example, declining earnings may be due to poor management, declining product demand, poor cost control, an inefficient sales force, and so on. By examining key items on financial statements, the analyst can make informed judgments on the probability of continued profitability or reversal of losses.

Companies do not operate in an economic vacuum. It is important to place financial statement analysis within an industry and economic environment context. Acceptable current ratios, gross margin percentages, debt to equity ratios, and so on, vary widely depending upon the industry in which the company operates and environmental conditions. Even within an industry legitimate variations may exist. For example, a retail discount store may operate at a relatively low gross profit percentage. This does not necessarily mean that its operating philosophy is inferior to that of its higher margin competitors. Also, within the same company over time, small percentage declines may indicate potential trouble. For example, a small percentage decline in gross margin percentage may be a danger signal because large dollar amounts may be involved. Conversely, if selling expenses are rising with respect to sales revenue, greater effort may be required to stimulate product demand which may be dwindling. Although the dollar amounts involved may be quite small, ignoring this ratio could prove costly. A change in the selling expense/sales ratio may be the first indicator of a long-term downward trend in profits.

The potential stock investor should realize that acquiring the ability to make informed judgments is a long process and is not acquired overnight. Professional financial analysts are eligible to join the American Society of Chartered Financial Analysts only after a seven-year "apprenticeship." Using ratios and percentages mechanically is a sure road to wrong conclusions.

Need for comparable data

Analysts must be sure that their comparisons are valid—whether the comparisons be of items for different periods or dates or for items of different companies. Consistent accounting practices must be followed from period to period if interperiod comparisons are to be made. It is the accountant's responsibility, of course, to disclose any changes in method or departures from consistent practice, if they are material. Footnotes to financial statements, for example, may be used to reveal the effects of any inconsistent practices.

Influence of external factors

Facts and conditions not disclosed by the financial statements may affect the interpretation of the statements. A single event of very great importance to the company may have been largely responsible for a

17¹¹
continued

given relationship. For example, a new product may have been unexpectedly put on the market by competitors, making it necessary for the company under study to sacrifice at drastically reduced prices its stock of a product suddenly rendered obsolete. Such an event would affect the percentage of gross margin to net sales severely. Yet, there may be little or no chance that such a thing would happen again.

The backdrop of general business conditions within the business or industry of the company under study must be considered. A downward trend in earnings, for example, is less alarming to a stockholder if the trend in the industry or in business in general is also downward rather than limited to the corporation in which he or she holds stock.

Consideration should be given to the possible seasonal nature of the businesses under study. If the statement of financial position date represents the seasonal peak in the volume of business, for example, the ratio of current assets to current liabilities may acceptably be much lower than if the statement of financial position date is one in a season of low activity.

Need for comparative standards

Relationships between financial statement items become much more meaningful when appropriate standards are available for comparison. Comparison with standards provides a starting point for the analyst's thinking and leads to further investigation and, ultimately, to conclusions and business decisions. Such standards consist of (1) those which the analyst has in his or her own mind, as a result of experience and observation; (2) those provided by the records of past performance and position of the business under study; and (3) those provided by accounting data of other enterprises – for example, data available through trade associations, universities, research organizations, and governmental units.

Indicate whether each of the following statements is correct or incorrect.

In making an evaluation of a firm, the financial analyst –

1. Can feel sure that the ratios computed from the financial statements represent the "normal" situation for that company for the period being evaluated.
2. Should use ratios as guides to further investigation rather than as absolute criteria by which to judge the financial condition and earning potential of a firm.
3. Must be alert to the economic climate in which that firm operates; the general economic conditions in the country, regional conditions, and conditions in the industry and related industries.
4. Must be sure that the data and techniques being used provide a basis for valid comparisons.

Refer to Answer Frame 17[11] on page 540 to check your answers.

Frame 18[11]

Effects of changes in the general purchasing power of the dollar

One of the most powerful factors influencing the comparability of financial statements in recent years has been the change in the general level of prices or the change in the general purchasing power of the dollar. General purchasing power refers to the ability to buy all goods and services with a specific quantity of money, say, one dollar. Actually, there is an inverse relationship between the general level of prices and the general purchasing power of the dollar. As the price level rises, the general purchasing power of the dollar declines – a situation commonly referred to as inflation. For example, if prices double within a certain period of time the purchasing power of the dollar declines by 50 percent or one half. Less frequently, the general level of prices declines and the general purchasing power of the dollar increases. That is, if prices decline by 50 percent or one half, the general purchasing power of the dollar doubles. This situation is usually called deflation. But inflation has been the most frequently encountered situation in the United States.

When analyzing financial statements for several years, one must keep

1. Incorrect. What is "normal" may vary from month to month in a seasonal business, so the analyst must keep the seasonal effects in mind. The analyst also must be aware of the effect of planned and unplanned transactions which occur just prior to the statement date. Temporary repayment of short-term loans or reductions in accounts payable can, for example, bolster a sagging current ratio since that ratio is particularly sensitive to changes in current liabilities. While the analyst may not be in a position to get details of this kind, he or she must be aware of these possibilities which can cause many of the ratios to be nonrepresentative at the statement date.

2. Correct. Analysis by ratios must be tempered with judgment grounded in knowledge about the firm, the industry, and business conditions.

3. Correct. War, the space program, steel strikes, recessions, new inventions, new products, a change in management, all have an impact on the ratios of business firms. The impact is greater or smaller depending on how strongly the firm's affairs are affected by the event, but an analyst cannot make an intelligent evaluation of any business without being aware of these events.

4. Correct. Conclusions based on data that are not comparable or adjusted to be made comparable can lead to incorrect decisions.

If you missed any of the above, restudy Frame 17[11] before proceeding to Frame 18[11] on page 539.

18[11]
continued

in mind the impact that inflation has on comparability; otherwise, incorrect conclusions may be drawn. For example, the dollar amount of sales appearing on the earnings statement may have doubled within ten years. But if the firm's selling prices have increased as much as the general level of prices which has doubled or tripled within the same ten years, then the physical volume of goods sold has either remained constant or decreased.

General price-level changes affect both the earnings statement (as evidenced by the discussion of sales) and the statement of financial position. Assets purchased in different years and with dollars representing different amounts of general purchasing power are all added together on the statement of financial position. Most of the items appearing on this statement are stated at historical cost. Suppose a company purchased a machine in 1975 for $20,000. Then in 1980, it purchased an identical machine for $30,000. Both of these assets appear on the statement of financial position at historical cost less accumulated depreciation—thus, 1975 dollars are added to 1980 dollars.

General purchasing power financial statements may someday be required in the United States. The objectivity of historical cost is maintained in these statements, but general price indices are used to convert the historical costs to dollars of current purchasing power. It is important for the reader to understand that general purchasing power financial statements do not intend to present replacement costs, appraisal values, or any other current value measurements. The historical costs are simply restated (by means of a price index) in terms of current dollars.

Choice of price index and conversion process

The Gross National Product Implicit Price Deflator is usually recommended as the price index that should be used to adjust or convert historical-dollar financial statements to general purchasing power financial statements. The conversion process is accomplished by (1) multiplying the historical-dollar amount by the price index existing on the date of the latest statement of financial position and (2) dividing the result obtained in step (1) by the price index existing on the date of purchase, incurrence, or issuance. For example, suppose land was purchased for $100,-000 when the price index was 105. At December 31, 1980, the price index is 147. The land would appear on the December 31, 1980, price-level adjusted statement of financial position at $140,000, computed as follows:

1. $100,000 \times 147 = \$14,700,000.$
2. $\$14,700,000 \div 105 = \$140,000.$

Monetary and nonmonetary items

When preparing general purchasing power financial statements, a distinction must be made between monetary items and nonmonetary items. Monetary items are those assets and liabilities whose dollar amounts are fixed by contract and do not vary with changes in the general price level. They include cash, notes and accounts receivable, notes and accounts payable, accrued receivables and payables, bonds payable, certain prepaid expenses and investments in debt instruments. The common characteristic of monetary items is their claim to a fixed amount of dollars. (Notice that the examples listed include both current and noncurrent assets and liabilities.) All other items are nonmonetary — their values change with changes in the general price level. Inventories, supplies, plant assets, investments in capital stock, capital stock, premium on capital stock, retained earnings, and intangibles are all nonmonetary items.

Purchasing power gains and losses

Purchasing power gains and losses result from holding monetary items while changes occur in the general price level. During inflation, purchasing power losses result from holding monetary assets and purchasing power gains result from maintaining monetary liabilities. During inflation, each dollar held will buy fewer and fewer goods and services.

But, if one pays off a debt during inflation, the dollars paid back are worth less than the dollars borrowed. On the other hand, during deflation, purchasing power gains result from holding monetary assets and purchasing power losses result from having monetary liabilities. Each dollar held will buy more real goods and services. To illustrate, if $15,000 cash is held as the price index increases from 100 to 120, there is a $3,000 purchasing power loss computed as follows:

Monetary item	Historical cost	Conversion	Purchasing power gain
Cash....................	$15,000	$15,000 \times \dfrac{120}{100} = $18,000	$3,000

But if a $10,000 note payable is held as the price index increases from 100 to 120, there is a $2,000 purchasing power gain, computed as follows:

Monetary item	Historical cost	Conversion	Purchasing power loss
Notes payable...........	$10,000	$10,000 \times \dfrac{120}{100} = $12,000	$2,000

Value of general purchasing power financial statements

In periods of rapid inflation, incorrect conclusions can be drawn from financial statements if general price-level changes are ignored. General purchasing power financial statements emphasize the effects of inflation on financial position and the results of operations. Therefore, when investors analyze financial statements, their attention is directed towards the impact of inflation. They can then evaluate the firm in dollars which represent the same purchasing power. In the case of comparative statements presented for 1979 and 1980, the 1979 statements would be expressed in 1980 dollars. Thus, all figures would represent dollars of equal purchasing power.

Indicate whether each of the following statements is correct or incorrect.

1. General purchasing power financial statements present replacement costs rather than historical costs.
2. Monetary items is a synonym for current assets.
3. During inflation, purchasing power losses result from holding monetary assets.
4. General price-level changes affect both the earnings statement and the statement of financial position.

Now turn to Answer Frame 18[11] on page 544 to check your answers.

Frame 19¹¹

Current value (or replacement cost) accounting

There is a possibility that financial statements containing current value information will be required instead of having purchasing power statements. Presently, the Securities and Exchange Commission (SEC) requires certain large companies to disclose current replacement cost information concerning inventory, cost of goods sold, plant assets (except land), and depreciation. The objectives of the disclosures are to help investors understand the current cost of operating the business and to indicate the current economic investment in inventory and plant assets.

Different methods can be used to estimate current values or replacement costs. They include (1) current price quotations for equal productive capacity, (2) current price quotations for specific assets, and (3) a cost index used as follows:

$$\text{Replacement cost} = \text{Historical cost} \times \frac{\text{Index of current replacement costs}}{\text{Index at acquisition}}$$

Currently, replacement cost information must be disclosed by only the largest companies. But it is possible that someday many companies will have to prepare financial statements reporting replacement costs.

Indicate whether each of the following statements is true or false.
1. General purchasing power financial statements are based on replacement costs.
2. Replacement costs can be estimated by several different methods.
3. Replacement cost financial statements are currently required of the largest 10,000 companies.
4. The SEC requires certain large companies to disclose the replacement cost of inventory and plant assets (except land).

Now turn to Answer Frame 19¹¹ on page 544 to check your answers.

Summary *chapter* 11

The usefulness of financial statements is enhanced considerably when they are presented in comparative form for two or more accounting periods. Trends may be quickly noted, and truly significant information may be obtained.

The analysis made possible through the presentation of comparative statements usually includes the computation of increases or decreases in financial statement items and in classes of items in both absolute dollar terms and percentages. Analysis is facilitated when both dollar and percentage changes are presented.

Analysis of comparative earnings statements usually consists of the

Answer frame 18[11]

1. Incorrect. General purchasing power financial statements do not present replacement costs. They simply restate historical costs (by means of a price index) in terms of current dollars to disclose the effects of changes in the general price level.
2. Incorrect. Monetary items include both current and noncurrent assets and liabilities. They are assets and liabilities whose dollar amounts are fixed by contract and do not vary with changes in the general price level.
3. Correct. During inflation, each dollar held will buy fewer and fewer goods and services.
4. Correct. General price-level changes affect items on both statements.

If you answered any of the above incorrectly, restudy Frame 18[11] before going on to Frame 19[11] on page 543.

Answer frame 19[11]

1. False. General purchasing power financial statements are based on historical cost.
2. True. Replacement costs can be estimated by current price quotations for (1) equal productive capacity or (2) specific assets. They can also be estimated by applying cost indices to historical cost.
3. False. Currently, such statements are not required by anyone.
4. True. Over one thousand large companies are required to disclose replacement cost information pertaining to inventory and plant assets (except land).

If you answered any of the above incorrectly, restudy Frame 19[11] before going on to the Summary on page 543.

---

computation of absolute and percentage changes between years as well as the presentation of the various items in the earnings statement as percentages of net sales. Attention is usually centered upon changes in net sales, gross margin, operating expenses, net operating earnings, and net earnings.

The analysis of comparative statements of financial position usually includes the computation of ratios such as the ones summarized in Illustration 11.15.

Ratios should be used with caution and as clues indicating areas requiring further investigation. Ratios should be computed from comparable data if intercompany or interperiod comparisons are to be made. Ratios should be interpreted in the light of known external factors, such as the introduction by a competitor of a superior product. One of the most serious limitations of ratio analysis is the failure to account for changes in the level of prices over a period of years. Since they emphasize the effect of price-level changes on financial position and results of operations, general purchasing power financial statements may be more valuable to an investor than historical-dollar statement in periods of inflation. Historical-dollar statements are converted to general pur-

Illustration 11.15

Ratio	Formula	Significance
SECTION 1:		
Current ratio	Current assets ÷ Current liabilities	Test of debt-paying ability
Acid test (quick) ratio	(Cash + Net receivables + Marketable securities) ÷ Current liabilities	Test of immediate debt-paying ability
Accounts receivable turnover	Net Sales ÷ Average Net Accounts Receivable	Test of quality of accounts receivable
Average collection period	Number of days in year ÷ Accounts receivable turnover ratio	Test of quality of accounts receivable
Inventory turnover	Cost of goods sold ÷ Average inventory	Test of whether or not a sufficient volume of business is being generated relative to inventory
Total assets turnover	Net sales ÷ Average total assets	Test of whether or not volume of business generated is adequate relative to amount of capital invested in business
Equity ratio	Owners' (Stockholders') equity ÷ Total equities	Index of long-run solvency and safety
SECTION II:		
Earning power	Net operating earnings ÷ Operating assets	Measure of managerial effectiveness
Net earnings to stock-holders' equity	Net earnings ÷ Average stockholders' equity	Measure of what a given company earned for its stockholders from all sources as a percentage of the stockholders' investment
Earnings per share (of common stock)	Net earnings available to common stockholders ÷ Average number of shares of common stock outstanding	Tends to have an effect on the market price per share
Number of times interest is earned	Net earnings before interest and taxes ÷ Interest expense	Indicates likelihood that bondholders will continue to receive their interest payments
Number of times preferred dividends are earned	Net earning after income taxes ÷ Preferred dividends	Indicates the probability that preferred stock-holders will receive their dividend each year
Earnings yield	Earnings per share ÷ Current market price per share	Useful for comparison with other stocks
Price-earnings ratio	Current market price per share ÷ Earnings per share	Index of whether a stock is relatively cheap or expensive

Illustration 11.15 (continued)

Ratio	Formula	Significance
Dividend yield	Dividend per share ÷ Current market price per share	Useful for comparison with other stocks
Payout ratio	Dividend per share ÷ Earnings per share	Index of whether company pays out large percentage of earnings as dividends or reinvests most of its earnings

chasing power financial statements by the use of a general price-level index. The Gross National Product Implicit Price Deflator is recommended in most cases.

The replacement cost of inventory, cost of goods sold, plant assets (except land), and depreciation must be disclosed by over 1,000 large companies in reports to the Securities and Exchange Commission.

To complete your review of this chapter, study the definitions of new terms introduced in this chapter contained in the Glossary which is given below. Then complete the Student Review Quiz beginning on page 547.

Glossary, *chapter* 11

Acid test ratio — the ratio of cash and near cash assets (net receivables and marketable securities) to total current liabilities.

Current ratio — the ratio of current assets to current liabilities.

Dividend yield — on common or preferred stocks, current annual dividend per share divided by current market price per share.

Earning power ratio — ratio of net operating earnings to net sales multiplied by the ratio of net sales to total operating assets. The result is equal to the ratio of net operating earnings to total net operating assets.

Earnings per share — usually computed for common stock; net earnings less annual preferred dividend requirements, if any, divided by the average number of shares of common stock outstanding.

Earnings yield — on common stock, ratio of current earnings per share to current market price per share.

Equity ratio — the ratio of stockholders' equity to total equities (or total assets).

Net earnings as a percentage of net sales — a ratio formed by dividing net sales into net earnings.

Net earnings to stockholders' equity — a ratio formed by dividing average stockholders' equity into net earnings; often called rate of return on stockholders' equity.

Net operating assets — the net book value of assets used to produce the major revenues of a company.

Net operating earnings — the principal revenues of a company less the expenses incurred in producing them; excluded are nonoperating expenses and revenues, extraordinary gains and losses, and federal income taxes.

Number of times interest earned — a ratio computed by dividing net earnings before interest expense and federal income taxes by interest expense.

Number of times preferred dividends are earned — a ratio computed by dividing net earnings after taxes by the annual preferred dividend requirements, whether declared and paid or not.

Payout ratio — the ratio of dividends to net earnings per share.

Price-earnings ratio – the ratio of the current market price of a share of stock to the earnings per share on the stock.

Quick ratio – same as acid test ratio above.

Turnover – the relationship between the amount of an asset and some measure of its use; thus: Accounts receivable turnover = Net sales divided by average net accounts receivable; Inventory turnover = Cost of goods sold divided by average inventory; and Total assets turnover = Net sales divided by average total assets.

Working capital ratio – same as current ratio above.

Yield – the annual revenue or earnings on an investment, expressed in either dollars or percentages; Earnings yield on common stock = Ratio of earnings per share to current market price; Dividend yield on common or preferred stocks = Ratio of current annual dividend to current market price.

Continue with the Student Review Quiz below as a self-administered test of your comprehension of the material presented in this chapter.

Student review quiz *chapter* 11

SECTION I

1 A firm's current ratio at the end of any given accounting period –

a Is generally larger than the acid test ratio of that firm for the same period.

b Is never smaller than the acid test ratio for the same period.

c Is always equal to the working capital ratio for that date.

d All of the above are true.

e Only **(a)** and **(c)** are true.

2 Which of the following transactions would result in an increase in the current ratio if the ratio presently is 2:1?

a Repaid a 90-day loan.

b Purchased merchandise on account.

c Liquidated a long-term liability.

d Received payment of an account receivable.

e None of the above.

f **(a)** and **(b)**.

3 Business enterprises obtain their assets from which of the following sources?

a Common and preferred stockholders.

b Stockholders and bondholders.

c Trade creditors.

d The federal government.

e All of the above.

f **(a)**, **(b)**, and **(c)** above.

4 The following selected data are taken from the Space Manufacturing Company statement of financial position dated May 31, 1979:

Accounts payable	$ 74,000
Accrued liabilities	26,000
Bonds payable..........................	400,000
Common stock (par $100).........	600,000
Paid-in capital in excess of	
par – common.......................	100,000
Retained earnings	300,000
Total Liabilities and	
Stockholders' Equity	$1,500,000

The owners' equity ratio is:

a 2.0 to 1.

b 1.75 to 1.

c 1.2 to 1.

d 66⅔ percent.

5 Which of the following statements is true?

a If a company can earn a 9 percent return on total assets and can borrow funds at 7 percent, it is desirable for the company to include a high percentage of long-term debt in its capital structure.

b A company that is successfully trading on the equity is earning a higher return per share for its stockholders than it would be if all of its long-term capital had been acquired from equity sources.

c Financing a company entirely with stockholders' equity is a desirable move from the viewpoint of the stockholder.

d None of the above.

547

6 The Drucker Dog Food Company accounts show the following for the fiscal year ended September 30, 1980:

Gross sales	$439,800
Sales returns and allowances	9,800
Net sales	$430,000

Accounts receivable (net):

On 9/30/79	$ 40,000
On 9/30/80	60,000

The turnover of accounts receivable is:
a 6.14 times per year.
b 8.4 times per year.
c 8.6 times per year.
d 8.8 times per year.
e 43 days.

7 Assuming relatively stable business conditions, a decline in the average number of days an account receivable is outstanding from one year to the next might indicate—
a A stiffening of the company's credit policies.
b That the second year's sales were made at lower prices than the first year's sales.
c A longer discount period and a more distant due date were extended to customers in the second year.
d A significant decrease in sales in the second year.
e None of the above.

8 The following selected data are taken from Goody Style Center's accounts.

Sales in 1979	$178,800
Cost of goods sold in 1979	108,000
Accounts receivable, 12/31/79	121,000
Accounts receivable, 1/1/79	110,000
Inventory, 1/1/79	65,000
Inventory, 12/31/79	35,000

The inventory turnover rate is:
a 2.16.
b 1.35.
c 3.56.
d 1.66.
e 5.12.

SECTION II

9 Given the following data, what are the net earnings per share of common stock? No shares were issued in 1979.

Net sales for 1979	$3,180,000	
Net earnings	194,000	
Common stock (par value, $100)	1,000,000	
Paid-in capital in excess of par —common	45,000	
Preferred stock	30,000	
Cash dividends:		
On preferred	$ 1,200	
On common	35,000	36,200

a $3.18.
b $3.62.
c $15.78.
d $19.28.
e $19.40.

10 The Elly Corporation stockholders earned a return of 12 percent on stock which had a market price of $60 per share. What was the price-earnings ratio?
a 12 to 1.
b 5 to 1.
c 8.33 to 1.
d .24 to 1.

11 You are given the following information:

Earnings before interest and taxes	$400,000
Less: Interest on bonds	30,000
Balance	$370,000
Less: Taxes (at 40% rate)	148,000
Earnings after taxes	$222,000
Less: Preferred dividends	10,000
Earnings Available for Common Stockholders	$212,000

The number of times the interest is earned is:
a $12\frac{1}{3}$.
b $13\frac{1}{3}$.
c $33\frac{1}{3}$.

12 A banker, examining comparative statements of financial position and other financial data relating to Company X and faced with the decision as to whether to approve a substantial 60-day loan to that company, would probably be *least* interested in which of the following ratios?

a   Acid test ratio.
b   Accounts receivable turnover.
c   Current ratio.
d   Inventory turnover.
e   Earnings per share of common stock.

13 Which of the following is not a monetary item?

a   Accounts payable.
b   Cash.
c   Delivery equipment.
d   Accounts receivable.
e   Bonds payable.

Now compare your answers with the correct answers and explanations on page 724.

Questions *chapter* 11

SECTION I

1 The higher the accounts receivable turnover rate the better off is the company. Do you agree? Why?

2 See if you can think of a situation where the current ratio is very misleading as an indicator of short-term debt-paying ability. Does the quick ratio offer a remedy to the situation you have described? Describe a situation where the quick ratio will not suffice either.

3 Before the John Company issued

$10,000 of long-term notes (due more than a year from the date of issue) in exchange for a like amount of accounts payable, its acid test ratio was 2:1. Will this transaction increase, decrease, or have no effect on the current ratio? The equity ratio?

4 Through the use of turnover ratios explain why a firm might seek to increase the volume of its sales even though such an increase can be secured only at reduced prices.

SECTION II

5 Indicate which of the relationships illustrated in Chapter 11 would be best to judge:
a   The short-term debt-paying ability of the firm.
b   The overall efficiency of the firm without regard to the sources of assets.
c   The return to owners of a corporation.
d   The safety of bondholders' interest.
e   The safety of preferred stockholders' dividends.

6 Indicate how each of the following ratios or measures is calculated:
a   Payout ratio.
b   Earnings per share of common stock.
c   Price-earnings ratio.
d   Yield on common stock.
e   Yield on preferred stock.
f   Times interest earned.
g   Times preferred dividends earned.
h   Return on stockholders' equity.

7 How is earning power on operating assets determined? Is it possible for two

companies with "operating margins" of 5 percent and 1 percent, respectively, to both have an earning power of 20 percent on operating assets? How?

8 Cite some of the possible deficiencies in accounting information especially as regards its use in analyzing a particular company over a ten-year period.

9 Distinguish between monetary items and nonmonetary items. Classify the following items as either monetary or nonmonetary:
1. Cash.
2. Retained earnings.
3. Bonds payable.
4. Merchandise inventory.
5. Accounts receivable.
6. Patents.
7. Common stock.
8. Land.
9. Accounts payable.
10. Buildings.

10 What are purchasing power gains and losses? When do purchasing power gains

549

occur? When do purchasing power losses occur?

11 How can replacement costs be estimated?

Exercises *chapter* 11

SECTION I

1 Under each of the three conditions listed below, compute the current ratio after each of the transactions described. Current assets are now $100,000. (Consider each transaction independently of the others.) Current ratio before the transactions is:

a 1:1.
b 2:1.
c 1:2.

Transactions:

a. $100,000 of merchandise is purchased on account.
b. Purchased $50,000 of machinery for cash.
c. Issued stock for $50,000 cash.

2 A company has sales of $912,500 per year. Its average accounts receivable balance is $182,500.

a What is the average number of days an account receivable is outstanding?
b Assuming released funds can be invested at 10 percent, how much could the company earn by reducing the collection period of the accounts receivable to 40 days?

c What assumption must you make in order for this earnings calculation to be correct?

3 From the following partial earnings statement calculate the inventory turnover for the period:

Net sales...................		$521,450
Cost of goods sold:		
Beginning inventory	$ 50,000	
Purchases..................	370,000	
Goods available for sale...................	$420,000	
Less: Ending inventory.............	58,000	
Cost of Goods Sold..............		$362,000
Gross margin		$159,450
Operating expenses.....		75,000
Net Operating Earnings.................		$ 84,450

SECTION II

4 The Korner Company had 40,000 shares of common stock outstanding on January 1, 1979. On April 1, 1979, it issued 10,000 additional shares for cash. The earnings available for common stockholders for 1979 were $200,000. What amount of earnings per share of common stock should the company report?

5 A company paid bond interest of $4,000, incurred federal income taxes of $11,000, and had net earnings (after taxes)

of $21,000. How many times was the bond interest earned?

6 The Field Company had 4,000 shares of $100 par value, 5 percent, preferred stock outstanding. Net earnings after taxes were $120,000. The market price per share was $80.

a How many times were the preferred dividends earned?
b What was the yield on the preferred stock assuming the regular preferred dividends were declared and paid?

Problems, Series A *chapter* 11

SECTION I

11–1–A

From the following data for the Edwards Company compute **(a)** the working capital, **(b)** the current ratio, and **(c)** the acid test ratio, all as of both dates, and **(d)** comment briefly on the company's short-term financial position.

	December 31, 1980	December 31, 1979
Notes payable (due in 90 days)	$ 47,000	$ 38,500
Merchandise inventory	200,000	176,200
Cash	63,310	78,350
Marketable securities	31,000	18,750
Accrued liabilities	12,000	13,800
Accounts receivable	117,500	115,000
Accounts payable	69,400	45,300
Allowance for doubtful accounts	14,800	9,600
Bonds payable, due 1985	92,500	98,000
Prepaid expenses	4,050	4,650

11–2–A

Dobson Products, Inc., has a current ratio on December 31, 1979, of two to one. If the following transactions were completed on that date, indicate (1) whether the amount of working capital would have been increased, decreased, or unaffected by each of the transactions; and (2) whether the current ratio would have been increased, decreased, or unaffected by each of the transactions (consider each independently of all of the others).

a. Sold building for cash.

b. Exchanged old equipment for new equipment. (No cash was involved.)

c. Declared a cash dividend on preferred stock.

d. Sold merchandise on account (at a profit).

e. Retired mortgage notes which would have matured in 1987.

f. Issued stock dividend to common stockholders.

g. Paid cash for a patent.

h. Temporarily invested cash in government bonds.

i. Purchased inventory for cash.

j. Wrote off an account receivable as uncollectible.

k. Paid the cash dividend on preferred stock.

l. Purchased a computer and gave a two-year promissory note.

m. Collected accounts receivable.

n. Borrowed from bank on a 120-day promissory note.

o. Discounted a customer's note. A financial expense was involved.

11–3–A

The following are comparative statements of financial position of the Happer Corporation on December 31, 1979, and 1980:

HAPPER CORPORATION
Comparative Statements of Financial Position

	December 31, 1980	December 31, 1979
Assets		
Cash	$ 75,000	$ 85,000
Accounts receivable, net	65,000	75,000
Merchandise inventory	45,000	55,000
Plant assets, net	100,000	45,000
Total Assets	$285,000	$260,000
Liabilities and Stockholders' Equity		
Accounts payable	$ 40,000	$ 25,000
Notes payable	35,000	43,000
Common stock	110,000	110,000
Retained earnings	100,000	82,000
Total Liabilities and Stockholders' Equity	$285,000	$260,000
Other data:		
Sales	$460,000	$400,000
Gross margin	190,000	170,000
Selling and administrative expense	120,000	110,000
Interest expense	4,000	2,000
Cash dividends	38,000	15,000

During 1980, a note in the amount of $25,000 was given for equipment purchased at that price. Unlike the company's other notes, which are short term, the $25,000 note matures in 1984.

Required:

a Prepare comparative earnings statements which show for each item its percentage of net sales.

b Prepare comparative statements of financial position which show for each item its percentage of total assets.

c Prepare a schedule which shows the percentage of each current asset to the total of current assets as of both year-end dates.

d Compute the current ratios as of both dates.

e Compute the acid test ratios as of both dates.

f Compute the percentage of stockholders' equity to total equity (or total assets) as of both dates.

SECTION II

11–4–A

The following condensed statement of financial position and supplementary data are for the Carradine Company for 1980:

Analysis and interpretation of financial statements

CARRADINE COMPANY
Statement of Financial Position
December 31, 1980

Assets

Current Assets:

Cash	$ 400,000	
Marketable securities	250,000	
Accounts receivable	650,000	
Inventory	420,000	$1,720,000

Property, Plant, and Equipment:

Plant assets, cost	3,000,000	
Less: Allowance for depreciation	550,000	2,450,000
Total Assets		$4,170,000

Liabilities and Stockholders' Equity

Current Liabilities:

Accounts payable	$ 300,000	
Bank loans payable (due in six months)	80,000	$ 380,000

Long-Term Liabilities:

Mortgage notes payable, due in 1986	$ 175,000	
Bond payable, 8%, due December 31, 1988	800,000	975,000

Stockholders' Equity:

Common stock, par value $50 per share	$2,300,000	
Reserve for bond sinking fund	115,000	
Retained earnings	400,000	2,815,000
Total Liabilities and Stockholders' Equity		$4,170,000

Supplementary data:

a. 1980 interest expense, $80,000.

b. 1980 net sales, $3,000,000.

c. 1980 cost of goods sold, $2,100,000.

d. 1980 net earnings after taxes, $200,000.

e. 1980 earnings before interest and taxes, $400,000.

f. Inventory, December 31, 1979, $625,000.

Required:

Calculate the following ratios. Where you would normally use the average amount for an item in a ratio, but the information is not available to do so, use the year-end balance. (Analysts sometimes have to do this.) Show computations.

a   Current ratio.

b   Percentage of net earnings to stockholders' equity.

c   Turnover of inventory.

d   Average collection period of accounts receivable (366 days in 1980).

e   Earnings per share of common stock.

f   Number of times bond interest was earned.

g   Stockholders' equity ratio.

h   Percentage of net earnings to total assets.

i   Turnover of total assets.

j   Acid test ratio.

11-5-A

	Operating assets	Net operating earnings	Net sales
Company 1	$ 150,000	$ 20,000	$ 220,000
Company 2	900,000	65,000	2,000,000
Company 3	4,000,000	525,000	3,750,000

Required:

a Determine the operating margin, turnover of operating assets, and earning power on operating assets for each company.

b In the subsequent year the following changes took place (no other changes occurred):

Company 1 bought some new machinery at a cost of $25,000. Net operating earnings increased by $2,000 as a result of an increase in sales of $40,000.

Company 2 sold some equipment it was using which was relatively unproductive. The book value of the equipment sold was $100,000. As a result of the sale of the equipment, sales declined by $50,000 and operating earnings declined by $1,000.

Company 3 purchased some new retail outlets at a cost of $1,000,000. As a result, sales increased by $1,500,000 and operating earnings increased by $80,000.

1. Which company has the largest absolute change in—
   a. Operating margin ratio?
   b. Turnover of operating assets?
   c. Earning power on operating assets?
2. Which one realized the largest dollar change in operating earnings? Explain this in the light of the earning power changes.

11-6-A

You have managed to determine the following data:

	1980	1979
Net sales..	$550,000	$425,000
Net earnings before interest and taxes	90,000	30,000
Net earnings after taxes	45,000	15,000
Bond interest expense..	12,000	5,000
Stockholders' equity, January 1	375,000	250,000
Stockholders' equity, December 31.........................	400,000	375,000
Common stock, par value $50. December 31.............	300,000	180,000

Additional shares of common stock were issued on January 1, 1980.

Required:

Compute the following for both 1979 and 1980:

a Earnings per share of common stock.
b Percentage of net earnings to net sales.
c Rate of return on stockholders' equity.
d Number of times bond interest was earned.

Compare and comment.

Problems, Series B *chapter* 11

SECTION I

11-1-B

The following account balances are taken from the ledger of the Toynbee Company:

	December 31, 1980	December 31, 1979
Allowance for doubtful accounts....................	$ 32,000	$ 25,000
Prepaid expenses..	15,000	20,000
Accrued liabilities.......................................	70,000	62,000
Cash in Bank A	365,000	325,000
Bank overdraft in Bank B (credit balance)	–0–	42,500
Accounts payable.......................................	238,000	195,000
Merchandise inventory...............................	595,000	658,000
Bonds payable, due in 1985.........................	205,000	198,000
Marketable securities	72,500	49,000
Notes payable (due in six months).................	151,000	91,000
Accounts receivable....................................	469,500	433,000

Required:

a   Compute the amount of working capital as of both year-end dates.
b   Compute the current ratio as of both year-end dates.
c   Compute the acid test ratio as of both year-end dates.
d   Comment briefly on the company's short-term financial position.

11-2-B

On December 31, 1979, the Brandy Company's current ratio was three to one. Assume that the following transactions were completed on that date and indicate (1) whether the amount of working capital would have been increased, decreased, or unaffected by each of the transactions; and (2) whether the current ratio would have been increased, decreased, or unaffected by each of the transactions. (Consider each transaction independently of all the others.)

a.   Purchased merchandise on account.
b.   Paid a cash dividend declared on November 15, 1979.
c.   Sold equipment for cash.
d.   Temporarily invested cash in marketable securities.
e.   Sold obsolete merchandise for cash (at a loss).
f.   Issued ten-year bonds for cash.
g.   Wrote off Goodwill to Retained Earnings.
h.   Paid cash for inventory.
i.   Purchased land for cash.
j.   Returned merchandise which had not been paid for.
k.   Wrote off an account receivable as uncollectible.
l.   Accepted a 90-day note from a customer in settlement of customer's account receivable.
m.   Declared a stock dividend on common stock.

11-3-B

From the following data of the Prader Company:

a Prepare comparative earnings statements which show for each item its percentage of net sales.

b Prepare comparative statements of financial position which show for each item its percentage of total assets.

c Prepare a schedule which shows the percentage of each current asset to the total of current assets as of both year-end dates.

d Compute the current ratios as of both dates.

e Compute the acid test ratios as of both dates.

f Compute the percentage of stockholders' equity to total assets as of both dates.

THE PRADER COMPANY
Comparative Statements of Financial Position

	December 31, 1980	December 31, 1979
Assets		
Cash	$ 25,000	$16,000
Accounts receivable, net	45,000	23,000
Merchandise inventory	35,000	28,000
Plant assets, net	36,000	27,000
Total Assets	$141,000	$94,000
Liabilities and Stockholders' Equity		
Accounts payable	$ 19,000	$13,000
Notes payable	25,000	14,000
Common stock	65,000	46,000
Retained earnings	32,000	21,000
Total Liabilities and Stockholders' Equity	$141,000	$94,000
Other data:		
Sales	$190,000	$145,000
Gross margin	115,000	95,000
Selling and administrative expense	60,000	53,000
Interest expense	2,000	700

Cash dividends of $42,000 were paid in 1980. In 1980, plant assets were increased by giving a note of $4,500 for machinery of the same cost. The note matures October 1, 1983. All other notes are short term.

SECTION II

11-4-B

The following statement of financial position and supplementary data are for the Yeomen Corporation for 1980:

Analysis and interpretation of financial statements

YEOMEN CORPORATION
Statement of Financial Position
December 31, 1980

Assets

Current Assets:

Cash	$ 150,000	
Marketable securities	80,000	
Accounts receivable	130,000	
Inventory	110,000	$ 470,000

Property, Plant, and Equipment:

Plant assets, cost	$1,700,000	
Less: Allowance for depreciation	125,000	$1,575,000
Total Assets		$2,045,000

Liabilities and Stockholders' Equity

Current Liabilities:

Accounts payable	$ 85,000	
Bank loans payable	35,000	$ 120,000

Long-Term Liabilities:

Mortgage notes payable, due in 1983	$ 45,000	
Bonds payable, 6%, due December 31, 1982	215,000	260,000
Total Liabilities		$ 380,000

Stockholders' Equity:

Common stock, par value $50 per share	$1,100,000	
Reserve for bond sinking fund	40,000	
Retained earnings	525,000	1,665,000
Total Liabilities and Stockholders' Equity		$2,045,000

Supplementary data:

a. 1980 net earnings after taxes amounted to $150,000.
b. 1980 earnings before interest and taxes, $300,000.
c. 1980 cost of goods sold was $400,000.
d. 1980 net sales amounted to $750,000.
e. Inventory on December 31, 1979, was $75,000.
f. Interest expense for the year was $15,000.

Required:

Calculate the following ratios. Where you would normally use the average amount for an item in a ratio, but the information is not available to do so, use the year-end balance. (Analysts sometimes have to do this.) Show computations.

a Current ratio.
b Percentage of net earnings to stockholders' equity.
c Turnover of inventory.
d Average collection period of accounts receivable (366 days in 1980).
e Earnings per share of common stock.
f Number of times bond interest was earned.
g Stockholders' equity ratio.
h Percentage of net earnings to total assets.
i Turnover of total assets.
j Acid test ratio.

11-5-B

The Lake Company has net operating earnings of $80,000 and operating assets of $400,-000. Its net sales are $800,000.

The accountant for the company computes the rate of earning power on operating assets after first computing the operating margin and the turnover of operating assets.

Required:

a Show the computations the accountant made.
b Indicate whether the operating margin and turnover will increase or decrease and then determine what the actual rate of earning power on operating assets would be after each of the following changes. The events are not interrelated; consider each separately starting from the original earning power position. No other changes occurred.
  1. Sales are increased by $20,000. There is no change in the amount of operating earnings and no change in operating assets.
  2. Management found some cost savings in the manufacturing process. The amount of reduction in operating expenses was $5,000. The savings resulted from the use of less materials to manufacture the same quantity of goods. As a result average inventory was $2,000 lower than it otherwise would have been.
  3. The company invested $10,000 of cash (received on accounts receivable) in a plot of land it plans to use in the future (a nonoperating asset); earnings are not affected.
  4. The federal income tax rate on amounts of taxable income over $50,000 was increased from 48 percent to 60 percent. The taxes have not yet been paid.
  5. The company issued bonds and used the proceeds to buy $50,000 of machinery to be used in the business. Interest payments are $2,500 per year. Operating earnings increased by $10,000 (net sales did not change).

11-6-B

	1980	1979
Net sales	$420,000	$260,000
Net earnings before interest and taxes	110,000	85,000
Net earnings after taxes	55,500	63,000
Bond interest expense	9,000	8,000
Stockholders' equity, December 31 (on		
December 31, 1978, $200,000)	305,000	235,000
Common stock, par value $50, December 31	260,000	230,000

Additional shares of common stock were issued on January 1, 1980.

Required:

Compute the following for both 1979 and 1980:
a Earnings per share of common stock.
b Percentage of net earnings to net sales.
c Rate of return on average stockholders' equity.
d Number of times bond interest was earned.

Compare and comment.

12

Reporting changes in financial position; cash flow statements

Learning objectives

Study of the material in this chapter is designed to achieve the following learning objectives:

1. An understanding of the uses of the statement of changes in financial position.

2. An ability to prepare a schedule of changes in working capital and a statement of changes in financial position.

3. A conceptual understanding of statements of changes in financial position which use the all-resources concept of funds but emphasize either working capital flows or cash flows.

4. An ability to prepare a cash flow statement.

5. An understanding of the T-account method for preparing a statement of changes in financial position (Appendix).

The conventional financial statements of a company—the earnings statement, the statement of retained earnings, and the statement of financial position—often have not provided answers to questions that users have been asking. These questions include: How much working capital was generated by operations? Why is such a profitable firm able to pay only such meager dividends? How much was spent for new plant and equipment and where did the funds come from to purchase it?

The statement which provides this desired information is called the statement of changes in financial position and is the topic of this chapter. The Accounting Principles Board decided that such a statement is to be provided as a basic financial statement for each period for which an earnings statement is presented.[1]

The statement of changes in financial position

Basic objectives and content

The broad objectives of the statement of changes in financial position are (1) to summarize the financing and investing activities of the enterprise including an indication of the amount of working capital provided by operations; and (2) to help explain and disclose the changes in financial position that occurred during the period. The statement provides information relating to the management of the financing and investing activities of the enterprise since these are a vital part of the successful administration of the enterprise.[2]

Currently, the concepts, terminology, and even the form of the statement of changes in financial position are in a transitional stage. *APB Opinion No. 19* permits considerable flexibility in form. The statement of changes in financial position presented in this text will be similar in format and terminology to those widely used in recent practice.

Typically, these statements contain two major sections. One is headed "Financial Resources Provided" and shows the sources of the flow of financial resources (funds) into the enterprise. The other is headed "Financial Resources Applied" and shows how the financial resources flowing into the enterprise were used. (Refer to Illustration 12.5, page 577, to examine the format of the statement.)[3]

In the past, such statements often were broadly referred to as funds flow statements and carried the formal titles of "statement of sources and applications of funds" or "statement of sources and uses of funds."

---

[1] Accounting Principles Board, "Reporting Changes in Financial Position," *APB Opinion No. 19* (New York: AICPA, March 1971), par. 7.

[2] The statement of changes in financial position may highlight the amount of cash provided by operations and still be in accord with *APB Opinion No. 19*. But current practice tends heavily to emphasize working capital from operations, and we will do the same.

[3] A schedule of working capital (to be illustrated later) may either appear as a third part of the statement of changes in financial position or may appear as a separate schedule. We have used the latter approach.

Reporting changes in financial position; cash flow statements

On other occasions, because such statements usually showed the flows of working capital into and out of the firm, the statement was entitled "statement of sources and uses of working capital." Following the definite preference expressed by the Board in *APB Opinion No. 19,* this text will use the broader title "statement of changes in financial position."

Uses of the statement of changes in financial position

The information contained in the statement of changes in financial position is useful to many parties for a variety of reasons.

Management uses. Management may, for example, after studying such information, decide to change its dividend policy in order to conserve working capital. Or it may decide that in the light of the large amount of working capital generated by operations that a certain amount of working capital can be safely invested in plant and equipment. Or the information may clearly show the need for additional financing to take advantage of capital expenditure opportunities that promise to be highly profitable. And the statement highlights the all-important relationship between working capital generated by operations, all other sources and uses of working capital, and financial resources provided and applied which did not affect working capital.

Creditor and investor uses. Information contained in the statement of changes in financial position also may be used by creditors and investors. These groups make decisions on whether to invest (or disinvest) in the debt or equity securities issued by a given company. *Projections* of such information can provide valuable insights into such matters as (1) whether or not dividends are likely to be increased; (2) how future capital expenditures are likely to be financed; and (3) whether or not a firm appears capable of meeting its debts as they come due. Typically, projections of the future are based upon study of the immediate past.

Determine whether each of the following statements is true or false.

1. The statement of changes in financial position is optional in that it need not be provided along with the other financial statements.
2. The terms "where got" and "where gone" would describe the two major sections of the statement of changes in financial position.
3. If the dividends paid out by a corporation far exceeded its working capital provided by operations for a given year, a stockholder would have cause to wonder how long the current rate of dividends could be maintained.
4. The statement of changes in financial position only presents historical data and is, therefore, useless in predicting the future.

Now turn to Answer Frame 1[12] on page 562 to check your answers.

1. False. *APB Opinion No. 19 requires* that the statement of changes in financial position be provided for each period for which an earnings statement is presented.
2. True. These terms are synonymous with the terms financial resources provided and financial resources applied but are not as desirable.
3. True. Financial resources provided from operations are the usual source of dividend payments, and in the long run will normally be equal to, or will exceed, the dividends paid.
4. False. Just because it includes only historical data does not mean that it is useless in predicting the future. Typically, projections of the future are based on the study of past data.

If you missed any of the above, restudy Frame 1[12] before beginning Frame 2[12] below.

Frame 2[12] ──

Preparing the statement of changes in financial position

Illustration 12.1 shows the financial resources provided (inflows) and the financial resources applied (outflows) which are reported in the statement of changes in financial position. A careful study of this illustration should be helpful in understanding the concepts presented in the remainder of this chapter. Compare this illustration with Illustration 12.5, page 577, and refer to Illustration 12.5 periodically as you read about how to prepare the statement.

Working capital from operations. The amount of working capital generated by operations has long been recognized as one of the most important single figures that can be determined for most business enterprises. Over the long run, a successful business will acquire plant and other assets, retire long-term debt, and pay dividends largely from working capital generated by operations.

Typically, the measurement of working capital from operations begins with net earnings. This is because sales of goods and services bring new current assets into the business (usually cash or receivables), while expenses for the most part decrease working capital (either through decreases in current assets or increases in current liabilities). But because of the inclusion of expenses such as depreciation, which do not require the use of working capital, net earnings do not measure the amount of working capital generated by operations. Adjustments for revenues not producing working capital and expenses not consuming working capital must be made.

Reporting changes in financial position; cash flow statements

Illustration 12.1   Graphic illustration of flows represented in the statement of changes in financial position

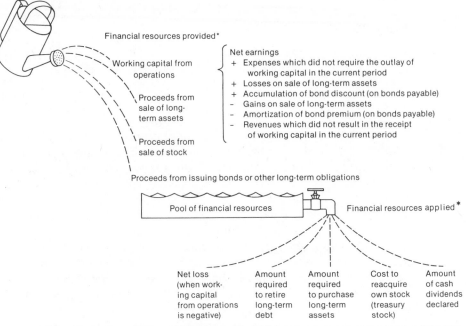

* If financial resources provided exceed financial resources applied, there is an increase in working capital, and vice versa. While financial resources provided and applied which did not affect working capital are included, the amounts offset each other.

The following illustration is presented to explain the adjustment needed when net earnings contain an expense not requiring working capital:

Sales (represented by receipts of cash and receivables)...............		$230,000
Less: Operating expenses consuming working capital (represented by credits to current asset or current liability accounts)	$180,000	
Depreciation (recorded by credits to allowance for depreciation accounts, which are related to plant assets and are *not* current assets or current liabilities)...................	12,000	192,000
Net Earnings		$ 38,000

The parenthetical expressions above indicate that one item presented — depreciation — does not result in either an increase or decrease in working capital. Unlike most expenses, depreciation does not decrease current assets or increase current liabilities. Since this is true, it follows that the amount of working capital generated by operations is not $38,000 (the net earnings amount) but $50,000. This amount is found as follows:

Working capital from sales	$230,000
Less: Working capital consumed by expenses......................................	180,000
Working Capital from Operations	$ 50,000

563

A more common way of showing the working capital generated by operations in the statement of changes in financial position is as follows:

Working Capital Provided:
By operations:

Net earnings	$38,000
Add: Expenses not requiring the outlay of working capital in the current period – depreciation	12,000
	$50,000

Because the purpose of the statement of changes in financial position is to show gross flows rather than simply net changes, the first method of reporting has considerable merit. But the second method is almost always used because it is brief and can be tied in with reported net earnings.

Depreciation is one example of an expense that does not require an outflow of working capital. Others are the amortization of patents, leases, and leaseholds, and the recording of depletion. In fact, an adjustment is required for any expense that is recorded by a debit to an expense account and a credit to a long-term asset account. The asset may be credited directly or by means of a credit to an allowance account (e.g., allowance for depreciation).

The periodic amortization of recorded amounts of bond premium or bond discount also affects net earnings through its effect on interest expense. The following situation illustrates the use of a premium. Assume that a company received $102,000 for $100,000 face value of 20-year, 9 percent, semiannual interest-bearing bonds ($4,500 of interest is paid each six months). The amount received in excess of the face value of the bonds is called a premium and is credited to Premium on Bonds Payable. The credit balance in this account is reported in the statement of financial position as an addition to Bonds Payable (a long-term liability). Since the premium is not paid back to investors at maturity date, it serves to reduce the interest cost on the bonds to less than 9 percent per year. The annual interest expense is determined as follows:

Total interest to be paid in cash ($100,000 × .09 × 20 years)	$180,000
Less premium received on issuance	2,000
Total Net Interest Cost	$178,000
Cost per year (divide by 20)	$ 8,900

An entry would be made annually debiting Premium on Bonds Payable and crediting Interest Expense for $100. The interest actually paid would be recorded by a debit to Interest Expense and a credit to either Cash or Accrued Interest Payable, both elements of working capital, for a total of $9,000 per year.

Thus, the amount of interest expense deducted in arriving at net earnings is $8,900, whereas the decrease in working capital is $9,000.

Net earnings will overstate the working capital from operations by this $100 difference. The $100 of bond premium amortized must therefore be deducted from net earnings in calculating working capital provided by operations.

When bonds are issued at a discount, the discount is also allocated over the life of the bonds. This amount is an addition to, rather than a deduction from, the amount of interest paid currently. The amount of expense recorded is therefore larger than the drain on working capital. The discount must be added to net earnings to convert it to a measure of working capital from operations.

Whether or not operations produce or consume working capital in a firm operating at a net loss depends upon the size of the items included in the net loss that did not require or produce working capital. For example, if a company reports a net loss of $50,000 occurring after deducting $80,000 of depreciation, then $30,000 of working capital was provided by operations. But if a loss of $50,000 is shown with only $15,000 of depreciation deducted, then operations have consumed (rather than provided) $35,000 of working capital. Typically, the $35,000 is reported as an application of working capital.

Is each of the following statements true or false?

1. Working capital is equal to assets minus liabilities.
2. Net earnings are equal to the amount of working capital generated by operations.
3. Conceptually, working capital from operations is equal to revenue that yields working capital, less expenses that consume working capital. But this figure can also be computed by adjusting net earnings for revenues and expenses that did not produce or consume working capital.
4. Adjustment to the net earnings figure is required for any expense that resulted from a transaction debiting the expense and crediting a noncurrent account.

Now turn to Answer Frame 2¹² on page 566 to check your answers.

Frame 3¹² ───

Other significant financing and investing activities. In addition to reporting the working capital provided by operations, the statement of changes in financial position should clearly disclose:

1. The use of working capital to acquire long-term assets — investments; property, plant, and equipment; and intangibles.
2. The other sources of working capital such as the sale of noncurrent assets and the issuance of long-term debt or shares of stock.
3. The use of working capital to pay dividends to stockholders.

3¹²
continued

4. All changes of a significant financial or investment nature which do not involve the use of working capital. These would include changes such as the conversion of long-term debt or preferred stock into common stock and the issuance of long-term debt or preferred or common stock for noncurrent assets.

Changes reported in the statement of financial position which are not significant investment or financial activities do not have to be reported in the statement of changes in financial position. Examples are stock dividends and stock splits.

The schedule of changes in working capital

APB Opinion No. 19, states that a statement or schedule showing the details of the net change in working capital should be presented when a statement of changes in financial position is presented. It is usually presented at the bottom of the statement of changes in financial position. But we will treat it as a separate schedule, as shown in Illustration 12.4, page 569.

The statement of changes in financial position illustrated

It is assumed in the following illustration that the accountant has prepared two of the financial statements for The United States Corporation (see Illustrations 12.2 and 12.3) and is now turning to the statement of changes in financial position. Additional information will be provided as

Illustration 12.2

THE UNITED STATES CORPORATION
Statement of Earnings and Retained Earnings
For the Year Ended December 31, 1979

Gross sales...		$1,475,000
Less: Sales returns and allowances		10,800
Net sales..		$1,464,200
Cost of Goods Sold:		
Inventories, January 1	$115,300	
Net purchases	883,450	
Cost of goods available for sale.................................	$998,750	
Inventories, December 31	127,600	
Cost of Goods Sold..		871,150
Gross margin		$ 593,050
Less: Operating expenses:		
Bad debts expense	$ 7,320	
Depreciation expense	34,300	
Salaries..	215,000	
Sundry selling expenses	90,000	
Taxes, payroll, and other..	26,000	
General administrative expenses..............................	123,780	
Total Operating Expenses		496,400
Net earnings from operations...		$ 96,650
Other revenue:		
Interest earned...	$ 1,950	
Gain on sale of long-term investments.............................	1,700	3,650
		$ 100,300
Other expense:		
Interest expense	$ 3,800	
Loss on sale of equipment...	900	4,700
Net earnings before federal income taxes..........................		$ 95,600
Deduct: Federal income taxes..		45,250
Net earnings to retained earnings....................................		$ 50,350
Retained earnings, January 1		84,100
		$ 134,450
Deduct: Dividends declared		18,000
Retained Earnings, December 31......................................		$ 116,450

---

required in order to illustrate the type of analyses undertaken in the preparation of the statement of changes in financial position.

The comparative statement of financial position in Illustration 12.3 has already been expanded to include a column showing the net increase or decrease in each item between December 31, 1978, and December 31, 1979. From the increase-decrease column it is a simple matter to prepare the comparative schedule of working capital shown in Illustration 12.4. Each of the current assets and current liabilities is listed along with its balance and its effect on working capital.

Each increase in a current asset results in an increase in working capital, as, for example, the $5,400 increase in cash. Similarly, a net decrease in any current asset results in a decrease in working capital. Con-

Illustration 12.3

			Increase
	1979	1978	*decrease**

THE UNITED STATES CORPORATION
Comparative Statement of Financial Position
December 31, 1978, and 1979

Assets

Current Assets:

	1979	1978	Increase decrease*
Cash	$ 46,300	$ 40,900	$ 5,400
Accounts receivable	119,980	107,000	12,980
Allowance for doubtful accounts	(7,820)	(6,000)	(1,820)
Marketable securities	3,000	–0–	3,000
Inventories	127,600	115,300	12,300
Prepaid expenses	3,100	4,700	1,600*
Total Current Assets	$292,160	$261,900	$30,260
Investments	$ 17,000	$ 25,000	$ 8,000*
Property, Plant, and Equipment:			
Land	$100,000	$ 80,000	$20,000
Buildings	175,000	130,000	45,000
Allowance for depreciation – buildings	(29,750)	(26,500)	(3,250)
Equipment	198,000	175,000	23,000
Allowance for depreciation – equipment	(57,650)	(43,100)	(14,550)
Total Property, Plant, and Equipment	$385,600	$315,400	$70,200
Total Assets	$694,760	$602,300	$92,460
Liabilities and Stockholders' Equity			
Current Liabilities:			
Accounts payable	$ 74,620	$ 64,900	$ 9,720
Notes payable	15,000	20,000	5,000*
Advances from customers	1,000	900	100
Accrued interest payable	800	1,070	270*
Other accrued liabilities	9,890	12,230	2,340*
Estimated federal income tax liability	12,000	14,100	2,100*
Total Current Liabilities	$113,310	$113,200	$ 110
Long-Term Liabilities:			
Mortgage note payable, 8% (on land and buildings)	$ 35,000	$ –0–	$35,000
Bonds payable, 9%, due 1983	40,000	40,000	–0–
Total Long-Term Liabilities	$ 75,000	$ 40,000	$35,000
Total Liabilities	$188,310	$153,200	$35,110
Stockholders' Equity:			
Common stock, stated value $50	$390,000	$365,000	$25,000
Retained earnings	116,450	84,100	32,350
Total Stockholders' Equity	$506,450	$449,100	$57,350
Total Liabilities and Stockholders' Equity	$694,760	$602,300	$92,460

versely, increases in current liabilities are decreases in working capital (accounts payable, for example), while decreases in current liabilities are increases in working capital.

The schedule of changes in working capital (Illustration 12.4) details the changes in the working capital of The United States Corporation.

Illustration 12.4

THE UNITED STATES CORPORATION
Comparative Schedule of Working Capital
December 31, 1978, and 1979

	December 31		Working capital	
	1979	1978	Increase	Decrease
Current Assets:				
Cash...	$ 46,300	$ 40,900	$ 5,400	
Accounts receivable	119,980	107,000	12,980	
Allowance for doubtful accounts.......	(7,820)	(6,000)	(1,820)	
Marketable securities.....................	3,000	–0–	3,000	
Inventories..................................	127,600	115,300	12,300	
Prepaid expenses	3,100	4,700		$ 1,600
Total Current Assets	$292,160	$261,900		
Current Liabilities:				
Accounts payable..........................	$ 74,620	$ 64,900		9,720
Notes payable	15,000	20,000	5,000	
Advances from customers...............	1,000	900		100
Accrued interest payable	800	1,070	270	
Other accrued liabilities..................	9,890	12,230	2,340	
Estimated federal income tax .liability......................................	12,000	14,100	2,100	
Total Current Liabilities.........	$113,310	$113,200		
Working Capital............................	$178,850	$148,700		
Net increase in working capital.........				30,150
			$41,570	$41,570

But it does not explain what caused the $30,150 net increase in working capital. One of the purposes of the statement of changes in financial position is to show these causes. As the analysis below explains, the reasons for the changes are found in the noncurrent accounts shown in the comparative statement of financial position. Bear in mind that the effect of net earnings and dividends is reported in retained earnings.

Determine whether each of the following statements is correct or incorrect.

1. Any time a transaction affects both a current account and a non-current account it is an item which affects working capital.
2. Transactions which do not affect working capital need not be reported in the statement of changes in financial position.
3. The comparative schedule of working capital (Illustration 12.4) shows the same information as the statement of changes in financial position.
4. The comparative schedule of working capital is prepared before the statement of changes in financial position.

Now turn to Answer Frame 3^{12} on page 570 to check your answers.

1. Correct. Conversely, whenever a transaction affects only current accounts or only noncurrent accounts it does not affect the total amount of working capital.
2. Incorrect. All changes which are of a *significant* financial or investment nature should be included *even* when they do not affect working capital. Examples are when long-term debt is converted into common stocks, or when common stock is issued in exchange for plant assets.
3. Incorrect. The schedule shows the details of the changes in the elements of the working capital but does not explain the *causes* of the changes in working capital. The statement of changes in financial position shows the causes.
4. Correct. It provides the net increase or decrease in working capital which is then used in preparing the statement of changes in financial position.

If you missed any of the above, reread Frame 3¹² before beginning Frame 4¹² below.

Frame 4¹²

Adjustment of net earnings to working capital provided by operations

Operations are a major source of working capital for most corporations. Modern financial analysis tends to highlight this source. Thus, a logical starting point in preparing the statement of changes in financial position is to convert reported net earnings to working capital provided by operations. As already noted, most of the items reported in the earnings statement either decrease or increase working capital. Depreciation is the most common item included in net earnings which does not. In the earnings statement in Illustration 12.2, $34,300 of depreciation was deducted in arriving at net earnings of $50,350. Thus, to arrive at the effect of operations on working capital, the $34,300 must be added back to net earnings.

The loss on sale of equipment of $900 does not consume working capital. It is similar to depreciation in that both are write-offs of part of the cost of a plant asset, so it is added back to net earnings. (The details of this transaction will be provided later. It is sufficient for now to note the similarity of the loss to depreciation.) In fact, working capital is increased by the proceeds from the sale of the equipment. Since the loss is not a part of operations and did not consume working capital, it is added back to net earnings.

A third adjustment is required to convert net earnings to working capital provided by operations; this time for a different reason. The comparative statement of financial position shows a decrease in investments of $8,000, while the earnings statement shows a gain from the sale of investments of $1,700. From this it follows that the investments were sold for $9,700. This is the amount that will be shown in the statement of changes in financial position as the working capital provided by the sale of the investments. But note that if the $1,700 gain is included in working capital provided by operations *and* in working capital provided by the sale of investments, it is counted twice. The sale of investments is not a part of operations. Thus, the preferred procedure is to deduct any gain from such sales from net earnings to arrive at working capital from operations. (Losses, of course, would be added back.) With these adjustments, the working capital provided by operations amounts to $83,850. This would be shown in the statement of changes in financial position as follows:

Working Capital Provided:
From operations:

Net earnings		$50,350
Add: Expenses not requiring outlay of working capital in the current period:		
Depreciation	$34,300	
Loss on sale of equipment	900	35,200
		$85,550
Deduct: Gain on sale of investments		1,700
Working Capital Provided by Operations		$83,850

Note carefully that the treatment given losses in the statement of changes in financial position depends upon the nature of the item causing the loss. Assume, for example, that the loss in the above illustration resulted from the sale of a current asset, such as temporary investments, and the loss was included in the determination of net earnings. No adjustment to net earnings would be required in deriving working capital provided by operations. The loss on the sale of a current asset is a loss that reduces working capital. The sale of part of a temporary investment in marketable securities having a cost of $2,000 for $1,800 cash reduces working capital by $200. Thus, no adjustment is needed.

To test your understanding, indicate whether each of the following would be added to net earnings, deducted from net earnings, or whether no adjustment is needed.

1. Gain on sale of building.
2. Gain on sale of temporary investments.
3. Loss on spoilage of inventory.
4. Loss on sale of land.

Now turn to Answer Frame 4¹² on page 572 to check your answers.

1. Deduct from net earnings.
2. No adjustment needed (current asset).
3. No adjustment needed (current asset).
4. Add to net earnings.

If you missed any of the above, reread Frame 4¹² before beginning Frame 5¹² below.

Frame 5¹²

Analysis of changes in noncurrent accounts

One of the items to be reported in the statement of changes in financial position is the net change in working capital. Consequently, once the change in working capital has been determined (see Illustration 12.4), no further attention need be paid to the individual items making up working capital—cash, accounts receivable, accounts payable, and so forth. The changes in all of these accounts are summarized and reported as one amount. Thus, in our analysis of changes in financial position, we need not concern ourselves with whether cash increased or decreased when we analyze the changes in the noncurrent accounts. All that we need to know is whether the change affected working capital or was part of a significant financing or investing transaction. If so, it must be reported in the statement of changes in financial position.

The changes which we must analyze to see whether they should be so reported are summarized below. They consist of all of the changes shown in the noncurrent accounts in the comparative statement of financial position for December 31, 1978, and December 31, 1979.

	Increase	*Decrease*
Investments...		$8,000
Land..	$20,000	
Buildings..	45,000	
Allowance for depreciation—buildings	3,250	
Equipment	23,000	
Allowance for depreciation—equipment	14,550	
Mortgage note payable..	35,000	
Common stock, stated value, $50 per share	25,000	
Retained earnings..	32,350	

Let us assume that the following information also is available:

1. There were no purchases of investments during the year. Investments with a cost of $8,000 were sold for $9,700.
2. One transaction took place in which land and buildings valued at $65,000 were acquired, subject to a 9 percent mortgage note of $35,000 on the building.
3. During the year the corporation disposed of equipment which had an original cost of $20,000 and which had been depreciated to the extent of $16,500 at date of sale.
4. All of the common stock was issued for cash.

We are now prepared to analyze each of the above changes in the noncurrent accounts to see if it affected working capital or was part of a significant investing or financing transaction. Changes of either type must be reported in the statement of changes in financial position.

Investments. We have already indicated that the gain on the sale of investments must be deducted from net earnings to show the entire amount received from the sale as a source of working capital. We know that the $8,000 change in investments actually produced $9,700 of working capital. The statement of changes in financial position would show:

> Other sources of working capital:
> Sale of investments................................. $9,700

Land and buildings. The increases in the land and buildings accounts were the result of a single transaction. In this transaction the acquisition of the building was financed in part by an increase in a long-term debt (the assumption of liability on the mortgage note of $35,000) and all of the land and part of the building were acquired by the use of working capital. The acquisition of these assets would be reported in the statement of changes in financial position as follows:

Working Capital Applied:
Acquisition of land $20,000
Acquisition of building 10,000

Financial resources applied which did not affect working capital:
Building acquired by assuming the liability on a mortgage note..................... $35,000

The assumption of the liability on the mortgage note would be reported:

Financial resources provided which did not affect working capital:
Assumption of liability on mortgage note to acquire building........................ $35,000

Before the issuance of *APB Opinion No. 19*, it was not uncommon to report only the $30,000 effect on working capital of transactions such as the above as an element of working capital applied. Such a procedure is now considered deficient. The merger wave of the 1960s showed very clearly that a company could engage in highly significant transactions which do not affect working capital. It could for example, double the amount of assets owned by issuing common stock for plant and equipment. Consequently, under *APB Opinion No. 19,* a transaction involving a change in a noncurrent asset and a noncurrent equity must be reported separately as both a provision of financial resources and an application of financial resources. Similarly, exchanges of one type of noncurrent asset for another and one type of noncurrent equity for another must also be reported separately as both financial resources provided and financial resources applied. Stock dividends and stock splits are exceptions.

Equipment. Since the equipment account shows a net increase of $23,000 in spite of the fact that some equipment was sold during the year, the net change in this account must be analyzed further to allow the reporting of the working capital provided and applied. The amount shown under "Other sources of working capital" from the sale of the equipment is the amount received at time of sale, computed as follows:

Cost of equipment sold	$20,000
Less: Allowance for depreciation	16,500
Book value of equipment sold	$ 3,500
Less: Loss on sale of equipment (from earnings statement)	900
Working Capital Received (sales price of the equipment)	$ 2,600

The equipment account must have been debited for purchases of equipment amounting to $43,000 if the account increased $23,000 in spite of a $20,000 credit to the account. Thus, the statement of changes in financial position would show working capital applied to purchase of equipment of $43,000.

Allowance for depreciation. The $17,800 net increase in the two allowance for depreciation accounts ($3,250 for buildings plus $14,550 for equipment) is the result of the credits from recording the depreciation charges for the year ($34,300) and the debit entered to remove the $16,500 applicable to the equipment sold. The effect of the change in these two accounts on working capital has already been explained in the adjustment of net earnings and in the treatment of the equipment sold.

Mortgage note payable. The manner in which the change in the Mortgage Note Payable account will appear in the statement of changes in financial position has already been presented.

Common stock. Since $25,000 of stated value common stock was issued for $25,000 cash, the statement of changes in financial position would show working capital provided by the issuance of common stock of $25,000. Had the stock been issued at an amount greater than stated value, the excess would appear as an increase in a separate stockholders' equity account. But the statement of changes in financial position would simply show the total amount received under "Other sources of working capital."

Retained earnings. The statement of retained earnings and the earnings statement reveal that net earnings for 1979 amounted to $50,350 and that dividends declared during the year amounted to $18,000. The difference between these two figures fully explains the $32,350 net increase in retained earnings. The net earnings amount has already been included as a source of working capital from operations. The dividends of $18,000 represent an application of working capital. They reduced working capital by $18,000 at the time of declaration (the creation of the current liability account, Dividends Payable, reduced working capital).

Had the Retained Earnings account changed for any other reason, the cause of the change must be determined in order to decide whether it should be reported in the statement of changes in financial position. The transfer of an amount from one stockholders' equity account to another does not affect working capital and usually is not a significant investment or financing transaction. Such transactions would not be reflected in the statement of changes in financial position.

Determine whether each of the following statements is true or false.
1. Losses on the sale of noncurrent assets are added back to net earnings and gains on the sale of these assets are deducted from net earnings in arriving at working capital provided by operations.
2. Current assets and current liabilities cannot be sources or applications of working capital.
3. Only changes in noncurrent accounts which affected working capital must be reported as sources or applications of financial resources.
4. Stock dividends and stock splits are significant and thus must be included in the statement of changes in financial position.

Now turn to Answer Frame 5¹² on page 576 to check your answers.

Frame 6¹² ————————————————————————————

The statement of changes in financial position illustrated

All information relating to working capital, the changes in working capital, and other significant financing and investing activities during 1979 has now been analyzed. The resulting statement of changes in financial position is shown in Illustration 12.5. This statement shows that of the total financial resources provided, over one half consisted

1. True. The gains or losses from these transactions are items that must be considered in arriving at working capital provided by operations. Since the proceeds of the sale are included as a separate item under "Other sources of working capital," not to deduct the gain would involve double counting. Not to add back the loss would be implicitly assuming that the loss was a consumption of working capital, while it was really a "consumption" of a noncurrent asset.

2. True. They *constitute* working capital and thus cannot be sources or applications of working capital. Only noncurrent accounts can be sources or applications of working capital.

3. False. Changes in the noncurrent accounts which affected working capital *or* were part of a significant investing or financing transaction must be included.

4. False. They do not affect working capital, and since they are not significant investing or financing transactions, they need not be included. Such transactions only involve the transfer of an amount from one stockholders' equity account to another.

If you missed any of the above, restudy Frame 5¹² before beginning Frame 6¹² on page 575.

6¹²
continued

of working capital provided by operations. The working capital provided by operations was adequate not only to cover the dividends for the year but also to finance approximately one half of the expansion in assets, including the increase in working capital. This latter increase may be a permanent increase necessary to support the corporation's expanded activity.

Assume the statement in Illustration 12.5 and a request for a $250,-000, five-year loan were presented to the United States Corporation's banker. The banker would be quick to note that the company has the ability to pay off the loan in about three years by using the working capital provided by operations. The banker would also note that the company pays dividends in an amount well under the amount of working capital generated by operations.

Note that the increase in working capital agrees with the change in working capital shown in Illustration 12.4.

See the Appendix at the end of this chapter for another method for discovering the amounts to be reported in the statement of changes in financial position. It is called the "T-account" method. It should be used by students who have difficulty in preparing the statement of changes in financial position using the method just illustrated.

Illustration 12.5

THE UNITED STATES CORPORATION*
Statement of Changes in Financial Position
For the Year Ended December 31, 1979

Financial Resources Provided:

Working capital provided:

By operations:

Net earnings..		$50,350	
Add: Expenses not requiring outlay of working capital in current period:			
Depreciation......................................	$34,300		
Loss on sale of equipment.....................	900	35,200	
		$85,550	
Deduct: Gain on sale of investments		1,700	
Working capital provided by operations.................			$ 83,850
Other sources of working capital:			
Sale of investments.....................................			9,700
Sale of equipment.......................................			2,600
Issuance of common stock...........................			25,000
Total Working Capital Provided............			$121,150
Financial resources provided which did not affect working capital:			
Assumption of liability on mortgage note to acquire building...			35,000
Total Financial Resources Provided			$156,150
Financial Resources Applied:			
Working capital applied:			
Acquisition of land			$ 20,000
Acquisition of building			10,000
Acquisition of equipment.................................			43,000
Payment of dividends......................................			18,000
Total Working Capital Applied			$ 91,000
Financial resources applied which did not affect working capital:			
Building acquired by assuming the liability on a mortgage note..			35,000
Total Financial Resources Applied.........			$126,000
Increase in working capital...................................			30,150
Total			$156,150

* Note: In published annual reports the information similar to that presented in Illustration 12.4 could be included at the bottom of this statement or could appear as a separate statement.

On a separate piece of paper prepare a schedule similar to that shown below, omitting for the sake of brevity the descriptions of the items. Indicate whether each is a source or an application of financial resources and enter the amount of financial resources provided or applied in the appropriate column. If any of the items described does not affect financial resources, indicate this by writing "Financial resources unaffected."

		Financial resources provided	Financial resources applied
1.	Net earnings for the year were $41,000............................	?	?
2.	Retired issue of 8 percent bonds due in 1984 by payment of $80,000 to the bondholders	?	?
3.	Purchased furniture and fixtures for the offices on account for $6,150...	?	?
4.	Declared a cash dividend of $9,000	?	?
5.	Sold old machinery for $15,000 cash; the book value was $10,000 at the date of sale, so the company realized a gain of $5,000 on the sale	?	?
6.	Issued 1,000 shares of stock, par $100, at $120 per share for cash..	?	?
7.	Purchased land for $300,000; no down payment; gave a ten-year mortgage note for full purchase price........................	?	?
8.	Issued new 9 percent bonds having a face value of $200,000 for $195,000 cash	?	?
9.	Bondholders exchanged their convertible bonds for common stock, paying $75,000 in addition to turning in bonds shown at $150,000 in the accounts	?	?

Turn to Answer Frame 6¹² on page 580 to check your responses.

Frame 7¹²

Statement of changes in financial position which emphasizes cash flow

The statement of changes in financial position may emphasize cash rather than working capital.[4] If so, the changes in other elements of working capital (all other current assets and the current liabilities) should be shown as sources or uses of cash in the statement.

As when the working capital concept was emphasized, the effects of other financing and investing activities should also be shown separately in such a statement of changes in financial position.

This form of the statement of changes in financial position is ideally suited to an entity which does not distinguish between current and noncurrent assets and liabilities (such firms are relatively rare). But it

[4] It may alternatively emphasize cash and temporary investments combined or all quick assets (see paragraph 11 of *APB Opinion No. 19*). But statements with this format are so rare that we will ignore them in our discussion.

may be used by any entity which believes this format will be the most informative in its circumstances. Since it is seldom used in practice, illustration of this form will be left to textbooks designed for more advanced courses. Thus, when we are discussing the statement of changes in financial position we will be using the working capital format.

The cash flow statement

The analysis of working capital as described in the first part of the chapter is particularly useful for long-range planning by management and for long-run analysis by external users. In making such plans management needs information about historical cash flows for the period. An adequate working capital position does not, in and of itself, imply an adequate cash position. Working capital may consist of accounts receivable, inventories, and so forth. On the other hand, the company's working capital may include too much cash in view of current cash needs. Some of the cash might be used to purchase marketable securities, to retire short-term debt, or possibly to increase inventory to provide better service to customers.

A cash flow statement provides information for planning the short-range cash needs of the firm. An analysis of cash flow shows whether the firm's pattern of cash inflow from operations will enable it to pay its debts promptly. If it cannot, it may seek short-term credit to meet current debts and planned purchases of plant, property, and equipment. Thus, cash flow analysis is another important management tool.

If this information is valued by external users, the firm may emphasize historical cash flows in its statement of changes in financial position. Otherwise, a cash flow statement may be prepared for internal use only.

A cash flow statement shows the cash receipts and disbursements leading to the net change in cash in a given period. It is easy in a computer-based system to code the input data on receipts and disbursements and to program the computer to prepare a cash flow statement. If such a system is not in operation, the information can be obtained by using an analysis similar to that for preparing the statement of changes in financial position. The major difference is that each earnings statement item is examined together with related changes in current asset, current liability, or other statement of financial position accounts to determine the cash flow from the item. Net earnings are converted to cash flow from operations. For example, the amount of cash paid to the owner of rented property in a period may differ from the amount of rent expense recognized in that same period. The amount of rent paid may have been $1,600, while rent expense was only $1,200. Also, those current accounts, other than cash, which do not enter into the adjustment of the earnings statement to a cash basis must be analyzed separately for their cash flow effects. For instance, if the Bank Loans Payable account increased by $30,000 during the year, this represents a cash receipt of $30,000. In other respects, the procedures used to determine cash flow

The correct responses for the blanks are:

	Funds provided	Funds applied	
1.	$ 41,000		
2.		$ 80,000	
3.		6,150	
4.		9,000	(Dividends payable, a current liability, increased.)
5.	15,000		(The gain of $5,000 would be deducted from net earnings.)
6.	120,000		(The par value is no indicator of the amount received.)
7.	300,000	300,000	(Two noncurrent accounts were affected but the transaction is significant.)
8.	195,000		
9.	225,000	150,000	(The $225,000 would be divided into the portion which affected working capital and the portion which did not.)

If you missed any of the above, restudy the first part of this chapter before beginning Frame 7¹² on page 578.

7¹²
continued

resemble those used in preparing the statement of changes in financial position under the working capital concept.

Net earnings and cash flow

The net earnings of a business seldom equal its net cash flow from operations. The earnings statement is prepared on the accrual basis of accounting. Hence the sales volume of a given month is not likely to produce an equal amount of cash inflow during that month. Credit sales result in accounts receivable which often are not collected until the following month. Thus a lag exists between sales and cash inflow. In addition, often a firm may purchase large quantities of goods to build up inventory to meet seasonal demands—the Christmas rush. The increased drain on cash during such periods may or may not be matched by cash inflows from customers. Also, short-term loans may be needed to take discounts and to meet cash outflows during inventory buildup. Conversely, in other periods, the inflow of cash from operations may be well in excess of current needs. Thus, analysis of the firm's *pattern* of cash flow is of great importance in setting up payment schedules, short-term borrowing and repayment schedules, and investment policies.

Cash outflow results also from acquiring property, plant, equipment, and other long-term assets, paying off long-term debt, and paying dividends. Similarly, cash balances are increased by selling marketable securities and borrowing on short-term loans. They are increased also by selling plant, property, and equipment, and by issuing long-term obligations and capital stock for cash. Thus, cash balances may decrease even though the firm is operating at a profit, or increase while the firm is operating at a loss.

Is each of the following statements true or false?

1. The analysis emphasizing working capital highlights the causes of changes in the working capital position of a firm, whereas the cash flow analysis concentrates on inflows and outflows of cash.
2. Cash flow analysis is not limited solely to current accounts but also includes long-term accounts.
3. For short-term planning, an analysis emphasizing working capital accounts would be more useful than a cash flow analysis.
4. Cash flow analysis is more useful for businesses with fluctuating seasonal sales patterns than those with stable sales patterns.

Now turn to Answer Frame 7^{12} on page 582 to check your answers.

Frame 8^{12}

Preparing the cash flow statement

Given below are the financial statements of the Delta Corporation and some related data. These will serve as a basis to illustrate the preparation of a cash flow statement.

THE DELTA CORPORATION
Comparative Statement of Financial Position
June 30, 1978, and 1979

	1979	1978	Increase decrease*
Assets			
Current Assets:			
Cash..	$ 30,000	$ 80,000	$ 50,000*
Accounts receivable	160,000	100,000	60,000
Inventory..	100,000	70,000	30,000
Prepaid rent	20,000	10,000	10,000
Total Current Assets	$310,000	$260,000	$ 50,000
Property, Plant and Equipment:			
Equipment	$400,000	$200,000	$200,000
Allowance for depreciation	(60,000)	(50,000)	(10,000)
Total Property, Plant, and Equipment.........	$340,000	$150,000	$190,000
Total Assets.....................................	$650,000	$410,000	$240,000

581

8¹²

continued

THE DELTA CORPORATION
Comparative Statement of Financial Position
June 30, 1978, and 1979

	1979	1978	Increase decrease*
Liabilities and Stockholders' Equity			
Current Liabilities:			
Accounts payable	$ 50,000	$ 40,000	$ 10,000
Notes payable—bank	–0–	50,000	50,000*
Accrued salaries and wages	10,000	20,000	10,000*
Estimated federal income tax liability	30,000	20,000	10,000
Total Current Liabilities	$ 90,000	$130,000	$ 40,000*
Stockholders' Equity:			
Common stock, $10 par	$300,000	$100,000	$200,000
Capital in excess of par	50,000	–0–	50,000
Retained earnings	210,000	180,000	30,000
Total Stockholders' Equity	$560,000	$280,000	$280,000
Total Liabilities and Stockholders' Equity	$650,000	$410,000	$240,000

Reporting changes in financial position; cash flow statements

THE DELTA CORPORATION
Statement of Earnings and Retained Earnings
For the Year Ended June 30, 1979

Sales...		$1,000,000
Cost of goods sold	$600,000	
Salaries and wages...	200,000	
Rent..	40,000	
Depreciation..	20,000	
Interest...	3,000	
Loss on sale of equipment..	7,000	870,000
Net earnings before federal income taxes............................		$ 130,000
Federal income taxes...		60,000
Net earnings		$ 70,000
Retained earnings, July 1, 1978..		180,000
		$ 250,000
Dividends...		40,000
Retained Earnings, June 30, 1979......................................		$ 210,000

Additional data:
1. Equipment with a cost of $20,000, on which $10,000 of depreciation had been recorded, was sold for cash.
2. Additional borrowings from the bank during the year amounted to $30,000.
3. Stock was issued for cash.

Cash flow from operations. The conversion of net earnings to cash from operations is the first step in the preparation of a cash flow statement. To do this, each item in the earnings statement is analyzed for its effect on cash. Since sales are usually recorded as debits to accounts receivable prior to the receipt of cash, the change in accounts receivable must be included in determining the amount of cash received from customers. This is done in the following manner for The Delta Corporation:

Accounts receivable at beginning of year	$ 100,000
Additions to accounts receivable for sales during year............	1,000,000
Total possible collections from customers	$1,100,000
Accounts receivable at year-end (amounts not yet collected)...	160,000
Cash collected from customers during year...........................	$ 940,000

The presence of notes receivable from customers does not complicate matters unduly. If the notes arose from sales to customers (directly or through accounts receivable), the notes and accounts receivable can be added together and treated as if they were one item and the analysis given above made. Assume, for example, that this is the case and that sales for the year were $500,000, accounts and notes receivable at year-end were $50,000 and $15,000, and at the beginning of the year were $40,000 and $10,000. The cash received from customers during the year was ___?___ .

Turn to Answer Frame 8¹² on page 584 to check your answer.

Frame 9¹²

Converting cost of goods sold to cash paid to vendors involves two steps. First, purchases must be determined by taking into consideration the change in the inventory. Then purchases must be converted from an accrual basis to a cash basis by including the change in accounts payable. For The Delta Corporation the computation is as follows:

Cost of goods sold	$600,000
Ending inventory	100,000
Goods available for sale	$700,000
Beginning inventory	70,000
Purchases during the year	$630,000
Accounts payable at beginning of year	40,000
Total possible payments to vendors	$670,000
Accounts payable at year-end	50,000
Cash Paid to Vendors	$620,000

To be sure that you understand the above analysis and to illustrate a short-cut technique, compute the cash paid to vendors from the following:

Cost of goods sold	$400,000
Decrease in inventory	4,000
Increase in accounts payable	7,000

Turn to Answer Frame 9¹² on page 586 to check your answer.

Frame 10¹²

The Delta Corporation's $200,000 of salaries and wages reported in its earnings statement is converted from its accrual basis amount to a cash basis in a similar manner simply by adding the decrease in accrued salaries and wages payable during the year to the earnings statement amount. In this instance, the accrued liability decreased from $20,000 to $10,000, or $10,000, which means that salary and wage payments during the year exceeded salaries and wages expense by $10,000. Thus, $210,000 was paid to employees.

The financial statements of The Delta Corporation show rent expense of $40,000, federal income tax expense of $60,000, and that prepaid rent increased from $10,000 to $20,000. The liability for federal income taxes increased from $20,000 to $30,000. From this information compute the amount of cash paid out as rent and for federal income taxes. Check your answers in Answer Frame 10¹² on page 586.

Frame 11¹²

There was no accrued interest payable at the beginning or end of the year. Thus, the amount of interest expense shown must have been paid in cash, and no adjustment is needed to convert interest expense to a cash basis. The $20,000 of depreciation expense and the loss on sale of equipment of $7,000 are both excluded in the determination of cash flow from operations since neither required an expenditure of cash.

All of the earnings statement items have now been analyzed, and their effect upon cash determined. Summarized, these items yield a net cash flow from operations of $7,000, computed as follows:

Sales ($1,000,000 + $100,000 − $160,000)		$940,000
Cost of goods sold ($600,000 + $100,000 − $70,000 + $40,000 − $50,000)	$620,000	
Salaries and wages ($200,000 + $20,000 − $10,000)	210,000	
Rent ($40,000 + $20,000 − $10,000)	50,000	
Interest	3,000	
Federal income taxes ($60,000 + $20,000 − $30,000)	50,000	933,000
Net Cash Flow from Operations		$ 7,000

The dollar amounts shown in parentheses in the above schedule are first the earnings statement amount of the item followed by the adjustments needed to convert it to a cash basis.

Other sources and uses of cash. To complete the accumulation of data for the cash flow statement, each of the remaining statement of financial position accounts must be analyzed for its effect on cash. This is done in a manner exactly like that used in the preparation of a statement of changes in financial position emphasizing working capital from operations. The changes in the accounts not yet analyzed are:

────────────────────────────

The cash paid to vendors amounted to $389,000. Since inventories decreased, more goods were sold than were purchased by an amount equal to the decrease in inventory. Thus, purchases must have been $396,000 ($400,000 − $4,000). Payments must have been $389,000, because in order for accounts payable to increase, purchases must have exceeded payments to vendors. Hence, the $7,000 increase in accounts payable is deducted from purchases to arrive at cash paid.

If you answered incorrectly, restudy Frame 9¹² before beginning Frame 10¹² on page 584.

Answer frame 10¹² ──

The required amounts can be computed as follows:

Rent

Expense for year	$40,000
Prepaid at year-end	20,000
	$60,000
Prepaid at beginning of year	10,000
Rent Paid	$50,000

Federal income taxes

Expense for year	$60,000
Accrued at beginning of year	20,000
	$80,000
Accrued at year-end	30,000
Federal Income Taxes Paid	$50,000

If you answered incorrectly, restudy Frame 10¹² before starting Frame 11¹² on page 585.

11¹²
continued

Notes payable—bank	$ 50,000*
Equipment	200,000
Allowance for depreciation	10,000
Common stock	200,000
Capital in excess of par	50,000
Retained earnings	30,000

* Decrease.

According to the data presented earlier, $30,000 was borrowed from the bank during the year. If $50,000 were owed to banks at the beginning of the year, $30,000 were borrowed during the year, and nothing is owed at year-end, $80,000 must have been paid on bank loans during the year. The cash flow statement must, therefore, show $30,000 of cash received from bank loans and $80,000 of payments on bank loans.

The additional data revealed that equipment was sold for cash. Since equipment costing $20,000 was sold during the year, $220,000 of equipment must have been purchased to cause the account to increase by $200,000. The $220,000 must appear in the cash flow statement as should the $3,000 of cash received from the sale of equipment. The $10,000 increase in the allowance for depreciation is the result of a $20,000 credit for depreciation recorded and the charge to the allowance for accumulated depreciation on equipment sold. It has no effect on cash.

Common stock was issued for cash of $250,000 – the total of the increases in the Common Stock and Capital in Excess of Par accounts – and this amount will appear in the cash flow statement. The $30,000 increase in retained earnings was caused by $70,000 of net earnings less $40,000 of dividends. Since the effect on cash of the net earnings has already been determined, only the cash paid out as dividends remains to be determined. This must be $40,000 since there were no dividends payable at either the beginning or end of the year.

The analysis is now complete. Every statement of financial position account has been analyzed for its effect on cash, and these effects have been classified into a number of major categories as is shown in The Delta Corporation's cash flow statement in Illustration 12.6.

Illustration 12.6 Cash flow statement

THE DELTA CORPORATION Cash Flow Statement For the Year Ended June 30, 1979		
Cash balance, July 1		$ 80,000
Add cash received from:		
Operations	$ 7,000	
Bank loans	30,000	
Sale of equipment.............................	3,000	
Common stock issued	250,000	290,000
		$370,000
Deduct cash paid out for:		
Payment of bank loans	$ 80,000	
Purchase of new equipment.................	220,000	
Dividends	40,000	340,000
Cash Balance, June 30		$ 30,000

Note also that the cash flow statement explains the major reasons for the decrease of $50,000 in the company's cash balance during the year.

While the above is overly simplified and kept deliberately brief, it serves to introduce knowledge of the nature and significance of cash flow and to indicate the general approach to cash flow statement preparation. As stated earlier, if this should be changed to a statement of changes in financial position, other changes of a significant financial or investment nature (even though they did not affect cash) must be included.

From the following information, what is the cash outflow and cash inflow to be reflected in a cash flow statement?

12/31/78	Equipment account balance...	$27,000
1/2/79	Sold equipment (cost, $8,000) for................................	3,000
4/1/79	Sold equipment (cost, $4,000) for................................	1,000
8/3/79	Bought new overhead crane for.....................................	?
12/31/79	Recorded depreciation on equipment for the year............	4,000
12/31/79	Equipment account balance...	20,000

Cash outflow _____?_____.

Cash inflow _____?_____.

Now turn to Answer Frame 11¹² on page 590 to check your answers.

Summary, *chapter* 12

The statement of changes in financial position has increased in importance in recent years. It is required to be included with the formal financial statements each time there is a formal reporting to external users. The statement is designed to provide information relating to the financing and investing activities of a firm. As such, the statement shows the sources and uses of working capital during the period, and all other significant financial or investment changes that took place during the period. Some of the main items presented include: (1) the amount of working capital generated through operations; (2) the other sources of working capital; (3) financial resources provided which did not affect working capital; (4) working capital applied; and (5) financial resources applied which did not affect working capital.

Current practice emphasizes the *changes* in *working capital* as the basic element of the statement. Preparation begins by identifying the total change in working capital. Net operating earnings are a source of working capital. But the earnings must be adjusted for certain expenses, such as depreciation, that do not have an effect on working capital. Likewise they must be adjusted for gains and losses on asset disposals, the net proceeds of which are reported elsewhere in the statement. In addition to changes in working capital, *APB Opinion No. 19* requires disclosure of all other changes which are of a significant financial or investment nature. The Appendix to this chapter provides an illustration of a method that is helpful in preparing the statement.

The statement of changes in financial position may emphasize cash provided from or used in operations rather than working capital. Under this format all changes in other current assets and in current liabilities would be shown as sources or uses of cash. Significant financing and investing activities not involving cash would also be included.

A cash flow statement may also be prepared for internal use only. Such a statement shows the sources of cash inflow and outflow for the period. The analysis required to prepare such a statement is quite similar to that for preparing the statement of changes in financial position. But changes in current accounts are also considered. Any activities which do not affect cash flows are excluded from such a statement.

To complete your review of this chapter, study the definitions of new terms introduced in the chapter, contained in the Glossary on page 592. Then complete the Student Review Quiz beginning on page 593.

APPENDIX 12: THE T-ACCOUNT METHOD

The purpose of this Appendix is to provide an alternative method for calculating the amount of working capital provided by operations and the amounts of other financing and investing activities. As already illustrated, the preparation of a statement of changes in financial position consists of a careful analysis of all of the changes in the non-current accounts. Consequently, we will first establish T-accounts for all non-current accounts and record in these accounts the change in each over the period. An example is The United States Corporation's Land account.

Land	
20,000	

We also will set up a T-account for Working Capital from Operations to help us analyze earnings statement data to arrive at this amount. And we will use one account, really a master account, entitled Financial Resources Provided and Applied which will, when completed, contain virtually all of the data needed for the statement of changes in financial position. In this account we will record the change in working capital for the period in the same manner as we have for land as shown above. The complete procedure is illustrated below using The United States Corporation data presented and analyzed earlier in this chapter.

The method illustrated

The complete set of T-accounts needed to analyze the activities of The United States Corporation for the year ended December 31, 1979, is shown on page 592. Each entry is keyed with a number and is discussed below.

We will start with data taken from the earnings statement. Entry 1 involves a debit to Working Capital from Operations and a credit to Retained Earnings. The reason for recording in this manner is that from a statement of financial position point of view, net earnings serve to increase retained earnings and working capital.

Entry 2 consists of a debit to Working Capital from Operations and

The effect of these transactions is a cash outflow of $5,000 and a cash inflow of $4,000. The cash outflow is determined from an analysis of the equipment account. The beginning balance of $27,000 less $8,000 and $4,000 for equipment sold leaves $15,000. Since the ending balance is $20,000, $5,000 must have been paid for the crane. The inflow is the total sales proceeds from the sale of equipment ($3,000 + $1,000). Depreciation does not enter the analysis at this time but is considered at the time when current expenses are analyzed.

If you answered incorrectly, restudy Frames 7¹²–11¹² before proceeding to the Summary on page 588.

a credit to a combined Allowances for Depreciation – Buildings and Equipment. Since the amount of depreciation expense recorded was not classified as between buildings and equipment, we simply combined the two allowance accounts. Recall that depreciation is an expense deducted in arriving at net earnings that does not reduce working capital. The amount of working capital from operations is larger than the amount of net earnings reported because depreciation was recorded.

Entry 3 consists of a debit to Financial Resources Provided and Applied of $2,600, a debit to Working Capital from Operations of $900, a debit to Allowances for Depreciation – Buildings and Equipment of $16,500, and a credit to Equipment of $20,000. Equipment costing $20,-000 and on which $16,500 of depreciation had been recorded was sold for $2,600, that is, at a loss of $900. The $2,600 must be recorded as working capital provided. The $900 is added to Working Capital from Operations because it did not reduce working capital from that source but did reduce net earnings – our initial measure of working capital from operations.

Continuing our analysis of earnings statement and retained earnings statement data, we come to dividends. As shown in entry 4, these are recorded as a debit to Retained Earnings of $18,000 and as a credit to Financial Resources Provided and Applied of a similar amount. As we have already noted, the declaration of cash dividends reduces working capital and retained earnings.

Turning to the remaining noncurrent accounts, we note that a net decrease of $8,000 occurred in the Investments accounts resulting, according to the additional data, from the sale of investments for $9,700. Entry 5 properly records this transaction in the T-accounts as a debit to Financial Resources Provided and Applied of $9,700, a credit to Investments of $8,000, and a credit to Working Capital from Operations of $1,700. As previously discussed, this latter credit is needed to remove funds provided by the sale of investments from Working Capital from Operations.

The next change is the $20,000 increase in the Land account. From the additional data we know that land and buildings were acquired for cash and the assumption of liability on a mortgage note. Because we wish to report all investing and financing activities, we record the assumption of liability on the mortgage note in a somewhat different manner. We debit Financial Resources Provided and Applied and credit Mortgage Note Payable for $35,000 (entry 6). Then, in entry 7, we debit Land for $20,000 and Buildings for $45,000 and credit Financial Resources Provided and Applied for $20,000 and $45,000. In this way, we include the effects of a significant financing and investing transaction that only partially affected working capital. As shown in Illustration 12.5 on page 577, on the statement of changes in financial position, the $45,000 amount of the cost of buildings is split into the $10,000 which consumed working capital and the $35,000 which did not consume working capital. Note that we have now fully accounted for the changes in the Land and Buildings accounts.

The next account is the Equipment account which shows a net change of $23,000 and in which we have already recorded a credit of $20,000. Since we have no additional information, we can only make the logical assumption that equipment was purchased at a total cost of $43,000. Entry 8 thus reflects a debit to Equipment and a credit to Financial Resources Provided and Applied of $43,000.

We have apparently fully accounted for the changes in the next account, Allowances for Depreciation – Buildings and Equipment, because the credit to the account of $34,300 when offset by the debit of $16,500 yields a net credit change of $17,800. The same is true for the Mortgage Note Payable and Retained Earnings accounts – the items entered account fully for the net change in the accounts.

Entry 9 records the issuance of common stock for cash by debiting Financial Resources Provided and Applied and crediting Common Stock for $25,000.

We have now completed the analysis of all of the noncurrent accounts. The data used in this illustration tie into the information contained in Illustration 12.5, on page 577. The entries in the accounts below reflect the net change in each account. We need only transfer the balance in Working Capital from Operations to Financial Resources Provided and Applied. This transfer is shown in entry 10. The Financial Resources Provided and Applied account now contains nearly all of the information needed to prepare the statement of changes in financial position. Only the details showing the conversion of net earnings to working capital from operations are missing. These are readily available in the Working Capital from Operations account. In the Financial Resources Provided and Applied account, the sum of the debits is $156,150 while the credits total to $126,000. The difference between these two amounts equals the change in working capital ($30,150) during the period.

Financial Resources Provided and Applied

	30,150		
(3) Sale of equipment	2,600	(4) Dividends	18,000
(5) Sale of investments	9,700	(7) Acquisition of land	20,000
(6) Mortgage note assumed to acquire building	35,000	(7) Acquisition of buildings (working capital)	10,000
(9) Issuance of common stock	25,000	(7) Acquisition of building (mortgage note)	35,000
(10) From operations	83,850	(8) Acquisition of equipment	43,000

Working Capital from Operations

(1) Net earnings	50,350	(5) Gain on sale of investments	1,700
(2) Depreciation	34,300	(10) Working capital from operations	83,850
(3) Loss on sale of equipment	900		

Investments		Land		Buildings	
	8,000	20,000		45,000	
	(5) 8,000	(7) 20,000		(7) 45,000	

Equipment		Allow. for Depreciation—Buildings and Equipment		Mortgage Note Payable	
23,000			17,800		35,000
(8) 43,000	(3) 20,000	(3) 16,500	(2) 34,300		(6) 35,000

Retained Earnings		Common Stock	
	32,350		25,000
(4) 18,000	(1) 50,350		(9) 25,000

Glossary *chapter* 12

Cash flow from operations – the net of cash receipts and disbursements for a given period as related to items which normally appear in the earnings statement; computed by adjusting each item in the earnings statement to a cash basis.

Cash flow statement – a statement or schedule showing beginning cash balance, sources of additions to cash, reasons for cash disbursements, and ending cash balance.

Comparative schedule of working capital – a statement showing the change in working capital as well as the change in each element of working capital as between two dates.

Nonworking capital charges or credits (items) – any change in any noncurrent account which does not involve a change in a current account; examples are depreciation and amortization of patents which ultimately offset retained earnings and long-term asset accounts.

Statement of changes in financial position – a statement which usually emphasizes the flows of working capital into and out of an enterprise in a given period of time; it also shows the effects of significant financial or investment transactions even though they involve only long-term accounts.

Working capital applied – the various uses of working capital in an enterprise during a given period.

Working capital provided – the various sources of working capital flowing into an enterprise in a given period.

Working capital from operations – working

capital arising from the regular operations of a business; computed as net earnings plus nonworking capital charges deducted in arriving at net earnings, less nonworking capital items added, and less certain gains which are included in the total proceeds received from the sale of noncurrent assets.

Continue with the Student Review Quiz below as a self-administered test of your comprehension of the material presented in this chapter.

Student review quiz *chapter* 12

To develop a permanent record of your responses, you may write them on the answer sheet provided in the *Work Papers* or on a separate sheet of paper.

1 Which of the following is most commonly emphasized in statements of changes in financial position?
a Cash.
b Cash and marketable securities.
c Quick assets.
d Working capital.
e None of the above.

2 An investor desiring to receive dividends over a long period of time would probably be most interested in which of the following statements of the company?
a The earnings statement for the year just ended.
b The statement of financial position as of the end of last month.
c The statement of changes in financial position for the past year.
d The cash flow statement for the year just ended.

3 Which of the following is *not* a major source of financial resources in the typical business concerned with selling merchandise if working capital is emphasized in the statement of changes in financial position?
a Operations (through the net earnings for the period).
b Issuance of additional capital stock.
c Collection of accounts receivable.
d Additional financing through the use of long-term debt.
e Sale of noncurrent assets.

4 Which of the following is *not* a major application or use of financial resources in a merchandising business if working capital is emphasized in the statement of changes in financial position?
a Acquisition of additional plant and equipment.
b Redemption of long-term debt.
c Declaration of dividends on outstanding stock.
d Acquisition of additional securities in affiliated companies.
e Repayment of a six months' bank loan.

5 Which of the following items is apt to be responsible for a difference between the increase in working capital generated by operations and the net earnings for the period?
a Unexpired insurance premiums charged to expense.
b Salary and other wage costs incurred.
c Cost of the merchandise delivered to customers.
d Amortization of premium on bonds payable.
e Interest expense for the period.

6 Which of the following transactions does not affect working capital but still must be reported in the statement of changes in financial position?
a The exchange of some of the company's capital stock for a building.
b Capital stock issued as a stock dividend.
c Capital stock issued for inventory.
d Inventory acquired with the proceeds of a short-term bank loan.
e Capital stock split two for one.

7 In the following circumstances what was the amount of cash received from customers during the year? Net sales, $500,000; accounts receivable increased by $3,000 but included in accounts receivable at the beginning of the year was an advance to an advertising agency of $4,000.
a $503,000.
b $497,000.
c $501,000.
d $507,000.
e $493,000.

8 Barker, Inc., purchased $100,000 of marketable securities as a temporary investment in 1979 and sold these securities in 1979 at a loss of $1,000 which was de-

ducted in arriving at net earnings. Which of the following statements is true?

a The cash flow statement would show cash applied to securities transactions of $1,000.

b The statement of changes in financial position (emphasizing working capital) would show working capital applied to purchase of securities of $100,000.

c In the statement of changes in financial position (emphasizing working capital), the loss on sale of securities would be added to net earnings in arriving at working capital from operations.

d The cash flow statement would show cash applied to acquisition of securities of $99,000.

e All of the above statements are false.

9 If it had been included in the determination of net earnings, which of the following items would *not* be added back to net earnings to arrive at working capital generated by operations?

a Depletion.

b Depreciation.

c Loss on sale of equipment.

d Amortization of patents.

e Amortization of bond premium.

f None of the above answers is correct.

10 The Equipment account of the Barlowe Company increased $15,000 during the year 1979, while the related allowance for depreciation increased $2,000. You are told that one piece of equipment, original cost $12,000 and on which $9,000 of depreciation had been accumulated, was sold at a loss of $1,000 and the loss was included in arriving at net earnings for the year.

Relative to the statement of changes in financial position (emphasizing working capital) for the year, which of the following statements is false?

a In the financial resources provided section of the statement the sale of equipment will be shown as bringing in $2,000 of funds.

b In the financial resources provided section of the statement the amount of depreciation added to net earnings in arriving at funds from operations will be $11,000.

c In the financial resources applied section of the statement, funds applied to

acquisition of new equipment will be shown at $15,000.

d In the financial resources provided section of the statement the loss on sale of equipment will be added back to net earnings in arriving at working capital generated by operations.

Now compare your answers with the correct answers and explanations on page 725.

Questions *chapter* 12

1 The term "funds" is used in many different ways in accounting. Indicate several of these usages other than that given in this chapter. What is the concept of funds as the term is used in a statement of changes in financial position?

2 If the net earnings for a given period amount to $25,000, does this mean that there is an increase in working capital of the same amount? Why or why not?

3 Give an example of how the analysis of working capital flow can aid management in its decision-making process.

4 What are the major sources of working capital in a business? What are the major uses of working capital in a business? What use of working capital might be called involuntary?

5 Does the declaration or the payment of dividends affect working capital? Why?

6 Why might a company have a positive inflow of working capital from operations in spite of operating at a net loss?

7 What effect, if any, does the amortization of premium on bonds payable have upon the statement of changes in financial position?

8 Why is an analysis of working capital flow apt to be unsuitable for short-run planning?

9 Why is it unlikely that the cash flow from operations will be equal to the net earnings for the same period?

10 What factors might cause cash to increase even though operations are conducted at a loss? What factors might cause cash to decrease even though operations are profitable?

11 In what respects does cash flow analysis differ from working capital flow analysis?

Exercises *chapter* 12

1 Indicate how the following data should be reported in a statement of changes in financial position. A company purchased land valued at $20,000 and a building valued at $40,000 by payment of $10,000 by check, signing an interest-bearing note due in six months for $15,000, and by assuming a mortgage on the property of $35,000.

2 A company sold for $5,000 equipment having an original cost of $7,000 and on which $4,000 of depreciation had been recorded. The gain was included in net earnings. How should these data be shown in the statement of changes in financial position and why?

3 The following data are from the Automobile and the Allowance for Depreciation—Automobile accounts of a certain company:

Automobile

		Debit	Credit	Balance
				$4,000
Jan. 1, 1979	Balance brought forward......................			$4,000
July 1, 1979	Traded for new auto		$4,000	–0–
	New auto...	$4,400		4,400

Allowance for Depreciation—Automobile

		Debit	Credit	Balance
				$3,000
Jan. 1, 1979	Balance brought forward......................			$3,000
July 1, 1979	One-half year's depreciation.................		500	3,500
	Auto traded......................................	$3,500		–0–
Dec. 31, 1979	One-half year's depreciation.................		550	550

The old auto was traded for a new one with the difference in values paid in cash. The earnings statement for the year shows a loss on the exchange of autos of $300.

Indicate the dollar amounts, the descriptions of these amounts, and their exact locations in a statement of changes in financial position.

4 Assume that the cost of goods sold for a given company for a given year is $350,000. Inventory at the beginning of the year was $51,000 and at the end of the year, $63,000; accounts payable for merchandise purchases were $38,000 and $42,000 at the beginning of the year and end of the year, respectively. What was the amount of cash paid to vendors during the year?

5 Use the data for Exercise 4 above. In addition, assume that one invoice for the purchase of equipment in the amount of $5,000 was unpaid at year-end, that the equipment account shows an increase of $40,000 during the year, and that equipment costing $8,000 was sold for $1,000 during the year. Compute the amount of cash paid to vendors during the year and the cash outflow for new equipment.

6 Dividends payable increased from $12,000 to $15,000 during the year. Dividends of $60,000 were declared during the year. What amount should be shown in the statement of changes in financial position for dividends? In the cash flow statement? If the amounts are not the same, why do they differ?

7 During the course of the year a company purchased $50,000 of marketable securities as a temporary investment. The securities were sold later at a loss of $1,500, and the loss was deducted in arriving at net earnings. How would these data appear on the cash flow statement?

Problems, Series A *chapter* 12

12-1-A

Following are comparative financial position data and a statement of retained earnings for the year ended May 31, 1979, for Beasley Company (000 omitted).

	May 31 1979	May 31 1978
Debits		
Cash	$ 70	$ 56
Marketable securities	20	24
Accounts receivable, net	116	144
Inventories	140	100
Investment in subsidiary	90	80
Land	60	50
Buildings and equipment	450	380
Patents	14	16
Total	$960	$850
Credits		
Accounts payable	$ 90	$ 64
Taxes payable	16	12
Allowance for depreciation	80	60
Bonds payable	200	200
Common stock, $100 par	400	400
Retained earnings	174	114
Total	$960	$850

Statement of Retained Earnings

Balance, May 31, 1978	$114
Net earnings	100
	$214
Dividends declared	40
Balance, May 31, 1979	$174

Additional data:

a. Additional shares of stock of the subsidiary company were acquired for cash.

b. A tract of land adjacent to land owned was purchased during the year.

c. Depreciation of $32,000 and patent amortization of $2,000 were charged to expense during the year.

d. New equipment with a cost of $82,000 was purchased during the year, while fully depreciated equipment with a cost of $12,000 was scrapped and discarded.

Required:

a Prepare a comparative schedule of working capital.

b Prepare a statement of changes in financial position (emphasizing working capital).

12-2-A

FISHER, INC.
Comparative Statement of Financial Position

	April 30	
	1979	1978
Assets		
Cash	$ 47,000	$ 26,000
Accounts receivable	141,000	134,000
Inventory	83,000	102,000
Prepaid expenses	9,000	11,000
Plant assets	300,000	280,000
Allowance for depreciation	(65,000)	(50,000)
Total Assets	$515,000	$503,000
Liabilities and Stockholders' Equity		
Accounts payable	$ 62,000	$ 48,000
Accrued expenses payable	17,000	19,000
Federal income taxes payable	23,000	21,000
Bank loan payable	60,000	80,000
Capital stock	300,000	300,000
Retained earnings	53,000	35,000
Total Liabilities and Stockholders' Equity	$515,000	$503,000

FISHER, INC.
Earnings Statement
For Year Ended, April 30, 1979

Net sales		$740,000
Cost of goods sold	$500,000	
Salaries and wages	130,000	
Depreciation	15,000	
Rent expense	15,000	
Other	33,000	693,000
Net earnings before taxes		$ 47,000
Federal income taxes		23,000
Net Earnings		$ 24,000

Additional data:

a. Dividends of $6,000 were declared during the year.

b. Prepaid expenses consist solely of rent.

c. Accrued expenses payable at April 30, 1979, and April 30, 1978, consist entirely of accrued salaries and wages.

d. During a high level of seasonal activity an additional $30,000 was borrowed from a local bank.

e. The accounts payable arose solely from the purchase of merchandise.

Required:

a Prepare a schedule similar to that on page 585 of the text showing the determination of the cash flow from operations.

b Prepare a cash flow statement.

12-3-A

CARDER COMPANY
Comparative Statement of Financial Position

	April 30	
	1979	1978
Assets		
Cash	$ 61,000	$ 61,000
Marketable securities	12,000	20,000
Accounts receivable, net	98,000	60,000
Inventories	250,000	100,000
Prepaid expenses	10,000	15,000
Total Current Assets	$431,000	$256,000
Land	60,000	65,000
Buildings and equipment	330,000	250,000
Allowance for depreciation	(80,000)	(65,000)
Total Assets	$741,000	$506,000
Liabilities and Stockholders' Equity		
Accounts payable	$100,000	$ 60,000
Bank loans	60,000	-0-
Accrued expenses payable	32,000	15,000
Federal income taxes payable	70,000	75,000
Total Current Liabilities	$262,000	$150,000
Bonds payable (5%)	200,000	200,000
Premium on bonds payable	1,800	2,000
Capital stock—common, $100 par	200,000	140,000
Capital in excess of par	10,000	-0-
Retained earnings	67,200	14,000
Total Liabilities and Stockholders' Equity	$741,000	$506,000

CARDER COMPANY
Earnings Statement
For Year Ended April 30, 1979

Net sales		$800,000
Less: Cost of goods sold	$500,000	
Selling and administrative expenses	148,000	648,000
Net earnings from operations		$152,000
Gain on sale of land		8,000
		$160,000
Loss on sale of marketable securities	$ 1,000	
Interest expense	10,800	
Loss on sale of equipment	4,200	16,000
Net earnings before income taxes		$144,000
Federal income taxes		70,000
Net Earnings		$ 74,000

Additional data:

a. Dividends of $20,800 were declared during the year.

b. Equipment sold during the year had an original cost of $20,000, and depreciation of $12,000 had been recorded to time of sale.

c. The capital stock was issued for a building valued at $70,000 erected on company property.

d. Premium on bonds payable of $200 was amortized during the year.

Reporting changes in financial position; cash flow statements

Required:

a Compute the change in working capital.

b Prepare a statement of changes in financial position (emphasizing working capital).

12-4-A

Use the data given in Problem 12-3-A and the following additional information:

a. Depreciation expense of $27,000 is included in selling and administrative expenses.

b. Accounts payable arose solely from the purchase of merchandise.

c. Prepaid expenses consist of prepaid store rent.

d. All of the accrued expenses payable relate to selling and administrative expenses except that the balance on April 30, 1979, includes $1,000 of accrued interest payable on bank loans.

Required:

a Prepare a schedule showing the cash flow from operations. (A schedule of the type found on page 585 of the text is sufficient.)

b Prepare a cash flow statement.

12-5-A

Use the data in Problem 12-6-A

Required:

a Prepare a comparative schedule of working capital for the year 1979.

b Prepare a statement of changes in financial position (emphasizing working capital) for the year ended December 31, 1979.

12-6-A

The earnings statement for the Mitchell Company for the year ended December 31, 1979, shows:

Net sales		$660,000
Cost of goods sold	$375,000	
Operating expenses	100,000	
Major repairs	60,000	
Interest expense	5,000	
Loss on sale of equipment	10,000	550,000
Net earnings before taxes		$110,000
Federal income taxes		48,000
Net Earnings		$ 62,000

Comparative statements of financial position for the company show:

	December 31	
	1979	1978
Assets		
Cash	$ 48,000	$ 40,000
Accounts receivable, net	105,000	76,000
Inventories	210,000	180,000
Prepaid expenses	16,000	6,000
Total Current Assets	$379,000	$302,000
Buildings	100,000	100,000
Allowance for depreciation – buildings	(55,000)	(50,000)
Equipment	185,000	130,000
Allowance for depreciation – equipment	(63,000)	(60,000)
Total Assets	$546,000	$422,000
Liabilities and Stockholders' Equity		
Accounts payable	$ 47,000	$ 75,000
Accrued expenses payable	16,500	14,500
Federal income taxes payable	48,000	45,000
Dividends payable	9,500	7,500
Total Current Liabilities	$121,000	$142,000
Bonds payable (5%)	100,000	100,000
Total Liabilities	$221,000	$242,000
Capital stock – par $100	$250,000	$150,000
Capital in excess of par	15,000	-0-
Retained earnings	60,000	30,000
Total Stockholders' Equity	$325,000	$180,000
Total Liabilities and Stockholders' Equity	$546,000	$422,000

Additional data:

a. Capital stock was issued for cash.
b. Accrued expenses payable relate solely to operating expenses.
c. The depreciation on equipment for the year amounted to $15,000. The equipment sold had an original cost of $30,000.
d. Dividends declared during the year total $32,000.
e. Accounts payable arose solely from purchases of merchandise.

Required:

a   Prepare a schedule of cash flow from operations. (See page 585 of the text.)
b   Present a cash flow statement.

12–7–A

Following are comparative account balances for the Sims Company:

	December 31	
	1979	1978
Debit balances		
Cash	$ 70,000	$ 20,000
Accounts receivable	54,000	52,000
Inventory	80,000	100,000
Land	50,000	50,000
Buildings	230,000	100,000
Equipment	250,000	200,000
Patents	75,000	100,000
Total	$809,000	$622,000
Credit balances		
Allowance for doubtful accounts	$ 4,000	$ 2,000
Allowance for depreciation – buildings	13,000	10,000
Allowance for depreciation – equipment	60,000	50,000
Accounts payable	80,000	50,000
Accrued liabilities	30,000	20,000
Bonds payable	200,000	200,000
Bond premium	4,000	5,000
Common stock	300,000	200,000
Capital in excess of par	20,000	10,000
Retained earnings	98,000	75,000
Total	$809,000	$622,000

Additional data:

a. Equipment with a cost of $30,000 on which $28,000 of depreciation had been accumulated was sold during the year at a gain of $5,000.
b. Net earnings for the year were $68,000 including the gain on sale of equipment, a special write-off of obsolete inventory of $17,000, and the write-off (in addition to the regular amortization) of a worthless patent of $20,000.
c. Cash dividends declared, $25,000.
d. An additional income tax assessment for 1976 of $20,000 was paid in cash and charged to retained earnings.

Required:

a Prepare a comparative schedule of working capital.
b Prepare a statement of changes in financial position (emphasizing working capital).

Problems, Series B *chapter* 12

12-1-B

ZABO CORPORATION
Comparative Statement of Financial Position

	June 30	
	1979	1978
Assets		
Current assets..	$ 340,000	$235,000
Investment in stock of affiliated company......................................	175,000	150,000
Buildings...	380,000	280,000
Allowance for depreciation—buildings..	(60,000)	(50,000)
Equipment..	470,000	400,000
Allowance for depreciation—equipment..	(160,000)	(120,000)
Total Assets	$1,145,000	$895,000
Liabilities and Stockholders' Equity		
Current liabilities...	$ 180,000	$120,000
Five-year note payable	100,000	-0-
Capital stock, par $100..	800,000	700,000
Retained earnings	65,000	75,000
Total Liabilities and Stockholders' Equity...........................	$1,145,000	$895,000

Additional data:

a. Net earnings for year ended June 30, 1979, were $30,000.

b. Dividends declared, $40,000.

c. Stock was issued at par for cash.

d. No equipment or building retirements occurred during the year.

e. The five-year note was issued to pay for a building erected on land leased by the company.

f. Additional shares of stock of the affiliated company were acquired for cash.

g. Equipment was also purchased for cash.

Required:

a State the change in working capital.

b Prepare a statement of changes in financial position (emphasizing working capital).

12-2-B

GEMS, INC.
Comparative Statement of Financial Position

	September 30	
	1979	1978
Assets		
Cash	$ 78,000	$ 23,000
Accounts receivable...	122,000	121,000
Inventory...	100,000	78,000
Prepaid expenses...	4,000	5,000
Equipment and fixtures..	75,000	60,000
Allowance for depreciation	(21,000)	(15,000)
Total Assets..	$358,000	$272,000

Reporting changes in financial position; cash flow statements

GEMS, INC.
Comparative Statement of Financial Position

	September 30	
	1979	*1978*
Liabilities and Stockholders' Equity		
Accounts payable..	$ 48,000	$ 40,000
Accrued expenses payable....................................	13,000	17,000
Federal income taxes payable................................	60,000	35,000
Dividends payable..	6,000	5,000
Capital stock	100,000	100,000
Retained earnings..	131,000	75,000
Total Liabilities and Stockholders' Equity	$358,000	$272,000

GEMS, INC.
Earnings Statement
For Year Ended September 30, 1979

Net sales		$750,000
Cost of goods sold..	$400,000	
Selling and administrative expenses	220,000	620,000
Net earnings before taxes		$130,000
Federal income taxes		60,000
Net Earnings		$ 70,000

Additional data:

a. Depreciation of $6,000 is included in selling and administrative expenses.
b. Dividends declared during the year amounted to $14,000.
c. Accounts payable arose solely from the purchase of merchandise.

Required:

a Prepare a schedule showing the cash flow from operations. (See page 585 of the text.)
b Prepare a cash flow statement.

12–3–B

POLASKY CORPORATION
Comparative Statement of Financial Position

	December 31	
	1979	*1978*
Assets		
Cash	$ 15,000	$ 20,000
Accounts receivable..	122,000	98,000
Inventories...	122,000	112,000
Unexpired insurance...	3,000	4,000
Total Current Assets	$262,000	$234,000
Land..	50,000	30,000
Buildings...	200,000	100,000
Allowance for depreciation – buildings	(25,000)	(20,000)
Equipment	225,000	215,000
Allowance for depreciation – equipment	(115,000)	(100,000)
Total Assets..	$597,000	$459,000

POLASKY CORPORATION
Comparative Statement of Financial Position

	December 31	
Liabilities and Stockholders' Equity	1979	1978
Accounts payable..	$ 82,000	$ 80,000
Dividends payable...	12,000	10,000
Federal income taxes payable...	38,000	30,000
Accrued salaries and wages payable	4,000	3,000
Accrued expenses payable..	6,000	4,000
Total Current Liabilities...	$142,000	$127,000
Bonds payable – 7%..	100,000	100,000
Total Liabilities..	$242,000	$227,000
Capital stock – common...	300,000	200,000
Capital in excess of par...	15,000	–0–
Retained earnings...	40,000	32,000
Total Liabilities and Stockholders' Equity	$597,000	$459,000

POLASKY CORPORATION
Earnings Statement and Statement of Retained Earnings
For Year Ended December 31, 1979

Sales (net)..		$900,000
Cost of goods sold...		600,000
Gross margin..		$300,000
Salaries and wages...	$150,000	
Depreciation...	27,000	
Insurance..	2,000	
Other expenses (including interest)...	50,000	
Loss on sale of equipment	1,000	230,000
Net earnings before federal income taxes		$ 70,000
Federal income taxes		38,000
Net earnings...		$ 32,000
Retained earnings, December 31, 1978		32,000
		$ 64,000
Less: Dividends..		24,000
Retained earnings, December 31, 1979		$ 40,000

Additional data:

a. Equipment having an original cost of $10,000 and on which $7,000 of depreciation was recorded was sold at a loss of $1,000. Equipment additions were for cash.

b. All of the additional capital stock issued during the year, plus $5,000 of cash, was exchanged for land and a building.

Required:

a Compute the changes in working capital.

b Prepare a statement of changes in financial position (emphasizing working capital).

12–4–B

Use the data given in Problem 12–3–B. Assume that the accounts payable at the end of 1978 and 1979 arose solely from the purchase of merchandise and that the accrued expenses payable arose from the accrual of expenses included in the other expenses shown in the earnings statement.

Reporting changes in financial position; cash flow statements

Required:

a   Prepare a schedule showing cash flow from operations. (See page 585 of the text.)
b   Prepare a cash flow statement.

12-5-B

Given below are comparative statement of financial position account balances and other data of the Brooks Corporation:

	June 30 1979	June 30 1978
Debit balances		
Cash	$ 64,000	$ 68,000
Accounts receivable, net	340,000	168,000
Notes receivable	42,000	54,000
Inventories	420,000	436,000
Unexpired insurance	2,400	2,800
Land	160,000	180,000
Buildings	1,120,000	620,000
Machinery and tools	440,000	240,000
Goodwill	-0-	200,000
Discount on bonds payable	4,200	5,000
Total	$2,592,600	$1,973,800
Credit balances		
Accrued liabilities	$ 14,000	$ 4,000
Accounts payable	65,000	90,000
Bank loans	29,000	33,600
Taxes payable	30,000	2,000
Allowance for depreciation of buildings, machinery and tools	442,000	262,000
Mortgage bonds payable	200,000	100,000
Common stock, $100 par	900,000	300,000
Retained earnings	912,600	1,182,200
Total	$2,592,600	$1,973,800

Additional data:

a.   Net earnings for the year ended June 30, 1979, were $35,400.
b.   A 5 percent cash dividend was declared and paid in June.
c.   Additional common stock was issued in April at $90, and the discount was charged to Retained Earnings.
d.   The mortgage bonds were issued in conjunction with the acquisition of a new building. The bonds were accepted by the seller of the building at their face value.
e.   The gain on the sale of land of $4,000 was credited to a miscellaneous revenue account.
f.   Fully depreciated machinery with an original cost of $30,000 was written off during the year and scrapped.

Required:

a   Prepare a comparative schedule of working capital.
b   Prepare a statement of changes in financial position (emphasizing working capital).   605

12–6–B

Given below is a condensed earnings statement for the Brooks Corporation for the year ended June 30, 1979:

Net sales	$2,700,000
Cost of goods sold	2,000,000
Gross margin	$ 700,000
Selling and administrative expenses	628,800
Net operating earnings	71,200
Gain on sale of land	4,000
	$ 75,200
Interest expense	9,800
	$ 65,400
Federal income taxes	30,000
Net Earnings	$ 35,400

Additional data:

a. Of the depreciation recorded for the year, $150,000 was charged to cost of goods sold and the balance to selling and administrative expenses.
b. The accrued liabilities relate solely to costs included in cost of goods sold. The accounts payable at year-end are all for material purchases except one account due of $10,000 for machinery purchased.
c. The total proceeds received from bank loans made during the year amount to $60,000.
d. The taxes payable shown consist only of federal income taxes.
e. The expired insurance premiums were charged to selling and administrative expense.
f. The notes receivable are from customers for merchandise sold to them.

Required:

From the above data and those in Problem 12–5–B, prepare:
a   A schedule showing cash flow from operations. (See page 585 of the text.)
b   A cash flow statement.

12–7–B

Following are comparative ledger balances for the Clayton Company:

	December 31	
	1979	1978
Debit balances		
Cash	$ 20,000	$ 25,000
Accounts receivable	42,000	31,000
Inventory	40,000	35,000
Land	45,000	40,000
Building	60,000	60,000
Equipment	190,000	150,000
Goodwill	80,000	100,000
Total	$477,000	$441,000

Reporting changes in financial position; cash flow statements

	December 31	
	1979	1978
Credit balances		
Allowance for doubtful accounts..	$ 2,000	$ 1,000
Allowance for depreciation—building..	20,000	18,000
Allowance for depreciation—equipment	35,000	32,000
Accounts payable..	50,000	30,000
Accrued liabilities..	20,000	15,000
Capital stock	210,000	200,000
Paid-in capital—stock dividends...	50,000	45,000
Paid-in capital—land donation	10,000	-0-
Retained earnings..	80,000	100,000
Total...	$477,000	$441,000

An analysis of the Retained Earnings account for the year reveals the following:

Balance, December 31, 1978...		$100,000
Add:		
Net earnings for the year...		85,000
		$185,000
Less:		
Cash dividends	$30,000	
Stock dividends..	15,000	
Goodwill written off...	20,000	
Additional income taxes for 1976...	40,000	105,000
Balance, December 31, 1979...		$ 80,000

Additional data:

Equipment with a cost of $20,000 on which $18,000 of depreciation had been accumulated was sold during the year at a loss of $1,000. Included in net earnings is a gain on the sale of land of $6,000.

Required:

a   Prepare a comparative schedule of working capital.
b   Prepare a statement of changes in financial position (emphasizing working capital).

part IV

AN OVERVIEW–BASIC THEORY AND REPORTING CONSOLIDATED RESULTS

13

The basic theory underlying financial statements

Learning objectives

Study of the material presented and discussed in this chapter is designed to provide:

1. Knowledge of how generally accepted accounting principles can be loosely structured into a framework consisting of (a) general objectives, (b) qualitative objectives, (c) underlying assumptions, (d) major principles, (e) modifying conventions, and (f) implementing and detailed accounting principles.

2. Knowledge of the nature of each of the above items and how each shapes and influences accounting thought and practice.

3. An understanding of how and why the principles guiding the determination of net earnings tend to dictate the nature and measurement of the items that appear in the statement of financial position.

4. An awareness of the fact that the historical cost basis of asset measurement is being seriously challenged and of the alternative bases being considered.

5. A workable knowledge of the nature and financial reporting of:
   a. Extraordinary items.
   b. Prior period adjustments.
   c. The effects of accounting changes.

Frame 1[13]

Some of the concepts discussed in this chapter have been dealt with directly in previous chapters, others only indirectly. But no attempt has been made to deal with concepts and principles as members of a conceptual framework of theory. This chapter deals with the conceptual framework underlying financial accounting and reporting.

Accounting theory has been defined as a set of basic concepts or assumptions and related principles and standards that explain and guide the accountant's actions in identifying, measuring, and communicating economic information.[1] What constitutes accounting theory and what its purposes are have been the subject of debate for years. And the issues are yet unresolved. But accounting practices are guided by a set of ideas that together are called "generally accepted accounting principles" (GAAP). This chapter deals with the nature of some of these principles and the objectives sought by their application.

The general objectives of financial accounting and financial statements

As the financial historians of business, accountants have provided a "history quantified in money terms of economic resources and obligations of a business enterprise and of economic activities that change these resources and obligations."[2] The information gathered is classified, interpreted, summarized, and reported to both internal and external users. Neither group would know much about the financial activities of a modern business corporation without such information.

For external users, the information is in the form of general-purpose financial statements (see the Appendix to Chapter 14 for examples). It is believed that such statements will serve the common needs of several classes of users if they provide the following:

1. Reliable financial information about economic resources and obligations.
2. Reliable information about changes in net resources (resources less obligations) of an enterprise that result from its profit-directed activities.
3. Financial information that assists in estimating the future capacity of an enterprise to generate earnings.
4. Information about changes in resources and obligations resulting from sources other than profit-directed activities, such as transactions between an entity and its owners, and information about working capital and other fund flows.

---

[1] American Accounting Association, *A Statement of Basic Accounting Theory* (Sarasota, Fla., 1966), pp. 1–2.

[2] Accounting Principles Board, "Basic Concepts and Accounting Principles Underlying Financial Statements of Business Enterprises," *APB Statement No. 4* (New York: AICPA, October 1970), par. 41.

5. Adequate disclosure of other information, such as accounting policies and depreciation and inventory methods, that is relevant to statement users' needs.[3]

Somewhat similar conclusions were tentatively reached by the Financial Accounting Standards Board (FASB):

> Financial statements of business enterprises should provide information . . . that is useful to present and potential investors and creditors in making rational investment and credit decisions. Financial statements should be comprehensible to investors and creditors who have a reasonable understanding of business and economic activities and financial accounting and who are willing to spend the time and effort needed to study financial statements.[4]

While recognizing the needs of other potential users of financial statements (e.g., employees, labor unions, and stock exchanges), the board designates "informed" investors and creditors as the primary parties to whom general-purpose financial statements are directed. To such parties, financial statements are a principal source of financial information about business firms. Recognizing that the decision process for such parties usually involves a comparison between present cash and future cash, the board further stated:

> Financial statements of business enterprises should provide information that helps investors and creditors assess the prospects of receiving cash from dividends or interest and from the proceeds from the sale, redemption, or maturity of securities or loans. These prospects are affected (1) by an enterprise's ability to obtain enough cash through its earning and financing activities to meet its obligations when due and its other cash operating needs, to reinvest in earning resources and activities, and to pay cash dividends and interest and (2) by perceptions of investors and creditors generally about that ability, which affect market prices of the enterprise's securities relative to those of other enterprises. Thus, financial accounting and financial statements should provide information that helps investors and creditors assess the enterprise's prospects of obtaining net cash inflows through its earning and financing activities.[5]

This statement of objectives ties the cash flows to investors and creditors to the cash flows of the enterprise. These latter flows are the source of cash for dividends and interest and for cash to redeem maturing debt. And the market's perception of an enterprise's ability to generate sufficient cash inflows to meet its needs may affect the price at which an investor can sell securities owned.

> Financial statements of a business enterprise should provide information about the economic resources of an enterprise, which are the sources of prospective cash inflows to the enterprise; its obligations to transfer economic resources to others, which are the causes of prospective cash outflows from the enterprise; and its earnings, which are the financial results of its operations and other events and conditions that affect the enterprise. Since that information is useful to investors and creditors in assessing an enterprise's ability to pay

---

[3] Ibid., pars. 77–81.

[4] FASB, *Tentative Conclusions on Objectives of Financial Statements of Business Enterprises* (Stamford, Conn., 1976), par. 8.

[5] Ibid. par. 14.

cash dividends and interest and to settle obligations when they mature, it should be the focus of financial accounting and financial reporting.[6]

This statement of objectives recognizes that investors and creditors often use information on an enterprise's past performance to assess its future prospects. It is the objective of financial accounting to provide such information, rather than direct predictions of enterprise cash flows. And despite the emphasis upon cash flows, earnings are to be measured under accrual accounting. Such earnings, which reflect the effects of events when they occur better than when cash is paid or received, are better indicators of ability to generate cash flows than are statements of cash receipts and payments.

Indicate whether each of the following statements is true or false.
1. Investment and credit decisions usually involve comparisons of present cash with future cash flows.
2. According to the FASB, general-purpose financial statements are intended primarily for investors and creditors.
3. The theory underlying financial statements is fairly well defined and generally accepted.
4. It is a function of financial accounting to provide information that will aid investors and creditors in assessing a firm's ability to generate future cash flows.
5. In its broadest sense, the objective of financial statements is to provide information useful to investors and creditors in making rational investment and credit decisions.

Now check your responses in Answer Frame 1[13] on page 616.

Frame 2[13]

Qualitative objectives

There is rather substantial agreement in the literature of accounting that, in order to be useful, the information contained in financial statements must possess certain qualities or characteristics.[7] These qualities are discussed below.

Relevance

For information to be relevant it must be pertinent or bear upon a decision. Relevance is the *primary* qualitative objective. If information is not relevant, it is useless even though it meets the other objectives

---

[6] Ibid. par. 16.

[7] For discussion and summarization of a number of lists of qualitative objectives, see FASB, *Conceptual Framework for Financial Accounting and Reporting: Elements of Financial Statements and Their Measurement* (Stamford, Conn., 1976), chap. 7.

fully. Relevant informations aids investors and creditors in assessing the possible returns (cash flows) and risks related to alternative investment or lending opportunities. It is for its lack of relevance that accounting information is under attack today. For example, it is argued that the fact that a tract of land cost its owner $1 million over 40 years ago is irrelevant (except for possible tax implications) to any user for any decision that must be made today. These attacks have encouraged research into the types of information that are relevant to users.

Relevance and materiality. Although often cited as a principle or a modifying convention, materiality is a part of the relevance objective. A statement, fact, or item is material if it is significant enough to influence the decisions of informed investors or creditors. Thus, material information is relevant information; immaterial information is irrelevant information.

One way of determining whether an item is material is to look at its relative size. A $10,000 item of expense in a firm with net earnings of $30,000 would seem to be material. But the same amount in a much more profitable firm may not be material. If an item is considered immaterial, it may be handled without regard to accounting principles. Thus, the cost of a minor asset, such as a wastebasket, may be charged to expense in the period in which it is acquired rather than set up as an asset and depreciated over its useful life. Material items must be handled in accordance with generally accepted accounting principles.

But there is more to materiality than dollar amounts. The very nature of an item may make it material. For example, it may be quite significant to know that a firm is securing its overseas business by bribing officials of a foreign government. Or that U.S. firms are making illegal political contributions. How to assess the significance of such actions is proving to be a serious problem for accountants.

Relevance and substance over form. In some instances the economic substance of a transaction may conflict with its legal form. For example, a contract which is legally a lease may, in fact, be a purchase. This is true for a three-year contract to rent an auto at a stated monthly rental, with the lessee to receive title to the auto at the end of the lease upon payment of a nominal sum (say, $1). Because it is likely to be relevant to economic decision making, the accountant records economic substance rather than legal form.

Understandability

This objective is important on the simple grounds that information must be understood if it is to be useful. Information should be presented in a form and expressed in terminology that investors and creditors understand. But the complexity of economic activity makes it impossible to reduce reports on it to simple terms. Investors and creditors must aid their own cause by acquiring knowledge of business and economic activity and of financial accounting and reporting. They must

Answer frame 1¹³

1. True. Such decisions typically involve comparing the amount of cash that must be given up now in order to receive certain future, expected cash flows.
2. True. While not overlooking other needs, the FASB does hold that financial statements are intended primarily for investors and creditors including stockholders, bondholders, and suppliers of short-term credit such as vendors and banks.
3. False. There is little agreement as to the conceptual framework of the theory of financial accounting, although some ideas have received general acceptance.
4. True. To be useful to investors and creditors, financial information must help them assess an enterprise's ability to generate cash.
5. True. This is a statement of the objective of financial statements in its broadest, most generalized form.

If you answered incorrectly, study Frame 1¹³ again before proceeding to Frame 2¹³ on page 614.

2¹³
continued

also be willing to devote time and effort to the study of financial statements.

Indicate whether each of the following statements is true or false.

1. Financial accounting information should be expressed in terms that all readers can understand.
2. An item may be of nominal dollar amount and still be material.
3. When economic substance and legal form conflict, the accountant records legal form because one must obey the law.
4. The historical cost of an asset is a relevant fact in deciding whether to sell or keep it.

Now check your responses in Answer Frame 2¹³ on page 618.

Frame 3¹³

Quantifiability

Financial accounting is primarily concerned with measurements of economic resources and obligations and changes in both. Those activities, resources, and obligations that can be quantified (expressed in numbers) are of primary concern to financial accounting. Quantified data are generally more useful than verbal data. It is generally more useful to know exactly how much cash one possesses rather than to know that one has some cash. This concern for quantified data means that accounting pays little attention to unmeasurable economic concepts of satisfaction, utility, and welfare. Nor is accounting directly concerned with the sociological and psychological aspects of economic activity.

Verifiability

Accounting information is considered verifiable when it would be substantially duplicated by other independent measurers using the same measurement methods. The requirement that accounting information be based upon objective evidence is based upon the demonstrated needs of users for reliable, unbiased financial information. This is especially needed when parties with opposing interests (credit seekers and credit grantors) rely upon the same information. The reliability of information is enhanced if it is verifiable.

But accounting information will never be free of subjective opinion and judgment. It will always possess varying degrees of verifiability. Some measurements can be supported by canceled checks and invoices. Others, such as periodic depreciation charges, can never be verified because of their very nature. Thus, financial information in many instances is verifiable only in that it represents a consensus as to what would be reported if the same procedures had been followed by other accountants.

Neutrality

Financial accounting information should be neutral—it should not favor one group over another. It should meet the common needs of many users rather than the particular needs of specific users. It is not sufficient that the information be verifiable, since biased information can be verified. For example, inventories under the lower-of-cost-or-market method can be verified. But, since only declines in, and not increases in, market value have been recognized, one may question whether they meet the objective of neutrality.

Timeliness

The utility of information decreases with age. It is likely to be much more useful to know what the net earnings for 1978 were in early 1979 than to receive this information a year later. And if information is to be of any value in decision making, it must be available before the decision is made. If not, it is useless. In determining what constitutes timely information, consideration must be given to the other qualitative objectives and to the cost of gathering information. For example, a timely estimated amount for uncollectible accounts may be more valuable than a later, verified actual amount.

1. False. Economic activity is often far too complex to be reported in terms that every one can understand. Financial statements are intended primarily for informed investors and creditors.

2. True. Knowledge of illegal acts, such as briberies, may constitute material information even though the dollar amounts are small.

3. False. Economic substance is reported because it is more likely to be relevant for economic decision making.

4. False. The decision would involve a comparison of the cash that can be received immediately with the future cash inflows expected from retaining and using the asset.

If you answered incorrectly, review Frame 2¹³ before continuing in Frame 3¹³ on page 616.

3¹³

continued

Indicate whether each of the following statements is true or false.

1. Reporting the results of operations for the calendar year 1978 by June 1, 1979, would comply with the timeliness objective.

2. Information that can be verified may yet be biased because of the measurement method selected.

3. Some accounting measurements can be verified only in the sense that another accountant using the same measurement methods would arrive at the same result.

4. Conflicts may exist between objectives. For example, relevance may conflict with verifiability.

Check your responses in Answer Frame 3¹³ on page 620.

Frame 4¹³

Comparability

When comparable financial information is presented, the differences and similarities noted will arise from the matters being reported upon and not from their accounting treatment. Comparable information will reveal relative strengths and weaknesses in a single firm through time and between two or more firms at the same point in time.

The accounting requirement of consistency leads to comparability of financial information for a single firm through time. Consistency generally requires adherence to the same accounting principles and reporting practices through time. It bars indiscriminate switching of principles or methods (such as changing depreciation methods every year). It does not bar changes in principles if the information needs of users are better served by the change. But disclosure of the change and, if material, its effects are required.[8]

Comparability between firms is more difficult to achieve because the same activities may be accounted for in different ways. For example, B may use the Lifo and accelerated depreciation methods, while C accounts for identical activities using Fifo and straight-line depreciation methods. A high degree of interfirm comparability will not exist until it is required that the same activities be accounted for in the same manner.

Completeness

Completeness requires that all financial accounting information meeting the other qualitative objectives be reported. Full disclosure is to be made of all significant information in a manner that is understandable to and does not mislead informed investors, creditors, and other users. Such full disclosure generally requires presentation of a statement of financial position, an earnings statement, a statement of changes in financial position and necessary supporting schedules. Such statements are to be complete with items properly classified and segregated, such as reporting sales revenue separately from other revenues. The required disclosures may be made in (1) the body of the financial statements, (2) in the notes to such statements, (3) in special communications, and (4) in the president's letter in the annual report.

In addition to changes in accounting principles, disclosure usually must be made of a number of other items. These include unusual activities (loans to officers); changes in expectations (losses on inventory); long-term obligations entered into that are not recorded by the accountant (a 20-year lease on a building); new arrangements with certain groups (pension and profit-sharing plans for employees); significant events that occur after the date of the statements (loss of a major customer); and the accounting policies (major principles and their manner of application) followed in preparing the financial statements.[9] Because of its emphasis upon disclosure, this objective is often called the full-disclosure principle. Much of what constitutes full disclosure has already been illustrated in preceding chapters. For a real world example, see the Appendix to Chapter 14, pages 684–698.

[8] Accounting Principles Board, "Accounting Changes," *APB Opinion No. 20* (New York: AICPA, July 1971).

[9] Accounting Principles Board, "Disclosure of Accounting Policies," *APB Opinion No. 22* (New York: AICPA, 1972).

1. False. This is an example of a situation in which the information presented would have little utility because of its age.
2. True. Pricing inventories at the lower of cost or market may be an example. Accelerated depreciation may be another.
3. True. Examples here are net earnings and depreciation.
4. True. An investor may find it most relevant to know the market value of an asset that is reported at a verified cost figure. The asset may be reported at cost because it is unique and there is no verifiable market price for it.

Review Frame 3¹³ if you answered incorrectly. Then continue in Frame 4¹³ on page 618.

4¹³
continued

Indicate whether each of the following statements is true or false.

1. Even though they differ, an investor can, by knowing each firm's accounting policies, place their financial information on a comparable basis.
2. The completeness objective may require disclosure of an event that happened after the closing date of the period covered by the financial statements.
3. Consistency and comparability are essentially the same objective.
4. Consistency requires that the same accounting principles be adhered to through time with full disclosure of changes made to "better" principles.

Check your responses in Answer Frame 4¹³ on page 622.

Frame 5¹³

Underlying assumptions or concepts

Every discipline is based upon certain fundamental assumptions or concepts (also referred to as axioms, features, or postulates). Our law, for example, assumes that a person is innocent until proven guilty; the physicist assumes that energy can neither be created or destroyed; the mathematician, that every integer has a successor. And parts of economic theory rely heavily upon the assumption of diminishing marginal utility. Many of these assumptions cannot be proven true. They are accepted as being logical and as a place to start an inquiry into a discipline.

Some of the underlying assumptions or concepts of accounting were presented and discussed briefly in Chapter 1. A more complete discussion is presented below.

Entity

All accounting information pertains to a specific unit or area of interest called the entity. This entity is viewed as having an existence apart from its owners, creditors, employees, and other interested parties. For the corporation, this separate existence is confirmed by law. But the boundaries of the accounting entity may differ from those of the legal entity, since financial information may relate to a corporation and its subsidiary corporations as a single business. An accounting entity may exist where it is not supported by a legal entity, as in a single proprietorship. Here the business, not the individual, is the accounting entity. Financial statements must identify the entity for which they are prepared; and their content must be limited to reporting the activities, resources, and obligations of that entity.

Continuity (going concern)

In financial accounting, the entity is viewed as continuing indefinitely in operation unless evidence to the contrary exists. This assumption is justified because experience shows that continuity at least until the end of another reporting period is highly probable for most entities. Yet if liquidation appears likely, financial information should not be reported based on the assumption of continuity.

The expectation of continuity is often used to justify the use of cost rather than market value as a basis for measuring assets. While significant for an entity in liquidation, market values are alleged to be of no significance to an entity that intends to use rather than sell its assets. On the other hand, the expectation of continuity permits the accountant to treat certain costs as assets. For example, printed advertising matter may be on hand to be used to promote a special sale next month. It may have little, if any, value to anyone but its owner. But it is treated as an asset because its owner is expected to continue operating long enough to benefit from it.

Indicate whether each of the following statements is true or false.

1. An entity for accounting purposes may or may not be a legal entity.
2. An accounting entity may include several legal entities.
3. The continuity assumption, by ruling out liquidation values, requires the valuation of assets at their historical cost.
4. When based upon past history, the assumption of continuity seems reasonable.

Check your responses in Answer Frame 5[13] on page 622.

Answer frame 4¹³

1. False. Even accountants cannot do this, and this is likely to be the case even if they are employed by one of the reporting companies. Such information simply is not likely to be available. For example, a company that uses Fifo to cost its inventories is not likely to compile information that would permit it to use Lifo at the same time.
2. True. It has long been a reporting principle that such events be disclosed, if they have a material effect.
3. False. Consistency is generally considered to relate to a single firm through time. Comparability relates to interfirm comparisons.
4. True. Changes in principles are permitted provided it is believed such changes will yield more relevant information and are fully disclosed.

If you answered incorrectly, restudy Frame 4¹³ before continuing in Frame 5¹³ on page 620.

Answer frame 5¹³

1. True. Single proprietorships and partnerships are not legal entities, while a corporation is. But all are accounting entities.
2. True. Consolidated financial statements report upon a corporation and its subsidiary corporations as a single entity, although each corporation is a legal entity.
3. False. The ruling out of liquidation values for assets does not, of and by itself, mean that assets are automatically to be valued at historical cost. Valuation at historical cost must be supported on other grounds.
4. True. The vast majority of accounting entities do exist until the accountant has another opportunity to report upon them, making the assumption seem reasonable. But enough do not survive each year so that the accountant should at least raise the question of the likelihood of survival if termination seems possible.

If you answered incorrectly, review Frame 5¹³ before proceding to Frame 6¹³ below.

Frame 6¹³

Money measurement

Accounting measurements normally will be expressed in money terms. The unit of measure (the dollar in the United States) is identified in the financial statements.

This does not mean that all measurements of economic activity must be stated in monetary terms to be useful. It may, for example, be pertinent to know that a plant is operating at 50 percent of its capacity. But the full economic significance of this bit of information cannot be known until it is translated into money terms.

The monetary unit, the dollar, also provides accountants with a common unit of measure in reporting upon economic activity. Think, for a moment, about preparing a statement of financial position without using the dollar as a unit of measure. Such a statement would probably be of little value.

Stable unit. In making money measurements, accountants have typically ignored fluctuations in the value of the unit of measure – the dollar. Thus, a portion of the cost of a building acquired in 1940 is deducted, without adjustment for change in the value of the dollar, from revenues earned in, and expressed in, 1979 dollars in arriving at the net earnings for 1979. The 1940 and 1979 dollars are treated as equal units of measure, even though substantial price inflation has occurred between the two years. The inflation experienced in the 1970s once again caused renewed interest to be expressed in the problem of adjusting financial statements for changes in the general level of prices. The question at issue is whether accountants should continue to report in historical, unadjusted dollars or adopt another unit of measure – a constant dollar of equal general purchasing power.

Periodicity (*time periods*)

To provide useful financial information to investors and creditors for decision making at various points in the life of an entity, accountants must subdivide the life of an entity into periods and prepare reports on the activities of those periods. In order to aid comparisons, the time periods usually are of equal length. The length of the period must be stated in the financial statements. Such financial statements are prepared under the accrual basis, which requires approximation and the exercise of judgment.

Accrual basis. Financial statements better reflect the financial status and operations of a firm when prepared under the accrual rather than the cash basis of accounting. Under the cash basis, which is used primarily in small service-rendering firms, revenues and most expenses are recorded at the time of cash receipt or cash payment. Under the accrual basis, changes in resources (assets) and obligations (equities), including revenues and expenses, are recorded much more nearly at the time that they actually occur. For example, revenues are recorded when services are rendered or products are sold and delivered, even if not paid for immediately in cash. Similarly, expenses are recorded as incurred in the period benefited – for example, employee services are recorded in the period received, which may not be the same period in which payment is made. The accrual basis reflects the fact that considerable economic activity can occur that is not matched by a concurrent cash flow.

Approximation and judgment. Accounting measurements are often estimates. To provide periodic financial information, estimates must often be made of such things as expected uncollectible accounts and the useful lives of depreciable assets. Periodic depreciation charges can never be anything but estimates. Because they depend on future events, estimates of the net realizable value of accounts receivable must be uncertain and tentative. This uncertainty precludes precise measurement and makes estimates necessary.

Yet, because they represent the exercise of judgment by an informed accountant, these estimates are often quite accurate. And it is this need to exercise judgment that prevents one from stating the financial accounting process as a set of inflexible rules, an example of which might be: Depreciate all trucks over three years.

Indicate whether each of the following statements is true or false.

1. A tract of land costing $10,000 in 1950 would be reported at $20,000 in 1979 if measured in 1979 dollars of constant purchasing power and prices, in general, have doubled between 1950 and 1979.

2. A serious conceptual flaw in accounting is its failure to take into consideration the changing value of its unit of measure — the dollar.

3. The need to provide financial information for relatively short periods of time is the cause of many accounting problems.

4. Under cash basis accounting collection of cash in 1979 in payment of services rendered in 1978 leads to the recording of revenue in 1979.

Now check your responses in Answer Frame 6[13] on page 626.

Frame 7[13]

Exchange prices

Because most goods and services are exchanged rather than consumed by their producers, accountants have long relied upon exchanges as indicators of, and exchange prices as measures of, economic activity. Typically, past exchange prices are used and called historical costs when applied to many assets. But, at times, a current exchange price or a future exchange price may be used. For example, both replacement cost and expected selling price are used in determining "market" under the lower-of-cost-or-market inventory method. But, on the whole, financial accounting is concerned largely with past exchange prices, that is, with historical costs.

But this appears to be changing. Due largely to the "double-digit" rate of inflation in the mid-70s, accountants are becoming more interested in "current value accounting." They are asking whether some other attribute of assets and liabilities, such as current market value, rather than historical cost should be measured and reported in providing relevant financial information. Among those in use or advocated are the following.[10]

1. *Historical cost/historical proceeds.* Initially, this is the amount of cash paid to acquire an asset (historical cost); for some assets, historical cost is subject to depreciation or amortization. For liabilities, this is the

[10] Adapted from FASB, *Conceptual Framework*, p. 193.

amount of cash received when a debt was incurred (historical proceeds); the amount may be subject to amortization as would be true for a premium on bonds payable.

2. *Current cost/current proceeds.* This is the amount of cash that would have to be paid currently to acquire an asset already owned. It is current reproduction cost for an identical asset; it is current replacement cost for an asset with equivalent productive capacity. Current proceeds refers to the amount of proceeds that would be obtained if the same obligation were incurred currently.

3. *Current exit value in orderly liquidation.* This is the amount of cash that would be obtained from an orderly, not rushed, sale of an asset. It is also the amount of cash that would have to be paid out currently to eliminate a liability. It is current market value for both assets and liabilities.

4. *Expected exit value in due course of business.* This is the amount of cash expected from conversion of an asset in the due course of business, less the direct costs of effecting the conversion. As applied to accounts receivable and inventories, this is the familiar net realizable value. It is also the amount of cash expected to be paid to eliminate a liability in the due course of business including the direct costs necessary to make those payments. Or, it is the nondiscounted amount of expected cash outlays.

5. *Present value of expected cash flows.* This is the present value of the future cash inflows expected from an asset in the due course of business less the present value of the cash outflows necessary to obtain those inflows. It is also the present value of the future cash outflows to eliminate a liability in the due course of business including the cash outflows necessary to make those payments. Several different rates of discount could be employed, including an historical rate, a current rate, or an average expected rate.

It is well beyond the scope of this text to attempt a full discussion of these attributes. But several points can be noted. Attribute No. 1 is the familiar historical cost upon which accounting has long been based and which is under attack currently. Attribute No. 2 has received considerable support in the literature and has been recommended for implementation in the United Kingdom. Also, as stated in its *Accounting Series Release No. 190,* the Securities and Exchange Commission requires that certain companies required to file financial statements with the Commission disclose in their annual reports (in footnotes or in a separate section) the current replacement cost of inventories, cost of goods sold, productive capacity (plant assets, except land), and depreciation, depletion, and amortization. Attribute No. 3 is currently used to value the marketable securities of investment companies and brokers and dealers in securities. As mentioned above, attribute No. 4 is actually net realizable value and is currently used for accounts receivable and inventories. Because it is based upon estimates of future cash flows, attribute No. 5 is highly subjective. Its use will very likely be restricted

1. True. If prices have doubled since 1950, one 1950 dollar would have bought as much as two 1979 dollars. Therefore, the ten thousand 1950 dollars had a purchasing power equal to twenty thousand 1979 dollars.

2. True. The economist would never present time series data (data relating to several years) that are expressed in dollars without adjusting for the change in the value of the dollar.

3. True. This is the reason why the accountant must make many of the estimates on which financial reporting is based.

4. True. Under cash basis accounting, revenues are recorded only when cash is received; it matters not when the services were or will be rendered. Since the cash was collected in 1979, revenue is recorded in 1979.

If you answered incorrectly, study Frame 6¹³ again before proceeding to Frame 7¹³ on page 624.

7¹³
continued

to assets and liabilities having fairly certain cash flows, such as U.S. government bonds.

The debate over which attribute of assets and liabilities should be measured is likely to be long and heated. But further departures from the historical cost/historical proceeds basis seem imminent.

Indicate whether each of the following statements is true or false.

1. Attributes other than historical cost are currently measured and reported by accounting.

2. Long-term bond investments are initially recorded at the present value of their expected cash flows.

3. While theoretically preferred, the subjectivity surrounding the measurement of the present value of future cash flows makes its widespread use unlikely.

4. The SEC requires certain companies to disclose the expected exit value in due course of business of their plant assets.

5. The cost of replacing an asset with an identical one is called its reproduction cost.

Check your responses in Answer Frame 7¹³ on page 628.

Frame 8¹³

The major principles

Although there exists no complete authoritative statement of generally accepted accounting principles, accountants agree that certain principles dominate their practice. These principles are presented and discussed below.

The initial recording (or cost) principle

Stated briefly, this principle is: Transfers of resources are recorded initially in the accounting system at the time of exchange and at the prices agreed upon by the parties to the exchange. Thus, for any firm, this principle determines to a large extent (1) what goes into the accounting system — transaction data; (2) when it is recorded — at the time of exchange; and (3) the amounts — exchange prices — at which assets, liabilities, owners' equity, revenues, and expenses are recorded. As applied to certain assets, this principle is often called the "cost principle," meaning that these assets are initially recorded at cost. But use of a term such as "exchange price principle" is to be preferred because it seems inappropriate to refer to liabilities, owners' equity, and certain assets such as cash and accounts receivable as being measured in terms of their cost. Note also that even if other attributes are reported in the financial statements, the data initially recorded in the accounting system will be exchange prices.

The matching principle

A most fundamental principle of accounting is that net earnings can be determined by matching the expenses incurred with the periodic revenues they generate. The logic of the principle stems from the fact that wherever economic resources are employed someone will want to know what was accomplished and at what cost. Every appraisal of economic activity will involve matching sacrifice with benefit. And knowledge of sacrifice and benefit is usually considered far more valuable than knowledge of the stock of resources. So it is in accounting. The earnings statement is generally considered more important than the statement of financial position.

In applying the matching principle, revenue is the independent variable. It is recognized through application of the realization principle, as discussed and illustrated below.

Revenue recognition

Revenue is defined as the product or service provided by a firm. It is best measured by the amount of cash expected from the customer. The generation of revenue usually consists of a never-ending stream of activity. A question thus arises as to when this revenue, this added utility, should be recorded, that is, credited to a revenue account. The general answer is that the revenue should be earned and realized before it is recognized.

The earning of revenue. In a broad sense, all of the activities of a firm to create additional utility constitute the earning process. The actual

8¹³
continued

receipt of cash from a customer may have been preceded by many events including (1) placing advertisements, (2) calling on the customer several times, (3) submission of samples, (4) acquisition of raw materials, (5) manufacture of the goods, and (6) delivery of the goods. Costs were undoubtedly incurred for these activities. And revenue was actually being generated by these activities, even though accountants refuse to recognize it until time of sale. This refusal is based upon their requirement that revenue be realized before it is recognized.

The realization of revenue. As a general principle, revenue is considered realized at the time of sale for merchandise transactions and when services have been performed in service transactions. Legally, a sale occurs when title to the goods passes to the buyer. As a practical matter, accountants generally record revenue when goods are delivered.

The advantages of recognizing revenue at time of sale include: (1) the delivery of the goods is a discernible event; (2) the revenue is measurable; (3) the risk of loss due to price decline or destruction of the goods has passed to the buyer; (4) the revenue has been earned, or substantially so; and (5) because the revenue has been earned, expenses can be determined thus allowing net earnings to be determined. As discussed below, the disadvantage of recognizing revenue at time of sale is that the revenue may not be recorded in the period in which the activity creating it occurred.

Indicate whether each of the following statements is true or false.

1. Even if equipment owned is to be reported in the statement of financial position at its replacement cost, it will be initially entered in the accounting system at its exchange price—its historical cost.

2. Generally speaking, information on stocks of resources is more valuable than information on flows of resources.

3. The realization of revenue generally means that a sale must have been made and cash received.

4. Virtually all of the activities undertaken by a firm are a part of the process of earning revenue.

Check your responses in Answer Frame 8[13] on page 630.

Frame 9[13] ───

Cash collection as point of revenue recognition. Some small firms record revenues and expenses at the time of cash collection and payment. This procedure is known as the cash basis of accounting. It is acceptable primarily in service enterprises which do not have substantial credit transactions or inventories, and in accounting for installment sales.

Installment basis of revenue recognition. When the selling price of goods is to be collected in installments and considerable doubt exists as to collectibility, the installment basis of accounting may be employed. Under this basis, the gross margin on a sale is treated as being realized proportionately with the cash collected from customers. If this gross margin rate is 40 percent, then 40 cents of every dollar collected on the installment accounts receivable represents realized gross margin. For example, assume a stereo system costing $300 is sold for $500, with payment to be made in ten equal installments of $50 each. If four installments are collected in the year of sale, the realized gross margin taken into net earnings is $80 (4 × $50 × .40). In the next year it will be $120 (6 × $50 × .40), if the final six installments are collected.

This method is accepted for tax purposes. But, because it delays the recognition of revenue beyond the time of sale, it is accepted for accounting purposes only when extreme doubt exists as to the collectibility of the installments due.

Revenue recognition on long-term construction projects. The revenue created by completing a long-term construction project can be recognized under two methods: (1) the completed contract method or (2) the percentage-of-completion method. Under the completed contract method, no revenue is recognized until the period in which the contract is completed, and then all of the revenue is recognized even though the contract may have required three years to complete. The costs incurred on the project are carried forward in inventory accounts and are charged to expense in the period in which the revenue is recognized. This approach is similar to recognizing revenue at the time of sale. It suffers from the disadvantage of recognizing no revenue or net earnings from a project in periods in which a major part of the revenue-producing activity may have occurred.

Under the percentage-of-completion method, revenue and net earnings are recognized periodically on the basis of the estimated stage of

1   True. Accountants are not likely to attempt to second-guess management by trying to find a value other than exchange price (cost) at which to record the transactions entered into by management.

2. False. Information on the flows of resources (uses and accomplishments) is far more valuable than information on amounts or stocks of resources.

3. False. Generally, a sale is required, but realization does not require that the asset received be cash and only cash.

4. True. In a broad sense all of the activities of a firm are taken to help it earn revenue.

If you answered incorrectly, study Frame 8¹³ again before continuing on in Frame 9¹³ on page 629.

9¹³
continued

completion of the project. To illustrate, assume that a firm has a contract to erect a dam at a price of $44 million. By the end of the first fiscal year, it had incurred costs of $30 million and expected to incur $10 million more. The contract would be considered 75 percent complete, since $30 million of an expected $40 million of costs have been incurred. Consequently, $33 million of revenue and $3 million of earnings would be recognized on the contract in the fiscal year.

Revenue recognition at completion of production. Recognizing revenue at the time of completion of productive activities is considered acceptable procedure for certain precious metals (gold) and for many farm products such as wheat, corn, and soybeans. The homogeneous nature of the products, the fact that they can usually be sold at their market prices, and the difficulties sometimes encountered in determining production costs are the reasons advanced to justify recognizing revenue prior to sale. Recognizing revenue upon completion of production is accomplished by debiting inventory and crediting a revenue account for the expected selling price of the goods produced. All of the costs incurred in the period can then be treated as expenses.

Collections of revenue before it is earned. Sometimes cash is collected before goods are delivered or services rendered; in effect, future revenues are collected. Such receipts should not be credited to a revenue account, since no revenue has been earned. Such receipts give rise to a liability, and they should be credited to an account that reveals their nature, such as Unearned Subscription Revenue or Advances by Customers. In the period in which the goods are delivered or the services performed, this account can be debited and the regular revenue account (Sales or Service Revenue) credited.

Indicate whether each of the following statements is true or false.

1. Revenue may not be recorded in the period in which the bulk of the activities creating it took place if it is recorded at the time of sale.

2. In limited circumstances where products are homogeneous and

markets are assured, revenue may be recognized upon completion of production.

3. If the gross margin rate on an installment sale is 35 percent and $400 of installment payments are collected from customers, the realized gross margin is $140.

4. If $16 million of an expected $20 million of costs on a $24 million contract are incurred in the first year of a contract, net earnings of $3.2 million before taxes are recognized in that year under the completed contract method.

Check your responses in Answer Frame 9[13] on page 632.

Frame 10[13] _____

Expense recognition

Expense is defined as the resources or service potentials consumed in generating revenue. Since resources and service potentials are assets, expense may also be defined as asset expirations voluntarily incurred to produce revenue. The television set delivered by a dealer to a customer for cash can readily be thought of as an asset expiration to produce revenue. Similarly, the services of a television station employed to advertise a product can be thought of as expiring to produce revenue. Losses, on the other hand, may be distinguished as involuntary asset expirations not related to the production of revenue. Fire losses are an example.

The measurement of expense. Since many assets used in operating a business are measured in terms of historical cost, it follows that many expenses, being expired assets, are measured in terms of the historical cost of the assets expired. Other expenses are paid for currently and are measured in terms of their current cost. Note that in a transaction recorded as a debit to Advertising Expense and a credit to Cash, it is not the asset, cash, that expires. The actual transaction consists of an exchange of cash for advertising services – an asset. The accountant, anticipating that the services will have expired by the end of the accounting period, records the expenditure as an expense. By this shortcut, an adjusting entry will be avoided. But this is merely an expedient accounting technique. No one knowingly buys expenses, that is, expired assets.

The timing of expense recognition.[11] The matching principle implies that a cause-and-effect relationship exists between expense and revenue, that is, expense is the cause of revenue. For certain expenses, the relationship is readily seen, as in the case of goods delivered to customers. When a direct cause-and-effect relationship cannot be seen, the costs

[11] For further discussion, see *APB Statement No. 4*, pars. 157–60.

631

10¹³
continued

of assets with limited lives may be charged to expense in the periods benefited on a systematic and rational allocation basis. Depreciation of plant assets is an example. In other instances, the relationship between expense and revenue can only be assumed to exist, as in the case of a contribution to the local community fund. Consequently, the recognition of expense, as a practical matter, is often guided by the concepts of product costs and period costs.

Product costs are those costs incurred directly and indirectly in the acquisition and manufacture of goods. Included are the invoice costs of goods, as well as freight and insurance-in-transit costs. For manufacturing firms, product costs include all costs of raw materials as well as the direct labor and indirect costs of operating a factory to produce goods (see Chapters 2, 3, and 4 of *Managerial Accounting: A Programmed Text*). Such costs are deemed to attach to the goods produced; are carried in inventory accounts as long as the goods are on hand; and are charged to expense when the goods are sold. Thus, a precise matching of the expense, cost of goods sold, and its related revenue is obtained.

Period costs are the remaining costs incurred and consist primarily of selling and administrative expenses. Under this concept, expenses are matched with revenues by periods because matching by transactions is simply not possible. Thus, period costs are expensed in the period incurred because (1) they relate to the current period's revenue — the local supermarket's weekly newspaper advertisement is an example; (2) the cost must be incurred every period and there is no measurable buildup of benefits — officers' salaries are an example here; (3) there is no measurable relationship with any segment of revenue, yet the cost must be incurred to remain in business — the cost of the annual audit is an example; and (4) the amount of cost to be carried forward cannot be measured in a nonarbitrary manner—as might be true for the costs of an employee training and apprenticeship program.

Indicate whether each of the following statements is true or false.

1. Most expenses are measured in terms of the historical cost of the assets that expired in the creation of revenue.
2. The cost of the cloth used in tailoring a suit is a product cost.
3. Period costs are treated as expenses of the period in which they are incurred.
4. Losses should be as carefully related to revenues as are product costs.

Check your responses in Answer Frame 10[13] on page 634.

Frame 11[13]

Earnings models. Since the 1930s the primary focus of financial accounting has been upon the determination of net earnings. This has led to increased attention to matching, including the recording of accruals and deferrals. And the accounting model for net earnings is:

Revenues (including gains) − Expenses (including losses and taxes) =
Net earnings

This focus upon earnings determination has been illustrated repeatedly in this text. But let us illustrate briefly how the earnings determination principles dominate what is reported in the financial statements. The initial recording (cost) principle directs that assets be initially recorded at cost. The realization principle requires that increases in the value of assets not be recorded until realized through an exchange. Thus, assets are reported at cost, or cost less accumulated depreciation if they are being systematically and rationally amortized in adherence to the matching principle. Also, in adhering to the matching principle, a firm may defer the cost of a major promotional campaign to introduce a new product. These costs are reported as assets and amortized over future periods even though they possess no value to anyone but the firm incurring them. And further, many firms include among their liabilities an item titled "Deferred federal income taxes (payable)." This item does not represent an obligation to transfer resources or to provide services. But, as discussed in Appendix 7B, it arises solely from a matching of federal income taxes expense with net earnings before taxes.

These effects upon the statement of financial position of the matching principle have caused concern among a growing number of accountants. And this, in turn, has led some of them to call for a different earnings model—one based upon the statement of financial position. It is similar to the economist's income model in that it is based upon the change in the value of the net assets (assets − liabilities) or owners' equity be-

1. True. This is clearly seen for depreciable assets. It is less obvious, but nonetheless true, for asset expirations that for practical reasons are recorded as expenses upon their payment in cash.
2. True. The cost is traceable to the product and, therefore, considered a product cost.
3. True. This is the accounting treatment for period costs.
4. False. Because a cause-and-effect relationship does not exist between losses and revenues, there is no need to match the two. Losses are recognized in the period in which it becomes rather evident that they exist.

If you answered incorrectly, restudy Frame 10^{13} before continuing on in Frame 11^{13} on page 633.

11^{13}
continued

tween two points of time, adjusted for dividends and capital investments and withdrawals. Sometimes referred to as the asset and liability view of earnings (to contrast it with the revenue and expense view), the model in equation form is:

$$OE_1 + D - CI - OE_0 = NE$$

where OE_1 is the ending owners' equity, D is dividends, CI is additional capital invested, OE_0 is beginning owners' equity, and NE is net earnings. To illustrate, a firm having a beginning owners' equity of $100,000, an ending equity of $200,000, $50,000 of capital invested for newly issued shares, and which paid a dividend of $20,000 would have net earnings for the period of $70,000.

The two earnings models will yield the same amount of net earnings if assets, liabilities, owners' equity, revenues, and expenses are defined the same and are based upon measurements of the same attributes. But the revenue and expense model is more likely to be based upon historical cost while the advocates of the change in owners' equity model are likely to support some type of "current value." This is but another aspect of the issue of what attribute of assets and liabilities should accountants seek to measure. It is an issue that must be resolved by the FASB.[12]

Indicate whether each of the following statements is true or false.

1. Revenues generally include gains such as those realized upon the sale of a truck used to deliver merchandise sold.
2. The reported assets of a firm may include items which would not be purchased by anyone external to the firm at any price.
3. $OE_8 + D - CI - OE_9 = NE$. (The terms stand for the items described above, except that the subscripts 8 and 9 stand for 1978 and 1979, respectively.)

[12] For further discussion, see FASB, *Conceptual Framework*, chap. 5.

4. The principles governing earnings determination also control to a considerable extent the items and amounts reported in the statement of financial position.

Check your responses in Answer Frame 11[13] on page 636.

Frame 12[13] ─────────────────────────────────────

Modifying conventions

For several reasons, called modifying conventions, accounting principles may not be strictly applied. These reasons reside in the environment in which accounting is practiced. We have already noted that immaterial items may be given a practical rather than a theoretical treatment. Materiality thus can be considered a modifying convention as well as a qualitative objective. We have also noted that construction revenues may be accounted for on a percentage-of-completion rather than the completed contract (sales) basis. This yields a clearer reflection of actual activities. It is also an example of the modifying convention calling for exercise of judgment by the accounting profession as a whole. It is also in accord with the emphasis placed by accountants upon earnings determination. But the primary modifying convention is conservatism.

Conservatism. Conservatism is the accountants' response to the uncertainty faced in the environment in which accounting is practiced. It embraces the idea of being cautious or prudent. Many accounting measurement are estimates and involve the exercise of judgment. In such cases, conservatism tells the accountant "to play it safe." Playing it safe usually involves making sure that, if in error, all estimates are in error in such a way as to yield lower reported net assets and net earnings than might otherwise be reported.

Conservatism may be applied with varying degrees of severity in different firms, causing decreased comparability in their financial information. This may cause investors to act in a manner not in their best interest. They may, for example, sell shares of stock in a firm because its earnings did not meet their expectations. But this failure may have been due solely to a conservative measurement of inventories. Thus, a fine line exists, in many instances, between conservative and incorrect accounting.

Implementing principles

Underlying the major principles discussed above is a set of implementing or broad operating principles. They guide the actual operation of the accounting system. They indicate which events are to be recorded and which are not, and how the selected events are to be measured. They show how the principle of initial recording of exchange prices is

1. True. Such gains are generally included in revenues.
2. True. The promotional costs incurred to introduce a new product would be an example. Such items are often referred to as deferred charges.
3. False. OE_8 and OE_9 must be reversed for the statement to be true.
4. True. Adherence to the matching principle results in the introduction of accrued and deferred items into the statement of financial position. The realization principle requires that assets be carried at not more than their historical cost until sold.

If you answered incorrectly, study Frame 11^{13} again before continuing on in Frame 12^{13} on page 635.

12^{13}
continued

to be applied to exchanges that affect assets, liabilities, owners' equity, revenues, and expenses. These principles also indicate the accounting to be applied to (1) transfers such as gifts, donations, lawsuit losses, fines, and thefts; (2) events favorable and unfavorable to the firm such as changes in the market values of assets owned; and (3) internal events such as the manufacture of goods. These implementing principles are not dealt with here because most of them are discussed in other chapters. For the same reason the procedures or detailed accounting principles underlying the implementing or operating principles will not be discussed here. Examples of these include the Fifo method of inventory costing and the straight-line depreciation method. One of the purposes of this chapter has been to put these detailed accounting principles or procedures in place in a loose framework of the theory of financial accounting. For an example of current financial reporting, see the Appendix to Chapter 14, pages 684–698.

Indicate whether each of the following statements is true or false.

1. Conservatism holds that if a liability must be estimated, the estimate should tend to the low side.
2. If experience shows that 1 percent of annual credit sales proves uncollectible, it would be conservative to estimate such uncollectibles at 2 percent of credit sales.
3. The recording of land acquired upon issuance of shares of stock at the market value of the shares issued is an example of the application of an implementing principle.
4. A procedure thought to be conservative in one accounting period may yield a nonconservative effect in a later period.

Check your responses in Answer Frame 12^{13} on page 638.

Frame 13¹³

Net earnings—inclusions and exclusions

Accounting has long been plagued by the problem of what should be included in the net earnings reported for a period. Should net earnings include only the revenues and expenses related to normal operations? Or should it include unusual, nonrecurring gains and losses? And further should the net earnings for 1979, for example, include an item that can be clearly associated with a prior year, such as additional federal income taxes for 1976? Or should such items, including corrections of errors, be carried directly to retained earnings?

APB Opinion No. 9 (December 1966) sought to provide answers to the above questions. It directed that unusual or nonrecurring items that have an earnings or loss effect be classified as extraordinary items (reported in the earnings statement) or as prior period adjustments (reported in the statement of retained earnings). To provide useful information, extraordinary items were to be reported separately after net earnings from regular continuing activities.

Extraordinary items

Abuses in the financial reporting of gains and losses as extraordinary items led to the issuance of *APB Opinion No. 30* (September 1973). In it extraordinary items are redefined as those which are unusual in nature *and* which occur infrequently. Note that both conditions must be met— unusual nature and infrequent occurrence. Whether an item is unusual and infrequent is to be determined in the light of the environment in which the firm operates. Examples include gains or losses which are the direct result of a major casualty (a flood), an expropriation, or a prohibition under a newly enacted law. Such items are to be included in the determination of periodic net earnings, but disclosed separately (net of their tax effects, if any) in the earnings statement. *FASB Statement No. 4* further directs that gains and losses from the early extinguishment of debt are extraordinary items. Gains or losses related to ordinary business activities are not extraordinary items regardless of their size. For example, material write-downs of uncollectible receivables, obsolete inventories, and intangible assets are not extraordinary items. But such items may be separately disclosed as part of net earnings from continuing activities.

Prior period adjustments

According to *APB Opinion No. 9*, prior period adjustments were to be reported in the statement of retained earnings. They consisted of those material adjustments which (1) are directly and specifically related to business activities of a prior period, (2) are not the result of economic

637

1. False. To report lower net assets, the estimate should tend to the high side.
2. False. This would be better described as incorrect accounting.
3. True. This would be a means of implementing the principle of initial recording at exchange price (cost).
4. True. Depreciating an asset with an actual realized useful life of ten years over six years will yield conservative net earnings for six years and nonconservative earnings for the last four years.

If you answered incorrectly, review Frame 12¹³ before continuing on in Frame 13¹³ on page 637.

13¹³
continued

events occurring after the prior period, (3) result primarily from determinations made by persons outside the business, and (4) could not be estimated with reasonable accuracy prior to this determination.

Examples of prior period adjustments included material assessments or settlements of income taxes, settlements of contracts through renegotiation, amounts paid to settle litigation or other similar claims, and corrections of accounting errors. But *FASB Statement No. 16* (June 1977) changed virtually all of this. Here the Board held that assessments of income taxes and settlements of contracts and litigations were economic events of the year of settlement and involved management determination as well as the actions of outsiders. These settlements then did not qualify as prior period adjustments. They are to be reported in the earnings statement, classified as extraordinary items only if they are unusual and nonrecurring. As a result of the Board's action, prior period adjustments will consist almost solely of corrections of accounting errors.

In the statement of retained earnings, prior period adjustments are treated as adjustments of the opening balance of retained earnings. But normal recurring corrections or adjustments, which follow inevitably from the use of estimates in accounting practice, are not to be treated as prior period adjustments.

Indicate whether each of the following statements is true or false.

1. The correction in 1980 of an underestimation of the bad debts expense for 1979 would be reported as a prior period adjustment in 1980.
2. A loss suffered from destruction by a tornado of a firm's manufacturing plant is probably an extraordinary item.
3. The correction in 1980 of the expensing in 1979 of the $1 million cost of a tract of land acquired in 1979 would be treated as a prior period adjustment.

4. Damage suffered by a Florida citrus grower's orange crop from a heavy frost would probably be reported as an extraordinary item.

Check your responses in Answer Frame 13[13] on page 640.

Frame 14[13]

Accounting for tax effects

Most extraordinary items and prior period adjustments will affect the amount of income taxes payable with the result that questions arise as to proper reporting procedure. To prevent distortions, *Opinion No. 9* recommends that extraordinary items and prior period adjustments be reported net of their tax effects, as shown in Illustration 13.1.

Illustration 13.1

ANSON COMPANY Earnings Statement For the Year Ended December 31, 1979		
Net sales		$41,000,000
Other revenues		2,250,000
Total Revenue		$43,250,000
Cost of goods sold	$22,000,000	
Administrative, selling, and general expenses	12,000,000	34,000,000
Net earnings before income taxes		$ 9,250,000
Federal income taxes		4,625,000
Net earnings before extraordinary item and the cumulative effect of an accounting change		$ 4,625,000
Extraordinary Item:		
Gain on retirement of debt	40,000	
Less tax effect	20,000	20,000
		$ 4,645,000
Cumulative effect on prior years' earnings of changing to a different depreciation method		20,000
Net Earnings		$ 4,665,000
Earnings per share of common stock:		
Net earnings before extraordinary item and the cumulative effect of an accounting change		$ 4.625
Extraordinary item		.020
Cumulative effect on prior years' earnings of changing to a different depreciation method		.020
Net Earnings		$ 4.665

Accounting changes

A company's net earnings and financial position can be materially altered by changes in accounting methods. A change in inventory valuation method (for example, from Fifo to Lifo) or a change in depreciation

14¹³
continued

method (for example, from straight-line to accelerated) would be examples of accounting changes. According to *APB Opinion No. 20* a company should consistently apply the same accounting methods from one period to another. But a change may be made if the newly adopted method is preferable and if the change is adequately disclosed in the financial statements. In the period in which an accounting change is made, the nature of the change, its justification, and its effect on net earnings must be disclosed in the financial statements. Also, the cumulative effect of the change on prior years' earnings must be shown on the earnings statement for the year of change.

Corrections of accounting errors are considered another type of accounting change. But in this case the financial reporting would be as shown in Illustration 13.2. And the journal entry to record the correction (assuming income taxes, at a 50 percent rate, were underpaid to the extent of $100,000 because of the error) is:

Land	200,000	
Federal Income Taxes Payable		100,000
Prior Period Adjustment—Correction of Error in Expensing Cost of Land		100,000

Illustrative statements

Financial statements reporting on the types of items discussed above are shown in Illustrations 13.1 and 13.2. They assume that the Anson Company had a taxable gain in 1979 of $40,000 from retirement of debt and that it expensed the $200,000 cost of land acquired in 1978 for both financial accounting and tax purposes. Also, the company changed depreciation methods in 1979, and the cumulative effect of the change amounted to $20,000. There are 1,000,000 shares of common stock outstanding. The current tax rate is 50 percent.

Note especially the following in Illustrations 13.1 and 13.2: (1) earnings of $4,625,000 before extraordinary item and cumulative effect of an accounting change are more representative of the continuing earning power of the firm because normal amounts of income taxes have

Illustration 13.2

```
ANSON COMPANY
Statement of Retained Earnings
For the Year Ended December 31, 1979
```

Retained earnings, January 1, 1979... $5,000,000

Prior period adjustment:
Correction of error of expensing land (net of tax effect of $100,000) 100,000

Adjusted retained earnings, January 1, 1979...................................... $5,100,000
    Add: Net earnings 4,665,000

                                                     $9,765,000
    Less: Dividends 500,000
Retained Earnings, December 31, 1979... $9,265,000

been deducted in arriving at this amount; (2) the gain on debt retirement is reported at its actual impact upon the company—that is, net of its tax effect; (3) the correction of the $200,000 error adds only $100,000 to retained earnings because income taxes were underpaid in prior years because the mistake carried over to the tax return; and (4) earnings per share are reported both before and after the extraordinary item and the cumulative effect of an accounting change.

In 1979 X Company has revenues of $10 million; expenses, excluding federal income taxes, of $6 million; and a loss from war destruction of $1 million. It also paid $400,000 of additional income taxes for 1976. The federal income tax rate is 50 percent. Indicate whether each of the following statements is true or false.

1. The additional income taxes for 1976 should be reported in the earnings statement for 1979.

2. Net earnings before extraordinary items would be reported at $1 million.

3. The net earnings for the year are $1.1 million.

4. The loss from war damage should be reported in the statement of retained earnings at a net-of-tax amount of $500,000.

Check your responses in Answer Frame 14[13] on page 642.

Summary *chapter* 13

Financial accounting and reporting are guided by a set of ideas collectively referred to as generally accepted accounting principles. Financial statements are presented with the objective of providing information that is useful to many users, but especially to investors and creditors, in making rational economic decisions. For the most part,

1. True. *FASB Statement No. 16* requires these taxes to be included in the determination of the net earnings for 1979. They can be classified as an extraordinary item only if unusual and nonrecurring. This is not likely to be the case. Thus, these taxes will be included with the income taxes on net earnings from continuing activities for 1979.

2. False. Net earnings before extraordinary items would probably amount to $1.6 million: $10 million of revenues minus $6 million of expenses and minus $2.4 million of income taxes. The taxes would amount to .5 ($10 million − $6 million) plus the $400,000 additional taxes assessed for 1976. This assumes such assessments are not unusual or nonrecurring.

3. True. From the $1.6 million computed in answer 2 above, deduct the $500,000 net of tax effects amount of the war damage loss. The result is $1.1 million of net earnings.

4. False. The loss is an extraordinary item and should be reported in the earnings statement (net of tax effects) at $500,000.

If you answered incorrectly, review Frame 14¹³ before continuing in the Summary on page 641.

information is needed about the prospects of receiving cash from an investment or a loan.

To be useful, information must meet certain qualitative objectives including relevance (materiality), understandability, quantifiability, verifiability, neutrality, timeliness, comparability, and completeness.

In providing information about assets, liabilities, owners' equity, revenues, and expenses, accountants rely upon certain assumptions. These include: (1) the existence of an entity to be accounted for; (2) indefinite life for the entity (continuity); (3) accounting elements are to be measured in money terms; (4) financial reports are needed for time periods shorter than the life of the entity; and (5) exchange prices are the primary data with which accounting is concerned. Much debate currently centers on whether accounting should continue to be based largely on past exchange prices—historical costs.

Some of the major principles of financial accounting are: (1) the initial recording of exchange prices or cost principle; (2) the matching principle of relating expenses and revenues; (3) the earning and realization principles of revenue recognition; and (4) the expense recognition principles of traceable cause and effect, systematic and rational allocation, and immediate recognition. Certain modifying conventions permit the accountant to depart from a strict, theoretical adherence to the above principles. These include materiality, conservatism, and exercise of judgment of the profession as a whole.

Underlying these major principles are the implementing or operating principles and detailed accounting principles or procedures. These are presented and discussed throughout this entire volume.

Every business encounters certain unusual and nonrecurring gains and losses and other adjustments such as the effects of accounting changes. Such items are to be classified as extraordinary items and reported, net of their tax effects, if any, in the earnings statement.

Prior period adjustments are to be reported as adjustments to the opening balance in the statement of retained earnings. They are reported net of their tax effects.

To complete your review, study the definitions contained in the Glossary which follows. Then go to the Student Review Quiz beginning on page 645 for a self-administered test of your understanding of the material in the chapter.

Glossary *chapter* 13

Accounting changes – changes in accounting data caused by accounting errors (expensing of an asset), mistaken estimates (depreciation), and changes in principles (change from Fifo to Lifo).

Accrual basis – a system or basis of accounting that assigns measures of economic activity to the periods it occurs rather than the period of cash inflow or outflow.

Cash basis (of accounting) – a basis of accounting for expenses and revenues in which they are recorded in the period of cash payment or receipt.

Comparability – a qualitative objective of accounting information; when information is comparable it reveals similarities and differences that are real and not the result of differing accounting treatments.

Completed contract method – a method of recognizing revenue on long-term projects in which no revenue is recognized until the project is completed; similar to recognizing revenue upon the completion of a sale.

Completeness – a qualitative objective of accounting information; requires disclosure of all significant information in a manner that aids understanding and does not mislead; sometimes called the full-disclosure principle.

Conservatism – the mental quality of being cautious or prudent; making sure that estimates, if in error, tend to understate rather than overstate net assets and net earnings.

Continuity (going concern) – the assumption that an entity will continue in operation indefinitely, thus allowing the accountant to avoid using liquidation values for assets.

Cumulative effect – the earnings or loss effect of an accounting change upon years prior to the year of change; an item reported in the earnings statement.

Current cost – the amount of cash that would have to be paid currently to acquire an asset already owned; called current reproduction cost when applied to an identical asset and current replacement cost when applied to an asset of equivalent capacity. The amount of cash that would be received currently from the incurrence of a liability is called current proceeds.

Current exit value – current market value; the amount of cash that would be received from an orderly sale of an asset.

Earning principle – the requirement that revenue not be recognized prior to the time that all of the activities to create it have been completed.

Entity (accounting entity) – the specific unit or area of interest to which accounting information pertains; entities have a separate existence from owners, creditors, managers, employees, and other interested parties.

Expected exit value – the net realizable of an asset; the amount of cash expected from an asset less any direct costs to be incurred in converting it.

Expense – service potential or economic resources consumed in the generation of revenue; matched with revenue under the principles of associating cause and effect, systematic and rational allocation, or immediate recognition.

Extraordinary items — items having an earnings or loss effect and which are unusual and nonrecurring; reported in the earnings statement net of tax effects, if any.

General objectives — the broad overriding goals sought by engaging in financial accounting and reporting; providing informed investors and creditors with information useful in making rational investment and credit decisions is an example.

Implementing (broad operating) principles — the guides relied upon in making the major principles (such as realization) operational.

Initial recording (cost) principle — the requirement that transfers of resources be initially recorded at the time of exchange and at the prices (cost) agreed upon in the exchange.

Installment basis or method — a revenue recognition procedure in which the gross margin on an installment sale is considered realized only in proportion to the cash collected on the installment receivable.

Loss — expired service potential or economic resources that produced no revenue or other benefit; usually involuntary in nature.

Matching principle — the principle that net earnings can be determined by associating or relating the revenues generated in a period with the expenses incurred to create them.

Materiality — a qualitative objective specifying that financial accounting report only information significant enough to influence decisions or evaluations; also a modifying convention that allows the accountant to deal with immaterial items in a nontheoretical, expedient manner.

Modifying convention — a custom emerging from accounting practice that alters the results that would be obtained from a strict application of accounting principles; conservatism is an example.

Money measurement — quantification in terms of a monetary unit of measurement — the dollar — as contrasted to quantification in terms of physical or other units of measurement — feet, inches, grams, and so on.

Neutrality — a qualitative objective that requires accounting information to be free from bias.

Percentage-of-completion method — a method of recognizing revenue on long-term projects according to the degree of completion attained; the degree of completion is often measured by comparing costs incurred with total costs expected to be incurred.

Period costs — costs incurred that cannot be traced to specific revenue and that are, as a result, expensed in the period incurred.

Periodicity (time periods) — an assumption of the accountant that the life of an entity can be subdivided into time periods for purposes of reporting upon its economic activities.

Present value — the amount obtained by discounting net future cash flows.

Prior period adjustments — material adjustments that have an earnings or loss effect and result from accounting errors made in prior accounting periods; they are reported in the statement of retained earnings net of their tax effects, if any.

Product costs — costs incurred in the manufacture of goods which are accounted for as if they were attached to the goods, with the result that they are charged to expense when the goods are sold.

Production basis — a method of revenue recognition used in limited circumstances and which permits the recording of revenue upon completion of production prior to sale.

Qualitative objectives — characteristics accounting information should possess to be useful.

Quantifiability (quantification) — description in terms of a scale of natural numbers.

Realization principle — a principle that directs that goods be sold or that services be rendered before revenue is recognized.

Relevance — a qualitative objective requiring that information be pertinent to or have a bearing upon a decision or an evaluation.

Stable dollar — an assumption that fluctuations in the value of the dollar are insignificant and may, therefore, be ignored.

Timeliness — a qualitative objective requiring that accounting information be provided at a time when it may be considered in reaching a decision.

Underlying assumptions – the basic concepts or premises regarding the environment which serve as a foundation for accounting principles.

Understandability – a qualitative objective requiring that the accounting information provided be comprehended, as to format and terminology, by the intended user.

Verifiability – a qualitative objective requiring that other accountants using the same measurement methods reach the same conclusion as to the magnitude of the measurements presented.

Continue with the Student Review Quiz below as a self-administered test of your understanding of the material presented in this chapter.

Student review quiz *chapter* 13

To develop a permanent record of your responses, you may write them on the answer sheet provided in the *Work Papers* or on a separate sheet of paper.

1 The results of the financial accounting process are reported in general-purpose financial statements intended for use primarily by –
a The firm's top management.
b The federal government.
c Potential and existing creditors and investors.
d The Internal Revenue Service.
e The firm's employees and customers.

2 Accounting principles or standards are used or relied upon by all of the following except –
a A single entity, to give its records consistency through time.
b External parties, who seek to compare financial information of different entities.
c The general public, as a means of increasing its confidence in the reliability of the information provided.
d The CPA, in appraising the information provided by management for its fairness.
e Management, in making special studies of its operations.

3 Of the qualitative objectives for financial accounting information, the most important one is –
a Verifiability.
b Timeliness.
c Relevance.
d Neutrality.
e Conservatism.

4 Which of the following is not a loss or an expense?
a The cost of newspaper advertising announcing a recent successful sale.
b Depreciation on trucks used in constructing a building for the constructor's own use.
c The salary of the president of the company.
d A drop in the net realizable value of inventory below cost.
e Shrinkage in the net realizable value of accounts receivable as measured by an estimate for uncollectible accounts.

5 The practice of overstating expenses in the current period to avoid handicapping future periods is –
a Acceptable because it is conservative.
b Acceptable if done consistently.
c Acceptable if fully disclosed.
d Acceptable if followed throughout the firms in the industry.
e Acceptable only if the amounts are immaterial.

6 Materiality is –
a Unimportant in determining whether or not there is adequate disclosure.
b Measured strictly by the dollar amounts of the individual items – for example, a $100,000 amount is always material.
c Measured by whether or not the manner in which the item is treated might influence decisions or evaluations.
d Always an aggregate consideration.
e Closely related to the convention of conservatism.

7 If the accountant were to attempt to arrive at an absolutely correct figure for periodic net earnings, which of the following would be most useful?
a Comparability.
b Matching.
c Materiality.
d Disclosure.
e Conservatism.

8 Revenue may under proper circumstances be recognized at all of the following moments in time except—

a After the earning process has been completed and an exchange has taken place.

b Upon the receipt of cash from the customer.

c As certain stages of completion of production are attained.

d When manufactured goods are acquired for resale.

e Upon the completion of the production process but before a sale has taken place.

9 Advertising costs incurred are typically treated as expenses of the period in which incurred under the expense recognition principle of—

a Associating cause and effect.

b Systematic and rational allocation.

c Immediate recognition of a period cost.

d Matching.

e Realization.

10 Which of the following would not be considered a major principle of accounting?

a Initial recording of assets and liabilities at their exchange prices at time of acquisition or incurrence.

b Matching.

c Realization.

d Associating cause and effect as an expense recognition principle.

e That assets received as gifts be recorded at their fair market value.

11 Which of the following statements is false?

a The realization of revenue generally means that an exchange has taken place in which another asset has been received for merchandise delivered or services rendered.

b Although accounting is often said to deal with costs, expired costs, and lost costs, what is really meant is that accountants often use cost as a measure of service potential in assets and it is really these potentials that exist and expire.

c Revenue is earned throughout the entire range of activities of an enterprise but usually is not recorded prior to sale because, for one reason, it is not easily measurable until time of sale.

d An expense is an involuntary expiration of an asset without any expectation of receiving benefits from the expiration.

e The term "cost" is sometimes used synonymously with "asset" and at other times with "expense."

12 Match the items in Column A with the proper description in Column B.

Column A		Column B
1.	Continuity (going concern)	**a** An assumption relied on in the preparation of financial statements that would be unreasonable if applied to the environment of many South American countries in recent years.
2.	Comparability	**b** Concerned with relative dollar amounts.
3.	Disclosure or completeness	**c** The usual basis for the recording of assets.
4.	Verifiability	**d** Required if the accounting treatment differs from that previously accorded a particular item.
5.	Conservatism	**e** An assumption that would be unreasonable to use in reporting on a firm that had become insolvent.
6.	Stable dollar	**f** None of these.
7.	Matching	**g** An objective achieved for a single entity's financial information by adhering to the requirement of consistency.
8.	Materiality	**h** A measurement that can be corroborated by qualified accountants using the same measurement methods.
9.	Exchange prices	**i** Discourages undue optimism in measuring and reporting net assets and net earnings.
10.	Entity	**j** Requires separation of personal from business activity in the recording and reporting processes.

13 The SEC, for certain companies, requires disclosure of which of the following attributes (bases of valuation) for inventories and plant capacity in addition to historical cost?
a Present value.
b Current cost.
c Current exit value.
d Expected exit value.
e Current selling price.

14 A company wrote down a substantial amount of obsolete inventory to its scrap value. This loss is to be reported in the year it was recognized in the—
a Earnings statement, net of its tax effect, as an extraordinary item.
b Earnings statement, net of its tax effect, as part of the expenses related to regular operations.
c Earnings statement, at full amount, as part of the expenses related to regular operations.
d Earnings statement, net of tax effect, as a cumulative adjustment from an accounting change.
e Statement of retained earnings, net of tax, as a prior period adjustment.

15 In 1979 a corporation had revenues of $50 million; total expenses related to the above revenues, exclusive of federal income taxes, of $40 million; and was subject to federal income taxation at a 50 percent rate. It also suffered a tax-deductible earthquake loss (its first such loss) of $2 million, sold investment securities (a recurring event) at a gain of $3 million (subject to income taxation at a 30 percent rate), paid additional federal income taxes for 1976 of $500,000, and settled for $800,000 (tax-deductible) litigation brought against it for failure to comply in 1975 with the provisions of a contract to overhaul a fleet of jet engine planes. The corporation discontinued this line of activity in 1977. Which of the following statements is false?
a Net earnings before extraordinary items are $6.6 million.
b The earthquake loss should be reported at $1 million ($2 million less tax effect) as an extraordinary item in the earnings statement.
c The gain on sale of securities should be reported in the earnings statement, not net of tax effects, as an element of earnings from normal operations.

d The additional income tax assessment should be reported in the earnings statement for 1979 as part of the income taxes relating to earnings from continuing activities if such assessments are routinely encountered.
e The litigation settlement should be reported in the statement of retained earnings as a prior period adjustment, net of its tax effects.

Now compare your answers with the correct answers and explanations on page 725.

Questions *chapter* 13

1 For whom are financial statements primarily intended? Why?

2 Investment and credit decisions generally involve a comparison of what two amounts? What is the primary role played by financial statements in such decisions?

3 What are generally accepted accounting principles? What are the sources of such principles? Where might one find a list of them?

4 Why might it be desirable to have an authoritative set of generally accepted accounting principles?

5 In general, what are the qualitative objectives? Which is the primary such objective? Why?

6 What is meant by the term accrual basis of accounting? What is its alternative?

7 What two requirements generally must be met before revenue will be recognized in a period? What would you consider the ideal time to recognize revenue? Why?

8 Under what circumstances, if any, is the receipt of cash an acceptable time to recognize revenue?

9 A firm reports its marketable securities at a cost of $100,000. You note from the stock price reports in your newspaper that they have a market value of $250,000. Why are the securities reported at $100,000 and the $150,000 not included in net earnings? Is not the firm better off by $150,000?

10 Define expense. What principles guide the recognition of expense?

11 Contrast the accountant's approach to determining net earnings with that of the economist. Are the two reconcilable? Explain.

12 What is meant by the accounting term "conservatism? How does it affect the amounts reported in the financial statements?

13 What is the principle of initial recording or cost principle? What is the significance of adhering to this principle?

14 Name the assumptions underlying generally accepted accounting principles. Comment on the validity in recent years of the stable unit of measurement assumption.

15 Many assets are reported in the statement of financial position at their historical cost. But the reporting of other attributes for some assets is now in use or has been recommended. What are these other attributes?

16 How are consistency and full disclosure related?

17 What does it mean to say that accountants record substance rather than form?

18 What are extraordinary items? Where and how are they reported?

19 What are prior period adjustments? Where and how are they reported?

20 Name two types of accounting changes. How is each reported?

Exercises *chapter* 13

1 A company purchased a building on January 2, 1975, for $80,000. By December 31, 1979, it had a net book value of $64,000 and a market value of $100,000. The building was completely destroyed by fire on January 1, 1980. Cash of $72,000 was received as full settlement from an insurance company. **(a)** Compute the gain or loss from the fire that the accountant would record. **(b)** Comment on whether the accountant's record is in accord with the facts and explain why it is or is not.

2 Cloyce Company sells its products on an installment sales basis. Data for 1979 and 1980 are:

	1979	1980
Installment sales	$100,000	$120,000
Cost of installment sales	70,000	90,000
Other expenses...........	15,000	20,000
Cash collected from 1979 sales..............	60,000	30,000
Cash collected from 1980 sales..............		80,000

a Compute the net earnings for 1980 assuming use of the accrual (sales) basis of revenue recognition.

b Compute the net earnings for 1980 assuming use of the installment method of recognizing revenue and gross margin.

3 A company follows a practice of expensing the premium on its fire insurance policy when it is paid. In 1979 it charged to expense the $720 premium paid on a three-year policy covering the period July 1, 1979, to June 30, 1982. In 1976 a premium of $660 was charged to expense on the same policy for the period July 1, 1976, to June 30, 1979.

a State the principle of accounting that was violated by this practice.

b Compute the effects of this violation on the financial statements for the calendar year 1979.

c State the grounds upon which the company's practice might be justified.

4 A company employs the lower-of-cost-or-market method of inventory measurement. Its beginning and ending inventories for 1979 on this basis were $20,000 and $24,000. On a strict cost basis they would have been $21,000 and $24,400. **(a)** State the grounds upon which the company's practice may be justified. **(b)** Compute the effect on net earnings for 1979 from use of the lower-of-cost-or-market method rather than the strict cost method.

5 The following relate to the X Company for 1979:

a Sales on account, $100,000 of which $80,000 were collected.

b Services rendered on account, $60,000 of which $50,000 were collected. In addition, services were rendered for which cash was received in 1978 in the amount of $1,800.

c Sold a truck with a book value of $1,000 on December 31, 1979, and received a $1,500, 8 percent, six-month note in exchange.

State the amount of revenue earned by the company in 1979.

6 B Company has revenues of $42 million, expenses of $36 million, a tax-deductible earthquake loss (its first such loss) of $1 million, a tax-deductible downward adjustment of $3 million resulting from renegotiation of a contract completed two years ago, and an income tax rate of 50 percent. The beginning retained earnings were $10 million, and a dividend of $500,000 was declared.

a Prepare an earnings statement for the year.

b Prepare a statement of retained earnings for the year.

7 The Barton Company had owners' equity of $500,000 on May 31, 1979, and $700,000 on May 31, 1980. Additional shares of common stock were issued during the year for $100,000 cash; treasury stock was acquired at a cost of $10,000; and a cash dividend was declared and paid in the amount of $50,000. Compute the net earnings for the year ended May 31, 1980.

Problems, Series A *chapter* 13

13-1-A

Given below are the contract prices and costs relating to all of the Boyd Company's long-term construction contracts (in millions of dollars):

	Contract price	Costs incurred Prior to 1980	In 1980	Costs yet to be incurred
On contracts completed in 1980	$16.0		$14.0	-0-
On incomplete contracts.....................	48.0	$8.0	16.0	$16.0

General and administrative expenses for 1980 amounted to $600,000.

Required:

a Compute the earnings before taxes for 1980 using the completed contract method.
b Repeat part (a) assuming use of the percentage-of-completion method.

13-2-A

Your audit client, Rappel Company, has prepared tentative financial statements for 1980 which are summarized as follows:

Statement of Financial Position		Earnings Statement	
Total assets	$500,000	Total sales revenue	$1,200,000
Total liabilities	200,000	Total expenses and taxes..............	1,150,000
Total owners' equity..............	300,000	Net earnings	50,000

In the course of your audit, you discover the following items:

1. Accrued salaries at the end of 1980 were not recorded.
2. Accrued rent receivable at the end of 1980 was not recorded.
3. The cost of a machine was charged to expense in 1980. The machine has a useful life of six years.
4. Your client has been bribing an official of a foreign country to secure an annual license to do business in that country.

Required:

State at what dollar amount you would consider each of the above four items to be material ($100, $500, $1,000, $2,000, $5,000, $10,000, $20,000, or some other amount). Also state the references or relationships used to arrive at your answer.

13-3-A

Floodplain, Inc., sells real estate lots under terms calling for a small cash down payment and monthly installment payments spread over a few years. Following are data on the company's operations for its first three years:

	1978	1979	1980
Gross margin rate...	45%	48%	50%
Cash collected in 1980 from sales made in.............	$80,000	$100,000	$120,000

Sales in 1980 amounted to $400,000, while general and administrative expenses amounted to $100,000.

Required:

a Compute the net earnings for 1980 assuming revenue is recognized at the time of sale.
b Repeat part (a) assuming use of the installment method of accounting for sales and gross margin.

13–4–A

In each of the circumstances described below, the accounting practices followed may be questioned. You are to indicate whether you agree or disagree with the accounting employed and to state the principles or concepts on which you would rely to justify your position.

1. The cost of certain improvements to leased property having a life of five years was charged to expense because they would revert to the lessor when the lease expires in three years.
2. The salaries paid to the top officers of the company were charged to expense in the period in which they were incurred, even though the officers spent over half of their time planning next year's activities.
3. A company spent over $4 million in developing a new product and then spent an additional $4.5 million promoting it. All of these costs were incurred and charged to expense prior to the sale of a single unit of this new product. The expensing of these costs was justified on the grounds that they had to be incurred every year—that new product development and promotion were regularly recurring.
4. No entry was made to record the belief that the market value of the land owned (carried in the accounts at $58,000) increased in value from $100,000 to $105,000, in keeping with the advance in the general level of prices.
5. No entry was made to record the fact that costs of $50,000 were expected to be incurred in fulfilling warranty provisions on products sold this year, the revenue from which was recognized this year.
6. The acquisition of a tract of land was recorded at the price paid for it of $108,000, even though the company would have been willing to pay $125,000.
7. A truck acquired at the beginning of the year was reported at year end at 80 percent of its acquisition price, even though its market value then was only 65 percent of its original acquisition price.

13–5–A

By following the most conservative accounting practices permitted, its accountant determined that the Blake Company can report a loss of $60,000 for income tax purposes in 1979, its first year of operation. But the top management of the company is concerned about reporting such a loss for financial reporting purposes because it is planning on seeking outside financing for some additional equipment. It calls upon you as an expert accountant to review the accounting practices followed. You discover the following information relating to the loss that can be reported for tax purposes:

1. Construction revenue has been recorded on a completed contract basis. Six contracts with a total price of $800,000 were partially completed during the year, with costs of $120,000 incurred out of total expected costs of $480,000.
2. Only $20,000 of gross margin realized through installment collections was included in arriving at the net loss of $60,000. Installment sales for the year were $400,000; cost of goods sold was $300,000. There is little doubt about the collection of the installment receivables.
3. The ending inventory was $62,000, using Lifo. Under Fifo it would have amounted to $70,000.
4. Accelerated depreciation for the year amounted to $24,000. Under the straight-line method it would have been $16,000.

Required:

Prepare a schedule showing how the above items would change the reported net loss to net earnings (before income taxes) if they were accounted for in an acceptable, yet less conservative way.

13–6–A

Selected accounts of the Hammond Company for the year ended December 31, 1980, are:

Sales, net	$960,000
Interest expense	80,000
Cash dividends on common stock	160,000
Selling and administrative expense	240,000
Cash dividends on preferred stock	80,000
Rent revenue	440,000
Cost of goods sold	640,000
Flood loss (has never occurred before)	240,000
Interest revenue	80,000
Other revenue	120,000
Depreciation and maintenance on rental equipment	160,000
Stock dividend on common stock	400,000
Litigation loss	480,000
Cumulative effect on prior years' earnings of changing to a different depreciation method	40,000

The applicable federal income tax rate is 50 percent. All above items of expense, revenue, and loss are includable in the computation of taxable income. The litigation loss resulted from a court award of damages for patent infringement on a product the company produced and sold in 1976 and 1977 and which was discontinued in 1977. The cumulative effect of the accounting change amounts to an increase of $40,000. Retained earnings as of January 1, 1980, were $5,600,000.

Required:

Prepare an earnings statement and a statement of retained earnings for 1980.

The basic theory underlying financial statements

Problems, Series B *chapter* 13

13–1–B

The following data relate to the John Construction Company's long-term construction projects for the year 1980:

	Completed project	Incomplete projects
Contract price..	$4,500,000	$24,000,000
Costs incurred prior to 1980	–0–	4,000,000
Costs incurred in 1980	3,700,000	8,000,000
Estimated costs to complete (at 12/31/80)	–0–	8,000,000

General and administrative expenses incurred in 1980 amounted to $500,000. Federal income tax rate is 40 percent.

Required:

Assume that the same accounting methods are used for financial accounting and for income tax purposes and—

a Compute net earnings for 1980 under the completed contract method.

b Repeat part (a) using the percentage-of-completion method.

13–2–B

For each of the numbered items listed below, state the letter or letters of the principles used to justify the accounting procedure followed:

A — Entity

B — Conservatism

C — Earning principle of revenue recognition

D — Going concern (Continuity)

E — Initial recording at exchange prices principle

F — Matching principle

G — Period cost (or principle of immediate recognition of expense)

H — Realization principle

I — Systematic and rational allocation principle of expense recognition

J — Stable dollar assumption

1. The ending inventory was recorded at $60,000 using the cost or market, whichever is lower, method. The cost of the inventory was $64,000.
2. A truck purchased in January was reported at 80 percent of its cost even though its market value at year-end was only 70 percent of its cost.
3. One half of the premium paid on January 2 for a two-year term of insurance coverage was charged to expense.
4. The collection of $10,000 of cash for services to be performed next year was reported as a current liability.
5. The president's salary was treated as an expense of the year even though most of the president's time was spent planning the next two years' activities.
6. No entry was made to record the fact that the company received an offer of $100,000 for land carried in its accounts at $60,000.

7. A stock of printed stationery, checks, and invoices with a cost of $2,000 was treated as a current asset at year-end even though it had no value to others.

8. A tract of land acquired for $35,000 was recorded at that price even though it was appraised at $40,000 and the company would have been willing to pay that amount if pushed.

9. Paid and charged to expense the $1,500 paid to Bill Bunker for rent of a truck owned by him. Bill Bunker is president of the company and also owns all of its outstanding stock.

10. Recorded the $5,000 of interest collected on $100,000 of 5 percent bonds as interest revenue even though the general level of prices increased 8 percent during the year.

13-3-B

The following data are for the Ace Company for 1980:

Services rendered in 1980: credit sales, $220,000; cash sales, $50,000; for cash received in 1979, $6,000.

Cash collections in 1980 in addition to the above cash sales: from 1979 credit sales, $20,000; from 1980 credit sales, $180,000; prepaid on 1981 sales, $4,000.

Expenses: 1980 cash expenses, $40,000; 1980 credit expenses, $130,000; from 1979 prepayments, $3,000.

Cash payments in 1980 in addition to the above cash expenses: for 1979 credit expenses, $35,000; for 1980 credit expenses, $100,000; prepayment on 1981 expenses, $2,000.

Required:

Prepare separate schedules showing total revenues, total expenses, and net earnings for 1980 under:

a The cash basis of accounting.

b The accrual basis of accounting.

13-4-B

Slick Company sells a teaching machine under terms calling for a small cash down payment and monthly payments spread over three years. Following are data for the first three years of the company's operations:

	1978	1979	1980
Sales	$200,000	$300,000	$400,000
Cost of goods sold	140,000	180,000	200,000
Cash collected in 1980 from installment sales made in 1978, 1979, and 1980, respectively	60,000	80,000	130,000

General and selling expenses amounted to $120,000 in 1980.

Required:

a Compute the net earnings before income taxes for 1980 assuming revenues are recognized at the time of sale.

b Repeat part (a) using the installment method of accounting for sales and gross margin.

c Do your answers to parts (a) and (b) suggest which method the company would prefer for tax purposes? Explain.

13-5-B

The Krull Company reported the following financial position as of December 31, 1980:

Assets	$750,000
Liabilities	150,000
Stockholders' equity	600,000

Net earnings before taxes were $100,000 for 1980. You discover in your audit of the company's records that:

1. The company wrote off $25,000 of its merchandise inventory to expense on the grounds that future selling prices might decline.
2. Sales orders of $20,000 were recorded as sales revenue and debited to accounts receivable.
3. No entry was made to accrue employee wages in the amount of $8,000 at the end of the year because these wages were not paid until 1981.
4. The net book value of a machine of $8,000 was charged to expense because the machine was used to make a special product which is now obsolete. The machine could be used for another ten years in the manufacture of this product. There is no other use for the machine at this time and no future use can be seen at this time.
5. The company had its buildings appraised on December 31, 1980, and as a result recorded a $50,000 increase in its buildings account and in a stockholders' equity account called Capital from Appreciation.

Required:

a Prepare a schedule starting with reported net earnings which shows the corrections to be made to arrive at the correct net earnings (ignore income taxes).
b Prepare another schedule with three columns in which are entered first the amounts for assets, liabilities, and stockholders' equity for December 31, 1980. Show by means of plus and minus the needed corrections for these items to arrive at corrected amounts.
c Justify the position you took on each of the above items by reference to generally accepted accounting principles.

13-6-B

Selected accounts and other data for the Williams Company for 1980 are:

Common stock – $10 par value	$1,000,000
Sales, net	4,000,000
Selling and administrative expenses	800,000
Cash dividends declared and paid	300,000
Cost of goods sold	2,000,000
Gain on sale of securities	350,000
Depreciation expense	300,000
Interest revenue	50,000
Loss on write-down of obsolete inventory	100,000
Retained earnings (as of 12/31/79)	5,000,000

655

| Earthquake loss .... | 240,000 |
| Cumulative effect on prior years of changing from straight-line to an accelerated method of computing depreciation .... | 80,000 |

The applicable federal income tax rate is 50 percent. All of the items of expense, revenue, and loss are includable in the computation of the amount of income taxes payable. The tax effects of the cumulative effect of the change in depreciation methods can be ignored. The gain on sale of securities is a common item for the company, while the earthquake loss resulted from the first earthquake experienced at the company's location. In addition, the company discovered that in 1979 it had erroneously charged to expense the $400,000 cost of a tract of land purchased that year and had made the same error on its tax return for 1979.

Required:

a Prepare an earnings statement for 1980.
b Prepare a statement of retained earnings for 1980.

14

Consolidated financial statements

Learning objectives

Study of the material in this chapter is designed to achieve various learning objectives. These include an understanding of:

1. The nature of parent and subsidiary corporations and the relationships that may exist between them.

2. The process of preparing consolidated financial statements via a consolidated statement work sheet on which elimination entries are made.

3. Accounting for investments in partially owned subsidiaries and the nature and composition of minority interest.

4. Accounting for the earnings, losses, and dividends of a subsidiary on the parent company's books.

5. The differences between purchase accounting and pooling of interests accounting and the circumstances under which each method is correct.

6. The uses and limitations of consolidated financial statements.

7. The consolidated financial statements of an actual company (Appendix).

Parent and subsidiary corporations

In many cases, one corporation owns a majority (more than 50 percent) of the outstanding voting common stock of a second corporation. In such cases, both corporations exist as separate legal entities; neither of the corporations is dissolved. The corporation which owns a majority (more than 50 percent) of the outstanding voting common stock of another corporation is referred to as the *parent* company; the corporation controlled by the parent company is known as the *subsidiary* company.

When a large enterprise is operated as a parent company and its controlled subsidiaries, each corporation maintains its own accounting records. But, since the parent and its subsidiaries are *controlled* by a central management and are related to each other, the parent company usually is *required* to prepare one set of financial statements as if the parent and its subsidiaries taken together constitute a single enterprise. The term *consolidated statements* refers to the financial statements that result from combining the parent's financial statement amounts with those of its subsidiaries. Preparation of consolidated statements is discussed in the following sections. Consolidated statements *must be prepared* when one company owns more than 50 percent of the outstanding voting common stock of another company (and, thus, exerts control over the other company) and the two companies are not engaged in markedly dissimilar businesses.

Indicate whether each of the following statements is true or false.

1. When a bank owns more than 50 percent of a manufacturing company's outstanding voting common stock, consolidated financial statements must be prepared.

2. A parent company is a corporation that owns more than 50 percent of the outstanding preferred stock of another company.

3. Consolidated statements are required when one company owns more than 50 percent of the outstanding voting common stock of another company and the two companies are not engaged in markedly dissimilar businesses.

Now turn to Answer Frame 1¹⁴ on page 660 to check your answers.

Eliminations

For the purposes of preparing consolidated financial statements, it is necessary to eliminate the amounts of intercompany transactions in order to show the assets, liabilities, and stockholders' equity accounts as if the parent and its subsidiaries were a single economic enterprise. The items remaining on the financial statements of the subsidiaries are combined with the corresponding items on the parent's financial statements (after eliminations have been made for intercompany transactions).

One elimination will offset the parent company's investment in the subsidiary against the stockholders' equity accounts of the subsidiary. Assume that P Company organized the S Company, receiving all of S Company's $100,000 par value common stock for $100,000 cash. If a consolidated statement of financial position is to be prepared, the required elimination is:

Common Stock – S Company	100,000	
Investment in S Company..		100,000

This elimination is required because the parent company's investment in the stock of the subsidiary actually represents an equity in the net assets of the subsidiary. Thus, unless the investment is eliminated, the same resources will appear twice on the consolidated statement of financial position (as the investment and as the assets of the subsidiary). The elimination is also necessary to avoid double counting the owners' equity.

Intercompany receivables and payables (due from and owed to companies in the consolidated group) are also items which must be eliminated during the preparation of consolidated statements. For example, assume the parent company owes the subsidiary $5,000 as evidenced by a $5,000 note receivable on the subsidiary's books and a $5,000 note payable on the parent's books. These balances would be eliminated by offsetting the note receivable against the note payable. No debt is owed to or due from any entity outside the consolidated enterprise. Similarly, other intercompany balances would be eliminated when consolidated statements are prepared.

When consolidated financial statements are prepared, one elimination entry offsets (select the correct answer) —

1. The parent company's investment account and the parent company's stockholders' equity accounts.
2. The parent company's investment account and the subsidiary company's stockholders' equity accounts.
3. The parent company's asset accounts and the subsidiary company's asset accounts.
4. The parent company's investment account and the subsidiary's asset accounts.

Check your answer in Answer Frame 2[14] on page 660.

Frame 3¹⁴

Consolidated statement of financial position at time of acquisition

Acquisition at book value

To combine the assets and liabilities of a parent company and its subsidiaries, a work sheet similar to the one shown in Illustration 14.1 is prepared. The first two columns show the assets, liabilities, and stockholders' equity of the parent and subsidiary as they would appear on each corporation's individual statement of financial position. The pair of columns labeled Eliminations allow intercompany items to be offset and consequently eliminated from the consolidated statement. The final column shows the amounts that will appear on the consolidated statement.

This particular work sheet (Illustration 14.1) was prepared to consolidate the accounts of P Company and its subsidiary, S Company, on January 1, 1979. P Company acquired S Company on January 1, 1979, by purchasing all of its outstanding voting common stock for $106,000 cash, which was the *book value* of the stock.

Two elimination entries are required in this example. When P Company acquired the stock of S Company from S Company's stockholders, P Company made the following entry:

Investment in S Company	106,000	
Cash		106,000
To record investment in S Company.		

Illustration 14.1

P COMPANY AND SUBSIDIARY S COMPANY
Work Sheet for Consolidated Statement of Financial Position
January 1, 1979 (date of acquisition)

	P Company	S Company	Eliminations Debit	Eliminations Credit	Consolidated Amounts
Assets					
Cash	26,000	12,000			38,000
Notes receivable	5,000			(b) 5,000	
Accounts receivable, net	24,000	15,000			39,000
Inventory	35,000	30,000			65,000
Investment in S Company	106,000			(a) 106,000	
Equipment, net	41,000	15,000			56,000
Buildings, net	65,000	35,000			100,000
Land	20,000	10,000			30,000
	322,000	117,000			328,000
Liabilities and Stockholders' Equity					
Accounts payable	18,000	6,000			24,000
Notes payable		5,000	(b) 5,000		
Common stock	250,000	100,000	(a) 100,000		250,000
Retained earnings	54,000	6,000	(a) 6,000		54,000
	322,000	117,000	111,000	111,000	328,000

The investment appears as an asset on P Company's statement of financial position. By buying the subsidiary's stock, the parent in effect acquired a 100 percent equity or ownership interest in the subsidiary's net assets. Thus, if both the investment and the subsidiary's assets appear on the consolidated statement of financial position, the same resources will be counted twice. The Common Stock and Retained Earnings accounts of the subsidiary also represent an equity in the subsidiary's assets. Therefore, it is necessary to offset P's investment in S Company against S Company's stockholders' equity accounts so that the subsidiary's assets and the ownership interest in these assets appear only once on the consolidated statement. This elimination is accomplished by entry (a) on the work sheet.

Entry (b) is required to eliminate the effect of an intercompany transaction (intercompany debt in this case). On the date it acquired S Company, P Company loaned S Company $5,000 — which is recorded as a $5,000 note receivable on P's books and a $5,000 note payable on S's books. If the elimination entry is not made on the work sheet, the consolidated statement of financial position will show $5,000 owed to the consolidated enterprise *by itself.* Actually from the viewpoint of the consolidated entity, neither an asset nor a liability exists. Therefore, entry (b) is made on the work sheet to eliminate both the asset and the liability.

In making elimination entries, it is important to understand that *the entries are made only on the consolidated statement work sheet; no elimination entries are made in the accounts of either P Company or S Company.*

Assume X Company acquired all the outstanding voting common stock of Y Company for $200,000 cash. Y Company's stockholders' equity accounts had balances as follows:

Common stock, $10 par............................ $150,000
Retained earnings 50,000

Prepare the journal entry to record the investment on X Company's books on the date of acquisition.

Check your answer by turning to Answer Frame 3[14] on page 664.

Frame 4[14]

Acquisition of subsidiary at a cost above or below book value

In the previous illustration, P Company acquired 100 percent of S Company at a cost equal to book value. But, in some cases, subsidiaries may be acquired at a cost greater than or less than book value. For example, assume P Company purchases 100 percent of S Company's outstanding voting common stock for $125,000. The book value of the stock is $106,000. Cost exceeds book value by $19,000. P Company may have paid more than book value for either or both of two reasons: (1) P Company may think that the subsidiary's earnings prospects justify paying a price greater than book value, or (2) P Company may believe that the fair value of the subsidiary's assets exceeds the assets' book values.

According to the Accounting Principles Board (*APB Opinion No. 16*), in cases where cost exceeds book value because of expected above-average earnings, the excess should be labeled as goodwill on the consolidated statement of financial position. On the other hand, if the excess is attributable to the belief that assets of the subsidiary are undervalued then the value of the assets should be increased to the extent of the excess.[1] In Illustration 14.2, it is assumed that the $19,000 excess of cost over book value is attributable to expected above-average earnings. As a result, the excess is identified as goodwill on the statement of financial position (Illustration 14.3). Elimination entry

[1] *APB Accounting Principles* (Chicago: Commerce Clearing House, Inc., 1973), vol. II, p. 6655.

Consolidated financial statements

Illustration 14.2

P COMPANY AND SUBSIDIARY S COMPANY
Work Sheet for Consolidated Statement of Financial Position
January 1, 1979 (date of acquisition)

	P Company	S Company	Eliminations Debit	Eliminations Credit	Consolidated Amounts
Assets					
Cash	7,000	12,000			19,000
Notes receivable	5,000			(b) 5,000	
Accounts receivable, net	24,000	15,000			39,000
Inventory	35,000	30,000			65,000
Investment in S Company	125,000			(a) 125,000	
Equipment, net	41,000	15,000			56,000
Buildings, net	65,000	35,000			100,000
Land	20,000	10,000			30,000
Excess of cost over book value			(a) 19,000		19,000
	322,000	117,000			328,000
Liabilities and Stockholders' Equity					
Accounts payable	18,000	6,000			24,000
Notes payable		5,000	(b) 5,000		
Common stock	250,000	100,000	(a) 100,000		250,000
Retained earnings	54,000	6,000	(a) 6,000		54,000
	322,000	117,000	130,000	130,000	328,000

(b) in Illustration 14.2 is the same as for the first illustration. Entry (a) involves debits to the subsidiary's common stock and retained earnings accounts and to an account labeled excess of cost over book value and a credit to the parent's investment account. After these elimination entries are made, the remaining amounts are combined and extended to the column labeled consolidated amounts. The amounts in this column are then used to prepare the consolidated statement of financial position shown in Illustration 14.3.

If the $19,000 excess of cost over book value is partially attributable to the belief that the equipment is undervalued by $8,000 and partly due to expected above-average earnings, then goodwill should be reported on the statement of financial position in Illustration 14.3 at—

1. $19,000.
2. $27,000.
3. $11,000.
4. $8,000.

Turn to Answer Frame 4[14] on page 666 to check your answer.

The journal entry to record the investment is:

Investment in Y Company... 200,000
    Cash 200,000
To record investment in Y Company.

If you answered incorrectly, reread Frame 3¹⁴ before going on to Frame 4¹⁴ on page 662.

4¹⁴
continued

Illustration 14.3

P COMPANY AND SUBSIDIARY S COMPANY		
Consolidated Statement of Financial Position		
January 1, 1979		

Assets

Current Assets:		
Cash	$ 19,000	
Accounts receivable, net	39,000	
Inventory	65,000	
Total Current Assets		$123,000
Property, Plant, and Equipment:		
Equipment, net	$ 56,000	
Buildings, net	100,000	
Land	30,000	
Total Property, Plant, and Equipment		186,000
Goodwill		19,000
Total Assets		$328,000

Liabilities and Stockholders' Equity

Current Liabilities:		
Accounts payable		$ 24,000
Stockholders' Equity:		
Common stock	$250,000	
Retained earnings	54,000	
Total Stockholders' Equity		304,000
Total Liabilities and Stockholders' Equity		$328,000

Frame 5¹⁴

Under some circumstances, a parent company may pay less than the book value of the subsidiary's net assets. In such cases, it is highly unlikely that a "bargain" purchase has been made. The most logical explanation for the price paid is that some of the subsidiary's assets are overvalued. The Accounting Principles Board requires that the excess of book value over cost be used to reduce proportionately the value of the noncurrent assets acquired.[2] If the noncurrent assets are reduced to zero before the excess of book value over cost is fully eliminated, the remaining amount of excess should be reported as a deferred credit on the consolidated statement of financial position. Deferred credits, which will be allocated to future operations, are often reported between liabilities and stockholders' equity on the statement of financial position.

Assume that AB Company purchases all of ST Company's outstanding voting common stock for $150,000. The book value of the stock is $160,000. The book value of the noncurrent assets acquired is $90,000. Based upon the above assumptions, the consolidated statement of financial position on the date of acquisition would show:

1. A reduction of $10,000 in the value of the noncurrent assets acquired.
2. Deferred credit, $10,000.
3. Goodwill, $5,000. Deferred credit, $5,000.
4. Either goodwill or a deferred credit, $10,000.

Refer to Answer Frame 5[14] on page 666 to check your answer.

Frame 6[14]

Acquisition of less than 100 percent of subsidiary

Sometimes a parent company acquires less than 100 percent of the outstanding voting common stock of a subsidiary. For example, assume P Company acquires 80 percent of S Company's outstanding voting common stock. P Company is the majority stockholder, but there exist minority stockholders who own 20 percent of the stock. These minority stockholders, usually referred to as the *minority interest,* have an interest in the subsidiary's net assets and share the subsidiary's earnings with the parent company.

When preparing a consolidated statement of financial position for a partially owned subsidiary, only part of the subsidiary's stockholders' equity is eliminated. That part of the common stock and retained earnings which relates to the minority stockholders is established on the consolidated work sheet as the minority interest.

Illustration 14.4 shows what elimination entries are required when P Company purchases 80 percent of S Company's stock for $100,000. The book value of the stock acquired by P Company is $84,800 (80 percent of $106,000). The excess of cost over book value amounts to $15,200 and can be attributed to S Company's above-average earnings

Answer 3, $11,000, is correct. The equipment should be reported on the consolidated statement of financial position at $64,000 ($56,000 + $8,000). The remainder of the excess of cost over book value, $11,000, ($19,000 − $8,000) should be labeled as goodwill on the consolidated statement of financial position.

If you answered incorrectly, reread Frame 4¹⁴ before continuing to Frame 5¹⁴ on page 664.

Number 1 is the correct response. The common stock cost is $150,000 and has a book value of $160,000. The excess of book value over cost of $10,000 should be deducted from the value of the noncurrent assets acquired.

If you answered incorrectly, reread Frames 4¹⁴ and 5¹⁴ before going on to Frame 6¹⁴ on page 665.

6¹⁴

continued

Illustration 14.4

P COMPANY AND SUBSIDIARY S COMPANY
Work Sheet for Consolidated Statement of Financial Position
January 1, 1979 (date of acquisition)

	P Company	S Company	Eliminations Debit	Eliminations Credit	Consolidated Amounts
Assets					
Cash	32,000	12,000			44,000
Notes receivable	5,000			(b) 5,000	
Accounts receivable, net	24,000	15,000			39,000
Inventory	35,000	30,000			65,000
Investment in S Company	100,000			(a) 100,000	
Equipment, net	41,000	15,000			56,000
Buildings, net	65,000	35,000			100,000
Land	20,000	10,000			30,000
Excess of cost over book value			(a) 15,200		15,200
	322,000	117,000			349,200
Liabilities and Stockholders' Equity					
Accounts payable	18,000	6,000			24,000
Notes payable		5,000	(b) 5,000		
Common stock	250,000	100,000	(a) 100,000		250,000
Retained earnings	54,000	6,000	(a) 6,000		54,000
Minority interest				(a) 21,200	21,200
	322,000	117,000	126,200	126,200	349,200

prospects. On the consolidated statement of financial position, the $15,200 excess will be identified as goodwill (Illustration 14.5).

The minority stockholders have an equity of $21,200 (20 percent of $106,000) in the net assets of the consolidated enterprise (Illustration 14.5). The amount of the minority interest appears between the liabilities and stockholders' equity sections of the consolidated statement of financial position. (Actually, there is some disagreement as to whether the minority interest is a liability or a part of stockholders' equity.)

Illustration 14.5

P COMPANY AND SUBSIDIARY S COMPANY	

P COMPANY AND SUBSIDIARY S COMPANY
Consolidated Statement of Financial Position
January 1, 1979

Assets

Current Assets:		
Cash	$ 44,000	
Accounts receivable, net..	39,000	
Inventory..	65,000	
Total Current Assets		$148,000
Property, Plant, and Equipment:		
Equipment, net	$ 56,000	
Buildings, net...	100,000	
Land...	30,000	
Total Property, Plant, and Equipment.........................		186,000
Goodwill...		15,200
Total Assets...		$349,200

Liabilities and Stockholders' Equity

Liabilities:		
Accounts payable...		$ 24,000
Minority interest		21,200
Stockholders' Equity:		
Common stock...	$250,000	
Retained earnings..	54,000	
Total Stockholders' Equity.......................................		304,000
Total Liabilities and Stockholders' Equity........................		$349,200

Assume that P Company purchased 90 percent (instead of 80 percent) of S Company's outstanding voting common stock for $105,000. The minority interest on the date of acquisition would be—

1. $10,600.
2. $9,600.
3. $1,000.
4. $15,200.

Check your answer in Answer Frame 6¹⁴ on page 668.

Number 1 is the correct response. The minority stockholders own 10 per-cent (100 percent − 90 percent) of the outstanding voting common stock. Thus, the minority interest is represented by 10 percent of the net assets of S Com-pany which amounts to $10,600 (10 percent of $106,000).

$9,600 is the excess of cost over book value ($105,000 − $95,400). The book value is $95,400 (90 percent of $106,000).

If you did not answer correctly, reread Frame 6¹⁴ before advancing to Frame 7¹⁴ below.

Frame 7¹⁴

Earnings, losses, and dividends of a subsidiary

If a subsidiary is operated profitably, there will be an increase in its net assets and retained earnings. When the subsidiary pays dividends, both the parent company and the minority stockholders will share in the distribution. Earnings and dividends will be recorded in the accounting records of the subsidiary just as they are recorded for other corpora-tions.

Two different methods can be used by an investor to account for in-vestments in common stock. They are the cost method and the equity method. The Accounting Principles Board has identified the circum-stances under which each method can be used. The *general rules* for determining the appropriate method of accounting are summarized below:

Percent of outstanding voting common stock of investee owned by investor	Method of accounting required by Accounting Principles Board in most cases
Less than 20%...	Cost
20%–50%..	Equity
More than 50%:	
Consolidated subsidiary	Cost or equity
Nonconsolidated subsidiary	Equity

According to the above table, the parent company can use either the cost or the equity method of accounting for its investment in a consoli-dated subsidiary.

Under the cost method, the investor company records its investment at cost (price paid at acquisition). Only subsidiary (investee) earnings that are distributed as dividends are recorded by the investor company (under the cost method). The investor company records dividends re-ceived from the subsidiary by debiting Cash and crediting Dividend Revenue.

Under the equity method, the parent (investor) company initially records its investment at cost. Subsequently, the investment account is periodically adjusted for the parent (investor) company's share of the subsidiary's (investee's) earnings or losses as they are reported by the subsidiary. The parent company's share of the subsidiary's earnings is debited to the Investment in S Company account and credited to an account labeled Earnings of S Company. For example, assume the subsidiary S Company mentioned in the preceding illustrations earned $20,000 during 1979; P Company owns 80 percent of S Company. P Company would record its share of the earnings in the following manner:

Investment in S Company..	16,000	
Earnings of S Company..		16,000
To record 80 percent of subsidiary's earnings.		

The $16,000 debit to the investment account increases the parent's equity in the subsidiary. The $16,000 credit to the revenue account will be closed to the Expense and Revenue Summary account and then to P Company's Retained Earnings account.

If the subsidiary incurs a loss, the parent company debits a loss account and credits the investment account for its share of the loss. For example, assume S Company incurs a loss of $10,000 in 1980. Since P Company still owns 80 percent of S Company, P Company would record its share of the loss as follows:

Loss of S Company	8,000	
Investment in S Company..		8,000
To record 80 percent of subsidiary's loss.		

The $8,000 debit is closed first to the Expense and Revenue Summary and then to Retained Earnings; the $8,000 *credit* reduces P Company's equity in the subsidiary.

Amortization of goodwill over a period not to exceed 40 years is required by the APB. Thus, the following entries would also be required on P Company's books in 1979 and 1980 to amortize goodwill ($15,200) over 40 years:

1979	Earnings of S Company	380	
	Investment in S Company		380
1980	Loss of S Company...	380	
	Investment in S Company		380

P Company actually records its share of the net earnings (loss) of S Company less (plus) the amortization of goodwill from consolidation. The amortization expense reduces the revenues and increases the loss. Changes in values of limited life assets are likely to require similar adjusting entries with calculations based on additional depreciation on revalued depreciable assets.

When a subsidiary declares and pays a dividend, the assets and retained earnings of the subsidiary are both reduced by the amount of the dividend payment. When the parent company receives its share of the dividends, it debits the asset received (cash, in this case) and credits the investment account. For instance, assume S Company declares a cash dividend of $8,000 in 1979. P Company's share of the dividend amounts to $6,400 and is recorded as follows:

Cash.. 6,400
    Investment in S Company... 6,400
    To record dividend received from subsidiary.

The receipt of the dividend reduces the parent's equity in the subsidiary as shown by the credit to the investment account.

On January 1, 1979, X Company acquired 90 percent of the common stock of Y Company for $212,000, the book value of 90 percent of the stock. Y Company incurred a net loss of $5,400 in 1979 and had net earnings of $8,100 in 1980. Also, in 1980 Y Company paid a cash dividend of $2,800. Assume X Company uses the equity method of accounting for its investment in Y Company. The balance in X Company's Investment in Y Company account on January 1, 1981, is—

1. $211,900.
2. $211,910.
3. $212,000.
4. $214,430.

Check your answer in Answer Frame 7^{14} on page 672.

Frame 8^{14}

Consolidated financial statements at a date after acquisition

The investment account on the parent company's books increases and decreases as the parent company records its share of the earnings, losses, and dividends reported by the subsidiary. Consequently, the balance in the investment account differs after acquisition from its balance on the date of acquisition. Therefore, the amounts eliminated on the consolidated statement work sheet will differ from year to year. As an illustration, assume the following facts:

1. P Company acquired 100 percent of the outstanding voting common stock of S Company on January 1, 1979. P Company paid $121,000 for an equity of $106,000. The excess of cost over book value (sometimes referred to as a *differential*) is attributable to S Company's above-average earnings prospects.
2. During 1979, S Company earned $20,000 from profitable operations.
3. On December 31, 1979, S Company paid a cash dividend of $8,000.
4. S Company has not paid the $5,000 it borrowed from P Company at the beginning of 1979.
5. Including S Company's earnings, P Company earned $30,250 during 1979.
6. P Company paid a cash dividend of $10,000 during December, 1979.

7. P Company uses the equity method of accounting for its investment in S Company.

The financial statements for the two companies are given in the first two columns of the work sheet for consolidated financial statements for December 31, 1979, Illustration 14.6.

In Illustration 14.6, notice that P Company has a balance of $19,250 in its Earnings of S Company account and a balance of $132,250 in its Investment in S Company account. The balances are the result of the following journal entries made by P Company in 1979:

Investment in S Company	121,000	
Cash..		121,000
To record 100 percent investment in subsidiary.		

Investment in S Company	20,000	
Earnings of S Company		20,000
To record earnings of subsidiary.		

Earnings of S Company	750	
Investment in S Company		750
To amortize excess of cost over book value over 20 years ($15,000 ÷ 20).		

Cash...	8,000	
Investment in S Company		8,000
To record dividends received from subsidiary.		

The elimination entries are explained below:

Entry (*a*): During the year, S Company earned $20,000. P Company increased its investment account balance by $20,000. P Company also reduced its investment account balance by amortizing $750 of the excess of cost over book value. The first entry (*a*) on the work sheet eliminates the subsidiary's earnings less amortization from the investment account and P Company's revenue. It reverses the entries made on the books of P Company to recognize the parent's share of the subsidiary's earnings less amortization.

Entry (*b*): When S Company paid its cash dividend, P Company debited Cash and credited the investment account for $8,000. The second entry (*b*) offsets parts of the entries originally made by P Company and S Company. That is, P's investment account is debited and S's dividends account is credited.

Entry (*c*): This entry is familiar. It eliminates the original investment account balance and the subsidiary's stockholders' equity accounts as of the date of acquisition. It also establishes an amount which represents the excess of cost over book value.

After the first three entries are made, the investment account contains a zero balance from the viewpoint of the consolidated entity.

Entry (*d*): According to *APB Opinion No. 17,* goodwill must be amortized over a period of time not to exceed 40 years. In this case, goodwill is being amortized over 20 years which results in $750 being written off as expense each year.

Entry (*e*): This entry is also familiar. It eliminates the intercompany debt of $5,000.

The correct answer is $211,910. X Company would have made the following journal entries:

Investment in Y Company...	212,000	
Cash..		212,000
To record 90 percent investment in subsidiary.		
Loss of Y Company..	4,860	
Investment in Y Company...		4,860
To record 90 percent of subsidiary's net loss.		
Investment in Y Company...	7,290	
Earnings of Y Company..		7,290
To record 90 percent of subsidiary's earnings.		
Cash..	2,520	
Investment in Y Company...		2,520
To record dividend received from subsidiary.		

The balance in the Investment in Y Company account can be computed as follows:

$$\$212,000 - \$4,860 + \$7,290 - \$2,520 = \$211,910$$

If you did not answer correctly, restudy Frame 7¹⁴ before going on to Frame 8¹⁴ on page 670.

8¹⁴
continued

After the eliminations have been made and goodwill has been amortized, the corresponding amounts are added together and placed in the Consolidated Amounts column. The entire net earnings row in the earnings statement section is carried forward to the net earnings row in the statement of retained earnings section. Likewise, the entire ending retained earnings row in the statement of retained earnings section is carried forward to the retained earnings row in the statement of financial position section. The final column of the work sheet is then used in the preparation of the consolidated earnings statement (Illustration 14.7), the consolidated statement of retained earnings (Illustration 14.7), and the consolidated statement of financial position (Illustration 14.8).

What effect does each of the following have on the investment account balance of the parent company?

1. Earnings of a subsidiary.
2. Dividends declared by the parent.
3. Dividends paid by a subsidiary.
4. Losses of a subsidiary.

Turn to Answer Frame 8¹⁴ on page 676 to check your answers.

Illustration 14.6

P COMPANY AND SUBSIDIARY S COMPANY
Work Sheet for Consolidated Financial Statements
December 31, 1979

	P Company	S Company	Eliminations Debit	Eliminations Credit	Consolidated Amounts
Earnings Statement:					
Revenue from sales	397,000	303,000			700,000
Earnings of S Company	19,250		(a) 19,250		
Cost of goods sold	(250,000)	(180,000)			(430,000)
Expenses (excluding deprecia- tion, amortization, and taxes)	(100,000)	(80,000)			(180,000)
Depreciation expense	(7,400)	(5,000)			(12,400)
Amortization of goodwill			(d) 750		(750)
Income tax expense	(28,600)	(18,000)			(46,600)
Net Earnings – Carried Forward	30,250	20,000			30,250
Statement of Retained Earnings:					
Retained earnings – January 1:					
P Company	54,000				54,000
S Company		6,000	(c) 6,000		
Net earnings – brought forward	30,250	20,000			30,250
	84,250	26,000			84,250
Dividends:					
P Company	(10,000)				(10,000)
S Company		(8,000)		(b) 8,000	
Retained Earnings – December 31 – Carried Forward	74,250	18,000			74,250
Statement of Financial Position:					
Assets					
Cash	38,000	16,000			54,000
Notes receivable	5,000			(e) 5,000	
Accounts receivable, net	25,000	18,000			43,000
Inventory	40,000	36,000			76,000
Investment in S Company	132,250		(b) 8,000	(c) 121,000 (a) 19,250	
Equipment, net	36,900	12,000			48,900
Buildings, net	61,700	33,000			94,700
Land	20,000	10,000			30,000
Excess of cost over book value			(c) 15,000	(d) 750	14,250
	358,850	125,000			360,850
Liabilities and Stockholders' Equity					
Accounts payable	19,600	2,000			21,600
Notes payable	15,000	5,000	(e) 5,000		15,000
Common stock	250,000	100,000	(c) 100,000		250,000
Retained earnings – brought forward	74,250	18,000			74,250
	358,850	125,000	154,000	154,000	360,850

Illustration 14.7

```
        P COMPANY AND SUBSIDIARY S COMPANY
             Consolidated Earnings Statement
           For the Year Ended December 31, 1979
```

Revenue from sales		$700,000
Cost of goods sold		430,000
Gross margin		$270,000
Expenses (excluding depreciation, amortization, and taxes)	$180,000	
Depreciation expense	12,400	
Amortization of goodwill	750	
Income tax expense	46,600	239,750
Net Earnings		$ 30,250

```
        P COMPANY AND SUBSIDIARY S COMPANY
       Consolidated Statement of Retained Earnings
           For the Year Ended December 31, 1979
```

Retained earnings, January 1, 1979	$54,000
Net earnings	30,250
	$84,250
Dividends	10,000
Retained Earnings, December 31, 1979	$74,250

Illustration 14.8

```
        P COMPANY AND SUBSIDIARY S COMPANY
        Consolidated Statement of Financial Position
                   December 31, 1979
```

Assets

Current Assets:		
Cash	$ 54,000	
Accounts receivable, net	43,000	
Inventory	76,000	
Total Current Assets		$173,000
Property, Plant, and Equipment:		
Equipment, net	$ 48,900	
Buildings, net	94,700	
Land	30,000	
Total Property, Plant, and Equipment		173,600
Goodwill		14,250
Total Assets		$360,850

Liabilities and Stockholders' Equity

Current Liabilities:		
Accounts payable	$ 21,600	
Notes payable	15,000	
Total Liabilities		$ 36,600
Stockholders' Equity:		
Common stock	$250,000	
Retained earnings	74,250	
Total Stockholders' Equity		324,250
Total Liabilities and Stockholders' Equity		$360,850

Frame 9¹⁴

Purchase versus pooling of interests

In the illustrations in this chapter, it has been assumed that the parent company acquired the subsidiary's common stock in exchange for cash. Such a business combination is classified as a *purchase*. A purchase would also result if the acquiring company issued debt securities or assets other than cash. But, in some cases, one company issues common stock in exchange for the common stock of another company. Here it appears that the stockholders of both companies maintain an ownership interest in the combined company. Such a business combination is classified as a *pooling of interests* (if it meets all the pooling criteria cited in *APB Opinion No. 16*).

Given the circumstances surrounding a particular business combination, only one of the two methods—purchase or pooling of interests—is appropriate. It should be emphasized that the purchase and pooling of interest methods are not alternatives which can be applied to the same situation. *APB Opinion No. 16* specified 12 conditions (only two of which will be described here) that must be met before a business combination can be classified as a pooling of interests. Two of the conditions are (1) that the combination be effected in one transaction or be completed within one year in accordance with a specific plan and (2) that one corporation issue only its common stock for 90 percent or more of the voting common stock of another company. If all 12 of the conditions are met, then the resulting business combination *must* be accounted for as a pooling of interests. Otherwise, the purchase method must be used to account for the combination.

When the pooling of interests method is used, the parent company's investment is recorded at the book value of the subsidiary's net assets and not at the market value of the parent's common stock given in exchange. This differs from the purchase method in which an investment is recorded at the amount of cash given up or at the fair market value of the assets or stock given up, whichever can be most clearly and objectively determined.

Since the investment is recorded at the book value of the subsidiary's net assets, under the pooling of interests method, there can be no goodwill or deferred credit from consolidation. The subsidiary's retained earnings at the date of acquisition become a part of the consolidated retained earnings, whereas under the purchase method they do not become part of consolidated retained earnings. Also, under the pooling of interests method all the earnings of a subsidiary for the year during which it is acquired are included in the consolidated earnings for the year of acquisition. On the other hand, only that portion of the subsidiary's earnings which arises after the date of acquisition is included in consolidated net earnings under the purchase method.

From the above discussion, it should be apparent that significant dif-

1. Earnings of a subsidiary *increase* the parent's investment account balance.
2. Dividends declared by the parent *do not affect* the parent's investment account balance.
3. Dividends paid by a subsidiary *decrease* the parent's investment account balance.
4. Losses of a subsidiary *decrease* the parent's investment account balance.

If you answered any of the above incorrectly, restudy Frames 7¹⁴ and 8¹⁴ before proceeding to Frame 9¹⁴ on page 675.

9¹⁴

continued

ferences exist between earnings statement and statement of financial position amounts when the different methods are used. (Remember only one method is appropriate for a given set of circumstances.) For instance, under the purchase method, any excess of cost over book value must be used to increase the value of any assets that are undervalued or be recognized as goodwill from consolidation. Thus, more depreciation and amortization will be recorded under the purchase method when cost exceeds book value with the result that consolidated net earnings are less under the purchase method than under the pooling of interests method. (Remember that under the pooling of interests method asset values are not increased and goodwill is not recognized upon consolidation.) Similarly, since the subsidiary's earnings for the entire year during which it was acquired are included in consolidated net earnings under the pooling of interests method, consolidated net earnings for the year of acquisition also would be larger under the pooling of interests method than under the purchase method (unless the combination occurred at the beginning of the accounting period). It is important that the appropriate method of accounting be used for a particular business combination.

Indicate whether each of the following statements is true or false with respect to the pooling of interests method of accounting.

1. There can be no goodwill or deferred credit from consolidation.
2. The parent company's investment is recorded at the market value of the common stock given up by the parent.
3. The retained earnings of the subsidiary at date of acquisition become part of consolidated retained earnings.

4. Only the subsidiary's earnings which arise after the date of acquisition are included in consolidated net earnings for the year of acquisition.

Now check your answers in Answer Frame 9[14] on page 678.

Frame 10[14]

Purchase versus pooling of interests illustrated

In this section, we will present a work sheet for consolidated statements using both the purchase and pooling of interests methods (under different sets of assumptions). We will then contrast the two sets of statements.

Assumptions (purchase method). Par Company acquired 100 percent of Sub Company's voting common stock on January 2, 1979. Par Company paid $200,000 cash for the stock, which had a book value of $190,000 ($150,000 common stock and $40,000 retained earnings). The $10,000 excess of cost over book value is attributed to the subsidiary's above-average earnings prospects. During 1979, Sub Company borrowed $8,000 from Par Company. The debt is evidenced by a note and has not been paid on December 31, 1979.

The work sheet for consolidated financial statements on December 31, 1979, is shown in Illustration 14.9.

Assumptions (pooling of interests method). Par Company acquired 100 percent of Sub Company's voting common stock on January 2, 1979. Par Company issued 15,000 shares of its own $10 par value common stock in exchange for the stock of Sub Company which had a book value of $190,000 ($150,000 common stock and $40,000 retained earnings). Par Company made the following entry to record its investment:

Investment in Sub Company...	190,000	
Common Stock (15,000 shares)....................................		150,000
Paid-In Capital—Pooling of Interests		40,000
To record investment in Sub Company.		

Notice that the investment is recorded at the book value of the subsidiary's stock, $190,000. The Common Stock account is credited for the par value of the shares issued (15,000 × $10). The remainder ($190,000 − $150,000 = $40,000) is credited to a paid-in capital account.

During 1979, Sub Company borrowed $8,000 from Par Company. The debt is evidenced by a note that has not been paid on December 31, 1979. The work sheet for consolidated financial statements on December 31, 1979, is shown in Illustration 14.10.

Notice that under the pooling of interests method the investment account balance is offset against the common stock of the subsidiary and paid-in capital—pooling of interests. The retained earnings of the sub-

1. True. Under the pooling of interests method, the parent s investment is recorded at the book value of the subsidiary's net assets. Thus, there can be no goodwill or deferred credit from consolidation.

2. False. See Answer 1.

3. True. Retained earnings of the subsidiary at date of acquisition do become part of consolidated retained earnings.

4. False. All the subsidiary's earnings for the year of acquisition are included in consolidated net earnings.

If you missed any of the above, restudy Frame 9¹⁴ before beginning Frame 10¹⁴ on page 677.

10¹⁴
continued

sidiary is included in consolidated retained earnings. The following differences are found when the two sets of statements are contrasted:

	Purchase	Pooling of interests	Difference
Amortization of goodwill	$ 1,000	$ –0–	$ (1,000)
Net earnings	119,000	120,000	1,000
Cash	180,000	380,000	$200,000
Excess of cost over book value	9,000	–0–	(9,000)
Total			$191,000
Common stock – $10 par	200,000	350,000	$150,000
Retained earnings	219,000	260,000	41,000
Total			$191,000

Net earnings are $1,000 more under the pooling of interests method because there is no goodwill to be amortized. Cash is $200,000 more under the pooling of interest method because common stock was issued whereas under the purchase method, $200,000 cash was paid. Under the pooling of interests method, common stock is $150,000 more because 15,000 shares of common stock were issued by Par Company to effect the combination. Retained earnings are $41,000 larger under pooling of interests accounting because of the $1,000 difference in net earnings and because the subsidiary's retained earnings at acquisition ($40,000) is included in consolidated retained earnings.

Illustration 14.9

PAR COMPANY AND SUBSIDIARY SUB COMPANY
Work Sheet for Consolidated Financial Statements
(purchase method)
December 31, 1979

	Par Company	Sub Company	Eliminations Debit	Eliminations Credit	Consolidated Amounts
Earnings Statement:					
Revenue from sales	400,000	150,000			550,000
Earnings of Sub Company	49,000		(a) 49,000		
Cost of goods sold	(250,000)	(75,000)			(325,000)
Expenses (excluding amortization)	(80,000)	(25,000)			(105,000)
Amortization of goodwill			(d) 1,000		(1,000)
Net Earnings — Carried Forward	119,000	50,000			119,000
Statement of Retained Earnings:					
Retained earnings — January 1:					
Par Company	200,000				200,000
Sub Company		40,000	(c) 40,000		
Net earnings — brought forward	119,000	50,000			119,000
	319,000	90,000			319,000
Dividends:					
Par Company	100,000				100,000
Sub Company		30,000		(b) 30,000	
Retained Earnings — December 31 — Carried Forward	219,000	60,000			219,000
Statement of Financial Position					
Assets					
Cash	100,000	80,000			180,000
Notes receivable	8,000			(e) 8,000	
Accounts receivable, net	17,000	28,000			45,000
Inventory	30,000	40,000			70,000
Investment in Sub Company	219,000		(b) 30,000	(c) 200,000	
				(a) 49,000	
Equipment, net	70,000	80,000			150,000
Excess of cost over book value			(c) 10,000	(d) 1,000	9,000
	444,000	228,000			454,000
Liabilities and Stockholders' Equity					
Accounts payable	25,000	10,000			35,000
Notes payable		8,000	(e) 8,000		
Common stock — $10 par	200,000	150,000	(c) 150,000		200,000
Retained earnings — brought forward	219,000	60,000			219,000
	444,000	228,000	288,000	288,000	454,000

Explanation of elimination entries:
  (a) To eliminate earnings of subsidiary less amortization.
  (b) To eliminate dividends received from subsidiary.
  (c) To eliminate investment in subsidiary and subsidiary's capital accounts.
  (d) To adjust excess of cost over book value by recording one year's amortization. (Goodwill is being amortized over ten years.)
  (e) To eliminate intercompany debt.

Illustration 14.10

PAR COMPANY AND SUBSIDIARY SUB COMPANY
Work Sheet for Consolidated Financial Statements
(pooling of interests method)
December 31, 1979

	Par Company	Sub Company	Eliminations Debit	Eliminations Credit	Consolidated Amounts
Earnings Statement:					
Revenue from sales	400,000	150,000			550,000
Earnings of Sub Company	50,000		(a) 50,000		
Cost of goods sold	(250,000)	(75,000)			(325,000)
Expenses	(80,000)	(25,000)			(105,000)
Net Earnings—Carried Forward	120,000	50,000			120,000
Statement of Retained Earnings:					
Retained Earnings—January 1:					
Par Company	200,000				200,000
Sub Company		40,000			40,000
Net earnings—brought forward	120,000	50,000			120,000
	320,000	90,000			360,000
Dividends:					
Par Company	100,000				100,000
Sub Company		30,000		(b) 30,000	
Retained Earnings—December 31—					
Carried Forward	220,000	60,000			260,000
Statement of Financial Position:					
Assets					
Cash	300,000	80,000			380,000
Notes receivable	8,000			(d) 8,000	
Accounts receivable, net	17,000	28,000			45,000
Inventory	30,000	40,000			70,000
Investment in Sub Company	210,000		(b) 30,000	(c) 190,000	
				(a) 50,000	
Equipment, net	70,000	80,000			150,000
	635,000	228,000			645,000
Liabilities and Stockholders' Equity					
Accounts payable	25,000	10,000			35,000
Notes payable		8,000	(d) 8,000		
Common stock—$10 par	350,000	150,000	(c) 150,000		350,000
Paid-in capital—pooling of interest	40,000		(c) 40,000		
Retained earnings—brought forward	220,000	60,000			260,000
	635,000	228,000	278,000	278,000	645,000

Explanation of elimination entries:
  (a) To eliminate earnings of subsidiary.
  (b) To eliminate dividends received from subsidiary.
  (c) To eliminate investment in subsidiary and common stock of subsidiary and paid-in capital from pooling of interests.
  (d) To eliminate intercompany debt.

XYZ Company issued 20,000 shares of its own $20 par value common stock for all of the outstanding voting common stock (20,000 shares) of ABC Company. The ABC Company common stock has a par value of $10 per share. The total book value of the ABC stock is $300,000 ($200,000, common stock, and $100,000, retained earnings). The market values on the date of acquisition are $30 per share for the ABC stock and $30 per share for the XYZ stock. The combination qualifies as a pooling of interests. On the date of acquisition, the XYZ Company should debit the Investment in ABC Company account for which of the following amounts?

1. $400,000.
2. $300,000.
3. $200,000.
4. $600,000.

Now turn to Answer Frame 10¹⁴ on page 682 to check your response.

Frame 11¹⁴ _____

Abuses of pooling of interests method

Prior to the issuance of *APB Opinion No. 16*, the pooling of interests method was used in cases where it really was not applicable. In other words, its use was subject to abuse. Four common abuses of pooling are indicated below:

1. Acquisition of smaller companies at year-end so that the earnings of the smaller companies can be combined with the parent's earnings (or used to offset the parent's loss) in order to increase net earnings and earnings per share.

2. Acquisition of a company having several plants whose fair market values are much greater than their book values. In this case the plants would be recorded as assets at their rather low book value, say, $200,-000. The next year, one of the plants would be sold for its fair market value of, say, $800,000. The result of the sale would be a $600,000 gain which would instantly increase net earnings and earnings per share.

3. Issuance of unusual convertible securities which could be traded in one year later for either common stock or cash. Such securities were issued so that (1) the combination could be accounted for as a pooling of interests and (2) stockholders of the subsidiary could receive cash shortly if they did not want common stock.

4. Accounting for an acquisition as "part-purchase, part-pooling." In some cases, a certain number of stockholders would refuse to accept common stock or unusual convertible securities. They wanted cash immediately. Thus, some companies accounted for part of the acquisition as a purchase and the other part as a pooling of interests.

APB Opinion No. 16 has helped to reduce these abuses of pooling. 681

Answer frame 10¹⁴

Answer 2, $300,000, is the correct response. Under the pooling of interests method, the investment is recorded at the book value of the subsidiary's net assets. In this case, the book value is $300,000 ($200,000, common stock, and $100,000, retained earnings).

If you did not answer correctly, restudy Frames 9¹⁴ and 10¹⁴ before proceeding to Frame 11¹⁴ on page 681.

11¹⁴   Uses and limitations of consolidated statements

continued

Consolidated statements are of primary importance to the stockholders, managers, and directors of the parent company. The parent company benefits from the earnings, asset increases, and other financial strengths of the subsidiary. Likewise, the parent company suffers from a subsidiary's losses or other financial weaknesses. The Appendix to this chapter includes significant portions of the consolidated financial statements of an actual company. They illustrate many of the concepts discussed in this text.

On the other hand, consolidated statements are of very limited use to the creditors and minority stockholders of the subsidiary. The subsidiary's creditors have a claim against the subsidiary alone; they cannot look to the parent company for payment. And the minority stockholders do not benefit or suffer from the parent company's operations. They benefit only from the subsidiary's earnings, asset increases, and financial strengths; they suffer only from the subsidiary's losses and financial weaknesses. Therefore, the subsidiary's creditors and minority stockholders are more interested in the subsidiary's individual financial statements than in the consolidated statements.

Indicate whether each of the following statements is true or false.

1. The creditors and minority stockholders of a subsidiary are more interested in the subsidiary's financial statements than the parent's statements or the consolidated statements.
2. The pooling of interests method of accounting can be used when the parent company issues cash or debt securities in exchange for the common stock of the subsidiary.
3. Prior to the issuance of *APB Opinion No. 16,* there were many abuses of the pooling of interests method.
4. When common stock is exchanged for common stock to effect a business combination, either the purchase or the pooling of interests method can be used.

Now check your responses in Answer Frame 11¹⁴ on page 684.

Summary *chapter* 14

A corporation that owns a majority of the outstanding voting common stock of another corporation is called a *parent* company; the corporation controlled by the parent company is known as a *subsidiary* company. Consolidated statements are the financial statements that result from combining the parent's financial statement amounts with those of its subsidiaries. When preparing consolidated statements, a work sheet is a valuable tool on which the necessary elimination entries can be made. Such entries are required to eliminate certain intercompany items to show the assets, liabilities, stockholders' equity, revenues, expenses, and dividend accounts as if the parent and its subsidiaries were a single economic enterprise. Included in the items to be eliminated are the parent's investment account, the subsidiary's stockholders' equity accounts, and intercompany receivables and payables as well as intercompany revenues, expenses, and dividends.

In certain instances, a parent company may acquire a subsidiary at a cost above or below book value. Any excess of cost over book value must be used to increase the value of undervalued assets or be recognized as goodwill from consolidation. Any excess of book value over cost must first be used to reduce the values of the noncurrent assets; the remaining excess should be recorded as a deferred credit.

When a parent company acquires less than 100 percent but more than 50 percent of the outstanding voting common stock of a subsidiary, the interest not acquired is called the minority interest and is held by minority stockholders. These minority stockholders have an interest in the subsidiary's net assets and share the subsidiary's earnings with the parent company.

The use of the equity method requires the parent company to account for its share of the subsidiary's earnings, losses, and dividends as they are reported by the subsidiary. Earnings increase the investment while losses and dividends reduce the investment.

Business combinations can be classified as purchases or poolings of interests. A purchase results when the acquiring company exchanges cash, other assets, and debt securities (and sometimes, preferred and common stock) for the net assets or common stock of another company. A pooling of interests results if the acquiring company issues common stock in exchange for common stock *and* if the business combination satisfies other conditions. Only one of the methods—purchase or pooling of interests—is appropriate (correct) given the circumstances surrounding a particular business combination. The two methods would yield different earnings statement and statement of financial position amounts if they could be alternatively applied to the same combination.

Consolidated statements are of primary importance to the stockholders, managers, and directors of the parent company. On the other

683

1. True. The parent company's statements are of no use in determining or assessing the financial position and results of operations of the subsidiary. The consolidated statements are of very limited use to the creditors and minority stockholders of the subsidiary because their claims and interests do not run to the consolidated entity. Thus, the subsidiary's creditors and minority stockholders are primarily interested in the subsidiary's individual financial statements.

2. False. The pooling of interests method can be used only when the parent exchanges its own common stock for the subsidiary's common stock and the business combination satisfies the 12 criteria specified in *APB Opinion No. 16.*

3. True. The pooling of interests method was often used in cases where it was not really applicable. *APB Opinion No. 16* helped to reduce the abuses of pooling.

4. False. The purchase and pooling of interests methods are not alternatives. If the business combination satisfies all 12 conditions specified in *APB Opinion No. 16,* the pooling method must be used. Otherwise, the purchase method must be used.

If you missed any of the above, restudy Frames 10[14] and 11[14] before proceeding to the Summary on page 683.

hand, the minority stockholders and creditors of the subsidiary company are more interested in the individual subsidiary's financial statements.

The Appendix to this chapter includes significant portions of the consolidated financial statements of an actual company.

To complete your review, study the terms introduced in this chapter in the Glossary on page 699. Then go on to the Student Review Quiz beginning on page 699 for a self-administered test of your comprehension of the material in the chapter.

APPENDIX 14: A SET OF CONSOLIDATED FINANCIAL STATEMENTS FOR AN ACTUAL COMPANY

Presented in this Appendix are significant portions of the Annual Report for 1976 of Interlake, Inc., and its consolidated subsidiaries. Included are: (1) 1976 Highlights, (2) Operating/Financial Review, (3) Statement of Consolidated Income and Retained Earnings, (4) Consolidated Balance Sheet, (5) Statement of Changes in Consolidated Financial Position, (6) Notes to Consolidated Financial Statements, (7) Report of Independent Accountants, (8) Five-Year Financial Summary of Operations, and (9) Management's Discussion of Summary of Operations. These items are presented as illustrative of the financial reporting practices of a modern business corporation in reporting to its stockholders and to other external parties. Several explanatory comments on the above items are needed.

1. Your authors prefer the terminology of earnings statement and net earnings in the statement reporting on operations and the title statement of financial position to balance sheet, although the terminology employed by the company is fully acceptable and, indeed, more widely used.

2. The item "Future Income Taxes" in the Consolidated Balance Sheet (page 692) and discussed in Note 1 and Note 11 (pages 694 and 695) is explained and discussed in Appendix 7B.

3. Particular attention should be paid to the rather substantial amounts of additional information and explanation presented in the Notes to Consolidated Financial Statements. Note 1 is especially informative since it discloses the accounting policies followed in developing the amounts reported in the various statements, such as the use of the straight-line method of computing periodic depreciation charges and principles of consolidation.

4. A strong trend has emerged in recent years toward making more informative disclosures in corporate annual reports. Many of these added disclosures are in response to SEC requirements. Examples include: (1) management's review of operations and financial results (page 698), (2) the reporting of quarterly data (pages 686 and 696), and sales and earnings by segments or major lines of business (pages 686–689). The premise underlying these added disclosures is that management more than anyone else knows what happened and why operating and financial results differ from period to period and, therefore, should be called upon to explain and to further enlighten readers.

5. Note 14 (page 696) shows that the company chose not to reveal detailed replacement cost information in its annual report. Rather, it elected to make only a general reference to replacement costs and to indicate that such detailed information is available to the public, as filed with the SEC.

Interlake, Inc.

1976 Highlights

Interlake, Inc. is a Chicago-based international company engaged in two major businesses: metals and material handling. In metals, we manufacture and sell iron, steel, silicon metal, ferroalloys, ferrous metal powders plus investment and die castings. Material handling includes packaging, shipping, storage, and handling products and systems.

For The Year (In thousands)	% Change '76–'75	1976	1975
Net sales of continuing operations	+10.6	$708,876	$640,831
Net income of continuing operations	− 4.5	37,905	39,706
Net income	+10.3	37,905	34,375
Cash flow	+10.5	57,884	52,388
Capital expenditures	−45.6	19,538	35,884
Cash dividends paid	+54.1	12,440	8,075
At Year End (In thousands)			
Working capital	+21.7	$133,151	$109,421
Current ratio	+ 5.0	2.1 to 1	2.0 to 1
Property, plant and equipment—net	+ .4	202,195	201,345
Long-term debt, less current maturities	− 7.9	78,828	85,599
Shareholders' equity	+14.3	301,818	264,046
Shares outstanding	+ 9.2	5,901	5,405
Per Share Statistics			
Income of continuing operations	− 9.9	$ 6.61	$ 7.34
Net income	+ 4.1	6.61	6.35
Cash dividends paid	+43.3	2.15	1.50
Shareholders' equity at year-end	+ 4.7	51.15	48.85

Quarterly Results—1976 and 1975 (In millions—except per share statistics)

	Sales*		Net Income				Stock Price Range				Dividends	
			Amount		Per Share		1976		1975		Per Share	
	1976	1975	1976	1975	1976	1975	High	Low	High	Low	1976	1975
1st	$164.6	$186.5	$ 8.5	$ 7.7	$1.57	$1.39	42½	25½	21⅝	18	$ .50	$ .33
2nd	181.2	153.9	9.7	5.4	1.70	1.02	40½	35	23⅜	19½	.55	.33
3rd	176.5	143.2	10.2	10.9	1.74	2.01	40⅝	35¼	25⅞	20⅝	.55	.34
4th	186.6	157.2	9.5	10.4	1.60	1.93	38	33⅝	26½	23¾	.55	.50
Year	$708.9	$640.8	$37.9	$34.4	$6.61	$6.35	42½	25½	26½	18	$2.15	$1.50

*Of continuing operations

Sales and Earnings by Business (In millions)

		Sales				Earnings*			
		1976	%	1975	%	1976	%	1975	%
Metals	**Iron**	$107.3	15	$110.1	17	$32.9	47	$50.7	66
	Steel	198.2	28	171.4	27				
	Silicon Metal/Ferroalloys	46.9	7	48.6	7	6.3	9	8.1	11
	Metal Powders	49.0	7	30.4	5	9.7	14	4.0	5
	Investment/Die Castings**	27.8	4	—	—	3.9	5	—	—
Material Handling	**Packaging**	128.0	18	109.1	17	10.3	15	5.7	7
	Material Handling/Storage	151.7	21	171.2	27	7.1	10	8.8	11
		$708.9	100%	$640.8	100%	$70.2	100%	$77.3	100%

*Of continuing operations before unallocated corporate items and income taxes
**Eight months

Operating/Financial Review

Interlake's geographic and product line diversification moves in recent years helped 1976 to be a good year—achieving another new sales record and yielding net income at the best level since the 1974 record. This performance was aided by record sales and earnings of metal powders, significantly improved earnings outside the U.S., and the acquisition of Arwood Corporation. Sales volumes were at or above 1975 levels in all product lines except material handling/ storage and ferroalloys. In the U.S., however, increased costs without adequate price relief and price pressures from imported products limited volume gain benefits.

The financial highlights of 1976 include:

□ **Net income** was $37.9 million, the best since 1974's record level and an increase of $3.5 million, or 10.3% over 1975. Net income per common share of $6.61 compared with $6.35 in 1975.

□ **Cash dividends** of $2.15 per common share were 65¢ or 43% higher than in 1975.

□ **Cash flow** and year-end **working capital** reached record levels —$57.9 million and $133.2 million, respectively—and the current ratio continued to improve, moving to 2.1 to 1 from 2.0 to 1 at the end of 1975.

□ **Net sales** increased $68.1 million, or 10.6%, from 1975 to a record $708.9 million.

□ **Arwood Corporation** was acquired on April 29, 1976 for 437,562 shares of Interlake common stock.

Results of Operations

Continued growth of metal powders, eight months results of Arwood's castings businesses, and improved profit performance outside the U.S. highlighted 1976 operating performance.

Except for the addition of Arwood, sales contributions in '75 and '76 remained relatively stable:

	Sales			
	1976		1975	
(In millions)	Amount	%	Amount	%
Iron/Steel	$305.5	43%	$281.5	44%
Silicon Metal/ Ferroalloys	46.9	7	48.6	7
Metal Powders	49.0	7	30.4	5
Investment/ Die Castings	27.8	4	—	—
Packaging	128.0	18	109.1	17
Material Handling/ Storage	151.7	21	171.2	27
	$708.9	100%	$640.8	100%

However, operating profit comparisons showed several changes:

	Operating Profit			
	1976		1975	
(In millions)	Amount	%	Amount	%
Iron/Steel	$32.9	47%	$50.7	66%
Silicon Metal/ Ferroalloys	6.3	9	8.1	11
Metal Powders	9.7	14	4.0	5
Investment/ Die Castings	3.9	5	—	—
Packaging	10.3	15	5.7	7
Material Handling/ Storage	7.1	10	8.8	11
	$70.2	100%	$77.3	100%

Income before unallocated corporate items and taxes was $70.2 million in 1976 or 9% below the '75 figure. However, '75 benefited from a $10 million settlement with a raw material supplier. In addition, foreign currency devaluations reduced '76 sales and income gains. Australia, United Kingdom, and Mexico experienced currency devaluations ranging from 13% to 37% in '76. Compared with foreign currency rates prevailing in 1975, '76 devaluations lowered international sales and operating profit by $10.7 million and $1.2 million, respectively.

Iron and Steel

The Riverdale, Ill. plant achieved record steel shipments and led this division's sales upswing to $305.5 million—a $24.0 million, or 9% gain over 1975. Total iron and steel tons shipped increased by 8%, but specific performances were mixed.

Flat rolled steel shipments reached 588,777 tons—21% over 1975 and 6% higher than in '74. Customers in the automotive, agricultural, and industrial machinery industries contributed most to this sales growth.

Iron shipments in 1976 were essentially at the 1975 level. A slight decline in total domestic iron consumption in 1976 was accompanied by comparable reductions in iron imports; however, low-priced imports remained at a high level, 28% of all domestic consumption, and continued to reflect excess world supplies. Low scrap prices also had a continuing adverse effect on iron demand.

Spiral weld and line pipe sales dropped 19% below '75 totals, continuing a decline since 1973. Demand slumped after a good first quarter, then picked up again in the fourth quarter. Uncertainty in our government's energy policy combined with an abundant supply of low-priced imports continued to undermine any sustained demand for U.S. products.

Iron and Steel '76 operating profit was $32.9 million, down 35%, or $17.8 million from a record $50.7 million established in '75. A major factor in the decline was a favorable $10 million settlement with a raw material supplier in 1975. The earnings drop in 1976 was limited, in part, by a rebound in equity income from our interest in Wabush Iron after an extended strike in 1975, and by effective cost reduction programs. Still, some declines took place in all major iron and steel product lines, primarily because overall price relief was inadequate to offset rising costs.

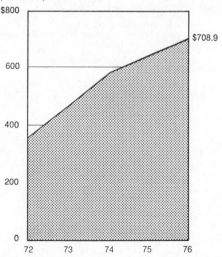

Net Sales
(in millions)

687

The lack of price relief was most pronounced for iron products where average selling prices remained at 1974's year end level. Competitive pricing from U.S. suppliers, plus low-priced imported iron held prices at this level during a period of low demand.

Earnings from steel products in '76 were also lower than a year earlier. Benefits from improved volume and sales mix were more than offset by the continuing cost/price squeeze.

Silicon Metal/Ferroalloys

Shipments increased 10% in 1976, but gains were offset by competitive price pressures. As a result, sales were $46.9 million, down $1.7 million, or 3%, from '75. Foreign imports had a compounding negative impact in 1976. Low-priced foreign ferrochromes generated deteriorating prices for domestic products and captured the major share of U.S. consumption. In addition, foreign stainless steel imports limited domestic production, and this reduced overall domestic demand for ferrochromes.

Silicon metal shipments increased 20% over 1975 and were 1% above record '74 volume. Demand continued high from our two major industry users: chemical and secondary aluminum. Prices remained relatively stable throughout the year. Silicon metal production increased at Selma, Alabama, because of the new furnace completed in late 1975.

'76 operating profit was $6.3 million, down $1.8 million, or 22%. The major reason for the continuing decline was the impact of lower selling prices for ferrochromes. Stable prices for other products with higher labor, material, utility, and other costs also contributed to lower profits. High production volume and strict cost controls only partially offset higher costs.

Metal Powders

Record sales and shipments in '76 resulted from high demand throughout the year. Shipments increased 46% over 1975 and were 12% higher than the previous record in 1974. This record volume and a mid-year price increase boosted sales to $49.0 million, or 61% above 1975 and 44% above the 1974 record level. Increased activity by automotive customers was the chief reason for achieving this performance. All grades of metal powders, except welding powders, shared the high growth rate with atomized powders representing an increasing proportion of sales.

Operating profit of $9.7 million more than doubled the record 1975 level and continued the earnings growth trend begun in 1973. High sales volume was the major factor contributing to this achievement.

Investment/Die Castings

The investment and die casting businesses became new dimensions of Interlake on April 29, 1976, with the acquisition of the Arwood Corporation. Eight months sales of $27.8 million were accounted for about equally by the two businesses. Die casting sales reflected high demand in consumer products industries in each of the three major geographic markets served: western, northeastern, and southeastern. Investment castings sales softened in '76 because aircraft manufacturers reduced their spending.

Arwood's eight months results added $3.9 million to operating profit, or 5% of Interlake's total. Earnings improvements in '76 were achieved by five of six plants. Higher volume helped the three die casting operations. Improved facilities and management controls allowed two of the investment casting plants to report income gains and limited the earnings decline at the third plant and the joint venture company.

Packaging

Worldwide sales improved in 1976:

(In Millions)	1976		1975	
	Amount	%	Amount	%
Domestic	$ 85.1	66	$ 72.5	66
Foreign	42.9	34	36.6	34
	$128.0	100%	$109.1	100%

This overall 17% gain reflected a modest increase in industrial activity and, more significantly, benefits from a high level of strapping equipment placements in 1975 and 1976. Steel strapping shipments increased 15% in 1976. Steel strapping prices followed general steel cost increases in domestic and foreign markets. Non-metallic strapping achieved substantial gains in all four major geographic markets, particularly in domestic corrugated paper and textile industries. Sales were adversely affected in '76 by $1.0 million due to discontinuation of A. J. Bayer's metal forming and bronze plaque businesses.

Stitching markets recovered during the year, as stitching wire shipments rose 19%. Exports to Central American banana plantations increased 12% over '75, but have not returned to '74's high levels. In the U.S., stitching wire sales rose 23%, and stitching equipment volume also increased.

Operating profit rose 81% to $10.3 million from $5.7 million in 1975. Domestic earnings increased as shipments rose in all major product groups. Earnings of foreign operations set a new record in 1976, but lower foreign currency values tempered these gains.

Results of Foreign Operations
(In millions)

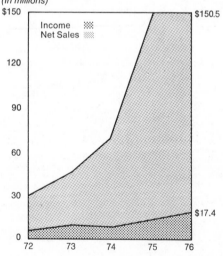

Material Handling/Storage

Recovery of foreign sales and income highlighted '76 results. Sales were $151.7 million, down 11% from 1975 results. Domestic activity was particularly weak for the second straight year, reflecting a continued low level of capital spending by customers. Foreign sales activity was stronger.

(In Millions)	1976 Amount	%	1975 Amount	%
Domestic	$ 44.7	29	$ 57.6	34
Foreign	107.0	71	113.6	66
	$151.7	100%	$171.2	100%

Two factors adversely affect year-to-year foreign sales comparisons. First: foreign currency devaluations lowered '76 sales by $8.3 million. Second: '75 sales included 13 months for the Dexion companies, which added $8.2 million. Adjusting for these items, foreign sales were 10% higher in 1976.

Shipments rose in the European Economic Community countries and Australia. Sales achievements in Europe have been significant, considering limited economic growth in EEC countries. Canadian volume was lower than '75 due to political and economic problems.

Domestic shipments were down in all areas, but most significantly in the area of engineered storage systems.

The systems business fell dramatically in 1976 as new project quotations were few in number and were usually accompanied by heavy competitive price discounting. Although the year ended with increased quotation activity, the number of projects awarded has remained low.

Material Handling/Storage operating profit was $7.1 million, down 19% from 1975. Negative effects of lower volume and price discounts reduced domestic earnings, particularly engineered storage systems. The A. J. Bayer conveyor business was reorganized during the year, and manufacturing was concentrated at Shepherdsville, Kentucky. Costs associated with relocations and product improvements also helped erode earnings.

Foreign earnings improvements helped limit the division's overall earnings decline from 1975. European Material Handling/Storage subsidiaries realized the greatest earnings gains. Higher '76 volume and benefits from sales and administrative reorganizations increased foreign income. Earnings improvements were achieved in each European company, with particularly significant increases in the United Kingdom and Germany.

Outside of Europe and the U.S., operating profit performance was mixed. Australia reflected improved earnings in part from the participation in an increasing number of major systems projects. The Japanese joint venture, Kawatetsu-Interlake Ltd. initiated production in March 1976; however, the economic downturn in Japan has caused the results to be below expectations. In Canada, lower earnings were reported in 1976 in the face of government imposed price contrpls, political unrest in Quebec, and an extended construction strike in Montreal.

Income

Net income was $37.9 million in '76, up 10% over $34.4 million in 1975. Net income per share rose 4% to $6.61 compared with $6.35 in '75. Interlake's average number of common shares outstanding increased 6% because 437,562 shares were issued to acquire Arwood Corporation in April.

Income from continuing operations declined 4.5% or the equivalent of 73¢ per share. This can be largely attributed to a settlement of $5 million after tax from a raw material supplier which added about 93¢ per share to 1975 earnings.

A lower effective tax rate improved 1976 earnings by 44¢ per share. Although investment tax credits trailed 1975 by the equivalent of 34¢ per share, this was more than offset by:

☐ Higher proportion of equity income from increased earnings of unconsolidated companies, primarily Wabush Iron, which rebounded from a strike-plagued 1975

☐ Increased foreign tax credits

Net income in 1975 was reduced by a $5.3 million loss from disposal and losses from operations, of the Howell Division (home furnishings and gas products) as of May 25, 1975.

Net Income and Common Dividends
(in millions)

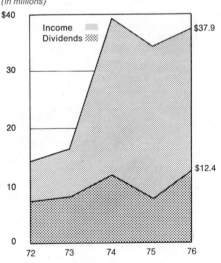

Capitalization
(in millions)

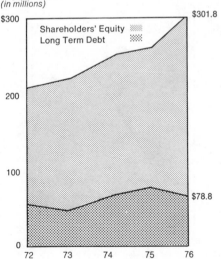

Dividends

Cash dividends on common stock were $12.4 million in 1976 compared with $8.1 million last year. The dividend payout rate increased to 32.8% of net income from 23.5% in 1975. The regular cash dividend was increased in November, 1975 to $.50 per common share on restated shares . . . and again in May 1976 to $.55 per common share. These actions brought total '76 payments to $2.15 per common share, compared with $1.50 per restated common share in 1975.

Financial Condition

The company's financial condition strengthened further in '76. Record cash flow of $57.9 million was sufficient to meet the normal business requirements, increase common stock dividends, and reduce a portion of long-term debt. Major funds requirements were:

☐ Capital expenditures of $19.5 million

☐ Increased working capital of $23.7 million

☐ Common stock dividends of $12.4 million

☐ Investments in coal and other ventures of $4.7 million

☐ Net reduction of long-term debt by $6.8 million

Shareholder's equity totaled $302 million at December 26, 1976 representing a 14.3% increase over the preceding year end. This increase held the return on shareholders' average equity to 13.3%, just below the 13.7% reported in 1975, but substantially above the 10.2% average return over the preceding five years.

A summary of the key financial ratios highlighted the strengthened financial condition:

	At 12/26/76	At 12/28/75
Working Capital Ratio	2.1 to 1	2.0 to 1
Quick Asset Ratio	.9 to 1	.8 to 1
Debt/Total Capitalization	21%	24%

Capital Expenditures

Capital spending in '76 was down considerably from record spending in 1975. '76 Capital expenditures of $19.5 million, were $16.4 million below $35.9 million spent in '75.

Replacement and improvement projects accounted for $16.1 million, or 83% of total '76 spending. The Iron and Steel Division continued the blast furnace rehabilitation programs started in 1975 and accounted for a significant portion of '76 spending.

Spending on environmental control was $1.8 million, or 9% of total '76 spending. Our Iron and Steel plus Silicon Metal/Ferroalloy businesses accounted for 90% of all environmental spending, primarily for fume and dust collection systems and water recycling projects. Although environmental control spending is below '75 levels, '76 projects represent our continuing commitment to upgrade facilities to meet or exceed multiple environmental standards imposed by governmental agencies.

Expansion projects accounted for $1.6 million, or 8% of '76 capital outlays. Several projects started in '75 were completed as were several smaller, new projects in our material handling/storage business.

Capital Expenditures and Depreciation
(in millions)

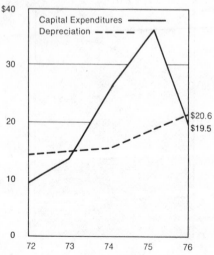

Capital Expenditures—By Type
(in millions)

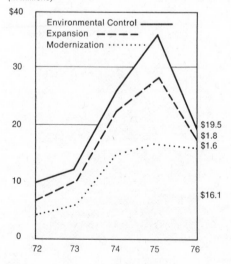

Interlake, Inc.
Statement of Consolidated Income and Retained Earnings

For the Years Ended December 26, 1976 and December 28, 1975

	1976	1975
Sales and Revenues:		
Net sales of continuing operations	$708,876,480	$640,831,084
Other revenues	9,767,080	9,492,783
	718,643,560	650,323,867
Costs and Expenses:		
Cost of products sold (Note 6)	528,234,922	457,733,049
Depreciation, depletion and amortization (Note 1)	20,960,421	19,287,194
Selling and administrative expenses	77,907,000	74,984,861
State, local and miscellaneous taxes	20,927,642	19,283,832
Interest expense	8,932,289	9,861,363
	656,962,274	581,150,299
Income of Continuing Operations before Taxes on Income	61,681,286	69,173,568
Provision for Income Taxes (Note 11)	23,776,000	29,467,000
Income of Continuing Operations	37,905,286	39,706,568
Loss from Discontinued Operations, net of applicable income taxes (Note 9)	—	5,331,238
Net Income for the Year	37,905,286	34,375,330
Retained Earnings at Beginning of Year	183,877,288	157,577,049
	221,782,574	191,952,379
Deduct Cash Dividends Paid ($2.15 per share in 1976 and $1.50 per share in 1975) (Note 4)	(12,439,597)	(8,075,091)
Retained Earnings at End of Year	$209,342,977	$183,877,288
Per Share of Common Stock (based on average number of shares outstanding— 5,736,424 in 1976 and 5,412,904 in 1975):		
Income of Continuing Operations	$6.61	$7.34
Loss from Discontinued Operations	—	(.99)
Net Income	$6.61	$6.35

(See notes to consolidated financial statements)

Interlake, Inc.

Consolidated Balance Sheet

December 26, 1976 and December 28, 1975

Assets	1976	1975
Current Assets:		
Cash	$ 2,756,719	$ 2,860,359
Certificates of deposit	3,372,136	5,728,920
Marketable securities, at cost which approximates market	4,783,358	149,441
Receivables, less allowance for doubtful accounts		
of $2,715,000 in 1976 and $2,470,000 in 1975	101,289,055	81,636,139
Inventories (Note 1):		
Raw materials and supplies	60,074,785	57,339,376
Semi-finished and finished products	70,964,264	60,790,986
Other current assets	11,423,278	7,986,684
Total current assets	254,663,595	216,491,905
Investments and Other Assets:		
Affiliated companies (Note 1)	15,891,955	12,057,200
Iron ore interests (Notes 1 and 12)	25,404,370	21,704,676
Other investments and deferred charges	12,755,588	11,182,920
Construction funds held by trustees	4,057,312	5,712,428
Goodwill (Note 1)	11,213,575	11,619,402
	69,322,800	62,276,626
Property, Plant and Equipment, at cost (Note 1):		
Land and mineral properties, less depletion	13,190,194	13,438,904
Plant and equipment	465,060,845	441,396,530
	478,251,039	454,835,434
Less—Depreciation and amortization	276,056,402	253,490,893
	202,194,637	201,344,541
	$526,181,032	$480,113,072

Liabilities and Shareholders' Equity	1976	1975
Current Liabilities:		
Accounts payable	$ 67,621,666	$ 58,567,310
Salaries and wages	19,688,659	15,890,461
Taxes other than income taxes	8,648,114	8,154,881
U.S. and foreign income taxes (Notes 8 and 11)	11,069,894	13,484,385
Notes payable (Note 2)	11,405,792	10,090,457
Current maturities of long-term debt (Note 2)	3,078,502	883,702
Total current liabilities	121,512,627	107,071,196
Long-Term Debt (Note 2)	78,828,443	85,599,287
Other Long-Term Liabilities	10,818,646.	10,202,481
Future Income Taxes (Note 1)	11,060,191	12,041,761
Minority Interests in Subsidiaries	2,143,377	1,152,494
Shareholders' Equity:		
Common stock, par value $1 a share; authorized 10,000,000 shares;		
issued 6,819,510 shares in 1976 and 6,381,948 shares in 1975 (Notes 4 and 7)	109,446,752	98,221,862
Retained earnings (Note 3)	209,342,977	183,877,288
	318,789,729	282,099,150
Less—Cost of common stock held in treasury		
(918,569 shares in 1976 and 976,919 shares in 1975) (Note 4)	16,971,981	18,053,297
	301,817,748	264,045,853
	$526,181,032	$480,113,072

(See notes to consolidated financial statements)

Interlake, Inc.
Statement of Changes in Consolidated Financial Position

For the Years Ended December 26, 1976 and December 28, 1975

	1976	1975
Financial Resources Were Provided By:		
Income of continuing operations	$ 37,905,286	$ 39,706,568
Depreciation, depletion and amortization	20,960,421	19,287,194
Equity in earnings of affiliates and joint ventures, less dividends received	(1,649,763)	(3,224,345)
Future income taxes	(981,570)	(1,274,444)
Loss from discontinued operations, net of applicable income taxes	—	(5,331,238)
Increase in other long-term liabilities	405,002	1,802,861
Working capital provided from operations	56,639,376	50,966,596
Decrease in construction funds held by trustees	1,655,116	3,856,500
Long-term borrowings	4,806,000	14,140,149
Common stock issued to acquire Arwood Corporation	11,267,221	—
Exercise of stock options	1,030,670	766,830
	75,398,383	69,730,075
Financial Resources Were Used For:		
Capital expenditures, less net book value of retirements and sales of $2,561,840 in 1976 and $1,161,892 in 1975	16,975,958	34,722,000
Reduction of long-term debt	13,114,381	2,757,036
Cash dividends	12,439,597	8,075,091
Purchase of Company common stock	—	5,080,950
Acquisition of Arwood Corporation, less working capital acquired	3,968,117	—
Investment in affiliated companies and joint ventures	4,705,689	2,551,463
Purchase of minority interests	—	1,925,925
Other	464,382	339,553
	51,668,124	55,452,018
Increase in working capital	$ 23,730,259	$ 14,278,057
Increase (Decrease) in Working Capital Comprises:		
Cash, certificates of deposit and marketable securities	$ 2,173,493	$ (1,538,352)
Receivables	19,652,916	(24,500,276)
Inventories	12,908,687	(8,323,024)
Other current assets	3,436,594	407,747
Accounts payable and salaries and wages	(12,852,554)	26,057,431
Taxes payable	1,921,258	13,719,923
Notes payable	(1,315,335)	6,610,025
Current maturities of long-term debt	(2,194,800)	1,844,583
	23,730,259	14,278,057
Working capital at beginning of year	109,420,709	95,142,652
Working capital at end of year	$133,150,968	$109,420,709

(See notes to consolidated financial statements)

Interlake, Inc.

Notes to Consolidated Financial Statements

For the Years Ended December 26, 1976 and December 28, 1975

Note 1—Summary of Significant Accounting Policies

Principles of Consolidation—The consolidated financial statements include the accounts of all majority-owned domestic and foreign subsidiaries. Investments in corporate joint ventures and companies owned 20% to 50% are accounted for by the equity method. Such investments are carried at cost plus equity in undistributed earnings.

Inventories—Inventories are stated at the lower of cost or market value. Cost of domestic inventories is determined principally by the last-in first-out method, which is less than current costs by $77,667,000 and $69,460,000 at December 26, 1976 and December 28, 1975, respectively. Cost of inventories of foreign subsidiaries is determined principally by the first-in first-out method.

Property, Plant and Equipment and Depreciation—For financial reporting purposes, plant and equipment are depreciated principally on a straight-line method over the estimated useful lives of the assets. Costs of significant renewals and betterments, including furnace relines, are capitalized. Depreciation claimed for income tax purposes is computed by use of accelerated methods. Income taxes applicable to differences in depreciation claimed for tax purposes and that reported in the financial statements is charged or credited to future income taxes, as appropriate. Provision for depletion of mineral properties is based on tonnage rates which are expected to amortize the cost of such properties over the estimated amount of mineral deposits to be removed.

Goodwill—Goodwill represents the excess of the purchase price over the fair value of the net assets of acquired companies and is amortized on a straight-line basis over a period of approximately thirty years.

Investment Tax Credits—The full amount of investment tax credits claimed for tax purposes is reflected in income in the year the related property is placed in service.

Pension Plans—The Company has various pension plans which cover substantially all employees. The majority of employees are covered by plans which follow the basic pension pattern of the steel industry. The provision for pension cost includes current costs plus interest on and amortization of unfunded prior service cost over periods not exceeding 25 years. The Company's policy is to fund pension cost accrued.

NOTE 2—Long-Term Debt and Credit Arrangements

Long-term debt of the Company consists of the following:

	December 26, 1976	December 28, 1975
8.80% debentures, due annually $2,500,000 1978 to 1995, and $5,000,000 in 1996	$50,000,000	$50,000,000
Obligations under long-term lease agreements	16,300,000	16,300,000
11-¼% notes payable, due annually in varying installments from 1980 to 1998	9,168,000	4,362,000
4⅞% debentures, due in 1977	2,429,000	2,683,000
Bank term loans, repaid in 1976	—	9,103,500
Other	4,009,945	4,034,489
	81,906,945	86,482,989
Less—Current maturities	3,078,502	883,702
	$78,828,443	$85,599,287

The long-term lease obligations relate principally to pollution control facilities which are being accounted for as plant and equipment as funds are expended. The interest rates on these obligations vary from 6.00% to 7.88%. Principal payments begin in 1981 ($500,000) and continue in varying annual amounts through 1999.

During 1975 the Company entered into a loan agreement to sell $10,000,000 of 11-¼% notes to finance the Company's share of construction costs for a coal mining venture.

The Company maintains informal domestic and foreign short-term bank credit lines of $51,000,000 against which $11,400,000 was borrowed at December 26, 1976. Domestic borrowings bear interest at the prime rate. Foreign borrowings bear interest at varying rates which are, generally, the overseas equivalent of the prime rate. In connection with the domestic lines of credit, the Company has entered into informal arrangements to maintain average compensating balances of 10% for the unused lines and an additional 10% for any borrowings. The Company's estimated average float exceeded the bank deposits required under these arrangements.

NOTE 3—Retained Earnings

Under the most restrictive terms of the Company's various loan agreements, the Company could not as of December 26, 1976 pay cash dividends or repurchase the Company's capital stock in amounts aggregating more than $107,500,000.

NOTE 4—Capital Stock

In August, 1975 the Board of Directors declared a three-for-two stock split effected in the form of a 50% stock dividend on all common shares outstanding and held in the treasury. Common stock data for 1975 have been restated to reflect the stock split.

In February, 1975 the Company purchased 241,950 shares of its common stock for $5,080,950. Shares purchased are being held in the treasury. During 1976 and 1975 the number of shares issued under a deferred compensation plan were 369 and 864, respectively.

At December 26, 1976, 101,716 treasury shares were reserved principally for outstanding options under the Company's 1965 Stock Option Plan.

The Company's authorized capital stock includes 1,000,000 shares of serial preferred stock, $1 par value per share, none of which has been issued.

NOTE 5—Stock Options

In 1965 the shareholders approved a Qualified Stock Option Plan for the Company's officers and key employees. Under the plan, options were available for grant until December 31, 1974 to purchase common stock for periods not longer than five years from the date of grant and at prices not less than the market value at date of grant. Options are exercisable 33⅓% annually, on a cumulative basis, beginning one year from date of grant. Options outstanding at December 26, 1976 expire at varying dates until 1979.

In April, 1975 the shareholders approved a non-qualified Stock Option Plan for the Company's officers and key employees. Under the plan, options may be granted until December 31, 1984 to purchase common stock for periods not longer than ten years from date of grant and at prices not less than the market value at date of grant. Options are exercisable 33⅓% annually, on a cumulative basis, beginning one year from date of grant. The total number of shares which may be issued pursuant to this plan may not exceed 375,000 shares. At December 26, 1976, 254,825 options were available for grant.

Changes in the number of shares of common stock under option related to these plans were as follows:

	1976	1975
Options outstanding at beginning of year	208,600	217,500
Options granted— Per share—$40.25 in 1976 and $22.00 in 1975	70,400	54,975
Options exercised— Per share—$15.79 to $22.00 in 1976 and $15.42 to $18.75 in 1975	(52,450)	(47,099)
Options cancelled	(6,875)	(16,776)
Options outstanding at end of year: Number of shares	219,675	208,600
Exercise price per share	($15.79-$40.25)	($15.79-$22.00)
Options exercisable at end of year	96,475	98,075

In connection with the acquisition of Arwood Corporation on April 29, 1976, existing Arwood qualified stock options were converted to qualified options to purchase 12,222 Interlake common shares at prices ranging from $8.26 to $31.16 per share. Of these options 5,531 were exercised prior to December 26, 1976 and 1,334 were cancelled. At year end 5,357 options were outstanding at prices ranging from $8.26 to $31.16 per share, of which 3,485 were exercisable.

NOTE 6—Significant Transaction

In 1975 cost of products sold includes a $10,000,000 favorable settlement from a supplier in connection with a long-term coal supply contract. The settlement, recorded in the third quarter of 1975, increased net income $5,000,000.

NOTE 7—Acquisition

On April 29, 1976 the Company acquired all of the outstanding common and preferred stock of Arwood Corporation, a manufacturer of investment castings and die castings, in exchange for 437,562 shares of Interlake common stock. The acquisition has been accounted for using the purchase method. Arwood's results of operations have been included in the consolidated financial statements from date of acquisition.

Following is a pro-forma summary of the consolidated results of operations for 1976 and 1975, assuming the acquisition had occurred at the beginning of 1975. Pro-forma earnings per share have been calculated based on the average number of shares of Interlake common stock outstanding during the related periods, adjusted for the shares issued to consummate the acquisition.

	1976	1975
Net sales	$721,133,000	$676,108,000
Net income	38,825,000	37,155,000
Net income per share of common stock	$6.60	$6.35

NOTE 8—Foreign Operations

The Company's foreign subsidiaries, affiliates and joint ventures are located principally in Canada and Western Europe. Net assets of foreign companies at December 26, 1976 and December 28, 1975 and results of operations for the years then ended were as follows:

	1976	1975
Net assets	$ 65,038,000	$ 56,435,000
Net sales	150,462,000	150,655,000
Earnings before taxes and unallocated corporate items	17,418,000	12,109,000

Foreign currency exchange adjustments were immaterial in amount and have been reflected in earnings. No provision for U.S. income taxes on unremitted earnings of foreign companies has been made as it is anticipated that any U.S. taxes on dividend distributions will be substantially offset by foreign tax credits.

NOTE 9—Discontinued Operations

In April, 1975 the Company adopted a plan to dispose of its Howell Division (furnishings and gas products) and, as of May 25, 1975, the Company sold substantially all of the assets of the business. Results of operations of the Howell Division and loss on disposition have been reflected under the caption of discontinued operations in 1975 and were as follows:

Loss from discontinued operations to measurement date, less related income tax benefits of $574,000	$ 565,238
Loss on disposal of assets (including operating losses of $643,000 during the phase-out period), less related tax benefits of $3,820,000	4,766,000
	$5,331,238

NOTE 10—Pension Plans

Pension costs were $18,992,000 in 1976 and $15,737,000 in 1975. The actuarially computed value of vested benefits per the latest actuarial reports exceeded the market value of the pension fund assets by approximately $78,000,000 and $64,000,000 as of December 26, 1976 and December 28, 1975, respectively. Pension costs and unfunded vested benefits increased in 1976 primarily as a result of improved benefits effective August 1, 1975 and vesting requirements of the Employee Retirement Income Security Act.

NOTE 11—Income Taxes

The provisions for taxes on income of continuing operations consist of:

	1976	1975
Currently payable:		
U.S. Federal (less investment credits of $1,540,000 in 1976 and $3,320,000 in 1975)	$15,873,000	$21,938,000
State and foreign	9,631,000	8,206,000
Deferred	(1,728,000)	(677,000)
	$23,776,000	$29,467,000

The effective tax rates are lower than the statutory rate due principally to investment tax credits, equity in earnings of affiliated companies and percentage depletion allowances.

As of December 26, 1976 U.S. Federal income tax returns for the years 1965 through 1973 have been examined. A number of adjustments have been proposed, one of which involves the determination of the cost of ore from one of the Company's iron ore interests and could result in certain of these costs being disallowed as a tax deduction. The Company believes that its position on this issue has merit and should not result in any significant adjustment.

NOTE 12—Commitments

With respect to the Company's interests in two mining joint ventures, the Company is required to take its ownership proportion of production for which it is committed to pay its proportionate share of the operating costs of these projects, either directly or as a part of the product price. Such costs include, as a minimum and regardless of the quantity of ore received, annual interest and sinking fund requirements of the funded debt of these projects of approximately $3,000,000 through 1983, and lesser amounts thereafter through 1991.

Noncancelable leases for pollution control facilities have been capitalized. All other lease commitments, considered in the aggregate, are not material in relation to the operations of the Company.

NOTE 13—Quarterly Results (unaudited)

Quarterly results of operations for 1976 were as follows:

| | Quarter | | | | |
	1st	2nd	3rd	4th	Year
	(in millions—except per share data)				
Net sales	$164.6	$181.2	$176.5	$186.6	$708.9
Net sales less cost of products sold	42.7	47.6	44.4	45.9	180.6
Net income	8.5	9.7	10.2	9.5	37.9
Net income per share of common stock	$1.57	$1.70	$1.74	$1.60	$6.61

Net income in the fourth quarter included $1,325,000 net gain on the sale of the Torrance, California plant and equipment and discontinuance of the metal forming and bronze plaque operations.

NOTE 14—Replacement Cost Information (unaudited)

The Company's Annual Report (Form 10-K), filed with the Securities and Exchange Commission, contains specific replacement cost information. In general, replacement cost of sales is not materially different from actual cost of sales and replacement cost depreciation expense is significantly higher than actual depreciation expense.

Report of Independent Accountants

Price Waterhouse & Co.

To the Board of Directors and Shareholders of Interlake, Inc.

In our opinion, the accompanying consolidated balance sheets and the related statements of consolidated income and retained earnings and the statements of changes in consolidated financial position present fairly the financial position of Interlake, Inc. and its subsidiaries at December 26, 1976 and December 28, 1975, and the results of their operations and the changes in their financial position for the years then ended, in conformity with generally accepted accounting principles consistently applied. Our examinations of these statements were made in accordance with generally accepted auditing standards and accordingly included such tests of the accounting records and such other auditing procedures as we considered necessary in the circumstances.

Price Waterhouse & Co.

Chicago, Illinois
January 31, 1977

Interlake, Inc.
Five Year Financial Summary of Operations

(Amounts in thousands—except per share statistics)

For the Year (1)		1976	1975	1974	1973	1972
Net Sales of Continuing Operations		$708,876	$640,831	$593,764	$425,999	$353,552
Other Revenues		9,767	9,493	9,278	7,034	1,532
		718,643	650,324	603,042	433,033	355,084
Cost of Products Sold and Operating Expenses		648,030	571,290	523,488	398,948	327,992
Interest Expense		8,932	9,861	5,934	5,322	5,497
		656,962	581,151	529,422	404,270	333,489
Income Before Taxes on Income		61,681	69,173	73,620	28,763	21 595
Provision for U.S. and Foreign Income Taxes		23,776	29,467	33,357	10,813	9,016
Income of Continuing Operations		37,905	39,706	40,263	17,950	12,579
Income (loss) from Discontinued Operations		—	(5,331)	(1,264)	(1,166)	393
Net Income	Amount	37,905	34,375	38,999	16,784	12,972
	% of Net Sales	5.3%	5.4%	6.6%	3.9%	3.7%
	% of Average Shareholders' Equity	13.3%	13.7%	17.2%	8.0%	6.3%
Earnings per Common Share (2)— Income of Continuing Operations		6.61	7.34	7.19	3.15	2.11
Net Income		6.61	6.35	6.97	2.95	2.17
Cash Flow (net income, depreciation and future income taxes)		57,884	52,388	53,678	30,713	26,982
Cash Dividends	Amount	12,440	8,075	11,013	7,373	7,158
	Per Share (2)	2.15	1.50	1.97	1.30	1.20
	% of Net Income	32.8%	23.5%	28.2%	43.9%	55.2%
Capital Expenditures (excluding assets of acquired businesses)		19,538	35,884	25,486	12,773	9,818
Depreciation		20,557	19,018	15,230	14,738	14,274

At Year End

		1976	1975	1974	1973	1972
Working Capital	Amount	$133,151	$109,421	$ 95,143	$ 98,021	$ 90,040
	Current Ratio	2.1 to 1	2.0 to 1	1.6 to 1	2.5 to 1	2.5 to 1
Property, Plant and Equipment (net)		202,195	202,621	188,746	155,265	153,697
Long-Term Debt (less current maturities)		78,828	85,599	74,216	60,367	62,923
Future Income Taxes		11,060	12,042	13,316	13,974	15,816
Common Shareholders' Equity	Amount	301,818	264,046	242,134	214,056	208,295
	Shares Outstanding (2)	5,901	5,405	5,603	5,597	5,820
	Per Share (2)	51.15	48.85	43.22	38.24	35.79
Common Stock Price Range (2)		42½—25½	26½—18	19⅝—13⅞	19⅜—13⅛	21⅜—17⅜
Price Earnings Ratio (based upon year-end stock price)		5.43	4.09	2.56	4.75	8.82
Number of Shareholders		24,970	24,504	24,624	24,898	25,036
Number of Employees		11,329	10,502	13,391	10,272	9,440

(1) 1974 and prior years have been restated to exclude operating results of the Howell Division (home furnishings and gas products), which was sold in 1975.

(2) Restated to reflect the 3-for-2 share split in October, 1975.

Management's Discussion of Summary of Operations

Sales

Interlake's sales history indicates the combined benefit from effective acquisition and development programs plus higher selling prices. This combination led to the ninth consecutive year of record sales in 1976.

(In millions)	1976	1975	1974	1973	1972
Iron	$107.3	$110.1	$103.0	$ 78.6	$ 62.7
Steel	198.2	171.4	202.6	142.4	131.3
Silicon Metal/ Ferroalloys	46.9	48.6	55.1	32.9	22.4
Metal Powders	49.0	30.4	34.0	26.5	17.2
Investment/ Die Castings	27.8	—	—	—	—
Packaging	128.0	109.1	119.2	95.6	77.9
Material Handling/ Storage	151.7	171.2	79.9	50.0	42.1
	$708.9	$640.8	$593.8	$426.0	$353.6

Significant sales increases in 1973 and 1974 reflected strong demand and higher selling prices. In 1974, sales were improved by price increases placed into effect after government price controls were lifted. The acquisition of Dexion-Comino International in late 1974 aided sales performance in 1974 and especially 1975, while the addition of Arwood Corporation benefited 1976 sales.

Other Revenues

Other revenues include primarily rent and royalty income, gains on sales of property and equipment, and interest income.

In 1973, sales of vacant land in Canada and an office building in London generated a pre-tax gain of approximately $3.5 million. Net gains on sales of domestic vacant land and idle equipment averaged $2.5 million in the 1973-1976 period.

The 1974-1976 period reflects increased rental income from our Erie Coke plant lease. Royalty income also increased in this period. Interest income reached a peak in 1974, up $1.9 million from 1973, but it declined in subsequent years because of lower yields and lower cash balances resulting from the Dexion acquisition and high capital investment.

Cost of Products Sold and Operating Expenses

Cost of products sold and operating expenses as a per cent of sales increased annually from 1974, but remain below the 1972-73 period average of 93.3%. In 1974, suspension of government price controls allowed recovery of cost increases experienced in 1972 and 1973.

Since 1974, lower demand, coupled with low priced imports, especially in iron, steel and ferroalloys, has limited price increases obtainable in the market place. However, raw material, labor, utility and other operating costs have increased throughout the five-year period. In 1975, costs did benefit from a $10.0 million settlement of a suit against a raw material supplier. For 1976, the cost/sales ratio increase was limited because of increased overall sales volume, despite stable or lower prices for products representing about 30% of total sales.

Interest Expense

Interest expense during the 1972-1976 period primarily reflects the issuance of $50.0 million of 8.8% debentures in 1971. The increase in 1975 was due to a full year of Dexion's financing requirements and higher average interest rates. Cost of financing pollution control facilities and the increasing investment in the Scotts Branch coal mining venture also caused interest expense to increase in 1975-1976. However, a decrease in other interest bearing debt and lower average interest rates in 1976 reduced total interest expense in 1976.

Earnings

Earnings during 1974-1976 have reached a new level, more than double the average of the 1972-1973 period. Earnings growth was shared by all product lines, but not uniformly—emphasizing benefits from diversification and development programs:

(In millions)	1976	1975	1974	1973	1972
Iron/Steel	$32.9	$50.7	$45.5	$16.7	$18.5
Silicon Metal/ Ferroalloys	6.3	8.1	13.3	2.1	1.3
Metal Powders	9.7	4.0	3.5	1.5	(.4)
Investment/ Die Castings	3.9	—	—	—	—
Packaging	10.3	5.7	9.8	8.6	4.3
Material Handling/ Storage	7.1	8.8	6.6	4.8	2.9
	70.2	77.3	78.7	33.7	26.6
Corporate items*	(8.5)	(8.1)	(5.1)	(4.9)	(5.0)
Income of continuing operations before taxes	$61.7	$69.2	$73.6	$28.8	$21.6

( ) denotes loss or expense
*Corporate items include interest expense discussed in preceding section.

In 1975, the $10.0 million settlement from a raw material supplier and the full year benefit of 1974 price increases aided earnings; however, shipments volume declined from 1974. The 1974 selling price increases, the addition of Dexion and Arwood, and the growth of powdered metals aided the 1974-1976 performance. However, escalating costs without adequate price relief since 1974 accounted for declining income in that period.

U.S. and Foreign Income Taxes

The effective income tax rate experienced in the 1972-1976 period was as follows:

Year	1976	1975	1974	1973	1972
Effective tax rate	38.5%	42.6%	45.3%	37.6%	41.8%

The effective tax rate is below the statutory rate principally because of available depletion allowances, investment tax credits, and equity in earnings of affiliated companies which varies in impact in the period. In 1973, the effective rate was further reduced by the foreign real estate sales mentioned previously which were subject to minimal income taxes.

Glossary *chapter* 14

Business combination – the joining together of all or nearly all of the operations of two or more firms under a single controlling management.

Consolidated statements – the financial statements that result from combining the parent's financial statement amounts with those of its subsidiaries (after certain eliminations have been made). The consolidated statements reflect the financial position and results of operations of a single economic enterprise.

Consolidated statement work sheet – an informal statement on which elimination entries are made for the purpose of showing the assets, liabilities, stockholders' equity, revenues, expenses, and dividends as if the parent and its subsidiaries were a single economic enterprise.

Deferred credit – an account, such as the excess of book value over cost, which has a credit balance but which cannot be properly classified as a contra asset, liability, or stockholders' equity account. The credit balance will be allocated to future operations.

Differential – the difference between the cost and the book value of an investment in a subsidiary.

Elimination entries – entries made on a consolidated statement work sheet, which are necessary to remove certain intercompany items and transactions in order to show the assets, liabilities, stockholders' equity, revenues, expenses, and dividends as if the parent and its subsidiaries were a single economic enterprise.

Goodwill – an intangible value attaching to a business firm due primarily to its above average earnings prospects.

Minority interest – the claim of the stockholders who own less than 50 percent of a subsidiary's outstanding voting common stock. The minority stockholders have an interest in the subsidiary's net assets and share the subsidiary's earnings with the parent company.

Parent – a corporation which owns more than 50 percent of the outstanding voting common stock of another corporation.

Pooling of interests – a business combina-

tion which meets certain criteria specified in *APB Opinion No. 16* including the issue of common stock in exchange for common stock; also, a method of accounting for business combinations classified as poolings of interests. Using this method, the parent company records its investment at the book value of the subsidiary's net assets.

Purchase – a business combination which cannot be classified as a pooling of interests. It results when the acquiring company issues cash or other assets, debt securities, and sometimes common or preferred stock for the subsidiary's common stock. Also, a method of accounting for business combinations classified as purchases. Using this method, the parent company records its investment in the subsidiary at the fair market value of the assets or securities given up or at the fair market value of the common stock received, whichever can be the more clearly and objectively determined.

Subsidiary – a corporation acquired and controlled by a parent corporation, with control established by ownership of more than 50 percent of the subsidiary's outstanding voting common stock.

Continue with the Student Review Quiz below as a self-administered test of your understanding of the material presented in this chapter.

Student review quiz *chapter* 14

To develop a permanent record of your responses, you may write them on the answer sheet provided in the *Work Papers* or on a separate sheet of paper.

1 A parent company –
a May use the equity method to account for an investment in a subsidiary.
b Cannot borrow money from a subsidiary.
c May own less than 50 percent of the outstanding voting common stock of another company and yet be considered a parent company.
d Does not have to prepare consolidated financial statements when it owns 100 percent of a subsidiary engaged in a

699

business similar to the parent's line of business.

e Cannot lend money to a subsidiary.

2 For the purpose of preparing consolidated financial statements, elimination entries are made on the—
a Parent company's books.
b Consolidated statement work sheet.
c Subsidiary company's books.
d Parent's and subsidiary's books.
e None of the above.

3 The Duke Company acquired 85 percent of the outstanding voting common stock of the Trap Company for $355,000. The book value of all the Trap Company's outstanding voting common stock is $400,000. Assuming that none of the Trap Company's recorded assets is over- or undervalued, the consolidated statement of financial position prepared on the date of acquisition would show—
a Goodwill, $75,000.
b Goodwill, $15,000.
c Deferred credit, $75,000.
d Deferred credit, $15,000.

4 Goodwill—
a Is a tangible asset.
b Has a credit balance.
c Must be amortized over 40 or fewer years.
d Does not have to be amortized unless management decides amortization is desirable.
e Is a current liability.

5 When a wholly owned subsidiary pays a cash dividend of $9,600, the parent company makes the following entry:

a Investment in
    Subsidiary 9,600
      Cash.....................   9,600

b Dividends Payable........ 9,600
      Cash.....................   9,600

c Cash.......................... 9,600
    Earnings of
      Subsidiary   9,600

d Cash.......................... 9,600
    Dividends
      Receivable..........   9,600

e Cash.......................... 9,600
    Investment in
      Subsidiary   9,600

6 When the pooling of interests method is used to account for a business combina-

tion, which of the following statements is false?
a The investment is recorded at the book value of the subsidiary's net assets.
b The earnings of the subsidiary reduce the investment account balance on the parent company's books.
c There is no goodwill or deferred credit from consolidation.
d The subsidiary's retained earnings at date of acquisition become a part of the consolidated retained earnings.
e The subsidiary's earnings for the entire year during which it was acquired are included in consolidated net earnings.

7 P Company owns 95 percent of X Company. Notes receivable amount to $8,000 on P Company's books and $15,000 on X Company's books. Included in X Company's notes receivable is a $3,000 note from P Company. On the consolidated statement of financial position, notes receivable would amount to—
a $20,000.
b $26,000.
c $22,250.
d $19,400.
e None of the above.

8 The subsidiary's creditors and minority stockholders are primarily interested in the—
a Parent's financial statements.
b Consolidated financial statements.
c Subsidiary's financial statements.
d Parent's statement of financial position and the subsidiary's earnings statement.
e None of the above.

9 Which of the following statements is incorrect?
a The purchase method of accounting is used when a business combination does not satisfy the conditions for use of pooling of interests accounting listed in *APB Opinion No. 16*.
b Using the purchase method of accounting, the parent company records an investment in a subsidiary at the book value of the subsidiary's net assets.
c Earnings of a subsidiary increase the balance in the parent's investment account.
d When the purchase method of accounting is used, there is a possibility that

goodwill or a deferred credit will appear on the consolidated statement of financial position.

e When a parent company acquires common stock of a subsidiary in exchange for cash, the purchase method of accounting must be used.

10 H Company acquired 75 percent of the outstanding voting common stock of W Company for $328,000. W Company's stockholders' equity consists of common stock, $300,000, and retained earnings, $120,000. The minority interest in W Company on the date of its acquisition by H Company amounts to—
a $13,000.
b $92,000.
c $100,000.
d $105,000.

11 The minority interest cannot be reported—
a As a liability.
b As an asset.
c As part of stockholders' equity.
d In a category between liabilities and stockholders' equity.

12 On January 1, 1979, B Company acquired 85 percent of the outstanding voting common stock of A Company for $275,000. During 1979, A Company had net earnings of $30,500 and paid out $20,000 in dividends on common stock. On December 31, 1979, the Investment in A Company account on B Company's books should have a balance of—
a $283,925.
b $285,500.
c $242,675.
d $288,500.
e None of the above.

13 On January 1, 1979, Penn Company acquired 95 percent of the outstanding voting common stock of Whit Company for $355,000. The cost exceeds the book value of the investment by $13,000. During 1979, Whit Company generated net earnings of $45,500. Whit Company did not declare or pay any dividends during 1979. The minority interest in Whit Company on December 31, 1979 is—
a $385,225.
b $342,000.
c $17,100.
d $20,275.

e $20,025.
f None of the above.

Now compare your answers with the correct answers and explanations on page 726.

Questions *chapter* 14

1 What is the purpose of preparing consolidated financial statements?

2 Why is it necessary to make elimination entries on the consolidated statement work sheet? Are these elimination entries also posted to the accounts of the parent and subsidiary? Why or why not?

3 Why might a corporation pay an amount in excess of the book value of a subsidiary's stock? Why might it pay an amount less than the book value of the subsidiary's stock?

4 The item "Minority interest" often appears as one amount in the consolidated statement of financial position. What does this item represent?

5 How do a subsidiary's earnings, losses, and dividends affect the investment account of the parent?

6 Under what circumstances must consolidated financial statements be prepared?

7 When must each of the following methods be used to account for a business combination?
a Purchase.
b Pooling of interests.

8 List three differences that exist between the purchase and pooling of interests methods of accounting for business combinations.

9 Why are consolidated financial statements of limited usefulness to the creditors and minority stockholders of a subsidiary?

Exercises *chapter* 14

1 On February 1, 1979, the Howard Company acquired 100 percent of the outstanding voting common stock of the Bowden Company for $250,000 cash. The

701

stockholders' equity of the Bowden Company consisted of common stock, $200,000, and retained earnings, $50,000. Prepare (a) the entry to record the investment in Bowden Company and (b) the elimination entry that would be made on the consolidated statement work sheet on the date of acquisition.

2 The Ramsey Corporation acquired 80 percent of the outstanding voting common stock of Peacock Company. On the date of its acquisition, the Peacock Company's stockholders' equity consists of common stock, $175,000, and retained earnings, $65,000. The cost of the investment exceeds book value by $9,000. Prepare (a) the entry to record the investment in Peacock Company and (b) the entry to eliminate the investment for purposes of preparing consolidated financial statements on the date of acquisition.

3 On January 1, 1979, Company A acquired 85 percent of the outstanding voting common stock of Company B. On that date, Company B's stockholders' equity section appeared as follows:

Common stock, $20 par;
  10,000 shares authorized,
  issued, and outstanding....... $200,000
Retained earnings................. 50,000
    Total Stockholders'
      Equity.................... $250,000

Compute the difference between cost and book value in each of the following cases
a Company A pays $212,500 cash for its interest in B.
b Company A pays $250,000 cash for its interest in B.
c Company A pays $195,000 cash for its interest in B.
d Company A issues some of its own common stock; the resulting business combination must be accounted for as a pooling of interests.

4 Company Y purchased 90 percent of Company Z's outstanding voting common stock on January 2, 1979. Company Y paid $150,000 for an equity of $135,000 — $90,000, common stock, and $45,000, retained earnings. The difference was due to undervalued land owned by Z. Company Z earned $18,000 during 1979 and paid cash dividends of $6,000.
a Compute the balance in the investment account on December 31, 1979.
b Compute the amount of the minority interest on (1) January 2, 1979, and (2) December 31, 1979.

5 The Meadow Company owns 75 percent of the Foy Company. The Foy Company reported net earnings of $52,000 for 1979. On December 31, 1979, the Foy Company paid a cash dividend of $14,000. In 1980 the Foy Company incurred a net loss of $10,000. Prepare entries to reflect these events on Meadow Company's books.

6 On January 1, 1979, the stockholders' equity section of the Floyd Company's statement of financial position is as follows:

Paid-In Capital:
Common stock — $10 par
  value: authorized, 100,000
  shares; issued and out-
  standing, 75,000 shares $750,000
Paid-in capital in excess of
  par value........................ 125,000
    Total Paid-In Capital... $875,000
Retained earnings............... 75,000
                  $950,000

Ninety percent of Floyd Company's outstanding voting common stock was acquired by Duncan Company on January 1, 1979, for $835,000. Compute (a) the book value of the investment, (b) the difference between cost and book value, and (c) the minority interest.

7 On June 1, 1979, the Weeks Corporation issued 5,000 shares of its own $20 par value common stock for 70 percent of the outstanding voting common stock of the Wages Company. The business combination does not qualify as a pooling of interests. The book value of Wages Company's net assets is $320,000. The market value per share of Weeks Corporation stock is $50. Give the journal entry to record the investment on Weeks Company's books.

Problems, Series A *chapter* 14

14–1–A

Farr Company acquired 75 percent of the outstanding voting common stock of Daley Company for $172,000 cash on January 1, 1978. During 1978, 1979, and 1980, Daley Company reported the following:

	Net earnings (loss)	*Dividends paid*
1978	$42,600	$34,600
1979	$ (5,400)	–0–
1980	$12,900	$ 8,600

Required:

a Prepare general journal entries to record the investment and the effect of the subsidiary's earnings, losses, and dividends on Farr Company's accounts.
b Compute the balance in the investment account on December 31, 1980.

14–2–A

The Robins Company acquired 100 percent of the outstanding voting common stock of the Warner Company on January 1, 1979, for $76,000 cash. On the date of acquisition, the statements of financial position for the two companies were as follows:

	Robins Company	*Warner Company*
Assets		
Cash	$ 6,000	$14,000
Accounts receivable	14,000	18,000
Notes receivable	10,000	6,000
Inventory	25,000	15,000
Investment in Warner Company	76,000	
Equipment, net	22,000	28,000
Total Assets	$153,000	$81,000
Liabilities and Stockholders' Equity		
Accounts payable	$ 16,000	$ 5,000
Notes payable	12,000	
Common stock – $20 par	100,000	60,000
Retained earnings	25,000	16,000
Total Liabilities and Stockholders' Equity	$153,000	$81,000

Also on January 1, 1979, Robins Company borrowed $6,000 from Warner Company; the debt is evidenced by a note.

Required:

Prepare a work sheet for a consolidated statement of financial position on the date of acquisition.

14-3-A

On January 1, 1979, Medlin Company acquired 80 percent of the outstanding voting common stock of the Hamby Corporation for $90,000 cash. The January 1, 1979, statements of financial position for the two companies are shown below:

	Medlin Company	Hamby Corporation
Assets		
Cash..........	$ 12,000	$ 9,000
Accounts receivable....................	10,000	12,000
Inventory........................	30,000	26,000
Investment in Hamby Corporation	90,000	
Equipment, net.............	15,000	9,000
Buildings, net.........	45,000	32,000
Land	8,000	10,000
Total Assets	$210,000	$98,000
Liabilities and Stockholders' Equity		
Accounts payable	$ 10,000	$ 5,000
Common stock – $10 par.............	160,000	80,000
Retained earnings	40,000	13,000
Total Liabilities and Stockholders' Equity...............	$210,000	$98,000

Medlin Company was willing to pay an amount greater than the book value of Hamby Corporation's stockholders' equity for two reasons:

1. It believed that the equipment owned by Hamby Corporation was undervalued. It was felt that the equipment should be valued at $12,000 as opposed to $9,000.
2. The company believed that the remaining excess of cost over book value could be justified on the basis of the subsidiary's excellent earnings expectations.

Required:

a Prepare a work sheet for a consolidated statement of financial position on the date of acquisition.

b Prepare a consolidated statement of financial position for January 1, 1979.

14-4-A

The Adams Company acquired 100 percent of the outstanding voting common stock of the Belcher Company on January 2, 1979, for $300,000 cash. On the date of acquisition, the statements of financial position for the two companies were as follows:

	Adams Company	Belcher Company
Assets		
Cash	$ 35,000	$ 20,000
Accounts receivable........	26,000	16,000
Notes receivable	40,000	10,000
Inventory........	55,000	26,000
Investment in Belcher Company	300,000	
Equipment, net	72,000	50,000
Buildings, net........	210,000	110,000
Land	85,000	45,000
Total Assets.....	$823,000	$277,000

Consolidated financial statements

	Adams Company	Belcher Company
Liabilities and Stockholders' Equity		
Accounts payable...	$ 13,000	$ 15,000
Notes payable..	10,000	12,000
Common stock—$10 par	600,000	200,000
Retained earnings..	200,000	50,000
Total Liabilities and Stockholders' Equity	$823,000	$277,000

The excess of cost over book value is attributable to the above-average earnings prospects of Belcher Company and to the belief that Belcher Company's equipment and buildings are undervalued. The fair values are believed to be $70,000 for the equipment and $120,000 for the buildings. On the date of acquisition, Belcher Company borrowed $8,000 from Adams Company; the debt is evidenced by a note.

Required:

a Prepare a work sheet for a consolidated statement of financial position on the date of acquisition.

b Prepare a consolidated statement of financial position as of January 2, 1979.

14–5–A

Refer back to Problem 14–4–A. Assume the following are the adjusted trial balances for the Adams Company and the Belcher Company on December 31, 1979.

	Adams Company	Belcher Company
Cash	$ 39,000	$ 35,000
Accounts receivable...	42,000	20,000
Notes receivable	35,000	5,000
Inventory, December 31..	55,000	31,900
Investment in Belcher Company	307,600	
Equipment, net	68,400	47,500
Buildings, net..	201,600	105,600
Land...	85,000	45,000
Cost of goods sold...	200,000	70,000
Expenses (excluding depreciation, taxes, and amortization)..............	80,000	30,100
Depreciation expense..	12,000	6,900
Income tax expense..	65,000	21,000
Dividends declared...	60,000	12,000
Total Debits..	$1,250,600	$430,000
Accounts payable...	$ 15,000	$ 20,000
Notes payable..	16,000	10,000
Common stock—$10 par	600,000	200,000
Retained earnings—January 1..	200,000	50,000
Revenue from sales	400,000	150,000
Earnings of Belcher Company	19,600	
Total Credits...	$1,250,600	$430,000

There is no intercompany debt at the end of the year.

Required:

Prepare a work sheet for consolidated financial statements on December 31, 1979. (On January 2, 1979, the equipment and buildings had remaining lives of 20 and 25 years, respectively; goodwill is to be amortized over 20 years.)

14-6-A

Required:

Using the work sheet prepared for Problem 14-5-A, prepare the following items:
a Consolidated earnings statement for the year ended December 31, 1979.
b Consolidated statement of retained earnings for the year ended December 31, 1979.
c Consolidated statement of financial position for December 31, 1979.

14-7-A

Hasty Company acquired 100 percent of the Boland Company's voting common stock on January 2, 1979. Hasty Company issued 20,000 shares of its own $10 par value stock in exchange for all the stock of Boland Company which had a book value of $220,000 ($200,000 common stock and $20,000 retained earnings). On the date of acquisition, the statements of financial position for the two companies were as follows:

	Hasty Company	Boland Company
Assets		
Cash	$ 50,000	$ 30,000
Accounts receivable	32,000	15,000
Notes receivable	23,000	
Inventory	90,000	50,000
Investment in Boland Company	220,000	
Equipment, net	82,000	30,000
Buildings, net	190,000	120,000
Land	60,000	20,000
Total Assets	$747,000	$265,000
Liabilities and Stockholders' Equity		
Accounts payable	$ 37,000	$ 25,000
Notes payable		20,000
Common stock—$10 par	500,000	200,000
Paid-in capital—pooling of interests	20,000	
Retained earnings	190,000	20,000
Total Liabilities and Stockholders' Equity	$747,000	$265,000

On the date of acquisition, Boland Company borrowed $10,000 from Hasty Company. The debt is evidenced by a note.

Required:

a Give the journal entry Hasty Company made on January 2, 1979, to record its investment in Boland Company.
b Prepare a work sheet for a consolidated statement of financial position on the date of acquisition.
c Prepare a consolidated statement of financial position as of January 2, 1979.

14–1–B

Mincey Company acquired 68 percent of the outstanding voting common stock of Shelley Company for $510,000 on January 1, 1979. During the years 1979–81, Shelley Company reported the following:

	Net earnings (loss)	Dividends paid
1979	$86,600	$51,900
1980	22,200	13,300
1981	(1,400)	3,325

Required:

a Prepare general journal entries to record the investment and the effect of the subsidiary's earnings, losses, and dividends on Mincey Company's accounts.

b Compute the investment account balance on December 31, 1981.

14–2–B

The Smith Company acquired all of the outstanding voting common stock of the Boyer Company on January 3, 1979, for $84,000. On the date of acquisition, the statements of financial position for the two companies were as follows:

	Smith Company	Boyer Company
Assets		
Cash	$ 14,000	$12,000
Accounts receivable	27,000	25,000
Notes receivable	15,000	4,000
Inventory	39,000	18,000
Investment in Boyer Company	84,000	
Equipment, net	72,000	33,000
Total Assets	$251,000	$92,000
Liabilities and Stockholders' Equity		
Accounts payable	$ 26,000	$ 8,000
Common stock – $10 par	120,000	58,000
Retained earnings	105,000	26,000
Total Liabilities and Stockholders' Equity	$251,000	$92,000

Required:

Prepare a work sheet for a consolidated statement of financial position on the date of acquisition.

14–3–B

On February 1, 1979, Landon Company acquired 75 percent of the outstanding voting common stock of the Greene Corporation for $70,000. The February 1, 1979, statements of financial position for the two companies show:

	Landon Company	Greene Corporation
Assets		
Cash	$ 22,000	$17,000
Accounts receivable	18,000	14,000
Notes receivable	9,000	
Inventory	32,000	18,000
Investment in Greene Corporation	70,000	
Equipment, net	28,000	12,000
Buildings, net	42,000	28,000
Land	6,000	5,000
Total Assets	$227,000	$94,000
Liabilities and Stockholders' Equity		
Accounts payable	$ 17,000	$ 8,000
Common stock—$10 par	115,000	50,000
Retained earnings	95,000	36,000
Total Liabilities and Stockholders' Equity	$227,000	$94,000

The price paid by Landon reflects its belief that its 75 percent interest in the undervaluation of Greene's equipment and buildings was $2,000 and $3,500, respectively.

Required:

a Prepare a work sheet for a consolidated statement of financial position on the date of acquisition.

b Prepare a consolidated statement of financial position for February 1, 1979.

14-4-B

The Noel Company acquired all of the outstanding voting common stock of the Holly Company on January 1, 1979, for $240,000. On the date of acquisition, the statements of financial position for the two companies were as follows:

	Noel Company	Holly Company
Assets		
Cash	$ 50,000	$ 15,000
Accounts receivable	24,000	20,000
Notes receivable	10,000	6,000
Inventory	76,000	48,000
Investment in Holly Company	240,000	
Equipment, net	68,000	41,000
Buildings, net	185,000	92,000
Land	78,000	25,000
Total Assets	$731,000	$247,000
Liabilities and Stockholders' Equity		
Accounts payable	$ 44,000	$ 20,000
Notes payable	12,000	14,000
Common stock—$20 par	530,000	198,000
Retained earnings	145,000	15,000
Total Liabilities and Stockholders' Equity	$731,000	$247,000

The cost of the investment differs from its book value because the Noel Company thinks that the Holly Company's assets are undervalued. The Noel Company thinks the equipment, buildings, and land are undervalued by $6,000, $12,000, and $9,000, respectively.

On the date of acquisition, Holly Company borrowed $10,000 from Noel Company; the intercompany debt is evidenced by a note.

Required:

a Prepare a work sheet for a consolidated statement of financial position on the date of acquisition.

b Prepare a consolidated statement of financial position for January 1, 1979.

14–5–B

Refer back to Problem 14–4–B. Assume the following are the adjusted trial balances for the Noel Company and the Holly Company on December 31, 1979:

	Noel Company	Holly Company
Cash	$ 48,000	$ 20,238
Accounts receivable	30,752	23,000
Notes receivable	19,000	5,000
Inventory, December 31	85,000	56,000
Investment in Holly Company	250,100	
Equipment, net	63,750	38,437
Buildings, net	175,750	87,400
Land	78,000	25,000
Cost of goods sold	448,000	120,000
Expenses (excluding depreciation and taxes)	120,000	45,000
Depreciation expense	13,500	7,163
Income tax expense	31,648	6,862
Dividends declared	26,500	9,900
Total Debits	$1,390,000	$444,000
Accounts payable	$ 40,000	$ 21,000
Notes payable	15,000	10,000
Common stock – $20 par	530,000	198,000
Retained earnings	145,000	15,000
Revenue from sales	640,000	200,000
Earnings of Holly company	20,000	
Total Credits	$1,390,000	$444,000

There is no intercompany debt at the end of the year.

Required:

Prepare a work sheet for consolidated financial statements on December 31, 1979. (At the beginning of 1979, the equipment and buildings had remaining lives of 16 and 20 years, respectively.)

14-6-B

Using the work sheet prepared for Problem 14–5–B, prepare the following items:

a   Consolidated earnings statement for the year ended December 31, 1979.
b   Consolidated statement of retained earnings for the year ended December 31, 1979.
c   Consolidated statement of financial position for December 31, 1979.

14-7-B

Lavin Corporation acquired 100 percent of Allen Corporation's voting common stock on January 3, 1979. Lavin Corporation issued 50,000 shares of its own $5 par value stock in exchange for all the stock of Allen Corporation which had a book value of $300,000 ($250,000 common stock and $50,000 retained earnings). The following are the adjusted trial balances for the Lavin Corporation and the Allen Corporation on December 31, 1979:

	Lavin Corporation	Allen Corporation
Cash	$ 50,000	$ 20,000
Accounts receivable	80,000	40,000
Notes receivable	25,000	15,000
Inventory, December 31	130,000	80,000
Investment in Allen Corporation	330,000	
Equipment, net	180,000	75,000
Buildings, net	300,000	120,000
Land	205,000	100,000
Cost of goods sold	540,000	180,000
Expenses	200,000	65,000
Dividends declared	75,000	25,000
Total Debits	$2,115,000	$720,000
Accounts payable	$ 100,000	$ 80,000
Notes payable	60,000	40,000
Common stock	750,000	250,000
Paid-in capital — pooling of interests	50,000	
Retained earnings, January 1	200,000	50,000
Revenue from sales	900,000	300,000
Earnings of Allen Corporation	55,000	
Total Credits	$2,115,000	$720,000

Required:

Prepare a work sheet for consolidated financial statements on December 31, 1979.

Chapter 4

Problem

4-1-A
(a) Annual rate of interest = 21.6%
(c) Annual rate of interest = 14.4%

4-2-A Example:

Purchases...............	7,200	
Accounts Payable....		7,200

4-3-A Example:

Purchases.............	13,500	
Accounts Payable...		13,500

4-4-A Net Cost:

Freeman....................	$	4,611.56
Klein......................		4,571.03

4-5-A Case A, Buyer's Books:

1/15 Purchases......... 4,000		
Transportation-In... 216		
Accounts		
Payable......		4,216

4-6-A Seller's Books:

8/1 Accounts		
Receivable....... 3,860		
Cash..........		80
Sales..........		3,780
8/8 Sales Returns........ 630		
Accounts		
Receivable....		630
9/9 Cash.............. 3,167		
Sales Discounts..... 63		
Accounts		
Receivable...		3,230

4-7-A

(c) Cost of Goods Sold..........	149,000	
(d) Net Earnings.................	20,500	
(e) Total Assets................	157,900	

4-8-A

(e) Total Debits................	226,944	
(f) Gross Margin...............	7,906	

4-9-A

Sales.....................	98,750	
Total Expenses...............	33,125	
Stockholders' Equity, 12/31/78..	31,875	
12/31/79..	35,000	

4-10-A

(c) Accounts Receivable,		
control, balance...........	6,025	

4-11-A

Net Earnings.................	36,830	
Retained Earnings, 12/31/79....	71,920	

4-1-B
(a) Annual rate of interest = 36%
(c) Annual rate of interest = 14.4%

4-2-B Example:

Purchases............ 6,686.10		
Accounts Payable.		6,686.10

4-3-B Net Cost in Each Bid:

E...........................		2,053.30
M...........................		2,160.32
W...........................		2,100.00

4-4-B Company S, example:

Accounts Receivable... 24,000		
Sales............		24,000

4-5-B Buyer's Books, example:

3/1 Purchases........ 2,493.75		
Accounts		
Payable....		2,493.75
Accounts Payable.. 124.00		
Cash.........		124.00

4-6-B

(a) Net Earnings.................	14,100	
(b) Total Assets.................	97,650	

4-7-B

(d) Net Earnings.................	30,240	
(e) Total Assets................	200,240	

4-8-B

(b) Net Earnings.................	26,250	
(c) Total Assets.................	344,750	

4-9-B

Sales........................	106,000	
Total Expenses...............	46,000	
Owners' Equity, 12/31/78......	30,000	
12/31/79......	35,000	

4-10-B

(c) Accounts Payable, control,		
balance...................	$	8,655

4-11-B Net Loss.................... 40,616
Retained Earnings, 12/31/79.... 19,204

Chapter 5

Problem

5-1-A Net Earnings, corrected:

(a) 1979.....................	$	135,000
1980.....................		127,000
1981.....................		148,000
(b) Total Net Earnings...........		410,000

5-2-A

(a) 3/11 Purchase Discount......		80
(b) 3/21 Discount Lost..........		100

5-3-A Ending Inventory:

(a) FIFO....................		3,630
(c) Weighted Average..........		3,567.50

5-4-A Gross Margin, 1979:

FIFO....................		2,500
LIFO....................		2,100

5-5-A Net Earnings under LIFO:

1979.....................		67,600
1981.....................		66,900

5-6-A Lower of Cost or Market:

(a) Total Inventory...........		44,200
(b) Individual Items...........		42,400

5-7-A

(b) Inventory, April 30, 1980......		110,000

5-8-A

(b) Estimated Inventory, 7/31/79...		36,096

5-9-A Inventory, December 31, cost.. 48,000

5-10-A

(a) Correct Net Earnings, 1976.....		275,000
1978.....		360,000
(b) Errors, 1976:		
Inventory Understated......		40,000
Retained Earnings		
Understated.............		40,000

5-1-B Net Earnings, corrected:

(a) 1979.....................		123,400
1980.....................		120,000
1981.....................		113,200
(b) Total Net Earnings...........		356,600

5-2-B Gross Margin............... 18,400

5-3-B

(a) Ending Inventory:		
FIFO....................		4,000
Weighted Average..........		4,119.54

5-4-B

(a) Cost of Goods Sold:		
FIFO, 1979................		28,875
LIFO, 1979................		27,930

5-5-B

(a) Net Earnings under LIFO:		
1980.....................		1,022,000
(b) 1981.....................		1,014,000

5-6-B

(b) Lower of Cost or Market,		
individual.................		11,800
(c) Net Earnings, $150 less		

5-7-B

(b) Net Earnings, first quarter.....		68,000
second quarter...		75,000

5-8-B

(a) 6/15 Purchase Discount......		200
(b) 6/12 Discount Lost..........		210

5-9-B Inventory, June 30, cost....... 13,600

5-10-B

(a) Correct Net Earnings, 1976....		18,400
1978....		99,000
(b) Errors, 1976:		
Inventory and Retained		
Earnings Overstated......		20,000

FINANCIAL ACCOUNTING, Fourth edition

Edwards, Hermanson, and Salmonson

CHECK FIGURES

Chapter 1

Problem			
1-1-A	Total Assets.................	$	21,500
1-2-A	Assets after Transactions:		
	Cash.....................		9,640
	Accounts Receivable........		3,600
	Equipment.................		32,000
1-3-A	Total Cash Provided..........		46,000
	Total Cash Applied...........		36,360
1-4-A	Net Earnings.................		9,640
1-5-A	Net Earnings.................		192,600
1-6-A			
(b)	Net Earnings.................		8,120
(c)	Retained Earnings, 10/31/79....		20,120
(d)	Total Assets.................		64,400
1-7-A	Cash: $10,000 + $12,000 (cash from customers — $8,000 (salaries) — $2,000 (payment of liabilities) — $1,000 (dividends) = $11,000		
1-1-B	Total Assets.................		57,465
1-2-B	Assets after Transactions:		
	Cash.....................		9,470
	Accounts Receivable........		230
	Equipment.................		11,550
1-3-B	Total Cash Provided..........		59,265
	Total Cash Applied...........		49,600
1-4-B	Net Loss....................		2,000
1-5-B			
(a)	Net Earnings.................		4,450
(b)	Retained Earnings, 6/30/79....		18,600
(c)	Total Assets................		48,000
1-6-B			
(a)	Net Earnings.................		40,000
(b)	Retained Earnings, 5/31/79....		104,000
(c)	Total Assets................		274,000
1-7-B			
(b)	Cash from Operations........		2,000

Chapter 2

Problem			
2-1-A			
(a)	Cash......................	$	33,500
(b)	Total Debits.................		48,225
2-2-A			
(a)	Cash......................		2,400
(b)	Total Debits.................		72,250
2-3-A	Example:		
	Cash.................. 40,000		
	Capital Stock......		40,000
	Issued capital stock for cash.		
2-4-A			
(b)	Net Earnings.................	$	10,400
(c)	Retained Earnings, 6/30/79....		33,100
(d)	Total Assets.................		68,500
2-5-A			
(c)	Cash Balance................		16,480
(d)	Total Debits.................		72,755
2-6-A			
(d)	Total Debits.................		478,800
(f)	Net Earnings.................		37,980
(h)	Total Assets................		138,780
2-1-B			
(a)	Total Cash.................		19,300
(b)	Total Debits.................		30,200

2-2-B			
(a)	Total Cash..................	$	3,800
(b)	Total Debits................		8,750
2-3-B	Example:		
	Cash.................. 60,000		
	Capital Stock......		60,000
	Issued capital stock for cash.		
2-4-B			
(b)	Net Earnings.................		7,300
(c)	Retained Earnings, 12/31/79....		8,400
(d)	Total Assets.................		52,400
2-5-B			
(c)	Cash Balance.................		12,440
(d)	Total Debits.................		49,200
2-6-B			
(d)	Total Debits.................		571,860
(f)	Net Earnings.................		102,570
(h)	Total Assets.................		207,430

Chapter 3

Problem			
3-1-A	Case 1:		
(d)	Allowance for Depreciation....	$	24,000
(e)	Depreciation Expense.........		17,000
3-2-A	Example:		
	Insurance Expense...... 1,216		
	Unexpired Insurance		1,216
	Expired insurance since Sept. 1.		
3-3-A			
(b)	Unexpired Insurance, balance..		1,700
3-4-A			
(b)	Accounts Receivable, 9/30.....		92,000
3-5-A	Example:		
	Store Salaries Expense... 270		
	Accrued Stores Salaries Payable........		270
	To record salaries earned but not paid in 1978.		
3-6-A			
(c)	Net Increase in Earnings under Accrual Basis........		750
3-7-A	Net Earnings.................		36,830
	Retained Earnings, 12/31/78....		71,920
3-1-B	Case 1:		
(d)	Allowance for Depreciation....		176,000
(e)	Depreciation Expense.........		16,000
3-2-B	Example:		
	Insurance Expense...... 14,000		
	Unexpired Insurance		14,000
	To record insurance expired.		
3-3-B			
(b)	Prepaid Rent, balance.........		1,800
3-4-B	Net Earnings, 1977...........		18,225
	1978...........		121,375
3-5-B	Example:		
	Bad Debts Expense....... 925		
	Allowance for Doubtful Accounts.		925
3-6-B			
(c)	Net Decrease in Net Earnings under Accrual Basis		
3-7-B	Net Loss....................		40,616
	Retained Earnings, 12/31/78....		19,204

Chapter 11—*Continued*

11-5-B
(a) Operating margin = 10%
     Turnover of operating
        assets = 2 times
     Earning power on operating
        assets = 20%
11-6-B 1979:
(a) Earnings per share = $13.70
(c) Rate of return = 28.97%

Chapter 12

Problem

12-1-A
(a) Working Capital, 1978 .... $ 248,000
(b) Total Financial Resources
        Provided 134,000
12-2-A
(a) Cash Flow from Operations.... 67,000
(b) Cash Balance, 4/30/79 47,000
12-3-A
(a) Increase in Working Capital ... 63,000
(b) Total Financial Resources
        Provided 183,800
12-4-A
(a) Cash Paid Out 100,000
(b) Cash Balance, 4/30/79 61,000
12-5-A
(a) Increase in Working Capital ... 98,000
(b) Total Financial Resources
        Provided 215,000
12-6-A
(a) Cash Applied to Operations.... 0
(b) Cash Balance, 12/31/79 48,000
12-7-A
(a) Decrease in Working Capital ... 10,000
(b) Total Financial Resources
        Provided 245,000
12-1-B
(a) Increase in Working Capital ... 45,000
(b) Total Financial Resources
        Provided 280,000
12-2-B
(a) Cash Paid Out 217,000
(b) Cash Balance, 9/30/79 78,000
12-3-B
(a) Increase in Working Capital ... 13,000
(b) Total Financial Resources
        Provided 177,000
12-4-B
(a) Cash Flow from Operations.... 40,000
(b) Cash Balance, 12/31/79 15,000
12-5-B
(a) Increase in Working Capital ... 131,200
(b) Total Financial Resources
        Provided 906,200
12-6-B
(a) Cash Paid Out 1,859,000
(b) Cash Balance, 6/30/79 64,000
12-7-B
(a) Decrease in Working Capital ... 15,000
(b) Total Financial Resources
        Provided 115,000

Chapter 13

Problem

13-1-A
(a) Completed Contract $1,400,000
(b) Percentage-of-Completion 4,600,000
13-3-A
(a) Point of Sale 100,000
(b) Installment Method 44,000
13-4-A
(1) Disagree

(4) Agree
(7) Agree
13-5-A Net Earnings, alternative
        methods .... $ 116,000
13-6-A Net Loss .... (80,000)
     Retained Earnings, 12/31/80.... 4,880,000
13-1-B
(a) Completed Contract 180,000
(b) Percentage-of-Completion 1,140,000
13-2-B
(1) B and F
(4) C and E
(7) F (and E and possibly D)
13-3-B
(a) Cash Basis Net Earnings 77,000
(b) Accrual Basis Net Earnings.... 103,000
13-4-B
(a) Net Earnings (before taxes).... 80,000
(b) Net Loss 5,000
13-5-B
(a) Corrected Net Earnings 97,000
(b) Corrected Assets 705,000
13-6-B
(a) Net Earnings 400,000
(b) Retained Earnings, 12/31/80.... 5,300,000

Chapter 14

Problem

14-1-A
(b) Investment Account Balance,
        12/31/80 .... $ 177,175
14-2-A Consolidated Total Assets 152,000
14-3-A
(a) Excess of Cost over
        Book Value 13,200
(b) Total Assets 233,600
14-4-A
(a) Excess of Cost over
        Book Value 20,000
(b) Total Assets 842,000
14-5-A Excess of Cost over
        Book Value 19,000
     Investment in Belcher,
        12/31/79 307,400
14-6-A
(a) Net Earnings 62,600
(b) Retained Earnings, 12/31/79.... 202,600
(c) Total Assets 863,600
14-7-A
(a) Investment in
        Boland Co 220,000
        Common Stock... 200,000
        Paid-In Capital
        —Pooling..... 20,000
(b) Notes Receivable 13,000
(c) Total Assets 782,000
14-1-B
(b) Investment Account Balance,
        12/31/81 536,435
14-2-B Consolidated Total Assets 259,000
14-3-B
(a) Equipment, net 42,000
(b) Total Assets 256,500
14-4-B
(a) Equipment, net 115,000
(b) Total Assets 755,000
14-5-B Depreciation Expense 21,638
     Investment in Holly, 12/31/79 .. 250,100
14-6-B
(a) Net Earnings 46,852
(b) Retained Earnings, 12/31/79.... 165,352
(c) Total Assets 781,352
14-7-B Net Earnings 215,000
     Retained Earnings, 12/31/79.... 390,000
     Total Assets 1,420,000

Chapter 6

Problem

6-1-A			
(a)	Adjusted Balance, 8/12/79	$	5,903
6-2-A	Adjusted Balance, 6/30/79		37,900
6-3-A	Adjusted Balance, 7/31/79		16,926
6-4-A			
(a)	Unadjusted Cash Balance,		
	8/13/79		28,670
(b)	Adjusted Balance, 8/13/79		28,663
6-5-A			
(b)	Corrected Cash Balance,		
	12/31/79		5,750.95
6-6-A			
(a)	Corrected Cash Balance,		
	4/30/79		44,365
(c)	Undeposited Receipts		5,070
(e)	Corrected Balance, 5/31/79		(7,510)
6-7-A			
(b)	Actual Balance, 6/30/79		745
(c)	Corrected Balance, 6/30/79		745
6-9-A			
(a)	12/31 Realized Loss		560
6-10-A	Example:		
	Petty Cash ... 500		
	Cash		500
	To establish petty cash fund.		
6-11-A	Total, Vouchers Payable....Cr.		34,086
6-1-B			
(a)	Adjusted Balance, 4/14/79		11,207
6-2-B	Adjusted Balance, 7/31		28,501.86
6-3-B	Adjusted Balance, 7/31/79		23,167
6-4-B			
(a)	Adjusted Balance, 3/31/79		13,346
6-5-B			
(a)	Adjusted Balance, 5/31/79		10,330
6-6-B			
(a)	Cash Balance, 5/21/79		43,760
(c)	Check Drawn by Treasurer		73,000
6-7-B	Example:		
	Payroll Checking		
	Account ... 1,000		
	Cash		1,000
6-8-B			
(a)	Adjusted Balance, 7/31/79		20,200
(c)	Cash Disbursements		39,480
6-9-B			
(a)	11/2 Gain on Sale		1,602
6-10-B			
(b)	12/31 Realized Loss		3,850
6-11-B	Example:		
	Petty Cash ... 400		
	Cash		400
	To establish petty cash fund.		
6-12-B	Total, Vouchers Payable....Cr.		64,774

Chapter 7

Problem

7-1-A			
(a)	Bad Debts Expense	$	22,000
7-2-A			
(a)	Required Allowance		3,794
7-3-A			
(a)	Maturity Date, 10/22		
(c)	Discount to Maturity Date,		
	60 days		
(e)	Cash Proceeds		30,135
7-4-A			
(a)	Interest		72.45
(c)	Interest		4.17
(e)	Interest		30.00
7-5-A	Example:		
	Cash ... 11,800		
	Notes Payable—		
	Discount ... 200		
	Notes Payable		12,000

7-6-A			
(a)	Employees' FICA Tax	$	15,420.60
(b)	Federal Unemployment Tax		1,512.00
7-7-A			
(b)	Employer's FICA Tax		579.15
(c)	State Unemployment Tax		267.30
7-8-A			
(a)	Taxable Income		83,800
(c)	Federal Income Tax Expense		18,794
7-1-B	Example:		
	Bad Debts Expense ... 9,000		
	Allowance for		
	Doubtful Accounts		9,000
7-2-B			
(a)	Amount Uncollectible		3,095.50
7-3-B			
(a)	Maturity Value		6,160
(c)	Discount		92.40
7-4-B	Example:		
	Notes Payable—		
	Discount ... 100		
	Cash ... 9,900		
	Notes Payable		10,000
7-5-B	Example:		
	Cash ... 20,661.33		
	Interest Revenue		661.33
	Notes Receivable		
	Discounted		20,000
7-6-B			
(a)	Taxable Income		217,600
(b)	Total Tax		93,648
7-7-B			
(a)	Employer's FICA Tax		27,202.50
(b)	State Unemployment Tax		8,100
7-8-B			
(a)	FICA Tax Liability		2,293.20
(c)	Federal Unemployment Tax		274.40
7-9-B			
(a)	Taxable Income, year 1		60,000
	year 3		80,000
(b)	Net Earnings after Taxes,		
	years 1-4		45,000

Chapter 8

Problem

8-1-A	Net Cost of Land	$	657,400
8-2-A			
(b)	Depreciation Expense		10,444.44
(c)	Depreciation Expense		12,500
8-3-A			
(a)	Double-Declining-Balance		16,200
(b)	Depreciation Expense		4,860
8-4-A	Machine C		26,900
8-5-A	Depreciation		6,200
8-6-A	Land		105,000
8-7-A			
(a)	New Auto		5,500
(b)	New Auto		5,200
8-8-A	6/30 Depletion Charge		410,000
	Depreciation Expense—		
	Equipment		201,000
8-9-A	Amortization Expense		8,000
8-1-B	Building		247,280
	Land		294,320
8-2-B			
(a)	Building, 12/31/80		455,300
8-3-B	Sedan No. 3		1,700
	Truck No. 5		3,360
8-4-B			
(a)	Loss on Replacement		6,000
(b)	Annual Depreciation		1,800
8-5-B	Example:		
	Rent Expense ... 5,600		
	Cash		5,600
8-6-B	Moving Van, new		20,000
8-7-B	Autos, new		7,846
	Loss on Exchange		100

8-8-B
(a) Depletion, 1979.............. $ 245,000
(b) (4) Units of Production........ 42,000
8-9-B 12/31/79 Amortization........ 2,450
12/31/80 Amortization........ 3,700

Chapter 9

Problem

9-1-A
(a) 12/1 Accrued Bond
Interest
Payable....... Cr. $ 18,750
12/31 Accrued Bond
Interest
Payable....... Cr. 3,750
(b) 12/1 Accrued Interest
Receivable..... Dr. 3,750
12/31 Accrued Interest
Receivable.... Dr. 750
9-2-A 1/1/80 Bond Interest Expense
(Laundon)......... 4,750
1/1/80 Bond Interest
Expense (Mann).... 4,250
9-3-A 12/31/79 Bond Interest
Expense....... Dr. 4,500
9/30/80 Sinking Fund.... Dr. 20,900
3/31/81 Bond Interest
Expense....... Dr. 4,050
8/1/81 Gain on
Redemption... Cr. 50
9-4-A 9/1/79 Cash (Dahlberg).. Dr. 207,720
Premium........ Cr. 4,720
3/31/80 Premium........ Dr. 280
12/1/79 Cash (Lauer)..... Dr. 199,766.67
Discount........ Dr. 6,900.00
Discount........ Cr. 240.00
9-5-A 9/1/79 Investment in
Bonds
(Dahlberg)..... Dr. 102,360
12/1/79 Investment in
Bonds (Lauer).. Dr. 96,550
3/31/80 Investment in
Bonds
(Dahlberg)..... Cr. 140
3/31/80 Investment in
Bonds (Lauer).. Dr. 120
9-6-A 9/1/79 Accrued Bond
Interest
Payable....... Cr. 1,500
2/1/80 Premium on
Bonds
Payable....... Cr. 2,260
9-7-A 6/30/79 Bond Interest
Expense....... Dr. 43,750
1/1/84 Loss on Bond
Redemption... Dr. 5,000
9-8-A
(a) 9/30/84 Interest Expense.. Dr. 4,050
9-9-A
(a) Cash Received (Johnston)...... 123,114.79
(c) Interest Expense
(Johnston)............. Dr. 3,693.44
9-10-A 7/1/79 Investment in
Bonds......... Dr. 12,311.48
1/1/80 Interest Revenue.. Cr. 369.34
6/30/80 Accrued Interest
Receivable.... Dr. 400.00
9-11-A 1/1/79 Equipment........... Dr. 337,950
12/31/79 Interest Expense...... 28,795.00
Depreciation Expense. 22,530
9-1-B
(a) 6/1/79 Accrued Bond
Interest
Payable....... Cr. 12,000
4/1/80 Accrued Bond
Interest
Payable....... Dr. 35,920

(b) 6/1/79 Accrued Bond
Interest
Receivable..... Dr. $ 4,000
9/30/79 Interest Revenue.. Cr. 8,000
9-2-B 12/31/79 Bond Interest
Expense
(Yates)........ Dr. 8,200
12/31/79 Bond Interest
Expense
(Wyatt)....... Dr. 7,200
9-3-B 12/31/79 Bond Interest
Expense....... Dr. 6,000
6/30/80 Sinking Fund.... Dr. 10,600
12/31/80 Bond Interest
Expense....... Dr. 5,400
6/1/81 Gain on Bond
Redemption... Cr. 50
9-4-B 12/1/79 Discount on
Bonds Payable
(Wright)....... Dr. 6,960
Accrued Bond
Interest
Payable....... Cr. 6,000
3/31/80 Interest Expense
(Wright)....... Dr. 240
9-5-B 8/1/79 Accrued Interest
Receivable,
Armstrong
bonds......... Dr. 150
1/1/80 Interest Revenue,
Armstrong
bonds......... Cr. 750
3/31/80 Investment in
Bonds
(Armstrong)... Cr. 64
9-6-B 8/1/79 Premium on
Bonds Payable. Cr. 3,570
Accrued Bond Interest
Payable.......... 750
3/1/80 Discount on
Bonds Payable. Dr. 2,240
6/30/80 Net Interest
Expense.......... 7,250
9-7-B 7/1/79 Premium on
Bonds Payable. Dr. 150
1/1/84 Loss on Bond
Redemption... Dr. 200
Premium on
Bonds Payable. Dr. 1,800
9-8-B 7/1/84 Bonds Payable... Dr. 40,000
9/30/84 Bond Interest
Expense......... Dr. 3,200
9-9-B
(a) Whitley, Price received........ 90,103.61
(b) Discount on Bonds
Payable.............. Dr. 9,896.39
(c) Interest Expense........... Dr. 3,604.14
9-10-B 10/1/79 Investment in
Bonds......... Dr. 9,010.36
4/1/80 Interest Revenue.. Cr. 360.41
9/30/80 Investment in
Bonds......... Dr. 10.83
9-11-B Equipment............... Dr. 640,500
Depreciation Expense..... Dr. 51,240

Chapter 10

Problem

10-1-A
(a) 7/7/79 Subscriptions
Receivable—
Common...... Dr. $ 54,000
Common Stock
Subscribed..... Cr. 40,000
(b) 7/31/79 Common Stock
Subscribed..... Dr. 60,000
Common Stock... Cr. 60,000

10-2-A

(a)	Total Assets.................		$	54,000
	Paid-In Capital in Excess			
	of Par....................			24,000
(c)	Common Stock, subscribed			
	but not issued..............			54,000

10-3-A

(a)	7/1/79	Subscriptions		
		Receivable—		
		Common......	Dr.	210,000
	7/10/79	Subscriptions		
		Receivable—		
		Common......	Dr.	96,000
	7/11/79	Land............	Dr.	64,000
	9/1/79	Paid-In Capital in		
		Excess of Stated		
		Value—		
		Common......	Cr.	250,000

10-4-A Part 1.

(a)	1975	Preferred...............	8,000
		Common...............	89,000
	1978	Preferred...............	12,000
		Common...............	10,000
(b)	1977	Preferred...............	4,000
		Common...............	0

Part 2.

(a)	Preferred....................	210,000
	Common....................	270,000
(b)	Preferred....................	160,000
	Common....................	320,000

10-5-A	6/30/79	Retained Earnings		
		(or Dividends)..	Dr.	60,000
		Stock Dividend		
		Payable.......	Cr.	60,000
	7/31/79	Dividends		
		Payable.......	Dr.	60,000
10-6-A	1/3/79	Building.........	Dr.	400
	8/4/79	Reserve for Plant		
		Expansion.....	Dr.	200,000
		Paid-In Capital—		
		Stock		
		Dividend......	Cr.	10,000
10-7-A	Total Stockholders' Equity.....			2,712,000

10-8-A

(b)	Retained Earnings,	
	unappropriated balance,	
	12/31/79..................	181,080
(c)	Total Stockholders' Equity.....	928,535

10-9-A

(b)	Net Earnings.................	36,800
(c)	Total Assets.................	240,800

10-10-A

(b)	Capital Accounts, 12/31/79:	
	Slim......................	47,000
	Fat......................	49,000

10-11-A

(b)	Net Earnings.................	12,790
(c)	Capital Accounts, 12/31/79:	
	Salt......................	22,295
	Pepper....................	38,995

10-1-B

(a)	1/5/79	Common Stock		
		Subscribed.....	Cr.	26,000
	5/1/79	Subscriptions		
		Receivable		
		—Common....	Dr.	10,500
(b)	Total Assets.................			47,000

10-2-B

(a)	Paid-In Capital in Excess of	
	Stated Value:	
	Preferred..................	198,000
	Common..................	312,000
(b)	Dividends: Preferred..........	24,000
	Common..........	26,000

10-3-B

	Total Assets..................	455,000
	Retained Earnings............	43,000

10-4-B

(b)	Total Stockholders' Equity.....	1,607,000

(c)	6/30/83	$5 Cumulative			
		Preferred			
		Stock........	Dr.	$	100,000
10-5-B	12/31/74	Retained			
		Earnings......	Dr.		300,000
	1/2/77	Land............	Dr.		125,000
	3/10/79	Reserve for Plant			
		Expansion.....	Dr.		1,500,000

10-6-B

	Retained Earnings,	
	unappropriated balance,	
	12/31/79..................	704,000

10-7-B	8/4/79	Retained Earnings		
		(or Dividends) .	Dr.	2,500
	11/16/79	Paid-In Capital		
		—Stock		
		Dividend......	Cr.	3,400

10-8-B

(a)	(1) Treasury Stock........	Dr.	30,000
	(3) Dividends Payable—		
	Preferred..............	Cr.	1,750
(b)	Total Stockholders' Equity.....		666,250

10-9-B

(b)	Net Earnings.................	20,500
(c)	Total Assets.................	39,500

10-10-B

	Capital Accounts, 12/31/79:	
	He.......................	25,000
	She......................	17,000

10-11-B

(b)	Net Earnings.................	46,600
(c)	Capital Accounts, 6/30/79:	
	Pickle.....................	41,420
	Onion.....................	35,180
(d)	Total Assets.................	137,600

Chapter 11

Problem

11-1-A

(a)	Working Capital, 1980........	$	272,600
(c)	Acid test ratio, 1980 = 1.53:1		

11-2-A

	1.	2.
(a)	Increased	Increased
(e)	Decreased	Decreased
(k)	Unaffected	Increased

11-3-A

(d)	1980, 3.7:1
(e)	1980, 2.8:1
(f)	1980, 73.68%

11-4-A

(a)	Current ratio = 4.53:1
(e)	Earnings per share = $4.35
(i)	Turnover of total assets =
	.72 times

11-5-A Company 1:

(a)	Operating margin = 9.1%
	Turnover of operating
	assets = 1.47 times
	Earning power on operating
	assets = 13.38%

11-6-A 1979:

(a)	Earnings per share = $4.17
(c)	Rate of return = 4.8%

11-1-B

(a)	Working Capital, 1979........	$1,069,500
(c)	Acid test ratio, 1979 = 2:1	

11-2-B

	1.	2.
(a)	Unaffected	Decreased
(e)	Decreased	Decreased
(k)	Unaffected	Unaffected

11-3-B

(d)	1979, 2.48:1
(e)	1979, 1.44:1
(f)	1979, 71.28%

11-4-B

(a)	Current ratio = 3.92:1
(e)	Earnings per share = $6.82
(i)	Turnover of total assets =
	.37 times

Solutions to student review quizzes

Following are the solutions to the Student Review Quizzes contained at the end of each chapter. It is assumed that before you check the solutions for a particular chapter you will have already answered the questions in the quiz. So that you will have a permanent record of your responses, you should have recorded them on the answer sheet provided in the *Work Papers* to this volume or on a separate sheet of paper.

Chapter 1

1 e Since Assets = Liabilities + Stockholders' Equity, it must also be true that Stockholders' Equity is equal to Assets less Liabilities as shown below:

$$A = L + SE, \text{ so } A - L = SE$$

2 c Delivery equipment is an asset. Therefore, assets would be increased by $4,000. Since no payment has been made as yet, liabilities are also increased by $4,000. There is no effect on stockholders' equity.

3 a Revenue is properly defined as the total flow of products or services delivered to or performed for customers by an entity. The difference between selling price and cost is called the margin or markup. Revenue represents an element which tends to *increase* stockholders' equity. Net earnings are calculated by deducting expenses from revenues.

4 b The advertising services were received during the month and were used in securing revenue from customers.

Since the services were not paid for, a liability must be increased for the debt owed. Since the services were used up during the month, their cost should be shown as an expense. And expenses tend to offset the increase in retained earnings brought about by the recording of revenues as increases in retained earnings. Actually, it is only the excess of revenues over expenses which increases retained earnings.

5 c Collecting accounts receivable reduces the amount of these accounts still outstanding. Cash is increased by the same amount as the decrease in accounts receivable. Since both of these are assets, response **(c)** correctly describes the effect.

6 e The changes in assets and liabilities which occurred during the period of operation would have to be determined by comparing the statements of financial position prepared at the beginning and end of the period. The earnings statement would not give this information.

7 b The earnings for 1979 would be included in the total shown for retained earnings on the statement of financial position dated December 31, 1979. Also included in the total would be the cumulative earnings in past years less amounts paid out in dividends during the life of the firm.

8 f Net earnings appear as the last figure on the earnings statement. They also appear as an addition to beginning retained earnings (in arriving at ending

711

retained earnings) on the statement of retained earnings.

The account Retained Earnings appears as the last figure on the statement of retained earnings. It also appears on the statement of financial position as part of the stockholders' equity.

9 c Although such activity may be undertaken by a CPA as part of the CPA's management advisory services, executive recruitment is not an accounting function. All of the others involve financial information and are regularly engaged in by accountants.

10 c Generally, the right to express an opinion attesting to the fairness of published financial information is restricted by law to CPAs (and a few other public accountants in some states). All of the other indicated activities are regularly undertaken by accountants and others who are not CPAs. Many individuals offer their services in preparing tax returns; management consulting firms render management advisory services; many large companies have internal audit staffs; and the preparation of budgets is regularly undertaken by non-CPA accountants in private business.

11 d While a valuable part of the overall management of resources, reporting on the outcome of a decision is not part of the decision-making process.

12 e Since all of the statements are true, this is the best answer.

13 e Since all of the statements are true, this is the best answer.

14 a Since financial accounting information generally relates to the entity as a whole and is historical in nature, it is not likely to be useful or relevant in this type of decision. Note that all of the other types of decisions listed require information relating to an entity as a whole.

15 a The change in the Retained Earnings account is usually caused by the addition of net earnings and the deduction of dividends. It is not the primary purpose of the statement of changes in financial position to report such information.

Chapter 2

1 b Debits are entries on the left side of an account. Since assets and expenses normally have a balance on the left side, debits increase their balances. Liabilities, revenue, and stockholders' equity accounts normally have balances on the right side. Therefore, debits decrease their balances.

2 c Revenues, not expenses, operate to bring about an increase in the Retained Earnings account. Expenses normally have debit balances and represent the costs of producing revenue in an accounting period. They are reported in the earnings statement.

3 b An asset must be debited, since the company has a right to receive cash in the future for services already performed. It does not have a written promise from customers to pay a sum certain as of a particular date. Therefore, a debit to Cash or Notes Receivable is incorrect. Rights to receive an amount from customers are called Accounts Receivable, and this account should be debited (increased). The credit should be to Service Revenue. This indicates that revenue has been earned by performing services for customers and thus is the source of the accounts receivable.

4 a The receipt of the bill (or invoice as it is often referred to) indicates that the recipient owes the vendor for something already delivered or for a service performed. Since the service performed was advertising and it is billed only after performance, an expense has been incurred and an expense account must be debited, in this case Advertising Expense.

Since the bill has not yet been paid, the liability for future payment must also be recognized and recorded. The Accounts Payable account is the liability which should be increased. To increase a liability account, the account must be credited.

5 c Since cash was received, it is necessary to debit Cash for $825. To increase an asset account, the account must be debited.

Customers are paying amounts they owe. These amounts have been carried as accounts receivable. When the amounts are paid, the reduction in the asset accounts receivable is recorded by crediting that account. To reduce an asset account, that account must be credited. Notes receivable would be an incorrect debit unless these customers had signed written promises to pay a particular amount as of a given date. This is not normally required of customers.

6 d Two types of assets have been purchased. Therefore, this transaction requires that a compound entry (one with more than one debit or credit) be made. Office Machines should be debited (to show an increase in an asset) for the amount of the electric calculator. Office Furniture and Fixtures should be debited for the cost of the new typists' chairs.

Since the items were purchased on open account (meaning that cash was not involved nor was a note signed), the credit must be to Accounts Payable.

7 b In this transaction cash was received and revenue was earned. To record the receipt of cash (the increase of an asset), the Cash account must be debited. To record the earning of revenue, a revenue account must be credited. The account title Service Revenue adequately describes the revenue earned.

8 e In this transaction an expense has been incurred and paid for. To increase an expense account, it must be debited. The account title Salary Expense adequately describes the expense which should be debited. Since cash was given up, Cash must be credited. (To reduce an asset account, it must be credited.)

9 c A trial balance in balance fails to prove that no errors of any kind have been made in the accounts. For instance, if a debit were made to the wrong account, the trial balance would not aid in discovering the error. Total debits would still be equal to total credits.

10 e A ledger is a collection of all accounts, including both statement of financial position accounts and earnings statement accounts. Response (a) more nearly describes a journal. Response (d) describes a trial balance.

11 d For every entry that is made, total debits must equal total credits. Unless this is done, the ledger, the trial

balance, and the statement of financial position will be out of balance. The double-entry system is based on an equality of debits and credits.

12 d Cross-indexing accomplishes all of these things (**a, b,** and **c**). In the journal it shows the account to which an amount was posted. In the ledger it shows the journal source of all amounts entered. This provides a link between the journal and the ledger accounts, facilitates finding errors, and reduces the likelihood of errors in posting.

13 c Posting is the act of recording amounts in the ledger accounts as indicated in the journal. It is sometimes referred to as a transfer of amounts from the journal to the ledger. Response (e) would be correct if it said "from the journal to the ledger."

14 c The totals of all the debits and all the credits in the journal will be greater than the total debit and credit balances in the ledger if any account in the ledger has both a debit and a credit. For instance, if the Cash account had a debit of $10,000 and a credit of $8,000, it would have a debit balance of only $2,000, since the credit is offset against the debit. In the journal the $10,000 debit would be included in total debits and the $8,000 credit would be included in total credits.

Chapter 3

1 e An example of each situation is:

a Insurance Expense (an expense)
Unexpired Insurance (an asset)

To transfer the expired portion of the asset, unexpired insurance, from the asset account to an expense account.

b Wages Expense (an expense)
Accrued Wages Payable (a liability)

To record wages earned by employees but not yet paid. The expense and liability accounts are both increased.

c Rental Payments Received in Advance (a liability)
Rent Revenue (a revenue)

To transfer the portion of rent which has been earned from a liability account to a revenue account.

d Accrued Interest Receivable (an asset)
Interest Revenue (a revenue)

713

To record interest that has been earned but not yet received. The asset and revenue accounts are both increased.

2 b The information given tells you that 5 percent of the accounts receivable are estimated to be uncollectible. Thus, the amount of the entry is $340 (5 percent of $6,800). The amount must be charged to an expense account. In this manner, an expense is recognized and an asset reduced.

3 c Two things are missing from the accounts—they do not show the asset, the right to receive interest to be received later, and the revenue earned, the interest. Assets are increased by debits and revenues are increased by credits. Thus, entry **(c)** is correct.

4 a The policy is for three years and costs $900. The expense applicable to each year is one third of the $900, or $300. Since only one half of the first year of the policy falls within the current accounting year of the company, the amount of the entry is $150. The entry must transfer $150 of the asset, unexpired insurance, to the expense, insurance expense. To do so, the expense must be debited and the asset credited.

5 a An expense and a liability must be increased. Both responses **(a)** and **(d)** accomplish this. The liability increased in **(d)** is accounts payable, which is usually used to show only amounts owed to trade creditors. Since the liability increased is for amounts owed to employees, response **(a)** is preferable.

6 d Computation of amount:

Cost	$3,400
Less estimated salvage value	200
Amount to Be Depreciated	$3,200

$$\text{Depreciation per year} = \frac{\$3,200}{4} = \$800.$$

October 1 to December 31 is only one fourth of a year, so the current amount of the entry is $800/4, or $200. An expense account, Depreciation Expense—Office Furniture, must be debited (increased) and the contra asset account, Allowance for Depreciation—Office Equipment, must also be increased (credited). The latter account will be shown on the statement of financial position as a deduction from the asset, Office Equipment. Response **(e)** has the debit and credit reversed.

7 d The liability accrued wages payable would be understated because of the failure to include the debt owed to employees. The stockholders' equity of the company would be overstated because retained earnings would be overstated (as the result of an understatement of wages expense).

8 e Under the accrual basis of accounting, the timing of cash receipts is unimportant. Revenue recognition does not depend on the receipt of cash, nor does expense recognition depend on cash payment.

9 b and e No bad debts expense would ever appear if revenues were not recorded until cash is received. Recording service revenue on an accrual basis necessitates recording bad debts expense on an accrual basis. Entry **(e)** is also required under accrual accounting to bring about proper matching of expenses and revenues.

10 c Expenses are closed by debiting the Expense and Revenue Summary account and crediting the expense account (Rent Expense in this instance). Items **(b)**, **(d)**, and **(e)** are all statement of financial position accounts and are not closed. Item **(a)** is a revenue account and is closed by crediting the Expense and Revenue Summary account and debiting Service Revenue.

11 d Statement of financial position accounts are never closed (although it is possible that they may have zero balances for other reasons). As a result of closing, all expense and revenue accounts and the Expense and Revenue Summary account always are reduced to zero balances.

12 e The work sheet is an informal schedule. The accounting process could (although not as easily) be completed without preparing a work sheet. The work sheet may contain as many columns as the accountant wishes to use. The more conventional work sheets contain 8, 10, or 12 columns, depending on whether they include or exclude columns entitled Adjusted Trial Balance and Statement of Retained Earnings. It would be helpful to include explanations of each adjustment at the bottom of the work sheet, but it is not required.

13 d Depreciation is recorded by an entry that debits Depreciation Expense and credits the Allowance for Depreciation—Store Fixtures for $400. Note that the credit is to the allowance account rather than to the Store Fixtures account. This asset account will consequently continue to show a $4,000 balance throughout the period and throughout the life of the fixtures. But because the allowance is increased by periodic depreciation, the net book value of the fixtures decreases. So it is the allowance that changes, not the Store Fixtures account, with the result that the Statement of Financial Position debit column in the work sheet shows a $4,000 amount for store fixtures.

14 a The Supplies on Hand account is an asset. The adjustment for supplies used during the month is:

Supplies Expense	290	
Supplies on Hand		290

The original debit balance of $315 less the credit of $290 leaves a balance of $25 to be carried to the statement of financial position debit column.

15 d By reversing the effects of the adjusting entry to which it relates, it makes easier the subsequent entry to record the receipt or payment of cash relating to that item. See Appendix B for an example.

Chapter 4

1 e All of the arguments or reasons stated are deemed to support recording revenue at the time of the making of a sale.

2 d They are usually debited, not credited, to a Sales Discounts account when taken.

3 a The amount is computed as $2,000 - (.25 \times \$2,000) = \$1,500$; $\$1,500 - (.20 \times \$1,500) = \$1,200$; and $\$1,200 - (.10 \times \$1,200) = \$1,080$.

4

Accounts Payable	1,080.00	
Purchase Discounts		21.60
Cash		1,058.40

5 Three percent for 20 days is the equivalent of 54 percent per year: $.03 \times (360/20)$. Savings are equal to $150 (.03 \times \$5,000) - \$21.56 (\$4,850 \times .08 \times 20/360)$, or $128.44.

6 c Transportation-In is an addition to the cost of purchases rather than a reduction from this cost. All of the other accounts are contra or reduction accounts.

7 b The major disadvantage of periodic inventory procedure is that it fails to provide an inventory amount in the books against which the cost of a physical inventory can be compared. Thus, the element of control is missing.

8 e The Bunetta Company paid the freight bill merely as a convenience for the seller. The freight charge is the responsibility of the seller, since the goods were shipped f.o.b. destination.

9 a Trade discounts are granted regardless of whether an invoice is paid within the period specified in order to claim a cash discount.

10 e If legal title has passed, a sale has been made and the goods are the property of the buyer even though still in the seller's possession. Since they are not owned by the seller, they cannot be included in inventory.

11 All of the statements are correct. Net sales are $15,000 ($15,900 - $600 - $300). Net purchases are $9,100 ($9,000 + $700 - $400 - $200). Cost of goods available for sale is $14,100 ($9,100, net cost of purchases, plus $5,000, beginning inventory). Cost of goods sold is $11,100 ($14,100, cost of goods available for sale, less $3,000, ending inventory). Gross margin is $3,900 ($15,000, net sales, less $11,100, cost of goods sold).

12 d This entry correctly reduces the Accounts Payable account balance to zero, records the cash discount of $40 taken in the Purchase Discounts account, and records the decrease in the Cash account of $1,960.

13 a The company was entitled to, and took, a discount of $40 (.01 × $4,000), which meant that it paid $3,960. Since the goods were shipped f.o.b. shipping point, the transportation charges are the responsibility of the buyer.

14 a Ending inventory is a deduction from total goods available for sale to arrive at the cost of goods sold. If it is overstated, cost of goods sold will be understated. Cost of goods sold is a deduction from revenues in arriving at net earnings. If it is understated, net earnings will be overstated.

In reference to response (e), gross margin is equal to sales revenues less cost of goods sold. If cost of goods sold is understated, gross margin will be overstated rather than understated.

15 d Response (a) would be correct if it had indicated that transportation-in was added rather than subtracted. Response (b) is incorrect for two reasons. Transportation-in should be added rather than deducted. Ending inventory should be deducted rather than added. Response (c) is incorrect because purchase returns and allowances should be deducted rather than added in determining the cost of the goods sold.

16 d The use of special journals facilitates the use of accounting machines.

17 c The general journal is used to record all entries which are not suited to the other journals. Adjusting and closing entries generally are not suited to the design of the special journals.

18
  1 c
  2 e
  3 d
  4 a
  5 b
  6 b
  7 e
  8 e (notation only)
  9 b
  10 e
  11 d
  12 e
  13 No entry.
  14 d

19 b The individual accounts supporting a controlling account appear in a subsidiary ledger.

20 b The totals of Sundry columns are never posted. Only the individual items in the columns are posted.

21 d and f The beginning inventory must be credited in the adjustments credit column in order to transfer it to the Cost of Goods Sold expense account. The ending inventory is entered in the Adjustments debit column, since it is credited to the Cost of Goods Sold expense account. The ending inventory must also appear in the Statement of Financial Position debit column, since it is an asset.

Chapter 5

1 b The cost of goods sold is:

Inventory, January 1	$ 4,000
Purchases	$14,000
Less: Returns and allowances, $800, and discounts, $150	950
	$13,050
Add: Transportation-in	350
	$13,400
Cost of goods available for sale	$17,400
Less: Inventory, December 31	5,600
Cost of Goods Sold	$11,800

2 c All of the other costs incurred are necessary to having the goods in the condition and location desired for sale and, therefore, should be inventoried and matched against revenues secured upon sale.

3 a If the ending inventory is overstated, an excessive amount was deducted from the cost of the goods available for sale, leaving cost of goods sold understated. As cost of goods sold is an expense, expenses would be understated and the net earnings for the year would be overstated. The effect of overstating ending inventory in 1979 may be represented as follows:

  1979   Ending inventory overstated.
       Cost of goods sold understated.
       Net earnings overstated.
  1980   Beginning inventory overstated.
       Cost of goods sold overstated.
       Net earnings understated.

4 d Because taking discounts is considered a matter of routine, failure to take discounts is best looked upon as a mark of inefficiency rather than as part of the cost of the merchandise purchased.

5 b Since the inventory of 300 units is less than the 1,200 units acquired at $4.50 each in the most recent purchase, the 300 units are all priced at $4.50.

6 c The inventory under the weighted-average method is the weighted average cost per unit multiplied by the number of units on hand. The Fifo method results in the very latest items being included in ending inventory.

7 Only **(b)** of the three statements is false. Under Lifo, the 1,100 units in inventory will be priced at $2; all remaining purchase costs will be charged to cost of goods sold. In this instance, cost of goods sold consists of 100 at $2, 800 at $2.50, and 400 at $2.75. The cost of the February 12 sale is 100 at $2 and 600 at $2.50 —a total of $1,700.

8 a Under Fifo the most recent costs are included in the ending inventory. The earliest costs are charged to cost of goods sold.

9 All of the statements are true. The method can be applied to total inventory or to individual items, so both **(a)** and **(b)** are true. One of the modifications of the general method is that if there is no decline in selling price, there should be no write-down to market as this serves only to increase the amount of net earnings on the sale. A further modification of the general rule is that goods should not be priced for inventory purposes at an amount in excess of their net realizable value, since this would entail inventorying losses.

10 c The method is generally not accurate enough to be used as the sole means of determining year-end inventories.

11 c The cost of the goods available for sale is $77,000. The cost of the goods sold is estimated as $63,000 ($90,000 less 30 percent of $90,000). Thus, the inventory is estimated at $14,000 ($77,000 less $63,000).

12 c The total cost of the goods available for sale is $388,000 ($28,000 + $360,000). This amount is related to the retail value of the goods, $485,000 ($35,000 + $450,000).

Chapter 6

1 c It is highly unlikely that the information needs of stockholders will include a more detailed classification of cash than that given top management. Stockholders generally will need information as to the total cash resources of a company in making their evaluation of the overall financial position of the company. Management must have information as to individual account balances and the locations where funds are held on deposit in order to provide sufficient cash to support normal operations and to prevent the accumulation of excessive amounts of idle cash.

2 c Time certificates of deposit are not cash and are not available for immediate disbursement.

3 e All of the procedures stated are desirable features in a system designed to make the misappropriation of cash difficult to perpetrate or, if perpetrated, difficult to conceal.

4 c The bank reconciliation statement accomplishes its stated purpose by reconciling both the balance per the bank statement and the balance per the ledger with the adjusted ledger balance for cash.

5 b Only those items which the bank has entered in error or has yet to record should be entered as additions to, or deductions from, the balance per the bank statement. Of those listed, only outstanding checks are yet to be recorded by the bank as deductions from the balance it carries in its records for the depositor.

6 b Of the items listed only two have not been recorded by the company: (1) the return of the N.S.F. check deposited and (2) the service charges deducted by the bank from the company's balance. Entry **(b)** correctly restores the balance in accounts receivable and recognizes the expense incurred.

7 e The correct answer is $2,785. The solution to the problem is derived in the following manner:

Balance per bank statement.............	$2,750
Add: Deposit in transit................	1,200
	$3,950
Less: Checks outstanding............	1,625
Adjusted Balance...........................	$2,325

This adjusted balance will be reached on the other side of the bank reconciliation statement by adding the $45 error and deducting the N.S.F. check of $500 and the bank service charges of $5. Therefore, the unadjusted beginning balance can be obtained by reversing the procedure and adding the last two items and deducting the first. Thus, $2,325 + $500 + $5 − $45 = $2,785.

8 c A certified check is one drawn by a depositor in a bank on the bank and given to the named payee. The bank certifies that funds will be available to honor the check when it is presented for payment, but the check is not actually drawn by the bank.

9 c Capital stock results in dividend revenue rather than interest revenue. All of the others could earn interest.

10 d When a company purchases a long-term obligation as a short-term investment, it runs the risk that when it must convert back to cash (before the maturity date) the market price will be depressed.

11 a Stock investments are recorded at cost of acquisition. The broker's commission is not an expense of this period but a cost which continues to render benefits as long as the stock is held. There is no need to segregate the amount paid for the stock over its par value, since it is cost, not par value, that is significant to the investor.

12 d The dividend declared should be recorded as revenue for the year 1979, since the stock was held during that period and the dividend becomes unquestionably the company's when the date of record passes with the company still owning the shares. No entry need be made for the stock dividend which is to be received, since it will not be recorded via a formal journal entry when actually received.

13 c Under the imprest method of handling a petty cash fund, a debit is entered in the Petty Cash account only when the fund is established or increased in size. The amount of any check issued to replenish the fund is charged to expense (and possibly other accounts). Obviously, since the fund is an asset, it would not be debited if the goal were to decrease its size.

14 b The total of the vouchers in the fund is $77 and this amount must be charged to the proper expense and revenue contra accounts. The fund is also short $3, and this shortage must be charged to an expense account, Cash Short and Over.

15 b The voucher system is designed to provide close control only over cash disbursements.

16 d It shows more than the total amount of outstanding liabilities for merchandise purchased. All liabilities which will require the payment of cash will be included at some time before payment is made. Various types of liabilities may be included at any point in time (for example, the principal payment on long-term bonds).

17 d Only after the quantity and quality of the goods have been verified is the voucher authorizing payment filed in the unpaid voucher file.

18 e Attention is focused only on the discounts lost rather than on the discounts taken. When a discount is missed, a new voucher must be prepared because the original voucher is for a smaller amount than would actually be due. The necessity for preparing a new voucher and the use of the Discounts Lost account bring to the attention of management those discounts which were missed—an example of management by exception.

Chapter 7

1 b This method of estimating uncollectible accounts is based on sales rather than a statement of financial position amount. Thus, estimates of uncollectible accounts are directly related to revenues and the best matching possible is obtained. If uncollectible accounts are charged off when they are found to be bad, then the bulk of these accounts would be written off in the period following the period of sale.

2 c The amount received should be debited to the Cash account and credited to Accounts Receivable in the usual fashion. Then part of the entry to write off the account should be reversed, to the extent of the cash received. Mr. Poole indicates a willingness to pay, but so far has shown the ability to pay only to the extent of $50.

3 e After writing off the account of Backus Corporation, the accounts receivable total $200,000 and the allowance has a debit balance of $1,500. Since it is to be adjusted to a credit balance of $4,000, the amount of the credit to the allowance must be $5,500, and this is the amount charged to bad debts expense.

4 e When the collection of a non-trade receivable is in doubt, the receivable should not be shown in the current asset section of the statement of financial position. The information given suggests that collection is in doubt.

5 d The calculation is:

Life of note (days)		90
Days remaining in February, not counting the date of origin (28 − 15)	13	
March	31	
April	30	74
Days in May, counting the due date		16

The maturity date is May 16, 1979.

6 a The payee is the one who will receive payment. In this instance, the payee is Omsted Wholesalers. The note receivable and sales should each be recorded at the face value of the note.

7 b The Dishonored Notes Receivable account should be established at the total amount T. R. Baxter owes at the maturity date. This includes the face value of $400 plus interest of $10 ($400 × 10/100 × 90/360). The debit used by some accountants is to Accounts Receivable. This is a personal choice.

8 a

Notes Receivable	410	
Dishonored Notes Receivable		410
b Cash	410	
Dishonored Notes Receivable		410

9 d The effective rate of interest may be computed as follows:

$$\frac{\text{Discount}}{\text{Cash proceeds}} \times \frac{360}{60} = \text{Rate of interest}$$

$$\frac{\$270}{\$17,730} \times \frac{360}{60} = .0914$$

Thus, the effective rate is 9.14 percent; **(a), (b),** and **(c)** are all true.

10 a and b The discount period is 21 days, and the discount is computed on the maturity value of $304.50, not on the face value of $300. Thus, **(d)** should read: $304.50 × .10 × 21/360. Therefore, both **(c)** and **(d)** are false.

11 a The cash proceeds are computed as follows:

Face amount	$1,000.00
Interest, 9% for 60 days	15.00
Maturity value	$1,015.00
Discount of bank on $1,015, 10% for 60 days	16.92
Cash proceeds	$ 998.08

The difference between the cash proceeds and the face value plus accrued interest is the amount of the financing expense. In practice this would be debited to Interest Expense ($1,000.00 − $998.08 = $1.92). There was no accrued interest at the date of discount.

12 d The amount receivable from R. T. Johns includes the interest and protest fee ($3,060) and is debited to Dishonored Notes Receivable. The bank would deduct the maturity amount from the company's Cash account. The second entry is necessary to remove the note and the contingent liability from the records, since the note no longer exists as an asset and no contingent liability remains—it became an actual liability and was paid.

13 e All of the items may cause a difference.

14 Either **(c)** or **(e)**. If the employer does not choose to record his or her share of the F.I.C.A. tax liability at the time of payment, **(c)** is correct. If the employer does, **(e)** is correct.

15 c The figures are:

F.I.C.A. tax expense:

12 × $6,000 × .0585	$4,212	
4 × $16,500 × .0585		$3,861
Unemployment tax expense:		
12 × $6,000 × .034.........	2,448	
4 × $6,000 × .034.........		816
Total for 12 employees.......	$6,660	
Less: Total for 4		
employees	4,677	$4,677
Difference	$1,983	

Unemployment tax expense includes federal and state portions.

16 d The entry to be made reads:

Federal Income		
Tax Expense............	70,000	
Federal Income		
Taxes Payable ...		60,000
Deferred Federal		
Income Taxes		
Payable.............		10,000

To determine the amount of federal income tax expense chargeable to the year, the 50 percent rate should be applied to $140,000 of pretax earnings. The $10,000 of bond interest should be excluded because it will never be taxable.

Chapter 8

1 e In general, accountants subscribe to the idea of measuring earnings by matching revenue with the expenses incurred to secure that revenue. Thus, the purpose of depreciation accounting is to allocate the service potential of depreciable assets (measured in terms of cost) used to produce revenue to the period in which the revenue is recorded in the accounts.

2 d The cost of the land consists of the following items:

Cash payment	$30,000
Mortgage assumed	8,000
Property tax liability	
assumed	200
Legal fees	280
Removal of old structure	
and grading	5,400
Total Cost	$43,880

3 a The cost of disposing of an expired asset should not be considered a cost applicable to the future if the matching concept is to be applied. Such a cost is a cost of benefits already received. Because such costs can rarely be estimated

accurately and are often nominal in amount, they are usually ignored until incurred and then charged to expense. The cost of demolishing the old tenement building and the payments to the tenants of the building are costs incurred to place an asset in the condition necessary to operate it. The purpose of the allowance for depreciation is that of a temporary resting place for the credits to the asset indicating the expiration of service-rendering ability. Thus, the allowance is charged when the asset is retired. The cost of excavation must be incurred to get the building in operating condition (not the land).

4 d Interest is considered a cost of borrowing funds, not of acquiring assets. Thus, it is typically treated as a financial expense at the time it is incurred.

5 e Total cost of the machine is $12,000 − $240 + $250 + $590 = $12,600. The depreciation per unit of production is ($12,600 − $400) ÷ 100,000 = $0.122. The depreciation for the period then is 6,000 times $0.122, or $732.

6 d The accountant does not subscribe to the idea that a business can produce revenue simply by building a machine for its own use. Therefore, the depreciation charge for the first year under the double-declining-balance method is $11,700 times 40 percent, or $4,680. For the second year it is ($11,700 − $4,680) × 40 percent, or $2,808. Under the sum-of-the-years'-digits method, the depreciation for the first year is ($11,700 − $200) × 5/15, or $3,833. For the second year it is $11,500 × 4/15, or $3,067. Thus, **(a)** is true since $4,680 is greater than $3,833; **(b)** is true because $3,067 is greater than $2,808, and **(c)** is true − the depreciation for the year ended June 30, 1979, under the sum-of-the-years'-digits method is $3,833. Thus, **(d)** is the correct answer.

7 b Depreciation should be recorded on the equipment up to the date of sale. The straight-line method is being used, since $2,700/6 = $450 per year and $450 for four years equals $1,800. The amount for the two months in 1980 is 1/6 × $450, or $75. The depreciation accumulated to the date of sale is then $1,800 plus $75, or $1,875. The book value of the equipment at date of sale is $2,700 less $1,875, or $825. Since $850 was received, the equipment was sold at a gain of $25.

8 b The new truck should be recorded at the amount of cash paid plus the fair market value of the old truck. The amount of cash paid is $7,400 less $1,800, or $5,600, and the fair market value of the old truck is $1,500. Therefore, the new truck should be recorded at $7,100. The cost of the old truck is $6,400 (which must be removed from the accounts, as must the accumulated depreciation); its accumulated depreciation is $4,400, leaving a net book value of $2,000; and at time of trade it was worth $1,500, resulting in a loss on exchange of $500 which must be recognized.

9 b According to income tax regulations, the new typewriter will be carried in the accounts at the net book value of the old machine ($60) plus the amount of cash paid ($400).

10 a The amount of leasehold improvement expense chargeable to each year is $1,400 ($14,000/10 years). The annual rent expense is $15,000, consisting of $12,000 payable in cash and $3,000 from amortization of the advance payment ($30,000/10 years).

11 a The depletion cost per unit is $0.50 ($1,300,000/2,600,000), and since 300,000 tons were mined, the depletion to be recorded is $150,000.

12 c The cost of a patent should be allocated to the years in which it produces benefits. Thus, the cost of the patent ($180,000 + $2,000 + $8,000 = $190,000) should be charged to the five-year period of useful life at the rate of $38,000 per year.

13 e Statement **(a)** is false; payment for goodwill may be in other media than cash. Statement **(b)** is false; goodwill cannot be purchased separately. Statement **(c)** is false; goodwill must be amortized. Statement **(d)** is false; the existence of goodwill can be determined only with reference to the relative earnings of a business.

Chapter 9

1 a A bond sells in the market at a price less than face value when the rate of interest offered by the bonds is con-sidered by investors to be inadequate relative to the face value of the bonds (the amount paid if there is no premium or discount). Changing the price at which a bond sells is the market's way of changing the rate of interest actually earned on a bond, since an investor cannot change the rate in the face of the bond.

2 a The accrued interest payable is $30,000 ($1 million at 12 percent for three months). The amount of discount applicable to the period is $3,000 [($120,000 ÷ 10 years) × $1/4$]. Since the effect of issuing bonds at a discount is to increase the interest above the stated amount, the $3,000 must be added to the interest accrued to get the total expense for the period, $33,000.

3 e Cash must be debited for the $575,000 received. It is customary to carry bonds (notes, stocks, etc.) at their face value in a separate account. Thus, the bonds should be recorded in a separate account for their face value of $500,000. The remaining $75,000 is credited to a premium account, which in reality is an adjunct account to Bonds Payable. Together these accounts show the liability to the bondholders.

4 d Issuing bonds at a premium means that the rate of interest offered was higher than the going market rate for bonds of this type and quality. Thus, the total interest paid each period must be reduced by a part of the premium paid, because the premium paid represents the bondholders' purchase of a part of the interest payments. This part of the periodic payment is neither expense to the issuing company nor revenue to the bondholders.

5 d Of the $100,750 received, $2,000 is the amount of accrued interest for the period July 1 to September 1, 1979, which must have been collected by the company. Deducting this amount from $100,750 leaves $98,750 as the amount paid for the bonds and indicates issuance at a discount of $1,250.

6 b The amount of cash paid is 105 percent of the face value of the bonds redeemed, or $105,000 (plus accrued interest payable of $5,000). Since the face value of the bonds redeemed is $100,000, the loss on redemption is $5,000 plus any remaining discount, which in this instance is $1,500, computed as follows: original discount of $9,000 less $4,500 as the amount charged to the first 10 years of the 20 years of life of the bonds equals $4,500. Since one third of the bonds were retired, one third of the $4,500, or $1,500, must be written off at time of redemption.

7 e The correct answer is to debit Sinking Fund or Sinking Fund Trustee and credit Cash for $10,500. The entry to debit the Bonds Payable account and the Interest Expense or Accrued Bond Interest Payable account will be made after the trustee reports acquisition and cancellation of the bonds and payment of the interest.

8 a Cash is paid out to the extent of $75,000 to redeem $50,000 worth of bonds and to pay the $25,000 semiannual interest on all of the bonds ($500,000 × 0.10 × $\frac{1}{2}$ = $25,000).

9 a If for some reason a minor cash balance is left in the sinking fund, it is classified as a current asset if it will be used to redeem bonds classified as current liabilities. If not, it should be shown as part of the long-term assets, preferably in the investments section of the statement of financial position.

10 d Accrued interest purchased is $3,000 (.09 × $100,000 × $\frac{4}{12}$). Therefore, the bonds themselves were purchased for $99,000 (a discount of $1,000). The net price of the bonds is recorded in the Investment account of the purchaser.

11 c The present value of the promise to pay $100,000 in 40 periods at 2 percent is $100,000 times .45289042, or $45,289.04. The present value of the promise to pay $2,500 at the end of each of the next 40 periods at 2 percent is $2,500 times 27.35547924, or $68,388.70. These sums added together equal $113,677.74. It is customary to speak of interest rates as rates per year. Actually, the more accurate description of the yield rate, or effective rate of interest, on the bonds is 2 percent (per period) rather than 4 percent (which is understood to be per year). It is evident from the present values given that 2 percent per semiannual period (which means that interest is compounded semiannually) for 40 periods

is somewhat different than 4 percent per year (which means that interest is compounded annually) for 20 years.

12 c and e Some long-term leases are treated as rental agreements rather than as installment purchases. In the rental agreement type, the cash paid is debited to Rent Expense or Prepaid Rent as circumstances dictate. When pension benefits are paid by the company under an unfunded pension plan, the debit should be to Pension Plan Liability.

Chapter 10

1 b All of the other statements describe attributes of the corporation. But it is easier to transfer ownership because the ownership is represented by readily salable shares of stock.

2 c A common stockholder possesses all of the other rights listed but does not directly own the assets of the corporation, as these are owned by the corporation.

3 e Par value is a nominal and arbitrary amount printed on a stock certificate and has very little significance except possibly as an indicator of the amount of capital which must be legally maintained.

4 d This set of entries is correct because it reduces the Subscriptions Receivable account by the amount of cash received and also records the certificates which would be issued because subscribers making the payment have paid their subscription balances in full. Response (c) has the same effect but, technically, the cash received is in collection of the subscriptions receivable — the asset received when the stock was subscribed.

5 c The land should be recorded at its fair market value of $12,000. The assets received had a fair market value of $2,000 more than the par value of the shares issued, so Paid-In Capital in Excess of Par is recognized.

6 a Since the stock has a stated value of $20 per share, this amount should be carried in the Common Stock account for each share issued, a total of $800,000. The amount received in excess of stated value, $1,200,000, should be recorded in a Paid-In Capital in Excess of Stated Value account. The $2.0 million of cash received must, of course, be recorded in the Cash account.

7 b Since the stock is stated as being 6 percent preferred stock (noncumulative), the holders of this stock are entitled only to the basic preference rate applied to the par value of the stock (6 percent of $800,000) before dividends may be paid to the common stockholders.

8 d Preferred dividend requirements are $45,000 per year; total requirements are for two years' dividends, or $90,000, since the preferred stock is cumulative. Thus, only $20,000 ($110,000 − $90,000) is available for common dividends.

9 a Generally, the purpose of a retained earnings reserve is to indicate that not all of the existing retained earnings are available as a source of dividends. In some instances, reserves will be established with a balance left in the Retained Earnings account sufficient to maintain the regular dividends. Thus, the procedure does not always operate to limit dividends. For this reason retained earnings reserves can be looked upon as being ways of disclosing information as well as being restrictions upon the amount of dividends declared.

10 d If total stockholders' equity is less than paid-in capital, some account must have a debit (negative) balance. Only two possibilities exist—a discount account or a negative balance in the Retained Earnings account. Since the discount would be deducted in arriving at paid-in capital, the only account which can cause total stockholders' equity to be less than paid-in capital is Retained Earnings with a debit balance. A debit balance in the Retained Earnings account is called a deficit.

11 f The act of declaring a cash dividend creates a liability on the part of the corporation to pay. Thus, the credit must be to Dividends Payable. The debit must be charged to Retained Earnings since, by the act of distributing assets as dividends, the amount of earnings retained is reduced. The use of a temporary Dividends account to accumulate all of the dividend charges during the year is proper accounting if the account is closed to Retained Earnings. Thus, either (b) or (e) is correct.

12 c Since a stock dividend merely transfers retained earnings to paid-in capital, it does not change the total of the stockholders' equity in the corporation. But it does increase the number of shares outstanding. Thus, the book value per share is reduced.

13 c The amount of the dividend is $130,000 (10 percent of 10,000 shares equals 1,000; 1,000 times $130 equals $130,000). This is the amount to be charged to Retained Earnings. Since the shares to be issued have a par value, it is customary to set up the Stock Dividends Payable account at the par value of the shares to be issued, in this case $100,000. The difference represents the amount above par value to be capitalized, for which the source must be indicated— stock dividends.

14 e The correct entry is:

Cash............................	2,200	
Retained Earnings.............	200	
Treasury Stock.........		2,400

The $200 deficiency of reissue price from acquisition cost should be charged against Paid-In Capital—Treasury Stock Transactions until the balance in that account is exhausted. But in this case, there were no previous transactions in treasury stock, so no Paid-In Capital—Treasury Stock Transactions account exists.

15 d The cost of treasury shares should be shown as an unallocated debit against the total amount of paid-in capital plus retained earnings. The restriction on retained earnings should also be shown. It cannot be viewed as double counting of the cost of treasury shares, since the stating of a restriction is not the same as an actual reduction of the account.

16 d The only correct answer is (d). Answer (a) is incorrect because the amount of the dividend is $59,500, since 500 of the common shares are in the treasury. Answer (b) is incorrect because the common treasury stock acquired by purchase cost $45 per share ($18,000/ 400). Answer (c) is incorrect because the corporation is free to issue 500 shares of common treasury stock to whomever it wishes, but the other 40,000 shares must be offered to the existing stockholders (common) on a pro rata basis unless these

723

stockholders have waived their preemptive rights.

17 c The drawing or current account is usually closed to the capital account at the end of the period, so only this latter account has a balance at statement date.

18 b The $27,000 should be allocated 4/9 to Reeves and 5/9 to Hayes. Since net earnings existed, the Expense and Revenue Summary account had a credit balance before being closed.

Chapter 11

1 d If you got this one wrong, you probably selected statement **(e)**. The denominators of the two ratios are the same. The numerator of the current ratio is larger than the numerator of the acid test ratio unless there are no prepaid expenses or inventory. The current ratio, therefore, can be equal to, but not smaller than, the quick ratio.

2 a For questions of this type it is advisable to set up the ratio as follows:
A ratio of 2:1 would be the same as having

$$\frac{\text{Current assets}}{\text{Current liabilities}} = \frac{\$6}{\$3}$$

If you use $2 of cash in the numerator to pay a short-term note payable of $2, the ratio becomes

$$\frac{\$6 - \$2}{\$3 - \$2} = \frac{\$4}{\$1}, \text{ or } 4:1$$

3 e You may believe that the federal government should not have been included. When a firm incurs federal income taxes and does not pay them immediately a current liability is created. All items on the right side of the statement of financial position can be considered to be sources of assets. Thus, the federal government has been, at times, a source of some of the cash in a firm's Cash account. If it had been required to pay the tax immediately, the cash would not have appeared as an asset on its financial statements.

4 d

$$\frac{\text{Owners' equity}}{\text{Total equity}} = \frac{\$1,000,000}{\$1,500,000} = 66\tfrac{2}{3}\%$$

5 b (a) is not necessarily true. Other forms of financing growth may be less costly (i.e., retained earnings) and less risky. **(b)** is true. The use of favorable financial leverage means that trading on the equity has increased the per share return to its stockholders. **(c)** This may be a safe policy but not necessarily a profitable one.

6 c

$$\frac{\text{Net sales}}{\text{Average accounts receivable}}$$

$$= \frac{\$430,000}{\$50,000} = 8.6$$

Some analysts would hold that **(e)** is also correct since it is obtained by dividing 365 days by 8.4. We prefer to speak of the turnover of accounts receivable as being so many times per year.

7 a A stiffening of credit policies would be accomplished by turning away customers with relatively poor credit ratings and probably also by actively "going after" customers who were not paying amounts when due. If sales remained fairly constant in spite of this action, the average number of days an account receivable is outstanding would decline.

8 a Inventory turnover rate

$$= \frac{\text{Cost of goods sold}}{\text{Average inventory}}$$

$$= \frac{\$108,000}{\$50,000} = 2.16$$

9 d Net earnings per share of common stock

$= $ Net earnings less preferred dividends $\div$ No. of shares of common stock.

$$= \frac{\$194,000 - \$1,200}{10,000 \text{ shares}}$$

$$= \frac{\$192,800}{10,000 \text{ shares}}$$

$= \$19.28$ per share

10 c Twelve percent of $60 is $7.20 which is the amount of earnings per share.

$$\text{Price-earnings ratio} = \frac{\text{Current market price per share}}{\text{Earnings per share}}$$

$$= \frac{\$60}{\$7.20} = 8.33 \text{ to } 1$$

11 b Times interest is earned

$$= \frac{\text{Earnings before interest and taxes}}{\text{Interest on bonds}}$$

$$= \frac{\$400,000}{\$30,000} = 13\frac{1}{3} \text{ times}$$

12 e On a 60-day loan application the banker would look at the short-term debt-paying ability. The banker does not expect to receive payment from earnings but rather from conversion of accounts receivable and inventory into cash (even if the inventory were to be sold at cost, which is usually not the case).

13 c Delivery equipment is a nonmonetary item. All the other items are monetary items.

Chapter 12

1 d Published statements of changes in financial position usually emphasize working capital. But *Opinion No. 19* requires that all significant changes resulting from financial or investment transactions be disclosed in the statement even though a current account was not affected.

2 c The statement of changes in financial position would show whether working capital generated by operations was sufficient to cover dividends.

3 c The collection of accounts receivable is merely the transformation of one working capital item into another—accounts receivable to cash—and thus is not a source of working capital in the statement.

4 e The repayment of the loan reduces current assets and current liabilities by the same amount, and transactions which affect only current accounts can have no affect on working capital in a statement of changes in financial position unless a gain or loss is involved.

5 d Because it involves a noncurrent account in the determination of net earnings, the amortization of premium on bonds payable will cause the amount of working capital generated by operations to differ from net earnings. All of the other items listed affect both earnings and working capital.

6 a The issuance of the stock would be listed among the financial resources provided which did not affect working capital, while the acquisition of the building would be an application of financial resources which did not affect working capital.

7 e Accounts receivable due from customers actually increased $7,000 since the beginning amount included the advance to the advertising agency. Since accounts receivable increased by $7,000, more sales were made than cash collected and the increase must be deducted from sales to arrive at cash from customers.

8 e All of the statements are false. The cash flow statement would show cash applied to the acquisition of marketable securities of $100,000, not $1,000 or $99,000. The statement of changes in financial position would not show a $100,000 application of working capital since working capital did not decrease as a result of the acquisition of the securities and only the net change in working capital is reported. The sale of the securities at a loss of $1,000 did decrease working capital; therefore, it should not be added back to net earnings in converting net earnings to working capital from operations.

9 e The amortization of bond premium would be *deducted* from, not added to, net earnings in converting net earnings to working capital from operations. The amortization of bond premium reduces the amount of interest expense included in arriving at net earnings to an amount less than the amount of cash that must ultimately be paid.

10 c New equipment acquired must be more than $15,000 since that is the amount by which the account increased while equipment having an original cost of $12,000 was removed from the account. Thus, equipment acquired apparently amounted to $27,000.

Chapter 13

1 c General-purpose financial statements are intended, according to the FASB, primarily for existing and potential investors and creditors.

2 e Accounting principles and standards are needed in the provision of general-purpose financial information. Such information is hardly useful to managements engaging in special studies of their operations.

3 c Relevance is by far the most important. Information that is not relevant is useless.

4 b The depreciation on the trucks is considered the cost of valuable services received and used in construction on the building.

5 e If the amounts are immaterial, no real damage can be done. If the amounts are material, it is simply incorrect accounting.

6 c An amount is material only if it would make a difference to an informed reader in his evaluations and decisions.

7 b Presumably the accountant would try to perfect matching. If attained, this would provide comparability. Disclosure would become less meaningful because of the absolute consistency followed in the matching process. And materiality and conservatism would not be involved, since all items would be handled in the theoretically correct manner.

8 d No accounting principle permits revenue recognition at this point.

9 c Such costs are typically treated as period costs because of the difficulties encountered in measuring the amounts to be deferred or the benefits to be received in future periods.

10 e This is considered an implementing principle showing how the major principle of initial recording is made operational.

11 d An expense is a voluntary, not an involuntary, expiration of an asset.

12 1. **e**
  2. **g**
  3. **d**
  4. **h**
  5. **i**
  6. **a** (Many of these countries have experienced severe inflation recently.)
  7. **f**
  8. **b**
  9. **c** (The typical basis is initial exchange prices.)
  10. **j**

13 b For certain companies, the SEC requires disclosure of the current replacement cost of inventories, cost of goods sold, plant capacity, and depreciation.

14 c The loss is so closely related to regular or normal operations that it cannot be considered a prior period adjustment or an extraordinary item. The tax effects of regular revenues and expenses are not determined for each individual item; therefore, the amount should be reported gross (without deducting its tax effect).

15 e *FASB Statement No. 16* bars the reporting of such items as prior period adjustments because they result from an economic event of the current year and because management usually is involved in such settlements. If the settlement is unusual and not expected to recur, it should be reported as an extraordinary item, net of its tax effects because it is tax-deductible. Net earnings before extraordinary items do amount to $6.6 million. They consist of $10 million of the excess of revenues over expenses, plus the $3 million gain, less income taxes of $6.4 million—$5 million (.5 × $10 million) plus $900,000 (.3 × $3 million) plus $500,000 (the additional taxes for 1976).

Chapter 14

1 a In order to be a parent company, a corporation must own more than 50 percent of the outstanding voting common stock of another company. The parent must prepare consolidated financial statements when a subsidiary is engaged in a business similar to the parent's. The parent-subsidiary relationship does not prohibit the parent from lending money to or borrowing money from the subsidiary.

2 b Elimination entries are made only on the consolidated statement work sheet. The parent's and subsidiary's ledger accounts are not affected. Elimination entries are required to show the assets, liabilities, stockholders' equity, revenues, expenses, and dividends as if the parent and subsidiary constitute a single economic entity. The items eliminated for consolidated statement purposes would still appear on the parent's and subsidiary's separate financial statements.

3 b The book value of Duke's investment in Trap Company is 85 percent of $400,000, or $340,000. Cost exceeds book value by $15,000 ($355,000 − $340,000). Since the subsidiary's assets are not undervalued, the excess of cost over book value is labeled goodwill.

4 c According to *APB Opinion No. 17,* goodwill must be amortized over 40 or fewer years. Goodwill is an intangible asset and, thus, has a debit balance.

5 e A cash dividend received from a subsidiary reduces the parent's equity in the subsidiary's net assets. Thus, Cash is debited and the investment in subsidiary account is credited for $9,600 since the parent owns 100 percent of the subsidiary.

6 b All the other statements are true. The earnings of a subsidiary increase, not decrease, the parent's equity in the subsidiary's net assets. When earnings are reported by a subsidiary, the parent debits the investment account, thereby increasing the balance.

7 a The note received from P Company by X Company would not be included in notes receivable on the consolidated statement of financial position. From the viewpoint of the consolidated entity, notes receivable amount to $20,000 ($15,000 + $8,000 − $3,000 = $20,000).

8 c The subsidiary's minority stockholders and creditors benefit and suffer only from the subsidiary's financial position and results of operations. The parent's statements are not useful, and the consolidated statements are of limited usefulness to the subsidiary's creditors and minority stockholders.

9 b The other statements are correct. Under the purchase method of accounting, an investment in a subsidiary is recorded at the fair market value of the assets or stock given up or at the fair market value of the stock received, whichever is the more clearly and objectively determinable. This treatment agrees with the cost concept.

10 d The minority stockholders have a 25 percent interest in the subsidiary.

$$\$420,000 \times .25 = \$105,000$$

11 b The minority interest represents the equity of the minority stockholders in the net assets of the subsidiary. Thus, the minority interest cannot be classified as an asset. But it has appeared as a liability, as part of stockholders' equity, and in a category between liabilities and stockholders' equity. Its treatment in this text has been in a category between liabilities and stockholders' equity.

12 a The answer is computed as follows:

$275,000	original investment
25,925	(85% of A Company's net earnings)
(17,000)	(85% of dividends paid by A Company)
$283,925	

13 d At the beginning of the year, the book value of all the common stock was $360,000 ($355,000 − $13,000 = $342,000; $342,000 ÷ .95 = $360,000). The minority interest on January 1, 1979, was $18,000 (5 percent of $360,000). The minority stockholders have a 5 percent equity in the net earnings of the subsidiary which amounts to $2,275. Thus, minority interest in Whit Company on December 31, 1979, is $20,275 ($18,000 + $2,275).

Index

This book has been set in 10 point Times Roman, leaded 2 points and 9 point Times Roman, leaded 1 point. Part numbers are in 24 point Helvetica Bold and 48 point Times Roman. Part titles are in 18 point Times Roman Bold. Chapter numbers are in 66 point Weiss Series I and chapter titles are in 18 point Times Roman. The size of the type page is 33 by 48 picas.